CONTEMPORARY CHINA

BILL BRUGGER

CROOM HELM   LONDON

BARNES & NOBLE BOOKS   NEW YORK
(a division of Harper & Row Publishers, Inc.)

Croom Helm Ltd, 2-10 St John's Road, London SW11

ISBN 0-85664-388-2 (hardback)
ISBN 0-85664-480-3 (paperback)

Published in the U.S.A. 1977 by
Harper & Row Publishers, Inc.
Barnes & Noble Import Division
ISBN 0-06-490759-7

951.05
B891

Printed in Great Britain by Biddles Ltd, Guildford, Surrey

CONTENTS

47929

ACKNOWLEDGEMENTS

To those of the hundred-odd students who read the first draft of this book and felt able to break through the student culture of deference and apathy. To N. Blewett, S. Chan, D. Corbett, J. Hall, P. Schwartz, B. Thomas, A. Watson, D. Woodward and G. Young for their detailed comments on a highly condensed text. To H. Leng for saving me from too much arrogance and to N. Wintrop for helping me, in a dialectical sense, to preserve just a little. To N. Hunter, D. Jaensch and G. O'Leary who, from very dissimilar political and intellectual standpoints, combined to persuade me that I was not wasting my time. To M. Grieve for her help with indexes and style. To G. Willoughby and A. Little for map-work. To C. Cameron for the logistic support necessary to mount the original operation. To L. Koop, S. Stewart and the secretarial staff of the School of Social Sciences, Flinders University, for typing and retyping various barely intelligible drafts with a conscientiousness and good humour that the drafts scarcely deserved. Finally, to my wife Suzanne whose sharp criticism has always protected me from being eroded by academic complacency.

It is presumptuous to claim responsibility for a work that is ninetenths plagiarism, but I cannot avoid carrying the burden for the many errors that must remain. Perhaps the slogan I am looking for is that beloved of the Chinese radicals, 'collective initiative and individual responsibility'.

Bill Brugger

The Flinders University of
South Australia

July 1975

ABBREVIATIONS

ACFL	All China Federation of Labour
ACFTU	All China Federation of Trade Unions
APC	Agricultural producers' co-operative
CB	Current Background
CC	Central Committee
CCP	Chinese Community Party
CPSU	Communist Party of the Soviet Union
CQ	*The China Quarterly*
ECMM	*Extracts from China Mainland Magazines*
EEC	European Economic Community
FBIS	Federal Broadcast Information Service
FEER	*Far Eastern Economic Review*
GAC	Government Administration Council
HK	Hong Kong
JPRS	Joint Publications Research Service
KMT	Kuomintang
PFLP	Peking Foreign Languages Press
PLA	People's Liberation Army
PR	*Peking Review*
RMRB	*Renmin Ribao*
SC	State Council
SCMM	*Selections from China Mainland Magazines*
SCMP	*Survey of China Mainland Press*
SW	*Selected Works*
SWB	Summary of World Broadcasts (British Broadcasting Corporation)
UN	United Nations
URI	Union Research Institute

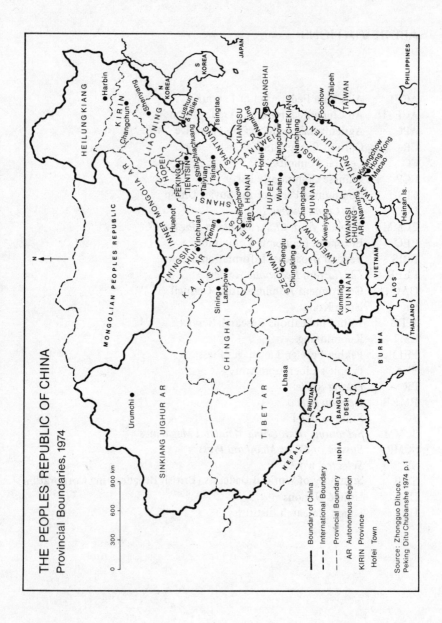

THE PEOPLES REPUBLIC OF CHINA
Provincial Boundaries, 1974

N

0   300   600   900 km

Boundary of China
International Boundary
Provincial Boundary
AR Autonomous Region
KIRIN Province
● Hofei Town

Source: Zhongguo Dituce.
Peking Ditu Chubanshe 1974 p.1

HEILUNGKIANG

KIRIN
● Harbin
Changchun ●
Shenyang ●
LIAONING
Lushun & Talien

MONGOLIAN PEOPLES REPUBLIC

S KOREA
N KOREA
S KOREA
JAPAN
PHILIPPINES

INNER MONGOLIA AR
Huehot ●
HOPEI
PEKING ●
TIENTSIN ●
Shihchiachuang ●
Taiyuan ●
SHANSI
Tsinan ●
SHANTUNG
Tsingtao ●
Nanking ●
SHANGHAI ●
KIANGSU
ANHWEI
Hofei ●
Hangchow ●
CHEKIANG
Nanchang ●
Foochow ●
FUKIEN
Taipeh ●
TAIWAN

NINGSIA HUI AR
Yinchuan ●
Yenan ●
SHENSI
Sian ●
HONAN
Chengchow ●
HUPEH
Wuhan ●
Changsha ●
HUNAN
Kweiyang ●
KWEICHOW
Hainan Is.

KANSU
Lanchow ●
Sining ●
CHINGHAI

SZECHWAN
Chengtu ●
Chungking ●

YUNNAN
Kunming ●

KWANGSI CHUANG AR
Nanning ●
KWANGTUNG
Kwangchow ●
Hong Kong
Macao

Urumchi ●
SINKIANG UIGHUR AR

TIBET AR
Lhasa ●

NEPAL
BHUTAN
BANGLA DESH
INDIA
BURMA
LAOS
THAILAND
VIETNAM

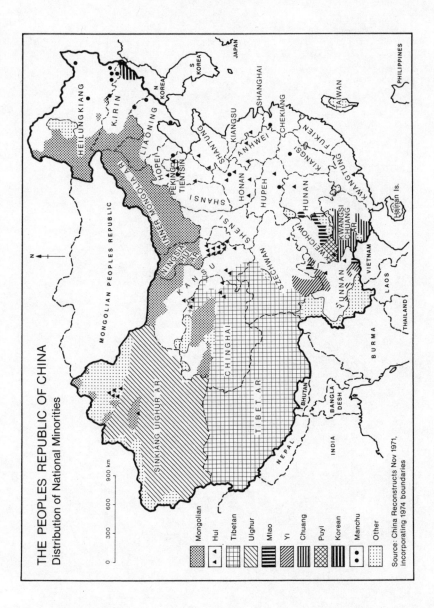

THE PEOPLES REPUBLIC OF CHINA
Distribution of National Minorities

Source: China Reconstructs Nov 1971,
incorporating 1974 boundaries

Mongolian
Hui
Tibetan
Uighur
Miao
Yi
Chuang
Puyi
Korean
Manchu
Other

PREFACE

In writing this simple history of contemporary China, I do not aim at originality but base myself firmly on secondary sources. It is perhaps inevitable, therefore, that I shall be open to the charges of plagiarism and over-simplification. In my defence, all I can say is that there is a need for a chronological account of events in China from the 1940s and, pending the arrival of some sinological E.H. Carr, a synthetic account must rely directly upon the work of others.

My aim is to produce a textbook to accompany a course in contemporary Chinese politics or history. I am not attempting to write an introductory history complete in itself and which may be read in isolation. The original intention to write such a book grew out of student complaints about the excessive amount of factual material I was compelled to include in my lectures. In introducing China to students, however, I was unable to avoid presenting a large amount of empirical data. On the other hand, I felt that the function of lectures should be not to inform but to entertain and to stimulate thought. A course of lectures should ideally serve to keep a group of students oriented to a field of study and to maintain their interest in it. Once such a course usurps the function of the written word, it inevitably becomes dull. I decided, therefore, to transfer the bulk of the empirical data used in my lectures to a textbook which hopefully would provide the take-off point for further reading.

Having transferred a mass of empirical data from lectures to a textbook to prevent the former from becoming too dull, there is always the possibility that I have also similarly transferred the dullness. Perhaps the notion of an exciting textbook is utopian, but I hope that the profoundly exciting nature of my subject matter will save me from too harsh a censure.

It is part of the liberal academic tradition that, in writing introductory textbooks, one should present as many different interpretations of each event as one can and argue which are the most plausible. The assumption is always that there is basic agreement on the paradigm that underlies these different interpretations. If there were basic differences of paradigm, such a product would be unreadable. Amongst students of China, there are Cold War power-struggle analysts, economic reductionists, psychological reductionists, Trotskyist bureaucratic reductionists,

classical sinologues, medieval theologians who claim to be Marxists and
not a few populists to whom 'truth' is revealed. I am not quite certain
of the utility of balancing all these views or of my ability to do so. I
shall therefore in general argue a line.

Throughout this book, I shall take very seriously what the Chinese
say they are doing and will operate according to a policy paradigm.
Though I shall consider power-struggles, the focus will be on differences
of line. One might argue, in the manner of Trotskyists, that Chinese
politics might be boiled down to Mao's attempt to remove all opposition
whether from the left or the right (arbitrarily defined), in the manner
of Joseph Stalin. If such is one's view, then there can be no argument
about principles and policies for these are seen merely as rationalisations
of a basic drive for power. One might also argue, in the manner of the
psychological reductionists, that what lies at the core of Chinese politics is a concern for identity or even Mao's search for a mode of
symbolic immortality. If such is one's view, then principles and policies
are merely sublimations of some deeper reality. One might also, in
vulgar Marxist vein, argue in terms of a one-to-one correspondence
between class and consciousness, assigning to Mao a peasant mentality
and to others an urban mentality. If one pushes this view to its logical
conclusion, then the whole Chinese revolution becomes populist rather
than socialist. In this book, I shall attempt to reject reductionism in
terms of power, psyche or crude class categorisation.

The main theme that runs through this book is the battle between
'conservatives', 'radicals' and 'ultra-leftists'. Though all three would
probably agree as to the nature of socialism and communism, they
emphasise different means to achieve them. The 'conservatives' see
socialist transition as an orderly process in which economic development is a precondition for social change. Adhering to a mechanical
notion of 'rationality', they all too easily create a state machine which
insulates them from those they seek to lead and which attempts to
process people into socialist society. The 'ultra-leftists' tend to see all
disorder as creative, at least until communist society is achieved. In-
toxicated by the idea of instant communism, they readily become
impatient with all state forms and all gradualist policies and try to
hector people into becoming socialist. The radicals see socialist transition as a process of alternating order and disorder in which economic
development and social change interact dialectically. They criticise the
'conservatives' for allowing economic development and social order to
become ends in themselves rather than means to achieve socialism and
describe the insulation of leaders from led as 'bureaucratism'. They

criticise the 'ultra-leftists' for basing operational programmes on a view of society not as it is but as they would like it to be and regard their unworldly fundamentalism as 'dogmatism'.

In talking about 'conservatives', 'radicals' and 'ultra-leftists', I may be criticised for not always stating who exactly fitted into which category on which issue. My primary aim, however, is to illustrate the various positions taken in each debate rather than document the orientation of individual people. It is inevitable, however, that I shall undertake some exercises in Kremlinology and, at times, will dwell upon the alleged perfidy of individuals. Such is unavoidable when much of the material I have used (which dates from the Cultural Revolution) seeks expressly to document that perfidy.

It is possible also that I may be criticised for 'sociologism' since I use sociological tools such as models and cycles. The word 'model' is an emotive symbol. Some people will declare that the very idea of a model is static and that models are inevitably defective in accommodating change. They are correct in pointing out the static nature of models but wrong in the suggestion that they should not be used. Analogously, short shrift would be given to anyone who abjures abstraction and simplification in science on the grounds that such exercises inevitably involve distortion. The truth is that we cannot avoid constructing models and it is better to be explicit about what we are doing than to believe that we are, in some mysterious way, hooked on to History. I shall talk, therefore, about the Yenan model worked out by the Communist Party in the 1940s and the model of organisation and administration imported from the Soviet Union in the 1950s. I shall use also a number of foreign policy models, knowing well that none of them presents a full picture of reality. Their utility lies merely in providing a datum against which to measure change.

A similar problem lies in the use of the notion 'cycles'. The book is organised around nine cycles of radicalism, accelerated radicalism and consolidation. My aim is to present a dynamic view of developments within China and to avoid the static 'pendulum model' in which policy seems to alternate left and right of a fixed point. I am not adhering to the absurd notion that history repeats itself nor to the theory of 'compliance cycles' made popular by Amitai Etzioni.[1] According to this view, a regime applies in cyclic fashion 'remunerative', 'normative' and 'coercive' measures to achieve certain goals and these measures correspond to periods of radicalism and consolidation. Such a view is, in my opinion, too mechanical. It assumes that all key decisions are made by an élite which manipulates the political process. The cyclic

view of progress, which I shall discuss in this book, is one formulated
by the Chinese Communist Party itself during the 1950s and which has
already been discussed by such writers as Richard Solomon.[2] According
to this view, the relationship between central leadership and mass initiative is not causal but *dialectical*. Central policies do not simply cause
the masses to be active, any more than mass activism simply causes a
reformulation of central policy. Both central leadership and mass
initiative ideally interact to produce policies that are not simply the
effect of pressure from different directions nor a compromise solution
but something which is qualitatively different. As the Chinese see it,
one is not dealing with simple *causal interaction* but *dialectical interaction*. Though the Central leadership should not manipulate the
political process, it should influence the pattern of dialectical interaction according to cyclic patterns of radicalism and consolidation. In
the Chinese idiom, progress is 'saddle-shaped' (*maanxing*)[3] consisting
of a high point, a trough and an even higher point. The high points of
the 'saddle' represent periods of radicalism and the trough represents
a period of consolidation. Ideally, each synthesis should be at a point
higher than the last when measured against the yardstick of overcoming the division of labour inherited from the old society and inherent in any transitional period. Different people will disagree, however, as to the degree of radicalism, the point at which a period of
consolidation is to begin, the nature of consolidation and the precise
nature of the yardstick. Accepting a radical view of development within China, one might argue that, in the early 1960s, an increasingly
technological view of what the yardstick ought to be almost resulted
in a situation where cycles reversed themselves and the saddle appeared
back to front.

One might, of course, maintain that the notion of the dialectic is
metaphysical, that the whole can be no more than the sum of its parts
and that the relationship between leaders and led may be no more than
causal interaction. One might indeed eschew any notion of progress
altogether, be it linear or cyclical. Suffice it to say here that, in this
book, I shall take very seriously the Chinese cyclical view and that, in
using the term 'cycle', I am not attempting to impose a Western model
on the Chinese reality. Though the models and cycles I shall use will be
recognisable to the Chinese, there are many other sociological terms
which will not. Such terms are used here not to impress the reader but
because they might be useful in cross-cultural comparisons.

A further problem lies in my use of many Chinese terms which
might possibly inhibit the narrative flow. An important function of this

book, however, is to prepare the student to read original Chinese texts (be they in translation or not). With this in mind, I have placed *Hanyu Pinyin* transliterations in parentheses wherever possible but have expressed most proper nouns either in the form most commonly met with or according to the Wade Giles system.

One of the great difficulties I experienced in writing this book was in integrating a number of very diverse themes. Though the references to Mao and the use of his statements have been challenged by those who would like to see a work of 'history from below', they do serve to provide a link connecting, for example, rural policy, art and literature, military strategy and foreign relations. I have tried to avoid the short-coming of so many textbooks which skip about from subject to subject and present little more than a thematic *smorgasbord*. It is inevitable, however, that there will be some disjunction between adjacent sections which may only be avoided by reorganising the whole text on thematic lines. Such a thematic approach is that of H.F. Schurmann's excellent *Ideology and Organisation in Communist China*, on which I have drawn quite liberally. What I am aiming for here is chronological rather than thematic integration along the lines of E. Vogel's *Canton Under Communism*, to which I am also greatly indebted.

A final point concerns the extent to which I need narrate the historical background against which the events of the 1940s to 1970s took place. I originally undertook the task of summarising some 300 years of Chinese history in two short introductory chapters. The result was far from satisfactory. All I have attempted here, therefore, is to sketch very briefly the background against which the Communist Party developed and suggest the reader consult historians far more competent than I. He will discover that there rages a fierce polemic not merely over the inter-pretation of data but on the reliability of conflicting sets of data. It is a morass that a student of contemporary China, such as myself, feels incompetent to evaluate.

The utility of this textbook to the undergraduate student will depend upon the academic tradition and intellectual milieu in which he finds himself. A student brought up in the world of sinology will probably find it alien, for the stress is on change rather than continuity. Those emerging from the tradition of Cold War *realpolitik* will probably find my attempt at empathy naive. Those who seek modern *gurus* might be affronted by my contention that Mao Tse-tung did not fore-see the whole course of Chinese history. I might offend also those who have inherited the mantle of the eighteenth-century *philosophes* and see China as the culmination of everything that is progressive. Such people bring to the study of China a static view in which history becomes a series of 'now'. In my view, the Chinese experience offers us valuable lessons in the dynamics of socialist transition, in revolution as a *process* rather than an *act* and in actuality defined not so much in *being* as in *becoming*.

Notes

1. Such an approach has been applied to the Chinese situation by Skinner and Winckler 1969.
2. See Solomon 1971.
3. Mao Tse-tung 23 May 1958, in JPRS 61269-1, 20 February 1974, p. 116.
   Liu Shao-ch'i 5 May 1958, in Liu 1968, p. 19 (in the official English translation, the term is 'U-shaped'.)

INTRODUCTION

There was a time when most writing on contemporary China began with the statement that China had enjoyed a degree of social and political continuity for two millennia and that such continuity was unparalleled. We now know enough about the process of development to beware of using the residual category of 'traditional society' and indulging in the ahistorical assumption that basic features of a society had not been subject to radical change. In the two millennia that precede our century, China had experienced many changes in the system of land tenure, had at times been politically unified and at others fragmented, had for periods experienced a level of scientific and technological sophistication far in advance of the West and had been the object of both the praise and vilification of foreign observers.

Feudal Society

Change within China during the last three decades has been away from a society which the Chinese Communist Party describes as 'feudal' (*fengjian de*). Those Western historians who see feudalism essentially as a phenomenon that either precedes or follows a bureaucratic empire and in which land ownership is based upon a tradition of military service would disagree with the use of this term. They would assert that the real 'feudal' period in Chinese history occurred before the second century B.C. when a number of military states vied with each other for power in much the same way as in medieval Europe. These states were to be replaced by the empire of Ch'in, from which the English name 'China' is derived. Nowadays, however, when Chinese historians use the word 'feudal', all they mean is a social system based upon the primacy of land ownership, which applies to the warring states, the Ch'in empire and, for that matter, the following two millennia.

Whether properly classified as 'feudal' or not, early twentieth-century China was governed by a disintegrating traditional bureaucracy. In its heyday, the Chinese bureaucracy had constituted an élite of educated amateurs dedicated not to expertise but to virtuous models of the past. They had been recruited by an elaborate examination system[1] consisting of four degrees, for which some candidates might study for the greater part of their lives. The system had been abolished at the beginning of the twentieth century but the values which it enshrined were remarkably persistent and in many places local Confucian 'mandarins' remained in power until the 1940s.

Confucian philosophy meant different things to different social groups and had been subject to repeated change since the time of the Sage (sixth century B.C.). In its ideological form, however (that is in the form which legitimised the rule of a landed élite), Confucianism was a highly static value system. It reduced human behaviour to moral determinants. Social turmoil or prosperity was seen as due to the moral qualities of individuals and groups rather than material determinants. Indeed, in its extreme form, natural calamities such as flood or drought were seen as due to human wickedness. The *moral* was considered more important not only than the material but also than the *intellectual*. In short, it was better to be 'good' than 'knowledgeable'. Wisdom was not the knowledge of necessity nor the overcoming of necessity but the knowledge of what was prescribed by the Confucian classics which harked back to a 'golden age'.

The normative model was one of 'Great Harmony' (*Datong*) rather than struggle. In contemporary social science jargon, what was aimed at was not a mode of conflict resolution nor conflict stimulation but of *conflict avoidance*. Since the laws which governed Nature were essentially the same as the laws which governed men, men should be in harmony not only with themselves but with Nature.

Within the Confucian scheme, great stress was placed on education and the creation of 'superior men' (*junzi*) who labour with their minds rather than their hands. This did not mean that the system was geared to the creation of individualistic super-men, for the 'superior man' was one who realised the continuity of the Confucian tradition and subordinated himself to his peers. Freedom consisted in the subordination of the self to the community of good men and to Nature. Indeed, when the word 'liberty' was translated into Chinese, it was associated with licence, for the Western negative concept of liberty was freedom *from* rather than freedom *to*. In theory, the Chinese positive conception of freedom applied to all men, though in practice it applied to those 'superior men' who, through education, had reached élite status.

One's adherence to the moral precepts of Confucianism was measured according to outward behaviour. In terms made popular by Riesman[2] one measured an individual's moral commitment and moral rectitude not in terms of his *inner direction* (to what extent he had internalised the prescriptions of the classics) nor in terms of *other direction* (to what extent his public image corresponded to current values) but in terms of *tradition direction* (to what extent his conduct measured up to his worthy ancestors). In this kind of situation, we can talk of society being essentially a *shame* culture (where people did what they ought out of fear of being shamed) rather than a *guilt* culture (where people did what they ought because they would feel guilty for not doing so). One result of this tradition direction was a considerable respect for age (made practicable by the scarcity of old men) and a gerontocratic organisation of society. Another result was an essentially patriarchal form of organisation which gave women inferior status.

The establishment of an educational hierarchy based on Confucian ideology led to a view of this world and the next (when Confucians bothered to think about such problems) as essentially organised according to the same kind of traditional bureaucracy which characterised Imperial China. As far as most peasants were concerned, however, the ideology of Confucianism which percolated down to them found very little relevance in the notion of a celestial bureaucracy. At the village level, Confucianism took on more overtly religious forms such as ancestor worship mixed with animism (the vesting of spiritual qualities in inanimate objects). At different levels of society, Confucianism mixed also with Buddhism and Taoism (the fusion of the self with the indefinable 'way' and the total integration of the self with Nature). At times, these religions served to legitimise revolt, as did Islam amongst national minorities. On occasions, heterodox Christianity even took on a Confucian hue. It would be inappropriate to go into all these transmutations here. Suffice it to say that a society based on land developed a static ideology that stressed not challenging the status quo but was sufficiently elastic to accommodate a right of rebellion justified only by success.

Just as the values of the traditional bureaucracy changed little during the early twentieth century, rural social and political structure was also relatively static. The formal apparatus of Imperial government did not extend much below the level of the two thousand odd *xian* (or counties) into which China was divided. There existed, however, in places, the remains of a system of mutual responsibility known as *baojia* in which each group of families was organised into a unit collectively responsible for the conduct of its members. There was also a level of local government lower than the *xian*, known as the *xiang*, at which most local dignitaries or 'gentry' (*shenshi* or *shidafu jieji*) operated. Here the 'gentry', who consisted of official aspirants or their landowning relatives, undertook the task of local administration and the settlement of disputes according to customary law.

It is probable that most *xiang* were coterminous with what anthropologist G.W. Skinner has referred to as 'standard marketing areas'.[3] Applying a version of the central place theory of Cristaller and Lösch to the Chinese situation, Skinner divided the whole country into a number of these standard marketing areas, each of which consisted of a group of villages (divisible usually by six) arranged around a market. By 1949, he calculated that there were some 58,000 standard marketing areas which themselves were grouped into intermediate marketing areas and which, in turn, were grouped into central marketing areas at *xian* level. There has been much discussion as to the applicability of Skinner's theory and whether or not the marketing areas correspond to administrative divisions. It does seem reasonable to me, however, that the horizon of a peasant's existence would be bounded by the area in which he could sell his produce rather than simply by the natural village in which he lived.

Within the villages, grouped together as *xiang* or standard marketing areas, there existed a number of organisations which cut across class lines. An example of such an organisation would be the clan (or lineage) (*zu*) based on real or imagined family ties and usually dominated by those of its members who had larger holdings of land. One should note here that the popular myth of a traditional Chinese society characterised by huge extended families living under one roof is largely untrue. Such families did, of course, exist, particularly among the wealthy, but in general the most common form of family organisation was the *famille souche* (or stem family) which consisted of husband and wife, their children and one or two grandparents,[4] forming a unit that would fit very neatly into clan or lineage.

Though the family was quite small (consisting on average of between four and six persons),[5] the clan or lineage was a significant organisation (particularly in South China), occasionally providing a primitive system of social security and a forum for the settlement of disputes.

Another organisation which cut across class lines, though this time characterised by *simulated* rather than real kinship, was the secret society which fed upon a long tradition of anti-bureaucratic dissent. During the seventeenth and eighteenth centuries, many secret societies were organised around resistance to the alien Manchu dynasty and had as their professed aim the restoration of the last great Han dynasty — the Ming (overthrown in 1644). Whatever the original political aim, however, many of these societies became religious organisations in their own right, probably because a religious organisation is better able to survive periods of repression than a clearly political organisation. Like their Western counterparts, these quasi-religious bodies, based upon patterns of simulated kinship, easily turned to crime.

Though the bulk of the Chinese population still lived in the country-side in the early twentieth century, some 10 per cent did, in fact, live in towns. The development of the urban population in China had been markedly different from that in the West. There has been much discussion as to why China, which in the seventeenth century was technologically more advanced than the West, did not produce an indigenous urban bourgeoisie. One reason is quite clearly that Confucian ideology accorded the merchant a low status though this, I believe, is only a partial explanation. A more fruitful line of enquiry is to be found in the pattern of social mobility.

It has been suggested that the development of a bourgeoisie in the West and a quasi-bourgeoisie in Japan depended upon the fact that class structure was relatively closed. There were few mechanisms in England, for example, whereby merchant classes might be absorbed into the landowning aristocracy and this led to the development of a bourgeoisie in independent towns with a consciousness of itself as a class for itself. Similarly in Japan, the Meiji Restoration of the 1870s depended upon the association of merchants and *samurai* who constituted two unassimilated middle-class groupings in a closed-class situation who could do nothing but assert their independence. In both Britain and Japan, the absence of a violent revolution might be explained by the subsequent blending of aristocratic elements into the new bourgeoisie whereas, in France, non-assimilation resulted in violent upheaval.[6] In China, on the other hand, the class structure was more 'open'. By 'open', I do not mean that there was much upward peasant mobility, merely that the landowning class could co-opt merchants. It was not until the impact of Western imperialism that anything like a bourgeoisie developed and such a bourgeoisie as existed in the twentieth century was shaped by that imperialism.

The Impact of Imperialism

In the 80 or so years after the First Opium War in the 1840s, China was repeatedly humiliated by the Western powers. Over ninety 'treaty ports' were established in which foreigners were immune from Chinese law. Spheres of influence were created which at one time looked like being turned into actual colonies, and Japan manifested direct colonial ambitions. A Maritime Customs Service under foreign control ensured the payment of foreign debts and the infamous indemnities wrung out of China at bayonet point. The Chinese tariff was fixed by treaty at a low 5 per cent, favourable to foreign business. Missionaries reached over

half of the two thousand-odd *xian* and, regardless of individual goodwill
and intentions, were often the instruments of foreign powers. Overall, a
plethora of limitations on Chinese sovereignty caused resentment which
was frequently explosive.

Though food production may have kept pace with population
increase during the nineteenth century,[7] the various risings that took
place at that time, which cannot be dissociated from foreign impact,
produced areas of intense privation exacerbated by monetary inflation.
By the early twentieth century, there had been a sharp increase in the
numbers of poor peasants forced to mortgage their land to pay to warlord regimes taxes demanded often a decade in advance. The exactions
of these warlord regimes drove many peasants into the arms of bandits
who found it fairly easy to operate in the fragmented political structure.
Though one cannot directly assign the phenomenon of warlordism to
the foreigner, some warlord regimes were backed by foreign powers
who were not sympathetic to the forces that sought national reunifica-
tion.

As far as traditional handicraft industries were concerned, it is
probably true that foreign manufactured equivalents of Chinese handicraft goods did not seriously dent the domestic market overall but the
effect of foreign competition on certain industries was dramatic.
Between 1870 and 1910, for example, the handicraft spinning of
cotton yarn declined by over 50 per cent and, although weaving held its
own, it could only absorb one-tenth of the labour released from
spinning. Though, by the early 1920s, some 78 per cent of factory
output in China south of the Great Wall came from Chinese-owned
factories, the bulk of the extractive and transport industries was under
foreign control — a characteristic of early imperialist penetration.
Foreign mines produced 99 per cent of the pig iron, 99 per cent of the
iron ore and 76 per cent of the coal mined by modern methods. In
1920, 83 per cent of the steamer tonnage cleared through Maritime
Customs and 78 per cent of that on China's main waterway — the
Yangtze — was in foreign ships. Railway control was brought about
through foreign loans and, according to one estimate, foreign capital
controlled 93 per cent of China's railways in 1911.[8]

Such a situation, so different from Japan, is all the more remarkable
in that China had embarked upon her own version of the Meiji Restoration at the same time as her Eastern neighbour.[9] The modern industries
of the 1860s were set up with little capital. Most of them were initiated
by governor-generals (in charge of one or several provinces) with funds
milked from any available source (such as the local defence budget).

Government officials placed in charge of them were expected to be major shareholders in their own right and to sell shares in the treaty ports to raise more capital.[10] It was thus impossible to separate the state from the private sector of the economy, especially when these industrial concerns established tenuous links with individual manufacturers organised along traditional lines. There was pressure throughout the latter part of the nineteenth century (especially from Peking) to increase the size of private investment in state-run factories and this frequently led to a situation where foreigners became majority shareholders. Perhaps the paradigm case here was the Hanyehp'ing Coal and Iron Company which commenced operation before the first Japanese iron and steel works (Yawata) and which, within half a century, had become completely a Japanese subsidiary.[11]

The government officials who were also major capitalists became known in the twentieth century as 'bureaucratic capitalists' (*guanliao zibenjia*) and depended for funds on a new class grouping which began to develop in the treaty ports — the comprador capitalists (*maiban zibenjia*), oriented towards the economy of the overseas imperial countries. By the early twentieth century, however, there also began to develop a third group of domestic or 'national capitalists' (*minzu zibenjia*) whose links with foreign countries were much weaker.

The expansion of foreign-controlled industry contributed much to the growth of an industrial working class. Half a century after the establishment of state-run factories, there existed a small number of workers who had few ties with the countryside. But, as the bulk of industrial expansion took place during the First World War boom, the majority of workers had arrived recently from the rural areas. They had been recruited by the notorious 'gang-boss system' (*batouzhi*).[12] Gang bosses were not merely labour contractors but also remained as supervisors of their contractees after they had been signed on. They took a sizable cut from workers' wages[13] and developed personal relationships with members of their gangs, expressed in terms of 'family' with all the obligations which that word implied in contemporary Chinese society. As one might expect, the labour gangs established links with the larger and more powerful organisations characterised by the same patterns of simulated kinship — the secret societies. In fact some secret societies such as the 'Green Gang' (*Qingbang*) specialised in the field of labour control and provided major obstacles to the development of labour unions.

The Early Years of the Chinese Communist Party[14]

The China in which the Communist Party was founded in 1921 was
politically, economically, socially and ideologically fragmented.
Warlord regimes vied for power. Modern capitalism coexisted with a
'feudal' agrarian economy. The wealth and social position of rural
classes was subject to sudden and extreme variations as intermittent
civil war took its toll. The working class was divided by complex
patterns of simulated kinship and different types of capitalist continually swallowed each other up. Traditional Confucians mixed with
Western and Japanese trained intellectuals. Buddhists and Taoists
rubbed shoulders with Marxists and anarchists.

In such a confusing situation, there is little wonder that the ideological coherence of the young Party depended on the Comintern (Communist International) in Moscow whose advisers had helped set it up. By
the early 1920s, the Comintern was convinced that the struggle in
colonial and semi-colonial countries should be directed against
imperialism and that Communist parties should unite with the 'national
bourgeoisie'. It had some difficulty, however, in deciding who exactly
in China represented the 'national bourgeoisie'. By 1923, Sun Yat-sen's
Kuomintang (Nationalist Party) seemed to fill the bill but the Soviet-
Kuomintang alliance and the United Front between Communist Party
and Nationalists was to be short-lived.

Following the death of Sun Yat-sen in 1925, the Nationalists embarked upon a series of military campaigns against the warlords. These
were to give China some kind of unity. During the course of the campaigns, the Communist Party switched from its earlier concentration on
mobilising the industrial workers to developing a peasant movement
and a radical programme of land reform. This, amongst other things,
alienated the right wing of the Kuomintang and resulted in the massacre
of Communist Party members, first by the Nationalist commander
Chiang K'ai-shek in Shanghai and then by the official Kuomintang
government in the central Chinese city of Wuhan.

During the resulting Civil War (1927-37), the Communist Party went
from crisis to crisis. In 1971 Mao Tse-tung referred to ten major crises
in the fifty-year history of the Party.[15] Six of them occurred in this
first Civil War. The first crisis (1927) was the direct outcome of
Comintern advice to the Chinese Party to maintain an alliance with the
Kuomintang at all costs.[16] It resulted in the inauguration of a series of
military engagements in the countryside in anticipation of decisive
risings of the urban proletariat.[17] When the risings failed to develop, a
second crisis occurred (1927) which produced a new leadership but

continued much the same strategy.

By 1930, a guerrilla base area had been built up by Mao Tse-tung in Kiangsi province, defended by a Workers and Peasants Red Army. An attempt, however, to use this army to capture major cities resulted in military defeat, another change in leadership (the third crisis),[18] a breakaway movement of what was left of the urban Party (the fourth crisis) and eventually the consolidation of a Chinese Soviet Republic in Kiangsi. In the early years of the Kiangsi Soviet, Mao Tse-tung evolved a distinctive approach to fighting the Civil War. Three Kuomintang campaigns of 'encirclement and suppression' were beaten off by a strategy expressed as 'the enemy advances, we retreat; the enemy camps, we harass; the enemy tires, we attack; the enemy retreats, we pursue'. Large bodies of Red Army troops were concentrated to attack enemy units one by one and war along fixed fronts was avoided. By the fourth encirclement campaign in 1933, however, the Party leadership under Wang Ming, now in control of military affairs, switched to a 'forward and offensive line' on the grounds that Mao's strategy invited enemy reprisals. The result was to be disastrous.

The 'forward and offensive line' together with a new Kuomintang strategy led to the defeat of the Red Army in the fifth encirclement campaign of 1934. During the course of the ensuing Long March[19] the fifth and sixth of the major crises occurred. The fifth crisis centred on the unsuccessful policies of the Wang Ming leadership whose influence was drastically reduced at a Politburo meeting in Tsunyi in January 1935. The Tsunyi meeting elected Mao as Politburo Chairman, though arguments over strategy still continued and the sixth crisis occurred soon after the meeting when Chang Kuo-t'ao, the former Vice Chairman of the Kiangsi Soviet, broke with Mao over the destination of the march. It was, therefore, only part of the Red Army that reached an isolated soviet in Northern Shensi in the autumn of 1935 though, before long, Mao's main force was joined by troops who had made a detour through Szechwan.

Most of the crises outlined above concerned military strategy and several crucial lessons had been learned. Mao's principles of People's War had been vindicated and any future strategy would rely on flexible guerrilla tactics to build up a network of rural bases with which to surround the cities. There were to be no premature assaults on the cities and what was left of the urban movement would subordinate its activities to those of the rural base areas. Secondly, several of the crises had been, in no small measure, the result of faulty advice from the Comintern in Moscow. Though the Comintern could not have prevented

the massacres of 1927, its advice to maintain the United Front at all
costs had made the debacle much worse than it need have been. At least
one of the abortive risings of 1927 had been the direct inspiration of
Stalin[20] who seemed to have little appreciation of the actual Chinese
situation. The attempt to capture major cities in 1930 and an extravagant faith in the Chinese proletariat's willingness to rise in revolt was
due in some measure to the Comintern's mystical faith that a global
'high tide' was in the offing. Finally, the inexperienced Wang Ming
leadership which took over the Party in the Kiangsi Soviet had actually
been sent to China from Moscow together with its Soviet mentor Pavel
Mif. By 1935, Mao had developed a contempt for Soviet-trained
intellectuals who attempted to import into China prepacked models of
revolution.

The Second United Front

Although, by 1935, Mao was wary of Comintern advice, there was one
policy which the Comintern adopted in that year which was very welcome – the call for a broadly-based United Front against imperialism. In
1931, the Japanese had turned north-east China into the puppet state
of Manchukuo and, since that time, Chiang K'ai-shek had been under
pressure to make peace with the Communist Party in order to resist
Japan. As early as 1933, the Communist Party had called for a United
Front though they had been wary of uniting with Chiang K'ai-shek. In
December 1935, a series of demonstrations in Peking[21] protested
against Japanese attempts to establish a puppet regime in north China
and in 1936 Nationalist forces in north-west China refused to fight the
Red Army. When Chiang K'ai-shek flew to Sian to investigate the situation, he was captured by Nationalist generals and forced to enter into
negotiations with the Communist Party.[22] An agreement was finally
concluded in September 1937 after the inauguration of total war with
Japan. The Soviet regime in north Shensi was reorganised as a 'special
region' of the Republic of China. The Red Army was incorporated into
the national forces (at least in theory) under the new name 'Eighth
Route Army' and land reform ceased.

Immediately after the reorganisation, the Eighth Route Army
crossed the Yellow River and joined battle with the Japanese. Limited
in strength to 45,000, it fought in small units of 1,000 behind the
Japanese lines and helped create guerrilla units. In the south, a New
Fourth Army was also formed in September 1937 out of people left
behind in the old Kiangsi Soviet. As anti-Japanese sentiment swelled, a
solid base of recruitment was established amongst intellectuals in the

towns as well as among peasants in the countryside and an anti-Japanese
university (*Kangda*) was set up to train them. Meanwhile the
Kuomintang resistance crumbled and, after a holding operation at
T'aierhchuang, the Nationalist government pulled back to remote
Chungking.

By 1940, the United Front had begun to fall to pieces. The
Communist Party suspected that Chiang K'ai-shek was about to do a
deal with the puppet government which the Japanese had set up in
Nanking[23] and the Kuomintang government looked with alarm upon
the rapid growth of the Eighth Route and New Fourth Armies well
beyond the limit imposed by the 1937 agreement. In early 1941,
tension gave way to open hostilities as Kuomintang troops attacked the
headquarters of the New Fourth Army after it had proved slow in
obeying an order from Chungking to withdraw north of the Yangtze
River.

The United Front was effectively at an end and an already existing
embargo on goods transported to the Communist border regions from
areas under Kuomintang control was strengthened. At the same time, a
fierce campaign of suppression known as the 'Three All' (*san guang*)
(burn all, kill all, loot all) was launched by the Japanese. The result was
dramatic. The population of Communist-controlled areas in north
China fell from 44 million to 25 million and, in the country as a whole,
from 100 million to 50 million.[24]

The situation in the border regions was critical. The tightening of the
Kuomintang blockade, together with the Japanese policy of ringing
individual areas with blockhouses, resulted in a shortage of goods. Now
that the Communist government in Yenan (the capital of the major
border region of Shen Kan Ning) received no subsidies from Chungking,
a crushing burden of taxation was imposed upon the residents. In 1941
alone, taxes were doubled and such a situation could surely not be
tolerated if the government were to retain the support of the peasants
and continue to call itself revolutionary. Secondly, the political situation deteriorated considerably. The rapid expansion of the border
regions during the early part of the war had led to large numbers of
people moving to places such as Yenan out of purely patriotic motives.
They consequently did not have much understanding of Marxism-
Leninism or Communist Party policy. A top-heavy bureaucratic structure had been created which was staffed by unreliable personnel without much contact with ordinary people. The bureaucrats had imposed a
formal education system based on current practice in the coastal cities
without much regard for the special needs of the border regions and a

peasantry that had to be convinced that education was not a waste of time. Thirdly, with the abandonment of land reform in 1937, the former rural élite strove to regain not only its political influence but also its property and vied with the cadres from the cities in a struggle which left the peasants untouched.[25] New policies were called for and, in 1942, a process was instituted which resulted in a new and very different model of political administration and economic management — a model which went a long way towards guaranteeing success in the war and which has been the starting point for the policies of the radical leadership of the Communist Party ever since. The adoption of the Yenan model, which marked the maturity of the Communist Party, is the starting point of this book.

Notes

1. See Ho 1962.
2. Riseman 1953.
3. Skinner 1964.
4. See Levy 1949.
5. Buck 1964, p. 368.
6. Moore 1967.
7. This is the view of Myers 1970, p. 124, who held that such was the case until 1937.
8. Based on Esherick 1972.
9. For a discussion of the Chinese T'ung Chih Restoration, see Wright 1957.
10. See Feuerwerker 1958.
11. See Feuerwerker 1964.
12. Discussed in Brugger 1976, pp. 42-5.
13. Fong 1937, pp. 40-1.
14. A number of standard introductory histories exist for the period 1921-42. On the career of Mao Tse-tung, see Schram 1966, Ch'en 1965, Schwartz 1966, Snow 1961. On the career of Chu Teh, see Smedley 1972. On the early years of the Party, see Meisner 1967, Schwartz 1966. On the early labour movement, see Chesneaux 1968. On the student movement, see Israel 1966. On the events of 1927, see Isaacs 1961. On the Kiangsi Soviet, see Rue 1966, Swarup 1966, Waller 1973. For an interesting collection of excerpts from various writings see Schurmann and Schell, Vol. 2, 1968.
15. Schram 1974, p. 290 and *Issues and Studies*, September 1972, p. 65.
16. See Isaacs 1961.
17. See Guillermaz 1962, Wilbur 1964, Hofheinz 1967.
18. See Harrison 1963.
19. For a graphic account, see Wilson 1971.
20. See Hsiao Tso-liang 1967.
21. See Israel 1966, Chapter 5.
22. See Snow 1961, Part 12.
23. Schram 1966, p. 217.
24. Selden 1971, p. 179.
25. For a description of the crisis, see Selden 1971, Chapter 5.

1 FROM YENAN TO VICTORY (1942-50)

The first of the nine cycles discussed in this book began in 1942 with a moderate period of radicalism, accelerated in 1946, deradicalised after 1948 and ended about the time of the outbreak of hostilities in Korea. The period saw the formulation of what has been called the Yenan model of administration and participation (1942-3), victory over Japan (1945), the Civil War (1946-9) and the establishment of the Chinese People's Republic (1949).

The Yenan Model of Administration and Participation[1]

The crisis facing the border regions in 1942 had revealed a defective local leadership. The first and most important feature of the Yenan model, therefore, was the desire to improve that leadership in a process known as 'rectification' (*zhengfeng*). In the rectification movement of 1942, leaders learned how to apply Marxist-Leninist theory to their concrete environment and were made to answer for their conduct in the field. With the rapid expansion of the Party from some 40,000 in 1937 to some 800,000 in 1940, the quality of Party members and leaders deteriorated to the point that many merely mouthed slogans and behaved as bureaucratically as any Nanking official. Launching the rectification movement in February 1942, Mao was acutely conscious that the target should not only be intellectuals from the coastal cities, steeped in foreign knowledge, but 'dogmatists' such as Wang Ming who believed they had a Marxist-Leninist approach. As he was to remark during the course of the movement:

> We do not study Marxism-Leninism because it is pleasing to the eye or because it has some mystical value, like the doctrine of the Taoist priests who ascend Mao Shan to learn how to subdue devils and evil spirits. Marxism-Leninism has no beauty, nor has it any mystical value. It is only extremely useful. It seems that right up to the present quite a few have regarded Marxism-Leninism as a ready-made panacea; once you have it you can cure all your ills with little effort. This is a type of childish blindness and we must start a movement to enlighten these people. Those who regard Marxism-Leninism as religious dogma show this type of blind ignorance. We must tell them openly, 'your dogma is of no use' or to use an impolite phrase

31

'your dogma is less useful than excrement'. We see that dog excrement can fertilise the fields and Man's can feed the dog. And dogmas? They can't fertilise the fields nor can they feed the dog. Of what use are they?[2]

Clearly then, one of the major targets was those who blindly worshipped the Soviet Union. During the course of the movement, all cadres were submitted to 'struggle' within small groups under psychological stress; the object of struggle was then reincorporated into the group. The metaphor that was drawn was 'curing the sickness to save the patient' which was vastly different from the metaphor, often drawn by Stalin, of the surgeon amputating the diseased limb. The movement, therefore, was not a 'purge' but a method of internalising prescribed group norms. The mode of conflict management here was not the traditional conflict *avoidance* but conflict *stimulation* within the individual. Conflict within the individual was prescribed as was competition and conflict between groups and classes but not between individuals the dominant Western pattern).[3]

One of the primary aims of the rectification movement, which was centred around 27 documents[4] (of which only four derived from the Soviet Union), was to create a new leadership type – the 'cadre'. The nature of this second feature of the Yenan model may best be understood in terms of the characterisation made by Franz Schurmann. Whereas the traditional bureaucrat operated in a network of human solidarity (between human beings and groups of human beings), he was also directed towards the preservation of the status quo. The ideal cadre also operated within a network of human solidarity but was directed towards *change*. Both these types of leadership differ considerably from those types with which we are more familiar in our own society characterised by technological solidarity (between roles and structures) – the manager (directed towards change) and the modern bureaucrat (directed towards maintaining the status quo). In simple form, Schurmann's matrix is as follows:[5]

Type of social solidarity	Commitment to change	Commitment to status quo
HUMAN	CADRE	TRADITIONAL BUREAUCRAT
TECHNOLOGICAL	MANAGER	MODERN BUREAUCRAT

The ideal cadre should preferably be young. He should be a leader rather than a conciliator, but should persuade rather than command. He should participate in 'criticism and self-criticism' both as part of the rectification process and in the course of his normal work. He should be responsive to those amongst whom he operates and their reactions to him should be recorded in a dossier which might be scrutinised by the Party leadership during a rectification session.

The commitment of the cadre was to the Party as the symbol of a transition to socialism rather than to the Party as an *organisation*. Perhaps a religious analogy might clarify this notion. The cadre is like the Protestant whose commitment is directly to God rather than the Church and who seeks inspiration in the *Word* which is not interpreted for him but which only has meaning for him in practical life. He is not like the Catholic, whose commitment to God is through the Church and who deals with a number of agents who interpret the word for him and mediate between him and God. The cadre's guilt orientation is not absolved in the private confessional but in his work within a group.

Precisely because the cadre operates in a network of human solidarity, as opposed to technological solidarity, his commitment is first to 'virtue' (*de*) (self-awareness of action and motive) rather than 'ability' (*cai*) (knowing how to do things and having the talent to do them).[6] Though he may serve very different classes and groups in society, this pattern of commitment is precisely the same as the traditional bureaucrat and there is always a possibility that the cadre might slip back into this traditional leadership type. Hence the need for rectification.

This sociological characterisation of cadre leadership has been made only recently because of the dominant and erroneous assumption of the 1950s that institutional leadership and personal leadership are mutually exclusive. It leads us to the third feature of the Yenan model – the relationship between leaders and led known as the 'Mass Line'. In its 1943 form, the Mass Line was spelt out as follows:

> In all the practical work of our Party, all correct leadership is necessarily from the masses, to the masses. This means: take the ideas of the masses (scattered and unsystematic ideas) and concentrate them (through study, turn them into concentrated and systematic ideas), then go to the masses and propagate and explain these ideas until the masses embrace them as their own, hold fast to them and translate them into action, and test the correctness of these ideas in such action. Then once again concentrate ideas from the masses and once again go to the masses so that the ideas are perse-

vered in and carried through. And so on over and over again in an
endless spiral with the ideas becoming more correct, more vital and
richer every time. Such is the Marxist theory of knowledge.[7]

What this meant in practice was that each leader at each level of organisation was required, as part of his job, to explain policy to those he
operated amongst and to collect their opinions for processing into
future policy. The cadre was required to tread the narrow path between
'commandism' (relying too much on central policy directives) and
'tailism' (just doing what the masses wanted without regard to central
policy. Although (like all leadership strategies) this process was open to
manipulation, it was intended to prevent cadres behaving in a routine
manner. It provided material for the criticism and self-criticism to keep
the cadre on his toes. It also dealt squarely with what Mao felt was a
contradictory relationship between leaders and led and avoided the con-
venient assumption of Stalinists that, given the right class composition
and the right political line, one could assume identity between all members of an organisation who were not actively counter-revolutionary.
Indeed, it was this assumption that led Stalin to brand even minor
deviations as counter-revolutionary acts maliciously contrived.

To facilitate the operation of the Mass Line, there was the assumption of a dichotomy between broadly determined *policy* and routine or
specific *operations*. For this reason, policy tended to be kept general
and unspecific to allow for optimum flexibility and leeway. There was
also the assumption that cadres would not remain in their offices but
would go out and solicit mass opinions. This leads us to a fourth feature
of the Yenan model — the *xiaxiang* ('to the countryside') movement.
During the course of this movement, large numbers of office workers
and intellectuals were required to spend a period of time in the countryside to integrate with the people they were serving. As well as educating
the cadres, this movement fulfilled a number of other functions. It
helped get the harvest in when there was a manpower shortage. It provided personnel to counter the influence of those landlords and members of the old rural élite whose power had increased following the
cessation of land reform. It brought senior leadership into contact with
local poorly-educated cadres deprived of their leading position once the
great influx of new people began with the arrival of the Long March. It
helped form peasant organisations to replace the centrally controlled
work-teams that hitherto had constituted the major instrument for
dealing with rural problems and also provided a supplement to the
inadequate supply of teachers in the border region.

As one might have expected, the process of *xiaxiang* generated some hostility amongst members of the former rural élite and among local cadres who felt that the movement was aimed at usurping their position. Some of the rusticated personnel did not regard their new position with equanimity but most accounts of the time speak of the exhilaration of participating in a historic mission.

In addition to the above, one of the more important functions of the *xiaxiang* movement was connected with a fifth feature of the Yenan model — the movement to streamline administration (or as it was known the 'Movement For Crack Troops and Simple Administration'), since the *xiaxiang* process could absorb many retrenched cadres. During the streamlining movement, the number of full-time cadres in mass organisations (labour unions, Women's Federation, etc.) was halved. The number of cadres located at sub-region, *xian* and *qu* (the next level down) was reduced by 15 per cent and militia cadres were deprived of their separate salary. For example, of 55 cadres in Yen Ch'uan *xian*, 17 were retrenched of whom 11 resumed full-time work in production, four became heads of *xiang* and two were sent to Yenan to study.[8] As a consequence of this reduction of personnel, there was a partial move to what some sociologists refer to as *functional* as opposed to *staff-line* leadership. That is to say, there was a greater tendency for a person who had a particular skill to be deployed when and where he was needed rather than to locate him at a particular point in an administrative hierarchy where he could only advise a leader at one position in the direct line of command. One of the drawbacks of functional leadership in such a situation was that a person fulfilling a particular role might increasingly see his own position defined only according to that role and this would militate against social solidarity defined in *human* terms. Here again was need for constant rectification and constant retrenchment and at least temporary exchange of roles. Such was Mao's practical application of a commitment to socialism which attempted to reduce the alienation[9] caused by the division of labour; a problem which the Soviet Union never really solved.

The retrenchment of cadres made available people to penetrate the natural village.[10] Such a policy, which no government administration had succeeded in carrying out for many hundreds of years, was one of the major achievements of the Communist Party. To prevent, however, the development of a system of attenuated lines of command, which would have made the Mass Line unworkable, a sixth feature of the Yenan model was introduced — the principle of *dual rule*.[11] This system may best be understood by examining first what it replaced —

the system of *vertical rule*. Prior to 1942, specialised chains of command, staffed almost exclusively by 'outside' intellectuals, reached right down from top to bottom according to what was known as a branch (*bumen*) principle. In practice, this meant that the local education office or the local finance department was a subdivision of a higher-level education or finance department and responsible only to that level. Thus, if two offices at a local level wished to co-ordinate their activities, they could only do so through higher-level organs at that point where the matter in hand was authorised to be settled (which might be at the very apex of the hierarchy). As a result of such a system lateral co-ordination was difficult, resources tended to be concentrated at higher levels of administration and there was considerable delay in the transfer of materials across branch lines. Anyone who has studied Soviet administration will be familiar with such a system which, in that country, led to severe bottlenecks in production and delays in decision-making. In the wartime situation in China, such inefficiency and delay could not be tolerated, and the new principle of dual rule specified that each office at each level of administration should be responsible not only to higher levels in the same system but also to local government via a co-ordinating committee. These co-ordinating committees were, in practice, the local Party branch. Such a system would make local administration dynamic so long as the Party remained a directing organ with as little formal structure as possible. If the Party itself were to become bureaucratised or fuse with bureaucracy and management, then co-ordination would suffer. Similarly, the considerable powers now given to local Party branches might produce a situation where *co-ordination* became *direction* and specialised vertical chains of command atrophied. A careful balance had to be maintained therefore between, on the one hand, the fusion of Party with bureaucracy and, on the other, the Party organisation taking everything on to its own shoulders. Here was another important need for on-going rectification.

The decentralisation of decision-making power to local areas and the strengthening of the power of co-ordinating committees leads us to a seventh feature of the Yenan model — user control of an increasingly informal education system.[12] The pressing educational need in the border region was seen to be not skilled manpower but rather a literate work force. In the late 1920s, the literacy rate in the Shen Kan Ning area was between 1 and 3 per cent and superstition was widespread with over 2,000 spirit mediums in operation.[13] There was a long tradition of suspicion of the values of education in these rural areas especially for women who, by infanticide, were made relatively scarce and to whom peasants were unwilling to grant the means to independence. With the onset of fighting and the economic blockade, the exigencies of the war made the establishment of a formal education system very difficult, especially when imports of paper were cut off. Despite these difficulties, however, some progress was made, in the early years, in establishing a formal school system based on structures and methods currently employed in the eastern coastal ports and run by intellectuals from those areas. The stress was on formal lectures, strict entrance examinations and the standardisation of curricula. Despite the phenomenal rise in the numbers of students engaged in formal education (the number in primary schools in the region leapt from 5,600 in 1937 to some 22,000 in 1939),[14] the impact was inadequate and the peasant hostility towards book learning had not been overcome. In 1943, therefore, following administrative decentralisation, the bureaucratic educational hierarchy was broken down and a large portion of the educational effort handed over to *xiang* and village cadres. The number of courses was reduced and courses made more relevant to the needs of agriculture and the war effort.

The stress now was on mutual learning among the peasants who were invited not only to give talks based on their experiences but to take part in school administration and help establish schools attached to units of production. Such was the origin of the *minbangongzhu* ('people run, public help') schools. The idea was that everyone could in some way participate in the educational process as student or teacher. The peasant associations could assist with housing; the spinning and weaving co-ops could provide for the clothing of students and teachers; the schools could run their own agricultural enterprises and could thus attune themselves to the harmony of rural life. In short, the approach was to produce an education system which sought to *create* the environment for mass education rather than to *select* an educated élite. If formal standards suffered in the process, then surely these would be offset by the long-term gains in mass literacy, without which many other features of the Yenan model such as the Mass Line and the training of cadres would suffer.

There was, however, to be a serious problem. Although *minban* education was considerably expanded, the formal school system co-existed beside it. Such a 'two-track' system might make the *minban* idea merely subsidiary to the effort of selecting trained personnel who might increasingly see themselves in a privileged position. I shall return to this problem in the subsequent discussion of the 1960s, for this was to be one of the main bones of contention in the early Cultural Revolution of 1966.

The breakdown of the division of labour within the border region leads us to an eighth feature of the Yenan model. The severe economic privation in 1943 was countered by the insistence that, wherever possible, military and civilian organisations should merge and that each unit of administration, whether civilian or military, should engage in production and aim at self-sufficiency. Back in 1936, some moves had been made in this direction but it was not until 1943 that the Party insisted that *all* cadres should take part both in productive labour and management and that military units should seek self-sufficiency when not in combat. The model here was the 359th Brigade under Wang Chen (subsequently Minister of Land Reclamation) which opened up new land around Nanniwan and managed to recover 82 per cent of the cost of its upkeep. Enthusiastically, Mao called upon all units to strive for 80 per cent self-sufficiency and, although most units never got beyond one-third or one-half, this was nonetheless a remarkable achievement. Some indication of the achievement is provided in the 1944 budget which was worked out as the equivalent of 260,000 piculs of millet (this being the currency standard) of which 100,000 was to be produced by units and agencies of government themselves.[15] Though the stress on self-sufficiency and ingenuity was, in many ways, dictated by a particular objective situation, Nanniwan was to serve as a model for the next three decades.

But in the main agricultural field, any attempts at radical reform were hampered by the provisions of the United Front whereby outright confiscation of landlords' property had been replaced by periodic campaigns aimed at rent reduction. With the breakdown of the United Front, these campaigns became more significant and the strengthening of Party branches at village level made the campaign style of politics much easier, particularly since vertical bureaucratic barriers in administration had been weakened. Nevertheless, the rent ceiling was still set at the remarkably high figure of 37.5 per cent of crop (deliberately chosen, for this had been the stipulation of an old Kuomintang law which that party had been unable or unwilling to put into effect). If landlords resisted, occasional coercion was employed but a real problem remained whereby each campaign would adjust rent ceilings which might be raised again once the campaign was over. In such a situation, despite the view commonly held in the West at the time that the Communists were no more than 'agrarian reformers',[16] the original aim of the Party to break the power of the landlords remained in the background and, as an initial step towards its realisation, a programme of co-operativisation was launched.

In the early years of the border regions, attempts to effect a rudimentary form of co-operativisation had been undertaken by *work-teams* sent down from above which were regarded correctly by peasants as agencies of central government. With the reforms of 1942-3, newly formed *peasant associations* were given the task of forming co-operatives and the role of the cadre sent down from above was merely that of initiator. A policy of Mao, attempted in the Kiangsi Soviet, to transform existing patterns of organisation from within now came to the fore once again and traditional forms of labour organisation were incorporated into the peasant association structure with a minimum of interference from the outside. By the beginning of 1943, only some 15 per cent of the full-time labour power of the Shen Kan Ning border region had been organised into various forms of mutual aid team. By the summer of 1943, 25-40 per cent had participated in the co-operativisation movement and, in 1944, 50-75 per cent.[17] This figure declined in 1945 to 28-45 per cent with the rapid expansion of the region and the consolidation of previous gains. By that time, however, the institution of peasant associations had been firmly established and, once radical land reform was resumed again during the Civil War, these associations were to play an important part in restructuring the countryside. Co-operativisation, therefore, was the ninth feature of the Yenan model and indeed one of its most significant for we shall see again the conflict between the *work-team* and *peasant association* approach to rural mobilisation and shall dwell at length on one of the weaknesses of an approach which sought social transformation from within. Although such a policy may prevent alienation, there was always the possibility that the Party might fail to take over existing leadership and existing forms of organisation and those leaders and those organisations might, in some cases, take over the Party.

The final feature of the Yenan model we shall consider here concerns industry which was comparatively underdeveloped in the border regions during the war. I mentioned earlier that the operation of the Mass Line involved a separation between broadly defined *policy* and specific *operations* and the tendency in organisation towards functional patterns of leadership as opposed to the Soviet-style staff-line systems. In industry, this took the form of a policy known as 'concentrated leadership and divided operations' (*jizhong lingdao fensan jingying*), whereby general targets were set centrally but where scattered units of production were allowed operational independence. In such a system, expertise might be deployed over a wide area rather than concentrated in a particular location. The dispersal of industry was useful in time of war when

transport costs were high and there was a danger of enemy air attack.
More importantly, the dispersal of industry led to the spreading of
technical skills and the development of a rudimentary intermediate
technology which married in with the traditional handicrafts and what
little modern industry there was. Such a policy probably owed much to
experiments in industrial co-operation carried out independently of the
Communist Party.[18] It was to develop, however, into a cardinal element
of Mao's economic strategy. Bringing industry to the peasants and
decentralising operational decision-making was a significant break from
the Soviet tradition

Some features of the Soviet experience were, however, employed in
the Yenan area such as the fostering of labour models based on the
Stakhanovite system.[19] Though this policy was often individualistic,
the stress was usually on the *collective* dimensions of incentive rather
than the *individual* dimensions and the wartime situation generated a
significant degree of *moral* incentive to counter *material* incentive. In
subsequent chapters, we shall explore the extent to which the above
pattern was seen to be a temporary expedient and the extent to which
it offered a blueprint for the whole of a modernising society. All I
need say here is that the ten features of the Yenan model I have
enumerated above were all to reappear subsequently and to be the
subject of intense polemic.

In concluding this section, something must be said about the extent
to which the success enjoyed by the Communist Party during the war
was due to the implementation of the above Yenan model rather than
to 'peasant nationalism' engendered by Japanese brutality. The latter
position is articulated, in its clearest form, by Chalmers Johnson in his
Peasant Nationalism and Communist Power[20] which starts from the
assumption that the Kiangsi Soviet did not enjoy much peasant support
and it was mainly the policies of the Japanese that drove the peasants
into the arms of the Communist Party. In contrast, Mark Selden, in
The Yenan Way in Revolutionary China, stresses the success of domestic policies. In my view, Johnson's characterisation of the Kiangsi
Soviet is in the main incorrect although, to be sure, peasant support for
the Communist Party was much stronger in the Yenan period.
Johnson's weakness, I feel, lies in his concentration largely on Japanese
sources to prove the significance of Japan. There is no doubt, however,
that the Yenan model owed its very form to the Party's reassessment
of its position after the Japanese 'Three All' policy and that many of
its features were conditioned if not determined by the wartime situation. The Japanese might have provided the Chinese peasants with a

definable enemy they could fight *against* but the Yenan model gave
those same peasants something they could fight *for* — on the one hand
a fairer deal at the hands of landlords and on the other an opportunity
to participate in basic-level administration. Johnson's case would be
substantiated if only one could show that the Kuomintang offered an
alternative to the Yenan model, the implementation of which was frustrated by the war. I see no evidence that the Kuomintang did offer
such an alternative and the wartime land reform of the Kuomintang
seems to have been directed not so much against the institution of
landlords as against those landlords in south-west China whose primary
allegiance was not to the new arrivals from east China but to the former
local semi-warlord regime. It is my view, therefore, that the relative
contributions of Japanese brutality and Communist Party domestic
policy towards Communist Party success cannot be determined, for
they constitute a dialectical relationship and one cannot be dissociated
from the other.

The Japanese Surrender

The Yenan model constituted a rejection of alien models of development and prepacked strategies from which China had suffered all too
much in the past. In this sense, the model was implicitly critical of the
Soviet Union. The role of the Soviet Union as the first socialist state,
however, was consistently upheld and the writings of Lenin and Stalin
figured in the rectification campaign.[21] By the 1940s Mao had also
written a number of introductory philosophical works,[22] which meant
that the newly literate peasant's introduction to Marxism-Leninism
would henceforth be via the writings of Mao which were firmly rooted
in the Chinese situation. It was appropriately at this point that the
Comintern was dissolved (1943) and Stalin's major preoccupation
became, quite naturally, the war in his own country.

In 1943, the war in China was not a major concern of the Soviet
Union, which had yet to declare war on Japan. It was, however, of
crucial importance to the United States. In that year, the Americans
beheld an enigmatic Chiang K'ai-shek going through a Confucian meta-
morphosis[23] though in practice his military inactivity, in the mountain
fastness of Szechwan, was more akin to the Taoist doctrine of *wuwei*
(doing nothing). As the Kuomintang contribution to the Allied war
effort sank to almost zero, Chiang was challenged by an exasperated
American General Stilwell[24] and was prodded firmly, but more
diplomatically, by the American government. The Americans began to
realise that the brunt of the war with Japan in China was being borne

not by Chiang but by the forces led by the Communist Party in the
north.

Not long after the Yenan *Liberation Daily* (*Jiefang Ribao*) published
its 1944 4 July editorial on the parallel between the Communist Party's
struggle and that of George Washington,[25] an American mission was
sent to Yenan.[26] When President Roosevelt sought to achieve the
appointment of General Stilwell as supreme Allied commander, he was
supported by, of all people, Mao Tse-tung against the opposition of
Chiang K'ai-shek. In the end, however, Chiang was to be victorious.
Wedemeyer replaced Stilwell and a new American ambassador to China,
Patrick Hurley, proved singularly inept at negotiating between the
Kuomintang and the Communist Party. An agreement, concluded
between Hurley and Mao to support a coalition government, was
vetoed by Chiang to whose camp Hurley eventually gravitated. A chain
of events was then set in motion which culminated in increasing enmity
between the United States and the Chinese Communist Party and the
eventual purge of those American officials who had gone to Yenan in
1944.

By the Seventh Congress of the Chinese Communist Party in April
1945, it was clear that the Party depended on the support of no outside
body. The mood was confidently defiant. The Thought of Mao Tse-tung,
as the practical application of Marxism-Leninism to the Chinese situation, was given particular prominence in the new Party constitution[27]
and it was claimed that the oppressed peoples in all countries could
profit from a study of the experiences of the Chinese Revolution. Now
that the forces led by the Communist Party were approaching one
million and areas under the various Communist Party-led governments
contained a population of some 100 million, Stalin feared that once
the war with Japan was over, the Chinese Civil War would erupt once
again and go on for a very long time. In such a war he felt the Chinese
Communist Party had a very slim chance of success.[28] In the meantime, a weakened China would leave the long Sino-Soviet frontier
exposed to any future enemy. The best policy of the Soviet Union,
therefore, was to conclude an alliance with Chiang K'ai-shek and
attempt to prevent the Chinese Civil War.

With the dropping of atomic bombs on Japan and the Soviet declara-
tion of war, the Russian Red Army poured into the former state of
Manchukuo in an attempt to secure an area that had been strategically
important since the Russo-Japanese war of 1904-5. On the very day of
Japan's surrender (14 August), an alliance was concluded between
Moscow and the regime of Chiang K'ai-shek which stipulated that, once

Soviet troops were withdrawn from north-east China, the area would be handed over to the Kuomintang government.[29] To cap it all, the Soviet government had stressed the urgency of an alliance on the grounds that any delay would allow the forces led by the Chinese Communist Party to get there first.[30] Although this was clearly a diplomatic ploy, it did not attest to the reliability of the socialist ally of the Chinese Communist Party.

With the surrender of Japan, the Kuomintang and Japanese armies co-operated in preventing Japanese troops from surrendering to those led by the Communist Party. In some cases, the Japanese continued to fight Communist Party-led troops with the tacit support of the Kuomintang. As civil war seemed imminent, Mao and Chiang met in Chungking to negotiate a *modus vivendi*.[31] An agreement was concluded on 10 October 1946 but almost immediately Chiang's forces intensified their attack on the base areas and hurriedly availed themselves of American transport to ferry troops to the Soviet-occupied north-east. The Soviet response was inexplicable. Despite certain sympathy expressed to Chiang in August, the Red Army proceeded to give aid to the Communist forces until November and then changed to a policy of actively aiding Chiang K'ai-shek. By spring 1946, the Soviet position had changed yet again.[32] Meanwhile, vast amounts of industrial equipment in north-east China were dismantled and shipped off to the Soviet Union.[33] The American position was equally confusing. Considerable aid was given to Chiang K'ai-shek yet, at the same time, an American mission under General Marshall proceeded to negotiate between the two sides.[34] By mid-1946, however, the Civil War was on in earnest and the initial struggle centred on control over the north-east in the wake of the withdrawing Soviet troops.

It is not my intention here to go into the various campaigns of the Civil War.[35] I shall, however, devote some attention to the various and different policies put forward by the Communist Party during the war which provide a background for the establishment of the People's Republic. In the very early period, these policies were to be far more radical than any of those implemented in Yenan.

Rural Policy (1946-9)

With the onset of the Civil War, Mao's policies on 'People's War' emerged in their fullest form. In the early period, attention was devoted to building up strength in the countryside and the main focus of the fighting consisted of guerrilla engagements. To facilitate this, a huge militia was created[36] which fed recruits into the guerrilla forces and

these in turn provided recruits for the regular forces which in 1947
were to be renamed the Chinese People's Liberation Army (PLA). The
notion of unity of work and arms, which had been developed in Yenan
days, received a new emphasis but the situation was somewhat different
from the early 1940s. The co-operatives which had been formed at that
time were frequently identical with units of the people's militia and
such a situation facilitated the initial penetration of the natural village
and the financing of the war effort. Soldiers on the march had been
given work tickets which expressed a certain period of active service as
the equivalent of so many days' farm work and which were repayable
according to a millet standard of currency.[37] When no fighting was
necessary, soldiers might return to farm work or at least help train the
local militia units which were also engaged in political work. Such a
system worked best when the regular army was relatively small, when
its area of operations was concentrated and where armies remained near
to their place of original recruitment. But after 1946 it became increasingly difficult for troops to return to farm work. On the one hand,
there were fewer breaks in the fighting and on the other, troops were
moved over great distances with the result that their knowledge of the
area in which they operated was not as great as their old Eighth Route
Army predecessors. Consequently, the Party had to rely more and
more on the rapid development of village activists (jijifenzi) to insti-
gate rural reforms.[38] This was particularly important for three reasons.
First, the enemy was no longer a foreign aggressor but Kuomintang
troops who often had close relations with landowners in their areas of
operation. Secondly, at the beginning of the war, these Kuomintang
troops far outnumbered those of the Communist Party. In the old
Japanese occupation days, the enemy was greatly overextended and
resorted merely to periodic (though savage) 'mopping-up' (saodang)
operations. Now the resources at the disposal of the Kuomintang
allowed for permanent instruments of repression to be continually
buttressed by Kuomintang military force. Thirdly, as the Civil War
erupted, a new radical land reform policy was instituted which no
longer favoured the rich peasants. As the focus of attention switched
to 'poor and lower middle peasants', intensive mass mobilisation was
seen as imperative.

The new radical period of land reform commenced with a Party
directive of May 1946 and a draft Land Reform Law was passed at a
national agricultural conference in September of that year. In October
1947, this law was finally formally adopted. It stipulated that all
property of landlords and land owned by the (Kuomintang) state were

subject to confiscation; additionally all property above the general average (which included that of rich peasants) was confiscated and redistributed, but peasants still retained the right to buy and sell land.[39] The cadres recruited to implement this policy had first to seize power from village elders but, if they were to do this according to the Yenan principle, mass mobilisation had to come first; meanwhile village elders would do all within their power to frustrate this process. It was all too easy, therefore, for work-teams to descend upon the village and impose policies from above,[40] which was a violation of the Yenan principle and might generate mass hostility.

The above 'commandist' deviation could dampen mass enthusiasm but the opposite 'tailist' deviation could produce an equally unsatisfactory result. Traditional social structure within villages frequently cut across class lines. Organisations such as the clan (lineage) or the secret society would contain both landlords and rich peasants and the network of loyalties within them frustrated any attempt by an outside organisation to penetrate the villages, closed the ranks of the clan and caused fragmentation on a non-class basis. The Yenan pattern had been to utilise existing members of these organisations to weaken the structure of loyalties and, over a period of time, to heighten consciousness of class divisions within them. This task had been facilitated by the relatively mild land reform policy. Now with the occupation of vast expanses of new territory with a new land reform policy, cadres frequently encountered a situation where peasants were unwilling to be mobilised either because they did not perceive their class interests or because, in a wartime situation of rapidly shifting fronts, they feared Kuomintang reprisals once the PLA withdrew. Participation in land reform was a commitment to the whole process of revolution and was not made lightly.

Peasants, therefore, could not drift into the process of land reform as had been possible in Yenan days. A conscious act of repudiation of traditional loyalties was required. Such an act tended to be made suddenly and in a highly charged emotional atmosphere which the Communist Party cadres sought to create. Struggle sessions were held at which landlords stood with heads bowed and were humiliated. As more and more peasants joined in the process of denunciation, they symbolised their irrevocable commitment by burning land titles and mortgage agreements. The result was a snowball effect; or, as one writer put it, the process was a veritable 'hurricane'.[41] Peasants, who for a long period had resisted mobilisation, now took the law into their own hands and were often as unresponsive to Party cadres as they had been in the early days of mobilisation. The Land Reform Law had stipulated that only landlords guilty of certain crimes should be punished and that others should be given a share of land after redistribution. But what was the Party to do in a situation where decades of bottled-up hatred and resentment finally exploded and resulted in the victimisation or summary execution of landlords? A 'tailist' solution, whereby inexperienced rural cadres just went along with spontaneous peasant action and random seizure of land, was clearly not what was required. Yet if controls were applied harshly by work-teams sent down from above, peasants might be alienated and further administrative reform made difficult.

The problem was compounded by the fact that, due to the exigencies of war and the concentration on areas of actual conflict, the Party network in rural areas was weak. Moreover, a situation might occur where cadres adopted a radical approach to land reform and a highly conservative attitude towards other issues such as the rights of women.[42] Pending adoption of a Marriage Law, cadres had to deal with knotty problems such as what to do with a woman who was formerly half-owned by her husband and half-owned by a landlord. With the demise of the landlord, was she wholly owned by her husband or owned by neither? The answer was obvious, one might assume, but not to the cadre who had thought about nothing but the problem of land.

As one might expect, there was consensus in the Party that something had to be done about what the Party historian Ho Kan-chih called 'erroneous dispersionism, lack of discipline and anarchy at work' and situations where inexperienced cadres were guilty of 'free actions in political affairs, a dislike of Party leadership and supervision and a disrespect for the decisions made by the Central Committee and higher echelons'.[43] It was generally agreed that a rectification movement was necessary but the attitude towards the movement, which was launched in February 1948, varied amongst different cadres and different members of the Party leadership. The bone of contention seems to have been what was the permissible degree of central control. Party conservatives tended to favour a concentration on the use of work-teams from above while radicals stressed more the role of peasant associations and expressed confidence in the ability of these organisations to discipline themselves. The conservatives were eventually to prevail. With the Second Plenum of the Seventh Central Committee in March 1949, the Party announced that the main focus of its work was to shift from the rural areas to the cities[44] and, by late 1949 a new land law had been formulated which was less radical than the original 1947 one.[45] Stability was, for the moment, considered more important than radical reform. Such was the genesis of what was later referred to as 'The Rich Peasant Line'.

Urban Policy (1946-9)

In the urban and industrial sectors, a similar pattern of radicalisation followed by deradicalisation occurred, with rank and file cadres tending to be somewhat more radical than the centre. In the early part of the Civil War, a considerable amount of industrial equipment had been removed either by the Soviet armies occupying north-east China or by the retreating Kuomintang. Machinery too had been destroyed by Communist Party-led troops guilty of 'left deviation' or to prevent it falling into enemy hands once a particular town was abandoned. By December 1947, however, it had become clear that from then on, cities would be occupied permanently and a clear policy was enunciated by Mao Tse-tung that the takeover (jieguan) of industry was to cause as little disruption as possible.[46] Nevertheless, however mild the policy was after that date, the confused military situation still led to considerable damage. The mammoth Anshan Iron and Steel Works, for example, which was later to be the keystone of China's First Five Year Plan (1953-7), did not resume production after the war with Japan until 1947, after which it changed hands no less than seven times between February and November 1948.[47] As it had already been ransacked by occupying Soviet troops, this further damage was disastrous.

The increasingly mild policy towards industrial takeover was reflected in the resolutions of the Sixth Labour Conference which met in Harbin in August 1948[48] and which attempted to establish a transitional structure for industrial enterprises, but, even at that late date, the north-east bureau of the Party was reluctant to employ Kuomintang members in senior management positions.[49] The Party was particularly suspicious of those Kuomintang government appointees who had been sent to take over industrial concerns from former Japanese management in 1945.[50]

The great problem that faced the new administration in China's heavy industrial heartland, north-east China, was not only that much of industry was not operational but that many senior management personnel had been transferred to the south by the retreating Kuomintang forces. Regional government, therefore, was required to appoint new and inexperienced people to senior management positions often from outside the industrial sector. These people were occasionally attacked for maintaining 'the line of the poor peasant and hired hand' (they paid no attention to orderly planning).[51] But, as more senior

management and administrators were found still at their posts as the
PLA moved south, the policy of industrial and urban takeover became
more and more restrained. An urban equivalent of the 'Rich Peasant
Line' was apparent.

The Collapse of the Kuomintang

By the end of 1947, the numerical superiority of the Kuomintang over
the People's Liberation Army had been reduced from 4 to 1 (in 1945)
to 2 to 1 and, from then on, smaller towns tended to be occupied
permanently.[52] In late 1948, parity in forces had been reached in part
due to large-scale defection of Kuomintang forces to the side of the
PLA. Up to that year, two-thirds of recruits were from the peasants and
only one-third from Kuomintang defectors but the situation was to
change so drastically that, by the end of the war, it was reckoned that
two-fifths of the PLA strength of 5 million were from the Kuomintang.[53]
There was no course but to retain such troops since there was often
nowhere to demobilise them, and one of the plagues of China's history
had been demobilised troops who had turned to banditry.

To counter the influence of Kuomintang defectors and also as a consequence of the Yenan tradition, a system of 'military democracy' prevailed in the PLA ranks. When not in combat, the most important
figure in a military unit would be the political instructor or commissar
who was frequently also the secretary of a military Party branch. At
such times, soldiers were encouraged to criticise their officers and might
nominate non-commissioned officers (if that term has any meaning in
an army that had appointments but no ranks), though such nominations
were subject to ratification by higher levels. The old Eighth Route
Army tradition of not appropriating the property of civilians was maintained though it was often difficult to enforce at a time of rapid expansion and increasing defection from the enemy. Relations with the mass
of the people were, on the whole, very good and in the major campaigns, especially as the focus switched to east China, peasants provided
large numbers of auxiliaries.[54] Yet gradually the expanded army took
on a new character: a large conglomerate army was not the small, well-
disciplined force that had fought the Japanese.

The turning point of the Civil War came in the autumn of 1948. By
that time, not only had the PLA achieved parity in numbers with the
Kuomintang forces but the international environment had begun to
change. In the early stages of the Civil War, the United States had
given considerable aid to Chiang K'ai-shek and the degree to which that
country should prop up the Kuomintang became an important issue in

the United States presidential election. With the unexpected defeat of
the pro-Chiang candidate Thomas Dewey, Mao Tse-tung could see that
large scale aid was a thing of the past. In the United States, the talk was
of negotiations and peace and influential journals such as the *New York
Times* and *Business Week* urged that their government should stop
supporting Chiang for fear of driving the Communist Party further into
the arms of the Soviet Union.

The Chinese Communist Party's perception of the change in United
States policy was not that imperialism was any less of an ultimate
threat; merely that in the immediate future, the United States was
unlikely to intervene in China, in her offshore islands such as T'aiwan,
or for that matter in Korea. Indeed, by mid-1949, United States forces
had been removed from Korea and even such a 'hawk' as General
MacArthur, who had fostered policies such as the rearmament of Japan,
declared that it was not America's intention to fight a war on the Asian
mainland.[55] American intervention now was to consist largely of economic blockade and financial aid to Chiang; intervention was to be no
more active than it had been in Greece.

In the autumn of 1948, the PLA swung into a massive offensive in
north-east China. Following the capture of the north-eastern capital of
Shenyang, the policy was to seize the major cities. As the Communist
Party leaders constantly updated their estimate of the end of the war,
the Kuomintang regime crumbled. Peip'ing (soon to be renamed
Peking) negotiated a surrender and, in a last bid to negotiate a settlement, Chiang resigned in favour of his vice president, Li Tsung-jen. In
April 1949, the terms proposed by the Communist Party were rejected
and the PLA crossed the Yangtze. A demoralised south China, ruined
by catastrophic inflation and having lost its confidence in the
Kuomintang's military ability, fell rapidly to pieces. By the time of the
inauguration of the Chinese People's Republic on 1 October 1949,
Chiang K'ai-shek had retreated to the offshore island of T'aiwan.

A regime which had showed little inclination to fight the Japanese or
to ally itself effectively with forces that were fighting the Japanese,
which by 1949 was riddled with corruption and had allowed a catastrophic inflation to develop, which had been co-opted by old rural élites
and which had even convinced the United States that to continue aiding
it would mean casting money down a bottomless well, was indeed one
worthy of opposition. The opposition had come from many different
quarters – workers, peasants, nationalists, frustrated businessmen, dis-
pirited generals and even those who still maintained the ideals of the
'revolutionary Kuomintang'. The Communist Party did more than offer

just an alternative regime tried and tested in the wartime border regions. Like the Kuomintang in the 1920s, it also offered the vision of an alternative society which promised to redress the humiliations of a century. In such a situation, the decay of the Kuomintang probably hastened the birth of that society.

'Leaning to One Side'

As the Civil War reached its climax in 1949, the United States seemed, for the time being, to have cut its losses in Asia. As the fighting in Indo-China and in Korea itensified, it seemed to the Chinese Communist Party that a United States *cordon sanitaire* would be drawn far from China's borders and would not be sharply demarcated. The Party's long-term concern, which was treated with the utmost seriousness, concerned the activities of General MacArthur in Japan.[56] It is not difficult for us to imagine China's apprehension concerning a rearmed Japan, which, if anything, was greater than Soviet apprehension about a rearmed Germany. China, therefore, had misgivings about a future United States-Japanese threat, which led Mao Tse-tung to declare unequivocally that China would 'lean to the side' of the Soviet Union,[57] despite the treatment China had received at Soviet hands. In the immediate future, however, the United States seemed to pose little danger and it is possible that diplomatic relations might have been established, at least on the same partial basis that they were with Britain not long after the creation of the People's Republic. China showed no intention of intervening in Indo-China or Korea and it seemed that the progress of People's War in those areas would, before long, lead to a result similar to that which had occurred in China, without much danger of American intervention. This view was of course wrong but, as Edward Friedman has argued, it was not an irrational one.[58] One cannot blame the Chinese, not skilled at this stage in 'Washingtonology', for not understanding the erroneous view gaining currency in the United States that north-east China was in the grip of the Soviet Union and that what was happening in Asia was part of some international Communist conspiracy hatched by the Cominform[59] after its establishment in 1947.[60] To the Chinese, such a view was manifestly ludicrous especially since relations with the Soviet Union were not particularly good. One may compare Chinese views of the Soviet Union and of the United States. Just as the United States was potentially very dangerous while posing little immediate threat so the Soviet Union was potentially a source of great support, though this was not immediately obvious.

We have noted the ambivalent attitude of the Soviet Union during the occupation of the north-east at the start of the Civil War when a treaty was concluded with the Kuomintang government. But by 1949, an agreement had been signed between Moscow and the Communist Party administration in north-east China[61] although, even in late 1949 when Mao Tse-tung went to Moscow to conclude a new treaty, the atmosphere was cool.[62]

The thirty-year Sino-Soviet Treaty signed in February 1950[63] reflected clearly the fear of a rearmed Japan. The two sides agreed that if either ally were attacked by Japan or any state allied with it (a reference to the United States), the other partner would immediately render military and other assistance by all means at its disposal. In a separate agreement, the Soviet Union granted trade concessions and a $300 million loan.

In return, China agreed to preserve the special rights of the Soviet Union granted by the former Kuomintang government. Joint Sino-Soviet administration was established over railways in the north-east and over the port of Lushun and Talien pending the conclusion of a peace treaty with Japan or, failing that, until 1952. A number of joint-stock companies were established in petroleum, non-ferrous metals, shipbuilding and civil aviation and the *de facto* independence of the Mongolian People's Republic (Outer Mongolia — formerly claimed by China) was guaranteed.

Despite the apparently successful conclusion of the treaty, in Mao's view, it was not until the Korean War that Stalin developed confidence in the new Chinese leadership.[64] In late 1949 and early 1950, however, American intervention in Korea could not have been foreseen.

New Democracy or People's Democratic Dictatorship

Just as the Yenan reforms took place during a period of United Front, so the social, political and economic reforms that resulted from victory in the Civil War were also seen in a United Front context. The revolution which the Communist Party led was seen not as a socialist revolution in the Marxian[65] sense but as a New Democratic Revolution (*Xin Minzhuzhuyi Geming*). Under this formulation the workers were defined as 'masters' (*zhurenweng*) but were joined in their dictatorship over the landlords and bureaucratic capitalists by three other class groupings — peasants, petty bourgeoisie, and national capitalists. This four-class bloc was defined as the 'people' (*renmin*) and was represented as the four smaller stars on the new Chinese flag. It was a somewhat wider concept than Lenin's 'democratic dictatorship of workers and peasants'.

The New Democratic Revolution was seen as a process rather than an act. The act by which the regime changed was referred to as 'liberation' (*jiefang*) and, in its individual dimension, was known as 'turning over' (*fanshen*). Likewise the construction of socialism (*shehuizhuyi jianshe*) was also seen as a process during which the composition of the concept 'people' (95 per cent of the population at that stage) would change according to the pace of transformation (*gaizao*). The key questions then were how quickly should this process develop, what was the structure of the United Front during each of its stages, and what were the policy implications of that structure.

The Establishment of Government

The principles of New Democracy had first been articulated by Mao Tse-tung back in 1940 and reformulated again in 1949 in his 'On People's Democratic Dictatorship'.[66] They were formally enshrined in official state documents in September 1949, by a body known as the Chinese People's Political Consultative Conference. The members of this body were chosen to represent the current United Front and the formal delegates represented a number of political parties and groups sympathetic to the Communist Party, geographical areas, religious groups, national minorities overseas Chinese and mass organisations (such as the All China Federation of Democratic Women).

The three major documents passed by the Conference, which were to serve as an interim constitution, were the Common Programme, the Organic Law of the Chinese People's Political Consultative Conference and the Organic Law of the Central People's Government.[67] The first of these outlined the formal content of New Democracy, stating that citizen rights would be given only to those who formally qualified as the 'people' and prescribing dictatorship over the former exploiting classes and groups that constituted the remainder. The document stipulated the abolition of imperialist privileges, the pressing need for industrialisation and the importance of friendship with the Soviet Union. It stated that the Political Consultative Conference was only to serve as a temporary body until a National People's Congress might be elected by all citizens (such a body was to meet in 1954). Until such time, a Central People's Government Council would be elected by the Conference and a National Committee (with a smaller Standing Committee) would be set up to conduct Conference affairs while the larger body (with over 500 delegates) was not in session. The second document outlined the policies and functions of the Conference in the rehabilitation of the country and procedures for the selection of delegates, and the third prescribed the initial organs of state.

The supreme government organ of the new regime was to be the Central People's Government Council, which was simultaneously a legislative, executive and judicial organ. It supervised a number of committees, the most important being the Government Administration Council headed by the premier, Chou En-lai. This latter body, which consisted also of five deputy premiers, a secretary-general and 16 members, controlled all government ministries under three very powerful committees — Political and Legal Affairs, Finance and Economics, and Culture and Education. In addition, there ranked equal to these committees a People's Control Committee charged with checking up on the operation of all ministries. Alongside the Government Administration Council, the Central People's Government Council established a Revolutionary Military Council, a Supreme People's Court and a Supreme People's Procuracy. These institutions were based on Soviet models — especially the third of these bodies which was required to ensure the observance of the law by all government officials.

Until 1954, the powers of the central government were considerably limited by those of the six large administrative regions that were set up during and after the Civil War. Of these, the first to be established, and probably the most powerful, was that of north-east China under Kao Kang, a former leader of the North Shensi Soviet area before the arrival in that area of the Long March. Devastated by war, the north-east was still the centre of China's heavy industry and the area with the closest links with the Soviet Union. In 1949, part of the region (Lushun and Talien) was still occupied by Soviet troops and the administration in that area was to serve as a model of industrial rehabilitation for those who inclined towards the Soviet Union.[68] In this region, and later elsewhere, the initiative in creating a state structure was taken by the Army. The Fourth Field Army under Lin Piao, having successfully completed its campaign in the north-east, proceeded to the Kwangtung area in south China where a Central South Administrative Region was carved out with its capital in the central China city of Wuhan. Throughout the next 20 years, key government and Party personnel in these two regions remained Fourth Field Army men with, it has been alleged, a greater or lesser attachment to their former military commander, Lin Piao. A similar pattern has been posited for north-west China (the First Field Army under Ho Lung and P'eng Teh-huai), north China (the Fifth Field Army under Nieh Jung-chen), east China (the Third Field Army under Ch'en Yi and Su Yü) and south-west China (the Second Field Army under Liu Po-ch'eng).[69] The six large administrative regions, therefore, corresponded to the zones of operations of these armies. Below them came the traditional administrative divisions — province, special district, *xian* (or urban *shi*), *xiang* (or market town *zhen*), and village. At most of the higher levels, there was initially a military control commission which operated through a number of committees (Party, economic, educational, cultural, etc.) set up on an *ad hoc* basis. The control commissions at various levels sent out special task forces to take over various institutions and these task forces, before very long, became absorbed into the institutions themselves.

The life of the military control commissions was very limited. Their function, as described by A. Doak Barnett, was similar to receivers in bankruptcy. In Peking, where takeover proceeded very smoothly, the control commission was assisted by a joint administrative office consisting of Kuomintang officials and Communist Party cadres. Once the Kuomintang members of this office had made an inventory of the assets of former government organisations and those of organisations designated as 'bureaucratic capitalist', they handed over power to a newly formed People's Government. This consisted of personnel retained from the old regime, representatives of mass organisations ('red' labour unions etc.) and Party-military personnel.[70]

This triple alliance formula was repeated at lower levels of administration though the components of the alliance varied from area to area. In north-east China, since many Kuomintang government officials had been removed before the cessation of hostilities, the component of retained personnel was comparatively small. The south, where they had concentrated before the advance of the PLA, however, provided greater numbers of experienced personnel who might be retained. Here, many senior government officials and management personnel remained at their posts upon liberation[71] and consequently the triple alliance was more evenly balanced.

Within factories, the military representatives who had been sent down by military control commissions (or their sub-committees, when they were in existence) frequently remained behind and linked the retained personnel with the mass organisations.[72] These latter were frequently the worker pickets (*gongren jiuchadui*) whose function had been to maintain factory discipline while the fighting had been going on and to undertake policing and patrolling duties pending the arrival of the PLA.[73] Sometimes these pickets maintained a city-wide organisation such as the Shanghai People's Peace Preservation Corps (*Renmin Baoandui*) which was formed by the Communist Party and which consisted of some 60,000 people, of whom 60 per cent were workers. Its members were responsible for some remarkable feats of courage in keeping production going during the battle of Shanghai.[74]

In Shanghai, the resumption of production and the restoration of order was relatively smooth. In some areas, however, disruptions occurred due to what the Party conservatives felt to be excessive radicalism on the part of the worker picket organisations. In Tientsin, for example, which had been liberated during the last phase of the northeast campaign prior to the seige of Peking and where there were relatively few retained personnel, worker organisations often disregarded Party policy, took over factory management themselves and created a considerable amount of confusion.[75] In such a situation the vice chairman of the Party, Liu Shao-ch'i, delivered his famous Tientsin talks designed to restore discipline.[76]

The situation in Tientsin was perhaps an exception but it does reveal that, in an increasingly conservative mood, the Party leadership was prepared to curb radicalism and make concessions to the employees of the former government. When they were in existence, considerable autonomy seems to have been given to military control commissions or takeover groups in deciding who was suitable for re-employment, and the urgent need to establish the organs of state resulted in very elastic standards In public security work in particular, the disappearance of former policemen was initially made up for by the employment of PLA troops though a number of former Kuomintang government policemen were reinstated.[77] The credentials of these policemen were not always impeccable from a Communist Party point of view. Nor were the former civil servants who were now employed in civil affairs bureaux comparable to the former cadres of Yenan days and it was felt necessary to balance their influence by the recruitment of a large number of activists often drawn from the ranks of students.[78]

The new conservatism was also evident in the rural sector and took the form of the 'Rich Peasant Line'. During the Cultural Revolution, some 17 years later, the inauguration of the 'Rich Peasant Line' was directly attributed to Liu Shao-ch'i.[79] It was certainly Liu who made one of the key speeches elucidating the line on 14 June 1950, though perhaps here he was only reflecting a committee decision. In the speech, Liu called for a halt to land reform in all areas where it had not yet started and imposed restraints upon peasants who had already initiated the process.[80] Liu stressed that land reform should in no way harm production and that where it had been decided on for the winter of 1950-1 every effort should be made to get in the harvest and collect the public (tax) grain before launching the reform. Under no circumstances should land reform be allowed to lead to 'confusion' and on no account should the land of rich peasants be confiscated, for they had moved to a 'neutralist' position. The main theme, therefore, was that production should come before social change, nothing was to be done without authorisation from above and the work-team method of social control should replace the former peasant association approach. Now, 'enlightened gentry' were to be invited to participate in a United Front and all land reform trials were to be handled by the formal court structures.[81]

A new and complex class analysis was employed. The category of 'small landlords' was invented and defined as landlords who had supported the revolution, and, to avoid the opprobrium associated with the name 'rich peasants', a new term, 'prosperous middle peasant', became current. It was frequently the case that several of these different categories might be found in the same family and the problem of implementing the new scheme of categorisation led to a veritable bureaucrat's paradise.[82] We shall return to the problem of bureaucratisation later; in the meantime it should be noted that, by 1949, village administration tended to conform to the triple alliance model — 'enlightened gentry' or rich peasants corresponded with retained personnel; what was left of the radical peasant associations were classed as mass organisations and personnel remaining from the work teams sent down from above, around which Party nuclei to grow, provided the link.

The Democratisation of Enterprise Management

One of the most interesting manifestations of the triple alliance formula was in factory management.[83] Military representatives, or Party secretaries who replaced them, were required to establish factory management committees upon which worker delegates and senior management (often retained) also sat. These bodies were to formulate factory policy according to regional plans as they were drawn up, and were to provide an institutional form for worker participation in management.

The management committees, however, were not very successful for a number of reasons. First, industrial management (and especially in the north-east where much industry was located) was the one area in Chinese society where a Soviet model of organisation was introduced very early on. Although the management committees were similar to the Soviet workers' councils set up after the Bolshevik Revolution, the model of organisation emulated in Chinese industry after 1948 was a current Stalinist one which was extremely suspicious of 'parliamentary' (*yihui*) forms of management. The considerable powers given to line management meant that the effectiveness of other elements in the triple alliance formula was not great. Secondly, the Party representatives and worker delegates were often too inexperienced to curb management. Thirdly, many worker delegates were creamed off into management if they showed any particular skill. Fourthly, the worker component on the management committees often became the nuclei of labour union branches from which the more politically active were transferred to higher union posts. In such a situation, many management committees became little more than audiences for managment (*tingting hui*) and lacked any democratic spirit.

Other bodies which were set up in factories to curb the power of management and to foster worker participation were the worker and staff congresses at which factory general managers were required to defend policies, seek suggestions and if necessary undergo 'self-examination'. As time passed, however, these bodies met more and more infrequently and caused the Party some concern.

Although leading bodies in factories occasionally manifested some radicalism in early 1949, it was quite clear by 1950 that a more usual development was bureaucratism. At first sight, a manifestation of bureaucratism would seem strange in the atmosphere of euphoria that accompanied liberation but the transformation of an 'ultra-left' deviation into its opposite was probably quite familiar to cadres schooled in the dialectic. Undoubtedly the major cause of this change was that cadres were swamped by the complexity and size of the myriad tasks that had to be undertaken.

The Establishment of Control

The most immediate task that had to be undertaken following liberation was a general stocktaking of all resources both human and economic. Rudimentary census returns had to be made, births reported and residence units demarcated. Particularly active here were citizen groups such as the worker picket organisations who, through controlling grain supplies,[84] not only registered the population and established an elementary system of public security but also took measures to facilitate the regulation of labour and the relief of unemployment.[85]

As the registration of the population proceeded, local authorities were instructed to provide work for the unemployed and relieve the needy. China's cities had for long been afflicted by periodic influxes of rural vagrants (*youmin*) who were now organised to undertake huge labour-intensive construction tasks at low wages. At the same time, measures were taken to ensure that the swollen urban population was fed. Pending the establishment of an effective rural taxation policy, however, the government could do little but dispatch work-teams to the countryside to requisition grain and this policy occasioned sporadic peasant opposition.[86]

Along with the registration of the population, the new government made an inventory of all industrial and commercial institutions with a view to controlling resource allocation (in favour of the former). In the early post-liberation period, such control was best effected by the supervision of contracts between economic organisations both in the state and private sectors. The institution of controlled contracts, it was said, was to provide the rudiments of a planning system and local budgeting.

Perhaps the greatest headache was the catastrophic inflationary situation which the new government inherited. As far as wages were concerned, the first step was to extend the wage policy of the old liberated areas to the whole country. According to this policy, a system of wage-points (known either as *xi* or *fen* in various parts of the country) was in operation, whereby a day's labour was calculated in wage-points assessed in terms of bundles of commodities (rice, wheat, edible oil, coal, etc.).[87] In effect, this meant greatly extending the millet standard (north China) or rice standard (south China).

A second anti-inflationary policy was to impose strict control over the banking system and to subordinate all financial institutions to the People's Bank. Regulations were issued imposing limits upon private banks and increasing their indebtedness to the People's Bank. Similarly, insurance companies were required to deposit sums of money with the People's Bank and were forbidden to invest in industry.[88] Strict limits were imposed upon all state organs concerning the amount of ready cash they were to retain[89] and the inherited Kuomintang taxation system was used to soak up private funds, to channel resources into the public sector and to drive smaller, inefficient private concerns out of business. At the same time, the circulation of foreign currency was forbidden and propaganda teams were organised to persuade holders of foreign currency to pay it into branches of the People's Bank.

Another task of the propaganda teams was to promote the sale of government bonds. When first introduced, these bonds had been specifically designed to support the war effort but continued to be promoted as hostilities lessened. They were issued for five years with (by traditional Chinese standards) a low rate of return of 5 per cent per annum which was probably not very attractive to businessmen. Nonetheless, many were sold though we cannot be sure of the extent to which this was due to patriotic fervour or to pressure.[90]

On the whole, the new government's response to inflation was bold and imaginative and the above were merely the first of a whole series of measures that eventually stabilised the currency. Before long, new measures were adopted such as the provision of consumer co-operatives in which ordinary people invested at a low rate of interest but which provided daily necessities at low prices. At the same time, a whole stream of regulations was published to achieve economic ends not explicit in their provisions. Sanitation regulations, for example, were used to restrict the number of barbers' shops and other service establishments, though care was taken to see that such restriction did not lead to unemployment.

Policy was aimed at restricting the operations of the small shopkeeper and businessman and establishing clear lines of ownership and control. Similarly in private educational institutions, initial attention was focused not on the content of courses but the degree to which these institutions had any advantage over the government school system.[91] Many teachers did, however, institute new curricula in the new political climate and the degree to which they did so must surely have had some effect on the provision of government subsidies.

All of the above measures, of course, needed people to administer them and the retained personnel were inadequate both in numbers and in political consciousness. To provide such personnel, a massive educational campaign was launched in which the New Democratic Youth League (the youth wing of the Party) played an active part, especially since large numbers of these activists were students. To achieve a greater degree of national integration, the activists undertook a campaign for the teaching of the national language and attempted to spread their effect outside the ranks of intellectuals. More and more housewives, for example, were encouraged to form residents' groups and street committees.

Perhaps the most important sphere to involve housewives concerned the new Marriage Law of 13 April 1950[92] which abolished child marriage, polygamy and concubinage and provided the legal basis for what was to be a fundamental change in the status of women. The earlier Kuomintang Marriage Law, while quite progressive, had been a dead letter as far as most of China was concerned because legal reforms had not been matched by economic, social and ideological reforms. As a first step in the implementation of the new law, a propaganda campaign was launched, though traditional ideology and traditional forms of social organisation were to impose limits on the success of its implementation in the very early period.

The Chinese Communist Party had had a long history of successful propaganda. Now all the stops were pulled out. Millions of pamphlets were issued on every conceivable subject from choosing a marriage partner to the layout of a meeting hall. Mobile theatrical groups toured the country and local units of production organised plays and propaganda meetings to familiarise people with Party policy. It was an exhilarating experience but one that required a considerable amount of work, particularly by those organisations whose job it was to co-ordinate the whole process — the Party and the labour unions.

Party and Union Bureaucratism

We have noted that the structure of state administration was determined at the highest level by the principle of the United Front and at lower levels, to an increasing degree, by its specific variant — the triple alliance. What is important to look at here is not so much the components of the United Front but the linkages. The main body responsible for maintaining these linkages was the Party although in the very early period of military government, Army personnel performed the linkage function between retained personnel and mass organisations until a regular Party network could be established.

In linking up diverse elements, the Party was to impel policy in a particular direction without exactly giving administrative orders. It was the function of state bodies to formulate *operational* instructions; it was the job of the Party to establish broad *policy*, ideally according to the Mass Line formula. It was vital, therefore, that the Party, defined as embodying the long-term interests of a class, should be kept separate from the state defined merely as its instrument of repression. The state structure was characterised by a hierarchical bureaucratic organisation whose parts were linked by a network of technological solidarity. The Party should ideally be characterised not by structure and organisation (though indeed it must possess these) but by its *direction*. Its internal linkages should be 'human' rather than technological, ideological rather than routinised. The Party was to be rooted in society rather than in the state and, in the words of Schurmann, it was 'the instrument that forges the resolution of the contradiction between state and society in socialism'.[93]

Following liberation, the activities of Party branches had to adhere to the narrow path between the same opposing errors that figured in the rectification movement of 1942. The first of these errors was to usurp the power of the state structure and take everything on to their own shoulders.[94] This 'ultra-leftist' error stemmed often from extreme enthusiasm or from distrust or retained personnel. The second error was for a Party branch or committee to subordinate itself completely to the state structure and to do little more than invest the directives of bureaucrats or managers with moral force. In a situation where personnel were inexperienced, this latter error was probably more frequent than the former. Many Party branches had only come into existence following the end of military rule and the initiative in their formation had been taken by military representatives formerly attached to control commissions. These representatives had, at the same time, to supervise the establishment of regular administrative machinery and it is little wonder that they confused their functions. Such bureaucratism as developed was probably strengthened by the increasingly conservative atmosphere that prevailed after 1949, and was particularly marked in that most important of the transmission belts which were ideally to link the Party with the masses — the labour unions.

Although syndicalism (where unions actually took over the running of factories) occasionally occurred,[95] the newly formed labour unions[96] revealed themselves as extremely pallid bodies. Upon their formation, many union branches simply sided with management both in the state and private sectors.[97] This was due to the fact that many union cadres had concurrent management posts, were subject to repeated transfer (leaving their branches in the hands of inexperienced cadres), were too busy with the sheer paperwork involved in union registration and too busy studying technology to develop any independent position. Many of those who proved themselves to be competent technically were creamed off into management; similarly those who proved themselves to have a high level of political consciousness became specifically Party cadres. Unions were defined as 'schools for management' but, quite clearly, the educational principle that was applied was that described earlier as selective rather than creative. It is not surprising therefore that some union cadres bemoaned the fact that they were considered to be 'fourth class'[98] (the top three classes being 1. Party cadres, 2. government cadres and 3. engineers).

Just as the rapid expansion of union organisations in the period following liberation weakened union branches and the paperwork involved contributed to bureaucratism, so the Party itself was impaired by a similar process. The overall rise in Party membership between October 1949 and mid-1950 was only from 4.5 to 5 million[99] but these figures concealed the fact that, following the Party decision in March 1949 to switch the focus of its work from countryside to cities, there had been a decline in rural Party membership and a staggering increase in the urban areas. Many factories reported increases in Party membership from some 3 per cent to between 10 and 30 per cent, of whom large numbers were skilled workers and technicians retained from pre-liberation days.[100] In fact, policy was not just to increase the working-class component of the Party but in particular its skilled and managerial component. This process of recruitment, similar to Stalin's 'Leninist Levy', may perhaps have diluted the overall political consciousness of the Party. One must note also that, all too frequently, enthusiasm for production was taken as a sufficient indicator of political consciousness, particularly during China's first major production movement known as the 'Movement to Create New Records',[101] launched in north-east China in 1949 and designed to determine production norms.

By mid-1950 therefore, the composition of the Party, though more orthodox (in a Soviet sense), was very different from two years previously. In the following year when 11.4 per cent of the total industrial work force in north-east China was enrolled, it was announced that within five years the Party planned to recruit one-third of all the industrial workers.[102] Meanwhile, leaders began to worry about the political health of the Party which, according to Kao Kang, had been affected by 'the depraved ideology of remnant feudal elements and capitalists, petty bourgeois individualism and defects in ideological and educational work'. Kao noted that industrial idlers tended to rationalise their indolent attitude in political terms and, when admonished for relaxing, accused their critics of 'taking a rural viewpoint' and of not realising the importance of the United Front between workers, peasants, petty bourgeoisie and national capitalists.[103]

Clearly the low level of political consciousness was not just confined to new Party members. Many veteran cadres had neglected their political duties while studying new and unfamiliar technical and administrative problems. Others, after entering the cities, were said to be infected with the 'ideology of power and prestige'.[104] The major factor, however, which contributed to the new bureaucratism resulted from the rapid verticalisation of administrative control according to a scheme very different from the Yenan pattern of *dual rule*. As the power of central economic ministries grew, local Party and state organs began to abdicate all responsibility for economic enterprises and were reduced to merely functional agents in an increasingly staff-line pattern of organisation. They had either to kick against the system, as was done in Yenan, or succumb to it.

The Persistence of Simulated Kinship Structures

The simulated kinship structures such as secret societies and the gang-boss network proved to be difficult to eradicate for the simple reason that they had considerable success in permeating any government that impinged upon them. Indeed one of the principal reasons why Party and unions came under criticism in the period following liberation was because they had in fact been infiltrated.

Again, the situation varied from area to area. In north-east China, where there were fewer retained personnel, reconstruction could proceed almost from scratch in a somewhat more radical atmosphere than that which prevailed in areas further south which were not liberated until 1949. In the north-east, a Democratic Reform Movement (*Minzhu Gaige Yundong*) was launched immediately after liberation with, it would appear, much success.[105] South of the Great Wall, however, a policy of maintaining the status quo remained in force until mid-1950. In many mining enterprises, former gang bosses were still practising extortion at that time and had merely changed the name of their gangs to shifts and teams. In the construction industry, which was still largely dependent upon contract labour, the gang-boss system was rife with as many as seven levels of contractor each taking its cut. Cases are on record of gang bosses completely dominating mine Party committees and their position was justified on the ground that Party policy demanded the retention of skilled workers.[106] Many union branches were similarly dominated and some gang bosses had even managed to get themselves chosen as model workers. Various secret societies such as the notorious Green Gang and the *Yi Guan Dao* were still in existence and *banghui* (mutual aid groups), which had degenerated into protection rackets, still operated.[107]

Was the Yenan pattern of transformation from within adequate to deal with the situation? Although it had proved remarkably successful in generating commitment to the Communist Party during the war, it seemed inadequate to cope with the process of transformation with a diluted Party spread thinly on the ground over the country.

It was quite apparent that, in local situations where its organisation had been created from scratch out of very dubious personnel, the Party was far from taking over the existing structures from within. It was rather the simulated kinship structures that were taking over the Party. In such a situation, calls for a more radical approach for social transformation became louder.

Problems of Defence and the Outbreak of the Korean War

Anyone familiar with the history of the Soviet Union will observe that the conservative policies pursued during the first few months after the establishment of the People's Republic were similar to those of the Bolshevik government after October 1917 and before the commencement of the Russian Civil War. There was, however, one crucial difference: the moderate policies pursued by the Chinese government *followed* a protracted Civil War which did not come to an abrupt end. Throughout 1949 and into early 1950, Kuomintang air raids continued. In Kwangchow alone, from 3 November 1949 to 24 February 1950, there were 76 'plane incidents' at a time when a PLA Air Force hardly existed and when air defences were very poor. Indeed, in Kwangchow, it was not until March 1950 that the first enemy aircraft was shot down.[108] At the same time, China was particularly vulnerable to attacks by sea and the Kuomintang Navy maintained control over the Chinese coast well into 1950. Coastal defence was complicated by the fact that, in south China, communities of boat people had been infiltrated by Kuomintang agents. Inland, the Kuomintang still maintained a Military Secret Service (*Jun Tong*) which remained active in the anticipation of a Kuomintang counterattack on the mainland from T'aiwan.[109]

In early 1950, such a counterattack was not the remote possibility it seems today. Then, it appeared increasingly that General MacArthur's plans for T'aiwan went far beyond defence[110] despite the proclaimed American intention not to intervene further in the Chinese Civil War and American Secretary of State Acheson's assertion to that effect on 12 January.[111] Despite the massive literature on the origins of the Korean War, it is still not clear to what extent in early 1950 MacArthur was wagging the American Presidential dog. It is I.F. Stone's contention that the first shots in that war were fired by South Korea as part of an international conspiracy involving MacArthur, President Rhee of South Korea, John Foster Dulles and Chiang K'ai-shek to provoke a North Korean reaction, enlarge the war and so commit United States forces to a restoration of the Kuomintang within China.[112] Others would support the claim that South Korea opened hostilities and that the United States found it extremely difficult to restrain Rhee in early 1950 but the evidence for a conspiracy is rather weak. The conventional Western view, however, is that hostilities were opened by the North. Whatever the situation, it is my view that China was unaware of any intention of either side to cross the 38th Parallel and initiate full-scale war.

China's main military concern in early 1950 was the liberation of

T'aiwan. The Third Field Army had been mobilised under Su Yü and an intensive programme of training in amphibious operations carried out. Five thousand junks had been assembled, 30 airfields constructed, radar installations set up with Soviet help and 15,000 troops mobilised for the invasion.[113] The last thing surely the Chinese would have wanted was a war on two fronts.

Despite the intended T'aiwan operation, plans were under way in China for large-scale demobilisation. Two-fifths of the 5 million-strong PLA still consisted of Kuomintang defectors and the sheer size of the Army placed considerable burdens on the Chinese exchequer. Military expenditure in 1950 was estimated at 38.8 per cent of the draft budget for that year which was probably a gross underestimate since many military items were not included under the military heading. Gittings estimates that the figure was probably more like 60 per cent.[114] Though a large number of troops had been assigned to production work in their original place of recruitment[115] to ease the burden (units of the Fourth Field Army, for example, were transferred back to the north-east from Kwangtung), mass demobilisation was considered to be imperative. By a curious quirk of fate, the decision was taken for large-scale demobilisation on 24 June 1950,[116] the day before hostilities broke out on the 38th Parallel and the Korean War began. The surprised Chinese government could only cancel the demobilisation order and await events. It did not have to wait long, for one of the first acts of the United States was to order the Seventh Fleet into the T'aiwan Straits, allegedly to hold back Chiang K'ai-shek. The previous policy enunciated by Acheson was at an end; the United States was now a direct threat.

A fatal decision had been taken. An Asian Cold War which was to last 20 years had been inaugurated and China was to move closer to the Soviet Union. Internally, the conservative policy in force since 1948, and under increasing criticism, was now to give way to a more radical one. The new radicalism in China was not a direct consequence of the outbreak of the Korean War for many of its features antedate slightly the opening of hostilities. China's new concern with security, however, made an active campaign against counter-revolutionaries more urgent and perhaps silenced some of the conservatives. One thing was now certain, with the exception of Tibet where a Chinese military presence was established following negotiations later in 1950, the Civil War was, for the time being, over.

Notes

1. This section is based on Selden 1971, with some ideas from Schurmann 1966.
2. Mao Tse-tung 1 February 1942, in Compton 1966, pp. 21-2.
3. This idea courtesy of Bill Jenner.
4. Compton 1966.
5. Schurmann 1966, p. 236.
6. This was later redefined as 'red' (*hong*) and 'expert' (*zhuan*).
7. Mao Tse-tung 1 June 1943, in SW III, p. 119.
8. Selden 1971, p. 215.
9. Note, Mao did not speak specifically of alienation.
10. Schurmann 1966, pp. 415-6, 422-7.
11. Ibid., pp. 188-94.
12. See Seybolt 1971.
13. Ibid., p. 644.
14. Selden 1971, p. 269.
15. Ibid., pp. 253-4.
16. See Shewmaker 1968.
17. Selden 1971, p. 246.
18. These were the Chinese Industrial Co-operatives. At one time, these co-operatives received some support from the Kuomintang government but with the collapse of the United Front were frequently considered to be too radical. With the expansion of the Communist Party base areas during the war, many of these co-operatives were swept into the orbit of the Communist Party and given a new lease of life. See Alley 1952.
19. The Stakhanovite movement in the Soviet Union was named after A.G. Stakhanov whose team of three workers attained, in the mid-1930s, the remarkable output of 102 tons of coal in a shift of 5¾ hours at the Irmino Mine in the Ukraine. The team went on to break new records and a nation-wide movement was launched to emulate it. The term 'Stakhanovite worker' was applied thereafter to those who broke output records.
20. Johnson 1962.
21. Compton 1952, pp. x-xi.
22. E.g. 'On Practice', July 1937, (SW I, pp. 295-309), 'On Contradiction', August 1937 (SW I, pp. 311-47).
23. See Chiang 1947.
24. Tuchman 1970.
25. Schram 1966, pp. 225-6.
26. Barrett 1970.
27. Text in Liu Shao-ch'i 1950, pp. 155-204.
28 Mao Tse-tung 24 September 1962, in Schram 1974, p. 191. Djilas 1969, p. 141.
29. Tsou 1967, pp. 284-5.
30. Ibid., p. 283.
31. See Mao Tse-tung 17 October 1945, *SW* IV, pp. 53-63.
32. Tsou 1967, pp. 327-40, for one explanation.
33. During the 268 days' Soviet occupation, the value of installations damaged or shipped away from north-east China to the Soviet Union has been esti-mated at $U.S. 635,649,000 (Pauley's statistics cited in Cheng 1956, p. 266) and $U.S. 845,238,000 (statistics compiled by Japanese technicians cited in ibid., p. 266).
34. See Beal 1970.
35. See Chassin 1966.
36. Liu-cheng, *PR* 34, 21 August 1964, p. 22.
37. Lindsay 1970, p. 3.

38. Hinton 1966, p. 115.
39. Text with supplements in ibid., pp. 615-26.
40. Discussed in ibid., especially chapters 41-3.
41. The title of a novel by Chou Li-po.
42. Hinton 1966, p. 398.
43. Ho Kan-chih cited in Schurmann 1966, p. 433.
44. *Beiping Jiefangbao* 25 March 1949, p. 1.
45. Text in *CB* 42, 22 December 1950.
46. Mao Tse-tung 25 December 1947, '*Muqian Xingshi he Women de Renwu*',
    in collection of articles of same title, 1949, pp. 20-41.
47. Cheng Tsu-yuan 1955, p. 22.
48. *RMRB* 10 November 1948, p. 3.
49. *RMRB* 7 August 1948, p. 2.
50. Ibid.
51. *RMRB* 12 September 1948, p. 1.
52. *CCP.CC.* N.E. Bureau 10 June 1948, in Liu Shao-ch'i *et al.* 1949.
53. On KMT absorption see Gittings 1967, pp. 68-73.
54. Ibid., pp. 65-8.
55. Friedman 1971, p. 214.
56. Ibid., p. 210.
57. Mao Tse-tung 30 June 1949, in *SW* IV, p. 415.
58. Friedman 1971.
59. The Cominform was a much looser organisation than the old Comintern and
    was concerned largely with the dissemination of information throughout the
    International Communist Movement.
60. Gittings 1971.
61. Schurmann 1966, pp. 239-40.
62. Mao Tse-tung 24 September 1962, in Schram 1974, p. 191.
63. Text of treaty and associated documents in *CB* 62, 5 March 1951.
64. Mao Tse-tung 24 September 1962, in Schram 1974, p. 191.
65. The word 'Marxian' is used here to signify the writings of Marx rather than
    the much broader term 'Marxist'.
66. Texts in *SW* II, pp. 339-84 and *SW* IV, pp. 411-24.
67. These documents are discussed in Waller 1970, pp. 81-4. The Common
    Programme is in *CB* 9, 21 September 1950.
68. Discussed in Brugger 1976.
69. Whitson 1969.
70. Barnett 1963, p. 340.
71. It was said that as many as 90 per cent of old administrative personnel were
    retained in Shanghai.
72. Brugger 1976, pp. 74-5.
73. Shanghai . . . *Jiefang hou*, pp. 1-4.
    The institution of worker pickets had a very long history in China. They
    fulfilled an important role in the takeover of factories during the abortive
    revolution of 1926-7. They were again active following the Japanese
    surrender in 1945 and their very existence in 1948-9 attests to a very signi-
    ficant urban Communist Party underground that had been in existence
    during the Civil War.
74. Shanghai . . . *Jiefang hou*, pp. 1-4.
75. Lieberthal 1971, pp. 509-12.
76. The situation in Tientsin, in April-May 1949, occasioned a considerable
    polemic during the subsequent Cultural Revolution. As Party troubleshooter,
    Liu Shao-ch'i was sent to Tientsin to rectify the situation. It was claimed
    that Liu's 'Tientsin Talks' ended the previously moderate radical policy in

favour of a 'revisionist' policy which favoured the national capitalists in the private sector and precluded fundamental rearrangement of factory management in the public sector. As such, it was said to be a violation of the programme announced by Mao in his report to the second plenum of the Seventh Central Committee of the Party (5 March 1949). The implementation of reform in the spring and summer of 1949 was much less radical than in the earlier period and the 'Tientsin Talks' occupied an important place in the development of policy, but I am not convinced that these 'Talks' constituted a total break from previous policy. The 'Talks' seem only to be the culmination of the previously moderate policy dating from December 1947. What the 'Tientsin Talks' do reveal, however, is that Liu's view of the United Front was a much longer-term one than that of Mao (at least on the basis of speeches published in *Zhong Gong Yanjiu Zazhi she* 1970, pp. 200-20).

77.   Vogel 1971, p. 48. Schurmann 1966, pp. 371-2.
78.   Vogel 1971, pp. 49, 53-4.
79.   E.g. *SCMM* 652, 28 April 1969, p. 3.
80.   Liu Shao-ch'i 14 June 1950, in Liu 1969, pp. 215-33.
81.   Ibid., pp. 230-3.
82.   One might note here that it was extremely difficult to determine ownership in a situation where land had been informally divided amongst members of the same family. In such a situation, the terms 'poor' and 'lower middle' peasant may not have had much operational significance.
83.   Discussed in Brugger 1976, Chapter 7.
84.   Vogel 1971, pp. 72-3.
85.   On early labour regulation, see Howe 1971, pp. 88-94.
86.   Vogel 1971, pp. 78-9.
87.   See the examples in Brugger 1976, Appendix I.
88.   Vogel 1971, p. 75.
89.   *Xinhua Yuebao* No. 7, May 1950, p. 128.
90.   Vogel 1971, pp. 79-80.
91.   Ibid., p. 75.
92.   PFLP 1959, *The Marriage Law* . . .
93.   Schurmann 1966, p. 112.
94.   Ling Hua-ch'un, *Dongbei Gongye*, No. 56, 21 April 1951, pp. 19-21.
95.   Kao Kang 13 March 1950, *Dongbei Ribao*, 6 June 1950, p. 1.
96.   These unions were formed out of the underground unions of pre-liberation days, out of the worker pickets or sometimes *ex nihilo*.
97.   *Zhongguo Gongren*, No. 15, April 1951, p. 36.
98.   *Gongren Ribao*, 11 January 1952.
99.   Schurmann 1966, p. 129.
100   E.g. *Zhongguo Gongren*, Vol. I No. 3, 15 April 1950, pp. 32-3. Hsiao Feng, in *Laodong Chubanshe Bianshenbu*, 1951, pp. 55-67.
101. Brugger 1976, Chapter 4.
102. An Tzu-wen, *Gongren Ribao*, 31 August 1951, pp. 1 and 4.
103. Kao Kang 31 August 1951, reprinted in *Zhongguo Minzhu Tongmeng Zongbu Xuanchuan Weiyuanhui*, 1951, pp. 14-25.
104. Li Lung, *Xuexi*, Vol. 3 No. 7, 1 January 1951, p. 8.
105. E.g. *Gongren Chubanshe*, 1953, p. 36.
106. Lin Li, *Zhongguo Gongren*, No. 3, 15 April 1950, pp. 12-14.
107. Liu Tzu-chiu, *Gongren Ribao*, 12 September 1951.
108. Vogel 1971, pp. 61-2.
109. *Huadong Renmin Chubanshe*, May 1951 (for a catalogue of subversive activities).

110. Friedman 1971, p. 222.
111. Gittings 1967, p. 41.
112. Stone 1970.
113. Gittings 1967, p. 42.
114. Ibid., pp. 26-7.
115. Ibid., pp. 26, 29-32. For Mao's directive on this task (5 December 1949) see JPRS 61269-1, 20 February 1974, pp. 2-5.
116. Gittings 1967, p. 27

2 FROM MASS MOBILISATION TO THE SOVIET MODEL (1950-4)

The second of the nine cycles that will be considered here began in 1950 with a number of moderately radical measures designed to reverse the bureaucratic drift. In 1951, these measures gave rise to an unprecedented series of mass movements which continued into 1952. With their conclusion, a policy of 'regularisation' was adopted and an all-out attempt was made to implement a model of administration which derived from the Soviet Union.

Party and Union Rectification (Mid-1950)

The new radicalism of mid-1950 was ushered in by Mao Tse-tung at the Third Plenum of the Seventh Central Committee on 6 June,[1] 19 days before the commencement of hostilities in Korea. Directed against bureaucratism and commandism in economic and financial administration, the rectification movement assumed only modest proportions. Perhaps those most severely treated were many former guerrilla cadres who, unable to adapt to routine administration, were sent back to the countryside.[2] In general, however, cadres alienated from the masses, who had succumbed to the 'ideology of the meritorious' or the fleshpots of the cities, were merely required to undergo self-criticism.

Within industry in north China, the process of democratic reform was stepped up. Administrative orders were issued formally abolishing the gang-boss system in various sectors of industry[3] and reports began to appear in the press describing how stubborn and persistent gang bosses were dealt with.[4] It was soon apparent, however, that Party and union branches within economic enterprises were responding to the movement rather sluggishly. Cadres were unsure how to eradicate the gang-boss system without harming production, how to distinguish gang bosses among skilled workers[5] or how to deal with the informal structure within factories. I have argued elsewhere that, just as rich peasants in the countryside came to exercise some of the power that formerly belonged to landlords,[6] so a stratum of 'industrial kulaks' appeared in industry following the demise of the more obvious gang bosses.[7] Such was the consequence of a rectification movement that involved inadequate mass mobilisation.

Amongst labour union cadres the rectification movement of 1950 had results often contrary to what had been intended. In July 1950, Teng Tzu-hui, vice chairman of the Central South Finance and Economics Committee, criticised the excessive subordination of unions to management in both the public and private sectors of industry and demanded that both sides examine in what way their concrete 'standpoint' (*lichang*) might differ.[8] Teng's cautious speech sought to ensure that the interests of workers were not sacrificed to the goal of merely increasing production but was not 'economist' in the Leninist sense. The debate which followed, however, was not so cautious[9] and could indeed be described as 'economist'.[10] Some unions began to interpret the demand that they show greater independence as an injunction to devote greater attention to the immediate gratification of material desires. Unions' concentration on benefits for the working class as opposed to those of workers *and* peasants was to precipitate a major union crisis in the following year.

In view of China's increasing concern about developments in Korea, it was particularly serious that the beginnings of radicalisation in the summer of 1950 lacked vigour and had led labour unions into a reactionary position.

China's Participation in the Korean War (June-November 1950)

Even after the outbreak of fighting between North and South Korea, the possibility of an active Chinese involvement seemed remote. Opinion in Washington held that South Korea could at least hold her own and, with the sealing of the T'aiwan Straits, President Truman had silenced the pro-Chiang Republican 'China lobby' who had complained that he was 'soft on Communism'. At one fell swoop Truman seemed not only to have rescued his image but looked like securing a $50 billion military budget that had previously been resisted by conservative Republicans.[11]

But with the rapid collapse of the South Korean forces, Truman was forced to reassess the situation and could only explain his miscalculation in terms of 'external aggression'. Two grossly dangerous misconceptions vied for supremacy. In Truman's view, the source of 'aggression' lay in Moscow; this required a strengthening of the United States' position in Europe. In the view of General MacArthur, however, the source of 'aggression' lay in Peking whither the war should be carried.[12] When American bombers failed to halt the advance of the North Korean forces, the general secured the deployment of American ground troops and initiated a process of escalation which was increasingly rationalised according to his view of 'Chinese aggression'. The return of Korean forces which had fought with the PLA in China was interpreted in terms of such 'aggression' and China's warnings that it would contemplate the dispatch of troops if UN forces crossed the 38th Parallel were disregarded, presumably on the grounds that China was thought to be behind the whole operation anyway.

In October 1950, PLA forces moved silently into North Korea[13] accompanied by Chou En-lai's signal to the United States, via the Indian ambassador, that China would commit troops only if American forces invaded North Korea; in the event of South Korean forces crossing the parallel, China would not react. Though seemingly accepted by Truman, the Chinese position was ignored by MacArthur who continued to push towards the Sino-Korean border – the Yalu River. On 1 November, Chinese and UN forces were to clash.

Even at that point, however, full-scale war could have been averted. With the UN advance on the Yalu River checked, the Chinese forces 'faded away' to allow Truman, it has been argued, to resurrect an earlier idea for the establishment of a buffer zone along the Yalu. MacArthur's response was to escalate the war even further. In receipt of Truman's order not to bomb bridges across the Yalu, MacArthur lodged the 'gravest protest' and Washington gave way. All, however, was still not lost. On 13 November, MacArthur proposed hot pursuit into northeast China but his suggestion was apparently vetoed by six of the powers who made up the UN forces and who appeared to show more resolve than President Truman.[14] It was too late, however, to establish a buffer zone and, with MacArthur's offensive towards the Yalu River in November, China became effectively at war with the United States. In securing T'aiwan and occupying Korea, it could only seem to the Chinese that the United States had replaced Japan, which had embarked upon exactly the same strategy half a century previously, as the expansionist enemy.

Consolidation of Tibet (1950-1)[15]

Following its involvement in the Korean War, China became particularly concerned with the security of the frontiers. The pacification of south-west China had been proceeding steadily throughout 1950 but, with the possibility of invasion, all efforts had to be directed towards carrying pacification to a rapid conclusion.

Although the idea of Tibetan independence had been canvassed by some Americans during the Civil War, the position of President Truman (at least prior to his actions in June 1950) had been that the United States would make no commitment on the Tibetan question. As far as the British and Indian governments were concerned, the Simla agreement of 1913 was adhered to whereby Chinese 'suzerainty' over the region was recognised.

In early 1950, there appears to have been some disagreement within the traditional aristocratic governing body in Tibet — the *Kashag* — as to the nature of Tibetan sovereignty and Chinese 'suzerainty', and two courses of action were pursued. In February, Tibet's ruler, the Dalai Lama, dispatched a mission to Peking, via New Delhi, to see what terms would be offered by the Chinese government and, at the same time, a Tibetan army under Ngapo Ngawang-jigme set out for the Chamdo region on the border with Sikang province. The first course of action came to nothing since the Tibetan delegation never left India and the second resulted in a Tibetan defeat at the battle of Chamdo in October 1950. At that time, many Tibetans went over to the side of the People's Liberation Army and later the Tibetan commander was to achieve high rank in the Chinese government.

The victory of Chamdo was not, however, followed by a PLA advance into Tibet proper. On instructions from the Dalai Lama, Ngapo Ngawang-jigme proceeded to Peking to negotiate a settlement and this was concluded in May 1951,[16] after which PLA troops entered Tibet. For its part the Tibetan government recognised the region's inclusion into the People's Republic and accepted 'regional national autonomy . . . under the leadership of the national government and in accordance with the policy laid down in the Common Programme'. The *Kashag* remained in existence and agreed to institute a reform of the existing system of monastic serfdom. For its part, the Peking government agreed not to abolish the powers of the Dalai Lama or the other main religious and temporal ruler, the Panchen Erdeni. It also agreed not to carry out reform through compulsion and allowed for Tibetan forces to be rein-corporated into the PLA (though this, in fact, never happened). In other words, the frontier region of Tibet was now secured, although the domestic social structure remained unchanged with only a vague commitment to self-generated reform.

The Intensification of Land Reform (late 1950)

Active Chinese participation in the Korean War gave the rather pallid radicalism inaugurated in June 1950 a little more colour. This was nowhere more evident than in the rural sector. The new Agrarian Law that went into effect on 30 June was an extremely moderate one. Rich peasants were allowed to retain their property and landlords were given a share of land in a slow and orderly process of redistribution. Justifying the new situation, Liu Shao-ch'i argued that radical land reform policies had been necessary during the Civil War when landlords were siding with the enemy, but now landlords were to be encouraged to live by the fruits of their labours.[17] It was not, however, until the autumn of 1950 that the new land policy began to be implemented in the 'later liberated areas' of south China,[18] by which time the situation in Korea looked ominous. With the full-scale Chinese commitment of November 1950, agrarian policy became much tougher.

By that time, the main area embarking upon a programme of land reform was the Central South Administrative Region, based on Wuhan, whose leaders felt that landlord resistence might stiffen now that there was a possibility (however remote) of a renewal of the Civil War on the mainland. At the same time, the rectification movement in the urban sphere might have made them aware of the extent to which local cadres had been taken over by traditional organisations. Indeed it was discovered that landlords in the south had tried to preserve their position by bribing or making concessions to peasants in return for lenient treatment once land reform was undertaken.[19]

The situation in south China was particularly complex. Here land holdings were smaller than in the north. Some land was owned by overseas Chinese who, in the early years, were an important source of foreign currency. Many landlords were involved in commerce and had gone to the cities to sit out agrarian reform. Lineage organisations within the villages were much stronger than in north China which made identification on the basis of class extraordinarily difficult and, most important, there was a much larger number of local cadres within the Party who were related to landowners.

In such circumstances, the authorities in Wuhan were not completely in touch with the situation in rural areas and the further down the chain of command one went, the greater was the resistance to any new hard line.[20] The situation was further complicated by the fact that, at the basic level, many activists were former guerrilla cadres. Their experiences had been very different from the PLA cadres who were sent down in the work-teams from the north and who often did not speak the same language.[21] It was not, however, just a matter of cleavage between higher and lower levels since leaders at most levels divided on the degree of sympathy they showed for either the work-teams or the local cadres. The dimensions of administrative disputes were extremely complex, especially since constant pressure was placed on local cadres to speed up the whole process.[22]

By the end of 1950, this pressure was seen to have been only

moderately effective. Just as in the urban sphere, the initial moderate
radicalism foundered on the rocks of traditional connections, so in the
rural sphere, a somewhat more vigorous movement was similarly
obstructed. China's leaders could only pause to consider what to do
next.

The Beginnings of Mobilisation (late 1950-1)

Although more mass mobilisation was involved in the land reform campaign of late 1950 than in the urban sector, the movements at that time
were largely from the top down. The last of these early movements was
the Campaign for the Suppression of Counter Revolutionaries, the
urgency of which was dictated by security concerns in the new wartime
situation. The targets were secret agents (*tewufenzi*) who worked for
such organisations as the Kuomintang Military Secret Service or the
Nationalist Youth Corps (*San Min Tuan*).[23] Numerous accounts of the
sabotage of industrial plant had appeared in the press since liberation[24]
and now a massive campaign was launched to flush actual or potential
saboteurs out. The registration of all spies and Kuomintang party members was ordered. If they surrendered within a given period they would
be accorded lenient treatment especially if they gave lists of their
associates, but if they did not surrender, no mercy would be shown.[25]
In fact many people did register under these regulations in late 1950
and early 1951, and a rapid exercise in data collection was undertaken
to provide the basis for mass arrests in mid-year. True to their promise,
the Communist Party was quite ruthless in the trials and executions
which followed. It is said that 28,332 people were executed in
Kwangtung province alone (one in every thousand of the population);[26]
239 people, not classified as counter-revolutionaries, also lost their lives
and 5,467 were poisoned or injured during the campaign.[27]

One will never be able to ascertain to what extent local cadres broke
faith and executed some of those who had registered and who had been
promised leniency. It is my own feeling, however, that this latter category was small, since the whole campaign was loudly publicised and
much propaganda capital was made even to the point of broadcasting
public accusation meetings over the radio. We cannot ascertain either,
the extent to which the campaign might have been used to settle old
scores.

In March 1951, Mao demanded that the movement 'be carried out
precisely, cautiously and in a planned and methodical way . . . controlled from above'.[28] During the course of the movement, therefore,
ordinary workers were not mobilised to denounce gang bosses and

secret society elements that remained in the factories. A concurrent movement that was specifically directed to mass mobilisation, however, was a donation drive to raise funds for the Korean War effort.[29] The drive, which was launched in the autumn of 1950 and intensified in mid-1951, called upon individuals, families and units of production, residence and administration to donate specific sums of money to purchase armaments for Korea.

Contracting individuals or groups might make a donation plan which was expressed in terms of the armaments the contracted sum might buy.[30] The movement was as much political as economic, for it aimed to integrate macro-politics with the day-to-day concerns of ordinary individuals and stress was laid on its educative effect. As the movement unfolded, greater identification was made between donating units and units of work, and units of production competed with each other in concluding 'patriotic compacts' to support the war effort. [31] These compacts were at first somewhat vague but, as time went by, they began to express more and more production targets which were later included in Increase Production and Practise Economy Plans.[32] In this way the formation of production plans, mass mobilisation and mass education became fused into a single process.

The slow progress of the Party and union rectification movement and the limited success of the land reform campaign in south China, in the winter of 1950-1, were in part compensated for by increasingly successful mobilisation behind the slogan 'Resist American Aggression and Aid Korea'. Towards the end of 1950, following the freezing of foreign (including White Russian) assets, the formerly permissive attitude towards foreign residents hardened.[33] Prior to the Korean war, a few newspapermen and missionaries had been expelled but the majority of foreigners, who had left China at that time, went of their own accord. But with Chinese involvement in the Korean War, greater pressure was placed on foreign firms and businessmen as back debts were assessed and greater numbers of foreigners were persuaded to leave. Cultural, religious, welfare and educational institutions with foreign affiliations were investigated, and people were mobilised to criticise foreigners, a particular target being Roman Catholic convents.[34]

With increasing criticism of foreign religious bodies, the new government began to formulate a policy towards Christian churches.[35] All foreign ties were to be broken and allegiance to foreign organisations was proscribed. The Catholic Church, with an estimated 3.3 million believers was placed in a very difficult position once it was reorganised as a national body and forbidden to proselytise. It is likely, however, that a good number of the 3.3 million were in fact 'rice Christians' attracted to the Church because of its welfare services and with no lasting commitment. Nevertheless, following the expulsion of some senior prelates accused of espionage, the new national church remained in existence in an uneasy atmosphere of official tolerance and semi-official discouragement.

Accompanying the mass mobilisation against foreign influence was a mammoth drive to create a nationwide propaganda network.[36] In the very early period, activists were divided into 'propagandists' (*xuanchuanyuan*) and routine 'agitators' (*gudongyuan*) along Soviet lines,[37] though soon a new level of propagandist was instituted — the 'reporter' (*baogaoyuan*). He was usually a high-ranking cadre whose job was to invest with authority the activities of lower-level propagandists. Propaganda posts were set up throughout all the mass organisations as well as centres for disseminating a growing volume of literature.

Propagandists were to busy themselves in the escalating campaigns against opium smoking, prostitution, gambling and alcoholism. They faced particularly arduous tasks in the campaign against 'cultural imperialism' in the field of education. Jazz and romantic ('yellow') music came under attack. Kuomintang textbooks were removed and replaced by material which had been prepared in the liberated areas and in Hong Kong. Film circulation began to be controlled, though Western movies were shown throughout most of 1950. Mass criticism was instituted against the notion of 'art for art's sake' and Mao Tse-tung's 'Talks at the Yenan Forum on Literature and Art'[38] were widely disseminated. Attempts were made to introduce and standardise political training in institutions of tertiary education, though a more thorough campaign of thought reform (*sixiang gaizao*) did not really get under way until mid-1951, and then only in the older liberated areas. On all these measures, the Party pinned high hopes though, as we shall have cause to remark time and again, the influences it sought to eradicate were remarkably persistent.

In the new atmosphere of mass mobilisation, attempts were made to recapture the spirit of Yenan with its close bond between soldiers and civilians. An earlier system, whereby the dependants of servicemen were compensated by their neighbours for loss of labour power, was reintroduced and more and more cadres were transferred from the Army to help with mass movements such as land reform. Notable successes were achieved in building up a People's Militia which was expanded from 5 million in 1950 to 12.8 million by the autumn of 1951,[39] and this militia provided recruits for the PLA of which initially 700,000 were in active service with the Chinese People's Volunteers in Korea.[40]

The stress now was on the quality of China's armed forces and China's leaders felt sufficiently confident to resume the process of demobilisation, though at first this was probably confined to ex-Kuomintang garrison troops who did not form part of the field armies.[41] Success at the front had given the PLA a new élan, though this élan could not conceal the fact that the war constituted a tremendous drain on the Chinese economy which had hardly begun to recover from the ravages of the Civil War. The Soviet Union, convinced now that Mao was not another Tito,[42] provided some military aid particularly after the autumn of 1951. Furthermore China was not short of unskilled manpower. The country lacked, however, skilled workers, technicians and doctors. (The doctor-population ratio at that time was probably only some 1:10,000 of whom 7-8 per cent were enrolled for service in Korea).[43] New military academies were set up, enrolling students with technical and engineering qualifications who might have been employed elsewhere in the economy. The cost of the Korean War was quite considerable but perhaps what is more important, in the light of the subsequent history of the People's Republic, was that the Army was becoming more and more a professional body, unlike the old Army of Yenan and Civil War days.

The Further Intensification of Reform (1951)

Following the spring sowing of 1951 and flushed with a new confidence, the Party radicals attempted to bring urban and rural reform in line with the mass enthusiasm engendered by the war. Large numbers of ex-Fourth Field Army cadres were moved south from Wuhan in work-teams to speed up the process of land reform and, in May, criticism of the 'five kinds of personal relationships' (*wutong guanxi*) (loyalty to those of the same surname, same clan, same village, same school and same working place) was intensified.[44] Local cadres who tended towards conservatism were subjected to criticism and attitudes towards landlords (including those who had taken up business in the cities) hardened. As mass mobilisation in the rural areas got under way, schedules for the completion of land reform were brought forward.

In the urban areas, a major attempt was made in May 1951 to carry the Democratic Reform Movement to a successful conclusion,[45] this time by mass mobilisation. Conservatives still argued that such mobilisation should not exceed that of the Campaign for the Suppression of Counter-Revolutionaries, of which the current movement was but the sequel.[46] A commitment to gradualism led them to propose that it might be sufficient to flush out feudal elements during production competitions[47] or that registration of workers for labour insurance might reveal the parasitic.[48]

The Party leadership, however, adhered to its new commitment to mass mobilisation and set up Democratic Reform Committees to lead the movement. Three stages were designated — 'democratic struggle', 'democratic unity' and 'democratic construction'.[49] The first of these, launched by outside cadres' 'initiation reports' (*qifa baogao*), concentrated on general issues such as imperialism and the Chiang K'ai-shek regime. Before long, attacks became more specific as more and more workers found, through participation in the earlier meetings, sufficient confidence to accuse people with whom they were in daily contact. Once sufficient numbers of workers were involved, groups of activists were formed to conduct discussions and formulate specific accusations of selected targets. As the movement widened in its appeal and narrowed in its criticism, 'speak-bitterness' meetings were held which drew directly on the experiences of land reform. Nevertheless, though gang bosses were occasionally dragged through the streets,[50] the urban movement was much milder than its rural counterpart.

In both the Democratic Reform Movement and land reform, mass reaction tended to be similar. The fear of retaliation and a long tradition of deference resulted in an initial reluctance to denounce the accused, though once the accusations got under way a climate was created where the accused rapidly put an end to their anguish by repenting.[51] Despite the new stress on mass mobilisation, however, both movements proceeded more slowly than anticipated, not only because of the strength of traditional ties but also because of the weakness of lower level Party branches. In the towns, this situation led to even greater political movements and in the countryside, to an intensification of land reform in the autumn of 1951.

In most cases the 'struggle' stage of the Democratic Reform Movement went on until the autumn of 1951, though some units did commence the second stage, that of 'democratic unity'. Workers who had previously been forced to join reactionary organisations such as the Kuomintang Militia or police force, were required to confess their past misdeeds and submit themselves for criticism.[52] Struggle was now to be avoided and errant workers were reincorporated into the community. In such a situation, a new enthusiasm developed for labour union activities[53] though, as had been suggested, the labour unions were, from the Party's point of view, not particularly healthy. As for the final stage of the movement — 'democratic construction' — not much could be done until a whole series of mass movements had come to an end. The really radical ones were yet to come.

The Labour Union Crisis (1951)

With the radicalisation of May 1951, more attention was devoted to the 'economist' trend in the unions. After engaging in intensive debate on the different standpoints of unions, Party and management,[54] the All China Federation of Labour (ACFL) journal *Chinese Workers* (*Zhongguo Gongren*) was suspended and it became increasingly apparent that peaceful means of dealing with 'economism' (such as linking welfare demands with collective contracts between unions and management) were ineffective. In July 1951 it was estimated that, although over half of all union branches in north-east China were considered to be relatively successful in mobilising workers to fulfil plans and engage in production competitions, they were unable to co-ordinate welfare demands with productivity.[55] The great problem was that cadres, once censured for echoing the 'commandist' demands of management, had now drifted to a 'tailist' position whereby they merely put forward welfare demands without explaining the difficulties in their realisation.

Though 'economism' permeated all levels of the ACFL network, the problem was less serious at lower levels than it might have been.[56] First vertical links within the ACFL hierarchy were relatively weak and this prevented the effective transmission of an 'economist' line to all union branches. Secondly, labour union cadres were still subject to rapid transfer and were thus prevented from maintaining effective contact with lower levels.

By the second half of 1951, a full-scale reform of labour unions was under way. Now the theme of 'bureaucratism', which had dominated the earlier rectification movement, was joined by that of 'anti-feudalism' (which derived from the Democratic Reform Movement) and 'anti-economism'. A major programme of re-electing union branches was undertaken, though we are not clear with what success, since the key documents relating to the reform, such as Li Fu-ch'un's report to the Party faction (*Dangzu*) of the ACFL in December, were never published. All we may observe is the official (1953) comment on the proceedings of the second half of 1951 that most cadres had not followed the 'economist line' in the labour unions.[57]

In may ways, the labour crisis of 1951 was similar to the Soviet labour union crisis of 1920-1[58] and there were similarities in the approaches of Tomsky and the effective head of the ACFL, Li Li-san, who had returned from the Soviet Union in 1948 after a long exile following the debacles of 1930. There were, however, a number of differences, the most crucial of which was that in China the crisis took place in an atmosphere of growing centralisation of economic administration, whereas in the Soviet Union it originated in an opposition to economic centralisation and took place before the widespread decentralisation of the New Economic Policy.

The Centralisation of Economic Administration (1949-51)

Having outlined the major political movements from mid-1950 to the autumn of 1951, it is possible to draw a few conclusions about them. First, each movement was more radical than the one that preceded it and involved a greater degree of mass mobilisation. The movements ceased to be simple exercises from the top down and more and more involved the conscious participation of the masses. Secondly, movements of this latter type, led by the Party, were effective to the extent that horizontal links were stronger than vertical ones in the dual-rule scheme of organisation outlined in the last chapter. Thirdly, one might anticipate that the success of such movements would slow down the effective building of vertical ministerial chains of command and, conversely, would be impeded by such chains of command that already existed. We are confronted here by a classic contradictory situation — between administrative leadership directed towards managerial and bureaucratic goals and Party leadership directed towards political goals. Before considering the greatest of these horizontally mobilised movements, therefore, it would be useful to consider the degree of administrative centralisation by the autumn of 1951.

At the time of liberation, the Party inherited a fragmented administrative system and a mixed economy. As regional administrations were set up on an *ad hoc* basis, the model in the minds of cadres was that of the Soviet Union at the time of the New Economic Policy.[59] Indeed, south of the Great Wall this model was taken sufficiently seriously for people to advocate the establishment of semi-autonomous economic organisations similar to the Soviet NEP trusts. In Tientsin in 1949, for example, Liu Shao-ch'i had advocated the establishment of ten horizontally integrated corporations and the incorporation of sundry factories, which did not fall into clearly defined production criteria, into 'joint enterprises' (*lianhe qiye*).[60] Liu stated that private firms could enter these organisations, though it is difficult to imagine how this would have worked out in practice.

In the north-east on the other hand, the model of economic organisation which was followed was that of the contemporary Soviet Union,

actualised in the occupied areas of Lushun and Talien. A north-east
industrial department (*Gongyebu*) was set up which controlled nine
administrative bureaux and two corporations – the Anshan and Penki
Iron and Steel Works.[61] The administrative bureaux were the counterparts of Soviet organisational forms known as *glavki* and the corporations were the equivalent of Soviet combines. With the exception of the
corporations, the basic economic accounting unit was the economic
'enterprise' (*qiye*), again similar to its Soviet counterpart. In the
economy as a whole, the commercially-defined companies and
territorially-defined factories were redefined administratively according
to a process known as 'enterprisation' (*qiyehua*), whereby an internal
'economic accounting system' (*jingji hesuanzhi*) (*khozraschët*) meshed
in with the rudiments of a wider planning system.[62]

The aim was to create an integrated Soviet-style planning system,
first in the north-east and then throughout the country, though at first
this was extremely difficult. Vague annual plans had been in existence
in the north-east since 1948[63] but it is doubtful whether these general
plans were articulated to operational planning within factories until
much later. In the early days of its existence (after 1949), the north-
east Industrial Department operated according to ten-day operational
plans with controls far tighter than could ever be carried out in the
chaotic situation that prevailed.[64] Allocation problems restricted the
proportion of the market supply of products controlled by the state.
Planning was frustrated by wide cost disparities, even between sectors
of the same industry,[65] and supply problems remained serious. Nevertheless, by 1951 there had been established in the north-east a blueprint
for national planning that was intended to be implemented over the
whole country by 1953.

Reliance on Soviet models of planning was matched by reliance on
Soviet methods of industrial organisation. The prescribed model was
very clearly one of vertical rule with restricted scope for the operation
of the Party branches. Quite unashamedly, former advocates of the
Yenan-style 'dual rule' pattern of control and of 'concentrated leadership and divided operations' now looked sympathetically on Soviet-
style 'one man management' (*danyi lingdaozhi* or *yizhangzhi*).[66]
According to this system, each manager at each level of organisation
enjoyed exclusive authority and exclusive responsibility for everything
that happened in his area of jurisdiction. Cadres in other leading roles,
be they technical, financial or even political, were gradually reduced
to merely 'staff' status. Advocates of planning concentrated on balancing the books and tended to look askance at political movements

which destabilised their operations. Some people began to see production as more important than political awareness and this view militated
against movements such as Democratic Reform which sought to flush
out gang bosses who might also be highly skilled. The contradiction
was becoming acute, but the sheer momentum of the movements, set
in motion in the second half of 1950 and the first half of 1951, was
such that each failure and each shortcoming only spurred the drive for
more thorough mass mobilisation. The trend towards verticalisation
and the reduction in the role of horizontal (Party) linkages was, for the
time being, halted.

The Three Anti Movement (August 1951-June 1952)

The Movement to Create New Records had been launched in north-east
China in 1949 to formulate production norms. This grew into a Movement to Increase Production and Practise Economy which was formally
begun in August 1951. Like its predecessor, the movement originated in
the north-east.[67] It absorbed the drive for donations to help the Korean
War effort, merged with the three main political movements in the
urban sphere — Democratic Reform, Party Rectification and Union
Rectification — and linked up with a parallel campaign in progress in
the academic world dealing with Ideological Reform. This latter movement, under way since the spring of 1951, took on a new intensity
following Chou En-lai's report to a mass meeting of academics on 29
September, after which intensive discussion and criticism took place
concerning the 'standpoint' of adminsitrative and teaching staff. In
October, the movement was formalised by the Government Administration Council's 'Decision on the Reform of the Educational System'[68]
whereby the former *laissez-faire* policy towards educational institutions
was officially replaced by a greater emphasis on political and ideological
training.

By that time, it was impossible to separate all the various movements
and parts of movements that were going on. Everything had merged
into a nationwide upheaval known as the Three Anti Movement which
took as its main targets graft, waste and bureaucratism.[69] At first, an
attempt was made to examine the political factors that had led to waste
— bureaucratism, the rural viewpoint, and a cavalier attitude towards
planning. Then, the scope of the movement was widened to take in all
the post-liberation targets for reform — the tendency to relax after
victory, to feather one's own nest, tardiness in implementing democratic reform, etc. During the early stages one could often find the principal suspect targets of the movement actually leading it, but as the

campaign moved closer to the daily concerns of workers, large numbers
of activists outside the Party became involved in criticising urban and
industrial leadership.

Formal leadership in the movement was usually vested in Increase
Production and Practise Economy Committees (*Zengchan Jieyue
Weiyuanhui*) at municipal level, organised according to the United
Front principle.[70] In practice, however, leadership rested with the
Party who acted through these bodies. Within factories, local Party
committees took the initiative, though at higher levels Retrenchment
and Economy Committees (*Jingjian Jieyueh Weiyuanhui*) were set up
to flush out people guilty of bureaucratism[71] and, within the educational sphere, Austerity Inspection Committees began to organise
students.[72]

The initial stage consisted of mobilising industrial workers to detect
serious crimes and these were dealt with by the courts. In the east
China region during this stage, which lasted until mid-December 1951,
higher level courts and organs of the Procuracy dealt with 179 cases
of graft involving some ¥29 million and, according to the East China
People's Control Commission, the amount of money involved in cases
of graft and loss of state property in that region, from September 1950
to November 1951, was some ¥124 million. Convictions by the courts
in the region numbered 650, of whom 470 were employed in government departments or financial and economic enterprises. Of the 650,
356 were retained personnel and 133 new cadres.[73] These figures were
small, however, for by the end of the movement in mid-1952 it was
estimated that 4.5 per cent of all state officials in China had received
some form of punishment.[74]

Within the field of education in late 1951, the Austerity Inspection
Committees initiated the criticism of professors and other academics.
Their efforts culminated in mass criticism meetings, resulting in one or
more confessions from each of the accused. The objects of criticism
included worshipping the United States, placing research above teaching,
individualism, indifference to politics, neglecting political study and
clinging to old habits.[75] The results in retrospect were not remarkable
but it should be remembered that at that time the most urgent field for
reform was considered to be industry and civil administration and here
the movement was to reach new heights in the following year.

In January 1952, the movement was widened to include a larger
range of targets. It was discovered that former capitalists, now employed
in the state sector, were using economic information to help their relatives and colleagues in the private sector[76] and government officials

were said to be taking bribes to treat former capitalists leniently. In the view of Kao Kang the Party had been relying too much on the bourgeoisie and, unless this reliance was severed, the end of the Party was in sight.[77] By that time, the policy of placing targets of the movement in leading positions was beginning to reveal a situation in which a movement designed to combat bureaucratism, was being run itself with undue bureaucratism and Kao Kang was in a position to expose the guilty. At the same time, Li Li-san, under a cloud for advocating too 'economist' a line in the ACFL, castigated the unions for bourgeois thought, bad leadership and an undue concern for status[78] (which, as we have seen, led to union cadres complaining that they were 'fourth class').

By early 1952, all leading personnel in economic administration were involved in the movement in some way, often neglecting their production duties. Particular problems were created when those guilty of graft were flushed out of supply departments with no one to replace them.[79] As a consequence, planned targets for many commodities were not reached in the month of January 1952 and there was occasionally a decline in the quality of products.[80] In the following month, the movement entered a stage of consolidation. A concern for production led to the provision of detailed limitations on the amount of time management might devote to the movement.[81] 'Tiger bashing' (*dahu*) (the flushing out of principal targets) was now combined with production competitions and efforts were directed to making up for the decline in production. By March 1952, steady production in the state sector seems to have been resumed.

The Five Anti Movement (January-June 1952)

The extension of the Three Anti Movement, in January 1952, into the private sector gave birth to a parallel movement specifically aimed at that sector known as the Five Anti Movement.[82] Here, the five targets were bribery, tax evasion, theft of state property, cheating on government contracts, and stealing state economic information. Responsibility for running this movement again lay with the Increase Production and Practise Economy Committees, which included industrialists from the private sector, aided by similar committees set up in organisations of private capitalists such as the federations of industry and commerce. In the early stages of the movement, attempts were made to persuade selected businessmen to confess their misdemeanours and engage in 'self-examination', though predictably most of them did not participate willingly in this process and 'defensive alliances' began to form.

In February 1952, businessmen in the private sector were subjected to a number of regulations, such as being confined to their place of work and being forbidden to go out of business, to dismiss employees, withhold or lower wages or conclude alliances with dubious elements in the public sector. At the same time, labour unions were instructed to mobilise industrial and shop workers to investigate their employers and write letters of denunciation. Teams were organised to go into key areas where private management was suspect and to propagandise their findings. 'Five Anti battle headquarters' were set up, newspaper reading groups were organised and 'Five Anti broadcasting stations' proliferated, in an all-out attempt to involve the whole working class in the private sector — literate and illiterate alike.

The response of workers and industrialists was similar to the response of peasants and landlords in the agrarian struggle or workers and gang bosses in the Democratic Reform Movement. After some initial reserve and fear of reprisals the movement acquired a considerable momentum, often to the point of getting out of hand. Officially, specialist teams were to investigate suspected capitalists, though by February 1952 workers occasionally took the law into their own hands and initiated inspection themselves.

Paralleling the stress on orderly production in the public sector in March, the Five Anti Movement entered a planned stage. Direct action without the authorisation of the Increase Production and Practise Economy Committees was now forbidden and new inspection brigades set out on a process of 'key-point testing'. At the same time, 'Five Anti work-teams', organised on a three-tier basis (urban ward, sub-urban ward, and individual firm), mobilised the workers according to techniques with which we are already familiar — 'speak bitterness' meetings, confrontation meetings, etc. As workers gradually developed a confidence that at least they were 'masters', many employers began to change sides and form what was known as a 'Five Anti United Front'. Such actions split the ranks of the businessmen and gave a tremendous propaganda fillip to the campaign. Capitalists who had 'achieved merit' in this way were treated leniently and sent around the cities advertising the benefits of such action. By early May, the Party could claim 'basic victory' in the movement and, in June, a formal end was called to both the Three and Five Anti Movements.[83]

The description above has drawn much on the parallel with land reform but this is useful only in comparing patterns of mobilisation and response. The treatment meted out to capitalists and landlords was quite dissimilar, even if one considers the earlier, milder period of land

reform. All landlords at least lost their land whereas, according to
P'eng Chen, only 1 per cent of the business community was designated
as 'big robbing elements' and subject to imprisonment and labour
reform. Even then, some of these elements could 'achieve merit' by
confession. By May, people's tribunals had been set up to deal with
these elements and the most frequent forms of punishment were fines
or confiscation rather than more serious penalties.[84] This is not to say
that the effects of the campaign were not profound.

The movement increased the dependence of capitalists upon the
Communist Party and the People's Government in three important
respects. First, capitalists were now fearful of leaving the United
Front; they realised the immense power both of organised labour and
the state. Financial losses incurred in the movement were frequently
made up by loans from the People's Bank which produced indebtedness
and facilitated state financial control.[85] There could be no doubt that,
although 31 per cent of total production still came from the private
sector of the economy,[86] the state sector was supreme. Secondly, the
Five Anti Movement strengthened organisations designed to maintain
working-class control over private businessmen and industrialists.
Among these were the labour-capital consultative conferences which,
although set up before the movements, acquired a new importance.
These bodies brought unions and management together in the private
sector and facilitated the control of the former over the latter.[87] At a
national level one of the 'democratic parties', the China National Democratic Construction Association, promoted the extension of ideological
reform from the sphere of intellectuals, where it had begun in 1951, to
the world of private industry and commerce. The All China Federation
of Industry and Commerce, likewise, began to act as a 'transmission
belt' between Party and national bourgeoisie and to organise education
in New Democracy.[88] A third consequence of the Five Anti Movement
was the generation of a whole new corps of activitists who began to
replace the many defective cadres who had hitherto exercised leading
roles in the labour unions and who had been responsible for the slow
pace of union reform in 1950-1. Utilising the extensive propaganda network established during the movement, these activists advanced the
penetration of most aspects of urban life to a new level.

It is true that the Three Anti and Five Anti Movements had some
adverse economic effects and an unemployment problem in 1952 may
have influenced the date of their termination.[89] It is important to note,
however, that the subordination of the private sector to that of the state
facilitated the move towards more centralised planning already under

way before the movements began, and this, in the longer run, probably had a far greater effect on the economy. From an administrative point of view, the plethora of movements strengthened the horizontal component in the 'dual rule' pattern of administration and gave local Party organisations a much more effective role. In the years which followed, however, there was a gradual decline in that effectiveness to the point that, in the mid-1950s, movements of the Three Anti type had of necessity to be reinstituted.

The End of Radicalism (1952)

The return to a policy of consolidation in the urban sphere in mid-1952 was accompanied by similar moves in the rural sector. With the 'high-tide' of the land reform movement in south China in the autumn of 1951, a call had been issued for the completion of land reform in that area by the spring of 1952. After the arrival of the former Fourth Field Army cadre, T'ao Chu, in Kwangtung in early 1952, the official policy changed to rectifying conservative and localist (*benweizhuyi de*) cadres in the countryside. As land reform drew to a close, more and more former Fourth Field Army cadres, based on Wuhan, were moved south displacing local cadres and aiding an inexorable drive towards centralisation.[90]

In many other areas, policies which were initially quite radical took on a more cautious note by mid-1952. In December 1951, for example, the Central Committee of the Party had attempted to accelerate the pace of rural co-operativisation[91] but by mid-1952 not much had been achieved and policy became more gradualist. The implementation of the new Marriage Law underwent a similar change. The new law, which was to free people from the bondage of the traditional family system, had occasionally been promoted far too zealously with cadres actively engaged in propagandising divorce. One of the results of this was an increase in the suicide rate, while the murder rate also rose as a result of discarded spouses seeking revenge on those who had humiliated them by ending their marriage. It was reported in 1953 by the National Committee for the Thorough Implementation of the Marriage Law that over 75,000 deaths or suicides in one year could be attributed to marriage differences,[92] though we are not sure of the extent to which these were due to the implementation or non-implementation of the Law. As the new period of consolidation began, the keynote was caution. The Yenan style had been to bring about change from within existing institutions, not to smash them. The family revolution was to take some time.

The Lean to One Side Becomes More Pronounced (1952-4)

The new period of consolidation coincided with an improvement in
relations between the Soviet Union and China. Although the Korean
War brought China and the Soviet Union closer together, there was
initially a certain coolness between the two countries on the degree of
Soviet military aid. During the first phase of China's involvement in the
war (November 1950-June 1951), the Chinese People's Volunteers
were reported to have been very badly equipped.[93] Nonetheless,
demonstrating Mao's dictum that 'men are superior to weapons', considerable military successes were achieved. The first rapid Sino-North
Korean offensive captured Seoul on 4 January 1951. By mid-June,
however, vastly superior UN munitions and air power drove the Chinese
and North Korean forces back to the 38th Parallel. Truce talks began in
July 1951 and, from the end of that year to the armistice on 27 July
1953, both sides remained bogged down around the Parallel. The
Chinese forces found themselves fighting a positional war with which
they were unfamiliar.

Although some resentment may have been caused by the refusal of
the Soviet Union to involve itself in the fighting,[94] the cautious policy
of the Soviet Union prevented further escalation and at least China was now
protected by the Soviet nuclear shield. Following the military stalemate
in the second half of 1951, supplies of Soviet military aid to China
increased and an effective Chinese air force was created to fight a war
which was increasingly being carried on in the air.[95]

With the stepping up of aid, coolness between the two countries
dissipated somewhat but a number of bones of contention still
remained concerning the degree to which Chinese sovereignty was
limited by areas of joint Sino-Soviet control. In the autumn of 1952,
serious and hard bargaining began. During the visit of Chou En-lai to
Moscow in September 1952, the two governments announced that
control over the north-eastern railways would be returned to China by
the end of 1952 but the Russians would remain in Lushun and Talien,
allegedly at Peking's request.[96] (which is not unlikely since the Korean
War was still in progress). Upon Chou's departure from Moscow, a large
number of representatives remained behind to continue negotiations
and, in October, Liu Shao-ch'i arrived for the Nineteenth Congress of
the Communist Party of the Soviet Union (though we are unsure as to
whether he took part in the negotiations). Since China's first five year
Plan was to begin in 1953, there was a certain urgency about determining the degree of Soviet assistance. Negotiations, however, were to

drag on well into 1953 and were complicated by discussions concerning the termination of the Korean War and by the death of Stalin.

There has been much speculation on exactly how the Korean War was brought to an end and the extent to which nuclear blackmail might have been used. Suffice it to note here that the main opponent of armistice was South Korea's Syngman Rhee who still believed in mid-1953 that he could win.[97] With the Chinese attack on the élite Korean White Tiger Regiment (subsequently the subject of a famous revolutionary Peking opera), Rhee's hopes were dashed and an armistice was signed.

Meanwhile, after the death of Stalin in March 1953, the Sino-Soviet climate for negotiations improved. There is insufficient evidence to test the claim subsequently made by Nikita Khruschev that Stalin had actually impeded Sino-Soviet relations.[98] Nonetheless, it is true that before long the new Russian leadership committed itself to providing far greater aid and assistance to China. The Soviet Union promised to supply China with a number of key industrial projects to facilitate the development of the five year plan. Upon the visit of Bulganin and Kruschev to Peking in the autumn of 1954, it was finally agreed that Lushun and Talien should be handed back to China; the number of Soviet aid projects was increased; a new loan was negotiated and agreements on railway construction signed. In the words of Khruschev, China was now a 'great power' and 'after the Great October Socialist Revolution, the victory of the Chinese people's revolution is the most outstanding event in world history', one which has 'immense significance for the peoples of Asia'.[99] As a Soviet model of development began to be applied in China, Sino-Soviet relations acquired a new warmth, to the point that at the European Security Conference held in Moscow in December 1954, the Chinese observer Chang Wen-t'ien declared that China would be bound by the terms of the Sino-Soviet alliance to join in the defence of Europe if peace were threatened.[100]

With the Korean War over, improved Sino-Soviet relations and the change of Soviet foreign policy to one of accommodation with newly emerging nations, the government of the Chinese People's Republic, which now enjoyed unparalleled prestige in the socialist camp, began to formulate an independent foreign policy (though not too dissimilar to that of the Soviet Union). As attempts were made to drive United States influence out of Asia by winning over neutrals or quasi-neutrals, an era of peaceful coexistence was to begin.

The Establishment of a Nationwide Planning Network (1951-3)

In the aftermath of the turbulent movements of 1951-2, attention
began to be devoted to orderly planning. Indeed, as we have seen, even
while the Five Anti Movement was in progress, measures were taken to
see that mobilisation proceeded according to plan. A regional planning
commission had been set up in north-east China as early as 1951[101] but
it was not until the second half of 1952 that attempts were made to
reproduce the north-east model in the country as a whole. In August
1952, a State Statistical Bureau (*Guojia Tongji ju*) was set up, followed
by a State Planning Commission (*Guojia Jihua Weiyuanhui*) in preparation for the first five year plan. The priority given to the establishment
of a planning network is reflected in the fact that, on its establishment
in November 1952, the State Planning Commission was given status
equal to the Government Administration Council, which meant that its
head, Kao Kang, who had been transferred from the north-east, was
rated in the formal government apparatus equal to the Premier, Chou
En-lai (though his status in the Party remained lower).[102]

Together with the renewed stress on 'rational' planning went a stress
on 'rational' organisation. By late 1952, 'rational' very clearly meant
'Soviet' and large numbers of Soviet advisers were on hand to help
China implement its form of 'rational' organisation which had already
been introduced in north-east China. Kao Kang, said to be an arch-
exponent of the Soviet model, was elevated to new heights, though it
is perhaps worthwhile bearing in mind that another possible explanation
for his transfer might have been that his attempts to create an 'independent kingdom' in the north-east prompted Mao Tse-tung and others
to keep an eye on him in Peking. Whatever the explanation, Kao was
to be extremely influential in forging the new 'rationality' and articles
in the press were not stinting in his praise.

The prescribed procedure for drawing up a plan in 1952 was according
to the formula 'two up and two down'. The relevant ministry or industrial department would send control figures down through a long chain
of command to the enterprise. The enterprise would then work out a
draft plan for the approval of the higher level. After making amendments, the plan would descend once again to provide the basis of concrete work plans. Finally the resulting documents would be sent back
to the higher level for approval.[103] Such a procedure involved much
discussion which, in the immediate post-liberation period, might have
been initiated by factory management committees. By late 1952, however, these bodies were defunct and discussion either concerned merely

matters of operational detail or involved an inordinately long period of time. In an atmosphere in which efficient and speedy operation was the watchword, the former was more likely and, where discussions were thorough, they resulted in the late appearance of the final document.[104] The role of the Party organisation here was crucial. It could either promote the participation of workers in planning or act as the moral agent of management in securing compliance with predetermined targets. Increasingly the Party took this latter 'commandist' attitude, especially after the adoption in 1953 of the slogan 'The state plan is law' and after what seemed to be a lesson of the Five Anti Movement, that too wide a dissemination of 'economic secrets' encouraged corruption.[105] Rigidity in plan implementation seemed to be the order of the day,[106] as an all-out attempt was made to implement a model of organisation that derived from the Soviet Union.

The Soviet Model of Organisation and Administration[107]

The first feature of the Yenan model, described in the last chapter, was the concept of 'rectification'. The rectification movement of 1942 had been directed against foreign dogma and ready-made theories not adapted to the Chinese environment. Now in the early 1950s, Soviet forms of organisation and motivation were often adopted holus-bolus without adequate thought about the problem of adaptation. In the conservative atmosphere after 1952, conflict was avoided where possible but competition between individuals was actively encouraged. Production competitions rewarded the advanced producer with both prestige and money. Incentive policy was both material and individual with huge bonuses accruing to worker and manager alike if they fulfilled production goals. Conversely, a system of individual responsibility assigned all work tasks to specific individuals who were penalised if they failed to achieve them. One does not have to be much of a dialectician to see that such an individual incentive and responsibility system might grow over into what had long been denounced as 'bourgeois individualism' and militate against collective consciousness.

In such an organised individualised system, the concept of 'cadre' leadership gradually changed. 'Rational' organisation, according to the Soviet model, was characterised by technological solidarity with interrole relationships becoming more important than inter-personal relationships. The leadership type now was at best managerial, when committed to fast technological change, and at worst that of the modern bureaucrat who just went along with the system. The manager and the modern bureaucrat were less responsive to the opinions of those they worked

amongst and tended to confine criticism and self-criticism to meetings
of those they considered their peers. The commitment of leadership, in
this new situation, was still to the Party but increasingly to the Party as
organisation or to the Party mediated by other organisations. Operating
within a network of technological solidarity, the commitment of the
new leadership was more to ability (*cai*) than 'virtue' (*de*) or, in those
cases where the leader might explain that it was the contrary, the concept 'virtue' was interpreted increasingly in terms of expertise. Within
a network of human solidarity, the lax cadre could slip back into the
role of traditional bureaucrat — inert but occasionally accessible. In the
new network of technological solidarity, the lax 'manager' could slip
into the role of modern bureaucrat — inert perhaps, but quite
inaccessible.

Now that the operative slogans were 'regularise, systematise,
rationalise, and centralise', the Mass Line, though still proclaimed,
changed in content. The original idea of 1942 signified a process
whereby general policy was integrated with mass demands. By the early
1950s this formulation increasingly became the integration of general
policy with mass support for that policy. Workers participated less in
planning; they were more educated as to how to fulfil plans made
elsewhere. The Soviet view of the relationship between leaders and led
was that there were no contradictions. Thus they tended to see any conflict as counter-revolutionary. Increasingly the 'disease' was not cured
to 'save the patient' but diseased parts were amputated. Labour reform,
therefore, became less a process of remoulding than a form of punishment.

Under centralised leadership, the idea of the existence of a dichotomy between policy and operations became weaker. Leaders infrequently went down to the basic level or to the countryside to renew
their links with the masses and to discover to what extent policy and
operations might be at variance. The working-class identification of
leadership was assumed but rarely tested. As a result of this, the gap
between urban and rural areas grew not only in a political and ideological sense but also in an economic sense. An urban-oriented leadership now adopted the kind of economic strategy that is the bane of
most Third World countries. Though some attention was devoted to
industrialising medium-sized cities in the interior, considerable emphasis
was still laid on building up existing industrial areas, such as the north-
east and the old treaty ports, and an élite sector of industry consisting
of whole plants imported from the Soviet Union.

With centralisation came the adoption of a cumbersome staff-line pattern of administration organised according to the principle of vertical rule. Each leader at each level of administration tended to become exclusively responsible for activities within his sphere of jurisdiction. Within the factories, as we have noted, this pattern took the form of 'one man management' which replaced the earlier collegial system of decision-making now denounced as 'parliamentary'. Attached to each manager or bureaucrat on the line were a number of technical staff who now could not easily be deployed functionally where needed. It is axiomatic that when staff-line principles of organisation prevail, chains of command tend to elongate and the number of people attached to the line at middle levels of organisation tends to grow, effectively insulating the top of an organisation from its base. Even if the will to implement the Mass Line existed under such circumstances, organisational structures were not conducive to such implementation.

In 1953 industry, in the nation as a whole, was reorganised according to the structure of the north-east industrial department with ministries taking the place of the former administrative bureaux. Each ministry maintained its own hierarchy extending through the large administrative regions, provinces and cities down to individual productive units or offices. A network of parallel hierarchies was spawned, all subject less to lateral Party committee co-ordination than to further hierarchies of control. As the formal state control system (which culminated in a Ministry of State Control) extended down to the basic level, the nature of control changed from *internal* political control (as practised by the Party during the movements of 1951-2) to *external* economic control which consisted largely on checking up on economic performance after the event. In such a structure the Party, as the supreme co-ordinating body, found it increasingly difficult to operate. At a macro-political level, the Party was becoming fused with a state which it was designed to assist in withering away. As such it was guilty of bureaucratism.

A technological conception of solidarity, a stress on expertise with the engineer as the new culture hero, and a centralised administrative system, resulted in an overwhelming stress on a technocratic and formal education system. The old liberal universities modelled on a Euro-American pattern were not abolished but had the Soviet system of technical academies grafted upon them. In the new idiom of production, education was seen as a resource, just like coal or iron ore, which served as an input into a system which produced goods.[108] It was not seen in the wider sense, which I believe held in Yenan, as a qualitatively different type of resource which was itself resource-creating. The stress

was on quality above quantity and the *selection* of an educated élite
to serve the new needs of production. Mass fulfilment and other human
concerns were considered irrelevant. The school system was indeed
greatly expanded but it was the *school* system. Education was equated
with *schooling* and *urban schooling* at that. The children of the
bourgeoisie were not to be given preference *qua* children of the
bourgeoisie, but it so happened that those children more easily fulfilled
the entry standards of an examination-based technocratic system.

The Soviet Model in the Army

In the prevailing climate, the PLA was seen increasingly from a technological point of view. In the early days after liberation, the Army was
once again involved in agricultural production and, in some cases, the
old idea of achieving partial self-sufficiency in food was revived. As the
Korean War shifted from mobile to positional warfare, the old idea of
People's War atrophied. In his Army Day order on 1 August 1951,[109]
Chu Teh had called for modernisation but within the tradition of
People's War. In his national day (1 October) order of that year, Chu
made no mention of political tasks. One year later, the order called on
the PLA to master its profession and, on 1 October 1953, the order had
become 'learn from the advanced military science and techniques of the
Soviet Union'. The idea of a *professional* Army was a disturbing one. I
define a professional as one who is committed not just to the values of
his calling but one who increasingly uses them to interpret those of
other callings. In such a situation the notion of *ésprit de corps*, which is
defined in relation to other corps, was profoundly élitist and contra-
dicted the whole Yenan tradition of People's War.

The former political control system, with dual command exercised
by commander and political commissar, began to decline and as more
Soviet weapons became available towards the end of the Korean War and
thereafter, Mao's fundamental notion that the attitude of the men was
more important than the weapons they held was severely weakened. An
élitist air force was built up with Soviet help and military academies
began to train an officer corps with recruits no longer drawn from the
ranks.[110] In 1955, a whole panoply of ranks was borrowed from the
Soviet Union together with a system of orders and decorations.[111] By
early 1953 plans were well under way for introducing conscription to
replace the older militia system which had earned the scorn of professionals. The new conscription system was in force by 1954 with 3 years
for the Army, 4 years for the Air Force and 5 years for the Navy.[112]
The reason for its introduction was not that insufficient recruits were

forthcoming, but to make educated youth available for an increasingly technocratic army, to keep costs down and to create a trained reserved which was felt to be more 'modern' than the older militia system.

The last word on this fundamental change in the whole tradition of the People's Liberation Army was said by Minister of Defence P'eng Teh-huai when he noted that men 'fail to realise that past revolutionary experience, even experience in the Korean War, has a definitely limited value'.[113]

The Bureaucratisation of the Countryside

While we cannot speak of a Soviet Model in agriculture, we can speak of the effect on agriculture of a stress on stability and orderly government. With the winding-up of land reform in 1952-3, the structure of power in the Chinese countryside had undergone profound changes. In effect, a whole class had been neutralised though the bodies through which that neutralisation had been effected were but a shadow of their former selves. The poor peasant bands of Civil War days were now defunct and the peasant associations, which had once taken a radical lead in mass mobilisation, were formed into *xiang* people's congresses and *xiang* people's governments.[114] These organs operated largely through pro-liferating permanent and *ad hoc* committees. Schurmann has noted the case of one *xiang* in Shantung Province that had as many as eight permanent committees and 14 *ad hoc* committees, as well as Sino-Soviet friendship clubs, credit communes, statistical teams, tax teams, publi-shing stations and a few other *ad hoc* bodies designed to check up on the implementation of various policies.[115] By 1953, the press contained many accounts of rural over-bureaucratisation with widespread publica-tion of questionnaires. One memorable case, mentioned by Schurmann, was a questionnaire prepared by the Shansi Provincial Government with 74 pages and 6,307 items.[116] To be sure, 1953 was perhaps an atypical year since it was the year of China's first modern national census; nonetheless the sheer amount of paper being generated gives us some indication of the degree of rural bureaucratisation at a time when China's rural literacy rate cannot have been much over 10 per cent.

The new stress on 'rationalisation' resulted in a redrawing of the boundaries of local government in the countryside in accordance with 'ecological criteria'. This presumably meant that the *xiang*, which now consisted of some 2,000-3,000 people, approximated even more closely to the traditional standard marketing area or intermediate marketing area. Leadership at the next higher level of rural administration (the *qu* or district) was strengthened and provided a home for more cadres,

though the lowest level of all (the village), which had been so successfully penetrated since Yenan days, declined in importance as an
administrative unit.[117] A number of reasons have been suggested for
this. First, the location of authority at levels higher than the village
might have reduced the influence of traditional leadership and secondly,
there were probably not enough cadres to make village administration
a workable reality. What the retreat from the village did mean, however,
was that the old Yenan pattern of transformation from within existing
structures was very difficult to implement, especially as the militia
organisation began to deteriorate after the Korean war.

A problem more serious than rural bureaucratisation was a direct
legacy of land reform. Land reform had divided the country into small
plots of land individually owned and individually farmed. The Party left
no doubt that its ultimate policy was to promote co-operativisation,
though in the early years following land reform peasant atomisation
was quite prevalent. With the inauguration of the 'Rich Peasant Line'
and the removal of landlords, real political, social and economic power
resided with a stratum of rich peasants whose land holdings were larger
and better than those of the poorer peasants. They not only monopo-
lised village leadership in some areas but infiltrated a rather lax Party
organisation and sought to consolidate their economic position.[118]
Being able to manipulate loans and to buy out poorer peasants who hit
upon bad times (the right to alienate land had not been abrogated by
the land reform law), these rich peasants took the lead in a process of
land concentration.

The initial response of the Party to these developments was actively
to promote mutual aid teams and elementary co-operatives but, with
superior economic resources in the hands of rich peasants who were
reluctant to join, the private sector looked much healthier than the co-
operative sector. Though mutual aid teams continued to be formed,
many of the earlier co-operatives were dissolved,[119] especially when
richer peasants pulled out of them or conducted propaganda against
them. In Mao Tse-tung's view the situation was extremely serious[120]
and in the new 'regularised' atmosphere there was a danger that many
of the gains of land reform would be lost.

In the field of rural economic policy, the effect of a national plan to
emulate the Soviet Union was more direct. It was the peasants who had
to bear much of the burden of industrialisation and feed the rapidly
growing urban population. By 1953, pressure had been placed upon the
peasants to cultivate economic crops to support light industry, thus
reducing the amount of land given over to producing grain. At the same

time, in addition to the grain tax, the peasants had to bear the cost of compulsory grain purchases made by the state at fairly low prices. As the urban grain supply barely kept up with the growth of urban population, not only was rationing introduced in the cities but further pressure was placed upon the countryside.[121] The price of a lopside development strategy was beginning to show.

The Bureaucratisation of Urban Administration[122]

By the time of the Three and Five Anti Movements, parts of China's urban population had been organised in street committees which, in turn, were divided into residents' groups. These organisations undertook such tasks as settling disputes, sanitation, literacy work and, of course, mobilisation in connection with the mass movements of 1951-2. The committees tended to be dominated by housewives whose menfolk had been organised elsewhere by labour unions and other bodies and this resulted in some tension. Though never formally part of government, the street committees' functions were very wide, especially in the period of consolidation after 1952 and, in effect, they constituted the lowest level of government administration. Formally, however, the lowest level of government administration in the cities, introduced after the Five Anti Movement, was the street office (*jie gongso*) which was articulated to ward (*qu*) and municipal (*shi*) government and which maintained links with the urban police force.

It was these parallel bodies that were responsible for urban registration, made extremely difficult by the massive increase in urban population (40 per cent between 1950 and 1953). They replaced the multiplicity of *ad hoc*) committees which had resulted in a confusion of 'multi-headed leadership' (*duotou lingdao*) and, by 1954, the situation had stabilised to the point that formal regulations could be issued governing street committees and street offices. The provision of appointed street offices now became mandatory in cities of more than 100,000 people and optional in cities of between 50,000 and 100,000. Their area of jurisdiction was exactly coterminous with local police stations (*paichuso*) which maintained a system of permanent 'household register policemen' (*hujijing*) within each residential area. Each street office supervised a street committee which consisted of the representatives of some 100-600 households and was subdivided into a number of residents' groups of 15-40 households.

The above system was highly formal. However confusing the former system of 'adhocracy' that had been established by radical worker pickets in the days after liberation, it had a certain spontaneity and drive which had now been dissipated. Though the new system was more effective in spreading participation in government to a lower level, its main *raison d'être* seemed to be one of control. As such, Schurmann has noted, it was probably not welcomed by many local Party branches committed to lateral communication and mass mobilisation, and this might explain why the system was introduced slowly.

The Bureaucratisation of the Legal System

One of the great debates in the Soviet Union after the Bolshevik Revolution had been the extent to which a revolutionary society should possess law or be ruled by *policy*. The radicals argued that law was inherently conservative, since it is governed by precedent, and that the revolution should not be unnecessarily fettered, whereas the conservatives argued that a body of transitional socialist law might be drawn up. In the old days of Yenan, the Chinese Communist Party attempted to create a body of law but tried at the same time to make it flexible and amenable to mass interpretation. Mass mediation committees of 'fairminded people' had been set up by village governments.[123] In the confused situation of the Civil War, however, even such a semi-formal system broke down under the strain. Civil disputes were handled more and more on an *ad hoc* basis and criminal cases settled by hastily improvised courts.

Following liberation, the Party attempted to create a formal court system which required low litigation fees to make it accessible to the masses.[124] It was to become *too* accessible especially since a huge backlog of unsettled cases had piled up during the Civil War. When the formal courts almost broke down under the huge burden of work, the Party turned once again to *ad hoc* bodies, new people's mediation committees or to the street committees which sometimes employed mediators; within government organs comrades' courts were established. A whole plethora of legal bodies began to develop at different levels and predictably, in the new atmosphere of 1952-3, calls went out for 'rationalisation'.

In the Judicial Reform Movement of 1952-3, legal cadres were instructed to lead the masses in creating a single system of mediation to relieve the formal court system but before the year was out the new mediation bodies were functioning in much the same way as the increasingly bureaucratised formal court system. A 'Five Too Many' Movement was launched to simplify administration.[125]

It seems that battle had been joined between advocates of *Gesellschaft* (bargaining) law and formal bureaucratic regulation on the one hand and Yenan-type *Gemeinschaft* (community) law on the other.[126] The former was to triumph, and by 1954 a system of provisional rules for mediation was promulgated, whereby committees were set up consisting of 'representatives of the residents under the direction of the basic level people's court'. Apparently of a mass character, these regulations have been described as having more in common with Kuomintang legislation than that of Yenan.[127] The vagueness of the regulations, one commentator remarks, was probably not to allow greater flexibility but reflected the fact that they were seen as a stop-gap measure pending their replacement by a formal court system based on legal expertise and without much mass participation.

Centralisation and the Seventh Crisis in the Party (1953-4)

With the new mood of 'rationalisation' after 1952, attempts were made to centralise power at a national level by reducing the powers of the large administrative regions that had for a time functioned almost like separate governments. In the Electoral Law of February 1953, which was to prepare the way for the convening of a National People's Congress to replace the consultative bodies set up in 1949, no mention was made of these large administrative regions.[128] It will be remembered also that not long previously Kao Kang, the most important cadre in the most important of all these regions, had been transferred to Peking to reproduce the north-east experiences on a national scale. By early 1953, it seemed that the regions were to be abolished. This move was to lead to the seventh of the major crises in the history of the Party outlined by Mao Tse-tung in 1971.

The dimensions of the crisis are still very unclear and even their most shadowy outlines were not revealed until long after the event. It would appear, however, that at a meeting of the Politburo in December 1953 attempts were made to institute a system of 'collective Party leadership' at all levels, in line with similar developments in the Soviet Union since the death of Stalin earlier in the year.[129] These moves were resisted by Kao Kang and his counterpart in east China, Jao Shu-shih, who were also the most notable exponents of regional government. At the Fourth Plenum of the Party Central Committee in February 1954, the principle of 'collective leadership' was adopted, in opposition to Kao and Jao, and an attack seems to have been formulated against their 'independent kingdoms', north-east China and east China.

What was at stake here was not just regionalism but the degree to which the Soviet model was to be implemented. Kao Kang was identified as an exponent of the model in its extreme form. For years, he had

dominated the north-east where various features of the model had been
tried out. He had effectively led the Secretariat of the Party (a similar
position to Stalin's in the early history of the Communist Party of the
Soviet Union) and was now chairman of the all-powerful State Planning
Commission. Kao's removal from office sometime in 1954 was to usher
in an attack upon the whole Soviet model. In the meantime, however,
the focus of criticism of Kao and Jao centred on their creation of
'independent kingdoms'[130] and, to counter this tendency, the formation of a permanent central government structure was brought to a
head.

It was not until March 1955 that the removal of Kao and Jao was
formally announced and probably not until the Cultural Revolution of
the mid-1960s that the importance of the crisis became really apparent.
In the retrospect of the Cultural Revolution we might note that, when a
very long period occurs between plenums of the Central Committee,
there is usually considerable struggle within the Party. The Third
Plenum had been held before the outbreak of the Korean War and the
Fourth Plenum, which ousted Kao and Jao, was not held until February
1954. It is not unreasonable to suppose that the nature of that struggle
concerned the unfortunate consequences of the adoption of the Soviet
model which I have outlined above. The history of the Kao-Jao struggle
is yet to be written. Suffice it to note here that its immediate consequence was Kao's suicide and the strengthening of Party control to
remove his supporters. At this stage, the arch-exponents of the Soviet
model were being disposed of paradoxically by mechanisms that
belonged to that model. The return to mass movements was not to
occur until the following year.

The Establishment of a Permanent Central Government Structure (1954)

In June 1954, the large administrative regions were abolished in preparation for the restructuring of central government. The body which was
to ratify this process was a newly-elected National People's Congress
which was to take over most (though not all) the functions of the
Chinese People's Political Consultative Conference. The first step in the
formation of this body had been the Electoral Law of 1953 which
established a 'soviet' principle of election stretching right down to the
xiang and with each level electing the next highest.[131] The electorate
was that section of the 'people' over the age of 18 years and candida-
ture for election was scrutinised by appropriate level Party branches.
The operative principle of democracy that applied was, therefore, one
of controlled representation. Such a principle had existed in Yenan

days but, at that time, had perhaps been overshadowed more by a participatory principle of democracy. We are nowadays very familiar with the participatory criticism of representation; it surely applied to China also in 1954.

After some delay in electing lower-level committees, the First National People's Congress finally met in Peking in September 1954.[132] Its first task was to approve a draft constitution which had been prepared by a committee under the chairmanship of Mao Tse-tung set up in January 1953.[133] By the time the draft reached the Congress, it is claimed that it had been discussed by some 150 million people who suggested amendments. The constitution was an imposing document, similar in many ways to the Soviet constitution of 1936. It discussed types of ownership, policy towards classes, rights and duties of citizens, etc., but only mentioned the Chinese Communist Party in its preamble and then only with reference to its leadership before 1949. Such was the mood of 1954 that was very soon to change.

China was now (unlike the Soviet Union), established as a unitary multinational state with a single legislature, the National People's Congress. The Congress was elected for four years and was scheduled to meet once a year. It elected a chairman, Mao Tse-tung, who was constitutionally commander of the armed forces and chairman of a Council of National Defence. He could, whenever necessary, convene a Supreme State Conference consisting of the vice chairman (Chu Teh), the chairman of the Standing Committee of the National People's Congress (Liu Shao-ch'i) and the premier of the State Council (Chou En-lai). The Standing Committee of the National People's Congress was set up to conduct the routine business of the Congress when it was not in session and the State Council was the main executive arm of the government, consisting initially of the premier, a secretary general and the heads of 30 ministries and five commissions. Significantly, one of these commissions was the State Planning Commission which, in the days of Kao Kang, had been ranked equal to the predecessor of the State Council and had now been demoted. The only bodies ranking equal to the State Council in 1954 were the Supreme People's Court (under Tung Pi-wu) and the Supreme People's Procuracy.

Thus by the end of 1954, the government had been centralised with a hierarchy of congresses and governments extending right down to the level of the *xiang* and urban ward. Centralisation had been at the expense of the former large administrative regions which, paradoxically, harboured the most extreme exponents of centralisation within their own spheres of jurisdiction.

The First T'aiwan Straits Crisis

By 1954 it seemed that the Chinese government could chalk up notable
successes in the field of foreign policy. The Chinese People's Volunteers
had fought the United States and her allies to a standstill in Korea and
an armistice had been signed. With the battle of Dienbienphu and the
temporary ending of the Vietnam war, the socialist camp had been
strengthened, and at Geneva Chou En-lai had emerged as a statesman of
international standing. It is possible that the Kao Kang incident, which
paralleled the struggle between Malenkov and Khruschev in Moscow,
had some immediate effect on relations between the Chinese and Soviet
Parties but, whatever that effect might have been, relations between the
two states and the two Parties were particularly good by the autumn of
1954.

The internal consolidation of the People's Republic and her improved international position was, of course, a serious concern for the
Nationalist regime on T'aiwan which had attempted to frustrate these
developments since 1950. For four years, the Kuomintang regime had
maintained a blockade of Chinese shipping which was facilitated by its
control over a number of offshore islands, notably Quemoy and Matsu
off Fukien province and the Tachens off Chekiang province. By 1954,
the Kuomintang forces had been considerably modernised, with United
States help and were ready to reinforce garrisons on the offshore
islands.[134]

As reinforcement got under way, a clash occurred between United
States and Chinese aircraft in late July which promoted bellicose noises
from President Syngman Rhee of South Korea to the effect that a
general war was threatened. After the inauguration of Chiang K'ai-shek
for a second term as president in the spring of that year, the posture of
the Kuomintang regime appeared much more aggressive and talk of
Chiang's return became more frequent. In a manner similar to I.F.
Stone's treatment of the events of 1950 in Korea, one might construct
a conspiratorial scenario whereby, once the attempts by Syngman Rhee
and Chiang K'ai-shek to recover lost ground were frustrated by the
Korean armistice, they sought to create a new conflagration in the offshore islands to involve the United States once again to the same end.
Evidence, however, is sparse and we can only speculate.

Arriving back in China in August after the Geneva conference on
Indo-China, Chou En-lai was most vigorous in his expressions of determination that the current period of consolidation would be completed
by the liberation of T'aiwan[135] and, in September, a large-scale artillery
duel began on the islands off Fukien province. In December, the

Tachens were blockaded and the United States and the T'aiwan regime signed a mutual defence agreement.[136] Though there is some disagreement about exactly what the terms of this agreement meant, the upshot was that the Kuomintang regime evacuated the vulnerable Tachens in February 1955 with American support and the United States seemed to have committed itself to defending the other offshore islands if any threat to them could be constituted as a threat against T'aiwan.

In this dangerous situation, appeals were made from many sides for negotiations, though to little effect. Having been rebuffed by the UN Security Council in 1950 and having been branded an 'aggressor' in Korea, China was unwilling to send a representative to address the Security Council where T'aiwan was a permanent member, and the subsequent visit of UN secretary general Dag Hammarskjold to China bore little fruit. As late as March 1955, United States Secretary of State Dulles still spoke of the possibility of escalation and there have been some suggestions that the United States attempted to use nuclear blackmail to solve the issue. The Soviet Union, for its part, offered only lukewarm support for China and official Soviet statements carefully avoided any reference to T'aiwan.[137] There seemed little that any of the major parties to the dispute could do.

The attention of the United States and Soviet Union was now shifting to Europe and that of China to the wider field of relations with the states of south and south-east Asia. This had been China's major concern before the crisis and, as the situation in the T'aiwan Straits froze once again, China's long-term policy which sought ultimately to isolate both T'aiwan and the United States, was restressed. In April 1955, at the Afro-Asian Conference of heads of government held in Bandung, Indonesia,[138] Chou En-lai was most active in promoting the 'Five Principles of Peaceful Coexistence', namely:

1. Mutual respect for sovereignty and territorial integrity.
2. Mutual non-aggression.
3. Non-interference in each other's internal affairs.
4. Equality and mutual benefit.
5. Peaceful coexistence.

The Five Principles were not, of course, to cover relations between socialist and imperialist states and were seen essentially in a United Front context of rallying forces to oppose the United States. This is not to say, however, that China would not engage in dialogue with the United States on specific issues. At the conference Chou, in fact, offered to negotiate the relaxation of tension in the Far East and abortive talks at ambassadorial level began in August. In the meantime, China's new outward-looking foreign policy achieved tangible results as more and more contacts were made with newly emerging nations.

The End of the Second Cycle

In Chapter 1, I outlined the development of a cycle of radicalism and consolidation that came to an end in 1950. By 1955 a second cycle was complete. The second period of consolidation brought with it bureaucratism and managerial leadership. It shattered the organic unity of soldiers and civilians treasured since Yenan days and saw the rural revolution in danger of slipping backward. The issues at the core of Mao's view of development, the élite-mass and urban-rural gaps, had become serious but for all that the consolidation of 1952-5 was qualitatively different from that of 1948-50.

In early 1950 the Civil War was not yet over, the attitude of the Soviet Union was one of caution and a Kuomintang network of agents awaited the possible return of Chiang K'ai-shek. Land reform was only half finished and secret societies and gang-boss organisations were still operating even to the point of infiltrating a none too disciplined Party. Civil administration was in the hands of a plethora of *ad hoc* bodies with varying degrees of military control and there was not one economy but a whole series of regional economies of which only the north-east had attempted anything that could be remotely described as planning. By 1955, the defusing of the T'aiwan Straits crisis, the inauguration of the 'Bandung spirit' and good relations with the Soviet Union saw China as an independent force in the world. The Party was perhaps bureaucratised and maybe still in disarray over the Kao Kang incident but no one could say in 1955, as Kao Kang said in 1952, that if something were not done urgently, the end of the Party was in sight. Civil administration was now formalised and there was something more like a single economy with the beginnings of a nationwide planning system. The first five year plan was half over and in 1955 its provisions were finally published. Consolidation was complete.

Although the Soviet model was in practice dominant, the ideals of Yenan were still very much alive and were still propagated. Before long, many people were to test those ideals against reality and to set out to change that reality.

Notes
1. Mao Tse-tung 6 June 1950, *RMRB*, 13 June 1950.

2. Vogel 1971, pp. 59-60.
3. E.g. *Zhongguo Gongren*, No. 3, 15 April 1950, p. 15.
4. E.g. Lin Li, *Zhongguo Gongren*, No. 3, 15 April 1950, pp. 12-14.
5. Ibid.
6. Schurmann 1966, p. 445.
7. See Brugger 1976, pp. 97-9.
8. Teng Tzu-hui 30 July 1950, *Zhongguo Gongren*, No. 8, September 1950, pp. 1-5.
9. Li Nan-hsing, *Zhongguo Gongren*, No. 15, April 1951, p. 36.
10. See Harper 1969, pp. 89-99.
11. Friedman 1971, p. 224.
12. Friedman 1971.
13. Whiting 1968, Chapter VII.
14. Friedman 1971, p. 235.
15. Strong 1965, pp. 43-8.
16. Text in ibid., pp. 310-5.
17. Liu Shao-ch'i 14 June 1950, in Liu 1969, pp. 215-33.
18. Vogel 1971, pp. 95-8.
19. Ibid., p. 99.
20 Ibid., pp. 101-10.
21. Vogel 1971, p. 53.
22. Ibid., pp. 107-8.
23. *Ganbu Xuexi Ziliao*, No. 37, pp. 28-31.
24. E.g. *Huadong Renmin Chubanshe*, 1951.
25. Vogel 1969, p. 63.
26. Ku Ta-ts'un, in *CB* 124, 5 October 1951, p. 4.
27. Ibid., p. 4.
28 Mao Tse-tung 30 March 1951, in *JPRS* 61269-1, 20 February 1974, p. 8.
29. *RMRB*, 2 June 1951.
30. *SCMP* No. 112, 8-9 June 1951, p. 2.
31. Brugger 1976, pp. 175-80.
32. *Zhongguo Minzhu Tongmeng Zongbu Xuanchuan Weiyuanhui* 1951, pp. 126-7.
33. Vogel 1971, pp. 69-71.
34. Ibid., p. 70.
35. See Wilson 1968, pp. 76-7.
36. *CCP.CC*, 1 January 1951, *RMRB*, 3 January 1951, p. 1.
37. Shanghai *Zonggonghui Wenjiaobu*, October 1950, Preface, pp. 1-3.
38. 2 May 1942, Text in *SW* III, pp. 69-98.
39. Chou En-lai 23 October 1951, in *CB* 134, 5 November 1951, p. 8.
40. Gittings 1967, p. 75.
41. Ibid., p. 77.
42. Mao Tse-tung 24 September 1962, in Schram 1974, p. 191.
43. Gittings 1967, p. 83.
44. Vogel 1971, p. 113.
45. See the collection of articles in *Ganbu Xuexi Ziliao*, No. 37, September 1951.
46. Brugger 1976, p. 106.
47. *Ganbu Xuexi Ziliao*, No. 37, September 1951, pp. 28-31.
48. Ibid.
49. *CCP.CC Zhongnan ju*, 1 August 1951, in ibid., pp. 1-16. Expanded at greater length in Liu Tzu-chiu, *Gongren Ribao*, 12 September 1951.
50. *Gongren Ribao*, 30 August 1951, p. 1.
51. Liu Tzu-chiu, *Gongren Ribao*, 12 September, 1951.
52. Ibid.
53. Ibid.

54. See Li Nan-hsing, *Zhongguo Gongren*, No. 15, April 1951, p. 36. In ibid., No. 16 (24 May 1951) the correspondence column on the labour movement was closed. This was the last number of the journal to appear in 1951.
55. *RMRB*, 9 July 1951, p. 2.
56. Harper 1969 p. 96.
57. *Gongren Ribao*, 11 February 1953, p. 1.
58. See Carr 1966, Vol. 1, pp. 202-19.
59. *ACFL*, August 1950, *Zhongguo Gongren*, No. 8, September 1950, p. 6.
60. Liu Shao-ch'i May 1949, in *Zhonggong Yanjiu Zazhi she*, 1970, pp. 200-7.
61. Kuan Shui-hsin, *Zhongguo Gongye*, Vol. I, No. 11, 17 March 1950, pp. 18-22.
62. Brugger 1976, Chapter 4.
63. *RMRB*, 20 November 1947, p. 1. *RMRB*, 16 December 1947, p. 1.
64. N.E. People's Government, Industrial Department, 28 February 1950, in *Zhongguo Quanguo Zonggonghui Shengchanbu*, May 1950, pp. 207-17.
65. Perkins 1968, p. 605.
66. See Brugger 1976, pp. 188-90.
67. Kao Kang 31 August 1951, in *Zhongguo Minzhu Tongmeng Zongbu*, 1951, pp. 14-25.
68. *GAC*, 1 October 1951, in *SCMP* 192, 11 October 1951, pp. 13-16.
69. See *Zhongguo Minzhu Tongmeng Zongbu Xuanchuan Weiyuanhui*, 1951.
70. Jao Shu-Shih 17 December 1951, in *Xinhua Yuebao*, No. 1, 1952, pp. 19-20. The composition of the Shanghai municipal committee is discussed in Gardner 1969.
71. Jao Shu-shih 17 December 1951, loc. cit.
72. Vogel 1971, p. 85.
73. Jao Shu-shih 17 December 1951, loc. cit.
74. Ho Kan-chih, *Zhongguo Xiandai Geming shi* (*The Contemporary Revolutionary History of China*), Hong Kong 1958, pp. 366-7, cited in Schurmann 1966, p. 318.
75. Vogel 1971, p. 84.
76. Kao Kang 10 January 1952, *Ganbu Xuexi Ziliao*, No. 44, February 1952.
77. Ibid.
78. *Gongren Ribao*, 9 January 1952.
79. *CCP.CC Dongbei ju*, 20 February 1952, *Xinhua Yuebao*, No. 3, 1952, pp. 7-8.
80. Ibid.
81. Ibid.
82. The following is based on Gardner 1969.
83. *CB* 201, 12 August 1952.
84. Gardner 1969, p. 523.
85. Ibid., pp. 524-5.
86. Li Wei-han 27 October 1953, *CB* 267, 15 November 1953, p. 3.
87. Gardner 1969, p. 526.
88. *SCMP* 405, 29-30 August 1952, pp. 18-20.
89. Howe 1971, p. 96.
90. Vogel 1971, pp. 116-24.
91. Gray 1970, pp. 87-8.
92. Wilson 1966, p. 81.
93. Gittings 1967, pp. 119-20.
94. *PR* 19, 8 May 1964, p. 14.
95. Rees 1964, pp. 370-8.
96. Schurmann and Schell 1967, Vol. 3, p. 257.
97. Gittings 1967, p. 120, Friedman 1971, p. 242.
98. Gittings 1967, p. 129.
99. Schurmann and Schell 1967, Vol. 3, p. 259.

100. Gittings 1967, p. 129.
101. Kuo Cho-hsin, *ECMM* No. 204, 14 March 1960.
102. Klein and Clark 1971, pp. 211, 433-4.
103. Schurmann unpublished manuscript, II, 14-15 and 28.
104. *Zhonggongye Tongxun*, No. 30, 21 October 1953, pp. 30-1.
105. See Brugger 1976, p. 134.
106. See for example *Gongren Chubanshe*, 1953, p. 80.
107. The following account is based on Schurmann 1966, Brugger 1976.
108. Vogel 1971, p. 127.
109. The following account is based on Gittings 1967, pp. 117-18.
110. Ibid., pp. 152-5.
111. Ibid., pp. 154-5.
112. *CB* No. 314, 18 February 1955, pp. 2-8.
113. Cited in Gittings 1967, p. 157.
114. Schurmann 1966, p. 438.
115. Ibid., pp. 438-9.
116. Ibid., p. 440.
117. Ibid., pp. 440-2.
118. See Bernstein 1968.
119. Schurmann 1966, pp. 444-5.
120. Ibid., p. 445.
121. Vogel 1971, pp. 128-9.
122. This section is based on Schurmann 1966, pp. 374-80.
123. Cohen 1971, p. 35.
124. Ibid., p. 31.
125. Ibid., p. 32.
126. For a discussion of these concepts in a Chinese context see Kamenka and Tay 1971 and Thomas 1974.
127. Cohen 1971, p. 35.
128. *PFLP* 1953.
129. Schurmann 1966, p. 267.
130. *CCP.CC* March 1955, in Chai 1970, pp. 343-5.
131. *PFLP* 1953.
132. *SCMP* 889, 16 September 1954, pp. 1-11.
133. *PFLP* 1961.
134. Hinton H. 1966, p. 260.
135. Chou En-lai 11 August 1954, in *CB* 288, 16 August 1954, pp. 6-8.
136. Hinton H. 1966 pp. 261-2.
137. Ibid., p. 262.
138. Ibid., pp. 30-3.

3 THE GENERALISATION OF THE YENAN HERITAGE (1955-6)[1]

The third cycle began in early 1955 with a number of political movements. Some of them, which by mid-year became highly radical,
acquired such a momentum that they continued throughout the entire
period covered in this chapter (1955-6). By March 1956, however, there
was a general deradicalisation of the political climate. In each of the
periods of consolidation discussed so far, it has been evident that disagreements occurred among the top leadership. Though there can be no
absolute certainty it seems that 1948-50 saw such disagreements over
the Rich Peasant Line, the scope and duration of New Democracy and
the pace of socialisation in industry and commerce. In the period
1952-4, debate centred on the degree to which the Soviet model was to
be implemented, the pace of co-operativisation and the issue of regionalism. Though the Kao Kang affair was extremely serious, the disagreements that were to develop in this third cycle were ultimately much
more profound. Polarising around the degree to which China was to
move away from the Soviet model, these disagreements were ultimately
to constitute two different world views that were to split the International Communist Movement.

Sufan

The way in which political campaigns swept through intellectual circles,
agriculture, industry and the Communist Party in the years 1955-6 was
similar to what happened in 1951. Starting from the top down, these
campaigns involved increasing mass mobilisation and, as a result,
acquired a gathering momentum.

The first of them, known as *Sufan* (an abbreviation of *Suqing
Ancang Fangeming* — the Campaign to wipe out Hidden Counter-
revolutionaries) was well under way by the middle of 1955. It was a
parallel to the earlier campaign for the Suppression of Counter-revolutionaries of 1951. The origins of *Sufan* are unclear. Though there was
possibly some link between the campaign and the Kao Kang incident, I
have seen no evidence for such an association. It has been argued more
forcibly that the campaign grew out of a movement in the field of art
and literature against the author Hu Feng,[2] who in 1954 had written a
letter to the Party Central Committee protesting against restrictions on

111

literary activity. After much academic discussion, the Hu Feng debate became openly political as Chou Yang (later denounced in the Cultural Revolution as the 'literary tsar') mounted a full-scale attack against him. By January 1955 Hu had confessed his errors, but his confession was considered inadequate and a nationwide campaign of criticism began to unfold. In May, Hu Feng began to be criticised not merely as a 'petit bourgeois' writer but as a 'counter-revolutionary' and a number of documents appeared, annotated by Mao, which subjected him to severe criticism.[3] Such, it has been claimed, was the origin of *Sufan* which soon enlarged its scope to investigate other 'counter-revolutionaries'.

The Hu Feng issue is extremely obscure, particularly since it involved both Mao Tse-tung and Chou Yang, who later took very different lines on literary dissidents. Mao was soon to put forward a policy known as 'blooming and contending' whereby intellectuals and others were encouraged to criticise the Party, whereas Chou Yang was a partisan of bureaucratic control in the Soviet mould. In 1955, however, they seemed united in their attack, maybe because Hu Feng was something more than just a dissident intellectual, maybe because Mao had yet to formulate his policy of 'blooming and contending' or maybe because he felt constrained by the Soviet model. It is difficult to be sure of what went on in the Party at this time beyond the fact that, by mid-1955, a major process of investigation was in full swing particularly amongst those Party members whose pre-1949 background was suspect.

Apparently, in some areas, fixed quotas of cadres were singled out for investigation from above and chosen targets were required to write out their past histories and submit them for examination by higher authorities.[4] By September 1955, 2.2 million people were reported to have been investigated and 110,000 'counter-revolutionaries' unearthed. In Mao's view, at that time there were 50,000 major suspects still around and before the movement ended, 11-12 million people had to be investigated.[5] As it happened, very few people were finally designated as 'counter-revolutionaries'[6] and turned out of the Party and most of those were, at first, confined to their place of work and, at the end of the year, sent for labour re-education without sentencing by the courts.

In the view of one writer, who draws his evidence partly from statements by the Minister of Public Security, Lo Jui-ch'ing, the exercise was designed to get opponents of the socialist transformation of industry and commerce out of the way.[7] This would explain why court sentences were not imposed (with fixed time limits), why many people were wrongly accused[8] and why many of those sent for labour re-education were returned to their place of work once socialist transformation had been concluded.

One might, however, suggest less 'totalitarian' explanations. First, such a Soviet-style movement from the top down sought scapegoats for bureaucratism and yet by 1956, when the model was under full-scale criticism, it was seen that bureaucratism did not necessarily stem from active 'counter-revolutionaries'. Secondly, the movement might itself have generated hostility to the Soviet way of doing things;[9] it violated the earlier Chinese Communist tradition of 'curing the sickness to save the patient' and thus necessitated a reversal of policy the following year.

The Unified Purchase and Marketing Movement[10]

Whatever the real purpose behind the *Sufan* movement, it is true that the urgency of 'socialist transformation' of the economy had been foremost in cadres' minds since 1953. Within most sectors of the economy, 'The General Line of Transition to Socialism' put forward in October of that year was taken very seriously, even though it was not always clear whether that transition should be along Yenan or Soviet lines.

In agriculture, the situation was particularly confusing. Not only had new rich peasants emerged, but the general level of political consciousness of rural cadres, burdened with a multiplicity of tasks, was low. The cost of China's mammoth industrialisation drive had to be borne by the peasants, and yet the Yenan tradition of peasant support and peasant activism was still very much alive. This contradiction was nowhere more manifest than when the Party tried to implement Unified Purchase and Marketing of grain as a first step in socialist transformation. Following the decision in November 1953 to impose a state monopoly upon trade in grain, attempts were made to reconcile low state prices (in one area reportedly 40 per cent lower than prices available on the private market) with demands for higher exactions of grain. If implemented properly, the Unified Purchase and Marketing of grain could bring benefits to the peasants; they would no longer be fleeced by unscrupulous merchants, prices would be stable and the state could then mobilise relief grain more readily. On the other hand, if the process was handled bureaucratically or in a 'commandist' manner, peasants would suffer. In 1954, for example, grain quotas were often too high[11] and bureaucratically-minded cadres sometimes applied quotas arbitrarily to areas both where there was a surplus and where there was a shortage. The planning system sometimes seemed incapable of accounting for regional natural calamities and there was considerable dissatisfaction.

To counter arbitrariness, misclassification and disorder, a 'three fix'

(*sanding*) campaign was inaugurated in March 1955[12] whereby quotas
were set for each *xiang* with regard to output, surplus and sale of grain
and later in the year the assignment of quotas was extended down to
households. In this campaign, work-teams investigated the situation at
lower levels where it appeared that cadres could not be relied upon
because of family ties or rich peasant influence. Such cadres, unsure of
what to do in the new situation, had reacted to peasant dissatisfaction
and rich peasant opposition by shifting from a policy that was
'commandist' to one that was 'tailist'. Many peasants had claimed to
be in need of relief supplies of grain when they were not, and others
had had themselves classified as in need merely because such a classifi-
cation might help them resist grain exactions in the future. Such
occurrences were explained not only as due to poor leadership at the
local level but also due to the continuing influence of 'bad elements'
and 'counter-revolutionaries'.

By April 1955, tension existed between higher and lower levels of
rural administration. Each was suspicious of the other for being in the
case of the former, too harsh and in the case of the latter, too lenient.
The situation varied in different parts of the country and though in
general older liberated areas found the job of rural transformation
much easier than newly liberated areas, it was by no means certain that
serious problems in the Unified Purchase and Marketing of grain did not
occur there too. One reason for this might have been that, in the former
areas, the interval between land reform and the movement had been
much longer and the reassertion of conservative values that much more
developed.

On 28 April 1955, the Party Central Committee and the State
Council turned their attention squarely to the problem of excess supply
(relief grain) and work-teams busied themselves with mobilising
peasants to part with their surplus. First, cadres were summoned to
meetings at *xian* level away from unhealthy local influences. Then,
these cadres and work-teams went down, once again, to the villages to
link up with Youth League or other activists who had begun to per-
saude peasants not to hoard or make unreasonable demands. During the
course of the campaign, many peasants confessed their errors but in a
climate very different from land reform, for techniques of 'struggle'
were not used. At the same time, cadres who admitted their 'tailist'
leadership remained at their posts and few active counter-revolutionaries
were found. Despite the implementation of the Soviet model in society
the Party, in the rural areas at least, still adhered to the Yenan tradition
of not imposing change too harshly from without.

Co-operativisation of Agriculture: Stage One – Moderation (to July 1955

Experience in the Unified Purchase and Marketing Movement convinced many in the Party that insufficient attention had been paid to the livelihood of peasants. In the spring of 1955, therefore, the burden of grain exaction was reduced,[13] both to maintain peasant support and to prevent the switch away from economic crops to the production of grain. More attention was paid to encouraging peasants to participate in decisions which affected them and attempts were made to strengthen rural leadership.

Since land reform, the transformation of traditional temporary mutual-aid teams (*huzhuzu*) into permanent teams had been widespread but this development had not been matched by a growth in the rural Party network.[14] The Party was barely able to influence what happened in the teams, much less organise producer co-operatives.

The initial co-ops – subsequently referred to as 'lower-stage co-ops' (*chuji hezuoshe*) – were four or five times the size of the mutual aid teams and consisted of some two to three dozen households. Members pooled most machinery, draught animals and all but about 5 per cent of their land ('private plots'). They received a share of the harvest after the co-op had paid land tax and made its compulsory sale of grain to the state. Such a system was described as 'co-operative' rather than socialist since the allocation of produce and cash deriving from the sale of grain was made on the basis of not only the amount of labour put into the joint venture but also the resources pooled. Consequently richer peasants, able to put more resources into the co-ops, did much better than poorer peasants and acquired a new institutional framework to cement their leadership over the villages.

Though many richer peasants benefited from their position in the co-ops, there remained at this time an important rich private peasant sector where superior resources often resulted in higher productivity. Frequently these richer peasants outside the co-ops put pressure on the co-op members to withdraw their resources to the point that many co-ops simply collapsed. In Chekiang in 1953, for example, 15,000 out of a total of 53,000 co-ops had been dissolved at one blow. Despite such developments, however, the overall number of co-ops continued to rise. By 1954, there were some 114,000 but both the speed and nature of their development left much to be desired.

The need to strengthen Party branches in the rural areas being paramount, the First National Conference of the Party on Basic-level

Organisational Work in the Villages resolved, in March 1955, to redirect the focus of Party recruitment from the cities (where it had
rested since 1949) back to the countryside. Responsibility for a new
co-operativisation drive was located at *xiang* level and attempts were
made to ensure that at least one co-op existed in each of these administrative units as a model for the formation of others. We might surmise,
therefore, that the bulk of new recruits to the Party which jumped
from 7.9 million at the end of 1954 to 9.4 million by the end of
1955[15] might be found at *xiang* level.

Though, in the beginning, the new co-operativisation drive was
initiated from above, it was not as bureaucratic as that might suggest.
Since leadership at *xiang* level rested with the Party rather than the
formal administration, it seemed that the intention was to repenetrate
the villages and carry out mobilisation along Yenan lines. Initially, however, since leadership talent was scarce, the *xiang* was probably a better
unit to operate from than the village.

Shortage of leadership talent for the drive resulted also in the
employment of large numbers of ex-servicemen with rural backgrounds
who had been released from an increasingly technocratic Army. It was
felt that such cadres might achieve the correct balance between the two
errors of subordination to local 'feudal' interests and the imposition of
change from without. Perhaps the model was that of the immediate
post-liberation period where transferred military cadres had played the
midwife to local Party branches, since at least one of these transferred
cadres was attached by the *xiang* Party branch to each co-op.

We have seen already that May 1955 was a crucial month in the
development of this new period of radicalisation. It saw an upsurge in
the *Sufan* campaign, the re-designation of Hu Feng as 'counter-revolutionary' and an intensification of the campaign to propagate the
value of Unified Purchase and Marketing. By that time the Kao Kang
issue had been cleared up, the First Five Year Plan ironed out and
Party control committees established at various levels. With the Fifth
Plenum of the Seventh Central Committee in April, Lin Piao and
Teng Hsiao-p'ing, at that time considered to be radicals, were elected
to the Politburo and the tide was flowing against those who felt that
co-operativisation should wait upon mechanisation.

As radicalisation accelerated the formation of producer co-ops,
cadres involved in the 'three fix' campaign found themselves increasingly
preoccupied with problems of co-operativisation and training activists.
At the same time, attempts were made to ensure that the heads of co-ops
were Party members, and frequently meetings of *xiang* Party committees

consisted simply of such co-op heads. There were, however, considerable difficulties. Cadres were not always sure just how much pressure to
put on richer peasants not to leave the co-ops without endangering the
rural United Front. There were no clear directives on how to handle
tension between middle peasants who enjoyed a privileged position and
poorer peasants unable to negotiate loans to provide share capital for
entering the co-ops. Though credit facilities were provided at *xiang*
level, it was not always clear whether they could generate funds quickly
enough.[16]

The fact that directives were seldom specific was perhaps a consequence of the Yenan model which was in part revived here. For the
Mass Line to operate, policies had to remain general; only that way
could some of the errors of the Soviet collectivisation programme of
1928-9 be avoided. Indecision, therefore, was to be expected in the
early stages though, to be sure, it was due in part to the low political
consciousness of some newly recruited cadres.

Though the Yenan model stipulated that directives should be general,
they had to be consistent. It was clear, however, in the spring of 1955
that this was not always the case. Deep divisions existed at the highest
levels of the Party concerning the speed of co-operativisation. Though
the focus of Party work had been shifted to the countryside in preparation for accelerated co-operativisation, a rural work conference in May
endorsed a plan submitted by Teng Tzu-hui to cut back 200,000
co-operatives.[17]

Faced with conservative opposition, Mao Tse-tung decided to intervene directly in rural policy. After extensive talks with Party leaders
from various parts of the country, Mao was convinced that the 1955
harvest would be a good one, guaranteeing adequate storage of grain
to tide over any dislocations that rapid co-operativisation might cause.
It also seemed obvious that co-operativisation was necessary to facilitate grain collections to fulfil the now fully-formulated five year plan.
On 31 July, therefore, Mao delivered his famous speech on 'The
Question of Agricultural Co-operation' which set the tone for the whole
movement.[18] In the speech, Mao revealed that the original target for
co-operativisation had been one million co-ops. Now the figure was set
at 1,300,000 for China's 200,000-odd *xiang* so that each *xiang* might
have one or more semi-socialist co-operatives; the target date was the
autumn harvest of 1956. The immediate task of the Party was to
arrange for the campaign to go into operation after the autumn harvest
of 1955. Mao Tse-tung was clearly in charge and full-scale mobilisation
was to be undertaken; the conservatives were, for the time being,

silenced.

The Consequences of 'Collective Leadership'

In the last chapter, it was noted that much of the discussion concerning the Kao Kang issue dwelt upon the principle of 'collective leadership' which had been formally adopted by the Chinese Communist Party in December 1953. Collective leadership, however, applied not only at higher levels of organisation but at all levels. In some senses, it might have approximated to that kind of functional leadership which had been referred to contemptuously as 'multi-headed leadership' when the Soviet model was implemented.

In the light of subsequent revelations, it would seem that the more extreme patterns of vertical rule and one man management, prescribed by the Soviet model, were adopted reluctantly and then only in a few areas such as north-east China. This might explain the fact that one man management was seldom referred to by its name and was just called the 'system of sole responsibility by the factory general manager'.[19] In his excellent summary of the history of one man management in China in the 1950s, Schurmann remarks on the apparent lack of enthusiasm with which the system was received.[20] By mid-1954, articles had begun to appear which revealed disquiet with this total revocation of the Yenan tradition and the principle of Party leadership. Presumably under the protection afforded by the new principle of collective leadership, factories indicated their implementation of the principle of 'responsibility of the factory general manager under the unified leadership of the Party', *despite* current policy. Other articles described the opposition that existed towards one man management and the fact that the Party Committee in some enterprises had been reduced to merely 'staff' status. Contrary to normal practice, little attempt was made to refute the critics and an association was made between excessive vertical rule and (the yet unnamed) Kao-Jao attempt to create 'independent kingdoms'.

By 1955, positive references to one man management had virtually disappeared and criticism appeared of the extent to which the system had, in the past, been introduced too precipitately.[21] Though the demise of one man management was achieved quietly, the significance was as profound as anything that happened in the rural sphere. First, the principle of dual rule with all its implications for *horizontal* mobilisation was once again the order of the day. The Soviet stress on *managerial* as opposed to *cadre* leadership was under implicit attack. The process whereby institutional arrangements were created for the subordination of political to technological leadership was reversed. The 'virtue' and 'ability' (now referred to as the 'red and expert') dichotomy was given a new meaning and, with it, the orientation of educational policy. Finally, once the principle of vertical rule was questioned, it was possible once again to think of decentralisation of operations. The implications for a country pursuing a five year plan of Soviet inspiration, with its stress on heavy industry and the élite sectors of the economy, were shattering. It was to be some time, however, before all these implications became manifest and it was not until later in 1956 that one man management was formally abolished.

Criticism of the Control Structure

The decline of one man management was remarkably similar to the decline of the system of external economic control. One of the characteristic features of the Soviet model was the creation of an elaborate control structure under the Ministry of State Control (established in 1954). The clearest example of this was a model introduced into the north-east railway network in 1954 known as the Harbin system, whereby a hierarchy of accounting offices was set up to check up on the operation of railways in the north-east.[22] According to this system, the whole task of supervising economic performance was subordinated to a vertical chain of command which severed links with local Party and government organs.

Like one man management, the external control system was strongest in the north-east but that was not only because the north-east was the region where the Soviet model was most thoroughly implemented. The one man management system had been strengthened by Kao Kang, whereas external control was strengthened as a consequence of the *removal* of Kao Kang. Schurmann has suggested that, in 1954, control over the ministerial command structure centred on Shenyang required the strengthening of structures centred on Peking. Consequently, when control cadres were criticised for being impervious to local authorities, such criticism might be from the 'left' who demanded a return to dual rule or from the 'right' who resented an erosion of the vertically-organised ministerial structure based on Shenyang.[23]

By 1955, however, one might assume that north-east China was no longer an 'independent kingdom' and there was no need for strict vertical control over China's major centre of heavy industry. Secondly, with the dismantling of one man management, Party committees were ready once again to assume the task of control and to integrate this duty with the work of local government according to the principle of dual rule. The centralisation of external control in 1954 was, therefore, a temporary measure and is a beautiful example of Mao's dialectical proposition, put forward in 1949, whereby state forms might be strengthened to prepare for their own demise.[24]

By the Fourth National Control Work Conference in Peking in April 1955, control cadres were unsure as to their proper function. The report of the Minister of State Control, Ch'ien Ying, was contradictory.[25] She praised the work of control cadres in supervising the movement for the Unified Purchase and Marketing of grain; yet she must have realised that this movement was a preparation for the co-operativisation drive which eventually would reassign rural control duties to the Party. She praised also the 'Harbin system' (which had been introduced experimentally into various sectors of industry), mainly for its results in the railway network (which Schurmann takes as a reference to the north-east where five out of a total of 17 branch bureaux were located)[26] and textiles (located mainly in Shanghai — the former independent kingdom of Jao Shu-shih). Other industries were now largely to control themselves. Ch'ien Ying stressed that control cadres were to assist in a process of administrative simplification (which was to follow the completion of *Sufan*) and to work with local Party committees and the People's Procuracy, who were also engaged in the business of control. One wonders to what extent control cadres realised that administrative simplification might result in their own retrenchment once it was seen that there were perhaps too many bodies engaged in the same work.

By mid-1955, therefore, there was a shift from external back to internal controls and, with the *Sufan* movement, from a separation of economic and political control back to their integration under Party leadership. In industry, that Party leadership was already being strengthened with the demise of one man management. In a manner reminiscent of the current treatment of one man management, articles appeared in the press by August 1955 praising the Harbin system but in effect warning against adopting it *in toto*.[27] As Schurmann sees it, the whole idea of external control implied intolerable rigidity. A body which stamped out illegality would also stamp out flexibility. The Yenan model, which sought not to impose control from without but to effect change from within, was one that initially tolerated a certain amount of illegality but under a Party which would choose the right moment to counter it by mass mobilisation.

The Socialist Transformation of Industry and Commerce: Stage One — to October 1955

The Five Anti Movement of 1952 had left some 30 per cent of China's total production in private hands. With the 'General Line of Transition to Socialism' in 1953, however, it became clear that the private sector would soon be brought under state or joint public-private control. In September 1954, the State Council passed the Temporary Regulations on Joint State-Private Enterprises which established 'joint public-private' (or 'joint state-private') as the prescribed form of operation for formerly private concerns following socialisation.[28] Small traders or service concerns, however, would be co-operativised rather than socialised.

The normal method of joint public-private operation would be for the state or local government to take over ownership of a concern paying the former owner 1-5 per cent per annum 'fixed interest' (*dingxi*), while still employing him to manage the concern at a fixed salary. Though a former capitalist in this situation might not earn an income more than a few times that of the average worker (since un-socialised firms were usually quite small), and though he might be urged to spend his fixed-interest payments on government bonds,[29] the fact that he continued to enjoy the fruits of what was technically still 'exploitation', was later to cause some disquiet among radicals.[30] But before one could worry about such problems, the Party had to ensure that the socialisation process was achieved without too much disruption of production.[31]

Between 1952 and 1955, the state had made some headway in the process of socialisation but had been more concerned with establishing a planning network and articulating private concerns to it via contracts. Controls imposed over the distribution of certain goods effectively turned many private shops into agencies of the state marketing organs which had already come to control the bulk of wholesale outlets. Since price controls often left retailers small profit margins, a guaranteed 5 per cent per annum began to look attractive.

There were a number of problems, however, which suggested that the pace of socialisation should be forced. Shopkeepers, faced with eventual socialisation, were often unwilling to invest large sums of money in their businesses. Insufficient goods were purchased from wholesalers which led to stockpiling and waste. A black market for rural produce developed as 'capitalist-minded' peasants sought to bypass the state marketing system which paid low prices. Private industry tended to neglect quality as it sought to make as much money as possible before

the axe fell, and private entrepreneurs seemed unwilling to share
technical knowledge with those in the public sector. The planning
machinery found it difficult to articulate production and distribution
in both public and private sectors. At the same time, the general radicalisation in other areas of society highlighted these problems and led to
pressure for the solution once and for all of the socialisation of industry
and commerce.

By early 1955, the problems in the private sector were such that the
government found itself supporting all sorts of conservative policies just
to keep trade and industry moving. Trade fairs were organised which
bypassed the state marketing organs. State banks made loans to private
businessmen who were unwilling to continue investing capital in their
concerns. Goods were redirected from co-operatives to private concerns,
and regulations governing some goods were relaxed. Senior cadres were
so concerned that production and distribution would be disrupted by a
lack of business confidence that, once the rural sector radicalised after
Mao's speech of 31 July 1955, they tried to convince businessmen that
a similar radicalisation would not occur in the urban sector. They
soon, however, set about making sure that it did in fact occur. Such
action cannot be dismissed as hypocrisy. The situation is perhaps ana-
logous to a country facing the possibility of devaluation of its currency.
All rumours of devaluation have to be denied right up to the last
moment to prevent speculation, but unless those rumours are effectively squashed (and they rarely are), the rumours themselves bring
about devaluation.

By August, plans were being actively pursued to effect socialist
transformation. Investigation teams were formed. United Front-type
organisations of businessmen such as federations of industry and
commerce became active in preparing the ground and shops were
organised according to given lines of work (often through existing
guilds). Here the Yenan principle of transformation from within came
into its own. Adherents of the Soviet model would surely have condemned the guilds as 'feudal'; now cadres used them as the basis for
reorganisation of commerce under Party-led management bureaux. As
in the rural sector, there was a need for more and more cadres to supervise the work. Some might be found in the labour unions but many
were businessmen themselves who were retrained in numerous study
courses. With the old lesson of democratic reform in mind, they were
presumably somewhat suspect.

By October 1955, preparations were ready. In a way similar to the
radicalisation of rural policy, Mao Tse-tung himself, at a joint meeting

of the Politburo and Executive Committee of the All China Federation of Industry and Commerce, called for a radical speed-up in the socialist transformation of industry and commerce. Originally the target for completing the transformation had been 1962. In December, Mao called for 90 per cent completion by 1957.[32] The radical movements in countryside and city had joined.

Co-operativisation of Agriculture: Stage 2 — 'High Tide' (September 1955-March 1956)

The parallel between 1951 and 1955 will by now be apparent. Just as in the earlier year the process of radicalisation got under way in May and intensified in the late summer, so in 1955 a similar process occurred. The immediate consequence of Mao's speech of 31 July, however, was not, as one might have expected, an immediate drive to step up the rate of co-operativisation. A prior concern of both Mao and Party cadres was to initiate a thorough process of discussion and to draft plans which were to go into effect after the summer harvest. A 'backbone cadre' had to be created for each co-operative and a new drive begun to recruit students and ex-servicemen to help with the movement. Accountants had to be trained to manage the books and new schools were set up for that purpose. The propaganda network had to be enlarged and films and propaganda material prepared.[33]

At the Sixth Enlarged Plenum of the Seventh Central Committee in September 1955, Mao outlined his strategy.[34] In Mao's view 'socialist transformation' was to be seen from two perspectives. In the long run, some two or three five year plans were necessary before the process was complete. Accordingly, he drafted a twelve year plan for Agriculture which was accepted by the plenum. Mao called for the following quite spectacular increase in agricultural and industrial production:

	1955 output (official)[35]	12-year targets (annual output)[36]
Grain	175 million tonnes	300 million tonnes
Cotton	1.5 " "	6 " "
Steel	2.9 " "	18-20 " "
Coal	98 " "	280 " "
Tractors	—	183,000
Motor vehicles	—	208,000
Machine tools	14,000	60,000
Cement	4.5 million tonnes	16.8 million tonnes
Chemical fertiliser	0.3 " "	7.5 " "
Crude oil	1 " "	18 " "
Electricity	12 billion Kwh	73 billion Kwh

By the completion of the plan, the area under mechanical cultivation
was also to be increased to some 61 per cent of the total. Quite clearly,
if these targets were to be achieved, a 'great leap' in agriculture and
industry was called for and the first step in this process was the rapid
co-operativisation of agriculture.

Rapid co-operativisation, therefore, was the second of Mao's perspectives. In most areas in the country, co-operativisation was to proceed in three waves, each in the winter and spring periods of 1955-6,
1956-7 and 1957-8; in a few national minority areas, however, co-
operativisation might not be completed until 1960. Though the pace
was to be rapid, the experiences of the Soviet Union in the late 1920s
were to be studied and 'left' excesses guarded against. Up to 1955, however, the main obstacles had come from the right and there is every
indication that the plenum was characterised by intense debate, during
which Teng Tzu-hui and the Party's Rural Work Department came
under considerable criticism.[37] But by September 1955, the conservative line of the early 1950s had been repudiated and the notion that
collectivisation had to follow mechanisation was rarely heard. As Mao
saw it, the Chinese countryside was ready for a much more intensified
radical programme which should not and need not be forced. In Mao's
words:

> . . . we must attain our objective naturally and not by forcing our-
> selves. It is like a woman giving birth to a child. If we force the
> delivery after seven months, it is 'left'. If after nine months we do
> not permit the birth, it is 'right'.[38]

The radicalisation of the Party's line on co-operativisation was not just
a question of increasing the number of co-ops and the rate at which
they were formed but also of changing their class composition.
Although Mao continued to insist that reformed landlords and rich
peasants could join,[39] fewer efforts were in fact directed at patient persuasion. At the same time, more money was made available to lend to
peasants who wished to purchase co-op shares. In general, therefore, a
'poor peasant line' was reborn.[40]

Following the Sixth Plenum and the formulation of detailed plans in
local areas, the co-operativisation movement reached its 'High Tide'.
Quotas and targets were constantly updated to the point that, by the
end of the year, 75 million peasant households (or 63.3 per cent of the
total peasant population) had joined co-ops.[41] The sheer pace of change
found many cadres wanting and sometimes resulted in 'formalism'

where mutual aid teams were transformed into co-ops with very little other change. Once the breakthrough had been made, however, the process of strengthening and consolidation was relatively easy. Richer peasants could no longer resist the tide and began to join in ever greater numbers. An added incentive, perhaps was the fact that grain collection was first done in the co-ops and then the responsibility for the collection from other sectors was assigned to co-op members.[42]

Once middle peasants had joined co-ops, it became possible to move to a more 'socialist' form. The model for a new type of co-op – the 'higher stage co-operative' (*gaoji hezuoshe*) – was clearly the Soviet *kolkhoz* (or collective farm). Those that were formed in 1955 varied considerably in size from a few lower-stage co-ops to collectives as big as a whole *xiang*.[43] They were similar to the earlier co-ops in that all land, draught animals, major production materials, etc. were turned over to the collective and individual peasants retained a plot of land, a few animals and some tools. Members continued to pay share funds determined according to property and labour status but payment was now exclusively according to work, not according to resources originally pooled, although provision for some compensation was made for loss of property.

By the beginning of 1956, with the co-operativisation movement still escalating, the Party began to discuss long-term agricultural policy and the optimum organisation of the collective (or agricultural producers' co-op). It was clear that the current drive would not finish until all the Chinese rural population were brought into collectives. But at the very peak of this 'Socialist High Tide in the Chinese Countryside', a decision seems to have been taken to deradicalise policy.

The events of early 1956 are still obscure. It seems, however, on the basis of circumstantial evidence, that the decision to deradicalise was endorsed at an enlarged Politburo conference in early April. By this time, the sheer momentum of the collectivisation drive was such that, even if any decisions were taken with regard to the agricultural sector, they did not prevent the figure of 83 per cent of all households enrolled in co-ops being reached by the end of the year, rising to 97 per cent in the summer of 1957.[44] What is important in the agricultural sector is that Mao's Twelve Year Plan for Agriculture, already modified,[45] was quietly pushed aside and only resurrected in late 1957.

It is my impression that the deradicalisation decisions of March 1956 resulted from factors outside the agricultural sector, as I shall go on to suggest, since on the whole the co-operativisation drive of 1955-6 was a success.[46] It is true that occasionally compulsion was used and there was some slaughter of livestock before co-ops were organised, but, in general, the principle of voluntarism seems to have been adhered to and change brought about from within in the old Yenan tradition. This is attested to by the fact that, even in later years, peasants occasionally withdrew from co-ops.[47] What is particularly relevant to our discussion here is that, for the first time since the bureaucratisation of the early 1950s, the natural village had been penetrated. Herein lay one of the strengths of the Yenan model which was now generalised and adapted to a very new situation.

The 'High Tide' of the Socialist Transformation of Industry and Commerce

With the radicalisation of the socialist transformation of industry and commerce following Mao's speech of 29 October 1955, a process similar to that in the rural sector unfolded.[48] Meetings of businessmen were held at which they were persuaded to petition local government to reorganise their concerns into joint public-private enterprises and mass meetings were held to hear reports on the need for socialisation. By January, the rural picture was repeated as the target dates for collectivisation were progressively brought forward. United Front organisations, reminiscent of the Five Anti Movement, busied themselves in assisting the reorganisation of whole lines of business and attending parades to celebrate the successful completion of the task. The pace was often so rapid that transformation sometimes occurred before proper inventories could be made, though care was taken initially not to cause disruption by too rapidly transferring personnel.

There was very little resistance to the process of transformation but the sheer pace of change did create problems *after* transformation, especially since there were insufficient numbers of cadres to supervise reorganisation. Nonetheless, once again the Yenan principle of change from within was effected as businessmen themselves engaged in making inventories of each other's former firms. This task was often undertaken before the formal State Council Regulations for Inventories and Assessments of 8 February 1956 came into force. With the deradicalisation of March, the more difficult task of consolidation was to begin.

Criticism of Army Professionalism

The sovietisation of the PLA was virtually completed by 1955, by which time the new atmosphere of radicalism allowed those who resented the decline of old traditions to voice their complaints. They demanded that the Army practise once again the Mass Line, the 'three military democracies' (political, economic and financial) and set up soldiers' committees.[49] No one doubted that Army modernisation was very necessary but the aim was to gain experience, not to become isolated *professionals*.[50]

In response to Mao Tse-tung's Twelve Year Plan for Agriculture, the Political Department of the PLA drew up a plan to support agricultural co-operativisation.[51] On the average, each soldier was required, during the course of the year, to devote 5-7 free labour days to production,[52] though, in this period, it appears that this average was not reached. The PLA of some 2½ million was to devote 12½ to 17½ million work-days in 1956, though it only reached the figure of 4 million.[53] Nevertheless, this was a considerable improvement on previous years. Soldiers were instructed, in particular, to use their spare time in the drive to eliminate four pests (rats, sparrows, flies and mosquitoes), and to assist in afforestation even to the point of planting trees in their barracks. Gifts of Army 'night soil' were to be made to local peasants and military doctors were to make their services available to civilians. Army units in the countryside were instructed to raise livestock at a rate of one pig per 50 men and military engineering shops were to help repair agricultural machinery in the co-ops. Army units were to build electric power stations which were to be co-ordinated with local civilian requirements. Soldiers were to engage in propaganda and the Signals Corps was to set up broadcasting stations. Military units were to assist in the establishment of schools in the co-ops and soldiers had the duty of looking after the ideological training of their relatives. The Army was to conduct an economy drive to save money for equipping tractor stations and was to provide personnel to run them. Perhaps most important of all, specific military units were to identify themselves with specific co-ops and accept the leadership of the local Party committee. An all-out attempt, therefore, was undertaken to reintegrate the Army with society according to the Yenan tradition.[54]

A far greater emphasis was now placed on political training in the Army. Excessive and dogmatic reliance on the new disciplinary code was criticised as well as the dogmatic rejection of formality. Syllabuses for political study were prescribed for officers of certain rank and political night schools established. Training manuals were rewritten in accordance with Chinese geographical conditions, since handbooks produced in Moscow often said very little about tactics in rice-paddy country. In drafting these manuals, officers were to consult with the men in accordance with the old idea of military democracy.[55]

In all the discussions of the generalisation of the Yenan heritage in the PLA, however, there is one area about which virtually nothing seems to have been written – the people's militia. With the introduction of conscription, the militia seems to have atrophied and yet there was clearly some kind of militia in existence in early 1956, for reference was made to militia activities in PLA regulations.[56] In the plan to support agricultural co-operativisation, for example, provision was made for the militia to hunt wild animals, and yet not much was said about militia organisation in the various articles on organising co-ops and collectives. It was not until much later that elaborate plans were put forward to make 'everyone a soldier'.

Deradicalisation and Khruschev's Secret Speech

In attempting an explanation of the deradicalisation decisions of 1956, the most persuasive arguments focus on the central leadership of the Party itself. The Cultural Revolution revealed that there were serious differences between Mao Tse-tung, who had effectively led the radical drive since the summer of 1955, and Liu Shao-ch'i, who urged caution, but this does not explain the significance of the date March 1956. The single event which probably activated those differences at that time was the Twentieth Congress of the Communist Party of the Soviet Union.

At the Twentieth Congress in February 1956, Nikita Khruschev took the International Communist Movement by storm in his denunciation of the excesses of Stalin.[57] Communist parties the world over recoiled at the shock and entered into furious debate on how to respond. It seems highly likely that, at the very Politburo conference where the decision was taken to deradicalise, the main item for discussion was Khruschev's secret speech. In his concluding remarks at the April Politburo conference, Mao expressed disquiet at Khruschev's actions. He acknowledged that discipline within the Soviet Union had been too strict and, if China persisted with a system of tight control from above, it would be tantamount to 'letting Kao Kang hold sway for another year'.[58] Mao opposed excessive centralisation and later was to castigate Stalin for occasional 'metaphysics and subjectivism', 'making mistakes in dialectics', failing to see that the October Revolution, which had negated capitalism, could itself be negated[59] and for using the public security organs exclusively in dealing with counter-revolutionaries.[60] What Mao was opposed to, however, was making the whole issue public. He considered that parts of the mass criticism campaign in the Soviet Union was suitable neither to China nor the Soviet Union[61] and urged that discussion of Stalin's bad points should be kept within the Party.[62]

In April 1956, Mao's position was made much clearer with the publication of an essay entitled "On the Historical Experience of the Dictatorship of the Proletariat"[63] which signified the first step in a radical critique of Khruschev's position. In Mao's view, Stalin's errors should be seen not in terms of Stalin's *personal* aberration but in terms of 'internal contradictions' occurring in socialist society. The Chinese leadership was quite aware that the bureaucratic model they had begun to dismantle was essentially Stalinist but, as Marxists, they could not ascribe it merely to Stalin's *personality*. The April essay went to great pains to point out that, at the height of the Yenan movement of 1943, Mao had personally attacked any notion of the 'cult of the individual' of which Khruschev had accused Stalin. Furthermore, if it were true that Stalin were divorced from the masses, this only highlighted the importance of the Mass Line concept. The article also pointed out some of Stalin's achievements, thus making the message abundantly clear; Stalin should not shoulder all the blame for what happened in the Soviet Union and, even if he were guilty of certain errors, these errors were not paralleled in a China now engaged in a radical generalisation of the Yenan heritage.

Whether Mao's response to 'destalinisation' was shared by all the senior leadership in the Chinese Party is doubtful. It is highly likely that Party conservatives such as Liu Shao-ch'i endorsed Khruschev's speech[64] though I doubt whether Liu would have supported the open discussion of Stalin's errors. Both Khruschev and Mao wanted open discussion of the problems that the Stalinist administrative system had given rise to, though Mao felt that a concentration on Stalin's person would hamper any analysis of systematic contradictions. Whereas most of the leaders of the Chinese Party wished to take stock before deciding what to do next, Mao's mind was made up. At the April Politburo meeting, he called for a policy of 'letting a hundred flowers bloom and letting a hundred schools of thought contend'[65] whereby intellectuals and others were encouraged to voice their opinions and stand the full test of open criticism. At the same time, he analysed contradictions within Chinese society and laid down the blueprint for a new economic strategy in a speech known as 'On the Ten Great Relationships'.[66]

The conservative response to Mao's April initiatives was to call for the convocation of a Party Congress to legitimise the process of consolidation and head off further radicalisation. The groundwork for this congress seems to have been laid in March-April 1956[67] and to have been supported by Mao[68] (who probably had different views as to its function). Meanwhile, Mao's main attention was directed towards the new policy of 'One Hundred Flowers'.

The Problem of the Intellectuals

The focus of Mao's attention in the spring and early summer of 1956 was clearly upon the intellectuals. In January of that year, Chou En-lai had spoken at length upon the subject and stressed opposition to rightist conservative ideology.[69] As Chou saw it, Party attitudes towards the intellectuals were subject to two kinds of error — sectarianism and compromise. The former, associated with an 'ultra-left' position, was élitist and, from a Mass Line perspective, reactionary, while the latter, which led to passivity, was conservative. In practice then the 'ultra-left' could dialectically be linked with the right.

Chou had spoken in an atmosphere that was still radical when the campaign style of leadership was triumphant. Following the deradicalisation of March, however, though there was probably little disagreement about the disease that afflicted policy towards intellectuals, there appeared to be different methods of prescribing treatment. Mao's solution was one of 'blooming and contending'. Through open discussion, intellectuals could engage in frank debate and assist in reforming the Party from without. At the same time he called for a parallel movement known as 'long-term co-existence and mutual supervision' whereby 'democratic parties and groups' could also assist the Party by pointing out its errors and of course vice versa.

Following the Twentieth Congress of the CPSU, the issue of Party doctrinairism was given importance equal to that of the 'sectarian-passive' debate and such was the focus of a major speech by Lu Ting-i, Director of the Party Central Committee's Propaganda Department, in late May.[70] Lu's approach was a cautious one. Academic freedom, he felt, should clearly be under Party leadership and within prescribed lines. Though there might be limits to *political* freedom, 'as everyone knows, the natural sciences, including medicine, have no class character'. Though we are not absolutely certain what Mao's position at that time actually was, it is my impression that Lu's speech represented a far more conservative position. Though Mao has consistently opposed unrestrained freedom, he has never been as afraid of disorder as Lu seemed to have been in May 1956 and the notion that the natural sciences had no class character was, from Mao's point of view, liberal and erroneous. It would seem then that, not long after its promulgation, Mao's new policy began to be distorted by Party conservatives.

At the meeting of the National People's Congress in June and thereafter, there appeared to be a difference of opinion on exactly what the

'Hundred Flowers' movement involved. The situation was complicated by the fact that Party rectification was prescribed presumably to deal with the criticism raised during the movement but also to deal with the number of strikes and disturbances that had developed in China in the wake of the Khruschev revelations.[71] Though Mao did not think that such disturbances would reach the proportions of those in Eastern Europe,[72] they did call for some action by the Party. Should the rectification be from the top down in the old Soviet style or should it be combined with the more open policies of 'blooming and contending'?

In a situation of confused leadership, very few intellectuals or members of 'democratic parties', in fact, responded to Mao's call. It was not only unpopular with bureaucratically-minded Party cadres, who had yet to learn exactly what a return to the spirit of Yenan meant, but also with a conservative Party leadership who sought, by means of a Party Congress, to prevent any further upheavals. Like Mao's Twelve Year Plan for Agriculture, the two policies remained on the table until 1957.

Wage Reform

It has been argued that one of the consequences of the consolidation of 1956 was that not only was there a liberalisation of policy towards intellectuals but also towards the 'economist' demands of workers; this was perhaps a result of the industrial disturbances in mid-year. To state the situation thus glosses over important differences between radicals and conservatives on these two issues. I have suggested above that Party radicals probably supported the idea of 'blooming and contending' (described by some as 'liberal'); the same probably cannot be said for their attitude towards wage rises (also described as 'liberal'). 'Blooming and contending' was a way of invoking the Mass Line in dismantling the cumbersome Soviet model, whereas wage rises stemmed directly from the Soviet model and sought to benefit one sector of society at the expense of, and without consulting, another (the peasants).

The idea of wage reform[73] did not spring from the blue in 1956, but had been formulated in the heyday of the Soviet model. In the period up to 1953 there had been only regional wage reforms and, in the period 1953-5, no wage reforms at all. During those latter two years, the stress was on a high rate of domestic saving which led to a drive to limit wage increases, practise strict industrial discipline and implement strict financial control. The former policy had been enforced by comrades' judicial committees (*qiye tongzhi shenpanhui*) and the latter by a strengthening of accounting procedures (which might have led to friction between accountant and 'one man manager' and contributed to

the latter's demise).[74] While it lasted, the policy seems to have been
effective since the rise in wages for industrial blue and white collar
workers was only 5 and 3 per cent respectively compared with 17.4
per cent in the years 1950-3. In the atmosphere of centralisation after
the Kao Kang affair, attempts to iron out regional differences and
abolish non-monetary payment tended to lower wages and raise
demands for wage reform. The first steps in that direction were taken in
the state administrative system in October 1955 when formal salary
scales were worked out for all cadres according to some 30 salary grades
with quite steep differentials.[75] Such a policy, quite clearly in line with
the Soviet model, was now to be applied to the industrial sector in
general but, it was anticipated, without a major increase in the average
wage.

As policy was worked out in the deradicalised atmosphere of mid-
1956, wage reform along Soviet lines stipulated that the differential
between management/technical staff and workers should be increased,
that managerial staff should have wages higher than technical staff and
that differentials among skilled workers should widen. In addition, in
marked contrast to 1955, an across-the-board wage rise became the
primary object of reform. As *ad hoc* wage reform committees began
their work at enterprise level, tensions developed, particular resentment being felt by management who did not wish to lose their discre-
tionary wage powers along with other powers they had lost with the
decline of one man management.

By the completion of the wage reform in the autumn of 1956,
the average wage had increased by nearly 20 per cent. In a few months,
the reform had fulfilled the total rise in average wages planned for the
whole of the First Five Year Plan. From a radical point of view, the
results were alarming. Migration from rural areas intensified. The manifest gap between urban and rural incomes cancelled out some of the
intended effects of co-operativisation. There was a great consumption
boom in some of the major cities leading to packed restaurants and the
opening of clubs. Conflicts between labour and management over
economic issues multiplied as labour unions once again began to walk
the path of 'economism'.

Consolidation of the Rural Sector

Though co-operativisation went on right through the consolidation
period which began in March 1956, the new stress on orderly administration had an impact on the villages. We have seen that the main administrative unit that undertook the task of initial co-operativisation

was the *xiang*, from whence cadres were sent down to the villages. The immediate consequence of this was a shortage of cadres at *xiang* level and a pressure for *xiang* amalgamation. Such pressure was exacerbated by the amalgamation of agricultural collectives across lines of *xiang* jurisdiction. One will remember that the earlier Party policy was to reduce the size of the *xiang* to fit in with ecological criteria; now the policy was to increase it, though it was not always clear how the new *xiang* fitted in with traditional standard marketing areas.

In December 1955 the level of administration intermediate between *xiang* and *xian* (county), known as the *qu*, was abolished. In the spring of 1955, there had been some 219,000 *xiang* but by the autumn of 1956 the number had been reduced to some 117,000. *Xiang* were divided into three categories — those on the plains with a population of 10,000-20,000 people, those in hilly areas with a population of 5,000-8,000 people and those in the mountains with an ideal population of some 2,000-3,000 people.[76]

After fixing the size of the *xiang*, attempts were made to specify the size of the new collectives. In September 1956, this was to be 300 households in the plains, 200 households in hilly regions and 100 households in the mountains. Collectives were subdivided into *brigades* (corresponding often to the older co-ops and consisting of 20-40 households) and *teams* (often corresponding to the old mutual aid teams containing 7-8 households).[77] As time went on, the early very large collectives were reduced in size to correspond more nearly to the old natural villages where rich peasants still owned proportionally better land. With the old village reconstituted as a collective, there was understandable pressure to collectivise all its population. In the conservative political climate of mid-1956, it became easier for richer peasants to join, though, as we have seen, not all wanted to and they may have been subjected to pressure.[78] Some joined but then left again and were to be the butt of a later anti-rightist campaign. Still others assumed leading roles in the collective and propelled policy in a conservative direction.

The Model Regulations for Collectives promulgated in 1956 demanded that the collective divide its gross income into four parts.[79] First, state taxes were to be paid and compulsory grain sales made to the state at fixed prices. Secondly, a sum was deducted for future production costs and the repayment of debts. Thirdly, a public accumulation fund and public benefit fund (not to exceed 8 per cent and 2 per cent of income respectively) were set up and finally the remainder was divided according to the work done by collective members calculated as the amount of 'work-points' they had collected during the year. Payment to peasants, therefore, would consist of a small amount of cash which had accrued to the collective from the sale of grain and other goods plus a share of the harvest in kind. The calculation of individual income, however, was by no means an easy task, for every single job of work, day in and day out throughout the year, had to be assigned a definite number of work-points. Accountants and administrators were needed in ever greater numbers and the problem arose of how one determined *their* income. Other problems arose, such as how one worked out equivalents between different types of farm work and between farm work and work in subsidiary industries set up by the collective.

The collectives were run by an administrative committee of nine to 19 members which was elected by a members' council or members' delegates' council and was supervised by a control committee similarly elected. Wherever possible, a Party committee was also set up in the collective whose membership overlapped the management committee. Where the Yenan model was effective, these structures helped younger men to assume leading roles in the village for the first time. Where it was a failure, however, older rich peasant leadership remained and frustrated social change. This latter possibility was to occur quite frequently in the early period when problems of organisation led to bureaucratism and new young cadres were too inexperienced. These young cadres did not know how to advise peasants on the relative importance to give to collective work or work on their private plots, what kind of commercial network to set up in the collectives or how indeed to prevent the spread of the capitalist mentality. Bureaucratic directives from above appeared in profusion but it was difficult to apply them in concrete situations and, as we have seen, mid-1956 was not noteworthy for clear Party leadership. Faced by supply problems in September 1956, the government responded by reopening rural markets.[80] How was the inexperienced cadre, who had just gone through the radical process of co-operativisation, to react, especially since he had just been engaged in the redrawing of *xiang* boundaries in a way which might have cut across traditional marketing areas? A lot of serious rethinking needed to be done.

National Minorities Policy

In the fields discussed above, the conservative policy of 1956 was one of consolidation after the radical movements of 1955. With regard to policy towards national minorities, there had never been any radical movements. In a major work on the subject published in that year, Chang Chih-i,[81] one of the leading architects of the United Front, noted that the People's Republic of China differed from the Soviet Union in that it was a unitary and not a federal state. Although the Party had supported a policy of federalism from 1921 to 1940, the war had forced nationalities together so that by 1949 there was no need for a federal state. In any case, national minorities comprised less than 10 per cent of the population, whereas in Russia in 1917, more than half of the population were non-Great Russians, some of them more advanced than the Great Russians themselves. The 1954 constitution, therefore, accepted the principle of self-government but not separation. Such a policy, Chang admitted, was different from that of Lenin.

Although the Soviet Union had accepted the principle of separation, it was not permitted in practice and Soviet policy towards nationalities was, at times, quite brutal. In China on the other hand, although separation was not permitted, policy in the 1950s had been to interfere hardly at all. An assimilationist policy was ruled out, since such a policy could lead to national movements led by non-proletarian elements. Religion was to be tolerated, since any attempt to suppress religion only produced martyrs and a Marxist position held that it was pointless to attempt to destroy religion unless, at the same time, one destroyed its class basis.[82] In the early 1950s, there remained 5,000 Buddhist temples with 3,000 living Buddhas and 320,000 lamas. In Islamic areas there were 40,000 mosques and more than 100,000 imams and mullahs.[83] In some nationality areas, a system of slavery was still maintained (e.g. among the Yi),[84] in others there existed monastic serfdom (Tibet), nomadic pastoralism (Inner Mongolia and Sinkiang), headhunting (among the Wa in Yünnan) and slash and burn agriculture (among the Chingp'o in Yünnan).[85]

Attempts were made to define special national minority regions at provincial level, known as 'autonomous regions' (*zizhiqu*), at levels intermediate between province and *xian*, known as 'autonomous districts' (*zizhizhou*) and also at *xian* level and below. In these regions, cadres busied themselves with educational work though this sometimes involved first inventing a written script. Reform was in general very slow.

In the high tide of co-operativisation during 1955-6, some areas had experienced change. By March 1956, 72.7 per cent of herding families in Inner Mongolia were co-operativised though similar attempts to co-operativise the Kazakhs were less successful. In the Chuang area of Kwangsi, the Yenpien Korean Autonomous District and agricultural parts of

Tsinghai, 70-90 per cent of households were co-operativised by 1956 and, in the Hui autonomous *xian* in Hopei, over 90 per cent were so organised.[86] In other areas such as Tibet, however, social change was minimal.[87] Cadres were instructed not to antagonise local leaders and must have been extremely perplexed at how to deal with such practices as Yao 'witch vengeance' (like Voodoo) or mating festivals, how one pursued a non-interventionist policy when musical instruments were made out of human skin, how to draft a directive to the effect that bugs should not be killed in areas where a belief in reincarnation was prevalent or whether to forbid the use of iron ploughs where tradition said that iron poisoned the soil.

In a fascinating account of how the United Front policy worked among the slave-owning Yi,[88] Alan Winnington described the reforms of 1956, whereby only those who owned more than ten slaves were singled out as targets for reform. Even after the slave-owners had lost their slaves, however, they still enjoyed political rights and still remained influential in local government. Sometimes they were even paid compensation for the loss of slaves. In the Yi region, opium cultivation (the main agricultural activity) was still permitted for fear of damaging the local economy.

The extraordinarily moderate policy towards nationalities[89] could not but lead to resentment, especially among cadres who elsewhere had been active in land reform. They could not but feel disquiet at a policy of Party recruitment whereby, if Party committees refused membership to national minorities who refused to give up the customs and religions of their people, they were criticised from the highest level as 'great Han chauvinists'.[90] I am not arguing here that all cases of great Han chauvinism were false, for clear cases are on record of, for example, Muslims being forced to eat pork, etc. My point is that excessive moderation, in which attempts are made to effect the Yenan model of transformation from within, can lead to the Party's being taken over by the people whom it was trying to reform. There was perhaps little danger of that in 1956, but many cadres were apprehensive.

The Party in 1956

It was in an increasingly conservative climate that preparations were made for the Eighth Party Congress. On 6 July 1956, a Politburo conference worked out the Congress agenda and, in late August, a somewhat confused Seventh Plenum of the Seventh Central Committee examined a political report to be submitted to the Congress.

Much of what went on at the Eighth Party Congress, which met finally on 15 September, is speculation but in my opinion some of the speculation, based on careful documentary analysis, has a strong ring of plausibility. It has been suggested, for example, that the battle between the conservative and radical wings of the Party leadership may be discerned in the differing stands taken on current questions by Liu Shao-ch'i and Teng Hsiao-p'ing.[91]

In all the debates, MacFarquhar argues, Teng appeared as the radical attuned to Mao's ideas. In 1954, he had been appointed Party secretary general (*mishuzhang*), but now in 1956 was elevated to the new eminence of general secretary (*zongshuji*) at the head of a strengthened Secretariat. The promotion of Teng, however, in no way signified the victory of the radicals since the line of the Congress was conservative and more in tune with the views of Liu Shao-ch'i. Priority was to be given to economic development rather than political reform.

One of the most striking features of the Congress was its definition of the theoretical line guiding the Party. The last Party constitution of 1945 had established Marxism-Leninism and Mao Tse-tung Thought as the foundation of Party policy. In the 1956 constitution, the reference to Mao Tse-tung Thought was omitted.[92] MacFarquhar argues that Liu Shao-ch'i, in line with the criticism of the 'cult of personality' in the Soviet Union following the Twentieth Party Congress, wished to play down the role of Mao in the Chinese revolution. In his stress on 'collective leadership', Liu implicitly criticised Mao's possible failure to consult his colleagues on the speed-up in the co-operativisation drive of mid-1955. It is possible also that Liu played a part in the drafting of an internal Party directive to the effect that no mention be made to Mao Tse-tung Thought in Party communications though Mao Tse-tung's *works* should continue to be stressed. It would seem further that Liu accepted the recommendation of Defence Minister P'eng Teh-huai that no reference be made to Mao Tse-tung Thought in the Party constitution.[93] Teng Hsiao-p'ing, on the other hand, appeared to defend the position of Mao. In stressing Mao's symbolic importance, Teng insisted that there had been no problem of a 'cult of personality' in China and pointed to the fact that, before the founding of the Chinese People's Republic, the Party had forbidden the celebration of the birthdays of Party leaders and the naming of places after them. Teng subsequently admitted that he had withdrawn reference to Mao Tse-tung Thought from the Party constitution but this is probably true only in the sense that Teng was a member of the drafting committee.

By September 1956, Party membership stood at some 10.7 million.[94] Growth since 1949 had been somewhat erratic. Though the worker

component in the Party rose in the years 1950-3, the overall rise in
membership was only from 5 million to 6.5 million. Following the Kao
Kang affair, Party membership jumped 1.5 million in one year (1954)
and again soared during the radical period after mid-1955 as attempts
were made to establish a Party branch in each *xiang*. As a result of the
expansion of rural membership, 7.4 million out of the 10.7 million
membership at the time of the Congress were classified as peasants (of
whom 5.4 million were poor peasants and 2 million middle peasants).
With the new policy towards intellectuals, the intellectual component
was also expanded. By the autumn of 1956, there were 1.3 million
people classified as intellectuals within the Party (and this was to
expand to 1.9 million the following year). Though a Party of 10.7
million was very large in absolute terms, it only represented some 1.7
per cent of the total population and clearly there was room for far
greater expansion.[95]

Few changes were made in the structure of the Party in 1956. The
Congress remained as the source of authority which determined the
Party's general line and elected a Central Committee which was required to meet periodically in plenary session. These plenary sessions
rarely initiated policy but in the 1950s were extremely important in
making authoritative decisions.[96] Policy tended to be initiated either
by the Politburo or sometimes, when the Mass Line was working
effectively, at meetings of provincial Party secretaries. The two most
important of these in the current period had been held in July 1955
when Mao explored the ground for speeding-up collectivisation and in
April 1956 when it appeared that Mao attempted to head off deradicalisation with his speech on 'The Ten Great Relationships'.

The Politburo, along with the chairman (Mao Tse-tung), vice
chairman and general secretary, were elected by the Central Committee.
In 1956, a new body was created, the Politburo Standing Committee,
to manage the day-to-day business of this extremely important decision-
making body. Around the time of the Congress (though some sources
refer to an earlier date), Mao divided this Standing Committee into two
'fronts'.[97] The chairman proposed gradually to remove himself from
the day-to-day management of current affairs by the creation of a
'second front' to which he would eventually retire. When he finally took
that step, operational decision-making would rest with the 'first front'
consisting of Liu Shao-ch'i, Chou En-lai, Chu Teh, Ch'en Yün, Teng
Hsiao-p'ing (and later Lin Piao).[98] Mao was obviously concerned about
the issue of succession to the post of Party chairman. He noted that,
in the Soviet Union, Malenkov had been unprepared to assume the

supreme leadership and, to prevent a similar situation occurring in China, he created the institutional framework whereby others could assume greater responsibility.[99] In anticipation of Mao's retirement, the post of 'honorary chairman' was created but for the time being left vacant.[100]

A number of other bodies existed at the central level of which perhaps the most important was the Party Secretariat under Teng Hsiao-p'ing. This body, which handled the routine business of the Central Committee, served probably as an important link between the Politburo and local Party organisations. In the post-Twentieth Soviet Congress atmosphere of 1956, the fact was not lost on the Party leadership that it was from his position in the Secretariat that Stalin had risen to the supreme leadership in the Soviet Union and, although this body was strengthened by the Eighth Party Congress, there may be some truth in the suggestion that the Politburo Standing Committee was set up precisely to act as a curb on the Secretariat.[101] Another body was the Military Commission which was linked to a newly created General Political Department (*Zongzhengzhibu*) of the People's Liberation Army, the immediate task of which seemed to be to ensure that all PLA companies had established Party branches. Other committees existed to deal with propaganda and various branches of the economy, the latter running parallel to the state structure. There was also a Party Control Commission, headed by Tung Pi-wu, about which very little is known. It had been very active, however, in the aftermath of the Kao Kang affair and reference was made to it time and again in later movements.[102]

The local organisation of the Party[103] paralleled the state structure. With the abolition of the large administrative regions in 1954, the six associated central bureaux of the Party were also dissolved. There had existed, however, prior to 1954, a number of central branch bureaux in areas where there were particular problems (Inner Mongolia, Shantung, South China and Sinkiang). In 1954, the Shantung and South China branch bureaux were abolished and a new branch bureau created in Shanghai where the bulk of 'national capitalists' had lived and where problems of socialisation were most acute.[104] After the formation of the Sinkiang Uighur Autonomous Region and the Inner Mongolian Autonomous Region, the only Party organisation between centre and provinces left by the time of the Congress was in Shanghai and this remained in existence until 1958.

The organisation of the Party at provincial level was the same as at the centre. Provincial Party congresses elected committees headed by a first secretary who was usually a member of the Central Committee. They set up a number of specialist committees to supervise various aspects of political and economic work and to supervise the 'Party fractions' (*Dangzu*) at various levels of administrative organisation. In view of the continuity of leadership in the provinces, it is highly likely that close links were maintained with the local military. At *xian* and city level, efforts were directed to recreating much the same kind of structure by abolishing many of the *ad hoc* committees that previously had been directly responsible to the Central Committee.

Basic-level Party organisations had been formed according to both geographical and functional principles with particular emphasis on establishing Party committees in each *xiang*. By 1956, there were 538,000 of these basic-level organisations each headed by a secretary, though this number was to increase rapidly with renewed radicalisation. The Party organisation at *xiang*, factory, school, military company, street, state organ and maybe collective was referred to as 'basic', in that it was the lowest level at which the principle of committee organisation applied. Though basic organisations could be set up where there were as few as three Party members, some of them were quite large and were subdivided into cells.

The only other local level Party organisations that need concern us here are local control committees (which functioned in much the same way as the central control committee in checking up on the operation of lower levels) and the Party fractions which existed at most levels of administration.[105] Ideally, these fractions were the link whereby administrative organs were articulated to local Party committees according to the principle of dual rule. They had no decision-making function but could take the lead in any horizontal mobilisation campaign. As their functions were prescribed in 1956, they were responsible only for Party members within any organisation and not for the general work of the organisation, though little guidance was given on how one made the distinction. Very soon it was to be seen that one could not.

We have seen that the attempts to specify clearly Party structure in 1956 occurred in a tense political climate. The contradiction between the Party as a source of direction and the Party as a structured institution was still a very real one. One could straighten out Party organisation as much as one liked, but it would mean little if the Party were guilty of bureaucratism. The halt to radicalisation had left much work to be done and many errors to be combated. Both Liu Shao-ch'i and Teng Hsiao-p'ing saw the need for rectification (though not much head-

way had been made in this regard since the early preparation for rectification in June). They probably differed, however, on the methods to
be used. In the view of one commentator, Liu attributed the major
cause of error to 'subjectivism' which implied a stress on increased
training in Marxist-Leninist theory and rectification from above.[106]
Teng, on the other hand (and presumably Mao) attributed the major
cause to 'bureaucratism' which reinforced Mao's call for the supervision
of the Party from outside. To back up this point, Teng was most insistent on the need to reinvigorate the Mass Line in contrast to Liu's more
élitist approach. It was probably Mao's view that these problems could
only be solved by new radical movements rather than by structuralist
reform. Until he was sure that these problems were being solved, Mao's
departure to the 'second front' would be delayed.

The Formal End of One Man Management and the Effective End of External Control

Though the deradicalisation of 1956 halted some of the reforms set in
motion in mid-1955, there were certain processes that could not be
halted. Though rural collectivisation may have been slowed down, it
still continued throughout the year. One man management was by now
a dead issue which probably could not have been revived even if anyone
had wanted to. It was formally laid to rest at the Eighth Congress,
though the manner of its passing was quite remarkable. In calling for its
abolition, the head of the Party's Industry and Communications
Department, Li Hsüeh-feng, in effect, congratulated those cadres who
had maintained the Yenan tradition in resisting it.[107] A senior member
of the Party was congratulating Party cadres for disobeying Party
policy; the implications were profound.

The new policy in industry was the 'responsibility of the factory
general manager under unified Party leadership'.[108] In control work
also, Party leadership over the external control structure was prescribed;
this, in effect, meant internal political control according to the dual
rule principle. The only exception here was Shanghai where the restoration of order, in what was the main centre of the former private sector,
necessitated the continuance of external control.[109]

Major administrative simplification was to await a new radical upsurge in 1957. Although 'left' pressure had contributed to the decline
of the cumbersome control bureaucracy, there is good reason to
suppose that the conservatives were also happy about its demise. It is
not unreasonable to imagine that the conservatives were worried about
the growth of separate bureaucracies with powers of inspection. Stalin

had depended on such a bureaucracy (The *Rabkrin* or Commissariat of Workers and Peasants Inspection) and Stalin was currently the focus of their criticism. They were concerned also, as indeed the radicals must have been, that 'deviant tendencies' had developed in that other control organ, the public security network, which were noted by the Minister of Public Security Lo Jui-ch'ing at the Congress.[110] Neither side wished to tolerate independent bureaucracies. The radicals did not want bureaucracies; the conservatives did not want independent ones.

From Bandung to Hungary

Through much of the period covered in this chapter, China continued the foreign policy initiated after the Korean War and which was symbolised in the 'Bandung spirit'. At the Bandung conference of April 1955, China emerged as a major actor in the Third World and considerable cordiality was expressed by Chou En-lai towards India's Nehru and Egypt's Nasser as major representatives of more or less non-aligned countries. For many years, the Bandung spirit was to be the symbol of the growing unity of ex-colonial countries. Nevertheless, however successful Bandung might have been, it left no lasting organisation to promote that unity. In this respect, a more important conference, which took plate just prior to Bandung, was the Asian Countries conference in New Delhi. This meeting created a liaison group which, in January 1957, was to persuade Nasser to extend its scope to include Africa. Such was the genesis of the Afro-Asian Peoples' Solidarity Organisation based in Cairo in which China was to play a major role.[111]

In the whole enterprise, the position of Nasser was crucial. In the face of growing Anglo-French hostility and the intransigence of Israel, Nasser, in 1955, began to purchase arms from Czechoslovakia and to establish trade relations with the socialist camp. In January 1956, Sino-Egyptian relations had improved to the point that a permanent trade office could be established in Cairo, thus signifying the first Chinese presence in the Arab or African world. By May, diplomatic relations between the two countries were announced with Ch'en Chia-k'ang, a high ranking cadre in the Foreign Ministry, as ambassador.[112] This was an important step, since Cairo was to become the major communications centre between three continents, the headquarters of the Afro Asian Peoples' Solidarity Organisation, the political centre of the Arab world and the point at which African liberation movements made contact. Ch'en was to remain in this vital post until 1965.

The Chinese support for Third World unity was in many ways similar to current Soviet foreign policy. In his secret speech, Khruschev had argued that 'a vast zone of peace' existed in which the socialist camp was linked to the emerging non-aligned countries. Where China and the Soviet Union disagreed, however, was in the tactics to be used by the socialist camp to counter imperialism. In the Soviet view, the world balance was shifting in the direction of the socialist camp and, provided nuclear war could be avoided, the socialist system would spread all over the world by peaceful means. The current tactic, therefore, should be to extend the hand of friendship to non-aligned countries and engage in peaceful coexistence and peaceful competition with the imperialist nations. In the meantime, Communist parties everywhere should endeavour to come to power by 'parliamentary' means to prevent the advent of world war.[113]

To Chinese radicals wrestling with the problems of contradictions at home, the Khruschev formula was unsatisfactory. Though their criticisms at this time were muted, they began to feel that one cannot arbitrarily decide that all the contradictions in the world were 'non-antagonistic'. Any non-antagonistic contradiction might quite easily become antagonistic.[114] In Mao's view, the primary factor in change occurs because of contradictions inherent in a thing. External factors are only effective in as much as they act on internal contradictions.[115] One could not, therefore, decide arbitrarily that the structure of class forces and antagonisms in the world had now become different just because there was a danger of nuclear war. As for the 'parliamentary road to socialism', devotees of the Yenan model were all too aware that a Communist Party that wishes to effect changes from within can all too easily itself lose its independence once it plays by the rules of the host institution. It was the Soviet foreign policy stance of 1956 that the Chinese were later to denounce as 'revisionist' and this term was well chosen. As Marxists, the Chinese Party were all too aware of the 'revisionism' of the Second International where social democratic parties came to see themselves as *inheritors* waiting for the future that would inevitably be theirs. For the time being, however, the issue of 'parliamentary roads to socialism' was sidestepped in official Chinese pronouncements. The much clearer Bandung call for anti-colonialist struggle was the watchword. According to the Bandung formula, 'peaceful coexistence' was accepted only as a relationship between socialist and Third World countries and not in the Khruschevian sense of a relationship between socialist and *imperialist* countries.

By mid-1956, the eyes of the whole world were on Egypt. One week after the Chinese ambassador took up his post, the Egyptian government nationalised the Suez Canal. With the Anglo-French-Israeli invasion,

China's response was reminiscent of the Korean War. A special committee was set up to mobilise support and, in November, China began
enlisting volunteers to fight in Egypt though they were never called for.
China immediately granted a loan of 20 million Swiss francs to Egypt[116]
and it seemed quite clear that she envisaged a protracted struggle of the
Korean type. By Christmas, however, Egypt had scored a major diplomatic victory and the dissension in the ranks of the imperialist powers
took everyone by surprise. Mao had always felt that 'imperialism was a
paper tiger' but surely the paper could not be that flimsy! A reassessment of the world balance was to be made.

However critical the Suez crisis looked from the Chinese point of
view, the simultaneous events in Hungary were of more immediate
importance. Having begun the task of dismantling the Soviet model,
China's radical leadership were probably quite happy to see devolution
of power within the socialist camp, provided the camp itself remained
intact. The position of the conservatives was probably not dissimilar,
though, as we shall see, they differed on the nature of decentralisation.
Accordingly, when the Soviet Union contemplated using force to overthrow the increasingly independent Gomulka regime in Poland in
October 1956, it is said that the Chinese restrained them.[117] Later in
the year, the Chinese leadership also attempted to mediate between the
Soviet Union and Yugoslavia.[118] Hungary, however, was a different
matter. As the Chinese saw it, the Hungarian leadership had in the past
committed much the same kind of error as the leadership in Poland or
the Soviet Union. Agriculture had been neglected, there had been no
Hungarian equivalent of the Mass Line and a policy of greater national
independence was to be welcomed. But what could not be tolerated
was a government whose reaction against Stalinist bureaucratism looked
like taking Hungary out of the socialist camp and playing into the
hands of external imperialist powers. It was in the interests of the unity
of the socialist camp that China had made no official criticism of the
new Soviet foreign policy line. Once that unity was seriously threatened,
the Chinese leadership decided that it had no course but to urge Soviet
invasion.[119] We do not know whether or not there was any serious
division of opinion within China on this issue but we can map out
possible differences of opinion as to the causes of the events in Hungary.
This will figure in the first part of the next chapter, since the aftermath
of Hungary was to see a revival of radicalism within China.

The End of the Third Cycle

The consolidation period of 1956 was a relatively short one and unlike the previous one (1952-4) was highly unstable, with radicals and con-servatives arguing alternative strategies in a rapidly changing interna-tional environment. The earlier cycle saw an exacerbation of the urban-rural gap which the events of 1955 did not really do much to solve. On the other hand the élite-mass gap which had grown in the early 1950s was narrowed by the simplification of complex bureaucratic mechanisms and by the reaffirmation of the Mass Line in industry, agriculture and the Army. The socialisation of industry and commerce and the collec-tivisation of agriculture with comparatively little disruption were con-siderable successes. With the affirmation of the Yenan principle of dual rule and the new policy of 'collective leadership', the Party was invigo-rated and ready once again to engage in the task of mass mobilisation horizontally across bureaucratic structures. There was a possibility, however, that the specification of a complex Party hierarchy in 1956 might lead to bureaucratism.

The cycle ends with a set of contradictions very different from those at the end of the last cycle in 1954. Now there was no doubt that the Soviet model had to be modified; but in what way? By late 1956 there had emerged 'two lines' or two ways of adapting the Soviet model to a new situation and two ways of overcoming problems. The embyonic features of these 'two lines' had of course existed from Yenan days but by late 1956 it was possible to be much clearer in identifying them.

Notes

1. This term was coined by Benjamin Schwartz.
2. Vogel 1971, pp. 135-7; Goldman 1962.
3. Mao's annotations in *CB* 891, 8 October 1969, pp. 19-21.
4. Vogel 1971, p. 136.
5. Mao Tse-tung September 1955, in *JPRS* 61269-1, 20 February 1974, p. 16.
6. Mao Tse-tung (8 December 1956 in ibid., p. 40) notes that, by December, 4 million people had been investigated and only 38,000 designated as counter-revolutionaries.
7. Vogel 1971, pp. 137-8.
8. Mao apologised for people being wrongly accused in December 1956. (Mao Tse-tung 8 December 1956, in *JPRS* 61269-1, 20 February 1974, p. 41).
9. For a Cultural Revolution criticism of excessive Soviet influence during the campaign, see Hsieh Fu-chih, in SCMM 641, 20 January 1969, pp. 20-2.
10. The following is taken from Bernstein 1969.
11. See Mao Tse-tung's criticism. Mao Tse-tung 13 January 1958, in *JPRS* 61269-1, 20 February 1974, p. 84.
12. *SC* 3 March 1955, in *CB* 318, 15 March 1955, pp. 1-7.
13. Mao Tse-tung September 1955, in *JPRS* 61269-1, p. 18.
14. The following is taken from Schurmann 1966, pp. 442-7.
15. Ibid, p. 129.
16. Vogel 1971, pp. 144-8.
17. Liu Shao-ch'i summer 1967, in Liu 1969, Vol. 3, p. 366.

18. Mao Tse-tung 31 July 1955, in Mao Tse-tung 1971, pp. 389-420.
19. e.g. *Zhonggongye Tongxun*, No. 16, 1 June 1953, pp. 1-5.
20. Schurmann 1966, p. 263.
21. Ibid., pp. 272-8.
22. Ibid., pp. 327-39.
23. Ibid., pp. 331-5.
24. Mao Tse-tung 30 June 1949, p. 418.
25. Schurmann 1966, pp. 340-4.
26. Ibid., p. 342.
27. Ibid., pp. 346-9.
28. Vogel 1971, p. 157.
29. Ibid., p. 170.
30. Mao Tse-tung 8 December 1956, in *JPRS* 61269-1, 20 February 1974, pp. 41-4.
31. The following description is taken from Vogel 1971, pp. 156-64.
32. Mao Tse-tung 6 December 1955, in *JPRS* 61269-1, 20 February 1974, p. 27.
33. Vogel 1971, pp. 149-53.
34. Mao Tse-tung September 1955, *JPRS* 61269-1, 20 February 1974, pp. 14-26.
35. *PFLP* 1960, *Ten Great Years*, pp. 95-8, 119.
36. Mao Tse-tung September 1955, *JPRS* 61269-1, 20 February 1974, p. 16.
37. Ibid., p. 22.
38. Ibid., pp. 24-5. My translation from Mao Tse-tung 1969, p. 23.
39. *JPRS* 61269-1, 20 February 1974, p. 23.
40. Vogel 1971, pp. 152-3.
41. Schurmann 1966, p. 454.
42. Vogel 1971, pp. 154-5.
43. Schurmann 1966, p. 455.
44. Ibid., p. 454.
45. The earliest version available, dated 23 January 1956 (Bowie and Fairbank 1965, pp. 119-26), does not mention the targets stated in Mao's speech of September 1955.
46. For an interesting comparison of campaigns in the Soviet Union (1929-30) and China, see Bernstein 1967.
47. Schurmann 1966, pp. 453-4.
48. See Vogel 1971, pp. 164-73.
49. These are summed up in T'an Cheng, in *PFLP* 1956, Vol. II, pp. 262-4.
50. See Gittings 1967, Chapter 8.
51. *SCMP* 1234, 24 February 1956, pp. 3-7.
52. Ibid.
53. *SCMP* 1443, 4 January 1957, p. 9.
54. *SCMP* 1234, 24 February 1956, pp. 3-7.
55. Gittings 1967, pp. 164-71.
56. Ibid., p. 207.
57. Text in Rigby 1968, pp. 23-84.
58. Mao Tse-tung April 1956, in *JPRS* 61269-1, 20 February 1974, pp. 30-5. On Kao Kang and Stalin, see Mao Tse-tung 10 March 1958, in Schram 1974, p. 100.
59. Mao Tse-tung January 1957, in ibid., pp. 49-50.
60. Mao Tse-tung 8 December 1956, in ibid., p. 40.
61. Mao Tse-tung April 1956, in ibid., p. 34.
62. Ibid., p. 35. For further views on Stalin, see Mao Tse-tung 10 March 1958, in Schram 1974, pp. 96-103.
63. Text in Bowie and Fairbank 1965, pp. 144-51.
64. See MacFarquhar 1973.

65. Mao Tse-tung April 1956, in *JPRS* 61269-1, p. 33.
66. Mao Tse-tung 1956, in *CB* 892, 21 October 1969, pp. 21-34.
67. *CB* 411, 27 September 1956, p. 3.
68. Mao Tse-tung 6 December 1955, in *JPRS* 61269-1, 20 February 1974, p. 28.
69. Chou En-lai 14 January 1956, text in Bowie and Fairbank 1965, pp. 128-44.
70. Lu Ting-i 26 May 1956, in *CB* 406, 15 August 1956, pp. 3-18 and Bowie and Fairbank 1965, pp. 151-62.
71. Mao Tse-tung 27 February 1957, in Mao Tse-tung 1971, p. 470.
72. Mao Tse-tung 8 December 1956, in *JPRS* 61269-1, 20 February 1974, p. 40 and January 1957, in ibid, p. 48.
73. The following account is taken from Howe 1973, *Wage Patterns . . .* , pp. 89-95.
74. On the role of the accountant, see Schurmann 1966, pp. 248, 250, 328.
75. Vogel 1967, p. 51.
76. Schurmann 1966, pp. 452-3.
77. Ibid., pp. 455-6, *CCP.CC.* 12 September 1956, in *URI* 1971, pp. 407-30.
78. Ibid., p. 457.
79. The following is taken from Schurmann 1966, 457-64.
80. Vogel 1971, p. 185
81. Chang Chih-i's work has been translated in Moseley 1966.
82. Moseley 1966, pp. 113-14.
83. Ibid., p. 41.
84. For a fascinating account of the Yi slave system, see Winnington 1959, Part I.
85. Ibid., Part II (*Wa*), and Part III (*Chingp'o*).
86. Moseley 1966, pp. 104-5.
87. Strong 1965, p. 51.
88. Winnington 1959, Part I.
89. The most succinct statement of this may be found in Moseley 1966, p. 132.
90. Moseley 1966, pp. 144-5.
91. The following section is based on MacFarquhar 1973.
92. For a side-by-side comparison of the two constitutions, see *CB* 417, 10 October 1956, pp. 32-76.
93. *URI* 1968, *The Case of P'eng Teh-huai*, pp. 119-20 and MacFarquhar 1973, pp. 619-24.
94. Schurmann 1966, p. 129.
95. Ibid., pp. 129-36.
96. On the loci of top-level decision-making, see Chang 1970.
97. Mao Tse-tung 25 October 1966, in *CB* 891, 8 October 1969, p. 75. See also the discussion in MacFarquhar 1973, pp. 629-34.
98. Lin Piao was appointed to the Politburo Standing Committee after the 2nd session of the 8th Party Congress in May 1958.
99. Mao Tse-tung 24 October 1966, in *CB* 891, 8 October 1969, p. 71.
100. See MacFarquhar 1973, p. 631.
101. Schurmann 1966, p. 146.
102. Ibid., p. 145.
103. The following is taken from Schurmann 1966, pp. 147-56.
104. The precise functions of central branch bureaux are somewhat vague. They seem, however, to have been specifically designed to deal with areas in which particular problems existed and where it might be necessary to adopt an approach to social transformation different from other parts of the country.
105. Ibid., pp. 156-62.
106. MacFarquhar 1973, p. 635.
107. Li Hsüeh-feng, in *PFLP* 1956, Vol. II, p. 306.

108. See Schurmann 1966, pp. 284-93.
109. Schurmann 1966, pp. 352-3.
110. Lo Jui-ch'ing, in *PFLP* 1956, Vol. II, pp. 98-124.
111. Larkin 1971, p. 20.
112. Ibid., pp. 20-1.
113. Discussed in ibid., pp. 21-4.
114. Mao Tse-tung 27 February 1957, in Mao Tse-tung 1971, pp. 432-79.
115. Mao Tse-tung August 1937, in *SW* I, pp. 312-3.
116. *SCMP* 1411, 15 November 1956, pp. 42-4.
117. Zagoria 1966, p. 56.
118. Ibid., pp. 58-65.
119. On Chinese reaction to events in Hungary, see Solomon 1971, pp. 285-8. For
      an interesting but jaundiced account, see Radvanyi 1970.

4 THE GREAT LEAP FORWARD (1957-9)

We have examined, so far, three cycles in the history of contemporary China. Each of these cycles began with a period of moderate radicalism, escalated into a much more thoroughgoing radicalism and then entered a period of consolidation in which Party conservatives became more powerful. As Mao would see it, each cycle gave rise to its own contradictions, some of which may have negated the collectivist ethos of Yenan days. A fourth cycle was to begin in 1957, which not only re-affirmed the Yenan principle but created new forms of social organisation. The Soviet leaders were eventually to see these social forms as 'utopian' and the Chinese Party radicals to see the Soviet leadership as proceeding down an involutionary[1] *cul de sac*, the end of which was capitalism. The period considered here, however, merely saw a growth of the Sino-Soviet dispute which had begun at the Soviet Twentieth Party Congress back in 1956, and which, in this early period, was concerned mainly with the direction of the International Communist Movement.

'The Correct Handling of Contradictions Among the People' (February 1957)

China's initial response to the events in Hungary in late 1956 was to stress the unity of the 'socialist camp', and yet it was quite obvious that those events had great significance for China's domestic politics. As Mao saw it, the Hungarian uprising was a reaction against a regime that had mechanically copied the experiences of the Soviet Union. It had been a rightist reaction against rightist oppression. Unless one struggled against the mechanical adoption of Soviet forms, therefore, the Mass Line would be ineffective and a pro-capitalist reaction might occur. Such was Mao's concern as the Chinese Party published its first important editorial after the incident, entitled 'More on the Historical Experiences of the Dictatorship of the Proletariat'.[2] It was felt that Soviet 'doctrinairism' should be countered not by 'revisionist' capitulation to capitalism but by the Mass Line. In Hungary the Petöfi Club, a clandestine group of dissident intellectuals who had been denied the opportunity to voice their complaints, had played an important part in the rising. To prevent the formation of similar groups in China, the answer was not more repression but open criticism of the Party.[3]

149

Since the slogan 'let a hundred flowers bloom, let a hundred schools of
thought contend' was first put forward in April 1956, it had been
closely associated with the idea of Party rectification and documents to
assist such rectification had been issued in June 1956.[4] But in the conservative climate which followed, not much had been done to rectify
the Party, at least in the old Yenan sense, for the stress in Party work
had been on the regularisation of Party structure. After Hungary, Mao
felt himself in a position to press once again for 'blooming and contending' for, as he saw it, the party had nothing to fear from criticism.

It is correct to let a hundred flowers bloom and a hundred schools of
thought contend. Truth develops in the struggle with falsehood.
Beauty develops in comparison with and in struggle against ugliness.
Good things and good men develop in comparison with and in
struggle against bad men. Fragrant flowers develop in comparison
with and in struggle against poisonous weeds. Materialism develops
in comparison with and in struggle against idealism. Many people
hate Chiang K'ai-shek but everyone is ignorant as to what kind of bad
man he is. We must publish, therefore, *The Collected Works of
Chiang K'ai-shek*, also *The Collected Works of Sun Yat-sen* and *The
Collected Works of K'ang Yu-wei*[5] . . . We people in the Communist
Party know too little of our opponents. We are somewhat simplistic
and consequently cannot speak persuasively.[6]

The Collected Works of Chiang K'ai-shek, however, were never to my
knowledge published by the Chinese Communist Party since other
Party leaders such as Liu Shao-ch'i and P'eng Chen, the mayor of
Peking, did not share Mao's confidence in the efficacy of mass criticism.
When in January 1957, attempts were made to get the Hundred
Flowers Movement under way, an article appeared in the Party Central
Committee's newspaper *People's Daily* expressing considerable reserve
towards the movement.[7] The implication was that it was the intellectuals who should be rectified rather than employed to rectify the Party.
Whether the principal author, a certain high-ranking political commissar
in the PLA by the name of Ch'en Ch'i-t'ung, represented the views of
Liu and P'eng we cannot say but the very fact that the article was published suggests division within the top leadership. It would seem also
that Ch'en's views enjoyed wide support within the Party at large; in
fact Mao was to remark (perhaps ironically) that Ch'en represented 90
per cent of the comrades in the Party and that he (Mao) did not have
any mass base.[8] It was to be some time, however, before Mao put for-

ward the slogan that 'going against the tide' was a Marxist-Leninist principle.[9]

According to Solomon's interpretation of events, a formula for the Hundred Flowers Movement was hammered out early in 1957 whereby rectification might proceed. It was, however, to be *internal* Party rectification based on a careful study of the (rather conservative) documents of the Eighth Congress.[10] Evidently Mao was most dissatisfied and set about writing what is perhaps one of his most important speeches entitled 'On the Correct Handling of Contradictions Among the People'. The speech was presented formally on 27 February 1957, not to any Party body, but to a session of the Supreme State Conference which only Mao, as state chairman, had the authority to convene. Though I have met people who have heard the full text of this speech, no copy of it exists outside China to my knowledge. What does exist, however, is an abridged version which, dilution notwithstanding, is still an extremely significant document. In 'On the Correct Handling . . .',[11] Mao elaborated on the occurrence of contradictions in socialist society. These contradictions, Mao maintained, may under certain circumstances become 'antagonistic' and require a process of 'struggle' before they are resolved; for to treat all contradictions as 'non-antagonistic' and amenable to resolution through debate is to court trouble. On the other hand, to treat all contradictions as 'antagonistic' (between an 'enemy' and oneself) is the surest way to tyranny and a violation of the Mass Line. In the context of the Hundred Flowers, open discussion was essential, precisely to prevent 'non-antagonistic' contradictions becoming 'antagonistic' and endangering the revolution. In short, unity did not imply absence of conflict, and the suppression of criticism could be potentially explosive. Conflict was a force for progress but it had to be kept within bounds. If suppressed, it would build up and the eventual eruption would be beyond control.

Though Mao did not say so in his speech, there was a great similarity between the actions of those cadres who were everywhere rooting out 'counter-revolutionaries' and those of Stalin. Such actions, Mao felt, endangered the very life of the Party and perhaps obscured the real counter-revolutionaries. The Party, then, was oscillating between 'left' dogmatism of a Stalinist variety and 'right' revisionism where all group struggle and all class struggle was discouraged. Under such circumstances the Yenan Mass Line formula was the appropriate remedy. In a vein reminiscent of the Yenan rectification movement of 1942-3, Mao expressed his confidence:

Marxism is scientific truth and fears no criticism . . . If it did, and if
it could be overthrown by criticism, it would be worthless . . .
Marxists should not be afraid of criticism from any quarter. Quite
the contrary, they need to temper and develop themselves and win
new positions in the teeth of criticism and in the storm and stress of
struggle. Fighting against wrong ideas is like being vaccinated — a
man develops greater immunity from disease as a result of vacci-
nation. Plants raised in hot houses are unlikely to be sturdy.
Carrying out the policy of letting a hundred flowers bloom and a
hundred schools of thought contend will not weaken but strengthen
the leading position of Marxism in the ideological field.[12]

The Hundred Flowers

With his speech 'On the Correct Handling . . .' Mao threw down the
gauntlet for the more conservative Party leaders whether of a 'left' dog-
matist or 'right' revisionist variety. In the next two months, he busied
himself seeing that organisational means existed for making his
'blooming and contending' policy a reality. In early March, the Chinese
People's Political Consultative Conference, which had been eclipsed by
the National People's Congress on the formation of that body in 1954,
was revived as the most appropriate United Front body to initiate discussion. Before long, the various 'democratic parties and groups' also
engaged in discussion of the policy of 'long-term coexistence and
mutual supervision'[13] and in March, at a National Party Conference on
Propaganda Work, Mao sought active support from rank and file Party
cadres for his policy of 'blooming and contending'.[14]

The response of Party cadres was mixed. Chang Chih-i, who as we
have seen was one of the more outspoken conservatives, expressed
fears that Mao's policy would endanger the United Front[15] and others
echoed People's Daily in its denunciation of people like Ch'en Ch'i-t'ung
who had suggested that intellectuals were unreliable. In fact People's
Daily, in April, engaged in self-criticism for its tardiness in criticising
Ch'en.[16] As the movement unfolded, even bureaucrats such as the
'literary tsar' Chou Yang echoed the call for 'blooming and contending'.[17] Mao found himself in strange company.

By April, local Party branches were urged to open themselves for
criticism and lead the movement. They were not to bury their heads in
routine tasks and fear a loss of prestige.[18] Progress at lower levels of the
Party was, however, slow, probably because Party secretaries knew that
there were senior leaders of the Party who did not support the move-

ment. In the words of Ch'ien Wei-ch'ang, a member of the Central
Committee of the China Democratic League (one of the 'democratic
parties'), ' "blooming and contending" will not work because it is not
supported by the line of Liu Shao-ch'i through P'eng Chen'.[19] At one
time, Mao was said to have been so angered by Party resistance that he
declared he would rather not be chairman so that he himself could
participate more actively in the movement.[20]

According to Solomon, a new formula was arrived at by the highest
levels in the Party in late April[21] whereupon Liu Shao-ch'i publicly gave
modest support to Mao's position in a speech in Shanghai on 27 April.
As Liu saw it, the Party leadership 'does not love struggle' and should
adopt the method of 'gentle breezes and mild rain'.[22] On the same day,
first secretaries of the Party organisations above *xian* level were
instructed to assume personal leadership of the movement.[23] By early
May, senior leaders of the Party were seen to be actively involved in this
rather watered-down version of the Hundred Flowers[24] and stern
warnings were issued to those in the Party who found even the 'gentle
breeze and mild rain' compromise too radical.

Until May 1957, the Hundred Flowers Movement was quite clearly
from the top down, but following the 27 April directive, the slow
trickle of criticism changed gradually into a steady flow and the movement began to take on the form of a mass movement. Forums of an
increasing animation were convened and big character posters (*dazibao*)
began to appear, specifying Party and government malpractice. Complaints were voiced that *Sufan* had been too harsh. Some critics maintained that the United Front was ineffective. Examples of corruption
and favouritism were pointed out. There was criticism of the socialist
transformation of industry and commerce, of blockages in the flow of
information and victimisation of the national bourgeoisie. Instances of
dogmatism and bureaucratism were given, especially the blind copying
of Soviet practices, and leading cadres engaged in 'self-examination'
(*jiantao*).[25]

The criticisms that began to be voiced in May 1957 were not just
confined to intellectuals. Even the PLA, which was undergoing a reassessment of the hastily imposed Soviet model, was affected. In the
period 1955-6, attempts had been made to strengthen the Party system
within the Army and to impose limits on the professionalisation of
what was rapidly becoming an 'officer corps'. With the Hundred
Flowers Movement, further criticism of these developments was voiced,
though this time some counter-criticism appeared to the effect that
too much time was being spent on political study. In Gittings' view, no

one opposed Party leadership over the Army as such; a few conservatives merely objected to what they felt to be excessive political study. In his words, politics was fine, as long as it did not get in their way.'[26] Pending further research, we are unable to assess to what extent criticism in the Army came from the left or the right, though one should note that it was senior Army personnel such as Ch'en Ch'i-t'ung who were most vocal in their doubts that people outside the Party could assist in its rectification.

These doubts were also shared by the All China Federation of Trade Unions (formerly known in English as the All China Federation of Labour).[27] During the period of the First Five Year Plan, the labour unions had undergone a process of professionalisation not dissimilar to that of the Army. The old local craft unions had been replaced by large industrial unions with special functional division of labour. Within the industrial network, specialist staff functions were paralleled by specialist union bodies increasingly committed merely to technical expertise. Within enterprises, managerial wages and welfare sections were often joined by similar union bodies, charged with the same functions and articulated to a rigid staff-line system.[28] In such a system, union activism was played down, except perhaps in the former private sphere where unions assisted in the process of socialist transformation. By 1956, the vertically organised unions, no longer very responsive to local general labour unions, had been very active in promoting the 'economist' wage reform. The unions were hardly the most radical section of Chinese society.

The great problem in the first labour union crisis of 1951 (discussed on pp. 81-2) had been the fact that 'economist' labour unions would not subordinate themselves to Party leadership, and it was for this reason that Li Li-san was replaced as effective head of the ACFL by Lai Jo-yü. Instead of implementing dual rule, however, Lai had built up an ACFTU hierarchy characterised by vertical rule and impervious to local Party influence. In this situation, it is not surprising that any criticism put forward by the official union hierarchy during the Hundred Flowers Movement would reflect demands for greater independence from the Party.

In early 1957, Lai's criticism of the current situation took the form of a protest that, during the First Five Year Plan, unions had once again become 'tails of management'.[29] Though this was probably true, the alternative was not necessarily independence from the Party. Lai argued that, although unions should submit to supreme policy directives from the Party, they should maintain operational independence within their own hierarchy. At a time when official management policy was 'the responsibility of factory general managers under the unified leadership of the enterprise Party committee', such a policy could not but lead to friction. In early 1957, the ACFTU sent out investigation teams to study the relations (contradictions) between Party and unions at local levels. In some cases, Party leadership was found to be weak and in others (from an ACFTU perspective) too strong. In Shanghai, for example, the local Party committee under K'o Ch'ing-shih (identified with the Party radicals) insisted most strongly on the principle of dual rule and this led to friction between Shanghai and the ACFTU centre, where it is likely that Liu Shao-ch'i backed the vertical rule policy of Lai Jo-yü.[30] In other areas, investigations discovered a general lack of union influence among the working class. In the words of Li Hsiu-jen, Deputy Director of the ACFTU General Office, who was sent on an inspection tour of the Peking-Kwangchow railway, everywhere 'unions had been cast aside by the workers'; they were 'workers control departments' or again 'tails of management'; union cadres did not know whether to listen to the directives of the Party or the demands of the masses; many union cadres were again complaining that they were 'fourth class' and Party members with union affiliations were said to be guilty of the 'three don't comes' (*san bulai*) (they did not come to union meetings, they did not come to make reports and they did not come to pay union dues). Unions were once again being used as a vehicle for promotion to management or the Party and had little life of their own.[31]

Though the diagnosis of the disease affecting unions was probably correct, the cure was not necessarily the strengthening of vertical controls and a repudiation of 'blooming and contending'. The fact that the views of the mass of union members were 'economist' and apathetic was not a negation of the value of the Mass Line. Nevertheless, on 9 May 1957, Lai Jo-yü declared his opposition to the Hundred Flowers. In his view, it was not possible to formulate one's own school of thought in labour union work and the views of the masses were not always correct.[32] The revised formula for the Hundred Flowers Movement, worked out in late April, was under attack and it is doubtful if Lai would have been so forthright had it not been for powerful support, presumably from Liu Shao-ch'i.[33] In its reply to Lai's criticism, *People's Daily* was most critical of labour union leadership[34] but Lai remained at his post.

Undoubtedly the most dramatic criticisms came from the élite universities. Complaints began to be voiced that academic work was

being interfered with by political work and, by the end of May, some
of these complaints grew into a criticism of the socialist system itself.
Despite the undue attention given to them by western observers, such
criticisms were probably a very small part of the movement as a
whole;[35] nevertheless they were strategically important in that they
played into the hands of Party conservatives who wished to bring the
whole process of 'blooming and contending' to a close.

By late May, the conservatives were poised to act. A session of the
National People's Congress scheduled to meet on 2 June was postponed,
it has been argued, in order to give P'eng Chen time to prepare his
ground for a new policy to be presented at the meeting.[36] Some circumstantial evidence exists that at a Politburo Standing Committee
meeting on 25 May, a decision was taken to reverse policy even though
Mao still felt that 'rightism' within the Party was more dangerous than
the 'rightism' that had been voiced outside it. Two weeks were to elapse,
however, before the movement was finally terminated, though we are
not sure whether this was because of radical opposition or because the
conservatives wanted to give the non-Party 'rightists' enough rope to
hang themselves.

With the termination of the movement on 8 June, it would seem
that the policies of the Party radicals had been defeated. The movement
had begun to take on the characteristics of a mass movement and was
probably much more than the protests of what has been called the
'non-power élite'.[37] Nonetheless the movement surely did not go nearly
as far as Mao would have liked.

In June 1957, the Hundred Flowers Movement turned into an 'Anti-
Rightist Movement' in which the Party turned on its critics and not
long after the delayed session of the National People's Congress met
finally on 26 June, Mao departed for Shanghai. There has been much
speculation on exactly why Mao left Peking.[38] One explanation is that
he went to investigate the 'rightist' editorial policy of the Shanghai non-
Party newspaper *Wenhuibao*, then under criticism by the soon to be
famous Yao Wen-yüan. A second explanation is that he wished publicly to dissociate himself from the policies of Liu Shao-ch'i and P'eng
Chen who were now directing the struggle against critics of the Party.
There is probably much truth in both these suggestions. The Shanghai
Party Committee, under the leadership of K'o Ch'ing-shih, seemed to
be firmly on the side of the radicals and Shanghai, therefore, was an
excellent place to regroup. It was probably no accident that a photo-
graph appeared in the 11 July edition of *People's Daily* showing Mao
engaged in intimate conversation with non-Party Shanghai intellectuals.[39]

In the same month, however, the same newspaper published criticisms of Mao made by rightists.[40] Though these criticisms were subjected to severe attack, their very publication may have aided Mao's critics. Whether *People's Daily* was, in fact, being used as a battleground one cannot be sure, and to avoid falling into a Kremlinological morass, let us leave the question open.

If the above description of the general contours of the Hundred Flowers Movement, which I have taken from Solomon, is correct, two important questions need to be answered. First, if Liu Shao-ch'i and P'eng Chen opposed the whole thing, why were they not accused of this in the Cultural Revolution? Secondly, if Mao's policies were defeated, how did he still manage to regain the initiative in the late summer of 1957? Again Solomon's answers have a strong ring of plausibility. First, Liu and P'eng were not attacked for their opposition to the Hundred Flowers precisely because their opposition, unlike that of Kao Kang in 1953, was not conspiratorial and conformed with the spirit of inner Party democracy. Secondly, although the Party, for the time being, was not going to allow too much criticism from outside, it was still firmly committed to the struggle against 'rightists'. Mao was soon to be in a position to steer the Anti-Rightist Movement to oppose 'rightist' economic policy.[41] Intellectuals had proved themselves to be unreliable but it had been precisely the influence of some intellectuals that had resulted in the conservative economic policies of 1956. If one set of intellectuals could not be employed in the service of the Mass Line, then a more sweeping Mass Line policy could be used to bring pressure on a different set of intellectuals with whom Liu Shao-ch'i and P'eng Chen might be in accord.

The Anti-Rightist Movement

It is perhaps ironical that the Anti-Rightist Movement, which followed the reversal of the policy of 'blooming and contending', should have been initiated with the publication of the revised version of Mao's speech 'On the Correct Handling . . .' which had played such a major role in the earlier movement. A number of reasons have been suggested for the publication of Mao's speech on 18 June. Perhaps the most convincing of these is that the Party wished to show a continuity in policy before the important meeting of the National People's Congress which was to be a forum for attacks on 'rightists'. A further plausible reason is that it is said that an unofficial copy of the original speech had found its way into the hands of the Soviet Party who were unhappy with the whole idea of 'blooming and contending'.[42] An official version, therefore, had to be published before any further leak occurred.

The Anti-Rightist Movement was to last well into 1958 but the initial stage, which dealt specifically with 'rightist' critics who had become vocal during the Hundred Flowers, was brief. Forums at which certain intellectuals and businessmen had spoken up were hastily reconvened and fresh judgements were made of the 'correctness' of the earlier criticisms. Newspapers published editorials outlining criteria for the evaluation of 'rightism' and organisational meetings were held to discuss how to deal with certain individuals. By late July, the denunciation of these original targets was virtually complete and those who had been 'capped' (i.e. designated as 'rightists') were usually sent for indefinite periods of manual labour.[43]

After the initial stage, however, progress was slow. Within the labour unions all that could be done at first was to criticise 'economism'. It was impossible to designate specific individuals as 'rightist' since leading cadres of the ACFTU were also ranking Party members. By September, however, a decision was taken at the Third Plenary session of the Eighth Central Committee to reactivate the earlier rectification movement, and from then on it was possible to remove labour union officials. Lai Jo-Yü, however, was spared for he became ill and died in May 1958.[44]

Within the Army, there was also a mild Anti-Rightist Movement though the 'poisonous weeds' that were discovered were given less publicity. Perhaps the main focus of attack in the PLA were those who had sought to weaken Party leadership and who insisted on a 'purely military viewpoint'. It was said that certain military cadres stressed only technical modernisation and were guilty of a modern form of 'warlordism'. It was apparent that the movement to return to the revolutionary tradition of People's War had been resisted and that certain senior military commanders might have been involved.[45]

By August 1957, it was clear that the Anti-Rightist Movement was not just a reflex action on the part of the Party conservatives but had also been embraced by the Party radicals in their attempts to dismantle the Soviet model. Late in that month, serious criticisms began to appear in the press of that archetypical Soviet form of organisation, the Ministry of State Control.[46] Initial attacks centred on one P'eng Ta, who was accused of opposing the Party fraction in the ministry and the principle of dual rule. By December, criticism of 'rightism' in the ministry had escalated to include Wang Han, a deputy minister who had played an important part in the introduction of the Harbin system. In March 1958, most control work was handed down to local authorities which, in effect, meant being handed over to the Party and, by mid-year, references to the external control network disappeared. The ministry was not to be formally abolished until April 1959 but clearly the Anti-Rightist Movement sealed its fate and signified the beginning of the end of Soviet-style central planning.

The Anti-Rightist Movement was also to prepare the ground for the decentralisation of authority to local areas. But before this could be done, it had to destroy 'localism', defined here in a more traditional sense than the concept 'independent kingdom'. One of the most striking examples of such 'localism' in this period was that of Feng Pai-chü in Hainan Island. Feng had for long resisted the influence of cadres from the north and had complained to the Eighth Party Congress in September 1956 about outside interference in Hainan affairs.[47] In December of that year, the situation had got so bad that minor armed incidents took place. Some 'localists' had made much of the 'blooming and contending' policy, but by August 1957 full-scale criticism of 'localism' was in progress. Feng and other 'localists' elsewhere were to be removed from office.

The Socialist Education Movement

The Hundred Flowers Movement never reached rural cadres still busy with the tasks of collectivisation. In the countryside, policy was still unclear and there was much confusion.[48] Throughout 1956 some cadres discriminated against the private sector while others did little to restrain peasants who wished to leave the collectives. Occasionally rural leaders permitted a decentralisation of power to individual households (*baochan dao hu*) or ignored what was happening provided that grain quotas were met. They permitted peasants to spend an increasing amount of time on their private plots and even began to act like 'rich peasants' themselves.[49]

To help retrieve the rural situation, a process of *xiafang* (sending down) was employed. The notion of *xiafang* had been put forward by Chou En-lai in his report to the Eighth Party Congress[50] though, in the conservative atmosphere of that time, it meant little more than the disposal of personnel made redundant by administrative streamlining; retrenched cadres did not usually take part in manual labour.[51] In his speech 'On the Correct Handling . . .' Mao hinted that rusticated cadres should 'share the sufferings of the masses' by engaging in productive labour[52] and this became official policy upon the promulgation of the 27 April directive which inaugurated the Hundred Flowers Movement.[53] In May, photographs appeared in the press showing leading Party figures doing manual work[54] and a Party directive was issued demanding that all Party members regardless of rank should assume the work of ordinary toilers.[55] As the movement developed, specific reference began to be made to the Yenan *xiaxiang* (down to the countryside) tradition. By June 1957 the *xiafang* movement had expanded from a process of retrenchment and self-education into one which might help clean up the countryside.

What, however, were retrenched cadres and educated youth to do? A programme of 'blooming and contending' was clearly not on the agenda but the Anti-Rightist Movement could be extended into the rural areas. At a conference of provincial-level Party secretaries in Tsingtao in late July, Mao took the initiative once again.[56] He proposed a Socialist Education Movement whereby excesses and shortcomings in rural work might be checked.

The Socialist Education Movement of 1957 was not a mass movement. It bore some superficial resemblance to land reform in that 'monsters and demons' (*niugui sheshen*) were criticised but there were no 'struggle sessions' or 'speak bitterness' meetings. Peasant associations were not reactivated and the initiative in detecting obstacles to collectivisation was taken by work-teams sent down from above. Despite its limited nature, the movement was to achieve some successes. In August, the State Council moved effectively to restrict rural markets. By September, rural Party rectification could be undertaken in earnest and work was begun on co-ops with the most serious problems (the so-called 'third category' co-ops). Aiming to reduce the size of collectives to about 100 households, the work-teams were able to bring the average down from 246 households in 1956 to 169 in 1957.[57] By the autumn, rural petty-capitalism had been checked, much of the power of the traditional village elders had been broken and leadership was in the hands of younger cadres. More and more the collectives began to resemble the Soviet *kolkhoz*.

Major problems, of course, still remained. In slack seasons there was temporary underemployment. In many areas women were excluded from the main agricultural work force except at harvest time. Perhaps most important of all, peasants had still not been mobilised to effect major changes for themselves. So much of what had been done was merely institutional engineering. The dead hand of bureaucratism was still apparent when in September 1957 a Party directive declared that once the size of the collectives and brigades had been fixed, there should be no further changes for ten years.[58] Mao Tse-tung was not to be so easily satisfied.

From the countryside, the Socialist Education Movement spread to the cities in a milder form. In September and October, capitalist influences in industrial and commercial enterprises[59] were attacked and the 1956 wage reform reassessed.[60] Individual piecework, bonuses and an exclusive concentration on material incentive were denounced and moral incentive affirmed. In universities and schools, special 'Socialist Education' sections resolved to undertake the task of training 'revolutionary successors'.[61] As the elements of education in the Socialist *Education* Movement received belated stress, it was seen that reforms could not be carried out effectively in watertight compartments. Students and teachers had to integrate with ordinary people.

Perhaps the most notable achievement in 1957 was not so much the rectification of shortcomings by the Socialist Education Movement but the success of the *xiafang* movement.[62] What started as mere administrative retrenchment had grown, by the end of 1957, into a major developmental policy. By the end of November, 303,000 out of a total of 575,000 cadres from 18 provinces and municipalities had gone to the 'labour front'. By February of the following year, the figure was to reach 1,300,000. A major attempt was under way to close the gap between those who labour with their hands and those who labour with their minds. *Xiafang* was no longer a remedial measure but a continuous process. Labour reform was no longer seen as a punishment but as an education and, although not all cadres were happy with their lot, most seemed content not merely to 'dismount and look at the flowers'.

Towards a New Economic Strategy

As the *xiafang* and Socialist Education Movements unfolded and the First Five Year Plan drew to a close in the summer and autumn of 1957, an intense debate arose, precisely on the question of development and economic strategy. The First Five Year Plan (1953-7) had given investment priority (over 50 per cent) to capital goods industries with a much smaller planned investment in consumer goods industries. Only 6.2 per cent of the state budget was devoted to agriculture though a considerable proportion of agricultural investment was not included in the state budget. The Soviet Union had agreed to provide about 300 modern industrial plants during the course of three five-year plans at an estimated total cost of $3 billion and by 1957, 68 of these projects had been completed. The bulk of Chinese indebtedness to the Soviet Union, however, resulted not so much from economic assistance as from the liquidation of Soviet shares in the former joint-stock companies in Lushun and Talien and payment for Soviet military supplies delivered during the Korean War. Though there was some Soviet assistance in key areas, the bulk of capital investment was provided by the Chinese themselves and gross fixed investment rose from an estimated 5.5 per cent of GNP in 1950 to some 18 per cent in 1957.[63]

As one might expect, the annual growth rate of industrial output during the Plan was spectacular. A rate of 14-19 per cent was higher than virtually every other country in the world and surpassed the industrial growth rate of the Soviet Union during her first two five-year plans (1928-37).[64] As a result of adherence to a Soviet economic model, heavy industry constituted as much as 48 per cent of total industrial output by 1957. In comparing China with the Soviet Union, however, one should remember that China started from a much lower base at the start of her plan.

Though economists differ as to their estimates of China's industrial growth during the period 1952-7, the differences in estimates are nowhere near as great as in the agricultural sector. Official figures claim that total farm output increased during the period by some 25 per cent, giving an annual growth rate of over 4 per cent, though it has been argued that these figures underestimate output for the early years. One estimate, that of Liu and Yeh, states that production increased by less than 9 per cent giving an annual growth rate of less than 2 per cent.[65] Economists argue amongst themselves as to the relative merits of estimates placed between these two extremes. It would seem, however, that the majority agree that food production roughly kept pace with the total population increase of from 11 to 12.5 per cent but did little more than that.[66] If this is so, two conclusions emerge. First, during a Plan which only allocated 6.2 per cent of the state budget to agriculture, a major collectivisation of agriculture was carried through without a significant decrease in output per capita; this was no mean achievement. Secondly, with the bulk of capital investment being financed domestically, agricultural output had to increase quite substantially to avoid a major investment crisis. Since investment in heavy industry derived in large measure from agriculture via light industry, a Soviet-style concentration on heavy industry alone was inappropriate.

In the field of foreign trade, there was considerable expansion during the period, mainly with countries of the socialist camp. The average annual growth rate was some 20 per cent for exports and 16 per cent for imports.[67] It seems, therefore, that trade was growing faster than industrial production. From a developmental perspective, it may be argued, such a situation could be potentially dangerous as the Chinese economy became plugged into a world economy whose prices she was in no position to control. In the radical atmosphere of the late 1950s, China was to move to a more autarchic view of development.

The key question, therefore, in the autumn of 1957 was how to increase agricultural output to pay for industrialisation. The Soviet answer, which had been found wanting, was to predicate rural transformation on industrialisation. Mechanisation of agriculture was to precede social transformation. We have seen, however, that after the relatively poor harvests of 1953-4, Mao and the Party radicals had taken the initiative in reversing this order of priorities. Social mobilisation itself was to increase productivity and thus generate funds for agricultural mechanisation which would make possible savings for industrial investment. As Mao saw it, collectivisation was not an end in itself but was the first step in a process whereby a 'Great Leap Forward' would take place in production, according to the slogan of producing 'more, better, faster and more economically'. Such had been the basis of Mao's Twelve Year Plan for Agriculture, so unceremoniously shelved in 1956. With the renewed radicalisation during the various movements in the summer of 1957, Mao was in a position to voice his strategy once again.

A second question concerned the location of operational economic decision-making. The Soviet answer lay in centralisation of both policy and operations. The revelations of Khruschev had shown how wasteful such a system had been and, in China, one could also discern similar (though perhaps less serious) problems.[68] The question to be answered was, if there was to be decentralisation, what kind of decentralisation and to what level? The Yugoslav solution (which Schurmann designates 'decentralisation 1'),[69] was to transfer decision-making power down to the units of production themselves. This view, which Schurmann believes was advocated in China by Ch'en Yün and to a lesser extent by Hsüeh Mu-ch'iao,[70] looked very attractive from the point of view of involving all enterprise and co-operative personnel in decision-making, but there were considerable drawbacks. In a system where units of production were atomised, the only possible structure that could hold the economy together was the market and not the plan. Once free play was given to market forces, the radicals believed there would be an inevitable tendency for industrial and agricultural units to produce solely for self-gain, the internal effects of which would be a stress on material incentive. In such a system, the articulation of the economy to regional and local government would break down, thus making the Party as ineffective as when it was subordinated to vertical decision-making structures. Far more attractive from a radical point of view than 'decentralisation 1' was the decentralisation of policy and operational decision-making power to *local areas* (Schurmann's 'decentralisation II'), if only one could make it work. This was the strategy adopted in the Soviet Union in 1957 when regional economic councils (*sovnarkhozy*) were set up with broad powers.[71] The Soviet experiment, however, was not to be a success. Ministries were abolished and their powers transferred to branches of the State Planning Commission which then proceeded to function in much the same way as the old ministries. On the one hand then, there was partial recentralisation and on the other, the adoption of what some call more 'liberal' economic policies (the Chinese were to call them 'revisionist'), which resulted in a partial 'decentralisation' and the growth of the market at the expense of the plan. In 1957, however, these problems that were to plague the Soviet Union were but dimly seen.

By the autumn, a modified version of 'decentralisation II' became the accepted strategy. Not only was power decentralised to local areas but a programme of decentralisation of power was also to be carried out *within* economic units.[72] The great virtue of 'decentralisation I' over 'decentralisation II' lay precisely in the scope that was given for mass participation in decision-making. The modified 'decentralisation II' adopted in China gave scope for that participation but located power both above and below the level of the productive unit.

It has been remarked that one of the decisive features of the Chinese planning system is that non-economic goals are fed into it.[73] I would argue, however, that the Chinese planners, as Marxists, would not accept such a description, since to them there is no such things as a non-economic goal. All goals are both political and economic. The Great Leap Forward strategy was not aimed just at increasing productivity, with some human considerations taken into account. Rather it was aimed at the closure of the élite-mass and urban-rural gaps in both their economic and non-economic dimensions and this within an atmosphere of expanding productivity whereby greater investment funds could be provided for all sectors of the economy. It was not to be, as it has sometimes been described, a shift from material to moral incentive but was rather a shift from the individual to the collective dimensions of both material and moral incentive. It was not merely to be an acceleration of the existing pattern of the modern-oriented First Five Year Plan with a slightly greater stress on agriculture, but was an exercise in creative imbalance or dynamic disequilibrium whereby sectors of the economy were thrown out of gear just to find out what the potential was. As a theoretical underpinning of the Leap, Mao articulated the

theory of 'uninterrupted revolution',[74] which he saw, not as Trotsky's
theory of 'permanent revolution' whereby the socialist revolution might
be launched before the democratic revolution was completed,[75] but as
a continuous succession of revolutionary stages during which periods of
consolidation did not endure long enough for institutionalisation to
occur. As Mao put it in early 1958:

> Imbalance is a universal objective law. Things forever proceed from
> imbalance to equilibrium, and from equilibrium to imbalance, in
> endless cycles. It will be forever like this, but each cycle reaches a
> higher level. Imbalance is constant and absolute; equilibrium is tem-
> porary and relative.[76]

For Mao, even 'communism' was not an end but a revolutionary process.[77] The Great Leap Forward, then, was envisaged as part of this
process of 'uninterrupted revolution' and there was nothing that was
not to be pressed into its service. A policy of 'walking on two legs'
was not just a device to utilise the old as well as the new, but implied
a continuous state of flux in which the old became something even
newer. It implied that both worker and peasant and both nuclear
physicist and traditional practitioner of acupuncture and moxibustion
were equally relevant. The Soviet-style planners, in many ways as conservative as any Western accountant, could not but be alarmed.

The Third Plenum (20 September – 9 October 1957)

The Third Plenum of the Eighth Central Committee confirmed the
victory of the Party radicals. By that time, Mao felt in a position to
criticise the line of the Eighth Party Congress which held that the main
contradiction in Chinese society was between the advanced social
system and the backward productive forces.[78] As Mao saw it, there
could be only one main contradiction – between the people and the
bourgeoisie. In the new radical atmosphere, Mao Tse-tung's Twelve
Year Plan for Agriculture was adopted,[79] though in a revised form.[80]
Notwithstanding the revisions, the symbolic importance of the Plan was
such that its adoption revivified the radical approach to social transformation and economic development adopted in 1955. At the same
time, a decision was taken in favour of 'decentralisation II' and the
process of rectification intensified. There is evidence, however, that
these decisions were not taken without some opposition. It will be
remembered that, less than a week before the plenum, on 14
September, a Central Committee directive had struck a very conserva-

tive note on rural organisation declaring that, once the current programme of scaling down the collectives had been completed, there
should be no change for the next ten years. This directive, which
probably resulted from the conclusions of a National Conference on
Rural Work which met in early September, was the complete negation
of Mao Tse-tung's Twelve Year Plan for Agriculture. There had quite
clearly been a reversal of policy probably during the course of the
plenum itself. Further evidence for disagreement lies in the fact that
Mao's plan was only 'basically' adopted (signifying only in broad outline) and that the speeches to the plenum by Ch'en Yün (on economic
administration) and Chou En-lai (on wages and welfare) were never
made public.

The Moscow Conference

The Great Leap Forward strategy was based upon the old Yenan principle of 'self-reliance' in all aspects, except for a portion of heavy
industry which was not decentralised. Here, a continued reliance on the
Soviet Union for the supply of capital goods was maintained and paid
for by expanded exports of primary products and the products of light
industry. The expansion of Sino-Soviet trade had become possible with
a marked improvement in Sino-Soviet relations, once again in 1957,
after the coolness following the Twentieth Congress. In June, Khruschev
had triumphed over an 'anti-Party clique' headed by Molotov and
Kaganovitch. We cannot be sure as to the precise Chinese reaction to
this development[81] but whatever China's leaders felt, Khruschev was
much more conciliatory towards the Chinese in the aftermath of the
crisis. *Pravda* declared that Mao's position, put forward in the essay 'On
the Correct Handling . . .', constituted a development of Marxist-
Leninist theory, and Khruschev himself declared that China *especially*
had the right to build socialism in accordance with her national
characteristics.[82] On 26 August 1957, the Soviet Union successfully
tested an intercontinental ballistic missile, followed on 4 October,
while the Chinese Third Plenum was in session, by the launching of her
first *Sputnik*. On 15 October, China and the Soviet Union signed an
'agreement on new technology for national defence' (perhaps involving
nuclear weapons)[83] and, as the fortieth anniversary of the Bolshevik
Revolution approached, it seemed that the balance of the world's forces
was shifting in the direction of the socialist camp. In Moscow for a
Conference of Representatives of Communist and Workers Parties in
November 1957, Mao was to make his famous remark that 'the East
wind prevails over the West wind', referring here not to China but to

the socialist camp.[84]

It is the view of some commentators that the outward cordiality expressed between China and the Soviet Union in November 1957 is evidence that one should not date the origins of the Sino-Soviet dispute from the Twentieth Party Congress in 1956.[85] There is much evidence, however, that fundamental disagreements still existed and that Mao's role in Moscow in November 1957 was much the same as Chou En-lai's role as conciliator after the Hungarian events in January 1957.[86] There is no evidence that the Chinese were prepared to accept the notion of 'peaceful competition' or 'peaceful coexistence' with *imperialist* countries; nor were they prepared to support Khruschev's partial rapprochement with Tito, who developed a 'diplomatic illness' at the time of the Moscow Conference.[87] In fact, the atmosphere of Sino-Soviet conciliation at the time of the Conference hardened the attitude of the CPSU towards Yugoslavia, then in receipt of American aid.

In the subsequent Sino-Soviet polemic on the General Line of the International Communist Movement, much was made of the conference declaration jointly sponsored by China and the Soviet Union with only Yugoslavia dissenting.[88] Khruschev probably felt that the tone of the declaration was much the same as the position he had adopted at the Twentieth Party Congress, though some concessions had been made on wording. The declaration still held that war was not 'fatally inevitable', though there was now no reference to any change of heart on the part of western leaders. 'Peaceful transition' to communism was still held to be possible, but only in advanced capitalist countries. There was also a new stress on wars of national liberation in the Third World. The notion of 'different roads to socialism' was still maintained, though in a watered-down form. Mao, on the other hand, though perhaps not completely at ease with the new formulation, probably saw Khruschev as coming to a slightly more revolutionary position. The declaration insisted that imperialism was still the major enemy and that 'revisionism' was more of a danger than 'dogmatism'. What is perhaps most important from Mao's point of view was that there was now agreement that the national liberation struggle in the Third World should not be underestimated. The declaration had every appearance of a strongly debated compromise but one that both China and the Soviet Union could accept without very much departure from principles. Under the surface, however, the same divergencies that had existed since the Twentieth Congress remained and were soon to re-emerge.

Despite the fact that the fundamental differences between the Soviet and Chinese Parties still continued to rankle, the atmosphere of conciliation in October and November 1957 did ensure the prospects of increased trade and, therefore guaranteed one crucial aspect of the Great Leap strategy.[89]

Decentralisation

Exports to the Soviet Union were to depend upon the development of agriculture and light industry. Light industry, as defined here, did not just mean the consumer goods industries but all medium and small-scale industry whether concerned with producer or consumer goods.[90] Such industries obtained some 80 per cent of their raw materials from agriculture and were the important link through which agriculture provided investment in heavy industry.[91] Their development necessitated the rapid expansion of intermediate technology in rural and semi-rural areas in accordance with a policy known as 'get the best out of each area (*yindi zhiyi*). With the decentralisation of control, the state was not going to provide much investment in this sector and local light industries were required to practice self-reliance (*zili gengsheng*). Finally, the very life of these light industries depended upon radical agricultural reorganisation. Unlike the radicalisation of 1955 which followed a good harvest, the radicalisation of 1957 came after a not very impressive harvest. Unless something drastic was done immediately to boost agricultural productivity, rural light industries were not going to generate enough funds for heavy industrial development. Thus radical rural reorganisation, the development of light industry and the continued growth of heavy industry were all linked in a programme of 'simultaneous development on all fronts'.

When, on 18 November 1957, the State Council published the decentralisation provisions, all light industry was transferred to provincial control. In addition, all non-strategic heavy industrial enterprises, the timber industry, ports, many construction enterprises and some industries formerly under the Ministry of Communications were likewise transferred. Now, more of the revenue of industrial enterprises (20 per cent) could be retained locally as could the proceeds of a number of taxes, though the Central government could, if it wished, compensate for this loss of revenue by altering its budget allocation to the local area the following year. Local governments could now raise funds by floating their own bonds and far greater provincial or municipal financial autonomy was enjoyed.[92]

At the same time, the planning system was simplified. Enterprises had now only to report on four instead of 12 planned targets and the former cumbersome 'two up and two down' planning procedure was replaced by a simpler 'two down and one up'. (This meant that the interval between the drafting of a plan and its final authorisation was shortened).[93] There was also a decentralisation of personnel, which in effect meant an intensification of *xiafang*. As local power was strengthened, the dual rule system became more effective and even industries still under central control became subject to far greater regional co-ordination.[94] The commercial network was reorganised with far greater power to determine prices being located in the regions; even the railways, where centralisation had been the main purpose of the Harbin system, were transferred to local authorities.[95]

The picture which emerged at the end of 1957 was one of far greater provincial and municipal independence, though some centralised financial controls (such as those exercised by the People's Bank) remained. In the following year, there was much discussion about the divisive effects of such a system and various plans were put forward for large economic co-operation regions,[96] though we are not sure how effective they were. With the strengthening of dual rule, the Party was stronger than ever and capable of effective horizontal mass mobilisation. If Kao Kang had been alive, he would have been astonished.

Rectification

According to the Yenan tradition, any programme of administrative decentralisation must be accompanied by a centralisation of key policies. If local leaders are to be given greater power, then there is a corresponding need to invoke the process of rectification. In the period following the Third Plenum, any hesitancy about criticising Party cadres disappeared. During the eleven months after December 1957, a number of very senior cadres at provincial level were removed from their posts. The reasons for their dismissal were many and varied. Some had supported 'rightist' criticism during the Hundred Flowers Movement, some advocated co-op decentralisation, some had communicated false statistics and information to higher levels, some had favoured too conservative a policy in national minority areas and some had even sought to create 'independent kingdoms'. Two features, however, link most of them. They had nearly all, in a major or minor way, committed errors of rural policy and, in the Great Leap Forward situation, this could not be tolerated. Furthermore, most of them failed to keep up with the increasing radicalisation.[97]

At lower levels, the rectification movement in late 1957 and 1958 was very closely linked with production. A 'conservative' attitude often signified a reluctance to raise production quotas or a 'tailist' pandering to peasant superstitions. Some cadres were accused of wasting scarce investment funds which led to a brief 'two anti' campaign (against waste and rightist conservatism) in early 1958.[98] As the movement blossomed in that year, almost all cadres engaged in criticism and self-criticism and, as part of the routinised *xiafang* system, spent some time in manual labour. Though excesses were to occur in the single-minded pursuit of production which was to characterise the Great Leap, there was more importantly a reaffirmation of the spirit of Yenan in a process whereby ongoing self-criticism and regular participation in manual labour became the norm.

The Water Conservancy Campaign

By December 1957, an economic strategy for the Great Leap had been worked out, power had been decentralised and an intense rural rectification movement launched. The next task was to initiate the process of mass rural mobilisation. Back in September, the Party had announced a policy to build and extend water works.[99] By December, the Central Committee and the State Council announced that this was to be a major movement to be undertaken before the spring ploughing.[100] At first, the movement was confined to individual collectives, but it was soon seen that the nature of water conservancy was such that the labour of several collectives had to combine to complete major tasks. There was but a short step from this to the amalgamation of collectives into large units which divided out the work according to a rational division of labour. In many areas peasants, for the first time, found themselves working far away from their familiar land and yet still within the same collectively administered area. The term 'brigade' and 'team' now meant something more than just a collective subdivision. The brigades and teams began to develop something like the spirit of a military unit engaged in a common struggle where the reward was collective benefit and from which they could not easily retire to till their private plot.[101]

As the pace of rural mobilisation intensified, a whole series of conferences of provincial Party secretaries and some Politburo members met to plan strategy. At the Hangchow Conference (early January 1958)[102] and the Nanning Conference (late January),[103] Mao and others engaged in endless discussions on Great Leap strategies and put forward guidelines in the form of 'Sixty Work Methods'.[104] As the atmosphere became more and more heated, it became clear that the Second Five Year Plan (commencing 1958) would be drastically revised. In late 1957, national plans called for an increase of 4.7 per cent in

agricultural production and 8-10 per cent in industrial production
during the coming year.[105] These figures were soon to be substantially
altered.

The Threat from T'aiwan

The Great Leap Forward took place in an atmosphere of growing international tension and any evaluation of the fervour engendered at that
time must take into account sentiments of patriotism. The first T'aiwan
crisis had resulted in stalemate, though in 1956-7 tension had been
somewhat eased. The opening of the port of Chankiang in late 1956
and the extension of a rail link between there and Amoy had done
much to break the Kuomintang blockade.[106] Throughout 1956 and
early 1957, there had been much talk of negotiations between Peking
and T'aipei and it is said that, in the original version of the speech 'On
the Correct Handling . . .', Mao had indicated the possibility of an
agreement with the Kuomintang. In May 1957, however, an agreement
was signed between T'aiwan and the United States whereby Matador
missiles were to be placed on the island. These weapons could carry
nuclear warheads and had an effective range of 1,000 kilometres. Faced
with this military threat, China could only press even more strongly for
some kind of diplomatic settlement, but Kuomintang positions were
hardening. The T'aipei government was particularly worried that some
kind of deal might be worked out between China and the United States
at the Geneva ambassadorial talks. It felt also that T'aiwan was now
beginning to acquire the capability to invade the mainland and that this
had to be carried out before China acquired nuclear weapons. As the
United States greatly expanded its programme of military aid in early
1958, the Kuomintang government embarked upon a 'forward looking'
foreign policy.[107]

The T'aiwan question began to look even more ominous when, in
early 1958, the United States reduced its representation at Geneva below
the ambassadorial level. In the view of one writer, it is possible that the
Chinese government interpreted this move as a preparation for a bid by
Chiang K'ai-shek to return to the mainland before the expiration of his
second term as President, the last allowed to him under the Republic of
China's constitution. The fear, then, was a Kuomintang invasion
supported by American tactical nuclear weapons. In such a situation, the
production drive of 1958 was geared not only to solving sectoral imbalance in the economy and reviving the Yenan tradition of greater mass
involvement and commitment but also to increasing defence potential
and reaffirming the Yenan tradition of People's War.

The Great Leap Forward: Stage One (January-March 1958)

By early 1958, most of the features of the old Yenan model were being actively promoted. Rectification of cadres was being undertaken to criticise not only 'rightist' thought but also the worship of foreign models. In the new radical climate, it was seen that one of the major errors of Stalin's policies in the Soviet Union had been a neglect of the Mass Line[108] and 'walking on one leg'[109] (an excessive concern with modern urban industry). As the principle of the Mass Line was given new stress, it was combined with the latter-day version of *xiaxiang* and decentralisation of authority. The decentralisation of 1957-8 placed much greater stress on the old ideal of 'cadre' leadership, dual rule and 'centralised policy and divided operations'.[110] As the T'aiwan threat loomed large, and the old idea of People's War was restressed, Mao was soon to note that the Communist Party could be grateful once again to Chiang K'ai-shek for helping the process of militia formation.[111] At the same time, the mass mobilisation effected during the water conservancy campaign led to a further reduction in the size of private plots,[112] the amalgamation of collectives and the redeployment of troops in the civilian rural sector.[113] Campaigns came thick and fast in the Chinese countryside and following the promulgation of an 'eight character constitution' for agriculture, further mobilisation became possible in a mass campaign to collect manure.[114]

As war was declared against natural obstacles, all efforts were bent in the direction of encouraging mass activism. Grain quotas were fixed at 1957 levels and were no longer to be adjusted annually; this meant that everything that was achieved above the quota could go into collective investment, to be decided by the collective itself.[115] Everyone was now instructed to help agriculture[116] and thus bring to an end the resentment felt by peasants that they were poor cousins of the industrial workers. By February 1958 there was every indication that the harvests in that year would be much better than in 1957 and this prospect added to the mood of tremendous optimism surrounding the launching of the Great Leap.

An immediate consequence of this optimism was the continual raising of planned targets. In Kwangtung for example,[117] the plan for 1958 decided on in October 1957 called for a 6.6 per cent increase in agricultural production during the year. By December this figure had been raised to 8 per cent with a planned rise in yields from 400 *jin/mu*[118] to 700 *jin/mu* by 1962 and 900 *jin/mu* by 1967. In January, however, the target was raised to a 26 per cent increase in one year and a planned yield of 800 *jin/mu* to be reached in the same period. Industrial plans

underwent the same escalation. In the same province, planned industrial
increase for 1958 stood at 5.8 per cent in October 1957, 12.4 per cent
in early January 1958, 15.0 per cent later in January and 33.2 per cent
in early February. It was, however, not only enthusiasm that accounted
for this escalation. With the decentralisation of authority and the
xiafang of statisticians, the mechanisms for reporting statistics were not
all they might have been and occasionally resulted in serious errors.
Secondly, since no one wanted to be criticised as a conservative,
planning organs tended to accept the highest possible estimate of pros-
pective output.

In a situation characterised by creative imbalance, it was extremely
difficult to determine exactly what could be planned. When every single
unit of organisation was encouraged to set up some kind of subsiduary
plant, when factories were encouraged to till and sow any bit of land
they might have, when schools took on productive functions, how
could one possibly know what potential output might be? A mammoth
drive was launched to discover oil (for China had hitherto been considered very poor in this crucial source of energy) and large new oil
deposits were, in fact, discovered causing a dramatic revision of China's
future energy programme.[119] More and more seemed possible and more
and more, in fact, became possible. It would be a very brave (or fool-
hardy) man who felt able, in the first few months of 1958, to make
anything like a reasonable estimate of exactly what could be done.

Just as intensified *xiafang* aimed at the closure of the gap between
mental and manual labour, between the leaders and the led, so attempts
were made to deal with that other major concern of the Party radicals,
the urban-rural gap. Steps were taken to establish some kind of industry
in each *xiang* to manufacture agricultural tools, to produce fertiliser
and to process food.[120] Attempts were also made to set up small
furnaces at *xian* level and lower to turn out steel.[121] Here, however, the
results were not successful and were admitted not to be by Mao. A lot
of steel was produced but it was of low quality and not very service-
able.[122] The failures were on a mammoth scale but so were the successes.
The growth of rural industries and intermediate technology in the first
few months of 1958 was an irreversible process and one which was late:
to account in large measure for the success of the Chinese developmental model.

The policy of closing the urban-rural gap was aimed at the eventual
transformation of peasants into workers. This did not mean the
creation of factory-like organisations in the countryside, for socialist
collectives still formed the majority of rural organisations. But in some

areas, especially where land was being newly reclaimed, a 'state farm' form of organisation was set up where peasants became farm workers and received payment in the form of wages.[123] In general, however, peasants continued to receive a proportion of the harvest on the basis of work-points.

As the Leap intensified in early 1958, there was inaugurated what Mao referred to as a period of 'three years' hard struggle'.[124] Technical cadres were sent, in ever-increasing numbers, to the countryside to participate in labour and to train other technicians. To this end, plans were put forward to have a secondary school in every *xiang*.[125] The schools were to pay particular attention to the experiences not of model organisations in the Soviet Union but to models within China itself. The Honan model, for example, was specified as an example of what could be done in the way of labour-intensive programmes on wheat lands[126] and was given particular support by the influential T'an Chen-lin. Similarly, the Swatow model was put forward in the field of rice cultivation.[127] A mammoth study programme was introduced with an urgency dictated by the ominous storm clouds over the T'aiwan Straits. Plans for study or increased production were no longer just 'plans'. They were 'battle plans'.[128]

The Great Leap Forward: Stage Two (March-August 1958)

In March 1958, in a manner similar to that of almost exactly two years previously, there were moves to begin a period of consolidation. Complaints of excesses began to appear in the press. Materials were said to be in short supply. The centre had begun to lose its grip on local developments. Local governments, finding it extremely difficult both to remit funds to the centre and to finance the burgeoning local investment, further decentralised authority to *xian* and minor municipalities. There was much talk of 'reckless advance' (which were precisely the words used by Party conservatives to describe the 'High Tide' of 1955-6) and of 'overcoming the ill wind of empty talk and false reports'.[129] Clearly some mistakes had been made but did this mean that the overall strategy was wrong (which was probably the position of the Party conservatives) or that some cadres had been found wanting (which was the view of the radicals)?

In March 1958, all kinds of meetings were held to discuss how the new policies were working. Of these, the most important was one held in Ch'engtu where Mao suggested that the experiences in mass mobilisation already undertaken in Honan province might tentatively be emulated in other areas.[130] Though the tone of Mao's speeches was cautious

it was much less so than those of some other Party leaders. When the
Eighth Party Congress was reconvened in May, Liu Shao-ch'i in particular, while repeating some of Mao's statements on the virtues of imbalance, revealed a far from radical position:

> Leaders must combine revolutionary enthusiasm with business-like
> sense. They must be able not only to put forward advanced targets,
> but also adopt effective measures in time to ensure the realisation
> of the targets. They must not engage in empty talk and bluff. The
> targets we put forward should be those that can be reached with
> hard work. Do not lightly publicise or plan that which is not really
> attainable lest failure dampen the enthusiasm of the masses and
> delight the conservatives.[131]

What Liu called for was not renewed radicalisation but investigation
and more investigation, and to this end Party leaders spent much of the
summer touring the country[132] to make an assessment of what in fact
was happening now that mass enthusiasm and local initiative were the
order of the day.

However much the Party conservatives may have wished to slow
down the Great Leap, the movement had acquired a momentum of its
own and the position of the radicals was still very strong. Immediately
after the Congress, at the Fifth Plenum of the Eighth Central Committee, Lin Piao (then considered to be a radical) was elected Party vice
chairman. K'o Ch'ing-shih, who had resisted the erosion of the principle of dual rule in Shanghai, was elected a member of the Politburo
and T'an Chen-lin, the architect of the ambitious Great Leap Forward
agricultural programme in the model province of Honan, was promoted
to that body.[133]

In the field of foreign affairs, policy remained radical. Back in
November 1957, Mao Tse-tung had been particularly concerned about
how much Yugoslavia had weakened the 'socialist camp' and the extent
of its 'revisionism'. Now, in May 1958, China's objections were stated
quite openly[134] and, in retrospect, it is not too difficult to read in
them a possible criticism of the direction in which the Soviet Union
was heading. The crucial question which faced China's leaders in the
early summer of 1958 was the extent to which Soviet aid might be
forthcoming in the event of a war in the T'aiwan Straits. It was this
question that probably dominated discussions at an extraordinary
meeting of the Party Central Committee's Military Commission from
27 May to 22 July 1958. The Soviet Union had apparently pressed for a

joint Sino-Soviet naval command in the Far East, integrated air
defences and perhaps the stationing of Soviet troops and emplacement
of weapons on Chinese territory.[135] If this were acceded to, China
would become no more than a Soviet dependency. In pressing for the
rejection of the Soviet demand, Mao was quite adamant:

> We must not eat ready-made food, for if we do so we will be
> defeated in war. This point should be conveyed clearly to our Soviet
> comrades.[136]

It was probably at this meeting of the enlarged Military Commission
that a new Chinese defence strategy was worked out. Chinese independence had to be secured as soon as possible by the development of an
independent nuclear capacity. At the same time, institutions should be
created within China to undertake the task of People's War should the
need arise. The Great Leap Forward then was not just to 'overtake
Britain within fifteen years'[137] (in those days that seemed a goal worth
attaining), not just to solve the fundamental contradictions between
élite and mass and city and countryside, not just to put China once
again on a People's War footing but also to break her dependency on
the Soviet Union once and for all.

There is evidence that the long meeting of the Military Commission
was particularly tense. Its final communiqué stated that the meeting
had been carried out 'using the method of the rectification campaign'.[138]
Apparently there were some senior commanders of the PLA who still
maintained the 'exclusively military viewpoint',[139] notably, it would
seem, Chief of Staff Su Yü who was dismissed in October.[140] By the
close of the meeting, tension hardly abated for, on 29 July, air clashes
occurred over the T'aiwan Straits and two days later no less a person
than Nikita Khruschev himself arrived in Peking accompanied by
Defence Minister Marshal Malinovsky.[141] We are not sure what
happened at the meeting except that no agreement was reached on
T'aiwan; in fact the press communiqué did not even mention it. There
was probably considerable disagreement, not only between Mao and
Khruschev but also between Mao and Chinese Defence Minister P'eng
Teh-huai,[142] on both Sino-Soviet relations and response to the T'aiwan
crisis. Whatever happened, less than three weeks after Khruschev
returned to Moscow, the shelling of Quemoy began (23 August) and a
United States task force was sent to the area.[143] Just as this crucial
juncture, the Great Leap entered its third and most radical phase.

The Great Leap Forward: Stage Three (August-December 1958) – Rural People's Communes

It was the extended debate on defence in the summer of 1958 that was to lead to a qualitatively new stage in the Great Leap Forward. The campaign to build waterworks, in the winter of 1957-8, had resulted in the amalgamation of some collectives and the advancement of the principle of a mobilised and potentially transferable rural work force. At that time, the absence of men in the work brigades had resulted in more and more women being engaged in agricultural tasks in the slack season and in the provision of communal mess facilities. The establishment of some industrial plants in the countryside had demanded the resources of more than one collective and had aided the process of collective amalgamation. The provision of secondary schools at *xiang* level had led people to consider that perhaps the *xiang* might be a more suitable collective unit than the smaller agricultural producers' co-operative. The final step in this whole process was when considerations of defence suggested the merger of productive units with militia organisation.[144]

We have seen that, in the old days of the Soviet model, the people's militia had been allowed to atrophy. Even the co-operativisation movement of 1955-6 had done little to revive militia organisation in the countryside. In 1957, however, as part of the radicalisation of the PLA, the militia was merged with the reserve. Demobilised soldiers and those eligible for conscription but not chosen were organised into a new 'backbone militia' which, in 1957, expanded quite considerably.[145] Doubtless one of the key issues in the defence debate of 1958 was the role of the militia and it was stated that:

> Some comrades take a purely military viewpoint in the militia organisation and overlook the part played by the militia organisations in promoting socialist construction; or else they take the view that the war for national defence and against aggression is the business of the army and not the whole people.[146]

The new slogan was to be 'everyone a soldier' (*quanmin jiebing*),[147] resulting in a militia enrolment by January 1959 of 220 million people. The way was now open for the creation of new units in the countryside which would combine agricultural and industrial production, administration, education and defence. These were to be the people's communes.

As we have seen, the amalgamation of collectives dates from, at the

latest, early 1958 and 'communes' began to appear in the model Honan
province as early as April.[148] It is perhaps ironical that the first model
commune in that province was named after one of the Soviet achievements that initiated the radicalisation of late 1957 — *Sputnik* (*weixing*).[149]
By the end of July, 5,376 agricultural collectives in the Honan region
had become 208 large people's communes with an average population
of 8,000 households.[150] It would appear that a 'High Tide' of communisation had taken place without any directive from Peking and, on his
inspection tour in August, Mao, while approving of amalgamation, did
not appear to have grasped all the intricacies of this development.

> In Shantung, a reporter asked me 'is the commune good? I said
> 'good' and he immediately published it in the newspaper. This might
> be due to some petty-bourgeois fervour. Hereafter newspaper repor-
> ters should leave (me alone).[151]

Mao was soon in little doubt, however, that the idea of the 'commune'
was in fact 'good' and at an enlarged Politburo conference, attended by
provincial Party secretaries and others at Peitaiho from 17 to 30 August,
a 'Resolution on the Establishment of People's Communes in the Rural
Areas' was adopted.[152] The term 'commune' (*renmin gongshe*) was well
chosen. Before the Peitaiho conference, Ch'en Po-ta, the editor of the
Party Central Committee's new journal *Red Flag (Hongqi)* had pointed
out that industry, agriculture, commerce, education and militia should
be combined into single large 'communes', the inspiration for which
could be found in Mao's report of November 1956, 'On the General
Line for the Building of Socialism'.[153] As Schurmann has pointed out,
the fundamental principle of the people's commune was the unity of
work and arms; such the radicals considered had also been the principle
of the *Paris Commune* of 1871.[154] The people's commune (together
with the General Line and the class struggle) was henceforth to become
one of the 'Three Red Banners' of China's radical developmental programme.

  Although the Peitaiho conference accepted the idea of communes,
the communiqué which followed was a very cautious document. Cadres
were instructed not to disturb the villages too much and to take
existing collectives as communal sub-units.[155] Though transformation
from within was an essential feature of the Yenan model, it is possible
that Party conservatives were worried about the destabilising effects of
new rural organisations. Ideally, it would seem the commune was to
replace the *xiang* as the basic level of rural administration and the

former collectives would become its brigades and the former brigades
its teams. In addition, specialist teams might be formed to undertake
light industrial or special agricultural work. The *xiang*-level school
system, separate tractor stations and marketing co-ops were merged
into a single organisation under the leadership of a Party committee
and an elected management committee. Now, with everything
happening in an area consisting of a number of villages under the
control of a tangible authority, much closer identification of the
peasant with the collective might be made. Some peasants were reluctant to give up their private plots and some complained that the food
in the communal mess halls was not very palatable. The point was, however, that the provision of communal messing facilities, communal
child-care centres and 'homes of respect for the aged' freed a lot of
people for productive labour who could now be absorbed in the subsidiary industries, not only at harvest time but also in the slack season.
The formal economic basis for equality between the sexes was laid.
With payment at harvest time made to individuals and not to families,
the structure of the former paternalist gerontocratic family life could
undergo change.

The radicals were understandably excited. To them, the commune
was a fusion of state and society and the beginnings of a process whereby the state would begin to wither away.[156] To Nikita Khruschev,
convinced that the most advanced form of rural organisation to date
was the Soviet *kolkhoz*, this was a very unwelcome suggestion. Even
more disturbing was the intention to introduce a partial free-supply
system within the communes, whereby a process could be initiated of
transition from the 'socialist' principle of 'payment according to work'
to the 'communist' principle of 'payment according to needs'. From the
vantage point of the Soviet Union or of its Chinese sympathisers, the
shift in incentive policy from individual material incentive to, at least,
group material incentive and, at most, group moral incentive was premature. Many of the proposed changes, however, were seen as long-
term. Although the structure of share-payment was altered, the family
and the concept 'family head' (*jiazhang*) remained much as before.[157]
The original idea of 30 per cent payment according to labour and 70
per cent according to needs was never really carried out. The intention
remained, however, to create an organisation whereby the end of
communism should not be perverted by the means used to reach it.

In the autumn of 1958, everything was in a state of experimentation.
With no clear directives on commune size, the initial communes became
bigger and bigger. The largest commune, to my knowledge, embraced a

whole *xian*[158] though, in general, the size of most communes was
roughly equivalent to the old *qu* (or intermediate level between *xiang*
and *xian*) with populations of some 30,000-60,000.[159] As such, they
may have cut across the old 'standard marketing areas' and contributed
to rural dislocation.[160]

Another problem that came to the fore in the autumn of 1958 was
the contradiction between the commune as a do-it-yourself exercise
in organisation and as a process whereby the Party organisations mobilised people to undertake tasks that they were unprepared for. The situation was new and cadres could quite easily fall into one of the two
extremes of 'commandism' or 'tailism'. In general, however, peasant
morale was very high and seemingly quite impossible construction tasks
were undertaken. We shall perhaps never know just how spectacular the
production increases in the bumper harvest year of 1958 actually were,
for statistics continued to be inflated and unreliable. Whatever the
shortcomings and errors, and there were many, China had embarked
upon a course that has radically altered all existing theories of development.

The Great Leap Forward: Stage Three (August-December 1958) – Urban People's Communes

The rural people's communes sought to bring some degree of industry
to the countryside – in short to make the countryside just a little bit
more like the city. Not long after their formation, some experiments
were undertaken to achieve the reverse – to make the cities or parts of
the cities a little more like the countryside.[161] In the countryside, a
major economic problem had been low productivity. In the urban areas,
the problem was a rapidly expanding drift of people from the countryside, many of whom were dependent relatives who could not find
employment. Since 1949, urban population had increased from some
58 million (out of 540 million) to 92 million (out of 657 million).[162]
In a survey of some 15 cities, it was found that from 1953 to 1956 the
basic population had increased by 28 per cent, the service population
by 5 per cent and the dependent population by 70 per cent.[163] The
rural people's communes were seen eventually as a way of stemming the
drift to the cities (though initially they were unsuccessful in this
respect). The *urban* communes were to rapidly expand the opportunities
for urban employment.

The model put forward in 1958 was the Chengchow urban people's
commune.[164] Here a factory became the nucleus of a people's commune
which took in the entire surrounding urban population of 10,500

people. New satellite factories were set up around the core factory to employ dependants and process waste. All commercial and service facilities in the area (formerly run by the city) were now taken over and run by the commune. A 'red and expert' university was set up together with elementary and night schools. The entire neighbourhood was organised into a militia unit and, perhaps most significant, two agricultural production brigades and one sheep milk station were attached. The keynote was 'self sufficiency'; not that the agricultural land was expected to feed the entire population but it could at least help. Since a primary aim was to provide full employment for all able-bodied people, the same kind of communal facilities that existed in the rural communes were organised, though probably with much greater ease, for restaurants, barbers' shops, etc. already existed before communisation. With the formation of urban communes, the shift in policy was away from control to activism, and it is significant that the old residents' committees and street offices did not seem to play a large part, at least in this type of urban commune.

The Chengchow commune was of course just a model and most of the communes formed in late 1958 fell short of its ideals. It had been possible to undertake such an ambitious venture in a city like Chengchow because it was in Honan, which had stood at the forefront of the rural communisation movement. Also, funds were available for the relocation of housing where necessary, and furthermore most of the city was not very old with established residential, commercial and industrial districts. Not much, for example, could have been done with Shanghai without colossal expense, amongst other things because there was just no agricultural land available in many industrial areas. A lot of communes, therefore, were just simply amalgamations of the former network of street administrations which, although useful in generating employment, were nothing like as comprehensive as the Chengchow-type and in some cities it seemed that no attempts were made to establish communes at all.

Even the model Chengchow commune experienced serious problems. The Chengchow factory was technically provincially-owned whereas the other property was collectively-owned. There were thus conflicting lines of authority. Secondly, there were wide disparities in wage structures; the workers in the core factory were paid at a much higher rate than those in satellite factories and the peasants still operated according to a work-point system. All these problems could, in theory, be solved though it would take time. One could just not ask the workers to reduce their wages immediately. There was not, however, to be enough time and the urban commune experiment was to be given up.

The Great Leap Forward: Stage Three (August-December 1958) — Other Aspects

Reforms in urban and rural administration in the autumn of 1958 were accompanied by reforms in industrial management. The demise of 'one man management' had led to the system of 'responsibility of the factory general manager under the unified leadership of the Party committee'. In 1958, this was supplemented by a policy known as the 'two participations and triple combination'.[165] The 'two participations' were of the cadre in manual labour and of the worker in management, and the 'triple combination' consisted of teams of workers, technicians and management cadres who made technical innovations and operational decisions. The idea was that Party committees should confine themselves to overall questions of *politics* (to see that the activity of factories was in harmony with long-term strategies), whereas the factory general manager should now share *operational* decision-making power with these 'triple combination' teams, which would hopefully cut through bureaucracy and implement some kind of functional leadership. Congresses of white and blue collar workers had been revived to discuss broad questions, but democracy within the plant was now seen to be better served in a *participatory* sense rather than in the *representative* sense that had failed so miserably in the early 1950s. As far as incentive policy was concerned, piecework was, in general, abolished and the ratio of highest to lowest paid in factories reduced to about 3:1 or 4:1.[166] Though there was some talk of greater egalitarianism and even of the introduction of a 'free-supply element', I know of no case where this was actually carried out.[167]

Though it is probably true that the Army was the area in which Great Leap policies were most strongly resisted, 1958 saw a massive involvement of the Army in civilian activities. In 1956, the PLA had contributed some 4 million work days to agricultural and industrial production. In 1957, this had risen to 20 million. The planned figure for 1958 was 30 million though, in fact, the figure actually claimed was 59 million (but along with other figures this might be an exaggeration).[168] Whether it was an exaggeration or not, however, some military commanders probably suggested that, in the face of the T'aiwan Straits crisis, far too much time was spent on production work.[169] In one city alone (Nanking), 82 factories were said to have been built with PLA aid.[170] As well as participating in normal civilian economic activities, the Army also engaged in its own economy drive, considerably reducing its logistics departments and economising on fuel.[171] The aim of all this was, of course, not just economic; great stress was laid on maintaining harmonious relations with civilians according to the Yenan tradition and civilians were urged to voice their grievances against the military.[172] The military was now compelled to pay overdue rent, to return land appropriated during the Korean War, and to compensate for requisitioned property. As a result, 72,400 civilian houses were returned.[173] Within the Army itself, the soldiers' committees were strengthened and a movement launched known as 'officers to the ranks'. Every serving officer was required to serve for a time in the ranks as an ordinary private soldier,[174] though this was said to have been unpopular and to have resulted in a backlash the following year associated with the Minister of Defence, P'eng Teh-huai.[175]

Foreign Policy in 1958

The sheer scope of the reforms undertaken in the autumn of 1958 was quite staggering. They took place in a quasi-wartime situation but by September it was fairly clear that the T'aiwan Straits crisis would not result in all-out war. On 6 September, Premier Chou En-lai proposed talks with the United States[176] and, once it was clear that neither America or China wanted armed confrontation, Khruschev announced that 'an attack against China is tantamount to an attack on the Soviet Union'. One does not know what would have happened to Sino-Soviet relations in 1958 had Khruschev made the announcement when he visited China. As it stood, however, the Soviet Union seemed only prepared to support China when it had nothing to lose.[177] It was probably with the Soviet Union in mind, therefore, that in October 1958 Mao's statements to the effect that all reactionaries were 'paper tigers' were given great stress.[178] Khruschev had been seen to bow before the 'paper tiger'.

Back in the old days of the Cold War, it used to be argued in the West that the Great Leap Forward brought to an end the Bandung period in Chinese foreign policy and somehow *caused* China to take a hard line in international affairs. Though quite clearly patriotic incentive served the interests of the radical Chinese leadership and the T'aiwan crisis gave the Great Leap its sense of urgency, there is ample evidence that, in general, many features of the Bandung period remained[179] and where there was a change in policy it was, more often than not, a reaction to circumstances beyond China's control. For example, China was alarmed at the attempts to bring down the elected

Communist government in the Indian state of Kerala, the right-wing reaction in Algeria and the American-backed attempted coup in Indonesia.[180] Sino-Indian relations were very cordial until well into the Great Leap period,[181] until Nehru expressed the intention of visiting Lhasa[182] and perhaps attempting to alter the People's Republic's policy towards Tibet. Before long, the Chinese government published a map showing that they had constructed a road, it is said, without the knowledge of the Indian government, across the remote disputed frontier region of Aksai Chin.[183]

What worried the Chinese above all in 1958 was that not only did imperialism (whether in the form of the 'Eisenhower doctrine' or not) seem suddenly more aggressive but that the Soviet Union did not appear to be doing anything about it. In Syria, for example, in September the Soviet government repeated its performance over T'aiwan by supporting the left-wing government only after the United States government had declared that it would probably not invoke military action under the 'Eisenhower doctrine'. When the Syrian crisis blew up again in October, the main result of Soviet interference was to drive Syria into the arms of an increasingly anti-Communist Egypt which was no longer the object of Chinese admiration.

Following the American landing in Lebanon in the summer of 1958, the stand of the Soviet Union was hardly decisive and after the revolution in Iraq on 14 July when it was rumoured that the United States might intervene, all the Soviet Union could do was attempt to convene a conference, which at one time might even have included T'aiwan in its capacity as a permanent member of the UN Security Council.[184]

It would be somewhat misleading to suggest, however, that Chinese foreign policy in 1958 was completely reactive. It must surely be partly due to the reaffirmation of the concept of People's War that China was the first major power to grant recognition to the Algerian Provisional Government proclaimed by the FLN in the autumn[185] and to express support for the victories of Fidel Castro in Cuba. Here the Soviet Union remained cautious, for Fidel's Communist credentials were still unproven.[186]

It would perhaps be wrong to suggest also that the implementation of Khruschev's policy of 'peaceful coexistence' had, by 1958, resulted in a complete sellout to the United States. The truth of the matter was that Soviet eyes were firmly riveted on Berlin with the aim of eliminating it as a possible source of war. Though Soviet pressure on Berlin was, in the long run, linked to the policy of 'peaceful coexistence' and 'peaceful competition' with the United States, Khruschev was still bold enough to offer the western powers a six-month ultimatum in November 1958. What the Chinese felt to be the real Soviet sellout was yet to come.

The Wuch'ang Plenum (28 November-19 December 1958) and its Aftermath

After the 'High Tide' of the Great Leap Forward in the summer and autumn of 1958, a number of serious problems had been encountered. One of the aims of the Leap had been to deal with rural underemployment. It had perhaps been too successful in that, by September, China was plagued by a labour shortage.[187] At the same time, inexperience occasionally resulted in a waste of labour power and cadres undertaking construction tasks which later proved worthless. There were sometimes severe dislocations in the supply and marketing network now that power was decentralised to commune level[188] and, once again, cases of excessive 'commandism' were noted. Occasionally richer collectives had refused to combine with poorer ones and friction had resulted. Perhaps the most serious problems resulted from the very enthusiasm for the Leap itself. Inflated statistics of grain production led to a consumption boom in late 1958 and the belief that the problem of food supply had been solved. Overconfidence caused many communes to believe they could implement immediately a ten-year plan to reduce the area sown in grain by 30 per cent.[189]

How serious were the problems and what were their causes? In his speech to the Sixth (Wuch'ang) Plenum in December 1958, Mao was quite prepared to admit that a number of problems had arisen with the formation of communes and that cadres had exaggerated production statistics.[190] He felt, however, that only some 1-5 per cent of cadres were guilty of violating discipline and had resorted to 'commandism'. In his view, the original aim to 'basically transform the country within three years' was overoptimistic. He, therefore, cautioned cadres not to be in so much of a hurry. At the same time, Mao urged that they should devote more time not only to practical investigation but also the study of economics and dialectics. He firmly refuted the idea that pockets of communism should develop in socialist society but not that communist elements should be incorporated into socialist policy. Though he welcomed changes in the orientation of the Army in 1958, he acknowledged that there was a tendency to disregard military training. Mao's speech to the Wuch'ang Plenum was, therefore, a cautious appeal for a period of consolidation. In no way, however, did he call for the abandonment of the Great Leap. The new stress on the principles of

Yenan was welcomed and the shortcomings had by no means negated the growth in mass enthusiasm which promised even more spectacular results in the future.

The Party conservatives on the other hand, who had lost their grip on the situation with the collapse of the old system of 'rational' balanced planning, were anxious to restore control and probably saw the need for a much more durable period of consolidation. Whereas Mao welcomed the splits that had occurred in the leadership in half the provinces during 1958[191] (for only by struggle could one advance to a new stage of unity), the conservatives were probably very alarmed. At the plenum, therefore, they succeeded in reversing many of the Great Leap innovations. Concerned above all with restoring order in the countryside, they imposed limits on horizontal Party mobilisation, placed far greater powers in the hands of formal structures (such as commune management committees) and rejected the free-supply system and any notion of 'communist' methods of payment according to need rather than work.[192] Instead of strengthening the inter-commune distribution system, they sought to deal with the problem of dislocations in the supply and marketing system by the partial revival of free markets.[193] Moreover, by the New Year, the old (Soviet model) notion of no fundamental rural reorganisation before adequate mech-anisation began to be voiced once again.[194]

It was at the Wuch'ang Plenum that Mao finally decided to retire as state chairman[195] and withdraw to the 'second front'. There has been much debate as to whether the conservatives forced him into this position or whether his action was a voluntary one.[196] The following quote from Mao suggests, I feel, the latter explanation, though it is possible that Mao was simply voicing Central Committee policy.

As for my relinquishing the post of Chairman of the Republic, this time we must make a formal resolution and I hope comrades will agree. I ask that within three days the provinces hold a telephone conference to notify the regions, *xian* and people's communes. The official communiqué will be published three days later so that the lower levels will not find it a total surprise. Things in this world are really strange. One can go up but not come down.[197]

What is perhaps more important, however, was that Mao did not see his resignation as a total withdrawal.

The masses do not understand, saying that, whilst everyone is full of

boundless energy, you are withdrawing from the front. I want to
make it clear. This is not the case. I am not withdrawing. I want to
surpass the United States before I go to see Marx.[198]

In my view, therefore, the subsequent controversy about Mao's resignation centred not so much on the formal act itself but on the fact
that, in the early 1960s, the conservatives interpreted it as *total* withdrawal.

At an enlarged Politburo conference in early 1959, the main item on
the agenda seems to have been who would replace Mao as state chairman once his resignation became effective in April. At the same time,
rural policy was energetically debated.[199] By the beginning of February,
Mao and the Party radicals seemed convinced that the process of consolidation had gone far enough and that the time had come to reactivate the Great Leap.[200] Their demands, however, seem not to have
been heard and the Party concentrated on strengthening the planning
structure under the slogan 'take the whole country as a co-ordinated
chess game'.[201]

Though Mao was clearly to the left of the policy-makers in Peking
headed by Liu Shao-ch'i, there seems to be no evidence to support the
contention, long held by western analysts, that Mao had a dogmatic
faith in the commune as an inviolable form of economic administration. In fact, in February 1959 he noted that accounting at commune
level usually only comprised some 10-30 per cent of the total, with the
bulk of economic activity being run at brigade level. In opposing excessive accumulation quotas decided on at commune level, Mao
adopted a cautious position in favour of a *federal* commune structure
which would only be completely unified after several years.[202] It
would appear, therefore, that Mao supported the decentralisation of the
unit of account to brigade and even team level,[203] though one should
bear in mind that in 1959, when there were some 5,000 households per
commune,[204] the team was often as big as the old higher-stage agricultural collective. It was probably around this time, however, that
attempts were made to reduce the size of the communes to that of the
old *xiang* or standard marketing areas (which was probably the original
intention) and consequently the size of the brigade to the old natural
village.

By the spring of 1959, Mao was probably most dissatisfied with the
turn of events in the aftermath of the Wuch'ang Plenum and, through
the first two-thirds of 1959, issued a series of communications calling
for a reactivation of the Great Leap.[205] To Nikita Khruschev on the

other hand, exasperated by claims made for the Leap, these events were welcome. At the Twenty-First Congress of the CPSU in January 1959, Khruschev insisted that all socialist states would attain communism more or less simultaneously,[206] which was now perfectly in accord with the Chinese line and the position of Mao himself.[207] Nevertheless, though Mao rejected the notion of pockets of communism, he probably did not accept the implication in Khruschev's remarks that the communes were no better than the Soviet *kolkhoz*. What he probably found more disturbing was another Khruschevian implication that socialist states could not slip backward. Anyway, it is perhaps immaterial what Mao felt, since Party policy was now being made by conservatives who wished to repair the breach with the Soviet Union. It is significant, therefore, that not long after the Soviet congress, Khruschev made available to China more industrial aid[208] and Defence Minister P'eng Teh-huai went on a tour of eastern Europe where he found Party leaders most congenial. At the Seventh Plenum of the Eighth Central Committee in April 1959, which marked the high point of the period of consolidation and which probably gave approval for the nomination of Liu Shao-ch'i as state chairman,[209] Mao could only express the hope that eventually he might be able to convince the majority that the Great Leap should be reactivated.

An individual sometimes wins over the majority because truth is often in one man's hands alone. Truth often rests in the hands of a minority as when Marxism remained solely in the hands of Marx. Lenin said that one must have the spirit of going against the tide.[210]

The Tibetan Rebellion (March 1959)

Though in some national minority areas, exasperation with the previous gradualist policy and the demands for independence made by 'rightists' during the Hundred Flowers Movement resulted in radical policies in 1957-8,[211] Tibet remained relatively untouched.[212] In some minority areas during the Great Leap, communes were formed and cadres strove to bring about a situation where minority nationalities 'caught up' with Han areas in 3-5 years.[213] But in Tibet the old system of monastic serfdom was still supreme. In his speech 'On the Correct Handling . . .' Mao had expressly stated that no changes should take place in Tibet during the Second Five Year Plan (up to 1962) and it was an open question as to whether they should take place in the Third (up to 1967).[214] Little was done during the most radical period of the Great

Leap in 1958, and it is strange, therefore, that a major crisis did not
occur in Tibet until the more conservative period of early 1959. The
timing of the Tibetan rebellion of March 1959, in my opinion, has less
to do with any excesses of the Leap than to a changing international
environment. It has been reported that during the T'aiwan Straits
crisis in the second half of 1958, arms were dropped to dissident elements in Loka,[215] though this has not been confirmed. What the
Pentagon Papers tell us, however, is that a CIA-run air company had
made overflights of Tibet during that period[216] and the United States
was definitely interested in the area. We have seen also that, in April
1958, Nehru had expressed a determination to involve himself in
China's Tibetan policy and that by the end of the year, Sino-Indian
relations had deteriorated considerably. At the turn of the year, Nehru
and Chou En-lai exchanged notes on the Aksai Chin highway, each
claiming it was in their own territory[217] and it was in this tense atmosphere that the Tibetan rebels chose to act. The rebellion of March 1959
was put down quite rapidly[218] by Chinese troops and the Dalai Lama
fled to India (or was kidnapped, depending on which source one
takes)[219] but, although the rebellion was a relatively minor affair, it
was to have very profound repercussions. First, the former entente
between China and India was now well and truly dead. In subsequent
years, the idea of Indian non-alignment was to appear highly questionable and to have meaning only in the sense of India's attempts to play
off the Soviet Union and the United States. India's China policy was to
become implacably hostile. Secondly, and perhaps more important in
the discussion here, it was quite obvious that the involvement of the
Kashag and the large monasteries in the March rebellion meant that the
former gradualist reform policy had to be revised. At a time when the
rest of China had embarked upon a policy which was increasingly conservative, Chinese authorities in Tibet were to embark upon a policy
that was to be quite radical. The contradiction was one that demanded
a solution.

The End of the Fourth Cycle

By the spring and summer of 1959, China's countryside had undergone
perhaps the most profound changes yet. There was much argument
between conservatives and radicals as to what the preferred organisation and size of the communes was to be and whether the 1958 policy
of mass mobilisation was to be resumed. There had been a retreat from
the optimistic policies of August 1958 but, even in the conservative
climate of early 1959, it would be impossible to go back on the basic

idea of a communal 'self-reliant' structure in the Chinese countryside.
The conservatives were not tardy in pointing out that, as they saw it,
people's communes need not necessarily be self-reliant[220] but, whatever happened, the old idea of an urban-oriented Soviet-style developmental strategy could probably never be restored.

The Great Leap Forward had caused much dislocation and chaos
but some might argue that this was a small price to pay when one takes
the longer perspective, since tremendous creative potential had been
released. Small-scale plants had mushroomed. The reactivation of the
minban concept of education had resulted in a phenomenal rise in the
number of people striving to raise themselves from a state of illiteracy.
The notion of part-work and part-study schools had called into
question developmental strategies that give primacy to formal academic
education. The explosion of job opportunities in the cities had not
meant that the problem of rural-urban drift had been solved but the
communal strategy of transferring industry to the countryside offered
a glimpse of an eventual solution. There had been supply difficulties
due to bad communications between communes and between cities
and countryside, but the new egalitarian ethos in the countryside meant
that it would be unlikely that, in the future, the former problem would
recur in which there were great variations of wealth in the same locality.

In 1959, as in 1956, conservative thinking in the Party was triumphant but conservatives could not dissolve the communes as they had
dissolved collectives and co-operatives. They could restore the planning
apparatus but they could no longer recentralise the economy along rigid
branch lines. They could attempt to patch up the growing quarrel with
the Soviet Union but they could not stop more and more people asking
what were the roots of the decline in revolutionary fervour in that
country. Up to 1959, the lid had been kept very tightly on the Sino-
Soviet dispute; it could probably not remain on for much longer.

The period of consolidation of 1959 was inherently unstable. The
Leap had acquired a momentum that was very difficult to slow down.
What was happening in Tibet could not for much longer be completely
divorced from what was happening in the rest of the country. In this
situation Mao could only wait for the catalyst that was to bring about a
reactivation of the Leap. That catalyst was to be found in the growing
relationship between Khruschev and Defence Minister P'eng Teh-huai.
Some conservatives were soon to overplay their hand and to initiate the
eighth of the major crises in the history of the Chinese Communist
Party.

Notes

1. The term 'involution', coined by Clifford Geertz, signifies dead-end development.
2. Text in Bowie and Fairbank 1965, pp. 257-72. Note: In Mao's view this essay should never have been published in the form it was, since it argued in terms of inevitability. Mao Tse-tung January 1957, in *JPRS* 61269-1, 20 February 1974, p. 58.
3. See Solomon 1971, pp. 285-8.
4. MacFarquhar 1973, p. 634.
5. A late nineteenth and early twentieth-century reformer.
6. Mao Tse-tung January 1957, in *JPRS* 61269-1, 20 February 1974, p. 57. My translation, from Mao Tse-tung 1969, pp. 84-5.
7. Ch'en Ch'i-t'ung *et al., RMRB*, 7 January 1957.
8. Mao Tse-tung January 1957, in *JPRS* 61269-1, 20 February 1974, p. 67.
9. Mao was to advance this principle the following year. See later in this chapter.
10. Solomon 1971, p. 289.
11. Mao Tse-tung 27 February 1957, in Mao Tse-tung 1971, pp. 432-79.
12. Ibid., p. 465.
13. Solomon 1971, pp. 296-7.
14. Mao Tse-tung 12 March 1957, in Mao Tse-tung 1971, pp. 480-98.
15. Chang Chih-i 31 March 1957, *SCMP* 1522, 3 May 1957, pp. 1-9.
16. *RMRB*, 10 April 1957, p. 1.
17. *RMRB*, 11 April 1957, p. 7.
18. *SCMP*, 1512, 17 April 1957, p. 15; *SCMP* 1516, 25 April 1957, p. 2; *SCMP* 1518, 29 April 1957, p. 2.
19. *RMRB*, 17 July 1957, p. 2, cited in Solomon 1971, p. 304.
20. Ma Che-min, *RMRB* 18 July 1957, p. 10, cited in ibid., p. 305.
21. Solomon 1971, pp. 304-9.
22. Ibid., p. 307.
23. *CCP.CC*, 27 April 1957, in *URI* 1971, pp. 253-7.
24. *RMRB*, 10 May 1957, p. 4.
25. Vogel 1971, pp. 192-9.
26. Gittings 1967, pp. 173-4.
27. The following is based on Harper 1969, pp. 99-114.
28. See Brugger 1976, Chapter 7.
29. *SCMP* 1535, 22 May 1957, p. 12.
30. Harper 1969, p. 106.
31. *JPRS*, 665, pp. 33-6 and *SCMP* 1551, 17 June 1957, pp. 10-13.
32. *SCMP* 1535, 22 May 1957, pp. 8-11.
33. Liu Shao-ch'i was later accused of advocating union independence, see *PR* 26, 28 June 1968, pp. 17-21.
34. *SCMP* 1536, 23 May 1957, pp. 1-3.
35. E.g. T'ao Chu noted in June that 90 per cent of criticisms had been 'correct', Vogel 1971, p. 201.
36. Solomon 1971, p. 314.
37. Vogel 1971, p. 193.
38. See Solomon 1971, pp. 319-22.
39. Reproduced in ibid., p. 321.
40. Ibid., p. 322.
41. Ibid., pp. 325-7.
42. These explanations are discussed in ibid., pp. 290-1.
43. Vogel 1971, p. 202.

44. Harper 1969, pp. 106-14.
45. Gittings 1967, pp. 173-5, 226-7.
46. See the discussion in Schurmann 1966, pp. 353-63.
47. Vogel 1971, pp. 211-16.
48. Ibid., pp. 204-5.
49. Ibid.
50. Chou En-lai, in *PFLP* 1956, Vol. I, p. 324.
51. Lee 1966, p. 44.
52. Mao Tse-tung, 27 February 1957, in Mao Tse-tung 1971, p. 475.
53. Lee 1966, p. 44.
54. See Solomon 1971, p. 310.
55. *CCP.CC*, 14 May 1957, in *URI* 1971, pp. 259-63.
56. The following is based on Vogel 1971, pp. 205-9.
57. Schurmann 1966, pp. 456-7.
58. Cited in Schurmann 1966, p. 456.
59. Vogel 1971, p. 210.
60. For criticism dating mainly from 1958, see *JPRS* 1337-N, 12 March 1959.
61. Vogel 1971, p. 210.
62. The following is taken from Lee 1966.
63. Wheelwright and McFarlane 1970, pp. 35-6.
64. Eckstein 1973, pp. 223-4.
65. Ibid., pp. 214-19.
66. Ibid., p. 215.
67. Ibid., pp. 228-9.
68. See Chou En-lai, in *PFLP* 1956, Vol. I, pp. 263-328.
69. Schurmann 1966, pp. 175-8.
70. Ibid., pp. 196-208.
71. Ibid., p. 176.
72. See Andors 1971.
73. Wheelwright and McFarlane 1970, p. 14.
74. See the discussion in Schram 1971 and Starr 1971.
75. Mao Tse-tung 28 January 1958, in *Chinese Law and Government*, Vol. I, No. 4, Winter 1968-9, pp. 13-14.
76. Mao Tse-tung 19 February 1958. This is taken from an untitled Red Guard pamphlet, p. 33. Another translation may be found in *CB* 892, 21 October 1969, p. 7. For an earlier formulation see Mao Tse-tung, January 1957, in *JPRS* 61269-1, 20 February 1974, p. 49, and for a later one, 20 May 1958, in ibid., p. 112.
77. 'On the Historical Experience of the Dictatorship of the Proletariat' talks of the persistence of contradictions among the people even in communist society. Bowie and Fairbank 1965, p. 148. See also Mao Tse-tung 1959, in *JPRS* 61269-1, 20 February 1974, p. 221.
78. Mao Tse-tung 7 October 1957, in *JPRS* 61269-1, 20 February 1974, p. 75.
79. *URI* 1971, pp. 109-10.
80. The revised plan, dated 22 October 1957, is in Chao 1963, pp. 157-78. There were, in fact, few differences between this and the 1956 text. On the importance of the plenum, see Schurmann 1966, pp. 195-205.
81. Zagoria 1966, p. 378.
82. Clark 1967, pp. 97-8.
83. Gittings 1967, p. 228.
84. Speech to Chinese students in Moscow, 17 November 1957, in *CB* 534, 12 November 1958, p. 12. This was only Mao's second trip abroad.
85. Clark 1967, pp. 95-8.
86. See Gittings 1968, p. 70.
87. Zagoria 1966, p. 178.

88. Text in Hudson, Lowenthal and MacFarquhar 1961, pp. 46-54. See the highly imaginative discussion in Crankshaw 1965.
89. Schurmann 1966, p. 203.
90. For a discussion of the Chinese meaning of the terms 'heavy' and 'light' industry, see Donnithorne 1967, pp. 140-1, Schurmann 1966, p. 202.
91. The following discussion is taken from Schurmann 1966, pp. 202-10.
92. Vogel 1971, p. 225.
93. *SC* in *SCMP* 1665, 5 December 1957, pp. 4-5.
94. Schurmann 1966, p. 207.
95. Ibid., p. 209.
96. Ibid., p. 210. Mao Tse-tung 20 March 1958, in Schram 1974, p. 106.
97. Teiwes 1966.
98. *SCMP* 1734, 19 March 1958, pp. 1-4.
99. *CCP.CC*, 24 September 1957, in *URI* 1971, pp. 517-22.
100. Schurmann 1966, p. 466.
101. Ibid., pp. 466-7.
102. Referred to in *CB* 892, 21 October 1969, p. 1.
103. See Mao's speeches at the conference, 11 and 13 January 1958, in *JPRS* 61269-1, 20 February 1974, pp. 77-84.
104. Mao Tse-tung, 19 February 1958, in *CB* 892, 21 October 1969, pp. 1-14.
105. *SCMP* 1612, 18 September 1957, pp. 14, 16.
106. The following is based on Hinton H. 1966, pp. 263-70. The Kuomintang blockade had been in existence since 1949.
107. Kallgren 1963, p. 38.
108. Mao Tse-tung, May 1958, in *JPRS* 61269-1, 20 February 1974, p. 121.
109. Mao Tse-tung, November 1958, in ibid., p. 129.
110. Mao Tse-tung, 19 December 1958, in ibid., p. 143.
111. Mao Tse-tung, 30 November 1958, in ibid., p. 136. Mao was specifically referring to the summer crisis.
112. Vogel 1971, p. 231.
113. *SCMP* 1682, 2 January, 1958, p. 27.
114. *CCP.CC* and *SC*, 24 September 1957, in *URI* 1971, pp. 517-22.
115. Vogel (1971, p. 231) notes that this provision was often disregarded.
116. Ibid., pp. 228-9.
117. The following is taken from ibid., pp. 233-5.
118. Traditional Chinese measurements, now standardised. There are 2 *jin* to the kilogramme and 15 *mu* to the hectare.
119. The famous Tach'ing oilfield dates from this time; see *PFLP* 1972, *Tach'ing...*
120. Vogel 1971, p. 235.
121. Mao Tse-tung, 23 July 1959, in *URI* 1968, *The Case of P'eng Teh-huai*, p.25.
122. Ibid. Mao Tse-tung, 19 December 1958, in *JPRS* 61269-1, 20 February 1974, p. 147. Mao Tse-tung 1959, in ibid, p. 223.
123. Vogel 1971, p. 236.
124. Inaugurated at the Nanning Conference. See Mao Tse-tung, 19 December 1958, in *JPRS* 61269-1, 20 February 1974, p. 141.
125. Vogel 1971, p. 237.
126. Mao Tse-tung, 20 March 1958, in Schram 1974, p. 104.
127. Vogel 1971, p. 238.
128. Ibid., p. 237.
129. See ibid., pp. 241-3.
130. Mao Tse-tung, 20 March 1958, in Schram 1974, p. 104.
131. *PFLP* 1958, p. 61 and Liu Shao-ch'i, Vol. 2, 1969, p. 36.
132. Schurmann 1966, pp. 475-6.
133. *CCP.CC*, 25 May 1958, in *URI* 1971, p. 111.

134. *RMRB*, 5 May 1958, p. 1.
135. See *URI* 1968, *The Case of P'eng Teh-huai*, p. 202. Garthoff 1966, p. 90.
136. Mao Tse-tung 28 June 1958, in *Chinese Law and Government*, Vol 1, No. 4, winter 1968-9, p. 19.
137. Mao Tse-tung 20 March 1958, in Schram 1974, p. 111.
138. *SCMP* 1822, 30 June 1958, p. 1.
139. Chu Teh, in *CB* 514, 6 August 1958, pp. 1-2.
140. Hsieh 1962, p. 122.
141. Hinton, H. 1966, p. 266, Gittings 1967, p. 230. Clark 1967, p. 100.
142. *URI* 1968, *The Case of P'eng Teh-huai*, p. 202. See also the discussion in Solomon 1971, pp. 386-7.
143. Hinton, H. 1966, pp. 266-7. Clark 1967, p. 100.
144. Schurmann 1966, p. 478.
145. Gittings 1967, pp. 207-8.
146. Cited in ibid., p. 211.
147. *SCMP* 1856, 18 September 1958, pp. 17-19.
148. Mao Tse-tung 19 December 1958, in *JPRS* 61269-1, 20 February 1974, p. 140.
149. Bowie and Fairbank 1965, pp. 463-70.
150. Schurmann 1966, p. 473.
151. Mao Tse-tung 23 July 1959, in *Chinese Law and Government*, Vol. I, No. 4, winter 1968-9, p. 41.
152. *CCP.CC*, 29 August 1958, in *URI* 1971, pp. 299-304.
153. According to Ch'en Po-ta, 1 July 1958, in Bowie and Fairbank 1965, p. 453.
154. Schurmann 1966, pp. 477-8.
155. *CCP.CC*, 29 August 1958, in Bowie and Fairbank 1965, pp. 454-6.
156. This is not to say that there was much support for the idea that pockets of communism had already arrived. See Hsü Li-ch'ün, in Bowie and Fairbank 1965, pp. 479-83.
157. Vogel 1971, p. 251.
158. Ibid., p. 248. This was P'an-yü *xian* in Kwangtung province; population 276,358.
159. Ibid., p. 249.
160. Skinner 1965, Part III.
161. See Salaff 1967.
162. Schurmann 1966, p. 381.
163. Ibid., pp. 381-2.
164. The following description is taken from ibid., pp. 387-91 and Salaff 1967.
165. Andors 1971, pp. 406-7.
166. Ibid., p. 409.
167. See the various articles collected and translated in *JPRS* 1337-N, 12 March 1959.
168. Gittings 1967, p. 181.
169. Ibid., p. 195.
170. Ibid., p. 183.
171. Ibid., p. 185-8.
172. Ibid., pp. 188-91.
173. Ibid., p. 190.
174. Ch'en Tsai-tao, *CB* 579, 25 May 1959, pp. 5-8.
175. See Chapter 5.
176. Chou En-lai 6 September 1958, in *SCMP* 1851, 11 September 1958, p. 2.
177. *PRC* spokesman 1 September 1963, in Garthoff (ed.) 1966, p. 233.
178. *CB* 534, 12 November 1958, pp. 1-14.
179. Hinton, H. 1966, p. 34.

180. Ibid.

181. Chou En-lai 10 February 1958, in Bowie and Fairbank 1965, pp. 401-10.

182. Patterson 1963, pp. 159-60.

183. On the Aksai Chin road, see Maxwell 1972, pp. 82-4.

184. Hinton, H. 1966, pp. 36-7.

185. *SCMP* 1861, 22 September 1958, p. 42.

186. Hinton, H. 1966, p. 38. China, however, had no illusions about Fidel being a Communist at that time.

187. *CCP.CC.*, 10 December 1958, in *URI* 1971, p. 139.

188. Skinner 1965, Pt. III.

189. Walker 1968, pp. 444-5.

190. Mao Tse-tung 19 December 1958, in *JPRS* 61269-1, 20 February 1974, pp. 140-8.

191. Ibid., p. 146.

192. *CCP.CC*, 10 December 1958, in *URI* 1971, pp. 123-48.

193. *SCMP* 2055, 15 July 1959, p. 19.

194. Hsieh Yin-ch'i, *SCMP* 1986, 6 April 1959, p. 3.

195. *CCP.CC*, 10 December 1958, in *URI* 1971, pp. 121-2.

196. See Solomon 1971, pp. 373-5.

197. Mao Tse-tung 19 December 1958, in *JPRS* 61269-1, 20 February 1974, p. 148. My translation, from Mao Tse-tung 1969, pp. 268-9.

198. Ibid. My translation from p. 269.

199. This conference is mentioned in Mao Tse-tung, 16 August 1959, in *Chinese Law and Government*, Vol. I, No. 4, winter 1968-9, p. 45. The agenda items are the guess of Chang 1970, p. 188, based on information by R. MacFarquhar.

200. Mao Tse-tung 2 February 1959, in *JPRS* 61269-1, 20 February 1974, p. 151.

201. *RMRB*, 24 February 1959, p. 1. For Mao's comments, see Mao Tse-tung 21 February 1959, in *JPRS* 61269-1, 20 February 1974, p. 162.

202. Mao Tse-tung 21 February 1959, in ibid., p. 161.

203. Mao Tse-tung 15 March 1959, in ibid., p. 167.

204. Schurmann 1966, p. 493.

205. See *JPRS* 61269-1, 20 February 1974, pp. 164-74.

206. Zagoria 1966, p. 127.

207. Mao Tse-tung 19 December 1958, in *JPRS* 61269-1, 20 February 1974, p. 145.

208. Zagoria 1966, p. 128.

209. The communiqué notes that the plenum decided on candidates for leading posts in state organs. *CCP.CC,* 2-5 April 1959, in *URI* 1971, pp. 149-50.

210. Mao Tse-tung April 1959, in *JPRS* 61269-1, 20 February 1974, p. 176. My translation, from Mao Tse-tung 1967, p. 52.

211. Dreyer 1968, pp. 98-9.

212. See Strong 1965, Chapters 3-4.

213. Dreyer 1968, p. 99.

214. Mao Tse-tung 27 February 1957, in Mao Tse-tung 1971, p. 460.

215. Strong 1965, p. 67.

216. Gravel edition, Vol. 2 pp. 648-9.

217. See the collection of documents in *PFLP* 1962, *The Sino-Indian Boundary Question*.

218. Strong 1965, pp. 73-81.

219. Ibid., pp. 70-1.

220. *SCMP* 1939, 22 January 1959, pp. 29-30.

5 THE YEARS OF CALAMITIES (1959-62)

The fifth cycle began in mid-1959, accelerated following the settlement of a major crisis in the Party in the late summer of that year and entered a period of consolidation in late 1960. It was different from the four preceding cycles in three important aspects. First, debates were sharper than hitherto. The radicals were critical not just of a vaguely defined conservatism but more specifically of 'revisionism' (the advocacy of policies which negated class struggle and threatened to push China back in the direction of capitalism). This concern had, of course, been present before but now reached critical proportions. Secondly, with the worsening of the Sino-Soviet dispute, the domestic Chinese debates had clear international implications. Thirdly, the period 1959-61 was marked by the three worst harvests in decades. Climatic conditions, therefore, severely limited policy options.

Though it is difficult to determine which leader adopted which position, we may say with certainty that cleavages within the Party leadership centred on how to interpret the Great Leap Forward. The major question was no longer simply should the Soviet model be restored. It was rather, should policies be pursued which would facilitate mass mobilisation and collective action, or should the aim be restoration of production and economic growth at the expense of class struggle? Was the eventual goal of communism to be defined in terms of the contradictions existing between classes, or in terms of greatly improved material conditions seen by some as a *prerequisite* for the abolition of classes? Such issues were not specifically national. They lay at the core of a huge debate on the proper policies for the International Communist Movement. Many Chinese radicals were beginning to ask themselves about the social basis of a set of Soviet foreign policies that seemed to be becoming less revolutionary day by day.[1] More importantly, they were concerned about any parallel changes that might be occurring in their own society.

The Tibetan Reforms

In the period immediately after the Tibetan Rebellion of March-April 1959, a stream of condemnatory speeches were issued by the Dalai Lama and his entourage in India. Perhaps the strongest of these, on 30 June, denounced every act of Peking towards Tibet from the 1951 agreement onwards. The Dalai Lama now declared that he would no longer attempt to deal with China directly but only through a third power (India?).[2] The Chinese response to this was to publish his charges alongside the extravagant praise the Dalai Lama had lavished on Peking's policies since 1951. It was perhaps ironical that the source of all Tibet's ills should be assigned to Mao Tse-tung whose deeds the Dalai Lama had, less than five years previously, compared with the Lord Brahma, creator of the world.[3] The Dalai Lama seemed to have burned his boats and thrown in his lot with India but was nevertheless recognised in Peking as Tibet's titular head and member of the Standing Committee of China's National People's Congress until December 1964.

Upon the Dalai Lama's departure, the State Council moved, on 28 March, to abolish the traditional government (The *Kashag*) and transfer power to the Preparatory Committee for the Tibet Autonomous Region.[4] This body had been set up in 1955 with the eventual aim of replacing the *Kashag,*[5] though it is unlikely whether anyone at that time envisaged that it might do so as early as 1959. Though the titular head of the committee remained the Dalai Lama, its effective head was now to be the Panchen Erdeni who celebrated his installation by reciting *sutras* with two living Buddhas.[6] Hardly a radical act to commence a new stage in Tibet's history!

Nevertheless, the policies to be pursued by the new government were, by Tibetan standards, highly revolutionary. While the fighting was still going on, the PLA spread the slogan of 'land to the tiller' and the first 'law and order groups', which were formed under PLA auspices to round up rebels, were expanded into peasant associations.[7] Following the first session of the new government in April, the Panchen Erdeni left for Peking and, on his return in July, the second session approved a whole series of measures for 'democratic reform'. The operative slogan was *'sanfan shuangjian'* ('three abolitions and two reductions'). The 'abolitions' here referred to rebellion, forced labour and personal servitude and the 'reductions' to land rent and interest. The land of all rebels was confiscated and the crops handed over to the tillers. The land of other nobles was made subject to rent restrictions and later compulsory purchase.[8]

The abolition of serfdom was carried through rapidly with many of the techniques of the old land reform. Nobles implicated in the rebellion were made to stand with bowed heads and hear the former serfs 'speak their bitterness'.[9] As in land reform, the aim was to raise the level of class consciousness but here there were many more problems. During the Civil War, work-teams and peasant associations did not have

to contend with peasants anxious to protect their *karma*. The price of
overthrowing a Tibetan lord or abbot was felt to be reincarnation as a
lower being.

The task of education was perhaps made easier once the corruption
of the monastic élite was revealed. One might have reverence for a
'living Buddha' who claimed to have chosen to remain in the world of
men rather than advance to Nirvana, but not after one had heard that
he had purchased his title of 'living Buddha' from the *Kashag*.[10] One
might acquire a different view of monastic hierarchy once the leadership of monasteries became democratised.[11] With the confiscation of
monastic lands, it was surely only a matter of time before the number
of monks that each monastery could support would decrease.

Much ink has been spilled on the events in Tibet in 1959. It is
probably true that large numbers of Han were moved into the area but
it is a peculiar twisting of the word to call it 'genocide'.[12] It is probably
true that the abolition of serfdom and the suppression of rebellion were
occasionally brutal, but this should occasion no shocked surprise. It is
true also that sporadic fighting was to continue for many years, but
fighting in Tibet, especially where the Khambas were concerned, had
gone on for decades, whatever the government in Lhasa. It might perhaps be argued that the PLA did not have the right to take the action
it did in March-April 1959, and many jurists have belaboured precisely
that point, but then the *Kashag*, and for that matter the Indian government, had accepted the authority of Peking over Tibet.[13] Legal issues
aside, it may be said that no nation has the right to impose its will over
another but then one must establish an adequate non-legal definition
of 'nation'. Finally, I suppose, the debate must turn on questions of
actual and perceived interest and such a debate, though important, is
endless.

In conclusion, I can only make two points. First, it is the opinion
of most travellers to Tibet, in the period after 1959, that the material
lot of ordinary Tibetans had improved immeasurably;[14] the travellers,
of course, cannot speak for the Tibetans' *karma*. Secondly, and
crucial to the argument here, Tibet stood out in mid-1959 as the one
area in Chinese society where policies were getting *more* and not less
radical. What was going on in Tibet must surely have strengthened the
position of those who argued for a revival once again of Great Leap
policies.

The Case of P'eng Teh-huai

The reforms in Tibet took place at a time of very fierce debate between

Party conservatives and Party radicals on social and economic strategy. In the summer of 1959, conservative policies prevailed and there was strong opposition to the strategy of Mao Tse-tung. This opposition was later said to be centred on the person of Minister of Defence P'eng Teh-huai who, during the Cultural Revolution, was said to have had secret dealings with Nikita Khruschev.[15] The P'eng Teh-huai affair is shrouded in mystery and many points remain which have never been satisfactorily explained. Attempts to unravel the P'eng case have resulted in an intricacy of explanation which, even by Kremlinological standards, is quite bewildering. All I can do here, following Simmonds, is to give a brief chronological account of the case and outline the charges made against him.

Like most Chinese leaders, P'eng undertook tours of inspection in the autumn of 1958 to evaluate the progress of the Great Leap and probably attended the Wuch'ang Plenum for a short period of time in late November and early December. There is evidence, however, that P'eng was absent from most of the discussions at the plenum which, Simmonds suggests, calls into question the subsequent accusation that P'eng was a principal architect in the sabotage of the Great Leap.[16]

In the period immediately following the plenum, articles began to appear in the press criticising those who sought to sabotage the Great Leap, and charges were made that individuals had attempted to set up 'independent kingdoms' of the Kao Kang type.[17] People were warned not to look after their own sphere of interest at the expense of the whole,[18] and this was taken subsequently to have been a reference to P'eng's demand for greater independence of the Army from the rest of society. After January, the Minister of Public Security, Lo Jui-ch'ing, began to relinquish some of his duties, in preparation, it may be argued, for appointment to a senior position in the PLA; though one might also surmise that he did this in order to give himself more time to concentrate on problems of public security that had arisen during the Leap. Sometime in early 1959, key personnel changes also occurred in the PLA especially in the Peking Military Region, possibly to rid sensitive commands of those who sought greater Army independence. In April, P'eng was conspicuously absent from the meeting of the National People's Congress, which endorsed the new state leadership, though this may have been because he was preparing for a visit to the Soviet Union and East European countries.

P'eng left China on 24 April, before the newly elected National Defence Council, under the new chairman Liu Shao-ch'i, convened its first meeting and this has been taken as an indication that P'eng was

being sent out of the country to prepare for his removal. This sugges-
tion is supported by the appointment, just after P'eng's departure, of
Lo Jui-ch'ing (later to become Chief of Staff) as Vice Premier. In June,
Vice Foreign Minister Chang Wen-t'ien and Hunan Party first secretary
Chou Hsiao-chou (both later criticised as P'eng's accomplices) dis-
appeared from view[19] and P'eng's position became more isolated.

In his chronological recapitulation of the P'eng Teh-huai case,
Simmonds has suggested that the decision gradually to remove P'eng
from office was taken long before his departure abroad, though the
question remains, who took the decision? It could well be that P'eng's
position was far too conservative even for Liu Shao-ch'i, who is said to
have worked hard at persuading a reluctant Lin Piao to replace him.[20]
One could hypothesise that, although Liu was hostile to a continuance
of the Great Leap, he could not support P'eng's alleged desire for
greater independence for the armed forces and was anxious to avoid a
split in the Party.

While the value of such speculation is questionable, there is no doubt
of the significance of charges subsequently made against P'eng concerning his overseas trip. It is almost certain that one of the assignments
given P'eng was to explain to Khruschev why the enlarged meeting of
the Military Commission, the previous summer, had rejected the Soviet
plans for a joint Sino-Soviet defence arrangement — a rejection with
which P'eng was probably not in agreement. In the light of P'eng's
commission, senior Party leaders within China could not but be suspicious of the warmth of the reception P'eng received in the Warsaw
Pact countries, and in particular the cordiality between Khruschev and
P'eng at their meeting in Albania. At that time, Khruschev was
attempting to apply the big stick to a recalcitrant Albania and the last
thing Chinese radicals wanted was any suggestion of Chinese endorsement for Khruschev's position. The condemnation of P'eng's activities
in Albania, published much later during the Cultural Revolution, is
both crude and pithy.

He (P'eng) informed bald-headed Khruschev of the shortcomings of
the Great Leap Forward, and the latter encouraged the former to go
home and oppose Chairman Mao.[21]

Whether the above is an accurate description of what happened, one
can only guess; what we do know, however, is that many of China's
leaders had good cause to be dissatisfied with P'eng's tour. On 20 June,
less than one week after his return, the Soviet Union cancelled 'the

agreement on new technology for national defence'.[22] This agreement, which was said to involve the principle of nuclear sharing was a highly important one and its cancellation might be related to a possible Soviet-American understanding on halting nuclear proliferation, whereby the United States would resist West Germany's demand for nuclear weapons if the Soviet Union did the same with China.[23] If that interpretation is correct, it could surely not have been perceived by the Chinese in June 1959 and a more likely Chinese interpretation of the cancellation was that Khruschev was attempting to do to China precisely what he was trying to do to Albania — to force the country back into a Soviet-controlled bloc and to strengthen conservatives among the Chinese leadership. Among their number was undoubtedly P'eng Teh-huai.

P'eng had returned to China on 13 June to find that his position had been weakened *inter alia* by changes in the PLA command which had been initiated before he left. More radicals were in positions of authority and the Party leadership had embarked on one of its periodic series of inspection tours to assess the situation before the next Central Committee plenum. In fact, it is possible that P'eng himself may have undertaken a tour of the north-west at that time.[24] It was quite apparent that the forthcoming Central Committee plenum would be crucial in determining whether or not Great Leap policies would be revived and opponents of radicalisation became more vocal. In June, the influential T'ao Chu had suggested that perhaps people should be bolder in their discussions of Great Leap shortcomings even if nine-tenths of Great Leap policies had been correct.[25] At the same time, the deputy mayor of Peking (a confidant, it is said, of P'eng Chen) wrote a number of articles which purported to be discussions of history but which could be read as criticism of the Great Leap.[26] It was in this atmosphere that P'eng Teh-huai decided to act.

From 2 July to 1 August, an enlarged Politburo conference was held at Lushan, presumably to assess the results of its members' inspection tours and to draft a programme for the approval of the Eighth Plenum to meet on 2 August. It was here that, on 14 July, P'eng launched his attack on the Great Leap strategy in the form of a 'Letter of Opinion'. In this letter, P'eng avoided all mention of Sino-Soviet relations (which perhaps would not win him much support) and concentrated on an evaluation of the Great Leap. His tone was extremely forthright.

Petty-bourgeois fanaticism causes us easily to commit 'left' errors.

In the course of the Great Leap Forward of 1958, I, like many comrades, was led astray by its achievements and the ardour of the mass movement. 'Left' tendencies developed to an appreciable extent. All the time one wanted to leap into communism in one bound. The idea of taking the lead took possession of our minds and we pushed to the back of our minds the Mass Line and the style of seeking truth from facts which had been formulated by the Party over a long period. In our method of reasoning we often confused strategic dispositions with concrete operational measures, long-term policies with the minor collective.[27]

Though forthright, P'eng's letter was in some respects a cautious one. What he specifically repudiated were the mistakes made in 1958 before the Wuch'ang Plenum. He was apparently quite happy with current Party policy. It is quite possible, therefore, that P'eng's comments could have been accepted under the rules of inner Party democracy, as T'ao Chu's seem to have been,[28] had it not been for a number of important coincidental events. The letter had been addressed to Chairman Mao but was, in fact, circulated on 14 July, three days before the chairman received it.[29] As such, it could be considered as provocative. Far more serious than that, however, was the fact that in Poznan, Poland, on 18 July, Khruschev reversed his 21st Congress line on China and spoke of how 'The Co-operative Way is the Surest Way for the Peasant'. He implied that, in setting up communes, the Chinese had a 'poor understanding' of how to build communism and stated that, when the Soviet Union had experimented with communes, the communes had failed because the material and political prerequisites for their establishment had not existed.[30]

Upon the publication of Khruschev's speech on 21 July, the radical Chinese leadership could only place one interpretation on the events of 14-18 July; Khruschev was attempting to push the deliberations of the Politburo conference in a conservative direction and was probably in league with P'eng Teh-huai. It was precisely this foreign connection that made P'eng's criticisms impossible to accept according to the rules of inner Party democracy. Very soon China's leaders were to associate P'eng with Kao Kang, who was also alleged to have had secret dealings with Moscow in the early 1950s.[31]

As Mao saw it, P'eng was part of a 'Khruschevian' conspiracy and the contradiction between P'eng and the Party was 'antagonistic'. Two days after the public disclosure of Khruschev's speech, on 23 July, Mao counter-attacked.

. . . I never attack others if I am not attacked. If others attack me, I
always attack back. Others attack me first, I attack them later.[32]

In his speech to the enlarged Politburo conference on 23 July and subsequently in his speech to the Eighth Plenum, which met at Lushan
immediately after the conference, Mao proceeded to defend the Great
Leap Forward. He was concerned to explain what, in his view, constituted mistakes and shortcomings in Party work and readily recognised
that he personally had made mistakes. He urged other comrades to
make a similar acknowledgement.

The chaos caused was on a grand scale and I take responsibility.
Comrades, you must all analyse your own responsibility. If you have
to shit, shit! If you have to fart, fart! You will feel much better for
it.[33]

He rejected, however, the idea that the Party should be cowed into a
conservative position because of any 'mess' that might have been caused.

Whenever they speak, they say we are in a mess. This is fine. The
more they say we are in a mess, the better, and the more we should
listen . . . Why should we let the others talk? The reason is that
China will not sink down, the sky will not fall. We have done some
good things and our backbones are strong. The majority of comrades need to strengthen their backbones. Why are they not all
strong? Just because for a time there were too few vegetables, too
few hair grips, no soap, a lack of balance in the economy and tension in the market, everyone became tense. People became psycho-
logically tense. I did not see any reason for tension, but I was also
tense nevertheless; it would be untrue to say I wasn't. In the first
part of the night you may be tense, but once you take your sleeping
pills the tension will go away for the rest of the night.

Mao was most indignant that a movement based on mass activism
should be dismissed as (in P'eng's words) 'petty bourgeois fanaticism'.

The people in Honan and Hopei have created the truth from experience, they have smashed Roosevelt's 'freedom from want'. How
should we look upon such enthusiasm for communism? Shall we call
it petty bourgeois fanaticism? I don't think we can put it in that way.
It's a matter of wanting to do a bit more, it's nothing else but wanting

to do a bit more a bit faster . . . We must not pour cold water on this
kind of broad mass movement. We can only use persuasion and say
to them: Comrades, your hearts are in the right place. When tasks
are difficult, don't be impatient . . . They (the cadres) are very active
. . . Do you think this is petty bourgeois fanaticism? They are not
the petty bourgeoisie, they are the poor peasants, proletarians and
semi-proletarians.[34]

Mao admitted, however, that there had been some cases of 'petty
bourgeois fanaticism' but these had long since been corrected. He was
convinced that one should look on the bright side. Originally he had
been prepared for the collapse of up to one-half of the communes but
not one had, in fact, collapsed. True, he had expected more of the
movement than had been realised, but perhaps it was natural to be
impatient. In Mao's view, the lesson that had been learned was that one
could not apply the logic of the accountant to what had been a
supreme act of spiritual liberation. He was determined that the Great
Leap strategy should not be abandoned.

By the time Mao delivered his defence of the Great Leap at the
Lushan Plenum, many members of the Central Committee began to
desert P'eng Teh-huai. Even so, it is rumoured that two ballots were
necessary to unseat him.[35] There was probably little those Party conservatives, who may have been disposed to support P'eng, could do
without admitting that they supported Khruschev's attempt to domi-
nate the Chinese Party. P'eng Teh-huai could only confess:

> At the Group Meeting of the Lushan Conference, I expressed a
> series of Right opportunist absurdities, especially in my 14 July
> letter to Comrade Mao Tse-tung. I attacked the Party's general line
> of going all out and aiming high for greater, quicker and more eco-
> nomical results in the construction of socialism. At the same time, I
> attacked the activism of the broad masses of the people and cadres
> and damaged the prestige of the Party Central Committee and Com-
> rade Mao Tse-tung. I now understand that this was a crime.[36]

In its resolution 'Concerning the Anti-Party Clique Headed by P'eng
Teh-huai' of 16 August, the Eighth Plenum seemed particularly sensitive to P'eng's Soviet connections noting that his attack came at a time
when 'the reactionary forces at home and abroad were exploiting certain transient and partial shortcomings'[37] in the Great Leap Forward.
Much was made of a remark by P'eng to the effect that 'if the Chinese

workers and peasants were not as good as they are, a Hungarian Incident would have occurred in China and it would have been necessary to
invite Soviet troops in'.[38] It was stated also that, at the time of the Kao
Kang incident, P'eng had been warned for supported Kao's 'Anti-Party'
activities.[39] The message was very clear.

In a letter to Chairman Mao on 9 September, P'eng Teh-huai apologised to the chairman and begged to be allowed to participate in manual
labour on the communes. His appeal for leniency appears to have been
granted, due perhaps to the mediation of Liu Shao-ch'i,[40] and it was
not until the Cultural Revolution that P'eng was subjected to public
criticism. With the appointment on 17 September of Lin Piao as Minister
of Defence and Lo Jui-ch'ing as Chief of Staff of the PLA, it would
seem that the eighth of the ten crises in the history of the Party had
ended. We shall see, however, that the eighth crisis was but the harbinger
of the ninth and tenth for the ninth crisis was to remove the advocate
of leniency and the tenth, P'eng's allegedly reluctant replacement.

The Revival of the Great Leap

The Lushan Plenum which dismissed P'eng Teh-huai was able, to some
extent, to silence Party conservatives but the Great Leap policies, which
were resumed in the autumn of 1959, were by no means as radical as
those of 1958. The principle of commune decentralisation (according
to the three-tiered ownership formula) was officially endorsed.[41]
Although free markets were restricted once again, they were not totally
abolished, the policy being 'freedom but not disorder, control but not
strangulation'.[42] It was admitted that attempts to employ handcraft
workers in factories had been premature and many were returned to
their former trades.[43] Although cadres who had permitted the large-
scale restoration of private plots were criticised, moves to restrict private family activities were cautious.[44]

With the High Tide of communisation in August 1958, the original
Anti-Rightist Movement had come to an end. In the aftermath of the
P'eng Teh-huai case, however, attempts were made to revive it though
in a very watered-down form. The targets for rectification were now
not so much 'rightists' but those of 'rightist tendency'[45] such as cadres
who tended to justify their passivity by saying that they were adhering
to the wishes of the masses. But policy could not be other than relatively cautious since, in marked contrast to 1958, the summer harvest
of 1959 was poor and peasant ardour had declined.[46]

Perhaps the most difficult task facing any leader in the revived Leap
of 1959 was that which confronted Lin Piao, who was entrusted to

counter the 'purely military viewpoint' in the Army. In his first major statement as Minister of Defence in September 1959, Lin reasserted Mao's slogan that men were superior to weapons but also paid considerable attention to the importance of military technology. In defending the idea of military democracy, Lin also gave particular stress to combating anarchism and egalitarianism.[47] The reform of the PLA was evidently to be carried out under conditions of strict discipline.

The revival of the Great Leap, therefore, was to be a cautious one. None the less, there was a certain atmosphere of excitement in the autumn of 1959 which reached its high point by the tenth anniversary of the founding of the Chinese People's Republic on 1 October 1959, and it was in a moderately radical atmosphere that Mao greeted perhaps the most distinguished guest to attend the celebrations — Nikita Khruschev.

The Spirit of Camp David

Although Khruschev had been conciliatory towards China at the 21st Congress of the CPSU in January 1959, he could not disguise the fact that the Party programme had effectively thrown out the Leninist thesis on imperialism and had reinforced the notion of 'peaceful competition'. The Chinese leadership had never accepted Khruschev's formulation, although the conservative leadership in early 1959 had muted their disquiet. At a time when the Soviet press was full of Khruschev's 'creative development of Marxism-Leninism', all *Red Flag* could say, in February, was that Khruschev had made the creative suggestion that socialist countries would more or less simultaneously pass to the higher state of communist society.[48]

After the replacement of U.S. Secretary of State Dulles by Christian Herter in April 1959, Khruschev, having seemingly forgotten about the Berlin ultimatum, moved towards a détente with the United States, much to the chagrin of the Chinese. As the Chinese leaders saw it, American foreign policy did not depend upon personalities but upon the requirements of monopoly capital and détente would only be possible once the United States withdrew its forces from Europe and Asia. In the summer and autumn of 1959, Chinese suspicion of the Soviet Union grew as Kassem bore down on Iraqi Communists and the Soviet Union seemed to demand that Iraqi insurgents take a more conciliatory line.[49] As Nasser stepped up his anti-Communist crusade in Egypt, the Soviet Union showed no willingness to modify its programme of economic assistance.[50] On the Algerian question, the Soviet

Union seemed more concerned with winning de Gaulle away from NATO than supporting the FLN.[51] Perhaps most galling of all, as Sino-Indian relations worsened in the aftermath of the Tibetan rebellion, Soviet-Indian relations were never better. In this atmosphere of suspicion, Khruschev not only dropped his bombshell of 18 August when he declared his opposition to communes, but also announced his plan to visit the United States. On 16 September, the very day Khruschev arrived in America, a *Red Flag* article laid particular stress on the struggle against imperialism,[52] in marked contrast to the article prepared by Khruschev for the American establishment journal *Foreign Affairs.*[53]

Unlike President Eisenhower, who had embarked upon a European tour prior to his meeting with Khruschev, the Soviet leader had apparently consulted no one.[54] As far as China was concerned, he was probably convinced that any agreement he might reach on détente would automically be accepted by the Chinese, who were too dependent upon the Soviet Union to be anything but compliant. He was quite mistaken. Upon his arrival in China on 30 September, flushed with his new-found understanding with Eisenhower (referred to at the time as the 'spirit of Camp David'), Khruschev was faced with severe Chinese criticism. In his speeches within China, Khruschev reiterated the uncompromising version of his Twentieth and Twenty-First Congress lines,[55] and appeared impervious to Chinese criticism. In a speech to the Supreme Soviet on 31 October, the Soviet leader implied that the Chinese were taking much the same position as Trotsky who, at Brest Litovsk, was said to have opposed Lenin's moves to conclude a temporary peace with Germany.[56] Was Khruschev suggesting that the Chinese should do to T'aiwan what the Soviet government had done to parts of European Russia in 1918? In any case, the Trotsky analogy could only be a calculated insult. With regard to the Sino-Indian border dispute, Khruschev assumed a neutral stance and, in the same speech, endorsed De Gaulle's demand for a ceasefire in Algeria.

Khruschev had failed to bring China to heel during the P'eng Teh-huai incident. He had failed to subdue China during his visit to Peking in October and his Supreme Soviet speech could only provoke even further Chinese criticism. In the new year, Khruschev was to think of even more direct methods of applying pressure.

The Worsening Sino-Soviet Dispute

By early 1960, it seemed to the Chinese that the American moves towards détente were aimed at buying time to close what was believed to be a wide missile gap.[57] They were particularly wary of any moves towards disarmament or any negotiations which did not involve all members of the socialist camp. On the ninetieth anniversary of Lenin's birth in late April, the Chinese press produced a series of articles outlining in detail the Chinese position under the title 'Long Live Leninism',[58] to which the Soviet press replied. Both the Soviet Union and China adhered to the notion of 'peaceful coexistence', although the Chinese felt that this notion should not be used to impede wars of national liberation. Both sides felt that a general war was not inevitable, but the Chinese felt that at least it was possible as long as imperialism existed.[59] The Chinese were most dismayed at Kuuisinen's use of a quote from Lenin to the effect that wars would become so destructive as to be impossible, to negate Lenin's much more important thesis that so long as imperialism existed there would be a danger of war. The Soviet position was based on two notions — that technology had changed the nature of war and that there were more reasonable men in power on the other side. To the Chinese, technology might make war more destructive but it could not change the nature of imperialism and a general war would not be the outcome of the reasonableness or unreasonableness of certain individuals. The Chinese could not accept that a 'parliamentary road to socialism'[60] was to be preferred in the Third World and that all local wars should be avoided regardless of the reasons for their occurrence. The argument of Soviet spokesman Sovetov that the existence of the socialist camp had made local wars less likely was most unconvincing.

Following the polemics of April and May 1960 and the abortive Paris summit, the dispute entered its most intense phase yet. At a meeting of the World Federation of Trade Unions in Peking from 5-9 June, the Chinese delegate Liu Ch'ang-sheng attacked most strongly the Soviet Twenty-First Congress line, declaring that disarmament was an illusion[61] and this was followed by the publication in the Soviet press of discourses on Lenin's 'Left Wing Communism, An Infantile Disorder'.[62] A feature of such a 'disorder', it was claimed, was the advocacy of a policy of skipping over historical stages, which was one of the 'rightist' criticisms of the Great Leap.

At the Third Congress of the Communist Party of Rumania, which met in Bucharest in late June, it is reported that Khruschev himself attacked Mao Tse-tung by name, suggesting that he was guilty of Trotskyist deviations, and of knowing nothing of the military realities of the modern world.[63] Khruschev's Bucharest explosions were followed, in July, by a plenum of the CPSU where much discussion was given over to 'left-wing sectarianism' and the 'manifestation of narrow nationalistic tendencies'.[64] At about the same time, the journal of the Sino-Soviet Friendship Society *Druzhba* (Friendship) was suspended, and explicit attacks on China began to appear in the journals of Moscow-line Communist parties. The Indian paper *Blitz*, for example, published an article entitled 'Moscow "Boxes the Ears" of Peking Trotskyites'.[65]

The culmination of escalating Soviet attacks on the Chinese Party came in August with the unilateral withdrawal of Soviet aid, technicians and blueprints,[66] right at a time when China was about to experience her second year of poor harvests. The Chinese leadership would, however, not be brought to heel and the blunt response of Li Fu-ch'un, the chairman of the State Planning Commission, was to call for even greater 'self-reliance'.[67]

A final attempt was made to reach agreement on the General Line of the International Communist Movement in the autumn of 1960. As plans were under way for a World Conference of Communist Parties to meet in Moscow in November, a preparatory commission was set up which became yet another forum for polemic.[68] A final declaration was in fact agreed upon in Moscow but it in no way signified that a *modus vivendi* had been reached. The declaration dealt with four major questions – the character of the present epoch, problems of war and peace, paths of transition to socialism and unity of the International Communist Movement (including rules which regulated the relations between fraternal parties). On the first question, some concessions were made to the Chinese position that the era was one of the collapse of imperialism and national liberation struggle, but the Soviet insistence that transition to socialism would come about largely because of the (economic) strength of the socialist camp rather than revolution, was maintained. On the second question, the resolution accepted both the Chinese assertion that imperialists would continue to start local wars and the Soviet view that they could be deterred. The Soviet contention that there was a real possibility of excluding world war, even while imperialism still existed, was retained. On the third question, the Soviet version of the principle of 'peaceful coexistence' was retained though it was no longer referred to as the 'general line' and, on the fourth question, the Soviet Union was called the 'universally recognised vanguard of the International Communist Movement' rather than the 'head' (as in 1957).

The Moscow Declaration, therefore, was no more than a collation of views.[69] It implied, however, a far greater degree of independence for individual Communist parties. At least that was how the Albanian Party

leader Enver Hoxha interpreted it. On 16 November, he reportedly
affirmed the Chinese line and criticised Khruschev's accusations against
the Chinese made at Bucharest.[70] The split between Moscow and
Tirana was now final and, in subsequent months, the Soviet press
pointedly used the epithet 'Albania' when they really meant China.
Such was the international environment within which China faced her
most serious economic crisis since Liberation.

The Worsening Economic Situation

In 1959, China suffered from its worst natural calamities for several
decades. Farmlands affected by drought exceeded 600 million *mu*
(more than 30 per cent of the land under cultivation).[71] At the same
time, other areas experienced severe floods. In the years 1959-60,
approximately half the land under cultivation was hit by bad weather.
In 1957, the official figure for grain production had been some 185
million tonnes and this figure has been accepted by most Western
commentators. The official figure for 1958 was 250 million tonnes,
which in view of the current tendency to inflate statistics, most
Western observers feel to be an overestimate. Most of them agree,
however, that grain production for that year was well over 200 million
tonnes.[72] As for 1959, Li Fu-ch'un claimed that food production
reached 270 million tonnes.[73] Most foreign economists dismiss this
figure and some of them place grain production for that year as low as
170 million tonnes. Similar foreign estimates for 1960 are around 160
million tonnes with a slight rise in 1961.[74]

There can be no doubt that the official Chinese figures were inflated,
though I do not propose here to go into the bitter polemic that exists
among economists as to the degree of that inflation. What I must do,
however, is spell out the various positions taken in the debate about the
causes of the economic crisis.

A common attitude adopted in the West is that the crisis of 1959-61
was directly attributable to the Great Leap Forward.[75] Dislocations
which occurred during the formation of communes had been so severe
that the autumn harvest of 1958 was not gathered in entirely. A
reduction of the area sown in grain in the winter of 1958 led to a food
shortage and the situation was further exacerbated by the poor harvests
of 1959. Moreover, a premature reduction of material incentives and
the abolition of the private sector led to a loss of peasant confidence.
The boom of 1958 encouraged rather than reversed the drift of peasants
to the cities and resulted in a rural labour shortage which hindered production. According to this view, therefore, the Great Leap was respon-

sible for the crisis and the bad harvests of 1959-61 merely emphasised the problems.

A contrary radical view maintains that the primary cause of the crisis was flood and drought. It admits there had been dislocations, inflated statistics and an excessive reduction in the area sown in grain. It stresses, however, the commune organisation in the countryside which facilitated grain distribution, caused the burden of insufficient food to be shared and prevented mass starvation.[76] There was little evidence that material incentives had been reduced prematurely and a loss of peasant morale was to be expected at a time of extraordinarily adverse weather conditions. Such rural labour shortage as existed would in the long run be solved by the very commune organisation which had been designed (amongst other things) to facilitate rural industrialisation and halt the drift to the cities. In the meantime, an excess urban population must be compelled to return to the communes. I personally find this latter explanation quite convincing since, although there was widespread malnutrition across wide areas of China, there was nowhere the mass starvation that would surely have occurred in a similar natural catastrophe in the pre-1949 situation. If there had been much opposition to the reduction of individual material incentives, then surely this would have manifested itself in the period prior to the onset of the natural calamities. Furthermore, the Great Leap Forward did not, as far as I know, significantly reduce *collective* material incentives.

It is tempting to imagine that the Chinese conservatives' explanation of the economic crisis of 1959-61 was much the same as that of Western economists but we have insufficient published evidence to confirm this. Liu Shao-ch'i's remarks in early 1962, however, are suggestive. Liu was not slow in pointing out that in Hunan, peasants had told him that 30 per cent of the difficulties in production had been caused by natural calamities and 70 per cent by man-made factors.[77] He suggested that perhaps things might have been better had communes not been formed[78] and, as we shall see, he was associated with a policy of restoring individual material incentives.

Whatever the causes, the overwhelming problem that faced China's leaders from the beginning of 1960 to the end of 1962 was how to feed the population. Though people might disagree on their interpretations of the Great Leap Forward and on how to modify its policies, there was probably little disagreement that *some* modifications had to be made. The initial response to the food crisis was in line with radical policies. What remained of the private plots (restored and then restricted again in 1959) was, in 1960, frequently handed over to commune and brigade canteens in order to keep the supply of public meals going.[79] A major problem was that communes and production brigades had little surplus to distribute to peasants. Once the grain earmarked for animal fodder was consumed by humans, animals were killed and thus the supply of animal fertiliser was reduced. This, in turn, reduced the quality of the crops and further lowered output. The tremendous pressure to restore the level of food production led now to a reduction in the area of land given over to industrial crops. Since it was mainly these industrial crops that provided much of the raw material for local light industry, many small light industrial plants had their activities severely restricted. Industrial plants in the towns were also affected and factories, operating at reduced capacity, scoured the countryside for raw materials and, where possible, entered into contracts with local communes and brigades regardless of any local planning directive.[80]

Though the people's communes were originally seen as do-it-yourself exercises in organisation and although few people were particularly worried about planning in the period of creative imbalance in 1958, it was always anticipated that once communes had been consolidated, a new planning structure would be ironed out. Unfortunately, once the Party moved to consolidate the rural situation in 1959-60, food shortages had resulted in a mass of *ad hoc* contractual and other relationships which made control extremely difficult. The immediate response of the Party to the problems of 1959-60 was to greatly accelerate the process of *xiafang*. In 1959-60 large numbers of cadres, intellectuals, students and PLA soldiers were sent to the countryside to re-establish control and to reduce the food supply problems in the cities. In the countryside, all sorts of systems were publicised in the press whereby administrative cadres spent greater amounts of time at lower levels. According to the 'two-five' system in Hopei, for example, cadres spent two days engaged in study, attending conferences and undertaking research projects followed by three days actually working in the teams.[81] According to the 'three-seven' system of Kirin province, three levels of cadre (*xian*, commune and brigade) divided each ten-day period into three days' study, investigation and allocation of work with the remaining seven devoted to production.[82] In some areas, *xian*-level cadres were given administrative jobs within the brigades, but the problems were immense and often beyond the abilities of newly retrenched cadres. It was precisely in this critical situation that the Soviet Union withdrew its technicians, aid and blueprints, thus causing more of industry to run at reduced capacity and, indeed, preventing many uncompleted industrial plants from coming into operation at all.

1960: The Worsening Urban Situation

The worsening food supply situation in the cities led, in early 1960, to a new drive to create urban communes.[83] The communes of 1960 were very different, however, from the Chengchow model of 1958, which reveals the fact that they were less the product of organisational inspiration and more an attempt merely to solve the problem of food production and distribution and keep small industry in the cities alive. Wherever possible, city suburbs were combined with agricultural production brigades to produce communes more or less self-sufficient in food. Most of the 1960 communes were not combined with regular industrial enterprises and consisted largely of housewives and family dependants with many of the male residents leaving the commune every day to work in regular factories. Such a situation was perhaps not the best way to form integrated urban units generating mass commitment.

These later communes tended to be huge. The original Red Flag Commune of Chengchow expanded sevenfold from 4,684 households in 24 streets to 150,000 people, and consisted of subdivisions each larger than the original commune.[84] The process here was the exact opposite of what was happening in the rural areas, where communes were in fact getting smaller to correspond more with the old *xiang*. In the rural areas then, communes were narrowing down to fit in with ecological conditions whereas in the cities they were expanding more and more to correspond to artificial administrative areas. It is probably because of this that many of the urban communes, which continued in existence throughout the 1960s, were little more than synonyms for urban wards (*qu*).

Although the 1960 urban communes were not very successful *qua* communes, various policies with which they were associated continued to be very important throughout the 1960s. Many of the locally-run child-care centres and service points set up at that time remained and the urban commune policy, whereby urban residents combined and pooled their own funds to set up small industries, continued. Perhaps, in the really critical years of 1960-2 their activities were limited, but in the period immediately prior to the Cultural Revolution, I saw many such industries that seemed remarkably successful. One might argue that street co-operatives and street industries were sometimes inefficient but this would really be to miss the point. The resources that they mobilised would not usually be collected for use elsewhere.

Secondly, most of these industries were run by women who, for the first time in their lives, were liberated from the home and introduced to technology, however primitive. I can remember visiting a shoe polish co-operative run largely by women in T'aiyüan. Another observer of the same co-operative has described how chaotic the organisation was.[85] It is true that much money was wasted in the early years producing inferior shoe polish without any expert guidance at all but by 1965 a product was made which was exportable and this fact gave to a group of men and women a sense of pride of achievement that perhaps could have come from nowhere else. Such was the legacy of the urban commune movement or perhaps the legacy of the Great Leap Forward itself. With the decline of the urban communes in late 1960 and early 1961, the Great Leap Forward was really at an end but it had created a desire amongst many ordinary people to produce goods for themselves and to become inventors. It was the beginning of a process of emancipation that no amount of economic bungling, 'commandism' or utopian thinking could render less worthwhile.

The Reform of the People's Liberation Army

The food shortages of 1960-1 inevitably affected the People's Liberation Army. In early and mid-1960, the Army became heavily involved in agricultural work. As the situation worsened in November 1960, Army rations were cut.[86] In the winter of 1960-1, it was estimated that 5 per cent of personnel in the armed forces suffered from oedema.[87] Even in this critical situation however, Lin Piao, who noted that some 4 per cent of Army units had 'fallen into the hands of the enemy',[88] proceeded gradually to carry out the task with which he had been entrusted — to raise the morale and political consciousness of the PLA after the dismissal of P'eng Teh-huai. At an enlarged conference of the Military Commission in September and October 1960, a 'Resolution on the Strengthening of Political and Ideological Work in the Armed Forces' was adopted. Lin proposed a policy known as the 'four firsts' — 'man' first in the relationship between man and weapons, 'politics' first in the relationship between political and other work, 'ideology' first in the relationship between routine and ideological political education, and 'living thought' in the relationship between book learning and practice. What Lin strove to overcome was formalistic political training where military cadres went by the political book in the same way as they adhered to the military manual.[89] The 'four firsts' were to be the first of a series of numerical slogans such as 'five good soldiers', 'four good companies', the 'three-eight working style', etc., which were to form the basis for political training in the Army.[90]

The enlarged conference of the Military Commission noted that, despite the many policies to that end that had been put forward over the past four years, there were still no Party branches in one-third of all PLA companies and the Party organisation below that level was often non-existent.[91] In the winter of 1960-1, considerable attention was devoted to building up the Party network at lower levels in the Army and to restoring the old political commissar and company political instructor system that had existed from the days of the Civil War. By April 1961, it was reported that all companies now had Party branches and 80 per cent of platoons had organised cells.[92] Later in that year, the functions and duties of company Party branches were spelt out.[93] Party branches were given control not only over political training but also over promotions and were also given some say in military training and operations. At the same time, attempts were made to revive the soldiers' clubs with elected committees. Once the Party organisation had been strengthened, the structure of the Communist Youth League could also be built up to undertake the political education of the bulk of recruits who were aged about 18 or 19. Young privates were instructed to make a particular study of the revolutionary traditions of the Army and to interview old people and veterens about their experiences in the old society.[94] Under no circumstances was the old technocratic military élitism to be allowed to recur.

The Decision to Deradicalise – late 1960 and early 1961

Since the revival of the Great Leap after the Lushan Plenum in 1959, attempts had been made in both the military and civilian spheres to keep the radical policies in operation. In this respect, the Army had been much more successful than the civilian sector. Much of the credit for this belonged, of course, to Lin Piao, but one should note also that, if there was one area in which both conservatives and radicals were united, it was in the belief that deteriorating Sino-Soviet relations and increasingly serious border disputes demanded a strengthening of military discipline. The Army was to be made ready to stand on its own if China were attacked. Whatever the economic cost, nothing should be done to demoralise the troops nor to slow down China's determination to develop an independent nuclear deterrent. Whatever the options open to China's military leaders, there was one option that now seemed closed – the integration of the Chinese armed forces into the network of the Warsaw Pact.

In the civilian sphere, however, despite the renewed *xiafang* of

1959-60, it was extremely difficult to keep the spirit of the Great Leap Forward alive. By mid-1960, Great Leap policies were, in many areas, no longer implemented[95] and Mao could only protest that, by that time, building communism was 'unacceptable'.[96] He had certainly rejected the idea of pockets of communism but was not prepared to reject completely the principle of free supply. As we noted in the last chapter, Mao was no dogmatic believer in the instant application of commune-level accounting. He did believe, however, that, over a period of time, the unit of account should be switched from team to brigade and then to commune and that finally, communal ownership would be synonymous with state ownership.[97] In 1960 the reverse was happening. After the decentralisation of some powers to brigade and team levels in 1959 (which Mao seemed to see as a necessary first step in consolidation), further moves seem to have been taken, towards the end of 1960, to transfer the bulk of decision-making power to the (by now much smaller) teams.

With the publication of a twelve-article directive on rural work towards the end of the year,[98] *de facto* decentralisation to team level took place and this move was confirmed at the Ninth Plenum of the Eighth Central Committee in January 1961. The team (which usually corresponded to the old lower-stage co-op) was now given full rights over the use of labour, land, animals, tools and equipment. The key slogan of the Ninth Plenum was 'agriculture as the base and industry as the leading factor', which had been put forward in March 1960[99] and was precisely the policy pursued during the Great Leap. What was essentially different in the new policy was not that agriculture was considered to be primary but that industry was severely cut back. Secondly, the primacy of agriculture was interpreted in such a way that it amounted to a general concession to the development of petty capitalism in the countryside.[100] It would appear, therefore, that the gust of wind from the 'right' which Mao had perceived in 1960[101] continued to blow throughout 1961 and, in his speech to the plenum, Mao noted that the deradicalisation of 1969 had led to a restoration of the power of former landlords.[102] The policies of the Ninth Plenum seemed to offer little chance that this situation would be remedied.

One decision taken by the plenum, however, probably caused little contention. This was the ratification of an earlier proposal, made by a central work conference in July-August 1960, to re-establish six regional bureaux of the Central Committee.[103] This decentralisation of Party authority seemed in no way a return to the pre-1954 situation whereby local leaders might re-establish 'independent kingdoms'. It signified only

the Party's attempt to co-ordinate activities following the decentralisation of power to provincial levels after November 1957. The move was
probably an extension of the idea of large economic co-operation regions
implemented during the Great Leap.

'Revisionism' in the Countryside

The key slogan of the post-Ninth Plenum period was 'consolidation,
filling out and raising standards'.[104] There was much talk of 'balance',
for no longer was the old Great Leap Forward affirmation of the
positive role of disequilibrium heard. Stress was on the realisation of
short-term economic goals rather than any longer-term perspective.
Instead of mass mobilisation there was to be closer inspection; instead
of target-raising there was now to be sober book-keeping.[105] The new
conservative policies were spelt out in a new programme known as the
'Sixty Articles on Agriculture' which were issued on 12 May 1961 but
never released publicly, presumably because the Party conservatives
did not wish to advertise the fact that they had completely abandoned
the Great Leap Forward.

It was probably the local cadres who during this period were most
deserving of sympathy. Many of them had done their best to adhere to
modified Great Leap policies during the food shortages of 1960 and
had tried to keep the basic framework of the communes together. Now
communes were reduced in size, from an average of some 5,000 households in 1959 to less than 2,000 in 1951,[106] and more and more
decision-making power was transferred down to team level. Cadres were
uncertain as to what their precise decision-making function was and just
exactly what the line was between 'commandism' and 'tailism'. The
Urgent Directive on Rural Work of 3 November 1960 criticised these
local cadres for exceeding the spirit of directives from above, of pushing
too far the idea of canteens, of collectivising too much private property,
of resorting to 'commandism' and of being insufficiently concerned
with the livelihood of the masses. Though some of this criticism was
undoubtedly just, one cannot help but reflect that now cadres were to
be rectified for being too enthusiastic about the Great Leap Forward.
One would perhaps give the criticisms of late 1960 and early 1961 more
credence if they could be shown to have come from the masses. The
rectification movement of early 1961, however, was carried on strictly
from above by means of work-teams who often discredited local cadres
in the eyes of the peasants and suggested that the economic crisis might
be due, in some measure, to their excessive zeal.[107] Such, undoubtedly
was often the case, but the interests of fair appraisal would surely have

been better served if the peasants themselves had been involved in making it through the mechanism of Poor and Lower Middle Peasant Associations, for which Mao had called at the Ninth Plenum.[108]

Though the above rectification movement from the top down was hardly revolutionary, it would probably be going too far to call it 'revisionist' (in the sense of contributing to a restoration of capitalism). There were certain features of rural policy, however, which were subsequently called 'revisionist' and with some justification. In the Cultural Revolution, Liu Shao-ch'i was accused of proposing, during this period, a policy known as *sanziyibao*[109] (three 'self' and one 'guarantee'). He was accused of advocating the extension of plots for private use, the extension of free markets, the increase of small enterprises with sole responsibility for their own profits and losses and the fixing of output quotas based on the household. Whether Liu should be assigned responsibility for all these is an open question but, whatever the answer, we must note that all these policies were in fact pursued during the period.

First, many of the private plots, partially restored in 1959 then restricted in the same year, and perhaps handed over to mess halls during the revival of the Great Leap, were now, once again, handed back to private ownership. At first, some 5 per cent of land was reassigned for private cultivation, with peasants allowed to derive 20 per cent of their income from private business.[110] Although sources are unreliable, it has been claimed that, by 1962, the private grain harvest in Yünnan province was larger than the collective harvest and privately cultivated land rose to 50 per cent of the total, while in Kweichow and Szechwan provinces, concentration on private plots led to a situation in 1964 where there was more private than collective tilling.[111] Although I find the above figures hard to believe, it cannot be denied that the policies enunciated in 1961 led to some very unsatisfactory results from a radical perspective.

Once peasants were allowed to sell the produce of their private plots, there inevitably developed thriving rural markets. The new policies demanded that goods be divided into three categories. The first category consisted of those that were required to be sold to the state at fixed prices, the second category could be sold on the open market once the state plan had been met and the third category could be disposed of in any way the peasant saw fit.[112] Ideally the 'free' markets should have been subject to some kind of government control but, in a situation where it was impossible to know exactly what kind of transactions were going on, it became increasingly difficult for local cadres to keep their finger on the pulse.[113] In any case, after being criticised

once for 'commandism', many cadres were unwilling to do anything
except go along with what many presumably saw as a drift towards
rural capitalism.

According to the new economic policy[114] after 1961, attempts were
made, not to restore the planning system, but to link industry and agriculture via the market. Various departments of industry frequently
held 'commodity exchange meetings' where contracts were signed
directly with rural districts for the supply of raw materials and the sale
of industrial goods and direct 'hook-ups' were established between
customers and markets.[115] Occasionally local production brigades,
teams or communes entered into direct dealings with consumer co-
operatives or urban department stores, thus strengthening market
relationships. Such a situation, which corresponded to what Schurmann
described as 'decentralisation 1', had been the great fear of the radicals
in 1957 for, surely from their point of view, flexibility had been bought
at the price of a drift back towards capitalism. What must have been
particularly disturbing in this situation, however, was that the unit of
production in the rural areas, to which authority had been decentralised,
was increasingly not the commune or brigade but the production team
to which a revised 'Sixty Articles on Agriculture' gave in December
1961 *de jure* authority as the basic economic accounting unit.[116]

Although the *de facto* and later *de jure* decentralisation of economic
decision-making to production teams in 1961 weakened the commune,
the latter still maintained authority over some agricultural and industrial activities according to the three-level system of ownership.[117] This
point needs to be given particular stress here since, until quite recently,
it was the conventional wisdom in the West that the measures of 1961
destroyed the commune as anything but an administrative unit. In fact
the importance of the commune, even in 1961, is underlined by the
fact that all sorts of provisions had to be worked out for specifying the
permissable contractual relationships that could exist between the
various levels of rural organisation.[118] There were, however, a number
of serious consequences of decentralisation within the communes.
First, communes and brigades were more able to set aside sums of
money for capital accumulation whereas it was much more difficult for
teams to do the same; in fact, regulations forbade teams to set aside
more than 3 per cent in their accumulation fund. Similarly, it was
easier for welfare facilities to be co-ordinated at commune or brigade
level and regulations forbade teams to set aside more than 3.5 per cent
for this purpose.[119] In an increasingly 'economist' atmosphere, smaller
units were perhaps less likely to subscribe to a policy of delayed gratifi-

cation. A second consequence of decentralisation within the communes
was that leadership at team level was more likely to reflect old values
than at commune level, especially since many of the Great Leap
activists sent down to team level had been removed for alleged
'commandism'. This older leadership probably contained a sizable proportion of former 'prosperous middle peasants', oriented towards
making a profit on the market and not so much towards collectivist
goals.[120] They could ideally be checked by the large numbers of
younger people sent down to the countryside during the 1960 *xiafang*,
were it not for the fact that many of the latter were still 'wet behind
the ears' and were sometimes resented by peasants tired of the countryside being used as a dumping ground for urban intellectuals.[121]

The third aspect of 'revisionism' in the countryside was said to be
the increase of small enterprises with sole responsibility for profits and
losses. It was perhaps inevitable that enterprises of this type should
develop once economic decision-making power was located at team
level. Teams, in 1959, usually contained some 40 households though,
by 1961, their size had been reduced to 20-30 households, but with
considerable local variations.[122] It is very difficult to imagine just what
kind of control an organisation of that size could exercise over light
industrial undertakings and, in those areas where even the team was
bypassed as the basic economic accounting unit and output quotas
fixed upon the household (the fourth aspect of 'revisionism'), light
industrial undertakings which had survived the bad harvests must have
been almost autonomous.

It is probably not going too far to say that the rural policies adopted
in 1961 negated a large number of the gains of the Great Leap Forward.
The private sector was larger than for several years and a free market
existed which sometimes bordered on the black market. One way of
countering black market tendencies was to set up government markets
where off-ration goods were available at higher prices;[123] this may
have been effective but hardly socialist. The new stress on economic
'rationality' meant that organisations which did not pay were closed
down regardless of the services they performed. A lot of the *minban*
schools, set up on the old Yenan model during the Great Leap, were
deemed to require too much local expenditure and were abolished;[124]
as one might expect, the bulk of these were in poorer rural areas.
Unless something was done quite drastically, the urban-rural gap would
continue to grow.

The Party conservatives were probably not very worried about the
urban-rural gap in 1961-2 but there was one concern that they did

share with the radicals – the determination to stamp out growing corruption. They held that rectification from above and the judicious use of work-teams could restore order in the countryside and prevent graft and malpractice. The radicals, on the other hand, knew from bitter experience that such a policy could not work. There was no use just rectifying men if socio-economic conditions gave primacy to the profit motive. Work-teams were insufficient to do anything except rectify individual cases. The only answer lay in mass mobilisation and a revival of the spirit of the Great Leap. But in the political climate of 1962, the Great Leap was not on the agenda.

'Revisionism' in Industry

We saw above that the new policy towards agriculture after the Ninth Plenum and the promulgation of the 'Sixty Articles on Agriculture' resulted in what Schurmann has called 'decentralisation 1'. In industry, following the promulgation of a similar document known as the 'Seventy Articles on Industry', a similar pattern of decentralisation to the unit of production occurred, this time accompanied by a strengthening of central ministerial organs.[125] According to Cultural Revolution material, this situation was likely to lead to the worst of both the old policies of the Soviet model and modern Libermanism (the belief in a 'socialist market'). Although there was a partial revival of 'one man management'[126] as factory general managers acquired more powers, this was not matched by a strengthening of the planning structure and economists began to write about the virtues of the profit motive and market relationships.[127] Even from the point of view of a Party radical, there is, of course, nothing wrong with the criterion of profit as a success indicator; in fact such a success indicator is essential if accounting is to be in terms of money as well as gross output. The radical critique centres not on profit *per se* but on the 'profit motive', whereby the *raison d'être* of an industrial concern becomes the degree to which its sales exceed capital and labour inputs, regardless of the criteria of service to the wider community. By 1961, the Chinese were quite convinced that Yugoslavia was no longer a socialist country[128] and yet it was precisely the pattern of 'decentralisation 1' that had contributed to that country's lopsided development.

Though I many be wrong, it is my impression that, although the question of the profit motive was to become important subsequently, the main bone of contention between conservatives and radicals in the period 1960-2 concerned the extent to which 'politics' should be 'in command' in the factories and the extent to which 'experts' should make policy and operational decisions. What in Yenan days were referred to as the concepts of 'ability' (*cai*) and 'virtue' (*de*) had been revived in the mid-1950s as the concepts 'expert' (*zhuan*) and 'red' (*hong*).[129] Though Party secretaries may have been somewhat cavalier in their treatment of technicians and engineers in the days of the Great Leap,[130] there was never, to my knowledge, any condemnation of the notion of expertise. What was condemned were those *professionals* who neglected political questions and whose view of 'rationality' was limited to an excessively economic view of production and all that involved. These men had been the 'one man managers' of the early 1950s and had been subjected to Party control in the Great Leap. Anxious that this type of manager should not run industrial enterprises once again, Mao, at the tail-end of the Great Leap Forward, put forward on 22 March 1960 a constitution for the mammoth Anshan Iron and Steel Corporation which he hoped would be a model for industrial enterprises elsewhere. The Anshan constitution affirmed the notion of 'politics in command' and the importance of Party leadership. It called for the launching of vigorous mass movements, the implementation of cadre participation in productive labour and worker participation in management, the reform of irrational and outdated rules and regulations, the close co-operation between workers, cadres and technicians and a fostering of the movement for technical innovation.[131] The Anshan constitution, however, was not to be adopted until 1970.[132] It was apparently resisted by Party conservatives, notably Liu Shao-ch'i, who is said to have countered it by a constitution deriving from the Soviet city of Magnitogorsk.[133] With the promulgation of the 'Seventy Articles on Industry', it would appear that Liu, later accused of spawning the 'ten thousand rules of bureaucracy', had won the day.

Although some of the descriptions of the restoration of one man management in the early 1960s are quite lurid,[134] it is possible that, in the atmosphere of the Cultural Revolution in which they were written, there was some exaggeration. In his extremely interesting account of industrial management in China, Andors puts forward the view that, in general, many of the reforms of management instituted during the Great Leap were retained including the 'two participations' and the 'triple combination',[135] which both figure in the Anshan constitution. Perhaps the extremes of one man management were isolated occurrences, for, quite frankly, in the light of the unpopularity of that system in the early 1950s, it is highly unlikely that such a policy would have made much headway in China *after* the Great Leap, no matter how conservative industrial policy might have been.

The Huixiang Movement

Just as, in the industrial sphere, the period after January 1961 saw an odd combination of a return to Soviet-model practices, concessions to 'revisionism' and a retention of some of the reforms of the Great Leap, so, in urban administration, a similar situation prevailed. With the decline of urban communes, the old Soviet-style network of street offices with parallel street committees was revamped, even though the name 'commune' might be retained. At the same time, although the growth of market relationships (even verging on the 'black') consti- tuted a 'revisionist' tendency, many of the street industries and services (which were a radical legacy of the Great Leap) also remained. So long as the primary concern of urban cadres was food supplies, *ad hoc* policies were the order of the day.

As we have seen, a major problem which the Great Leap Forward set out to solve, but in fact did not, was the constant drift of peasants into the cities. By the spring of 1962, the government had no course but to transfer physically large numbers of the urban population to the rural areas. A campaign was launched in April 1962 known as *huixiang* ('back to the village') whereby people were urged to return to their native areas (even if they were 'ancestral homes' with which their connection was purely historical). The movement was very different from *xiafang* which had manifest educational aims and which trans- ferred cadres usually to places with which they were unfamiliar. All *huixiang* appeared to be was a last-ditch measure to solve the urban food problem. Although there was some propaganda associated with the movement, the process was uncharacteristic in that sometimes very crude techniques were used such as closing down small factories and leaving workers very little option but to return from whence they came. It was largely the *huixiang* movement, combined with a straitened situ- ation in the countryside, which, in Schurmann's view, led to the mass exodus to Hong Kong in April 1962 in itself made much easier by the relaxation of border controls.[136]

There has been much speculation as to why border controls were, in fact, lifted for a time in April 1962. It could be that local officials in Kwangtung just despaired of the situation or, as Vogel suggests, they knew that, once the Chinese side relaxed border controls, the British would immediately tighten them to prevent a rapid rise in the Hong Kong population.[137] Whatever the truth of the matter, about 15,000 got through and about 60,000 were rounded up by the British and sent back to Kwangtung. In Schurmann's opinion, what was really significant about the exodus to Hong Kong in April 1962 lay not in the sphere of macro-politics, nor in the fact that Hong Kong was a *capitalist* city, but simply that it was a city which extended kinship and quasi-kinship networks out into the surrounding countryside be it socialist, capitalist or feudal.[138] Thus, the rush into Hong Kong in April 1962 gives us a very good idea of exactly how serious pressure on the cities must have been during the economic crisis of the early 1960s.

A 'Revisionist' Foreign Policy

It was later claimed that Party conservatives 'capitulated' not only to 'domestic reactionaries' but also to modern revisionists (the Soviet Union) and to imperialism (mainly the United States) in the period 1961-2. The assertion of 'three capitulations' together with 'one annihilation' (of national liberation struggles) may have been some-what of an exaggeration.[139] None the less, there is evidence that, in 1961-2, the former hard line in foreign policy began to soften.

Let us look first at 'capitulation' to the Soviet Union. It has always seemed strange to me that the Chinese could possibly have accepted the Moscow Declaration of November 1960, which was largely a 'victory' for the Soviet Union. One might note, however, that it was accepted in the very month that a Politburo conference laid the ground-work for the deradicalisation of policy prior to the Ninth Plenum. By the new year, there was clearly an outward show of cordiality between the two countries and there was even talk of a return of Soviet tech-nicians.[140] In February 1961, a Soviet economic mission arrived in Peking and the eleventh anniversary of the Sino-Soviet alliance of 1950 was celebrated with great fanfare. In this new atmosphere of cordiality, the Chinese government seemed to be putting up with actions which the radicals must have found intolerable. In 1961, the Soviet Union and some East European countries strengthened economic sanctions against Albania,[141] while in February and April, China had concluded with that country economic aid agreements.[142] In June, the Soviet Communist Party put forward a new Party programme (the first since 1919) which declared that a socialist society had been created in the Soviet Union and the Soviet Party was now engaged in the building of communism. Communism, however, was defined very largely in economic terms and was later to be bitterly denounced by the Chinese as 'goulash commun-ism'.[143] But in mid-1961, the Chinese seem to have been strangely reticent with their criticisms. In October, at the Twenty-Second Con-gress of the CPSU, Khruschev bitterly denounced Albania for opposing destalinisation and departing from 'the commonly agreed line of the whole World Communist Movement'.[144] This attack, which was

directly aimed at China, did result in a walk-out by the Chinese delegate
Chou En-lai[145] and the partial resumption of polemics using the code-
words 'Albania' (meaning China) and 'Yugoslavia' (meaning the Soviet
Union). There were some clashes at international Communist forums
but by March 1962 the atmosphere was still surprisingly calm. Under
the surface, however, Party radicals were most indignant. At a talk to
an enlarged central work conference, attended by 7,000 cadres, on 30
January 1962 (but not made public until the Cultural Revolution) Mao
pulled no punches.

> The Soviet Union was the first socialist country, and the Soviet
> Communist Party was the Party created by Lenin. Although the
> Party and the state leadership of the Soviet Union have now been
> usurped by the revisionists, I advise our comrades to believe firmly
> that the broad masses, the numerous Party members and cadres of
> the Soviet Union are good; that they want revolution, and that the
> rule of the revisionists won't last long.[146]

Nevertheless, Mao's words were said *in camera* and policy remained
cautious. In the summer of 1962, however, the atmosphere became
somewhat heated when Khruschev sought once and for all to heal the
breach with Tito of Yugoslavia, but it was not until the Cuban missile
crisis of October that the full fury of Chinese indignation broke out and
resulted in the dispute becoming public in December 1962. In the
meantime, what had happened in China itself was the Tenth Plenum
which sought to reverse the conservative line and inaugurate a new
period of radicalism. If the above account of events is correct, then it
would indeed seem that the period January 1961 to September 1962
did constitute something of a 'capitulation' to the Soviet Union.

The second charge that Party conservatives 'capitulated' to the
United States is somewhat more difficult to evaluate, especially since
the Chinese were most critical of Kennedy, the new President.[147] In
my view, the charge of 'capitulation' to imperialism can only refer to
Indo-China. In Laos, in August 1960, a 'left neutralist' military officer
Kong Lae took control of Vientiane and invited Prince Souvanna
Phouma to resume the post of Premier to maintain Laotian neutrality.
United States aid, however, went in increasing measure to the rightist
General Phoumi, who proceeded to move against both the Pathet Lao
and the neutralists, and to drive Souvanna Phouma out into Cambodia.
By the end of December 1960, Phoumi was in control of Vientiane and
the neutralists and Pathet Lao made their headquarters on the Plain of

Jars. Despite massive American aid, the Phoumi regime suffered repeated defeats, forcing the Kennedy government to consider cutting its losses and to press for negotiations. Faced with the possibility of a second Dienbienphu, the American government pressed for a ceasefire and threatened the neutralists and Pathet Lao with the might of SEATO. The Chinese response to this threat was to declare that if SEATO became involved, and if Souvanna Phouma's government requested help, China would not stand idle.[148] In this tense situation, however, China agreed to participate in a 14-nation conference at Geneva which met intermittently from May 1961 to July 1962. The final agreement guaranteed for Laos a very precarious neutrality which did not in fact last very long. Laos was soon to become once again a sphere of American military activity and, in retrospect, the Chinese actions of 1961 might indeed have seemed like a 'capitulation' to the United States and an 'annihilation' of the national liberation struggle.

The Third T'aiwan Straits Crisis

However 'capitulationist' or 'annihilationist' the Chinese may have been in other areas of foreign policy in 1962, these epithets surely did not apply to Peking's relations with T'aiwan. Since the crisis of 1958, a state of stalemate had existed, with both sides dug in and the shelling of Quemoy and Matsu being carried on on alternate days. In 1962, however, the situation began to change as the Kuomintang began to think of taking advantage of China's natural calamities. Chiang K'ai-shek's New Year message in that year was more bellicose than usual and, in the early spring, large numbers of new recruits were taken into the Kuomintang army. In May, a new tax was imposed specifically to support the 'return to the mainland' and a number of American officials were seen to visit T'aiwan (whether to encourage Chiang or to restrain him we do not know). It was surely not just a coincidence that the new United States ambassador to T'aiwan, appointed in May, was none other than Admiral Alan G. Kirk, an authority on amphibious operations.[149]

The crisis came to a head in June, when both sides considerably reinforced their troops and a Chinese statement was issued assuring the American-supported Kuomintang army that any invasion would be crushed.[150] At a meeting of United States and Chinese ambassadors in Warsaw, however, the United States disavowed any intention to support Chiang and this was endorsed by President Kennedy. The Chinese appeared to believe the American assurance and the crisis began to subside. Then just as tension relaxed, Khruschev announced, on 2 July, that any attack on China would be rebuffed by the people of the socialist camp.[151] It was 1958 all over again!

The Growing Sino-Indian Border Crisis

Another area in which the charge of 'capitulationism' will not stand up was Sino-Indian relations. By the end of 1960, Sino-Indian border negotiations had broken down. Under military pressure, the Indian government proceeded to step up the reinforcement of her frontier posts which had begun back in 1959 as part of a 'forward policy' and which could not but provoke severe Chinese censure.[152] In mid-1960, India had purchased a number of aircraft from the United States and, in the autumn, even larger amounts of military hardware from the Soviet Union. In early 1961, Indian troops began to move forward in the Western sector claimed by China and had established 43 posts on disputed territory by the autumn of 1962.

As has been noted, June 1962 was a time of crisis for Chinese foreign policy. Not only was the economy still suffering the effects of natural calamities, there was also a danger of war over the T'aiwan Straits. At the same time, a rising had occurred among the Kazakhs in the Ining region along the Soviet-Sinkiang frontier,[153] allegedly at Russian instigation, which was to result in the closure of Soviet consulates in Sinkiang.[154] It is probably not too much of an exaggeration to say that China was faced with the awesome possibility of a war on three fronts. By late June, however, it seemed that the T'aiwan situation had reverted to stalemate and Khruschev seemed to be too preoccupied with his Cuban adventure to fully exploit the situation in Sinkiang. In this situation, the Chinese decided to attempt to halt the Indian advance into the disputed territory. On 21 July, the first major armed clash since 1959 occurred along the frontier and China demanded immediate negotiations.[155] But the minimum Indian condition for negotiations was complete Chinese withdrawal from the disputed territories and this the Chinese found completely unacceptable. On 20 October, full-scale war broke out.[156] After four days' fighting, which saw considerable Chinese successes, China proposed a ceasefire and a border settlement based upon its proposals of 1959.[157] These proposals were, however, formally rejected in mid-November and fighting was resumed. On 21 November, after a complete rout of the Indian forces, the Chinese unilaterally withdrew to the *de facto* border proposed in the original offer of a ceasefire.[158]

We shall return to the implications of the Chinese victory, which coincided with the Cuban missile crisis, in the next chapter. My point

here is simply to demonstrate that, although the fighting along the
Sino-Indian border took place during a new period of radicalism, the
decision to stand firm had been taken in the earlier, more conservative period prior to the Tenth Plenum of September 1962 and, on this
score, no section of the Chinese leadership seems to have been guilty of
'capitulationism'.

A 'Revisionist' Version of 'Blooming and Contending'

In 1961-2 the old slogan of 'Let a hundred flowers bloom; let a
hundred schools of thought contend' was once more put forward.[159]
The 'blooming and contending' of the early 1960s was, however, very
different from that of 1956-7. In the middle 1950s, it was quite clearly
Mao Tse-tung who inspired the movement, seeking widespread criticism
of the Soviet model throughout Chinese society. In 1961, however,
the inspiration seemed to come from the Party conservatives who may
have sought some kind of 'liberalisation' of science and art but who
seemed to be concerned mainly with discrediting the Great Leap
Forward. It is significant to note, in this respect, that some of the most
important material to be produced during this period came not from
non-Party intellectuals but from senior cadres in the Central Committee's Propaganda Department and the Peking Party Committee – the
very people who had launched the movement in the first place.[160]

The origin of the new policy may be traced back to the time of the
Ninth Plenum in January 1961 when particular stress was given to
scientific standards.[161] It was felt that the standards of scientific research had fallen during the Great Leap and that this situation ought to
be rectified. From an academic point of view, it was probably true that
standards had fallen during the Great Leap but, at that time, the stress
had been on widespread popularisation of scientific method and a radical could quite easily argue that a campaign for mass technological innovation was probably worth more than a particular breakthrough in pure
mathematics . . . at least in the context of the tasks to be undertaken at
that time. Nevertheless, the new policy in 1961 was designed to give
scientists more time for individual (as opposed to group) research,
greater material incentives and greater responsibility.

In the discussion above concerning industrial policy, it was noted
that 1961 saw a reassessment of the policy of combining 'red' and
'expert'. This, of course, had enormous implications for educational
and scientific work. The theme was stated best by Foreign Minister
Ch'en Yi, who noted in July:

At present we should stress specialised studies because failure to do so will keep our country perpetually backward in science and culture. In the early years of the liberation it was completely necessary for the Party and the government to stress political study. In the past several years, thanks to the correct leadership of the Party, our institutes of higher education have made outstanding achievements in political teaching . . . Today there is a need for us . . . to train a large number of specialists . . . This is our greatest political mission. To make efforts in the study of his special field is the political task of the student . . . The students . . . should devote most of their time and efforts to specialist studies. Of course, these students should also study politics to equip themselves with a certain degree of political consciousness.[162]

It might be useful at this point to compare Ch'en's remarks with Mao Tse-tung's Great Leap Forward formulation:

The relationship between redness and expertness, politics and work is the unity of two opposites. The tendency to pay no attention to politics certainly must be criticised and repudiated. It is necessary to oppose the armchair politicians on the one hand and the pragmatists who have gone astray on the other. There is no doubt whatever about the unity of politics and technology. This is so every year and will forever be so. This is red and expert. The term 'politics' will continue to exist in the future but the content will be changed. Those who pay no attention to politics and are busy with their work all the day long will become economists who have gone astray and are dangerous. Ideological work and political work guarantee the accomplishment of economic work and technical work and they serve the economic base. Ideology and politics are also the supreme commander and the soul. As long as we are a bit slack with ideological work and political work, economic work and technical work will surely go astray.[163]

From the above, one might conclude that the Party conservatives who were making policy in 1961 had 'gone astray and were dangerous'. There were evidently quite a few economists who seemed to have forgotten classical Marxist political economy, for this was the period when the first discussions of Liberman-type proposals on the profit motive began to be heard.[164]

The period 1961-2 also saw an attempt to revaluate parts of China's

cultural tradition. In the latter Great Leap atmosphere of July 1960,
Professor Feng Yu-lan, the author of *A History of Chinese Philosophy*,
had come under some criticism for making positive remarks about
Confucius.[165] In the atmosphere of 1961-2, however, the issue of
Confucius could be debated quite openly.[166] There had been a long
tradition in China of interpreting Confucius as a 'progressive' according
to whatever criterion of progressive was currently in vogue. Once again
in 1961, some philosophers declared that Confucius was a progressive
because he was a herald of the new feudal society of the sixth century
B.C. who opposed the old slave society that had existed up to that
time. Others argued, however, that Confucius, in fact, strove to maintain slave society against the inroads of feudalism and was therefore
reactionary. I have always regarded such debates, which turn on
obscure questions such as whether the Chinese word *ren* (man) referred
(in the sixth century B.C.) to all people or just the ruling class, as highly
academic and rather abstruse but, in the light of the current campaign
against Lin Piao and Confucius (1974-5), I have been forced to revise
my view. It would seem, in retrospect, that the Confucius debates of
1961-2 turned on the Great Leap Forward in exactly the same way as
the current debates turn on the Cultural Revolution and I can only
conclude that those who wished to rehabilitate Confucius were in
reality opponents of the reforms of 1958. This view is amply reinforced
by other, far more explicit attacks on the Great Leap made at the same
time.

There was also much debate at that time arising out of the issue of
'socialist realism' and 'revolutionary romanticism' in literature and art.
In the old days of the Soviet model, considerable attention had been
paid to stereotyped 'socialist realism', which in 1958 had been criticised
by Kuo Mo-jo (clearly a Party radical) who insisted that 'socialist
realism' should be combined with 'revolutionary romanticism'. In
1961-2, however, intellectuals insisted that neither of these two models
were wholly adequate and suggested experimentation with other
artistic forms.[167] In reality this often meant no experimentation at all
but a return to more traditional forms and genres in Chinese art.

More Specific Attacks on the Great Leap Forward

The relationship of the above features of the 'blooming and contending'
of 1961-2 with the 'Great Leap Forward is perhaps a little oblique. In
the fields of short story writing and drama, however, the criticisms of
the Leap are clearer. At Talien in August 1962, for example, a conference met under the aegis of the 'literary tsar' Chou Yang to discuss

short stories about the countryside and finished up denouncing mass campaigns, crash programmes and the general Great Leap Forward strategy. Writers, it would seem, were urged to portray the events of that time as a tragedy. They were to guard against 'excessive romanticism'. Officials in the Propaganda Department, who had denounced Hu Feng, now began to voice much the same criticism as Hu. Writers were urged to portray 'middle characters' and avoid painting everything in black and white terms as had been the fashion during the Leap.[168]

What was potentially more explosive than the efforts of short story writers, however, was the publication of plays which not only satirised the Leap but indirectly called for the rehabilitation of P'eng Teh-huai. It has been argued that, from January 1961 to September 1962, a determined effort was made by Party conservatives to rehabilitate the former Minister of Defence.[169] It is in this connection, some suggest, that Liu Shao-ch'i's book *On Self Cultivation* . . . (better known in English as *How to Be a Good Communist*) was republished, precisely because one of its major themes was the need to combat 'ultra-leftism' and the need for peace within the Party.[170] At the tail-end of the preceding radical period, there had been published with much fanfare the fourth volume of the *Selected Works of Mao Tse-tung.*[171] It may well be that the republication of Liu's work in 1962 was a conservative counterattack.

Perhaps the most famous play in defence of P'eng to be published at that time was by the deputy mayor of Peking, Wu Han, entitled *Hai Jui Dismissed From Office.*[172] Hai Jui had been a high official of the Ming dynasty stationed in the Soochow area from 1569 to 1570. At that time, according to Wu Han, the peasants were in a sorry plight because their land has been confiscated by local officials. Despite threats from these officials, the 'noble' Hai Jui took the side of the peasants and ordered the death of a landlord's son who had killed a peasant. The local landlords and officials, however, appealed to the Emperor against Hai Jui's verdict with the result that the landlord's son was spared and Hai Jui unjustly dismissed. The theme of this play, which was similar to Wu Han's essay published in *People's Daily* during the earlier conservative period on 16 June 1959, was held to be a direct satire on the Great Leap Forward. Hai Jui was allegedly P'eng Teh-huai; the Emperor who had lost touch with reality and might be approaching senility was supposed to be Mao Tse-tung, and the process whereby land had been unjustly taken away was in fact the Great Leap Forward.

Perhaps the most outspoken of the satirists of 1961-2 was Teng T'o, the former editor of *People's Daily* and director of ideological and cultural activities of the Peking Municipal Party Committee. In a series of articles entitled 'Evening Talks at Yenshan', published in the Peking Party press during this period, Teng T'o also criticised the Great Leap by historical analogy.[173] Like the others, he implied that Mao had been misled by flattery, that he was stubborn and cut off from reality. Together with Wu Han and another official of the Peking Committee, Liao Mo-sha, Teng T'o suggested that perhaps Mao suffered from a particularly acute form of amnesia which caused him to go back on his word and which, if not treated, would result in insanity. He prescribed a long rest.[174] The writings of Teng T'o during 1961-2 are full of implied criticisms of Great Leap policy,[175] grandiose schemes that could not be realised[176] and 'throwing out one's teacher'[177] (the Soviet Union). Finally Teng T'o may even have suggested reconciliation with the United States, for, since the Chinese discovered America in the fifth century, Sino-American relations were worth treasuring.[178] Though it is possible to read all sorts of things into Teng T'o's historical analogies, it does seem fairly clear that his writings were part of a concerted attack on Great Leap policies and, significantly, they ceased on 2 September, just prior to that historic meeting which sought to revive the radical spirit.

The End of the Fifth Cycle

The fifth cycle in the history of contemporary China came to an end at a central work conference held between August and September 1962, first at Peitaiho and then in Peking,[179] and a new period of radicalism was endorsed at the Tenth Plenum of the Eighth Central Committee in September. The period of natural calamities now seemed to be at an end and the harvest had improved. In contrast to earlier periods of consolidation, however, it was much more difficult to chalk up the successes.

. The people's communes in the countryside had been emasculated and those in the cities had virtually disappeared. The full employment of 1958 had given way to widespread underemployment. Many of the light industrial enterprises in the countryside had ceased to operate and some of the smaller factories in the cities had closed. Some of the large industrial enterprises, started during the Great Leap, remained uncompleted. Much of the economy seemed to be regulated more by the market than by either central or local planning and there were many cases of corruption and bureaucratic inefficiency.

The above, however, is only one side of the coin. Although the

people's communes were only a shadow of their former selves,
commune-type organisation had, it may be argued, helped to ward off
famine during the bad years. Now that the weather had improved,
one might anticipate that the communes would be strengthened.
Though urban communes, in their original form, had perhaps been
somewhat premature, they had helped to institute street
industries that, potentially at least, offered great prospects for generating employment. Above all, the spirit of do-it-yourself organisation
had been established. It could surely only be a matter of time before
small industries, closed during the bad years, would be reopened once
a sufficient agricultural surplus began to appear. It might be some time
before some of the larger industrial concerns, which had depended on
imports of technology from the Soviet Union, could operate according
to the spirit of 'self-reliance' but China had learnt the lesson of avoiding
dependency – a lesson which most countries have yet to learn. It had
been defiantly, and perhaps hopefully, that Li Fu-ch'un had uttered the
words 'self-reliance' following the Soviet withdrawal of technicians.
Whatever happened in the future, however, the words 'self-reliance'
must surely become less of a slogan and more of a programme.

As for the growth of the market, a tremendous battle had yet to be
fought to establish exactly what degree of market relationships might
be permissible at what stage of socialist construction. At the conference
attended by 7,000 cadres in January 1962, Mao expressed the gravity
of this task:

> If our country does not establish a socialist economy, what kind of
> situation shall we be in? We shall become a country like Yugoslavia,
> which has actually become a bourgeois country; the dictatorship of
> the proletariat will be transformed into a bourgeois dictatorship,
> into a reactionary fascist type of dictatorship. This is a question
> which demands the utmost vigilance. I hope comrades will give a
> great deal of thought to it.[180]

In the field of foreign policy, 1962 saw China standing much more
alone than in 1959. In 1962, she was faced with the possibility of war
on three fronts. The Sino-Soviet dispute was by that time insoluble
and the United States had cut its losses for the time being in Laos only
to strengthen its position in Vietnam. By the end of the year, India
had been rebuffed but that country seemed no longer non-aligned but
aligned to both the super powers at the expense of China and, as such,
was an intermediate source of danger to China's security. Nevertheless,

Mao would probably argue that there was no virtue in maintaining an alliance with an increasingly 'revisionist' Soviet Union. China had stood on her own and could do so again. After all, the one area of Chinese society that had manifestly repudiated a 'revisionist' path was the People's Liberation Army, now gearing itself not only to the old tradition of People's War but also to the possibility of China becoming an independent nuclear power. Yet here too there was a danger. Like Kao Kang before him, P'eng Teh-huai had been accused of attempting to create a 'Party of the Army'.[181] whereby the Army might take over the functions of the civilian Party. Could one be sure that this trend had been reversed?

In 1961-2, both the Great Leap Forward and Mao himself had been ridiculed by people in very senior positions within the Party. What P'eng Teh-huai had tried to do very clumsily in 1959, others were trying to do with perhaps greater skill. There was a battle to be joined and, to wage it, Mao could only return to the 'first front'. It was to be an incredible battle quite unlike anything yet seen. It was to last a full decade and in some ways still continues. In terms of its world significance, it was to be far more important than the Long March or the Civil War. It concerned not personalities but the very possibility of an alternative to a dependent model of social development. In January 1962, Mao expressed his intention:

> Those of you who shirk responsibility or who are afraid of taking responsibility, who do not allow people to speak, who think that you are tigers, and that nobody will dare to touch your arse, whoever has this attitude, ten out of ten of you will fail. People will talk anyway. You think that nobody will really dare to touch the arse of tigers like you? They damn well will![182]

Notes

1. The most complete exposition of Mao's ideas concerning changes in Soviet society may be found in his page-by-page criticism of the Soviet official textbook on political economy in *JPRS* 61269-2, 20 February 1974, pp. 247-313.
2. Strong 1965, p. 71.
3. Ibid., p. 65.
4. *SC* in *URI* 1968, *Tibet*, pp. 357-8.
5. Adopted 9 March 1955, in *URI* 1968, *Tibet*, pp. 141-3. It was formally established April 1956 (ibid., pp. 144-55).
6. Strong 1965, p. 77.
7. Ibid., p. 81.

8. Ibid., pp. 83-4. See also Ngapo Ngawang-Jigme in *URI* 1968, *Tibet*, pp 394-403.
9. Strong 1965, pp. 168-90.
10. Ibid., p. 235.
11. Ngapo Ngawang-Jigme, in *URI* 1968, *Tibet*, pp. 394-403.
12. International Commission of Jurists 1960, pp. 11-63.
13. As late as 7 September 1958, Nehru told the Indian Parliament 'So far as I know, there is not one country in the world which recognised the independence of Tibet. We definitely have not'; cited in Wilson 1966, p. 115. •
14. See for example Gelder 1964.
15. *URI* 1968, *The Case of P'eng Teh-huai*, p. 14.
16. Simmonds 1969, p. 124.
17. Shu T'ung 24 January 1959, in *ECMM* 169, 25 May 1959, pp. 1-18.
18. K'o Ch'ing-shih, *ECMM* 165, 20 April 1959, p. 39.
19. Simmonds 1969, pp. 124-31.
20. Gigon cited in Dittmer 1974, p. 41.
21. *URI* 1968, *The Case of P'eng Teh-huai*, p. 204.
22. See Gittings 1968, pp. 102-9.
23. Suslov noted that the Soviet Union considered it inexpedient to help the Chinese produce nuclear weapons because such a course would lead to the acquisition of nuclear power by West Germany and Japan. See Gehlen 1967, p. 286.
24. Simmonds 1969, pp. 132-4.
25. T'ao Chu, *RMRB* 3 June 1959, p. 7. For a discussion of T'ao's position, see Moody 1973, pp. 279-80.
26. *RMRB* 16 June 1959, p. 8 (under pseudonym Liu Mien-chih).
27. P'eng Teh-huai, in *URI* 1968, *The Case of P'eng Teh-huai*, p. 400.
28. Moody 1973, p. 280.
29. *URI* 1968, *The Case of P'eng Teh-huai*, p. 400.
30. Zagoria 1966, p. 134.
31. *URI* 1968, *The Case of P'eng Teh-huai*, p. 426.
32. Mao Tse-tung 23 July 1959, in *URI* 1968, *The Case of P'eng Teh-huai*, pp. 19 and 407. See also Schram 1974, p. 137.
33. Mao Tse-tung, in Schram 1974, p. 146.
34. Ibid., pp. 132-3.
35. Dittmer (1974, p. 40) reports that Li Hsien-nien confessed in early 1967 that he had switched his vote between ballots.
36. *URI* 1968, *The Case of P'eng Teh-huai*, p. 419.
37. Ibid., p. 423.
38. Ibid., p. 424.
39. Ibid., p. 426.
40. Dittmer 1974, p. 41.
41. *PR* 35, 1 September 1959, pp. 7-8.
42. *CCP.CC, SC*, 23 September 1959, in *SCMP* 2108, 2 October 1959, pp. 6-9.
43. *SCMP* 2078, 18 August 1959, p. 43.
44. *SCMP* 2099, 21 September 1959, p. 38.
45. Vogel 1971, p. 263.
46. Ibid., p. 264.
47. *PR* 40, 6 October 1959, pp. 13-20.
48. *ECMM* 159, 2 March 1959, p. 11.
49. Zagoria 1966, pp. 258-60.
50. Ibid., pp. 260-2.
51. Ibid., pp. 270-6.
52. Yu Chiao-li, *PR* 38, 22 September 1959, pp. 6-11.

53. Khruschev 1959.
54. Zagoria 1966, p. 277.
55. *PR* 40 1959, pp. 7-10, reprinted in Hudson, Lowenthal and MacFarquhar 1961, pp. 61-3.
56. Zagoria 1966, pp. 281-4.
57. Ibid., p. 238.
58. *PFLP* 1960.
59. For Mao's views on the likelihood of war, see *JPRS* 61269-2, 20 February 1974, p. 265.
60. For Mao's views on this, see ibid., p. 251.
61. *PR* 24, 14 June 1960, pp. 13-14, in Hudson, Lowenthal and MacFarquhar 1961, pp. 123-6.
62. Shevlyagin, D. 10 June 1960, in Hudson, Lowenthal and MacFarquhar 1961, pp. 127-9 and Matkovsky 12 June 1960, in ibid., pp. 129-31.
63. See Crankshaw 1965, pp. 107-9. I am not sure about the authenticity of Crankshaw's account. The official speech of Khruschev may be found in Hudson, Lowenthal and MacFarquhar 1961, pp. 132-9.
64. According to Mao, Khruschev's actions here were designed to strengthen his position at home. Mao Tse-tung 18 January 1961, in *JPRS* 61269-2, 20 February 1974, p. 238.
65. Zagoria 1966, pp. 327-8.
66. See Gittings 1968, pp. 129-43.
67. Li Fu-ch'un, *PR* 34, 23 August 1960, p. 15.
68. *PFLP* 1965, *The Polemic* . . . pp. 83-9.
69. Zagoria 1966, pp. 367-8.
70. Crankshaw 1965, pp. 131-2.
71. Li Fu-ch'un in *PR* 14, 5 April 1960, p. 7.
72. Eckstein 1973, p. 216.
73. Li Fu-ch'un, *PR* 14, 5 April 1960, p. 6.
74. Eckstein 1973, p. 216.
75. e.g. Walker 1968, pp. 444-5.
76. Robinson J. 1969, p. 35.
77. *SCMM* 652, 28 April 1969, p. 25.
78. ibid., p. 27.
79. Chao Tzu-yang, *SCMP* 2262, 20 May 1960, p. 23.
80. Vogel 1971, p. 272.
81. *RMRB*, 16 June 1960, p. 1.
82. *RMRB*, 29 June 1960, p. 5.
83. See Vogel 1971, pp. 266-8.
84. Salaff 1967, p. 108.
85. Fokkema 1971, pp. 103-4.
86. Cheng 1966, p. 37.
87. Information from Nanking and Foochow military regions and Army units under General (Rear Services etc.) departments. Cheng 1966, p. 296 (from report of General Rear Services Dept. 20 February 1961).
88. Mao Tse-tung 18 January 1961, in *JPRS* 61269-2, 20 February 1974, p. 240.
89. *PR* 42, 18 October 1960, pp. 7-8.
90. Gittings 1967, p. 246.
91. Cheng 1966, p. 81.
92. Powell 1963, p. 8.
93. Gittings 1967, p. 248.
94. Ibid., p. 249.
95. Vogel 1971, p. 271.
96. Mao Tse-tung 1960 (?), in *JPRS* 61269-1, 20 February 1974, p. 233.

97.   Mao Tse-tung 1961-2, in *JPRS* 61269-2, 20 February 1974, p. 256.
98.   Cheng 1966, p. 137. On the 12 articles, see Walker 1968, p. 446.
99.   Vogel 1971, p. 273.
100. Ibid., pp. 275-92.
101. Mao Tse-tung 18 January 1961, in *JPRS* 61269-2, 20 February 1974, p. 244.
102. Ibid., pp. 237-8.
103. Chang 1970, p. 189. The date of this decision is taken from a Red Rebel
      source.
104. Po I-po, *PR* 8, 24 February 1961, p. 5.
105. Vogel 1971, p. 275.
106. Schurmann 1966, p. 493.
107. Vogel 1971, pp. 277-8.
108. Mao Tse-tung 18 January 1961, in *JPRS* 61269-2, 20 February 1974, p. 244.
109. This policy may have been enunciated by Liu at the 7,000 cadres conference
      on 26 January 1962. See Domes 1973, pp. 126-7, after research by von
      Groeling.
110. Vogel 1971. pp. 279-80.
111. Wilson D, in *FEER*, Vol. LIX No. 5, 1 February 1968, p. 193.
112. Vogel 1971, p. 280 and *SCMP* 2421, 20 January 1961, pp. 1-3.
113. Vogel 1971, p. 281.
114. The similarity with the Soviet NEP was noted by Schurmann 1964.
115. *PR* 38, 20 September 1960, pp. 21-2.
116. Vogel 1971, p. 283.
117. On the different levels of ownership in 1965, see Burki 1970, esp. Chapter
      II.
118. Vogel 1971, p. 283.
119. Ibid., p. 281.
120. Mao observed that, in Hopei, some 15 per cent of teams were dominated by
      wavering middle peasant elements. Mao Tse-tung 1961-2, in *JPRS* 61269-2,
      20 February 1974, p. 244. See also Vogel 1971, p. 284 and Schurmann
      1966, p. 494.
121. In this regard, see the poster which appeared on 14 January 1967, translated
      in *CQ* 30, 1967, pp. 207-9. Though this belongs to a later period it is indica-
      tive of some peasant feeling.
122. On the different sizes of production teams in 13 communes in 1965 (from
      7 members to 153), see Burki 1965, p. 8.
123. Vogel 1971, pp. 290-1.
124. Ibid., p. 286.
125. Schurmann 1966, p. 218.
126. E.g. *SCMP* 4369, 5 March 1969, pp. 7-10.
127. Meng Kuei and Hsiao Lin, *SCMM* 539, 29 August 1966, pp. 1-12.
128. Mao Tse-tung 30 January 1962, in Schram 1974, p. 167.
129. Mao Tse-tung 19 February 1958, *CB* 892, 21 October 1969, p. 6.
130. Schurmann 1966, p. 295.
131. *PR* 16, 17 April 1970, p. 3. *PR* 14, 3 April 1970, p. 11.
132. *PR* 16, 17 April 1970, p. 3.
133. Ibid., See also Mao Tse-tung March 1960, in *JPRS* 61269-1, 20 February
      1974, p. 230.
134. E.g. *SCMP* 4369, 5 March 1969, pp. 7-10.
135. Andors 1974.
136. Schurmann 1966, pp. 399-402.
137. Vogel 1971. p. 295.
138. Schurmann 1966, p. 399.

139. Chou En-lai December 1964, in *PR* 1, 1 January 1965, p. 13.
140. Crankshaw 1965, p. 137.
141. Zagoria 1961, p. 7.
142. Ibid., p. 8.
143. *PFLP* 1965, *The Polemic* . . . p. 465.
144. Zagoria 1966, pp. 370-83.
145. Crankshaw 1965, p. 142.
146. Mao Tse-tung 30 January 1962, in Schram 1974, p. 181.
147. E.g. Tan Wen-jui, *PR* 15, 14 April 1961, pp. 11-13.
148. Ch'en Yi, *PR* 15, 14 April 1961, p. 5.
149. Hinton H. 1966, p. 271.
150. *PR* 26, 29 June 1962, pp. 5-7.
151. Hinton H. 1966, p. 272.
152. On the Indian forward policy, see Maxwell 1972, pp. 179-273.
153. Hinton H. 1966, pp. 318, 324-5, 328.
154. Ibid., p. 324.
155. *PR* 30, 27 July 1962, p.6.
156. Ibid., p. 387. Maxwell 1972, p. 387.
157. *PR* 43, 26 October 1962, pp. 5-6.
158. *PR* 47/8, 30 November 1962, pp. 5-7.
159. *PR* 12, 24 March 1961, pp. 6-9.
160. Goldman 1969 (p. 68) makes this point. Much of what follows is taken from her account, though I disagree with her analysis.
161. Ibid., p. 61.
162. Ch'en Yi 10 August 1951, in *CQ* 8, 1961, p. 231, from *SWB* Pt. 3 FE/W126 (*Zhongguo Qingnianbao*, 1 September 1961).
163. Mao Tse-tung 19 February 1958, *CB* 892, 21 October 1969, p. 6.
164. Goldman 1969, p. 63. For a criticism of their views see *PR* 44, 28 October 1966, pp. 32-5.
165. Goldman 1969, p. 63.
166. The culmination of the Confucius debate took place in late 1962 at a symposium organised by the Historical Institute of Shantung. See Wilhelm 1965, p. 130.
167. Goldman 1969, p. 64.
168. Ibid., pp. 69-73.
169. *URI* 1968, *The Case of P'eng Teh-huai*, pp. 206-7.
170. *PR* 22, 12 May 1967, pp. 7-11.
171. *PR* 40, 4 October 1960, pp. 7-19.
172. See Pusey 1969. In Pusey's view, the 1959 letter under the pseudonym Liu Mien-chih was a far more severe criticism than the play (p. 15). During the more radical period after Lushan, Wu Han's writings on Hai Jui struck a different note (ibid., p. 17) in which he obliquely criticised P'eng Teh-huai. The play was written in November 1960 and first staged in Peking in February 1961. It was suspended after only a few performances. Wu Han was subsequently held to be guilty of 'using the past to satirise the present' (*yi gu feng jin*) as opposed to Mao's slogan of 'making the past serve the present' (*qu wei jin yong*).
173. Teng T'o 1963 (I have taken the following references from Goldman 1969 and checked the original).
174. *CB* 792, 29 June 1966, p. 4.
175. Teng T'o 1963, pp. 78-80.
176. Ibid., p. 180 (ref. to Wang An-shih).
177. Ibid., pp. 34-6.
178. Ibid., pp. 97-9.

179. Chang 1970, p. 191.
180. Mao Tse-tung 30 January 1962, in Schram 1974, p. 167.
181. Mao Tse-tung 11 September 1969, in Schram 1974, p. 148.
182. Mao Tse-tung 30 January 1962, in Schram 1974, p. 167.

6 THE SOCIALIST EDUCATION MOVEMENT (1962-5)

The sixth cycle since the Yenan movements of the early 1940s began in 1962, accelerated in mid-1964 and wound down in 1965. It took place at a time of economic recovery and growing confidence on the part of both radicals and conservatives and yet in an increasingly unfavourable international climate. During this period, Sino-Soviet polemics became extremely fierce and the United States threatened China far more seriously than at any time since the Korean War. To what extent would intensified American and Soviet hostility modify both radical and conservative policies?

I have stressed time and again in this book that political movements in China may be divided into two types — those from the top down and those involving mass mobilisation. In this sixth cycle, the conservatives tried to implement the former and the radicals the latter. When launched in 1962 by the radicals, the movements were designed to revive the spirit of the Great Leap. They were all too often used, however, by a conservative Party machine to reassert its control without disturbing production. In such a situation, conflict became sharper and the Army, aligning itself with the radicals, became more and more involved in civilian affairs. Such an alignment one might indeed expect if the Yenan model were to be reactivated. And yet it still wasn't quite . . .

The Tenth Plenum

The Tenth Plenum of the Eighth Central Committee, held in Peking from 24 to 27 September 1962, was the culmination of two month's extensive discussions at a central work conference which met first at Peitaiho and then in Peking.[1] What went on in these lengthy discussions we do not know; the result, however, was a radical victory. The Party line was now clear — primary attention should be given to the problem of 'revisionism' and the class struggle.

As Mao saw it, the issues of 'revisionism' and class struggle were exactly the same both within China and internationally. Constant attention needed to be paid to the fact that classes would continue to exist in socialist society and imperialism was still as active on the world stage as ever. Party cadres were falling into the morass of 'revisionism' in exactly the same way as some socialist countries were drifting back into capitalism. Unless there was constant vigilance, therefore, China could slip backwards into becoming another Yugoslavia; such, he believed, was happening to the Soviet Union.

'Revisionism', in Mao's eyes, was not just a question of the attitudes of individuals but the reflection of objective class forces. 'Revisionism' did not just happen in the Soviet Union because of Khruschev. It had, in fact, a very long history that could be traced back to the days of Stalin. It was perhaps ironic, therefore, that Stalin should have thought Mao a 'Tito' back in 1949, and yet now Tito had been welcomed back into the Soviet fold at the expense of China. Mao interpreted the Soviet naval proposal as an attempt to blockade China, Khruschev's siding with India on the border question in 1959 as a betrayal of socialist solidarity, and the Bucharest conference as an attempt to annihilate the Chinese leadership.

Since imperialism was seen in a Leninist sense as 'the highest stage of capitalism', the same United Front principles that applied domestically should apply internationally. Just as various domestic classes had been united to isolate the landlords and comprador bourgeoisie, so a number of countries with different social systems could be united to oppose imperialism. The governments of Egypt and Iraq might be reactionary but they played a progressive role internationally. The fundamental yardstick in evaluating a country's foreign policy, therefore, was its attitude towards imperialism, and in this regard the Soviet Union was found wanting.[2]

If the principle of class struggle was now to be operationalised, there was a very obvious model for implementation – the Yenan model of 1942-3. Such a model was sufficiently radical to revitalise the rural areas but not so disruptive that work would suffer.[3] The immediate task was not to go round rooting out rightists everywhere, neither was it to reverse the verdicts on people already branded as rightists. In the past year, there had been just such a wholesale reversal, allegedly at the instigation of Liu Shao-ch'i, who had provided aircraft for 'rightists' to return to Anhui for rehabilitation.[4] In Mao's view, though the original rightists ought gradually to be rehabilitated, no purpose would be served by reversing the verdicts[5] upon them lest people might think that they had been wrongly designated. It was to be the Yenan model, therefore, that informed the new mass movement which took its name from the Socialist Education Movement of 1957. Though a Leap Forward was not on the immediate agenda, Mao presumably saw the Socialist Education Movement of 1962 as preparing the ground for such a development in exactly the same way as the movement of 1957 prepared the way for the Great Leap Forward. For this reason, he was anxious that the Great Leap Forward of 1958-9 should be correctly interpreted. The novelists, short story writers and historians who, right up to the opening of the Plenum, had continued to slander it, should desist. Mao was quite aware of what had been going on.

> Writing novels is popular these days, isn't it? The use of novels for anti-Party activity is a great invention. Anyone wanting to over-throw a political regime must create public opinion and do some preparatory ideological work. This applies to counter-revolutionary as well as revolutionary classes.[6]

Thus the slogan for the Party in the immediate future was to be 'never forget the class struggle' and, in operational terms, this boiled down to three policies: a continuation of the struggle against 'modern revision-ism' both internationally and domestically, the Socialist Education Movement, particularly in the countryside, and a campaign to revolutionise literature and art.

The Socialist Education Movement: Stage One — September 1962-September 1963

The Socialist Education Movement, launched in September 1962, was probably accepted in principle by both Party conservatives and Party radicals since very serious problems had arisen in the countryside. According to a set of documents pertaining to Lienchiang *xian* in Fukien province which found their way to the West via one of the many Kuomintang raids launched during this period, there was a general 'spontaneous inclination towards capitalism' in the countryside. Many peasants were devoting an excessive amount of time to their private plots or had abandoned farming to go into business. Party authority was weak with very low morale amongst cadres. Some cadres were corrupt and had appropriated public funds. Speculation and gambling were rife and there had been a revival of 'feudal' practices such as religious festivals, bride purchase, spiritualism and witchcraft.[7]

Though their diagnosis of the disease affecting the countryside was probably the same, the Party conservatives and radicals differed in their prescribed treatment . . . The conservatives were preoccupied with law and order and restoring production. They blamed the situation on the Great Leap Forward and sought to rectify it by movements from the top down using Party-led work-teams (*gongzuodui*). Though educa-tional reform was considered important, under no circumstances was priority to be switched away from technical training. The Party radicals,

on the other hand, sought to put 'politics in command', and, while
not reviving the Great Leap *per se*, they wished to continue many of its
mobilisational policies. As they saw it, the situation was the result not
of the Great Leap but of the concessions to capitalism made during the
previous conservative period. Committed to countering bureaucratism,
they believed the best organisation to correct decaying official morality
was not the Party-led work-teams from above, but the old peasant
associations of more radical days. The radicals tried, therefore, to form
Poor and Lower Middle Peasant Associations in the teeth of conservative
criticism. They furthermore took the educational content of the
Socialist Education Movement very seriously and tried to revive the old
minban concept through the establishment of part-work part-study
schools.[8] The Socialist Education Movement had been launched in the
spirit of the Yenan model; the radicals were determined to keep it in
that spirit.

As the movement got under way in the autumn of 1962, however,
differences had not yet polarised at lower levels. At first, the movement
was implemented in a number of trial areas, notably in Hopei and
Hunan[9] (also in Lienchiang *xian*),[10] but although some progress was
made in raising cadre morale there still remained the problem of
ineffective leadership. In January 1963, therefore, cadres were instructed to pay particular attention to the health of the leading group within
the brigades when carrying out the annual task of 'readjusting
communes'.[11] When promoting cadres, stress should be placed on those
from poor and lower middle peasant backgrounds (although others
should not be automatically excluded).[12] Policy seemed to be a mix-
ture of the radical and conservative positions. The former was reflected
in the fact that cadres were instructed to be severe in their ideological
criticism and the latter in another demand that organisational treatment
should be lenient. One might argue, however, that this contradiction
was in accord with the Yenan principle of operating through existing
organisations rather than pulverising them.

By the New Year, moderate progress had been made in the movement in some areas. A number of economies in administration had been
effected and a few private plots had been restricted but the peasants
had not been mobilised and in some cases cadres had insisted that the
amount of money available to peasants to spend in the free markets
should be increased.[13] Now that the spirit of Yenan had once again
become Party policy, some cadres sought to turn Mao's 1942 policies
on their head by judicious quoting from the documents of that time to
support a conservative position. For example, the conservative call to

'develop the economy and safeguard supplies', which was used to prevent mass mobilisation, was taken out of context from a speech by Mao
in 1942.[14] Such a tactic the radicals were later to refer to as 'waving
the Red Flag to oppose it'.

With the Party dragging its heels in the Socialist Education Movement, further impetus towards radicalisation came from the Army. In
January 1963 the Army, which under Lin Piao had undergone a kind of
socialist education movement of its own, actively sought to propagandise the spirit of the movement, and Army cadres addressed gatherings
of civilian leaders to stress the need to strengthen rural collective
organisation. As the Army press turned out more and more study
materials with obvious civilian application, Army cadres published
articles in the newspapers calling for greater radicalism. At the same
time, however, these same newspapers carried articles by Party conservatives urging caution.[15]

In January 1963, a considerable amount of Army propaganda
material centred on the conduct of a model soldier by the name of Lei
Feng. Lei Feng was remarkable in his devotion to the 'Three Red
Banners' of the Great Leap Forward, his selfless devotion to his comrades and the civilian population. After a short life of utterly devoted
service, Lei Feng died a rather unspectacular death but fortunately left
behind his diaries, which became study materials for the new campaign.
The point of the Lei Feng model was a fairly obvious one — that true
glory did not consist of spectacular deeds and dying conspicuously for
one's country but might be achieve in one's everyday activities. The
model was that of a 'rustless screw' in the revolution — obviously above
any form of corruption.[16] In February 1963, the Lei Feng documents
became basic study material for a newly revamped militia organisation[17]
and it was precisely this militia organisation that was to provide the
backbone of new Poor and Lower Middle Peasant Associations. Though
it is very difficult to generalise about the Lei Feng Movement, it is my
impression that it was very effective. To Western eyes, Lei Feng might
have appeared a prig. One might doubt the selflessness of a man who
had himself photographed so many times and kept a diary that seemed
written for a mass audience or even wonder whether he existed at all.
That, in my opinion, would be to miss the point, for Lei Feng was
presented as a normative model and it did not matter very much
whether he existed or not. Time and again I raised the Lei Feng
question with my students in Peking in 1964-5 and all seemed completely convinced that the study of Lei Feng was worthwhile; the
question of authenticity was not important. Of course, I cannot answer

for the bulk of the peasants enrolled in the militia though there is much evidence that, there too, the life-style of Lei Feng was taken extremely seriously as an anti-individualistic model.

A second feature of Army involvement in the Socialist Education Movement was the launching of a campaign for the 'living study and living use of Mao Tse-tung Thought'. This campaign, originally initiated in the Army, was later to lead to the publication of 'Quotations from the Works of Chairman Mao' in red plastic covers[18] which were to become famous in the subsequent Cultural Revolution. The aims of the movement were many. First, and most obvious, the movement was aimed at countering individualism and the 'spontaneous development of capitalism' by presenting as many people as possible with a radical view of China's development. Secondly, it was aimed at countering dog-matism in the Party whereby statements of Mao could be taken out of context to justify a conservative position while ordinary people, who had not read the *Selected Works of Mao Tse-tung* could not evaluate them. Thirdly, the movement might provide the ideological cement which the radicals hoped (in the Yenan tradition) would be much more effective than mere organisational engineering. On the other hand, it also promoted the person of Lin Piao who was now designated as the one who most creatively applied Mao Tse-tung Thought.[19]

A third feature of Army involvement was that many of the key slogans put forward during the Army reform after 1960 (such as the 'three-eight working style', etc.) were now seen as having applicability to the civilian sphere, though this came initially through the militia. The implication here was that the Army should be involved in civilian life in a way not seen for over a decade. Again, this was in accordance with the Yenan model which sought to prevent the growth of a gap between Army and civilians and to prevent military professionalism. Such a movement was, from a radical point of view, healthy so long as it did not violate one of the cardinal principles of Mao Tse-tung which held that although 'political power grows out of the barrel of a gun', it is the Party that wields the gun[20] and not vice versa.

With the partial radicalisation of the Socialist Education Movement in the New Year of 1963, attempts were made to specify guidelines for the movement. In February, at a central work conference, Mao Tse-tung commented on the relatively successful experiences of the movement in Hunan and Hopei and urged that it be extended to cover the whole country. Experience in those areas had shown that the move-ment should be conducted in three steps. First, devote some 20 days to train a group of cadres; secondly, use this core to train more cadres and activists among the poor and lower middle peasants (which I take to mean form the nucleus of Poor and Lower Middle Peasant Associations); thirdly, conduct all-out efforts (to mobilise the masses).[21] In this formula for mass mobilisation, Mao called for a movement which would go far beyond the simple process of work-team rectification favoured by the Party conservatives.

At another central work conference in May, the experiences of conducting the Socialist Education Movement were codified in a 'Draft Resolution of the Central Committee on Some Problems in Current Rural Work'.[22] This document, commonly known as the 'Early Ten Points', which was compiled under Mao's personal supervision, stressed the importance of class struggle. The notion 'four clean-ups' (*siqing*) was introduced which signified cleaning up accounts, granaries, properties and work-points and ending cadre corruption. Cadres were to participate in productive labour and, most important of all, the Party formally proposed to re-establish Poor and Lower Middle Peasant Associations at commune, brigade and team levels to lead the movement.

After the promulgation of the 'Early Ten Points', the Party could hardly drag its feet on *policy* but it could, and indeed did, drag its feet on operations. The crux of the problem was exactly how the Poor and Lower Middle Peasant Associations should be established, what their functions were to be and how these related to the work-teams sent down from above. When the first 'poor peasants' representative groups' (*pinnong daibiao xiaozu*) were set up after the directive, they were charged with fostering the collective economy but under the leadership of the Party and as assistants to management committees.[23] The key question was — under the leadership of the Party *at what level*? What were they to do when a local Party branch was corrupt, or when the work-team was excessively conservative? For their part, Party committees were enjoined to *submit* to the supervision of the peasant associations and yet also *lead* them. The scope for confusion was very great and could be capitalised on by conservatives.

There was very little, however, that conservative cadres could do about avoiding participation in manual labour, since very detailed regulations were issued setting quotas on the number of days they must work in the fields and reducing the number of subsidised workpoints they received for office duties. These latter were commonly reduced from 4 per cent to 1-2 per cent.[24]

By the summer of 1963, therefore, the main task in the Socialist Education Movement was to activate the Poor and Lower Middle

Peasant Associations. As work-teams, obsessed with not interfering too much with production, tried to keep the lid on the movement and as newly-formed militia organisations, often with Army instructors, pressed for further radicalisation of the associations, the situation was potentially explosive. There was a need, therefore, for distinct Party instructions on the degree of permissible activism. The radicals pressed for a maximum, the conservatives for a minimum.

Initial Reform in Literature and the Arts

May 1963 saw not only the publication of the 'Early Ten Points', which were designed to spread the Socialist Education Movement over the whole country, but also Mao Tse-tung's first attempt to promote a campaign to reform literature and the arts. The National Conference of Writers and Artists convened at that time sought to mobilise intellectuals to 'play their full militant role' in the struggle against 'modern revisionism' and to help them identify themselves with the 'broad masses of the labouring people, with the workers, peasants and soldiers'. They were instructed not to avoid conflict[25] or, in the terminology soon to become popular, they were to adhere to the proposition that 'one divides into two'.

The proposition 'one divides into two' was not, as it might seem, an esoteric philosophical point, but was to have considerable relevance in the following years. It signified an injunction to look at everything in terms of its internal contradictions and to separate out the contradictory elements. Once these elements were separated, one could determine whether the relationship between them was antagonistic or non-antagonistic and so formulate a policy for dealing with them. The contradictory premise, soon to be put forward by some philosophers, was 'two combines into one' whereby one looked not at the inherent division within a thing but at the way divisive elements ceased to be divided and came together in an entity. The former proposition, therefore, was an obligation to criticise, analyse and struggle whereas the latter was to smooth over differences. In politics, the former advocated the theme of the Tenth Plenum — class struggle, whereas the latter was held to concentrate on the way classes died away. In literature and art, the former portrayed heroic and villainous characters as models whereas the latter was merely a continuation of the conservative policy of portraying 'middle characters'.

About the same time as the May 1963 National Conference of Writers and Artists, Mao's wife Chiang Ch'ing began to take a close interest in the process of literary and art reform. She is said to have carried out

investigations into the intent of Wu Han's play about Hai Jui and to
have examined a series of stories allegedly written in early 1961 by one
of the 'Three Family Village' trio, Liao Mo-sha.[26] In retrospect, it
would seem that this collection, entitled *Stories about Not Fearing
Ghosts*, was particularly significant though the precise meaning of the
stories has yet to be satisfactorily explained. One explanation, put
forward by Ho Ch'i-fang (in the preface to the volume), was that the
aim was to publicise Mao's slogan that 'all reactionaries are paper tigers'
by showing that imperialists and reactionaries, like ghosts, were not to
be feared.[27] On the other hand, it has been argued that Ho's preface
and the intent of the book was to de-emphasise Mao's slogan by
declaring that imperialists and reactionaries were merely 'ghosts',[28]
in the same way that Teng T'o had implied that Mao's statement about
the 'East wind prevailing over the West wind' was merely 'wind'.

It was evident that the researches of Chiang Ch'ing and her supporters
in the Army would take some time. In the meantime, however, the
campaign for the reform of literature and the arts made little headway.
Most Party statements on the subject were usually qualified[29] and
traditional Peking operas continued to be played.

The Sino-Soviet Dispute — Open Polemics

At the Tenth Plenum in September 1962, Mao clearly associated the
domestic class struggle with the struggle against 'revisionism'. Predictably, therefore, the first stage of the Socialist Education Movement
and the first stage of the campaign in literature and the arts coincided
with an increasingly open polemic between China and the Soviet Union.
If the point of no return had not been reached before, it had certainly
been reached by mid-1963.

On 22 October, two days after the outbreak of the hostilities between China and India, President Kennedy announced that the Cuban
missile crisis had begun.[30] As Gittings points out, there is no evidence
that China sought to take advantage of Soviet and American distrac-
tions, since no one surely could have predicted the events in Cuba and
such an explanation avoids any consideration of the state of India's
'forward policy'.[31] Although *Pravda* cautiously endorsed the Chinese
proposal to negotiate with India on 25 October during the height of
the Cuban crisis, the Soviet Union soon swung back to its so-called
'neutral' attitude. Khruschev's 'neutrality' allegedly included an
apology to Nehru for supporting China's bid for negotiations[32] and a
continued supply of arms to India. China, for her part, had supported
the Soviet Union in the Cuban crisis, also significantly on 25 October,

but once the Soviet Union backed down under American threats, the Chinese began to analyse the Cuban situation and found the Soviet Union guilty of 'capitulationism' for withdrawing the missiles under threat.[33] The Chinese were particularly indignant at what they considered 'a betrayal of proletarian internationalism' during the Indian war and were probably particularly incensed that, having supported Soviet actions which they considered adventurist in Cuba for the sake of that internationalism, the Soviet Union should now actively aid China's enemy. Anyway, now that the Soviet Union could be seen to be guilty of bad faith, there was no point in masking Chinese disquiet concerning the whole Cuban adventure. The Soviet view of the Cuban crisis, however, was that in obtaining a guarantee from the United States not to invade Cuba, they had scored a victory and the Chinese tough line, if implemented, would have threatened world peace.[34]

In the winter of 1962-3, a whole series of Communist Party congresses were held in Bulgaria, Hungary, Italy, Czechoslovakia and East Germany which saw the continuation of the polemic and during this period *People's Daily*, on 15 December, openly criticised the behaviour of anti-Chinese delegates to the congresses.[35] Such was the beginning of a furious open polemic which reached a climax in March 1963. By that time, a number of Communist parties, anxious to bring about a compromise, proposed an international conference which both the Soviet Union and China accepted. On 30 March, a Soviet letter spelt out questions of principle to be discussed[36] and in May agreement was reached to hold bilateral talks on 5 July. On 17 June, the Chinese published a reply to the Soviet letter of 30 March,[37] setting out what they considered a suitable agenda, but this was taken by the Soviet Party to be a breach of the agreement to suspend polemics. The Soviet government, in response, demanded the recall of three Chinese diplomats from Moscow. On 5 July, the bilateral talks opened in a very strained atmosphere and by 13 July the publication of open polemics was resumed. Following the opening of the test ban treaty talks in mid-July, Sino-Soviet negotiations ceased.

As the Chinese saw it, the partial test ban treaty between the Soviet Union, Britain and the United States, signed on 25 July, was the ultimate sell-out. The Soviet Union had given up the idea of complete disarmament and a total ban on nuclear weapons in favour of a partial treaty which banned tests in the atmosphere. Such a treaty froze the nuclear *status quo* since, with the current state of technology, any country that had begun to manufacture nuclear weapons would be obliged initially to test them in the atmosphere, particularly since it was much cheaper. Most aspiring nuclear powers could therefore not sign the treaty, for those that did would be unable to produce nuclear weapons at all. In the meantime, both the super-powers could go on increasing their stockpiles. To the Chinese, the test ban treaty was a supreme example of great power collusion and China could only propose a total and universal ban on the production, stockpiling, testing and use of all nuclear weapons.[38] In the meantime, China's own nuclear weapons programme would continue and China fully intended to test in the atmosphere once she was ready. Few people foresaw in July 1963 that she would be ready in only 15 months.

'Liuist' Internationalism

The open publication of the Sino-Soviet polemics in the first half of 1963 led to a Chinese reappraisal of the structure as well as the orientation of the International Communist Movement. It has never, to my knowledge, been satisfactorily demonstrated that there were significant differences among the Chinese leadership on this question, though Jim Peck has suggested possible divergencies that deserve mention.[39] Mao, was a dialectician, was concerned primarily with orientations and the direction of change, whereas Liu Shao-ch'i was primarily an organisation man. It is probable, therefore, that Mao's and the Party radicals' view of the world in the early 1960s was one of a global United Front constantly shifting in composition while Liu's and the Party conservatives' view was one of tightly organised blocs. With the disintegration of the 'socialist camp', the radicals strove to unite with whoever could be united with to oppose the principal enemy — United States imperialism — whereas the conservatives seemed committed to the creation of a new and separate International Communist Movement.[40]

Within international organisations during this period, the Chinese delegates made much of United States-Soviet collusion and the Soviet Union attempted to capitalise on China's denunciation of the partial test ban treaty. Sino-Soviet clashes occurred within the World Peace Council, the World Federation of Trade Unions, and the Afro-Asian Peoples' Solidarity Organisation.[41] Amongst Communist parties, the issue of Soviet 'revisionism' was hotly debated and a number of new Marxist-Leninist parties were formed with enthusiastic Chinese support. In the next two years, such parties appeared in Belgium, Ceylon, Australia, Colombia, India, Lebanon, Nepal and Paraguay. In Brazil, an 'anti-revisionist' party had been set up as early as February 1962 and was now supported by the Chinese. In 1963-4 a number of established Communist parties also took a firm line against Soviet 'revisionism', among them those of New Zealand, Japan, Indonesia, Malaya, Thailand and Burma. Other parties took a more moderately critical line, among them those of the Democratic Republic of Vietnam and the Democratic People's Republic of Korea.[42] In subsequent years, the International Communist Movement was to experience further splits and realignments but it was fairly clear by 1964 that the movement was irreconcilably split into two. Indeed it was the philosophical principle that 'one divides into two' that provided the rationale.[43]

The Socialist Education Movement: Stage Two — September 1963 — September 1964

Although one cannot be at all sure as to whether 'revised Soviet internationalism' in foreign policy represented a conservative or a radical position, we can say with some certainty that, in the autumn of 1963, domestic policy towards the Socialist Education Movement moved towards the right, and an attempt was made to halt the process of radicalisation. In September, the Party centre attempted to satisfy the need for more specific instructions on the Socialist Education Movement by the publication of a set of directives known as 'Some Concrete Policy Formulations . . . in the Socialist Education Movement'.[44] The ostensible aim of these directives, commonly referred to as the 'Later Ten Points', was to clarify a number of general issues enunciated in the 'Early Ten Points'. In fact the 'Later Ten Points', which were said to have been issued under the general direction of Party general secretary Teng Hsiao-p'ing,[45] in 'clarifying' certain issues, actually negated the spirit of the earlier document and so constituted a subtle victory for the Party conservatives. Instead of 'struggle' (which was now confined to a very limited number of people), the later document preferred to speak of 'appropriate criticism'. Contradictions were to be seen as 'among the people' and 'non-antagonistic'. People were not to be branded as 'rightists'. 'Prosperous middle peasants' were not to be considered 'rich peasants'; more important still, the work-teams were to control the peasant associations and were not to disrupt existing organisations in the countryside. The 'Later Ten Points', which are riddled with contradictions, give one the overall impression that the new organisations created in the countryside were not to become vehicles for horizontal mobilisation but were to be ancillary 'staff' in a rigid vertical staff-line system of command which would carry out a disciplined movement from the top down. Such was the opposite of Mao's original intention. The detailed class analysis in the document, far from clarifying how to analyse class elements in the countryside, confused the situation and must have left cadres unsure of exactly what were the movement's targets.

Attempts were now made to ensure that leadership from above was strengthened by demanding that cadres 'squat on the spot' (*dundian*) in specific areas. On the surface, the demand that cadres spend more time in the countryside would seem to be a radical move yet one might also interpret the requirement to 'squat on the spot' as a desire to prevent any unruly actions by peasant activists. Cadres were now not to wander aimlessly about convening meetings here and there and occasionally participating in manual labour, but were to stay in one area and thoroughly understand the situation.[46] Such a policy would only be effective if the cadres were sufficiently oriented to radical policies according to the Yenan model. If they just sought a quiet life, there could be no more effective way of preventing peasants criticising them.

Faced with what looked like a conservative attack, the radicals launched a movement in February 1964 to 'Learn from the People's Liberation Army'[47] which led, in the spring, to the establishment of a system of political departments in various branches of the economy based on that of the PLA.[48] As the movement unfolded, meetings were held having particular relevance for the Socialist Education Movement. Units were encouraged to 'compare' themselves with advanced units, in particular in the Army, 'study' these units, 'catch up' with them and 'help' the less advanced (*bi xue gan bang*).[49] Large numbers of people were transferred permanently or temporarily out of the PLA to work in urban and rural economic units and militia training was given much greater stress. Army cadres transferred to help militia units now began to propagate more radical policies in the Socialist Education Movement in a spirit much more thoroughgoing than that of the 'Later Ten Points'. These cadres could easily call upon lecturers from the PLA to come down and give reports,[50] thus bypassing the regular administrative network. In this situation, it was only a matter of time before some work-teams came into conflict with newly radicalised Poor and Lower Middle Peasant Associations, which under Army inspiration gradually acquired a life of their own.

Even in the somewhat more radical atmosphere of 1964, however, most of the policy directives put out by the Party from Peking were markedly conservative. However much the Army pushed *political* emulation, the Party conservatives still pushed *economic* emulation. Industry all over the country was still urged to emulate Shanghai,[51] the most industrially advanced and yet the most bourgeois city in the country, and smaller towns were urged to emulate industrial achievements in the larger towns.[52] With greatly improved harvests after 1962, the Party conservatives were proud of the economic achievements obtained during their period of ascendancy since the Great Leap and wished to avoid any disruption. Significantly a much publicised pamphlet by T'ao Chu concerning people's communes, written in 1964, made no mention of the role of the Army precisely at a time when the whole country was being urged to study its experiences.[53]

During the Socialist Education Movement, meetings were held to recall the past and peasants compiled their 'three histories' (personal, family and village) so as more easily to compare the present with the past.[54] Peasant associations were strengthened and cadres conducted lessons in 'class education'. In this atmosphere, a central work conference and Politburo Standing Committee conference met in June 1964 to discuss progress in the Socialist Education Movement. During this conference, Mao Tse-tung, regaining the initiative, laid down six criteria for evaluating the Socialist Education Movement. The first of these was the degree to which poor and lower middle peasants had been truly mobilised.[55] They could surely not have been mobilised according to the 'Later Ten Points' but, by then, this document seems to have been brushed aside. Mao further went on to demand that when rich peasants, counter-revolutionaries and bad elements who engaged in destructive activities were discovered, they should be 'struggled against' by the masses rather than dealt with by higher authorities.

The June conference finally formulated an 18-point document entitled 'Organisational Rules for Poor and Lower Middle Peasant Associations'[56] but here the hand of Mao is not to be seen. Peasant associations were still circumscribed by the leadership of local Party committees. The tone, however, was somewhat less cautious, in that cadres were strictly warned not to 'strike retaliatory blows' against peasants who criticised them. In short, it seemed that Party conservatives were failing to keep the lid on a movement which looked like achieving the aim of the old Hundred Flowers Movement of 1956-7 to rectify the Party from without. Unlike the Hundred Flowers, however, it was not to be intellectuals who were to do the rectifying but poor and lower middle peasants.

The Intensified Campaign in Literature and the Arts

The significance of the Hundred Flowers Movement was made quite explicit by Mao at a meeting of the All China Federation of Literary and

Art Circles in June 1964 when he declared that unless Chinese intellectuals remoulded themselves they would, at some future date, become groups like the Hungarian Petöfi Club.[57] Mao was profoundly pessimistic about the lack of advance made in literature and art since 1949 and was particularly worried about the recent return to old 'feudal' themes. He commented:

> Problems abound in all forms of art . . . and the people involved are numerous; in many departments very little has been achieved so far in socialist transformation. The 'dead' still predominate in many departments . . . Isn't it absurd that many communists are enthusiastic about promoting feudal and capitalist art, but not socialist art?[58]

The June Party central work conference approved Mao's demand to rectify the field of literature and art and in the second half of 1964 the movement was to be vigorously promoted within the Federation of Literary and Art Circles. The question was, however, who was to do the promoting? After Mao had complained about literature and art in December 1963, Liu Shao-ch'i, Teng Hsiao-p'ing, P'eng Chen and Chou Yang had discussed the question and in January had declared that they would promote socialist art.[59] As of June 1964, however, classical theatre still flourished and nothing much seems to have been done. In this situation, Mao came to rely more upon the efforts of Chiang Ch'ing, her Army colleagues and the Shanghai radicals such as Yao Wen-yüan who had assisted her in denouncing *Stories About Not Fearing Ghosts*.[60]

Chiang Ch'ing's initial attempts to get the First Peking Opera Company to produce Peking operas with modern themes came to nothing. Apparently, her first attempt to get produced a piece, which subsequently became the opera *Shachiapang*, was rebuffed by the opera company who insisted on producing time-honoured classical pieces.[61] After the initial failure, however, Chiang Ch'ing was to have more success with modern ideas during and after a national festival of Peking opera on revolutionary themes in the summer of 1964.

Formal responsibility for the rectification movement in the field of literature and art which began in mid-1964, however, was not entrusted to Chiang Ch'ing but to P'eng Chen. One might wonder why the immediate superior of Wu Han, Teng T'o and Liao Mo-sha should have been chosen for such a task.[62] One might posit a number of explanations. First, and in my opinion most unlikely, it is possible that the Party radicals thought that P'eng might 'see the error of his ways' once he was put in the position of rectifying his subordinates. Secondly, P'eng could have been an appointee of the Party conservatives who were attempting to blunt the edge of the movement in literature and art in the same way as they had attempted to blunt the edge of the Socialist Education Movement with the publication of the 'Later Ten Points'. Thirdly, it is possible that Mao had observed P'eng's unwillingness to do anything after his call in December 1963 and had realised that, once a mass movement could be launched from below, P'eng would attempt to crush it and so expose himself. As to which, if any, of these explanations is correct we can only guess.

Closely allied with the movement for the reform in literature and the arts was an attempt to inject fresh radical blood into the propaganda network.[63] Teng T'o, Wu Han and Liao Mo-sha had quite easily found outlets for their writing in the Peking press and indeed at one time T'eng T'o had been the editor-in-chief of *People's Daily*. With the radicalisation of 1964, it was claimed later that attempts were made in the Peking press to check the dissemination of Mao Tse-tung Thought.[64] The fresh blood to be injected into the press was to come from the People's Liberation Army though it is my impression that the injection was initially rather unsuccessful, at least judging from the way certain newspapers remained highly cautious in the early days of the subsequent Cultural Revolution.

The Campaign to Cultivate Revolutionary Successors[65]

It was not, however, only the older intellectuals who worried Mao and the Party radicals. In different conversations with foreign visitors in 1964-5, Mao remarked time and again that the youth of today lacked real experience in class struggle and were becoming soft.[66] He felt that the youth should participate in a much more radical version of the Socialist Education Movement and actively prevent the rural revolution from slipping backward. The Communist Youth League seemed to be degenerating into a corps where youth were apprenticed to become members of an élite,[67] and clearly it was not only the Party that should be rectified from the outside.

As Mao saw it, the current education system, far from doing anything to rectify the situation, was geared to creating a technocracy[68] devoid of sufficient political consciousness. Mao was to tell Edgar Snow in early 1965 that it was possible that today's youth might:

make peace with Imperialism, bring the remnants of the Chiang K'ai-shek clique back to the mainland, and take a stand beside the small percentage of counter-revolutionaries still in the country[69]

Mao's view of current teaching practices was equally stringent:

> The present method of education ruins talent and ruins youth. I do
> not approve of reading so many books. The method of examination
> is a method for dealing with the enemy, it is most harmful, and
> should be stopped.[70]

Mao's answer, however, did not lie in educational reform from above.
Youth must be actively mobilised to reform their own educational
system even if it meant overthrowing the academic authorities. What
was required was to extend the Socialist Education Movement into the
sphere of formal education. For the time being, however, P'eng Chen
did not seem to be the kind of man who could take a lead in that process.

The Campaign in Philosophy

The first major explosion to take place in the field of education
occurred in the summer of 1964 and centred on the issue of 'two combining into one'. In May, a rather obscure article appeared in
Guangming Daily to the effect that such was the universal law of
materialist dialectics and the notion of 'one dividing into two' was
merely an analytical method used by Marxists in analysing society and
nature.[71] As I suggested earlier, the debate hinged upon the whole
question of handling social contradictions. What the *Guangming* article
seemed to be advocating was a class conciliationist position, which
echoed that of Khruschev and the, as yet un-named, Party conservatives
within China. The philosophical polemics were to rage unabated for
three months and occasioned a forum held by the Higher Party School
on the issue. The final result was to be the dismissal of the head of the
Higher Party School, Yang Hsien-chen, who was charged with provoking
the debate with ulterior motives.[72]

In retrospect, the debate in philosophy appears extremely significant.
It was probably too early at this stage to attack Wu Han's and Teng
T'o's treatment of history for having ulterior motives but it was
possible to attack Yang Hsien-chen for covertly adopting a class conciliationist line under the guise of academic debate, if indeed that was
what he was doing. The Yang Hsien-chen debate was to set a precedent
that was to become increasingly important in the subsequent Cultural
Revolution. In the meantime, however, opportunists such as Chou

Yang had 'tested the wind' and had become most vocal in their application of the principle of 'one divides into two'.

On Khruschev's Phoney Communism and its Historical Lessons for the World

In examining the various cycles of radicalism and consolidation in contemporary China since 1942, we have seen that the early period of
radicalism involves a whole series of discrete movements proceeding
side by side and the subsequent period of more thoroughgoing radicalism brings all the movements together. The point at which movements merge can usually be clearly identified – the onset of the Civil
War, the Three Anti Movement, Mao's 1955 collectivisation speech, the
Third Plenum of 1957 and the Lushan Plenum. In this sixth cycle the
point was reached, in my opinion, in mid-1964 with the publication of
the document 'On Khruschev's Phoney Communism and its Historical
Lessons for the World'.[73]

'On Khruschev's Phoney Communism . . .', published on 14 July,
was in fact, the ninth comment on an open letter of the Central
Committee of the CPSU. Allegedly written under Mao's guidance,[74] it
represented the culminating point of the Sino-Soviet polemics begun in
December 1962. But its significance went far beyond the question of
peace, war and relations with the United States and represented a
distillation of all the criticisms of 'revisionism' made both internationally and domestically in the preceding years. Even more important,
it put forward an action programme reaffirming the major principles of
the Great Leap Forward in all respects except the economic.

As its major theme, 'On Khruschev's Phoney Communism . . .',
took the Khruschevian notion of a 'state of the whole people' and a
'Party of the whole people' and compared them with the Marxist-
Leninist notions of 'dictatorship of the proletariat' and 'vanguard
Party'. It noted that, in the Soviet Union, capitalist vestiges still existed
and had existed in Stalin's day (even though he did not see them). The
fundamental difference, however, between Stalin and Khruschev was
that, though Stalin did not make the correct class analysis, he did in
fact adhere to the Leninist principle of dictatorship of the proletariat,
whereas Khruschev not only knew that capitalist vestiges still existed,
but actually profited by them and sought their preservation. More
important, there was developing in the Soviet Union a *new* stratum of
'capitalists' who were committed to a policy of material incentives, the
profit motive and high salary differentials. The document went on to
give many examples of corrupt practice in the Soviet Union, taken from

the Soviet press, and noted that these had been made possible by the
active connivance of the Soviet leadership. Since the state was, in
Marxist terms, an instrument whereby one class exercised power over
other classes, a 'state of the whole people' could only be the instrument
of this privileged stratum and not the proletariat. In class terms the
privileged stratum could only be defined as *bourgeois*. Under such
circumstances, the Soviet state, far from withering away, was becoming
stronger. It was precisely this privileged stratum representing a capitalist
class that controlled the Soviet Party. The Soviet Party, therefore, in
being designated as a 'Party of the whole people' was in fact becoming a
bourgeois Party. As for the declaration in Khruschev's new Party programme that the Soviet Union was building 'communism' which would
be attained within 20 years, this was an 'economist' fantasy, for
communism was surely much more than the provision of a 'plate of
goulash'! As 'On Khruschev's Phoney Communism . . .' remarked,
British Prime Minister Sir Alec Douglas-Home saw the real essence of
this 'communism':

> Mr Khruschev said that the Russian brand of communism puts
> education and goulash first. That is good; goulash communism is
> better than war communism, and I am glad to have this confirmation
> of our view that fat and comfortable Communists are better than
> lean and hungry Communists.[75]

Sir Alec, the last British Prime Minister to have been 'produced' (and
not elected) by the oligarchs of the British Conservative Party, had
evidently found a fellow.

In case anyone should have any illusions that 'On Khruschev's
Phoney Communism . . .' was merely a discussion of the Soviet Union,
the document went on to explain Mao Tse-tung's 15-point programme
to prevent the same sort of thing happening in China. The theme of
Mao Tse-tung's speech 'On the Correct Handling . . .' was reaffirmed.
Class struggle in socialist society was stressed with the warning that
socialism was not simply a matter of transforming the economy and
communism could not be reached until a very long period of struggle
had been experienced. During this period, the principle of dictatorship
of the proletariat should be maintained with an emphasis on 'democratic centralism' within the ranks of the 'people'. The Mass Line, mass
movements, great debates, the 'Hundred Flowers and Hundred Schools'
should be given full play. In the Socialist Education Movement, reliance
should be placed on the poor and lower middle peasants and cadres

should participate in manual labour. The socialist economy should be expanded upon a broad scale and wide salary differentials should be narrowed. The people's commune was hailed as an appropriate organisational form for effecting the transformation from collective ownership to 'ownership by the whole people'. The idea of 'everyone a soldier', anti-careerism in the Army, officers serving in the ranks and Party and mass supervision of the PLA and public security organs was reaffirmed. The necessity to train 'revolutionary successors' who were both 'red' and 'expert' and to develop a socialist culture were matters of prime importance. In foreign policy, cadres were warned to avoid 'great power chauvinism' and 'national egotism' (such as characterised the Soviet Union) and to replace them by genuine 'proletarian internationalism'. Finally, and perhaps most important, cadres were enjoined to watch out for hidden conspirators who sought to reverse this (the Great Leap Forward) programme.

We cannot say whether Mao had anyone in mind when he put forward this final warning though he claimed later it was around this time that he found Liu Shao-ch'i quite incorrigible,[76] and it is perhaps significant that one of the main epithets applied to Liu in the subsequent Cultural Revolution was 'China's Khruschev'. In Mao's and the Party radicals' view, the 15-point programme outlined in 'On Khruschev's Phoney Communism . . .' was absolutely indispensable if China was not to 'change its colour'. As a matter of principle, Mao had reaffirmed that a revolution could move backward. His speech 'On the Correct Handling . . .' had been perhaps the first formulation of a dialectical theory of progress under socialism. 'On Khruschev's Phoney Communism . . .' was an intermediate stage between that and the Cultural Revolution formulation of 'continuous revolution'. It embraced all the major themes of the movements that had been begun after the Tenth Plenum in 1962 and signified a new period of more thoroughgoing radicalism in this, the sixth cycle since 1942.

The Socialist Education Movement: Stage Three — September–December 1964

In the late summer and autumn of 1964, events came thick and fast. In July, the Chinese had spelt out the relevance of the Sino-Soviet polemic for domestic politics. Soon, the Tonkin Gulf incident provided ample proof that the United States was as predatory as ever and, as the Vietnam war escalated, the relationship between international tension and Chinese domestic politics began once again to resemble 1958. By mid-October, Khruschev had been forced out of office and the Chinese leadership began hastily to reassess the new situation. At almost the same time, China conducted her first nuclear test, signalling to the world that her foreign policy was now to be completely independent. It was to be in this rapidly changing environment that the Socialist Education Movement radicalised.

In September 1964, the conservative 'Later Ten Points', now defunct, was replaced with another document known as the 'Revised Later Ten Points'.[77] Here the Socialist Education Movement was seen not as a moderate rectification movement but as something which required long and bitter struggle and might perhaps last five or six years or even longer. The document warned against superficiality and called for the re-registration of Party members. For the first time since land reform in the early 1950s, a general reclassification in the Chinese countryside was to be undertaken and particular attention was to be devoted to those cadres who had degenerated into becoming class enemies and who had committed 'four uncleans'.[78] The 'Later Ten Points' had warned against excesses and, although this point was taken up again, a far more serious deviation was now seen to be excessive leniency. The 'Revised Later Ten Points' laid particular stress on mass mobilisation to criticise errant cadres at whatever level.

> Experience . . . has revealed that cadres in basic level organisations who have committed serious mistakes are usually connected with certain cadres of higher level organisations . . . and are instigated, supported and protected by them. In such cases we must go to the origin and get hold of the responsible persons. No matter to what level the cadres belong, or what positions they hold . . . they should be subjected to open criticism before the people . . .[79]

In the light of the above, one would be tempted to conclude that the 'Revised Later Ten Points' was a radical document which heralded the new stage in the Socialist Education Movement. In the Cultural Revolution, however, the 'Revised Later Ten Points' was denounced as a conservative document written by Liu Shao-ch'i[80] and designed to redirect the focus of struggle away from senior Party cadres 'taking the capitalist road' and towards cadres at the very basic level.

In any case, whatever the 'Revised Later Ten Points' was really designed to do, there can be no doubt that the autumn of 1964 saw a strengthening of the Poor and Lower Middle Peasant Associations. One way of effecting this was to expand the militia organisation in accordance with Mao's renewed call for 'everyone to be a soldier'. At a time of

growing tension in South-east Asia, militia expansion was felt to be particularly necessary.[81] As militia-backed peasant associations swung into
action, those who were found to be guilty of 'unclean practices' were
denounced, fined or dismissed from office.[82] The movement in the
latter part of the year was no longer confined to key points but became
general. The techniques of 'struggle' will by now be very familiar. At
first 'struggle' was directed against obvious targets such as counter-
revolutionaries and unregenerate landlords but gradually extended to
include most cadres. As in land reform, there was often initial reluctance to 'struggle' as peasants feared retaliation once work-teams left,
but soon the power of the peasant associations was such that critics
might be protected. The Poor and Lower Middle Peasant Associations
were further strengthened by the extension of their organisation above
brigade level to the communes and even higher.[83] It would appear that
such strengthening was necessary once cadres began to hit back and
utilise their organisational position to quell criticism and the *People's
Daily* constantly warned against retaliation. In the subsequent Cultural
Revolution I have heard it said that, during this period, cadre retaliation
sometimes took the form of using work-teams to stifle criticism and
work-teams and peasant associations sometimes came to blows, though
I have seen no documentary verification of this. Whatever the case,
'struggle' was now the order of the day.

One of the major criticisms during the more radical period of the
Socialist Education Movement of late 1964 was that cadres had permitted or even encouraged the earlier 'spontaneous development of
capitalism'.[84] There was now pressure for the restriction of free
markets in the countryside in the spirit of the Great Leap.[85] By
December, Mao Tse-tung was once again using the term Great Leap
Forward to describe future policy:

> We cannot follow the old paths of technical development of every
> country in the world, and crawl step by step behind the others. We
> must smash conventions, do our utmost to adopt advanced tech-
> niques and within not too long a period of history, build our
> country up into a powerful modern socialist state. When we talk of a
> Great Leap Forward, we mean just this. Are we boasting or shooting
> off our mouths? Certainly not. It can be done.[86]

The last Socialist Education Movement had been the harbinger of
the Great Leap of 1958-9. Was the movement in 1965 to see its
revival?

Resistance to Radicalisation

The second half of 1964 saw the merging of a whole series of movements which aimed at a revival of the spirit of the Great Leap. The
intensified Socialist Education Movement in the countryside expanded
into a new Five Anti Movement in the cities (about which little has
been written in the West). The campaign in literature and the arts had
merged with the movement to Learn from the People's Liberation
Army and a campaign to Cultivate Revolutionary Successors was in full
swing in all areas. There was, however, quite considerable resistance to
each of these movements.

We have seen that the more radical documents of the Socialist Education Movement were sometimes qualified out of all recognition by
operational instructions; and sometimes the implementation of these
operational instructions was even more conservative. In many areas, the
machinery created to implement the Socialist Education Movement was
slowed down and pressure was diverted to relatively unimportant
targets.

Resistance was perhaps nowhere more marked than in the field of
propaganda and education. It was the Propaganda Department of the
Party Central Committee, together with its Peking municipal counterpart, that had launched much of the criticism of the Great Leap in the
so-called 'blooming and contending' period of 1961-2. In the subsequent more radical period, propaganda organs still seemed unprepared
to have any confidence in mass consciousness and mass enthusiasm.[87]
The Movement to Cultivate Revolutionary Successors was consequently
far less thoroughgoing than Mao would have liked. In 1964, considerable stress was laid once again on the 'part-work part-study' principle
in education and the selection of people from worker, peasant and
soldier backgrounds for enrolment in tertiary institutions.[88] It is evident, however, that the 'two track' system of education still made the
'part-work part-study' schools poor cousins of the more traditional
·school system[89] and students with better academic records from hardly
proletarian backgrounds were still enrolled in universities in substantial
numbers.

The Learn from the People's Liberation Army Campaign likewise
was greeted with much fanfare and, with the establishment of political
work departments, PLA cadres became more frequently engaged in
what was formerly considered exclusively civilian Party work. Nevertheless, the fact that the political work departments found it difficult to
extend their network down beyond the central level might be taken to
reflect resistance on the part of civilian cadres[90] and the inability of

outside organisations to crack the very strong established Party structure. I pointed out earlier that the radical view of the Party was that, as
far as may be possible, the Party should be characterised by *orientation*
rather than formal *structure*. In Schurmann's terms the cement which
held the Party together should be *ideological* rather than *organisational*.
By the early 1960s, however, it was very clearly the opposite and the
Party was beginning to fuse with the state. Such a situation is clearly
revealed in the changes in the locus of decision-making at the highest
levels. In the more radical periods of the mid-1950s, key decisions were
frequently taken either by *ad hoc* bodies or joint meetings of provincial
Party personnel and the Politburo. It was felt, presumably, that the
Mass Line would be more effective if regional Party secretaries, with
greater contact with what was going on in local areas, took part in the
formulation of decisions. In the early 1960s, however, such *ad hoc*
meetings or indeed Central Committee plenary sessions were few and
far between (there was no plenum between 1962 and 1966). Decisions
were now taken at central work conferences which may have included
outsiders but which were characterised by the domination and control
of the increasingly powerful Party Secretariat headed by Teng
Hsiao-p'ing and influenced by the arch organisation-man, Liu
Shao-ch'i.[91] In such a situation, it is not surprising that radical measures
designed to cut through bureaucratic channels should have been distorted.

An equally important reason why the radical policies after mid-1964
were not as effective as they might have been was that, in general, the
principle of 'inner-Party democracy' had broken down.[92] In the mid-
1950s, people who opposed Party policy such as Ch'en Yün could quite
happily remain at their posts provided they reserved their opinions after
a decision had been finally taken and provided they did not seek institutional support in organisations outside the Party or functionally
specific sections of the Party. The significance of the Kao Kang and
P'eng Teh-huai cases lay precisely in that they did not fulfil these latter
conditions. By the early 1960s, however, with the crystallisation of the
'two lines', it was virtually impossible for anyone to formulate any
decision without violating those conditions and, as a result, plenary
sessions of the Party Central Committee just did not meet; the bureaucracy just chugged along, distorting any decision that might threaten its
routine. Very soon, Mao was to come to the conclusion that the only
answer to such a problem was to smash the Party *structure* from without and reinforce its *orientation* during the process of rebuilding.

Ambiquity in the Economy

It was not only in government administration that the effects of the Socialist Education Movement were mixed. In the economy also, radical policies coexisted with legacies of the former conservative period.

The new radical climate after 1962 seems to have prevented any of the Liberman-type proposals advanced at that time being put into practice. It is probable, however, that the issue of the profit motive was effectively squashed even before the new period of radicalism began. The 'Seventy Articles on Industry' was, as far as we know, a very cautious, conservative document in that it paid very little attention to political work in industrial enterprises but it did stress the priority of output targets over profit targets.[93] An out-and-out 'revisionist' policy, from the point of view of the Chinese radicals, would have been to allow enterprises to produce directly for the market and judge their performance according to the profit they made in that arena. Such was the policy attempted in the Soviet Union in 1965. In China, however, there seems to be no evidence that this kind of policy was ever introduced.[94]

Another conservative policy, put forward in 1962, was the reversal of the priority given by Mao Tse-tung to collectivisation over mechanisation. In that year, Liu Shao-ch'i is said to have advocated a policy of selective mechanisation based on tractor stations separate from the people's communes. Liu is reported to have selected some 100-130 *xian* in which full mechanisation was to be introduced. The initiative here would be taken by tractor stations which would work for a profit. The profits generated during this first stage of mechanisation would be used to provide mechanisation for a similar batch of *xian* after ten years.[95] As Jack Gray points out, since there were some 2,000 *xian* in China, this road to mechanisation would have taken an extraordinary long period of time. It was opposed not only to Mao's economic policy but, in fact, to Mao's entire programme for rural social change.[96] Again, this conservative policy does not appear to have been carried out during the radical Socialist Education Movement, although Liu is reported to have advanced his ideas several times during the years after 1962.

In 1963, Liu was said to have extended his ideas for rural mechanisation by advocating the establishment of an agricultural machinery trust[97] and later other trusts covering other sectors of the economy. We must distinguish here between horizontally integrated local trusts which were set up in ever-increasing numbers in China even during the radical

period of the middle 1950s (often known as 'joint-enterprises')[98] and
the vertically integrated trusts advocated by Liu. Liu's trusts were in
fact to be state corporations with monopoly control of the manufacture and distribution of certain products. They were to operate auto-
nomously, free from ministerial control and also free from the influence of local Party and government organisation.[99] Such organisations
were not only to be subject to vertical rule (thus negating the dual-rule
policies advocated by the radicals) but were profit-making concerns
that might quite easily grow into 'independent kingdoms'. Liu
Shao-ch'i's trusts only seem to have been effective at provincial
level,[100] but it is significant that the Socialist Education Movement
even allowed them to get that far.

Another feature of economic policy which perhaps caused some concern to the radicals centred on the question of employment and wages.
During the period 1957-63, average industrial wages fell by 0.8 per
cent,[101] which was encouraging from the point of view of those who
wished to close the urban-rural gap. In 1963, however, a mild wage
reform was carried out which raised industrial wages somewhat but the
effects were not very significant. In general, the average industrial wage
remained almost static[102] during the period 1957-63, which was a
remarkable achievement in countering inflation.

To look at average wages, however, may perhaps give on a somewhat
distorted picture since the first half of the 1960s saw an enormous
growth in the number of temporary contract workers recruited from
the rural areas. In 1958, there were about 12 million such workers,
whereas in the early 1960s this figure increased to some 30-40 per cent
of the total non-agricultural work force.[103] One might argue that the
employment of this cheap labour actually served to close the urban-
rural gap but it also created sharp *intra-urban* differentials which were
potentially very divisive. Furthermore, an excessive reliance on temporary labour unassimilated into any communal-type organisation was a
violation of radical policies.

Though wage reform and the growth of temporary labour were
hardly radical victories, there were some areas of economic administration during the Socialist Education Movement which radicals initially
must have found quite encouraging. Though vertical rule in industry was
much stronger than hitherto, workers and staff congresses were
revamped[104] and, in some enterprises, experiments were undertaken
whereby factory general managers were elected.[105] Although 'one man
management' was occasionally revived, experiments were undertaken in
1964 to introduce a non-bureaucratic functional system of management

that accorded well with the old Yenan principle of 'centralised policy and divided operations'.[106] Although, occasionally, Party committees and senior management were in fact the same people, the principle of 'responsibility of the factory general manager under the enterprise Party committee' was retained and, as Andors has pointed out, the Great Leap Forward legacy could never be completely negated.[107]

A second source of encouragement lay in the remarkable success with which China's petroleum industry had developed since the Great Leap Forward. The radicals were particularly proud of the Tach'ing oil-field in north-east China, named after the 'great celebration' of the tenth anniversary of the founding of the Chinese People's Republic and thus signifying the spirit of the Great Leap. It was held to be a model of self-reliance and improvisation and a triumph of the human spirit over the pessimism of technologists. Before 1949, Western sur-veys had shown China to be very poor in oil. She was soon to become self-sufficient in this vital energy source. Tach'ing became the symbol of that self-sufficiency, and its heroes, such as the famous 'Iron Man' Wang Chin-hsi, symbols of the right combination of 'red' and 'expert'.[108] Before long, the oilfield was also to become a model of social organisation as many of the features of the old urban commune were recreated.[109] Mao Tse-tung was most insistent in his call for industry to 'learn from Tach'ing'.[110]

The agricultural counterpart of Tach'ing was the Tachai production brigade in the poor loess lands of Shansi. Before liberation, there had only been some 800 *mu* of land in Tachai scattered over seven gullies, eight ridges and one mountain slope with a per *mu* yield of only 140 *jin*. Most of the output went to one landlord and three rich peasants. Of the village's 64 households, 48 were in the category of poor and lower middle peasant, many of whose members had to work outside the village and some of whom had been reduced to begging. After land reform, a fierce struggle had occurred between those who saw little chance of improvement without considerable state aid and those who believed that co-operativisation could be undertaken before mechanisa-tion. At one stage in the early 1950s, two mutual aid teams had existed embodying these different approaches to modernisation, though finally the radical team under the leadership of Party secretary Ch'en Yung-kuei was victorious and set about organising a co-op. The early life of the Tachai co-op was very precarious since a conservative local government had little confidence in its chances of success in such a climatically hazardous region. When the co-op wanted to expand beyond the limits set by the *xian* authorities, Ch'en Yung-kuei was

forced to keep two sets of accounts, one showing the production of a
co-op of 41 households, and one showing the production for a co-op
of 30 households as prescribed by the *xian*. By the early 1960s, yields
in Tachai had begun to surpass the average for the Yellow River region
but, in the autumn of 1963, there occurred the worst floods for a century and some brigade members again began to think of asking for state
aid. Resisting this demand, Ch'en Yung-kuei persuaded the brigade
members to adhere to the principle of self-reliance and to repair the
broken stone walls which held up the terraces. By 1964, Tachai's
harvest was a spectacular 620,000 *jin* with a yield of 826 *jin/mu*.[111]

Not only was Tachai held out as a model for 'self-reliance' (according
to the spirit of the Great Leap), it was also designated a model for the
'living application of Mao Tse-tung Thought'. A practical example of
what this meant lay in the reform of the work-point system. The old
system of designating a number of points for each job of work was
abolished and a new system introduced whereby each peasant said
what he thought his work deserved and the other members of his
team discussed and amended his appraisal. As a consequence, the
average number of workdays per person went up from 260 in 1963 to
280 in 1964. Thus, an attempt had been made to get away from the old
idea of piecework and to move nearer to the payment ideals of the
Great Leap. True, this was not payment according to 'need' such as
was advocated in some areas during the Great Leap. It was still the
'socialist' principle of payment according to work, but it reintroduced
the idea of labour attitude and consciousness and, as such, was said to
have contributed much to work enthusiasm.[112] Tachai was a remarkable model and was in no way a fiction. Visiting Tachai in the summer
of 1966 after another, though much less serious downpour of heavy
rain, I was impressed by the way very bit of land had been preserved
behind stout stone walls, and how, after the rains of that year, they
were being rapidly repaired. Tachai was an example of what could be
done relatively quickly and cheaply in many other regions.

Economic policy, therefore, was ambiguous. Revisionist policies
were still voiced though rarely implemented. At the same time, the
radicals put forward impressive models though one was not always
sure how to establish them on the ground. What probably preoccupied
rural cadres were simply petty instances of capitalism and the continued distortion of radical policies. They were never quite sure
whether the targets of their criticism ought to be their fellows or senior
people in authority.

The Socialist Education Movement: Stage Four — Bogged Down

In his report on the work of the government to the Third National People's Congress in late December 1964, Chou En-lai redefined the 'four clean-ups' as 'politics, economics, ideology and organisation'[113] (the so-called 'big four clean-ups'), rather than the earlier narrower concentration on things like accounts, granaries, properties and work-points. He implied that the movement was to be much broader in scope and should not confine itself to petty misdemeanours. Chou's theme was taken up by the *People's Daily* in the new year in its suggestion that the movement should also deal with *antagonistic* contradictions[114] and, on 18 January, the same theme was reiterated in a new policy document.

This document, 'Some Problems Currently Arising in the Course of the Rural Socialist Education Movement' (commonly known as 'The Twenty-Three Articles'),[115] was said to have been written by Mao himself. At the level of *policy* the document made the extremely radical demand that the Socialist Education Movement focus its attention on 'persons in authority taking the capitalist road' at all levels up to and including the Central Committee itself. At an *operational* level, however, the Twenty-Three Articles suggested merely that peasants combine with basic-level cadres and work-teams in a 'triple alliance' reminiscent of that organisational form that characterised the immediate post-Liberation period. In the villages the stress was now on patient persuasion.

In my opinion, the Twenty-Three Articles were intended to radicalise the Socialist Education Movement.[116] The central work conference, which adopted them, criticised Liu Shao-ch'i's handling of the movement[117] and inaugurated a programme of rectifying *xian* Party leadership.[118] At the same time, a campaign to study Mao Tse-tung Thought was launched to strengthen the educational component of the movement. Despite the radical intentions, however, what was to happen in 1965 was a general deradicalisation. Once the focus of attention shifted away from basic-level cadres to 'top persons in authority taking the capitalist road', the movement in the villages was blunted and, though 'spontaneous capitalist tendencies' were still criticised, it was with less vigour than before. It is possible that the radicals intended to open a new stage of mass mobilisation once 'top persons in authority taking the capitalist road' had been designated. In early 1965, however, the Party machine, dominated by conservatives, appeared too strong to allow its senior members to come under criticism.

Consolidation

By the spring of 1965, a new period of consolidation had been inaugurated. Though the Socialist Education Movement wound down over two or three months, a decision to deradicalise seems to have been taken quite abruptly. This was the only major deradicalisation decision the effects of which I personally experienced. Teaching at that time in Peking, I found quite suddenly that my teaching time was cut by a third and extensive discussions were held on combining work with leisure. Not only were work schedules cut but also the amount of time people spent attending political meetings.

I am still not certain how the decision to deradicalise was taken and exactly why it came about in 1965. I feel that the major reasons were internal and linked to the situation of stalemate in the Socialist Education Movement and the relative lack of success in reforming literature and the arts, though alternative explanations have been put forward which focus on the international situation.[119] In February 1965 the United States commenced large-scale bombing of the Democratic Republic of Vietnam and there was a fear that the war might escalate into China. It is possible that a conservative response to this threat was to call a halt to any radical programmes under way before mass initiative made it inevitable that any movement should run its course. It is equally possible that the radicals saw the threat of war as an even more urgent reason why the masses should be mobilised and the spirit of Yenan invoked once again. I shall return to the strategic debate of 1965 shortly. In the meantime, we must note a major consequence of deradicalisation.

In 1965, the Campaign to Cultivate Revolutionary Successors was dealt a heavy blow by a change in the policies of the Communist Youth League. In 1964, the League secretary, Hu Yao-pang, admitted that 'bad and degenerate elements had wormed their way into the League'.[120] Many of its leaders were clearly above the upper age limit for the League and new, younger leaders were not coming forward. In the radical period of 1964, an attempt had been made to impart new vigour to the League in the Campaign to Cultivate Revolutionary Successors but, in 1965, policy was reversed and a massive recruitment drive launched. In that one year, 8 million new members were taken into the League, (a jump of nearly 25 per cent) and many of these new recruits were from dubious class backgrounds.[121] Radicals, who had condemned Khruschev's 'Party of the whole people', could not but look askance at an organisation which was rapidly turning itself into an élite training corps. As concessions were made to petty capitalism in the

Chinese countryside and some of the reforms undertaken in industry proved ineffective in the summer and autumn of 1965, it seemed that the only hope for radical reform lay in mobilising the youth – but clearly not through the bureaucratised Communist Youth League. New organisations had to be established.

The Consequences of 'Revised Soviet Internationalism'

The adoption by the Chinese, in early 1963, of what Peck has called 'revised Soviet internationalism' convinced Khruschev that China had to be expelled from the International Communist Movement. But due to the efforts of the Rumanian and other Communist parties, Khruschev's two attempts at collective mobilisation to oppose China in October 1963 and the late summer of 1964 came to nothing, and it is possible that his fall in October 1964 was not unconnected with his handling of the International Communist Movement.[122]

In political style, the new Soviet leadership could not have been more different from Khruschev. Khruschev had been an irascible, unpredictable adventurer. From the radical perspective, he was clearly a 'revisionist', but at least he was concerned primarily with Marxist-Leninist theory (however distorted his interpretation) and it is probably for this reason that the Chinese coined the term 'Khruschevism'. They were not to honour any of his successors with the title 'ism' for they seemed dull grey pragmatists, committed to the same goals as Khruschev but perhaps not so worthy of the really eloquent invective that had been produced in the polemic of 1963-4.

The new Soviet pragmatists believed that, although there was not much that could be done on a party-to-party basis since they affirmed Khruschev's position from the Twentieth to the Twenty-Second Congresses, it might be worth while calling an international conference and attempting to improve state-to-state relations. Following the demise of Khruschev, the polemics ceased for a while and Chou En-lai led a high-powered delegation to Moscow in November 1964.[123] Neither side held out much hope for its success. The Soviet position on most of the contentious issues was adamant and the Chinese press continued to print Albanian and other criticisms of the Soviet Union.[124] On 21 November, a major *Red Flag* editorial entitled 'Why Khruschev Fell' attributed his demise to a 'revisionist' general line[125] and all that both sides felt able to do was to agree that a preparatory meeting for an international conference be held in Moscow in March 1965. The March meeting was to be 'a gloomy and forlorn affair'.[126] It affirmed the principle of holding an international conference but did not say when and called for united action on Vietnam but did not say what. While the March meeting was in session, clashes occurred between Chinese demonstrators and Soviet police outside the United States Embassy in Moscow[127] and, in this deteriorating atmosphere, open polemics were resumed.

Following the meeting in March 1965, one of the major bones of contention between China and the Soviet Union concerned the question of aid to Vietnam and exactly how unity of action might be achieved.[128] The Chinese rejected Soviet moves to use Chinese air bases to ship material to Vietnam. They did, however, allow the shipment of supplies by rail through Chinese territory although the Soviet Union accused the Chinese of causing delays.[129] The Chinese, for their part, were suspicious of earlier Soviet initiatives to limit the fighting in Vietnam by concluding a deal over the heads of the Vietnamese.[130]

Another major bone of contention, in the spring of 1965, concerned the convocation of a second Afro-Asian conference to mark the tenth anniversary of the Bandung conference of 1955. On an extended tour of Africa and Asia in 1963-4, Chou En-lai had lobbied actively for its convocation[131] and, in April 1964, a preparatory meeting in Jakarta fixed its date as March 1965. The importance of the conference lay in the fact that it might provide a forum for a Third World front against the United States and might give support to the more revolutionary movements in Africa and Asia. As the Chinese saw it, Africa in particular was 'ripe for revolution' and this had been demonstrated in the abortive Congo war of 1964. The conference, however, foundered on the issue of Soviet participation. It was first postponed until June 1965 to be held in Algiers and then, following the Algerian coup of 19 June 1965, postponed again. It was never held.[132]

The Algerian coup and the abandonment of the second Bandung conference was only one of a whole series of events in 1965 that spelt failure for the policy of 'revised Soviet internationalism'. Not only did the new Marxist-Leninist parties remain small but attempts to mobilise the Third World to resist United States domination and Soviet blandishments were in the main unsuccessful. Nkrumah of Ghana was overthrown while on a trip to China, the Indo-Pakistan war left India far closer to the Soviet Union than ever before and, perhaps most important of all, the Indonesian coup not only rendered Sukarno powerless but led to the massacre of the second largest Communist party in Asia and China's most consistent supporter. The time had come to rethink foreign policy.

The Strategic Debate of 1965

To understand the evolution of the Lin Piao position in foreign affairs, some attention must be given to the strategic position in 1965. Though I doubt that the major reason for the deradicalisation in the spring of 1965 was a response to events in Vietnam, it is impossible to deny that China's leaders, whether radical or conservative, looked with grave concern at events beyond China's southern frontier. It has been argued that, following the bombing of North Vietnam in February, a furious strategic debate occurred in China which was ultimately to see the demise of PLA Chief of Staff Lo Jui-ch'ing and the assertion of Lin Piao's version of Mao Tse-tung's concept of People's War. Different commentators have described the debate in different ways. Donald Zagoria, for example, has pointed to three tendencies amongst the Chinese leadership – the 'doves' (who favoured peace at any price), the 'hawks' (who pressed for a hard line and reliance on the Soviet Union if necessary) and the 'dawks' (who were prepared for war if it came but who believed that a national liberation war had to be waged by the country invaded and China should not be actively involved in Vietnam unless the war escalated).[133] Others have rejected this ornithological fantasia and have even denied that there is evidence for any strategic debate at all.

The argument that I find the most convincing, even though it is based on very shaky evidence, has been provided by Michael Yahuda and is summarised here.[134] In May 1965, China saw a massive American build-up in Vietnam and the bombing of targets very near the Chinese frontier. Faced with this situation, Chief of Staff Lo Jui-ch'ing wrote an essay in May 1965[135] commemorating the twentieth anniversary of victory in Europe in which he implied that the United States could be deterred by a United Front (with the Soviet Union). If invaded, the tactics China should employ were those used by the Soviet Red Army in defeating Hitler. The stress should not be on guerrilla-type engagements luring the enemy in deep but a kind of mobile war based on a defensive line within Chinese territory. In Yahuda's view, Lo thus revealed a kind of positional mentality out of keeping with Mao's notion of People's War, an undue confidence in the Soviet Union and far too excessive a stress on modern armaments as opposed to the human factor. It is possible that Yahuda has read too much into Lo's published speeches but what one can say with confidence is that, in the summer of 1965, Lo Jui-ch'ing's position in the Army was severely weakened at the same time as an exchange of notes between China and the Soviet Union revealed that no joint action on Vietnam was possible.

In late May, the radicalisation of the PLA, in which both Lin Piao and Lo Jui-ch'ing had been involved, was intensified with the abolition of ranks[136] and in August the veteran military commander Ho Lung warned against 'overlords' with heads 'stuffed full of foreign ideas'.[137] At the same time, P'eng Chen, in a speech in Indonesia, struck a new note revealing, it is claimed, the radical response to Lo's conservative position. P'eng took up a theme of Aidit, the Chairman of the Indonesian Communist Party that, in the current situation, 'the world's countryside was surrounding the world's cities',[138] which implied that Mao's theory of People's War could be generalised on a world scale in contrast to Lo's positional approach.

Significantly, in this changed situation, the speech commemorating the twentieth anniversary of victory over Japan was given not by Lo Jui-ch'ing but Lin Piao. This was his famous *Long Live the Victory of People's War*[139] which reaffirmed the idea of the world's cities being surrounded by the world's countryside and saw that the response to any American attack on China must be the same as the Eighth Route Army's response to Japanese attacks during the Second World War . . . not positional war but essentially a combination of guerrilla and mobile war, waged by armed forces with deep roots among the people. Such a war had been effective in the 1940s because the policy of the Party had been moderately radical. There could, therefore, be no strategic reason for continued deradicalisation. As such *Long Live the Victory of People's War* was one of the first shots in the Cultural Revolution.

I do not know how one would go about substantiating the above highly imaginative exercise in Kremlinology but even if it were only half true, it does explain the extraordinary importance given to Lin Piao's *Long Live the Victory of People's War* and the disappearance and subsequent criticism of Chief of Staff Lo Jui-ch'ing, who allegedly preferred military exercises to political work.[140] It also explains Mao's reported horror at a Japanese Communist Party question in 1966 as to whether joint action with the Soviet Union on Vietnam were possible.[141] Mao's point was fairly clear. Once you invite the Russians in, they come to stay. As things turned out, China and the United States came very close to war in late 1965 but they never had to put Lin Piao's essay to the test, at least in a military sense.

What is really significant about Lin Piao's *Long Live the Victory of People's War* was its effect on foreign policy. If China were attacked, Lin proposed very active measures to deal with an aggressor. If, however, China were not attacked, she would remain an isolated fortress waiting for the 'world's countryside' to complete its work. China was no longer seen as the centre of a revised Soviet International, but as a base area awaiting the outcome of national liberation struggles she could support morally but in which she could not intervene. Thus Lin had taken the theory of People's War, which applied very well to China internally, and had projected it on to the international arena where it became a recipe for *passivity*.[142]

The End of the Sixth Cycle

As 1965 drew to a close, radical and conservative policies still vied for supremacy. Although the Socialist Education Movement had lost some of its vigour, it still continued and, in their revised form, 'The big four clean-ups' were still implemented. By that time, the rural movement had taken the form of a rectification of *xian* level cadres and the many young PLA models that had been put forward since 1963 were now joined by a model *xian* Party secretary, Chiao Yü-lu. Whether the Party secretary Chiao Yü-lu, who died of hard work with a copy of Liu Shao-ch'i's book *On Self-Cultivation* under his pillow,[143] was a conservative answer to models of the Lei Feng type is somewhat debatable. Nonetheless, the stress laid on the movement does indicate the new importance attached to the rectification of middle-level cadres.

In 1965, the Socialist Education Movement had merged with the earlier Five Anti Movement in the cities and the Learn from the PLA Movement. As a result, urban economic departments were, like their national counterparts, frequently modelled on PLA political departments and even street committees sometimes employed political instructors (*zhengzhi jiadaoyuan*).[144] The plethora of parallel bodies attached to urban organs must have created organisational confusion. In addition to the formal office and its Party committee, there might also be a political department modelled on the PLA, a socialist education department and occasionally also a work-team.[145] Where these various bodies failed to co-ordinate their activities, it is perhaps understandable that the work-team might temporarily have taken over the administration[146] and thus have made the implementation of the Mass Line very difficult.

The above is a problem we have met time and again — the relationship between work-teams and mass organisations. In the Socialist Education Movement, the problem was perhaps more acute than at other times because the Party machine seemed bent on stopping the movement getting out of hand. It was eventually to fail but, in the period reviewed in this chapter, its successes accounted in large measure for the extraordinary ambiguities of both policy and operations. Nowhere were these ambiguities more obvious than in the economy. The idea of trusts and 'learn from Tachai' were pushed at the same time. The slogan 'learn from Tach'ing' was proposed at a time when the Anshan constitution was still very carefully buried under a mound of bureaucracy. Whilst Tachai had scrapped the work-point system, some industrial enterprises had reintroduced piecework. It was a very confusing situation.

By the autumn of 1965, the various campaigns to reform literature and the arts had met with limited success. Some modern Peking operas had been produced and a very fierce debate was in progress. Wu Han and Teng T'o were, however, still unmolested in their Peking offices and Chou Yang still had his hand very firmly on the controls. There was, as yet, no sign of the outpouring of mass creative work that had characterised the Great Leap.

Within the Army, the reforms of Lin Piao had borne fruit, and the PLA appeared as one of the most radical forces in society. It had helped propel forward both the Socialist Education Movement and the movement for literary reform and, with the transfer of cadres after 1964, had come to provide a lot of new personnel for economic administration too. And yet if Lo Jui-ch'ing took the position attributed to him, there were clearly a number of people in senior positions of command who were not at all happy about the reiteration of the theory of People's War.

In the field of foreign policy, the attempt to 'revise Soviet internationalism' was not a success and many Third World countries had lurched rather rapidly to the right. The Vietnam situation was very dangerous and the Soviet Union was now definitely unreliable in the event of American attack. Though China had had some initial successes in what was called 'the second intermediate zone' (notably France),[147] the end of 1965 saw China searching for a new interpretation of the balance of world forces along the lines of Lin Piao's Long Live the Victory of People's War.

Both from a conservative and a radical point of view, however, the situation in 1965 was much brighter than it had been in 1962. China was free of debt.[148] Grain production was approaching 1958 levels[149] and industry had recovered from the crisis of 1960-62.[150] Vast new energy sources had been brought into production and any Leap Forward in future[151] would surely be able to build on the very firm base of intermediate technology that had been one of the enduring features of the Great Leap of 1958-9. If China were to experience a new Great Leap, however, it would never be the same as that of 1958-9.

Many lessons had been learned by both radicals and conservatives. They had, however, learned *different* lessons as was to be quite apparent in the struggle to come.

It was perhaps *Long Live the Victory of People's War* that signalled the end of the sixth cycle, though formally what was later to be known as the Great Proletarian Cultural Revolution was the outcome of a central work conference held in September-October 1965. The time had come for a showdown, and Mao Tse-tung issued a call to criticise Wu Han and bourgeois reactionary thinking in the Party.[152] A new period of radicalism had begun.

Notes

1. Mao Tse-tung 24 September 1962, in Schram 1974, p. 188.
2. Ibid., pp. 188-96.
3. Ibid., p. 193.
4. *SCMM* 651, 22 April 1969, p. 39.
5. Mao Tse-tung 24 September 1962, in Schram 1974, p. 194.
6. Ibid., p. 195.
7. Chen and Ridley 1969, summarised in Baum and Teiwes 1969, p. 12.
8. Price 1973, p. 7. Gardner 1971, p. 247.
9. Baum and Teiwes 1969, p. 63.
10. Chen and Ridley 1969, pp. 140-8, and *passim*.
11. Ibid., p. 151.
12. *RMRB*, 11 January 1963, p. 1.
13. Vogel 1971, p. 302.
14. Ibid. Kao Hsiang, *SCMP* 2939, 15 March 1963, pp. 1-9.
15. Vogel 1971, pp. 303-4.
16. Chen Kuang-sheng 1968.
17. *SCMP* 2947, 27 March 1963, pp. 7-8.
18. The English edition of this is Mao Tse-tung 1966.
19. See Chapter 9.
20. Mao Tse-tung 6 November 1938, *SW*, Vol. II, p. 224.
21. Baum and Teiwes 1968, pp. 63-4.
22. Text in ibid., pp. 58-71.
23. Ibid., pp. 16-17.
24. Ibid., p. 18.
25. *PR* 22, 31 May 1963, p. 8.
26. *SCMP* 3686, 28 April 1966, p. 2.
27. Ho Ch'i-fang, *PR* 10, 10 March 1961, pp. 6-10.
28. See Solomon 1971, p. 414.
29. Vogel 1971, pp. 309-10.
30. For China's response to the Cuban crisis, see *PR* 44, 2 November 1962, pp. 3-7.
31. See Gittings 1968, p. 174. For a full treatment of India's forward policy, see Maxwell 1972, pp. 179-273.
32. Dallin 1963, p. 660.
33. Ibid., pp. 656-9.
34. Suslov, quoted in Gittings 1968, pp. 176-8.

35. *PFLP* 1962, *Workers of All Countries* . . .
36. Gittings 1968, p. 185.
37. Text in *PFLP* 1965, *The Polemic* . . ., pp. 1-54.
38. *PR* 31, 2 August 1963, p. 8.
39. Peck 1972.
40. See in particular p. 293.
41. Gittings 1968, pp. 193-5.
42. Ibid., pp. 200-1.
43. Chou Yang, *PR* 1, 3 January 1964.
44. Text in Baum and Teiwes 1968, pp. 72-94.
45. Baum 1969, p. 94.
46. Baum and Teiwes 1968, p. 23.
47. *SCMP* 3164, 24 February 1964, pp. 1-8.
48. *SCMP* 3200, 16 April 1964, pp. 3-7.
49. Vogel 1971, p. 310. *SCMP* 3179, 16 March 1964, pp. 1-5.
50. Vogel 1971, p. 316.
51. On the movement for 'comparing with, learning from and overtaking the advanced and helping the backward in industry' (*bi xue gan bang*), see *CB* 731, 11 May 1964.
52. Vogel 1971, p. 312.
53. T'ao Chu 1964. Moody 1973 (pp. 284-5) describes this pamphlet as 'left in form and right in essence'.
54. Hu Yao-pang, in *PR* 28, 10 July 1964, p. 15.
55. Mao Tse-tung June 1964, in Baum and Teiwes 1968, p. 27.
56. Text in Baum and Teiwes 1968, pp. 95-101.
57. Mao Tse-tung June 1964, in *CB* 891, 8 October 1969, p. 41.
58. Mao Tse-tung December 1963, in *CB* 891, 8 October 1969, p. 41.
59. Esmein 1973, p. 49.
60. Solomon 1971, p. 450.
61. The opera 'Spark in the Reed Field' was a Shanghai opera. It was allegedly called off one day before the opening night on the orders of P'eng Chen, *SCMM* 639, 6 January 1969, pp. 15 and 23.
62. See the discussion in Bridgham 1967, p. 12. Dittmer (1974, p. 70) argues the alternative thesis that there was no *necessary* connection between Wu Han's actions and P'eng's defence of them.
63. Ibid., p. 13.
64. *SCMP* 4253, 9 September 1968, p. 25.
65. See Mao Tse-tung 16 June 1964, in *JPRS* 61269-2, 20 February 1974, pp. 356-60.
66. Snow 1965, p. 21.
67. Gardner 1971, pp. 276-86. See also Funnell 1970.
68. See Mao Tse-tung 13 February 1964, in *JPRS* 61269-2, 20 February 1974, pp. 329-30.
69. Snow 1965, p. 23.
70. Mao Tse-tung 13 February 1964, in Schram 1974, p. 205.
71. Ai Heng-wu and Lin Ch'ing-shan, *CB* 745, 2 December 1964, pp. 1-5. (particularly p. 3).
72. A post-Cultural Revolution Chinese account of the debate may be found in *PFLP* 1973, *Three Major Struggles* . . . See also *PR* 37, 11 September 1964, pp. 9-12. For an early Western account, see Munro 1965.
73. Text in *PFLP* 1965, *The Polemic* . . ., pp. 417-80.
74. Johnson 1969, p. 24.
75. *PFLP* 1965, *The Polemic* . . ., p. 466.
76. According to Edgar Snow, it was not until a meeting of the Party leadership

on 25 January 1965 that Mao finally decided that Liu had to go. Snow, 10 April 1971, p. 19. Dittmer (1974, p. 59) argues that this may have been an *ex post facto* rationalisation.

77. Text in Baum and Teiwes 1968, pp. 102-17.
78. Just as there were 2 sets of targets for the 4 clean-ups: (1) accounts, granaries, properties and work points, and (2) politics, economics, ideology and organisation, so one might assume there were 2 sets of 4 uncleans. The reference here is almost certainly to the final set.
79. Baum and Teiwes 1968, p. 115.
80. *PR* 49, 1 December 1967, p. 17.
81. Mao Tse-tung 16 June 1964, in *JPRS* 61269-2, 20 February 1974, pp. 356-7.
82. Baum and Teiwes 1968, p. 33.
83. Vogel 1971, p. 318.
84. Ibid., p. 317. Baum and Teiwes 1968, p. 33.
85. Baum and Teiwes 1968, p. 33.
86. Mao Tse-tung December 1964, in Schram 1974, p. 231.
87. Neuhauser 1967, p. 22.
88. Ibid., p. 23.
89. See the collection of articles in *CB* 868, 31 December 1968. Also Bastid 1970, p. 20. Gardner 1971, pp. 247-50.
90. Neuhauser 1967, p. 25.
91. Chang 1970, p. 177.
92. Dittmer 1973, p. 720.
93. Perkins 1968, p. 607. The 70 Articles were reproduced from memory. No copy exists to my knowledge outside China.
94. Ibid.
95. Gray 1973, p. 144.
96. Ibid. For Mao's views on agricultural mechanisation, see Mao Tse-tung 12 March 1966, in *JPRS* 61269-2, 20 February 1974, pp. 373-4.
97. *SCMM* 644, 10 February 1969, pp. 35-8.
98. Schurmann 1966, p. 300.
99. Gray 1973, p. 145.
100. *SCMM* 644, 10 February 1969, pp. 35-8. Liu and T'an Chen-lin did set up the 'China Tractor and Internal Combustion Engine Industrial Corporation', with branch companies in 7 areas though it is uncertain how effective the corporation was (ibid., p. 28). According to *Nongye Jixie Jishu*, its activities were 'checked in time' by Mao and 'boycotted by the masses'.
101. Howe 1973, p. 237.
102. Ibid.
103. Ibid., p. 235.
104. *SCMP* 2604, 24 October 1961, pp. 15-17.
105. Richman 1969, pp. 255-6.
106. Chang Ta-k'ai and Sung Chin-sheng, in *Renmin Shouce* 1965, pp. 564-6.
107. Andors 1974.
108. *PFLP* 1972, *Taching . . .*, pp. 5-8.
109. *PR* 53, 31 December 1971, pp. 6-9.
110. Mao Tse-tung 13 February 1964, in Schram 1964, p. 199.
111. Pien Hsi 1972.
112. Ibid., pp. 191-2.
113. Chou En-lai, *PR* 1, 1 February 1965, p. 13.
114. Implicit in the statement 'the principal contradiction in China today is the contradiction between socialism and capitalism', *PR* 2, 8 January 1965, p. 21.
115. Text in Baum and Teiwes 1968, pp. 118-26.

116. Baum and Teiwes argue that the Twenty-Three Articles were possibly intended to ameliorate class struggle in the countryside. ibid., p. 36.
117. *CB* 884, 18 July 1969, p. 24.
118. Baum and Teiwes 1968, pp. 95-6.
119. E.g. Bridgham 1967, pp. 14-15.
120. Hu Yao-pang, *PR* 28, 10 July 1964, p. 19.
121. Israel 1967, p. 3. Oksenberg 1966, p. 4. *SCMP* 3554, 8 October 1965, pp. 4-9.
122. Gittings 1968, pp. 212-17.
123. *PR* 46, 13 November 1964, p. 6.
124. E.g. *PR* 6, 5 February 1965, pp. 22-5.
125. *PR* 48, 27 November 1964, pp. 6-9.
126. *PR* 13, 26 March 1965, p. 7.
127. *PR* 11, 12 March 1965, p. 15.
128. See Gittings 1968, pp. 256-8.
129. *PR* 1, 1 January 1966, pp. 16-17.
130. Ch'en Yi, *PR* 33, 14 August 1964, pp. 8-9, and Gittings 1968, pp. 254-60.
131. Adie 1964.
132. Gittings 1968, pp. 247-8.
133. Zagoria 1968, p. 67.
134. Yahuda 1972.
135. Lo Jui-ch'ing, *PR* 20, 14 May 1965, pp. 7-15.
136. *PR* 22, 28 May 1965, p. 4.
137. Ho Lung, *PR* 32, 6 August 1965, pp. 8, 9.
138. P'eng Chen, *PR* 24, 11 June 1965, p. 11.
139. Lin Piao, *PR* 36, 3 September 1965, pp. 9-30.
140. *SCMM* 641, 20 January 1969, pp. 4-6.
141. Yahuda 1972, pp. 70-1.
142. Peck 1972, pp. 294-5.
143. *PR* 9, 25 February 1966, pp. 5-8.
144. White 1972, p. 342.
145. Ibid., p. 344.
146. Ibid., p. 345.
147. Erasmus 1964.
148. Li Cheng-jui, *PR* 1, 1 January 1966, p. 19.
149. Eckstein 1973, pp. 216-17.
150. Ibid., p. 224.
151. In early 1966 there was talk of a new Great Leap. See for example *SCMP* 3628, 1 February 1966, p. 8.
152. *PR* 21, 19 May 1967, p. 6.

7 THE CULTURAL REVOLUTION IS LAUNCHED
(September 1965—February 1967)

The seventh and eighth cycles, which will be discussed in the next two chapters, deal with the Cultural Revolution. The first of these began in September 1965, accelerated in August 1966 and deradicalised in February 1967. What was fought out were not just questions of culture (with a small or large 'c') but the whole relationship between ideas and socio-economic structure.[1] The radicals went beyond Stalin's view that class struggle under socialism should be explained in terms of the resistance of *former* exploiters, since this had led him to speak of the completion of proletarian dictatorship in much the same way as Khruschev spoke of a 'state of the whole people'.[2] In the words of Rossanda, the radicals attacked the survival of a capitalist mode of production not only 'as a vestige of the past but as an intrinsic form of the present'.[3] When they spoke of 'persons in authority taking the capitalist road', they referred to those who exacerbated inequalities 'based on material possession of the instruments of production (possession which is not *legal* but *managerial*)' and who reinforced 'the selling of one's labour power as the sole means of livelihood'.[4]

The radicals rejected, yet again, the technological determinism of the Soviet model. They felt that material changes only determined human relations in the broadest historical sense. As far as concrete developmental policy was concerned, equal attention should be paid to both the material and the human. They challenged, therefore, the Soviet view that accumulation might be achieved by rapid industrialisation at the expense of the countryside. Such a view, in exacerbating the urban-rural gap, made the disappearance of classes impossible. It led to an undialectical separation of technology from human relations and to the notion that technology was neutral. From this, Khruschev's notion of 'peaceful competition' with the West on their terms naturally followed.[5] A major priority, therefore, was to develop a new education system which integrated technology with social change.

The radicals of 1966 also rejected the notion of an excessively monolithic Party. They developed that process begun in 1957 whereby it was no longer taken as axiomatic that the Party should act *on behalf of* the proletariat. Once the Party ceased effectively to reconcile the contradictions between state and society and began to fuse with the state, it was seen as 'right to rebel' (*zaofan youli*).[6]

Cultural Revolution: Stage One – The P'eng Chen Period

The first stage of the Cultural Revolution was initiated by Mao Tse-tung at a central work conference which met from September to October 1965, during which he criticised Wu Han and called for a rectification movement in the Party.[7] Mao's initial strategy consisted of three components. First, expose the whole issue of Wu Han to the light of day so that people could make the association between reform in literature and the arts and the various policies associated with P'eng Teh-huai. Secondly, conduct a rectification movement in the Army so that the PLA could give moral support to the Cultural Revolution without the obstruction of military technocrats. Thirdly, support movements amongst students for educational reform so that they could see that the Youth League and the Party machine had departed from the revolutionary goals of Yenan. Each of these strategies had been initiated by November. On 10 November, under Mao's personal guidance, the Shanghai literary critic Yao Wen-yüan published an article entitled 'On the New Historical Play "Hai Jui Dismissed from Office" ', in which he bitterly attacked Wu Han.[8] On 18 November, Lin Piao issued a five-point directive to the PLA to rectify its style of work and, probably as early as September, Mao Tse-tung reportedly gave his support to a group of students at Peking University who were critical of the Chancellor, Lu P'ing.[9] Predictably, each of the three components in this strategy met with opposition.

The publication of Yao Wen-yüan's attack on Wu Han was undertaken, not by the Shanghai Party press but by the non-Party newspaper, *Wenhuibao*. An attack on the deputy mayor of Peking, and by extension on his superior the mayor P'eng Chen (the very man charged with rectifying the literary and art world) was regarded by the conservatives in charge of the Party machine as unforgivable. The immediate response of the Peking Municipal Party Committee was an urgent telephone call to the Shanghai Party Committee demanding the reasons for the publication of Yao Wen-yüan's article and expressing doubts about that committee's 'Party character'.[10] Not only would the Peking municipal press not reprint the article but the Central Committee newspaper *People's Daily* remained silent. On 29 November, however, the organ of the PLA – *Liberation Army Daily* – reprinted the article and thus ensured it a nationwide readership.[11] On the following day, *People's Daily* was finally forced to reprint Yao's criticism and it immediately became study material for cadres and people throughout the country.

In Mao's view, however, Yao Wen-yüan had still not gone far enough.

> Yao Wen-yüan's article ... is ... very good; it has had a great impact
> on theatrical, historical and philosophical circles. Its defect is that it
> did not hit the crux of the matter. The crux of *Hai Jui Dismissed
> from Office* was the question of dismissal from office. The Chia
> Ch'ing emperor dismissed Hai Jui from office. In 1959 we dismissed
> P'eng Teh-huai from office. And P'eng Teh-huai is Hai Jui too.[12]

Faced with the wide dissemination of Yao Wen-yüan's attack, the
Peking municipal authorities still endeavoured to shield themselves. On
12 December, Teng T'o wrote in *Peking Daily* that the question of Wu
Han was an 'internal contradiction' and that the deputy mayor was not
to be treated as an enemy and, on 27 December, the same paper published Wu Han's self-criticism in which the deputy mayor tried to head
off his critics.[13] When 'the group of five', appointed to look into the
question of Wu Han, met under the chairmanship of P'eng Chen in the
new year, its members were apparently divided on whether the P'eng
Teh-huai issue should be reactivated and it is said that the final report
of the group, which was produced in February 1966, was actively
opposed by one of the members, K'ang Sheng.[14] The so-called
'February Outline' was in many ways reminiscent of the Later Ten
Points and specified the implementation of the Cultural Revolution
in such a way that negated its very spirit.[15] According to the 'February
Outline', the main issue was not the radical policies of the Great Leap
Forward but the correct interpretation of history; in short was Hai Jui
progressive or not? One should not resolve the debate by discussing the
political viewpoint of individual writers such as Wu Han but by raising
the level of competence of China's historians; to this end, a series of
draft model articles was to be published.

The strategy of the conservatives here was exactly the same as their
attempts to confine the 'two combines into one' debate of 1964 to
academic discussion. It was, at first, moderately successful. Following
the acceptance of the 'February Outline' in the name of the Central
Committee (presumably by the Politburo Standing Committee chaired
by Liu Shao-ch'i in Mao's absence),[16] a campaign of criticism was
launched against historians who were felt to have interpreted history
wrongly.[17] Here we see another conservative strategy which was later
to become common. The attack was deflected from 'persons in
authority taking the capitalist road' to relatively harmless historians.
By March 1966 it seemed that, for the time being, P'eng Chen had held

his own and had prevented the Cultural Revolution developing into a mass movement. He could not, however, halt the furious debate that had been going on in the press since December and was soon to face much sterner opposition.

The second component of Mao's September strategy was to rectify the PLA. We know little about the movement in the Army following Lin Piao's Five Points of mid-November but we may surmise that Lo Jui-ch'ing came under very severe criticism and *Long Live the Victory of People's War* became required reading. It was probably opposition to this renewed radical line that led, in February 1966, to a spate of rumours concerning a possible military coup. It was later alleged that the Peking military authorities, encouraged by Lo Jui-ch'ing, strengthened the Peking garrison under the pretext of war preparations.[18] At a time when government offices were being moved out of Peking in preparation for a possible American attack,[19] it is more likely that what went on at that time were *genuine* war preparations. Though we do not know whether an actual coup was planned in February 1966, we do know that the events of February led to a renewed rectification movement in the Army and the formal dismissal of Lo Jui-ch'ing. After an unsuccessful attempt to commit suicide on 18 March,[20] Lo is reported to have been denounced on 13 April, finally stripped of office on 16 May and replaced by Yang Ch'eng-wu.[21]

By the spring of 1966, the Army appeared to have been firmly committed to a radical line and its press actively propagated the radical interpretation of the Cultural Revolution. The Army had also become extremely active in the field of literature and art. A meeting of the Military Commission on 30 March approved a document summarising the discussions of a Forum on Literary and Art Work in the Armed Forces, responsibility for which had been assigned by Lin Piao to Chiang Ch'ing.[22] Another dimension had been added to the campaign to Learn from the People's Liberation Army.

The third component of Mao's autumn strategy was educational reform. At the September meeting, Party general secretary Teng Hsiao-p'ing is said to have opposed any cultural reforms and changes in the schools but,[23] at the same time, Mao reportedly backed some of the more militant members of Peking University who were pressing for a less élitist approach to education. In a speech at Hangchow in December, Mao insisted on the urgency for educational reform:

> We should reform university education. So much time should not be spent attending classes. Not to reform arts faculties would be terrible.

If they are not reformed, can they produce philosophers? Can they produce writers? Can they produce historians? Today's philosophers can't turn out philosophy, writers can't write novels and historians can't produce history. All they want to write about is emperors, kings, generals and ministers.[24]

By March 1966, a 'Red Flag Militant Team' had been formed in a secondary school attached to Peking University,[25] in response to Mao's call, and pressure on Peking University Chancellor Lu P'ing mounted. Since Lu P'ing was a close associate of P'eng Chen and the Peking Municipal Party Committee, it was only a matter of time before the first and third components in Mao's strategy merged.

Cultural Revolution: Stage Two — The Collapse of the Peking Party Committee

By April 1966, it was apparent to many leaders of the Party that P'eng Chen's handling of the Cultural Revolution had resulted in no Cultural Revolution at all. Consequently a meeting of the Secretariat, attended also by Chou En-lai, K'ang Sheng and the influential radical editor of *Red Flag*, Ch'en Po-ta, on 9-12 April, resolved to appoint a new leading group. After K'ang Sheng had conveyed Mao's personal criticism of P'eng to the meeting, the 'February Outline' was repudiated and a resolution adopted to set up the new group to direct the reforms.[26] We are unfortunately unable to answer the crucial and intriguing question how it was that the change in orientation of the Cultural Revolution was brought about at a meeting of the highly bureaucratic Secretariat. Nor can we be certain exactly what the position of Liu Shao-ch'i might have been since he was abroad on a state visit to Burma. In fact, Liu returned just in time for the final stages of a Politburo Standing Committee meeting in Hangchow. This meeting (16-20 April) resolved to turn the criticism of P'eng Chen into 'struggle' and Mao Tse-tung endorsed seven documents repudiating P'eng's 'crimes'.[27]

In early April, events occurred thick and fast. The conservatives still attempted to deflect the focus of criticism by selecting obvious old 'bourgeois' targets according to the radical injunction to repudiate the 'four olds' (old thought, old ideas, old habits and old customs). The radicals, on the other hand, also stressed the importance of the rectification movement of Party secretaries at *xian* level and above (the final stage of the Socialist Education Movement), and attempted to keep the focus very clearly on the Party. As warnings of a Petöfi club again began to be heard,[28] the Army renewed its call for a nationwide movement to study Mao Tse-tung's works. The famous *May Seventh Directive* stipulated that the whole of the PLA should be a school (of Mao Tse-tung Thought),[29] with the obvious implication that such a 'school' would not be limited to the Army. Now the radicals saw the whole of society as a school and the formal school system was de-emphasised.

In the spring of 1966, most of the authoritative editorials on the Cultural Revolution were carried first in *Liberation Army Daily* and only later taken up by *People's Daily*. On 8 May, attacks were launched against the Peking municipal press[30] which had carried the original articles by Wu Han, Teng T'o and Liao Mo-sha. Two days later, Yao Wen-yüan published the first definitive attack on Teng T'o,[31] who probably still had connections with *People's Daily*. The following day, the radical Ch'i Pen-yü published a definitive attack on the Peking municipal press[32] and the stage was set for the public repudiation of P'eng Chen's Cultural Revolution line.

At an enlarged meeting of the Politburo Standing Committee in Hangchow on 16 May, at which P'eng Chen acknowledged his guilt,[33] another famous document was approved — the 'May Sixteenth Circular'.[34] The Secretariat's resolutions of April were ratified, the 'February Outline' was formally countermanded and the five-man group under P'eng Chen dissolved. To take its place, a new Cultural Revolution Group of 18 members was established. Though we are unclear as to the initial composition of the group, it soon came under the leadership of Ch'en Po-ta who, as well as being editor of *Red Flag*, had for long been Mao's political secretary. Other leaders included Mao's wife Chiang Ch'ing, the only radical in the old group of five- K'ang Sheng, and two Shanghai radicals Chang Ch'un-ch'iao and Yao Wen-yüan the now famous critic. As I have noted, the meeting of mid-May also approved the report of an investigation into the mistakes of Lo Jui-ch'ing, who was formally dismissed, and Lin Piao warned against the possibility of a counter-revolutionary coup.[35]

Although Lin Piao's warning indicated that, even then, the situation in the Army was not all it might have been, P'eng Chen's position had been completely undermined and the Peking Party committee could be reorganised. By the end of May, the student movement in Peking had acquired a momentum of its own. Around 21 May, a secondary school attached to Tsinghua University had organised the first student group to call itself 'Red Guards'[36] and on 25 May Nieh Yüan-tzu, a philosophy teacher at Peking University, put up a large character poster (*dazibao*) denouncing Lu P'ing and the Peking University leadership.[37] A week later, on 2 June, this poster, with Mao's support, was hailed by a now

radical *People's Daily* as a major contribution to the revolution.[38] On
1 June, the official designation of the Cultural Revolution was changed
from 'Great *Socialist* Cultural Revolution' to 'Great *Proletarian* Cultural
Revolution',[39] signifying a new radical spirit and it was quite clear that
the various articles published in the press denouncing 'persons in
authority taking the capitalist road' were a summons for others to make
similar criticism. Nieh Yüan-tzu's *dazibao* was to be a model. As the
Cultural Revolution switched into high gear, it was announced on 3
June that Li Hsüeh-feng had taken over from P'eng Chen[40] and the
Peking Party and Youth League Committees had been reorganised. Just
at this crucial moment, when the first thorough mass movement since
the Great Leap Forward looked like getting under way, control in
Peking passed to Liu Shao-ch'i.

Cultural Revolution: Stage Three — Liu Shao-ch'i's Fifty Days

Following the dismissal of P'eng Chen (although at this stage he was not
named) and the reorganisation of the Peking Municipal Party Committee, a wave of criticism engulfed the country. Initial criticisms centred
on the Peking Committee but soon widened to include almost anything
about which people had a grievance. On almost every wall, *dazibao*
appeared in profusion. There were often just too many to read and
people under attack knew that one of the surest ways of diluting
criticism was to attack all and sundry, so that criticism of their individual actions was lost in the storm. Just as P'eng Chen had diverted the
attacks upon him by criticising historians, so Party officials sought
scapegoats and unimportant targets to turn the spotlight away from
themselves.

In this early period of the Cultural Revolution, the main activists
were students and it is understandable, therefore, that some of the most
intense debates centred on education and examinations. The key question was, how was politics to be integrated more fully into university or
school life? What was the proper relationship between study and
manual labour? What part should students play in the administration of
their place of learning? To facilitate the debate, the State Council
announced, in mid-June that entrance examinations for tertiary institutions the following year would be postponed[41] and in many places,
all formal teaching stopped. At the same time, the Communist Youth
League was dissolved because of its association with the academic
establishment.[42] Now students were free to form their own groups to
discuss educational policy and what lessons could be learned in their
own university or school. They could discuss the charges that Peking

and other universities had been unduly élitist and had favoured the
children of the well-to-do. One should, of course, avoid the mistake
of thinking that Peking University (or for that matter any of the other
15 or so old élite universities) was typical of tertiary education.
Certainly, in the institute in which I taught, the class origin of most
students was very different from Peking University. None the less, there
was much that could be learned from the Peking experiences.

Although the main activists in the Cultural Revolution in June 1966
were students and teachers, it was quite clear that the injunction to
struggle against 'monsters and demons'[43] applied to all sectors of
society. Up to that time, the Socialist Education Movement in the
countryside had been concerned largely with the study of Mao Tse-tung
Thought and the rectification of *xian* level cadres begun in 1965. Now,
Poor and Lower Middle Peasant Associations were called upon to join
the great 'blooming and contending' and criticisms were voiced once
again of basic-level cadres in suburban villages. Many of these lower-
level cadres who had escaped the pre-1965 'small four clean-ups' and
those whose misdeeds had been neglected, as targets shifted upwards
in 1965, were now required to answer for their 'economism' and other
deviations.[44] The Socialist Education Movement and the Cultural
Revolution were beginning to merge.

While the 'blooming and contending' developed, the newly formed
Cultural Revolution Group does not appear to have been very active,
perhaps because it saw mass spontaneity needing little leadership, perhaps it wanted to see just how Liu Shao-ch'i would react or perhaps
because it did not know what to do. The group's activities seem to have
been confined to intensifying the press campaign against what were
referred to as the 'Black Gang'. In July, criticisms began to be voiced of
the 'literary tsar' Chou Yang[45] and, in the same month, T'ao Chu
replaced Lu Ting-i as head of the Party Central Committee's Propaganda Department.[46] In the universities, however, the conservative
party machine strove earnestly to establish control.

In early June, under Liu Shao-ch'i's guidance, decisions were taken
to send work-teams into schools and universities and an eight-point
directive was adopted.[47] It seemed evident that Liu, the organisation
man, was attempting to control the Cultural Revolution in exactly the
same way that the Party machine had attempted to control the Socialist
Education Movement. The work-teams consisted usually of middle rank
cadres often advised by some very senior Party cadre. At Tsinghua
University, for example, the senior cadre was none other than Wang
Kuang-mei, the wife of Liu Shao-ch'i.[48] Having seen just how work-teams

inhibited mass spontaneity in the Socialist Education Movement, Mao
cautioned against the hasty dispatch of these teams as early as the
Politburo Standing Committee meeting of 9 June.[49] None the less, the
work-teams went into action and, in many cases, succeeded in stifling
mass spontaneity. Just as student radicals began to link up with similar
groups of industrial workers, attempts were made by the teams to confine criticism to the universities and schools. 'Excesses' were denounced
and 'unruly' students detained.[50] Work-teams were said to have aided
those in authority in diverting the heat of criticism away from themselves, either by broadening its scope to include the absolutely trivial
or by focusing it upon targets that had little operational significance. It
was now all right to attack P'eng Chen or Chou Yang but not one's
own school principal or university chancellor. It was all right to
denounce the bombing of Hanoi and Haiphong, but not to criticise
local Party cadres.

It is my impression that the work-teams were remarkably successful
in dampening down the struggle in the universities and schools in June
and July 1966 and the Minister of Public Security, Hsieh Fu-chih, was
later to remark that the Cultural Revolution in Peking was almost
snuffed out.[51] There were some student groups, however, that would
not toe the conservative line, and they were sometimes helped by members of the Cultural Revolution Group. Chiang Ch'ing, for example,
actively supported groups at Tsinghua University in resisting the
pressure of the work-team sent down under the leadership of Wang
Kuang-mei.[52] Though proto-Red Guard groups were in existence before
the dispatch of the work-teams, it was in those colleges where student
groups struggled hardest against the work-teams that Red Guards
developed their strongest organisation. In a sense, the Red Guards were
the product of that struggle.

The struggles of June-July 1966 were very confusing. In many
students, obedience to local Party committees was ingrained. Others
were not quite sure just how far they should go in opposing the power
holders (dangquanpai). Still others were infuriated at the way work-
teams were defusing the struggle. Further confusion was caused by the
fact that every group and every work-team claimed allegiance to Mao,
and Mao's works (more particularly the 'little red book' now produced
by the million) were used to justify almost any position. And yet Mao
was silent! For a long period he had remained in the Yangtze region
watching events in Peking and elsewhere. Suddenly, on 16 July, he gave
a signal that heralded the end of Liu Shao-ch'i's 50 days' management
of the Cultural Revolution. Mao Tse-tung went for a marathon swim in

the Yangtze, thus signifying that he was not ill or infirm but ready to take a lead in the movement.[53] The next day he was back in Peking and ready to inaugurate the most radical phase of the Cultural Revolution yet.

Three days later, on 20 July, a central work conference was convened, this time with Mao Tse-tung in the chair.[54] He was determined the student movement should not be suppressed. In a speech to the conference, the following day, he demanded the total mobilisation of youth:

> I say to you all; youth is the great army of the Great Cultural Revolution! It must be mobilised to the full. After my return to Peking I felt very unhappy and desolate. Some colleges even had their gates shut. There were even some which suppressed the student movement. Who is it who suppressed the student movement? Only the Peiyang warlords. It is anti-Marxist for Communists to fear the student movement. Some people talk daily about the mass line and serving the people, but instead they follow the bourgeois line and serve the bourgeoisie. The Central Committee of the Youth League should stand on the side of the student movement. But instead it stands on the side of suppression of the student movement. Who opposes the great Cultural Revolution? The American imperialists, the Soviet revisionists and the reactionaries.[55]

The conference, which went on to the end of July, finally criticised the current handling of the Cultural Revolution and probably resolved to recall the work-teams.[56]

By early August, the atmosphere radicalised once again. The *May Seventh Directive* was reiterated[57] and Yang Ch'eng-wu confirmed as Acting Chief of Staff of the PLA.[58] Although it is difficult to gauge the significance of the delay of his confirmation since the formal dismissal of Lo Jui-ch'ing in May, it is my belief that the fact that a formal announcement could now be made signified that any trouble that may have occurred in the PLA, and to which Lin Piao had alluded in May, had now passed. In the new atmosphere, attacks shifted to the field of economics. A press campaign was launched, in early August, against the economist Sun Yeh-fang and other followers of Liberman-type market socialism[59] and it is not unreasonable to associate the campaign with the eclipse of Liu Shao-ch'i. By August, it was a completely different kind of revolution. However cultural the revolution had been before, it was now 'Cultural' in the widest sense.

The central work conference of late July was to pave the way for a far more significant meeting — the Eleventh Plenum of the Eighth Central Committee — the first plenum to be held since 1962. Its communiqué affirmed the radical policies adopted since the Tenth Plenum and thus disavowed those of Liu Shao-ch'i.[60] It adopted a Sixteen Point Programme for the Cultural Revolution[61] and confirmed Lin Piao as Party vice chairman — 'Mao Tse-tung's close comrade in arms'. The plenum took place in the enthusiastically radical atmosphere previously noted, in which not only were the press attacks on revisionism stepped up but Mao Tse-tung joined the Red Guards. In a letter to the Red Guards of Tsinghua University secondary school on 1 August, Mao remarked:

> Here I want to say that I myself as well as my revolutionary comrades in arms all take the same attitude. No matter where they are, in Peking or elsewhere in China, I will give enthusiastic support to all who take an attitude similar to yours in the Cultural Revolution movement.[62]

Mao had, however, some words of caution to offer and the Sixteen Points were not a recipe for unrestrained struggle. None the less, Mao supported mass action against the instruments of the Party machine. On 5 August, he even put up his own *dazibao*:

> China's first Marxist-Leninist big-character poster and Commentator's article on it in *People's Daily* are indeed superbly written. Comrades please read them again. But in the last fifty days or so some leading comrades from the central down to the local levels have acted in a diametrically opposite way. Adopting the reactionary stand of the bourgeoisie, they have enforced a bourgeois dictatorship and struck down the surging movement of the great cultural revolution of the proletariat. They have stood facts on their head and juggled black and white, encircled and suppressed revolutionaries, stifled opinions different from their own, imposed a white terror, and felt very pleased with themselves. They have puffed up the arrogance of the bourgeoisie and deflated the morale of the proletariat. How poisonous! Viewed in connection with the Right deviation of 1962 and the wrong tendency of 1964 which was 'Left' in form but 'Right' in essence, shouldn't this make one wide awake?[63]

Cultural Revolution: Stage Four — The Emergence of Red Guards and Red Rebels

The fourth stage of the Cultural Revolution, heralded by the events of early August, got under way at a mass rally on 18 August where Mao reviewed a large number of Red Guards in T'ien An Men Square in Peking and himself donned a red armband.[64] From then on, Red Guard actions spread rapidly outside the universities and large numbers of new Red Guard groups formed. The nuclei of such groups had already been in existence for some time in the form of Cultural Revolution study groups (formed after the dissolution of the Communist Youth League) or more militant groups formed to oppose the work-teams. All that was needed to galvanise them into action was the dispatch of Red Guards from Peking following the 18 August rally.[65] As the campaign against the 'four olds' achieved nationwide proportions, many different kinds of Red Guard groups formed, all with different action programmes. Opinions differed amongst groups as to what attitude to take to the former work-teams, to the leading personnel in various organisations, to the criteria for membership and to the priority between old intellectuals and specifically Party targets. The degree of Red Guard spontaneity was such that they could choose their targets at will and could organise themselves however they saw fit. In such a situation, factionalism was bound to occur, at least initially, and Party authorities, who sought to limit their activities, strove to keep targets confined either to the already discredited P'eng Chen 'Black Gang' or harmless 'bourgeois' targets outside the Party. When Red Guards busied themselves changing the names of streets and shops, Party bureaucrats who sought only to preserve their position were probably delighted, since they hoped that such actions would keep the heat off themselves.

One of the few things that all Red Guards seemed agreed upon was that the Youth League had been hopelessly bureaucratic and, on 20 August, its organs *China Youth News* and *Children's Daily* ceased publication.[66] Disagreements on how to evaluate Liu Shao-ch'i's 50 days, however, resulted in two separate Red Guard headquarters forming in Peking. One group felt that the conservative activity of the work-teams was merely an unfortunate episode in the Cultural Revolution which should now return to the criticism of the line of P'eng Chen, while the other felt that a profound analysis of the reasons why the work-teams had been sent in the first place should be undertaken.[67] In this situation, Party conservatives willingly lent their support to those who wished to confine the Cultural Revolution to the matters under discussion in June and thus prevent the movement escalating to a wholesale condemnation of Liu Shao-ch'i, Teng Hsiao-p'ing and the Party machine.

Perhaps the most important figure in this debate was the new head of the Party Central Committee's Propaganda Department, T'ao Chu. Following the overthrow of the Propaganda Department after the demise of Lu Ting-i and Chou Yang, T'ao Chu had acquired an extraordinary importance in the Cultural Revolution and, like P'eng Chen and Liu Shao-ch'i before him, he tried to keep it within bounds. Clearly he could no longer advocate the dispatch of work-teams but what he could do was to make use of 'liaison personnel' to limit the targets and attempt to direct Red Guard activities through 'Cultural Revolution committees'.[68] Provision for such committees had been made in that rather cautious charter of the Cultural Revolution known as the Sixteen Points and thus this revised work-team approach had the stamp of radical legitimacy. At the same time, T'ao himself, who was not sparing in his criticism of all and sundry,[69] acquired the appearance of a radical. In practice, however, we have seen that such a procedure only confused issues and the more targets there were the harder it was for anyone to reach conclusions about any of them.

Though it is probably true that T'ao Chu abetted the confusion that occurred in September 1966, it was probably the dynamic of the movement itself that constituted its primary cause. As early as the mass movements of the early 1950s, it had been anticipated that any mass movement would initially be characterised by confusion but that eventually water would flow along clearly defined channels.[70] In September 1966, however, such channels were very difficult to discern. Almost anyone in a position of authority came under criticism and, at the highest level, not only did posters appear criticising P'eng Chen and his group but also Liu Shao-ch'i, Teng Hsiao-p'ing[71] and even the new first secretary of the Peking Party Committee, Li Hsüeh-feng.[72] Not only did senior cadres in the Party attempt to channel criticism in certain directions but different Red Guard groups formed their own control organisation[73] to impart a sense of discipline, to limit targets and prevent the movement becoming too generalised.

At this point, some of the more radical students in Peking, notably from Tsinghua University and the Aeronautical Institute (in which Lin Piao had considerable influence), became tired of the rather sterile debate about the épisode of the work-teams and sought once and for all to concentrate criticism on Liu Shao-ch'i and Teng Hsiao-p'ing. Such was the origin of Peking's Third Red Guard Headquarters which received the enthusiastic support of Ch'en Po-ta and the Central Cultural

Revolution Group.[74] The process of splitting and realignment characteristic of Peking's Red Guards was duplicated in the provinces and
municipalities and further confusion was caused by the injunction that
Red Guards should travel round the country spreading revolutionary
experiences. It was perhaps necessary that free travel should be granted
to Red Guards, if the mass movement should truly be nationwide, but
this revolutionary exchange (*chuanlian*) led to certain problems. There
were severe logistic problems (Peking's population swelled by some 2
million, some provincial bus services were denuded of vehicles and the
rail service became overloaded).[75] Furthermore, much criticism became
uninformed and ineffective since the constant movement of people
prevented Red Guards in any particular locality having a detailed knowledge about the leadership in that area. On the other hand, 'revolutionary exchange' did lead to links being formed between university-based
Red Guards and factory-based Red Rebels.[76]

The factory-based rebel groups that began to form in August and
September 1966[77] were once again very disparate in aims. The more
radical amongst them demanded a greater say in management and protested that the labour unions had once again become 'economist' to the
detriment of political goals. In the early rallies, after 18 August, a few
worker groups had become quite active in support of Red Guard
activities[78] although, once organisations became formalised the
following month, more conservative groups formed with labour union
support to protect the privileged position of workers as opposed to
some other groups in society. These latter groups came increasingly
to oppose radical Red Guard activity. In early September, the press was
most insistent in its demand that the Cultural Revolution should not
interfere with production and many of the radical workers were persuaded to return to the factories,[79] not to emerge again until later in the
year. There is evidence, however, that ferment within the factories continued throughout October and was seen as being particularly significant. In Mao's view, university and school students could only initiate
the revolution. The orientation of the working class would decide its
fate.

The process of 'revolutionary exchange' led also to the forging of
links between Red Guard groups and rural Poor and Lower Middle
Peasant Associations. Although the cautious Sixteen Points still saw the
Cultural Revolution's main target[80] as cultural and educational units
and that of the Socialist Education Movement as communes and
factories, that document did point out the complementary nature of
the two movements. Care had to be taken, however, not to launch the

Cultural Revolution in villages and urban enterprises 'where original arrangements for the (Socialist Education) movement are appropriate and where the movement is going well'.[81] Such an injunction confused the nature of the two movements. Though peasant associations were much stronger than hitherto, work-teams still played an important part in the Socialist Education Movement whereas, in the Cultural Revolution, work-teams were by August the object of much vilification. It was thus still possible to control the Socialist Education Movement from above. Was it possible to exercise the same kind of control over the Cultural Revolution without it ceasing to be a mass movement proceeding according to its own momentum? I can only conclude that instructions concerning the Socialist Education Movement in the Sixteen Points were the result of a hasty compromise.

Not long after the beginning of 'revolutionary exchange', urban-based Red Guard units acted as the catalyst for the formation of groups of indigenous peasant Red Rebels which sought resolution of economic and other issues left over from the Socialist Education Movement.[82] Like their urban counterparts, peasant Red Rebels were subject to splits and, like the small rebel groups in the universities before July, came into conflict with the still active work-teams.[83] The rural work-teams were probably no different from those in the cities and responded characteristically by branding many rebels as 'counter-revolutionaries'.[84] As conflicts began to occur in the suburban countryside, however, the Central Committee was concerned that the gathering of the autumn harvest might be affected. On 14 September, a directive was issued 'Concerning the Great Cultural Revolution in Rural Districts Below the *Xian* Level' stipulating that the Cultural Revolution in rural areas should be conducted in communes and production brigades 'in association with the original "four clean-ups" arrangements'.[85] This quite extraordinary order was tantamount to saying that, in the rural areas, work-teams were still permissible. Cadres were to remain at their posts, urban-based Red Guard units were forbidden to interfere in the communes and, to all intents and purposes, a halt was called to the Cultural Revolution in the countryside. But not long after the directive, *Red Flag*, realising probably what the 14 September directive implied, modified its terms by declaring that urban-based Red Guards were only forbidden to 'make revolution' in rural units where the "four clean-up" provisions were considered appropriate by the masses.[86] The boot was now clearly on the other foot. Earlier in the Socialist Education Movement, radical policies had been modified by conservative operational instructions. The *Red Flag* article indicated that the reverse was now the case.

Though the major slogan in the autumn of 1966 was 'grasp revolution and promote production' with a very clear emphasis on the second part of the slogan, propaganda teams still continued to operate in the countryside and the work-teams seemed to fade from view. By the time the Socialist Education Movement was formally brought to an end on 15 December,[87] nothing much had been heard of them for some time.

Cultural Revolution: Stage Five — The Focus on Liu Shao-ch'i

By October 1966, the degree of mass mobilisation had increased to such an extent that even Mao Tse-tung was surprised:

> I had no idea that one big character poster, the Red Guards and the big exchange of revolutionary experiences would have stirred up such a big affair.[88]

Amongst the Red Guards, there was still turmoil but it was a turmoil in which young people were receiving a practical political education which no formal classes could achieve. Large numbers of weapons, hoarded gold and even pictures of Chiang K'ai-shek were unearthed.[89] The continued payment of 'fixed interest' to former 'national capitalists' was criticised.[90] Excessive Party secrecy and the keeping of dossiers on people of dubious political background (the so-called 'black documents') were denounced.[91] Literally millions of Red Guards still toured the country spreading experiences and the influx of people into Peking to attend mammoth rallies created many headaches for the city authorities; in fact it may be argued that one of the functions of the rallies was to give the Red Guards a chance to see Chairman Mao and then go home.

With the publication (by the Military Commission and the PLA General Political Department) on 5 October of an 'Urgent Directive on the Cultural Revolution in Military Academies',[92] it was apparent that the Cultural Revolution had radicalised even further. Such schools (and by extension all schools) were required to do away with 'all the bonds that have shackled the mass movement' and 'daring' was to be 'put above everything else'. Cultural Revolution groups were now seen as 'organs of power'. It is possible, however, that at that time the PLA command and the Central Party press (under the influence of Ch'en Po-ta) took a line slightly to the left of Mao Tse-tung. After the appearance of the early October edition of *Red Flag* which noted that repression still continued and had to be combatted,[93] *dazibao* appeared critical of Liu Shao-ch'i and Teng Hsiao-p'ing.[94] Although Mao was undoubtedly determined to break the influence of the Liu Shao-ch'i line, he was probably a little more cautious than either the press or the radical Red Guards. At a central work conference on 26 October, he remarked:

> You find it difficult to cross this pass and I don't find it easy either.
> You are anxious and so am I. I cannot blame you comrades, time has
> been so short. Some comrades say that they did not intentionally
> make mistakes, but did it because they were confused. This is
> pardonable. Nor can we put all the blame on Comrade (Liu)
> Shao-ch'i and Comrade (Teng) Hsiao-p'ing. They have some respon-
> sibility but so has the Centre. The Centre has not run things properly.
> The time was so short. We were not mentally prepared for new
> problems.[95]

Mao was obviously alluding here to the 'self-criticism' made by Liu Shao-ch'i to the same conference when he admitted that his handling of the Cultural Revolution during the 'fifty days' had been inadequate. Liu was most contrite:

> Comrade Lin Piao is better than I in every respect; so are the other
> comrades in the Party. I am determined to abide by a Party mem-
> ber's discipline and do nothing before anybody that amounts to
> 'agreement by mouth but disagreement at heart'.[96]

But, unlike Mao, the radical Red Guards would not, in any way, accept the self-criticism of Liu and made every effort to escalate criticism. On 18 October, some senior cadres in the Central South Bureau of the Party came under attack[97] as part of a general denunciation of the alleged diversionary line pursued by T'ao Chu, and it seemed that what-ever reserve Mao and others may have felt, their only course was to let the revolution work itself out to its final conclusion.

In the last two months of 1966, attempts were made by local authorities to limit Red Guard activity, though it was by no means certain whether their motives constituted anything more than just a practical response to logistic problems. The vast influx of Red Guards into Peking in the autumn of 1966 had been partially solved by their participation in gathering the autumn harvest. In October and November, however, more stringent efforts were made to reduce the burden Red Guards had imposed upon the transport system. Announcements appeared curtailing free travel[98] and Red Guards were encouraged to spread revolutionary experiences by undertaking new 'Long Marches'[99] rather than going everywhere by bus and train; though, to be sure, there were educational objectives pursued here as well as the purely economic.

At the same time, warnings appeared threatening both authorities and Red Guards with punishment if they employed violence,[100] and stories began to circulate about a particularly violent Red Guard group in Peking known as the United Action Committee (*Lianhe Xingdong Weiyuanhui*).[101] The United Action Committee had been formed at a time of furious debate about the proper response to old cadres and about whether admission to Red Guard organisations should be limited to the sons and daughters of workers, peasants, soldiers and others with impeccable class or revolutionary backgrounds. The more radical groups had denounced any requirements concerning parental background as 'the reactionary theory of lineage', but there were still some Red Guard groups who considered themselves an elite and it was they who formed the backbone of the United Action Committee. The United Action Committee, which comprised former members of the Red Guards' First and Second Headquarters, tended towards a much more conservative position than the Third Headquarters whose parental credentials were less impeccable. They accused the Third Headquarters, which was supported by the Cultural Revolution Group, of violating the moderate Sixteen Points and significantly of being infiltrated by 'bourgeois elements'. This accusation the radicals considered to be 'waving the Red Flag to oppose it'. For a while, it was claimed that the United Action Committee imposed a reign of terror over Red Guard organisations in Peking and availed themselves of money and vehicles supplied by unnamed Party officials who saw in the committee a force which might contain radicalism. The United Action Committee demanded the dissolution of the Cultural Revolution Group, denounced Lin Piao as a 'conspirator'[102] and were joined in their opposition to the radicals by conservative worker organisations backed by the labour unions.

The above situation in Peking was duplicated many times with many different variations in the provinces. It has yet to be established what (if any) co-ordination existed between the various conservative groups that became active in the latter part of 1966. We may surmise, however, that whatever reservations Mao and other senior Party radicals may have had about pressing home the attack against Liu Shao-ch'i and the Party machine must surely have been dissipated once it became clear that any call for moderation of radical criticism would play precisely into the hands of these conservatives.

In early December, Chou En-lai emphasised the support of Mao Tse-tung and Lin Piao for the Central Cultural Revolution Group[103] and the mid-December edition of *Red Flag* called for a counteroffensive to crush the 'bourgeois reactionary line'.[104] Probably as a result of this support, the Third Headquarters, now greatly augmented in numbers, stepped up their denunciation of Liu Shao-ch'i and Teng Hsiao-p'ing, the work of 'liaison personnel' (organised by Wang Jen-chung with the support of T'ao Chu) and the United Action Committee.[105] Before long, the name of T'ao Chu had been joined to those of Liu Shao-ch'i and Teng Hsiao-p'ing as targets for overthrow[106] and China's radicals prepared for a new onslaught.

The further radicalisation of the Cultural Revolution in December 1966 had three consequences. First, the Cultural Revolution superseded the Socialist Education Movement in the countryside. Secondly, the workers' movement now became the main focus of 'struggle' and thirdly, the Army became much more involved in the revolution.

Following a very successful autumn harvest, the 15 December directive ending the Socialist Education Movement[107] cleared the way for a more thoroughgoing rural Cultural Revolution. An immediate consequence of the directive was the strengthening of Poor and Lower Middle Peasant Associations which were now to form their own Cultural Revolution committees.[108] The associations seemed no longer subject to the leadership of local Party branches and could transcend all the limitations imposed upon them by the earlier 'four clean-ups'.[109] Together with special groups formed to promote production,[110] the peasant Cultural Revolution groups could now go into action against local cadres. The situation was, however, highly confused. During the earlier Socialist Education Movement, large numbers of peasant rebels had been demoted by the work-teams and branded as 'counter-revolutionaries'. These rebels now demanded the reversal of verdicts but were joined in their demands by rightists, ex-landlords and 'genuine' counter-revolutionaries. The peasant Cultural Revolution committees were to find new evaluations extremely difficult.[111]

The new radicalisation in the industrial sphere was considerably influenced in late 1966 by events in Shanghai. The growth of worker Red Rebel groups in the autumn resulted in a massive outpouring of all kinds of grievances concerning conditions of work, bonuses, piece-rate systems, participation in management, the role of the labour unions, etc.[112] A major bone of contention was the status of temporary workers

recruited on contract from the countryside.[113] Some advocated that
the wages and working conditions of these workers should be raised to
the level of regular industrial workers while others could not see how
job opportunities could be created to accommodate such a demand. In
all these debates, it was extremely difficult to sort out what constituted
a radical and what a conservative position.

On 9 November, a radical alliance was formed between workers and
students in Shanghai known as the Shanghai Workers Revolutionary
Rebel Headquarters.[114] The headquarters, which promoted the
establishment of Revolutionary Rebel groups in factories, was opposed
by the conservative Shanghai Party Committee, which may have been
responsible for ensuring that a train carrying a delegation from the
headquarters to Peking was shunted into a siding 18 kilometres outside
Shanghai and left there. The radical Chang Ch'un-ch'iao, who had been
active in the Central Cultural Revolution Group in Peking, flew
hurriedly back to Shanghai to sort out the situation and signed a document acceding to the workers' demands. Though Chang may have gone
further than the Central Cultural Revolution Group may have wished,
they could only endorse his action, much to the chagrin of Shanghai's
mayor Ts'ao Ti-ch'iu. At first, there was little the Shanghai authorities
could do, but following the occupation by rebels of the editorial
offices of *Liberation Daily* (the Shanghai Party newspaper) in early
December, they came more and more to rely upon a conservative rebel
formation known as the *Scarlet Guards* (*Chiweidui*) which inaugurated
a period of intense conflict with the radical Red Rebel groups. As
clashes occurred in December, the Central Committee issued a directive
calling for the extension of the Cultural Revolution into factories and
mines and the toleration of criticism.[115] Faced with what seemed to be
Peking's endorsement of the Revolutionary Rebel position, the Scarlet
Guards now made a bid for power and attempted to consolidate its
hold over the city's factories. The result was a wave of strikes that
began in late December, to which the radicals could only respond by
demanding that the Revolutionary Rebels 'seize power' and run the
factories themselves. Before the end of the year, Chiang Ch'ing
endorsed demands for such 'power seizures' not only in factories but
in the Ministry of Labour and the 'economist' All China Federation of
Trade Unions,[116] whose local branches in Shanghai had supported the
Scarlet Guards.

The third consequence of the radicalisation of December concerned
the Army. Through the autumn, the PLA had been ordered time and
again to confine its support for Red Guards and Red Rebels to the

logistic and the symbolic. The Army was not to involve itself actively in the civilian Cultural Revolution.[117] By December, however, the Cultural Revolution had spread to military academies and some regular troops had taken up the rebel cause.[118] At the same time, worker rebel groups became active in factories under military control,[119] such as those under the Seventh Ministry of Machine Building. On 18 December, Chiang Ch'ing called for mass action to seize power over the public security network and the courts[120] and, where this was resisted by the police, the Army sometimes took over public security duties.[121] The PLA, therefore, was gradually being pulled into the Cultural Revolution and found itself in a curiously ambiguous position. Sometimes troops supported rebel organisations and at other times adhered to the official policy of non-involvement; occasionally troops actually tried to dampen rebel ardour.[122] Not only did troops find themselves in support of the radical Chang Ch'un-ch'iao[123] but also the 'opportunist' T'ao Chu.[124] There was clearly a need for some kind of specific directive on PLA involvement in the Cultural Revolution. It is perhaps significant to note here that in late December, when P'eng Chen was arraigned before a Red Guard rally, Lo Jui-ch'ing and P'eng Teh-huai were also arrested.[125] Those who arrested the former Minister of Defence and Chief of Staff were in fact students of military academies;[126] the Army's attitude could hardly be neutral.

By the end of 1966, it was clear that the Cultural Revolution was not to be allowed to run down. Attempts were made to fuse the rebel movement in the universities, schools, factories and perhaps also the countryside. There was probably some pressure also for greater PLA involvement. Rebels were now enjoined not only to 'seize power' and to 'struggle' actively against the 'handful of people in authority taking the capitalist road' but also to model their organisations on the Paris Commune of 1871.[127]

Cultural Revolution: Stage Six — The January Revolution

One of the immediate consequences of the policies announced in late December was the disintegration of the All China Federation of Trade Unions. It was charged notably by Chiang Ch'ing, with permitting the exploitative contract labour system,[128] but in January there seemed little that could be done given the employment situation.[129] Radical workers, who began to seize power in January 1967, however, were concerned immediately not with major economic questions but with how to take over and run their own factories. It was a period of great excitement.[130] Semi-literate workers now put pen to paper without the slightest reservation and almost every printing press was devoted to the publication of broadsheets and newspapers. The rather abstract notion of 'politics in command' now began to mean something very concrete as workers showed a genuine interest in the politics that affected them. Worker organisations themselves entered into heated discussion on exactly how factories were to be organised and how they could develop their own potential. No bureaucratic authority stood over them telling them what to do, for at last they had grasped the essence of a *proletarian* revolution.

In Shanghai, the seizure of power was carried out with frantic urgency because of the need to end the strike caused by the Scarlet Guards. The Scarlet Guards were, however, probably numerically superior to the Revolutionary Rebels and were supported to some extent by the Municipal Committee.[131] As we have seen, their motive in carrying out the strike was probably to prevent the Municipal Committee giving in to the pressure of the Peking Cultural Revolution Group and their Shanghai spokesman Chang Ch'un-ch'iao.[132] But the strategy of the Revolutionary Rebels, backed by Peking, was to create new organisations to get production moving and so discredit both the Municipal Committee and the Scarlet Guards. They were remarkably successful. In early January, the Shanghai *Wenhuibao* was seized by the Rebels[133] and an appeal made to the people of Shanghai denouncing both the Municipal Committee and the Scarlet Guards.[134] The appeal, which was immediately supported by Mao Tse-tung,[135] greatly swelled the ranks of the Revolutionary Rebels who, by 9 January, had the railways moving once again. Before long, production committees in power stations and shipyards restored operations there too[136] and conservative resistance crumbled.

The problem of 'economism'[137] still remained. It was perhaps inevitable that amongst the mass of demands put forward by workers in January 1967, there should be included those for shorter hours and better pay. It was also inevitable that these demands should have been fostered by what remained of the conservative labour unions and utilised by the Party machine to protect its own position. The 'economism' of January 1967 took the form of the advance payment of wages and an increase in bonuses, on the one hand to buy off a section of the workers and on the other to split them. This second objective had also been pursued in late 1966 by encouraging work stoppages[138] although, with the seizure of power in 1967, this option no longer remained. A third method of causing splits derived from the commitment of the new ACFTU Centre to rationalise the contract labour

system in a situation where it had not the economic resources to do so.
Not only could the resentment of contract workers be capitalised on
but so could that of the peasants, who feared that rural-urban mobility
might be restricted.

A further set of problems resulted from the difficulties of seizing
power in a situation where a number of different revolutionary rebel
groups coexisted (let alone organisations such as the Scarlet Guards).
It was never clear which rebel group was to seize power. Sometimes
repeated power seizures took place between rival rebel groups and, at
a municipal level in Shanghai, power was siezed four times before a
city-wide organisation was constructed.[139] Sometimes the old administration formed their own group to seize power through which they
could still manipulate the organisation from backstage. Such, the Red
Guards felt, was the policy of the Minister of Agriculture, T'an Chen-lin,
in Peking.[140] On other occasions, the old administration concealed
records and plans from rebel groups seizing power so that the new
administration would be unable to function and request the return of
old cadres. Sometimes a successful seizure of power might take place
but, following that seizure, the rebels would send too many cadres
down to the factory floor and leave themselves with insufficient technical advice to keep the organisation running.[141] The situation was sometimes chaotic and yet, for the first time, many ordinary workers were
being drawn into administration. If one wanted to learn something
about administration, there was surely nothing like engaging in it oneself, even if one initially made great mistakes.

Although the Shanghai strikes did not last for very long, they were
sufficiently serious for Chou En-lai and Ch'en Po-ta, while endorsing
the rebel seizure of power, to warn that the seizure and control of
everything on the Shanghai pattern should not be repeated elsewhere.[142]
At the same time, Chiang Ch'ing stressed that groups that had seized
power should *supervise* cadres but not dispense with them.[143]

Despite the warnings not to seize power indiscriminately and the
reprinting of one of Mao's earlier essays opposing egalitarianism, the
Shanghai pattern did repeat itself in some other areas. In the countryside, the movement to seize power was further complicated by the fact
that different kinds of proscribed elements (so-called 'five category
elements') had demanded the reversal of verdicts reached in the
Socialist Education Movement. Attempts were made to recall the original work-teams to undergo criticism.[144] To prevent proscribed elements
usurping the leadership of the new radical movement, the Central
Committee had no course but to endorse the (now defunct) Socialist

Education Movement, despite its shortcomings, and prohibit the reversal of any verdicts at all,[145] at least for the time being. With the rural Cultural Revolution now proceeding in low gear, the problem of 'economism' again reached serious proportions.[146]

A problem even more important than the seizure of power within production units concerned the links between organisations in which power had been seized. Somehow a structure had to be created which would prevent the cities, or for that matter the countryside, dissolving into atomised units. Since the summer of 1966, there had been much talk of modelling organisations upon the Paris Commune whereby leaders at various levels of city administration might be elected by popular assemblies and subject to immediate recall by their constituents. In Shanghai, there was to be more than just talk but the Shanghai People's Commune proved to be extraordinarily difficult to organise. After three weeks of discussions, a Preparatory Committee led by Chang Ch'un-ch'iao and Yao Wen-yüan was finally established on 5 February.[147] The Preparatory Committee which represented 38 Red Rebel organisations organised a Provisional Committee which was vested with supreme power. The Provisional Committee consisted of 11 permanent members plus the heads of a number of commissions. Two student organisations ran the Liaison and External Relations Commissions; revolutionary cadres from the old Municipal Committee ran the Control Commission, the Workers Revolutionary Rebel Headquarters ran the Organisation Commission and the Revolution and Production Front (set up to deal with the strike) ran the Operations Commission. The Provisional Committee consisted of seven workers, three students, two peasants, two cadres and two soldiers. It formally proclaimed the abolition of the Shanghai Municipal Committee and the Shanghai Party Committee, declared all their decisions since 16 May 1966 null and void and urged rebels to seize power in all units.[148] Provision was made for other rebel organisations to join the new government but negotiations concerning membership might be protracted since there were still serious ideological and organisational problems that had to be overcome. Although the original intention had been for the Commune Provisional Committee to be chosen by popular elections the body that was proclaimed on 5 February was really just an amalgam of revolutionary organisations. In fact, popular elections for the Shanghai People's Commune were never held since events in other parts of the country were beginning to overtake Shanghai and new organisational forms were emerging.

The events of Shanghai in January 1967 were profoundly exciting as more and more people were drawn into city and local administration yet the problems were serious and the pattern of power seizure elsewhere in the country was much less abrupt. As Mao saw it, there could only be one organisation that could provide the cement necessary to hold the various institutions together after power had been seized; there was only one institution that could prevent highly destructive faction fighting and negate the influence of proscribed elements while the rural Cultural Revolution developed — the PLA. Without Army involvement, rebel clashes would continue and localism would develop. Army-supported mass action had, after all, constituted the pattern of power seizure in 1948-9. At that time, worker picket organisations often took over the factories and peasant associations took over the villages but they were linked to municipal and *xian* government by the Army and guided by Army representatives. In the period immediately prior to January 1967, Army schools had undergone their own internal rectification under the leadership of a special Army Cultural Revolution Group and on 11 January this group was reorganised, presumably to prepare it for a greater civilian role. Significantly, the Army Cultural Revolution Group was now subordinated to the Central Committee's Cultural Revolution Group.[149] As we have seen, the Army had already to some extent been drawn into the civilian Cultural Revolution by the actions of its military academies and factories and its involvement in public security work. It had, however, performed somewhat ambiguously for sometimes it had backed rebels and at others had supported the status quo. By mid-January, Mao was determined that the involvement of the Army in the Cultural Revolution had to be on the side of the 'left' and called upon the Army to help in the seizure and consolidation of power.[150] On 23 January, a definitive order went out for the PLA to 'support the left'.[151]

Though excited by developments in Shanghai, Mao Tse-tung saw great problems in the Shanghai People's Commune. In February 1967, he is reported to have told the Shanghai radicals Chang Ch'un-ch'iao and Yao Wen-yüan:

With the establishment of a People's commune, a series of problems arises and I wonder whether you have thought about them. If the whole of China sets up people's communes, should the People's Republic of China change its name to 'People's Commune of China'? Would others recognise us? Maybe the Soviet Union would not recognise us whereas Britain and France would. And what would we do about our ambassadors in various countries? And so on. There is

another series of problems which you may not have considered.
Many places have now applied to the Centre to establish people's
communes. A document has been issued by the Centre saying that
no place apart from Shanghai may set up people's communes. The
Chairman is of the opinion that Shanghai ought to make a change
and transform itself into a revolutionary committee or a city
committee or a city people's committee.[152]

By February, Mao's preferred model of organisation was clearly that of
1949, now known as the 'revolutionary committee' based on a triple
alliance of revolutionary rebels, old cadres and People's Liberation
Army. Such a committee had already been set up at a provincial level in
Heilungkiang on 31 January[153] and a number of other committees were
soon established on the same model.[154] Mao, therefore, advocated a
limited support role for the military until the Party could be rebuilt
along more revolutionary lines. As Chang Ch'un-ch'iao reported:

> With the Commune inaugurated do we still need the Party? I think
> we need it because we must have a hard core whether it is called a
> Communist Party or a social democratic Party . . . In short we still
> need a Party.[155]

This statement was made just before the Shanghai People's Commune
itself was transformed into a revolutionary committee based on the
triple alliance formula.[156] The Chairman was convinced that mass
action should no longer be as anarchistic as some of the 'ultra-left'
manifestations in Shanghai had been.

> The slogan of doubt everything and overthrow everything is re-
> actionary. The Shanghai People's Committee demanded that the
> Premier of the State Council should do away with all heads. This is
> extreme anarchism, it is most reactionary. If instead of calling some-
> one the 'head' of something, we call him 'orderly' or 'assistant' this
> would really be only a formal change. In reality there will always be
> 'heads'. It is the content which matters.[157]

The radicals were now faced with an extremely serious problem. How
was one to define 'ultra-left anarchism' and how was one to deal with
it? They were soon to be faced with an even more serious problem. The
Army was to support the 'left' but how was one to define the 'left' and
how was one to prevent the Army actually exercising control?

The Foreign Ministry Drags its Feet

Before we discuss the short period of consolidation in February 1967, it might be useful to look at the 'seizure of power' in one particularly crucial ministry — Foreign Affairs.[158] The aim here is not to describe a typical case, since the Foreign Ministry was regarded as being responsible for a particularly sensitive area of government policy, but because an examination of the events of January 1967 will help us understand the peculiar direction Chinese foreign affairs took in mid-1967.

In mid-1966, Foreign Minister Ch'en Yi was personally responsible for the dispatch of some 15 work-teams to subordinate departments and schools attached to the Foreign Ministry. He was, therefore, accused by Red Guards of excessive conservatism. When pressure mounted in the autumn of 1966 to establish Cultural Revolution committees, Ch'en still resisted the Red Guards. Not only did he not condemn Liu Shao-ch'i's earlier work-teams but he refused to withdraw his own work-teams from departments of the ministry. At one point, Mao himself reportedly dispatched Chou En-lai to find out why Ch'en was still violating Cultural Revolution policy.

In November, when other conservatives were adopting covert means to protect their position, the irascible Ch'en Yi actually went on the offensive and accused the Red Guards of indiscipline. In fact, the impression one gets of Ch'en Yi, in the autumn of 1966, was of a man who was not terribly worried about Red Guard criticism at all and was more concerned about the deterioration of China's foreign relations during the escalation of the Vietnam War and the changed situation in Asia following the Indonesian coup. Between his foreign policy statements and his personal reaction to the Cultural Revolution, there seemed to be a severe contradiction. On the one hand, he embraced the Lin Piao thesis, welcomed the growing anti-imperialist struggle, noted that temporary setbacks were part of a 'zigzag' pattern of development and affirmed the importance of the Chinese Cultural Revolution internationally yet, on the other, regarded the growth of the Cultural Revolution in his own ministry as a tiresome interference.

By the end of 1966, however, Ch'en's position had been somewhat undermined. He could no longer maintain work-teams or work-team surrogates and all China's ambassadors were gradually recalled (with the one exception of Huang Hua in Cairo). By the beginning of January, the lack of progress of the Cultural Revolution in the Foreign Ministry began to result in 'ultra-leftist' pressure. A key figure here was the influential Wang Li (a member of the Central Cultural Revolution Group) who tried to get rid of Ch'en in defiance of Premier Chou En-lai.

On 18 January, a Ministry of Foreign Affairs Revolutionary Rebel
Liaison Station (*Waijiaobu Geming Zaofan Lianluozhan*) was established to inspect work and check conservative policies. Although a
radical body, its setting up hardly constituted a 'seizure of power'.

On 24 January, Ch'en Yi was forced to give a self-criticism before a
mass rally where he was accused of a number of 'crimes' involving
support of work-teams, bureaucratism and his conservative position
on education in 1961-2. Unlike many other confessions, however,
Ch'en's was accepted and the Foreign Minister retained his post. Confirmed in office, he then launched a counterattack, criticised the rebel
liaison station and reinstated a number of people accused of 'revisionism'. Admitting that his confession had been forced out of him, Ch'en
demanded that, if the Red Guards really wanted to make revolution,
they should leave him alone and go to Vietnam. Almost unbelievably,
he reportedly went on to say: 'Comrade (Liu) Shao-ch'i speaks
correctly . . . Comrade Shao-ch'i is my teacher.' After what amounted
to a declaration of war upon the Red Guards, one might have suspected
that Ch'en Yi would have been bitterly denounced and removed from
office. In fact, Ch'en's position was stronger in February 1968 than
ever before.

As I see it, there are two possible explanations for the extraordinary
tolerance accorded to Ch'en Yi in early 1967. First, he was protected
by Chou En-lai who was concerned that China's foreign relations might
deteriorate further and secondly, Ch'en's counterattack coincided with
the beginning of a new and short period of consolidation following
some of the 'ultra-leftism' of January. But the consequences of Ch'en's
declaration of war were to be very far-reaching. There was to remain,
within the foreign affairs network, tremendous resentment against
Ch'en, and his conservatism gave rise to an 'ultra-leftism' that was
eventually to cause more havoc than might have occurred in January
1967 had Ch'en been less instransigent. Perhaps the most implacable
of Ch'en's critics was a man still employed as chargé d'affaires in the
beleaguered embassy in Jakarta – Yao Teng-shan.

Cultural Revolution: Stage Seven – The February Adverse Current

Foreign Minister Ch'en Yi was probably saved by what became known
later as the 'February Adverse Current' which, in terms of our cyclic
model, constituted a period of consolidation. The order of 23 January
gave rise to a new policy for the PLA known as 'three supports and two
militaries' (support the workers, peasants and the 'left' and adopt leadership and training by the military). The policy of 'three supports and

two militaries' was not, however, intended to halt the Cultural Revolution but merely to hold the ring while mass organisations formed their own alliances, and this is what happened in a good number of places. In a study of PLA reaction to the order of 23 January, Jürgen Domes notes that the Army firmly supported Red Rebel groups in six out of 29 administrative units at provincial level, gave moderate support in four, remained neutral in nine but either refused to support the 'left' or acti‧ suppressed it in ten.[159] I do not know how accurate Domes' evaluation is, but it is certainly true that in some areas the military support for the 'left' was highly questionable. In Tsinghai[160] and Kwangtung in particular, military reaction seemed to be particularly harsh and the Kwangtung military commander, Huang Yung-sheng, earned the title of Kwangchow's T'an Chen-lin[161] after the Minister of Agriculture who was soon to be renowned for organising his own power seizures.

In many ways, subsequent literature has identified the 'February Adverse Current' with the person of T'an Chen-lin probably because he symbolised a type of leader quite unlike any of the more conventional conservatives. T'an, it will be remembered, was the principal architect of the bold experiments with people's communes in Honan in 1958. He was deeply committed to the idea of the Great Leap Forward and to the revival of the Great Leap spirit and probably supported most of the demands for radical reforms in education. From a radical point of view, however, his one error was a lack of confidence in mass action.[162] It is a trifle unfair, therefore, to associate him with Kwangchow's Huang Yung-sheng who, in my opinion, seemed a remarkably unintelligent military commander whose obsession with law and order blinded him to anything else.

Throughout February 1967, accounts appeared thick and fast of an extension of military control. On 26 January, the Army took control of civil aviation.[163] In late January, military representatives began to be dispatched to factories, mines and stores.[164] In early February, many public security organs were firmly placed under military control.[165] At provincial levels and below, military control commissions were formed[166] prior to the establishment of revolutionary committees in exactly the same way as in 1948-9. In the countryside, the Army also became increasingly involved in administration.[167] One should not conclude from the simple fact of military involvement, however, that the Cultural Revolution was being stifled any more than radical change had been stifled by military involvement during the war. What we must look at is the way the Army restored order and this was sometimes peremp-

tory. We must look also at policy. In late January, for example, the
Cultural Revolution was actually *postponed* (whatever that may mean)
in a number of military regions until order could be restored.[168] In the
countryside, peasants were forbidden to take any action against members of the former work-teams,[169] and leniency was stressed during the
spring planting season.[170] Long Marches of students exchanging revolutionary experiences were curtailed[171] and numbers of former officials
who had been considered to be 'revisionist' were returned to office.[172]

What makes the 'February Adverse Current' extremely hard to
analyse is the fact that it was very difficult to draw the line between the
radical-left' and the 'ultra-left'. I do not believe that this is an arbitrary
distinction any more than the line between 'commandism' and 'tailism'
need be arbitrary. It will be obvious from the preceding chapters that the
hallmark of Mao Tse-tung's approach to social mobilisation is to keep
one step ahead of the masses but never to push them. As Mao sees it,
there is very little difference between an 'ultra-leftist' who wishes to
kick people into socialism and a reactionary. It is true that the line
between an 'ultra-left' and a 'radical-left' position will vary according to
people's consciousness in a particular situation, but essentially it
should be the masses that decide the limits beyond which leftists
cannot go. Doubtless these limits were occasionally transcended by
over-zealous rebels in the January Revolution, but it is impossible
to imagine how a major city such as Shanghai could have organised
itself to resume production in the face of organised opposition had it
not been for the fact that, in general, the Mass Line was adhered to by
the rebel organisations. The difficulty in analysing February 1967,
therefore, lies not in the fact that large numbers of people in China
could not distinguish between the 'radical-left' and the 'ultra-left'
position but that any act of repression was justified on the grounds
that it was the 'ultra-left' that was being suppressed.

The End of the Seventh Cycle

By February 1967, many problems had occurred in the Cultural Revolution. In some places the hand of the Army had perhaps been a trifle
too heavy and there were quite a number of local leaders who had
carried out bogus power seizures. The revolutionary committees which
had begun to form on the basis of the 'triple alliance' were much less
ambitious than the radical schemes for a Paris Commune which had
been discussed in January, and occasionally the initiative in their
formation had come from the Army rather than the masses.

Despite this, however, something quite remarkable had been

achieved. Not only were students and teachers asking questions about
political power that they had never considered before, not only were
peasants now free from bureaucratic control from above but there had
occurred, in Shanghai and some other places, events that could only be
described as a *proletarian* revolution, more radical even than the Peking
Party radicals envisaged. The Party machine had been dismantled and
could be rebuilt on less bureaucratic lines and the way was open for a
complete rethinking of China's educational system. More people than
ever before had become involved not only in operational decision-
making, not only in policy formulation but also in macro-politics. In
some ways, the situation in China resembled that of 1949, though this
time there was a much more literate and politically conscious population.

The situation was similar to 1949 also in the sense that military
control commissions and military representatives were active in helping
(and occasionally forcing) the process of consolidating new forms of
political power. If the mistakes of the early 1950s were not to be
repeated, much depended on the support-role of the military. In
1949-50, soldiers turned themselves into civilian Party cadres and their
inexperience sometimes led to the adoption of organisational forms
which negated the ideals for which they had fought. Would this happen
again or would the Army merely hold the ring until new administrative bodies from the masses might be consolidated? If the Army representatives in the factories, schools and communes did retain their
military position, however, was there a danger that the Army might
replace the Party? What kind of support from Peking might be given to
mass organisations which felt that the Army had acted with too heavy
a hand? Faced with situations like those in Kwangchow where
Huang Yung-sheng had created his own 'left' to support, it was evident
to the Peking Cultural Revolution Group that this new period of consolidation must be rapidly ended. Large numbers of Red Guards and Red
Rebels were infuriated by such actions and it was their initiative that
must be sustained if a new order was to be built out of the confusing
situation. The Central Cultural Revolution Group was swift to act. With
the publication of a *Red Flag* editorial on 9 March, it was stated quite
clearly that the main component in revolutionary alliances was the
masses. [173] T'ar Chen-lin began to be condemned as the architect of
false power seizures and there was no more talk of postponing the
Cultural Revolution. The Army was now required to examine itself and,
on 6 April, was ordered not to take any action against mass organisations without prior clearance from Peking. [174] Another chapter in the
history of the Cultural Revolution was about to begin.

Notes

1. This discussion is taken from Rossanda 1971.
2. Note, the Chinese never made any explicit criticism of Stalin during the Cultural Revolution, probably because of its international implications.
3. Robinson J. (1969, pp. 11-12), argues in terms of the persistence of a capitalist superstructure on a socialist base. Though many Chinese accounts also take this position, I support Rossanda's criticism of it (p. 59).
4. Rossanda's formulation. No Chinese accounts, to my knowledge, discuss the relationship of legal to managerial possession.
5. See Chapter 3.
6. A common Red Guard slogan of 1966.
7. *PR* 21, 19 May 1967, p. 6.
8. Text in *URI* 1968, *The Case of P'eng Teh-huai*, pp. 235-61.
9. Israel 1967, p. 7.
10. Ch'i Pen-yü, *SCMM* 529, 20 June 1966, p. 2.
11. *SCMM* 640, 13 January 1969, p. 3.
12. Mao Tse-tung 21 December 1965, in Schram 1974, p. 237.
13. *SCMM* 640, 13 January 1969, pp. 3-4.
14. *SCMM* 640, 13 January 1969, p. 6. The 16 May circular absolved K'ang Sheng from any blame (*URI* 1968, *CCP Documents* . . ., p. 21). The final report was said to have been adopted on 4 February though the text gives the date 3 February when K'ang Sheng and the radical wing were in attendance. (*URI* 1968, *CCP Documents* . . . p. 7.)
15. Text in *URI* 1968, *CCP Documents* . . ., pp. 7-12.
16. *SCMM* 640, 13 January 1969, p. 7. Note, Dittmer (1974, p. 74) argues that there was no necessary connection between P'eng Chen and Liu Shao-ch'i.
17. See Yin Ta, *SCMM* 517, 28 March 1966, pp. 1-11. Ch'i Pen-yü, Lin Chieh, Yen Ch'ang-kuei, *SCMM* 521, 25 April 1966, pp. 28-44. (Note, these authors were hardly conservatives.)
18. Esmein 1973, p. 78.
19. *CCP.CC* 16 May 1966, in *URI* 1968, *CCP Documents* . . ., pp. 31-2.
20. *SCMM* 641, 20 January 1969, p. 11.
21. Yang Ch'eng-wu's appointment was not announced until 1 August, and it is not certain exactly when he was appointed.
22. Text in *PFLP* 1970, *Important Documents* . . ., pp. 201-38.
23. Bridgham 1967, p. 16.
24. Mao Tse-tung 21 December 1965 in Schram 1964, pp. 236-7.
25. Israel 1967, p. 7.
26. *SCMM* 640, 13 January 1969, p. 12.
27. Ibid., pp. 13-4.
28. *PR* 20, 13 May 1966, p. 42.
29. Mao Tse-tung 7 May 1966, in *CB* 891, 8 October 1969, pp. 56-7.
30. Kao Chü, 8 May 1966. Text in Schurmann and Schell 1968, pp. 603-6.
31. *PR* 22, 27 May 1966, pp. 5-18.
32. Ch'i Pen-yü, *SCMM* 529, 20 June 1966, pp. 1-10.
33. Dittmer 1974, p. 77.
34. Not published until 16 May 1967, *PR* 21, 19 May 1967, pp. 6-9.
35. Chang 1970, pp. 193-4.
36. Israel 1967, p. 7.
37. Mao apparently saw the poster on 1 June and ordered it to be published throughout the country. *SCMM* 648, 24 March 1969, p. 18. On the early stages of the Cultural Revolution at Peking University see Nee 1969.
38. *RMRB*, 2 June 1966, p. 1.

39. *PR* 23, 3 June 1966, pp. 4-5. The article 'Sweep away all Monsters' refers to Great *Proletarian* Cultural Revolution. The editor of *Peking Review* was probably unaware of the significance, ibid., p. 1.
40. *PR* 24, 10 June 1966, pp. 3-4.
41. *PR* 26, 24 June 1966, p. 3.
42. Dittmer 1974, p. 81.
43. The term 'monsters and demons' (literally ox-ghosts and snake-spirits) was the same term that was used in 1957.
44. Baum 1969, p. 99.
45. *PR* 33, 12 August 1966, pp. 32-8.
46. No formal announcement was made concerning Lu Ting-i's dismissal. The first reference to T'ao Chu's appointment was made by *NCNA*, 10 July.
47. *CB* 834, 17 August 1967, pp. 26-7.
48. Liu Shao-ch'i 23 October 1966 in *URI* 1968, *CCP Documents* . . ., p. 358 and *CB* 834, 17 August 1967, p. 27. For a detailed account of Wang Kuang-mei's activities see Hinton 1972.
49. Chang 1970, p. 194.
50. Liu Shao-ch'i, 9 July 1967 in Liu 1968, p. 371-2.
51. Daubier 1974, p. 56.
52. Hinton 1972, p. 65.
53. *PR* 33, 12 August 1966, pp. 17-19.
54. *CB* 891, 8 October 1969, pp. 58-60.
55. Mao Tse-tung 21 July 1966, in Schram 1974, p. 253. The Peiyang warlords were a group of graduates from a military academy of that name in Tientsin who exercised tremendous power in China in the second and third decades of the twentieth century.
56. Chang 1970, p. 194, based on *CB* 891, 8 October 1969, pp. 58-60. A conference was certainly held at which regional party secretaries and members of the Cultural Revolution Group were present. I am not sure, however, about the dates, nor am I sure that it was at that meeting that a decision was taken to withdraw the teams.
57. *PR* 32, 5 August 1966, pp. 8-10.
58. *PR* 32, 5 August 1966, p. 4.
59. *SCMP* 3765, 22 August 1966, pp. 4-13.
60. *PR* 34, 19 August 1966, pp. 4-8 and in *URI* 1968, *CCP Documents* . . ., pp. 62-70.
61. Text in *PR* 33, 12 August 1966, pp. 6-11 and in *URI* 1968, *CCP Documents* . . ., pp. 42-54.
62. Mao Tse-tung 1 August 1966, in Schram 1974, p. 260.
63. Mao Tse-tung 5 August 1966, in *PR* 33, 11 August 1967, p. 5.
64. *PR* 35, 26 August 1966, pp. 3-8. In some places such as Sian, this stage began a few days earlier. Personal information from A. Watson.
65. E.g. Chengchow (Hinton 1972, pp. 83-7) and Sinkiang (Hinton 1972, pp. 87-94), where the movement was initially unsuccessful. Also marked by initial resistance, Kwangchow (Bennett and Montaperto 1971, pp. 74-7) and Shanghai (Hunter 1969, pp. 88-110).
66. Soviet and Yugoslav reports, *CQ* 28, 1966, p. 187.
67. Hinton 1972, p. 72.
68. Daubier 1974, pp. 89-90.
69. Hinton 1972, p. 97. For an explanation of Tao's contradictory behaviour, see Moody 1973, pp. 288-91.
70. Chu P'u in *Zhongguo Gongye*, Vol. I, No. 12, 24 April 1950, p. 13.
71. The first posters to appear criticising Liu Shao-ch'i were probably those at Tsinghua University – late August (Hinton 1972, pp. 74-5).

72. Israel 1967, p. 16. Note, Liu Shao-ch'i claimed he had dispatched work teams through the *new* Peking committee (Liu Shao-ch'i 23 October 1966, in Liu 1968, p. 358).
73. Personal observation.
74. Daubier 1974, p. 100.
75. Personal information. See also Befinett and Montaperto, p. 105. Many different estimates of Peking's population were made at the time and the 2 million figure can be no more than a guess.
76. Daubier 1974, p. 82.
77. Ibid., p. 79.
78. Personal observation and Daubier 1974, p. 80.
79. Esmein 1973, p. 113. In some places such as Sian, many workers did not return to the factories. Personal information from A. Watson.
80 Baum 1971, p. 378.
81. *PR* 33, 12 August 1966, p. 11.
82. Baum 1969, p. 101. Wylie 1967.
83. *SCMP* 4128, 29 February 1968, pp. 22-4.
84. Ch'en Po-ta in *SCMM* 617, 29 April 1968, p. 8.
85. Text in *URI* 1968, *CCP Documents* . . ., pp. 79-80.
86. Baum 1969, p. 103.
87. *CCP.CC* in *URI* 1968, *CCP Documents* . . ., pp. 139-42.
88. Mao Tse-tung 24 October 1966 in Schram 1974, p. 268.
89. Israel 1967, p. 13: report of Hsieh Fu-chih, 3 October 1966.
90. Personal observation. These criticisms appeared as early as late August.
91. *CCP.CC* 16 November 1966, in *URI* 1968, *CCP Documents* . . ., pp. 103-5.
92. Military Commission and General Political Dept., 5 October 1966, in *URI* 1968, *CCP Documents* . . . pp. 89-91.
93. *PR* 41, 7 October 1966, pp. 15-17.
94. Daubier 1974, p. 93.
95. Mao Tse-tung 25 October 1966, in Schram 1974, p. 274.
96. Liu Shao-ch'i 23 October 1966, in Liu 1968, p. 363.
97. Notably Wang Kuang, *CQ* 29 1967, p. 184.
98. E.g. *CCP.CC and SC* 16 November 1966, in *URI* 1968, *CCP Documents* . . ., pp. 109-11, *CCP.CC and SC* 1 December 1966, in ibid., pp. 127-9.
99. E.g. *PR* 44, 28 October 1966, pp. 16-19. Hinton 1972, p. 100.
100. *CCP* Peking Municipal Committee 18 November 1966, in *URI* 1968, *CCP Documents* . . ., pp. 122-3 – forbidding specifically kangaroo courts. arrests, torture and detention.
101. Daubier 1974, pp. 102-5.
102. Ibid., p. 104.
103. Ibid., p. 106.
104. *PR* 51 16 December 1966, pp. 5-7.
105. Daubier 1974, p. 106.
106. Ibid., p. 107.
107. *CCP.CC* 15 December 1966, in *URI* 1968, *CCP Documents* . . ., pp. 139-42.
108. Ibid., p. 140.
109. Baum 1971, p. 406.
110. *CCP.CC* 15 December 1966, in *URI* 1968, *CCP Documents* . . ., p. 140.
111. Baum 1971, p. 410.
112. Esmein 1973, p. 174.
113. *Current Scene*, Vol. VI No. 5, 15 March 1968, pp. 1-28 and Esmein 1973, pp. 174-5.
114. The following account is taken from Hunter 1969, pp. 132-220, Esmein 1973, pp. 179-83.

115. *CCP.CC*, 17 November 1966, in *URI* 1968, *CCP Documents* . . ., pp. 116-19.
116. Bridgham 1968, p. 8.
117. Esmein 1973, p. 81.
118. Ibid., p. 83.
119. Ibid.
120. Bridgham 1968, p. 8.
121. Esmein 1973, p. 84.
122. Ibid., p. 85.
123. Hunter 1969, p. 238, Esmein 1973, p. 86.
124. Esmein 1973, p. 86.
125. P'eng Teh-huai was arrested in Ch'angsha (*URI* 1968, *The Case of Peng Teh-huai*, p. 391). Lo Jui-ch'ing seems to have been arrested in Peking (Esmein 1973, p. 83).
126. Esmein 1973, p. 83, *URI* 1968, *The Case of P'eng Teh-huai*, p. 391.
127. *PR* 1, 1 January 1967, p. 21.
128. *Current Scene*, Vol. VI, No. 5, 15 March 1968, pp. 9-10.
129. The joint notice of the National Rebel General Corps of Red Labourers, Ministry of Labour and ACFTU, 2 January, was repudiated by the *CCP.CC* and *SC* on 17 February 1967. *URI* 1968, *CCP Documents* . . ., pp. 305-6.
130. Esmein 1973, pp. 195-201.
131. According to *Asahi*, there were 800,000 Scarlet Guards and 600,000 Revolutionary Rebels (Esmein 1973, p. 184). On the limited support for the Scarlet Guards see Esmein 1973, pp. 182-5.
132. Esmein 1973, p. 183.
133. Hunter 1969, p. 208.
134. Text in *PR* No. 3, 13 January 1967, pp. 5-7.
135. Mao Tse-tung, 9 January 1967, in Schram 1974, p. 275. Message of support from *CCP.CC*., Military Commission and Central Cultural Revolution Group, in *PR* 4, 11 January 1967, p. 5., and *URI* 1968, *CCP Documents* . . ., pp. 157-8.
136. *PR* 4, 20 January 1967, p. 28.
137. *PR* 4, 20 January 1967, pp. 7 and 12-15. *URI* 1968, *CCP Documents* . . ., pp. 165-70.
138. Daubier 1974, p. 127.
139. On 14, 22, 24 January and 5 February 1967. Esmein 1973, p. 192 and *SCMP* 4147, 27 March 1968, p. 3.
140. Robinson T. 1971, 'Chou En-lai . . .', p. 217.
141. Daubier 1974, pp. 139-40.
142. Bridgham 1968, p. 10. Robinson 1971, 'Chou En-lai . . .', p. 203.
143. Ibid.
144. *CCP.CC* 25 January 1967, in *CB* 852, 6 May 1968, p. 52.
145. *CCP.CC* 25 January 1967, in *URI* 1968, *CCP Documents* . . ., pp. 204-5.
146. *RMRB*, 27 January 1967, p. 2. *RMRB*, 1 February 1967, p.2. Wylie 1967.
147. Esmein 1973, p. 187.
148. Ibid., pp. 187-90.
149. Ibid., pp. 87-90. For details of the reorganisation, see *URI* 1969, *Communist China* 1967, p. 201. There was a further reorganisation of this group in August 1967.
150. Mao Tse-tung 1967, in *CB* 892, 21 October 1969, p. 50.
151. *CCP.CC, SC,* Military Commission, Central Cultural Revolution Group 23 January 1967, in *URI* 1968, *CCP Documents* . . ., pp. 195-7.
152. Mao Tse-tung February 1967, in Schram 1974, p. 278.
153. *PR* 7, 10 February 1967, pp. 12-13.
154. See Chapter 8.

155. Esmein 1973, p. 189. *SCMP* 4147, 27 March 1968, p. 7. This remark was attributed to Mao.
156. *PR* 10, 3 March 1967, pp. 10-12.
157. Mao Tse-tung February 1967, in Schram 1974, p. 277.
158. The following is taken from Gurtov 1971, pp. 313-66. Ch'en Yi, Self-criticism in *Chinese Law and Government* Vol. I, No. 1, Spring 1968, pp. 52-3.
159. Domes 1973, p. 181.
160. *CCP.CC, SC,* Military Commission and Central Cultural Revolution Group 24 March 1967, in *URI* 1968, *CCP Documents* . . ., pp. 385-7.
161. Vogel 1971, p. 332.
162. Esmein 1973, pp. 155-6.
163. *SC* and Military Commission 26 January 1967, in *URI* 1968, *CCP Documents* . . ., p. 208.
164. Vogel 1971, p. 332.
165. Ministry of Public Security and PLA Peking Garrison H.Q. in *URI* 1968, *CCP Documents* . . ., pp. 667-8.
166. E.g. Vogel 1971, p. 332.
167. Baum, in Robinson 1971, pp. 422-41.
168. Military Commission 28 January 1967, in *URI* 1968, *CCP Documents* . . ., p. 216.
169. *CCP.CC* 17 February 1967, in ibid., p. 294.
170. *CCP.CC* 20 February 1967, in ibid., pp. 331-3.
171. *CCP.CC, SC,* 3 February 1967, in ibid., pp. 227-9. Military Commission, 8 February 1967, in ibid., pp. 244-5.
172. Robinson 1971, 'Chou En-lai . . .', p. 217.
173. *PR* 12, 17 March 1967, pp. 14-16.
174. Text in *URI* 1968, *CCP Documents* . . ., pp. 409-11.

8 RADICAL LEFT AND ULTRA-LEFT (March 1967-April 1969)

The dominant theme of the eighth cycle, which began in March 1967, accelerated in July and consolidated after September, concerned the limits of revolution. How might élitism of a rightist or leftist variety be contained? What constraints might be applied to military involvement? How might one establish the framework of a new revolutionary order within which alliances and new forms of administration could form without outside manipulation?

Although the Cultural Revolution in 1967-9 was *limited*, it was not, in my view, *manipulated*. Those who disagree with me claim that radicalism got more and more out of hand to the point where Mao Tse-tung called in the Army and imposed a new order.[1] Undoubtedly Army involvement in the Cultural Revolution increased sharply in 1967 under the slogan 'three supports and two militaries' and the PLA was called in to deal with serious factional fighting. The call for the military to 'support the left', however, was not an attempt to achieve by coercive measures what could not be achieved by normative ones. Excessive coercion would not only negate the educative and emancipatory goals of the Cultural Revolution but would provoke an 'ultra-left' reaction. Indeed it was largely due to the excessive force used by the military in February 1967 that the problem of the 'ultra-left' became as serious as it did.

It is appropriate at this point to stress once again that the category 'ultra-left' was neither static nor arbitrary. Since it was defined in terms of mass reaction, few people actually claimed to be 'ultra-left' although, as we shall see, those who did revealed an extraordinary intransigence.

Cultural Revolution: Stage Eight — The Growth of the 'Ultra-left'

By March 1967, what was left of the Central Committee reached a number of decisions on military over-reaction during the preceding February Adverse Current and tried to ensure that similar actions did not occur in future. Its most harsh criticism was directed against the military commander Chao Yung-fu who was accused of carrying out a coup in Tsinghai on 23 February and of deceiving both the Central Committee and the masses.[2] In the weeks which followed, documents were issued dealing with mistakes in PLA support to the 'left' in Anhui,[3]

317

Inner Mongolia,[4] Szechwan[5] and Shantung.[6] The mistakes of the Kwangtung commander Huang Yung-sheng, however, which seemed to provoke quite considerable resentment from the rebels,[7] were spared official censure, probably because he was protected by Lin Piao, his long-time associate.[8]

It would seem that the 'radical left' leadership in March-April 1967 sought to restrict military reaction and to correct some of the mistakes made in February while still adhering to a policy of military involvement. Army participation in the triple alliance formula for revolutionary committees was seen as essential. Some of the 'ultra-left' also believed that Army participation was essential but felt that the Army was too weak and had itself been infiltrated with 'capitalist roaders'. Before long, therefore, they sought to 'drag out the handful in the Army'. The Jacobins among them, such as Lin Chieh, wished to strengthen the power of provisional organs and infuse the ranks of the revolutionary rebels with a military-type iron discipline.[9] However appealing this might have been to a few Cromwellians in the ranks of the military, the imposition of an iron discipline from above was clearly a negation of the Mass Line and, in fact, of the Cultural Revolution. Still others of an 'ultra-left' persuasion bitterly resented the Army's mistakes in February and had no time for the Army at all. The 'radical-left' were, therefore, in a dilemma. They realised that the Army had sometimes gone too far in February but that if they criticised the Army too severely they would play into the hands of some very dangerous elements. They wanted the Cultural Revolution speeded up and yet they could not rely too heavily on those of a Jacobin mentality whose stress on discipline was no different from the military hardheads who had over-reacted during the February Adverse Current. Here we see precisely why Mao was later to make the association between the 'ultra-left' and the 'ultra-right'.

Perhaps the major difference between radicals and 'ultra-left' in the period March-April 1967 concerned the criticism of Liu Shao-ch'i. The radical line, which seemed to emerge from an enlarged meeting of the Politburo in March 1967, was that criticism should centre on Liu Shao-ch'i's *line* rather than his *person*.[10] What was being waged was a 'line struggle' and not 'unprincipled civil war'. The moderate radical position is seen most clearly in the various articles that appeared criticising Liu Shao-ch'i's book *On Self Cultivation* . . . Particularly singled out for denunciation was Liu's tendency to play down class struggle.[11] It was felt that the revisions Liu made to his book in 1962 were part of a concerted campaign to reinstate P'eng Teh-huai and his assertion that 'leftist dogmatism' was a more serious deviation than 'rightist revisionism' was an echo of Khruschev's attack on the Chinese radicals.[12] Bearing in mind the criticism of Wu Han and Teng T'o made at the same time as Liu's 1962 revisions, some people felt that *On Self Cultivation* . . . contained implied criticisms of Mao[13] though in retrospect they may well have been criticisms of Lin Piao's alleged 'cult of heroism'. The point which was perhaps of the greatest importance, however, was that the very notion of 'cultivation' (*xiuyang*) was individualistic and élitist. The aim was to create men of superior moral qualities who were essentially self-trained, whereas Mao's view was that the qualities of leadership were acquired in dialectical interaction with the masses. It was felt, therefore, that Liu's prescription for leadership had more in common with ancient Confucianism than with the Mass Line.[14]

The 'ultra-left' seemed, however, not to be satisfied with an analysis of 'revisionist' line and were more interested in disgracing Liu himself. One of their principal spokesmen, Ch'i Pen-yü, took a far more aggressive position in his opening press attack entitled 'Patriotism or National Betrayal'.[15] He accused Liu of propagating a film entitled 'The Inside Story of the Ch'ing Court' which portrayed the Kuang Hsü Emperor, at the turn of the century, as a progressive element struggling against the reactionary Empress Dowager and which painted the *Yihetuan* ('Boxers') in an unfavourable light. In Ch'i's view, the Ch'ing court was hopelessly corrupt from top to bottom and the *Yihetuan* were just about the only progressive anti-imperialist force in 1900. Ch'i was, however, unwilling to let the matter rest with a denunciation of the film. Having warmed himself up for a full-scale attack, he accused Liu of capitulating to the Kuomintang during the war against Japan, opposing the socialisation of industry and commerce, dissolving co-ops, liquidating the class struggle, attacking the Great Leap Forward, advocating *sanziyibao*, pursuing a revisionist foreign policy, propagating 'self-cultivation' to oppose Mao Tse-tung Thought, perverting the Socialist Education Movement and colluding with Teng Hsiao-p'ing to sabotage the Cultural Revolution. As Ch'i saw it, Liu was a 'sham revolutionary, a counter-revolutionary . . . a Khruschev lying right beside us'.[16]

Although both radicals and 'ultra-left' demanded that Liu answer Ch'i's accusations, there was a certain danger in Ch'i's 'ultra-left' style. It was possible to reduce the Cultural Revolution to a witch-hunt. An excessive concentration on the *subjective* villainy of a few people such as Liu Shao-ch'i hindered an analysis of the objective reasons for their standpoint. Ch'i's focus was on the *person* not the *line*.

Later, in the summer of 1967, Liu attempted to defend himself.[17] On the question of capitulating to the Kuomintang, he pleaded ignorance. He blamed Teng Tzu-hui for the dissolution of co-ops and others for the revisionist policies of the early 1960s. He admitted, however, that the Eighth Party Congress had made mistakes in line and that his book *On Self Cultivation* . . . contained errors. Though he had made mistakes in the Socialist Education Movement, he defended his own and Wang Kuang-mei's participation. Finally, in his handling of the early stages of the Cultural Revolution, he confessed an inability to see what he had done wrong and, if anything, went back on his earlier 'self-criticism'.[18] The 'ultra-left' could only see Liu's defence as perfidious lying whereas it would surely have been more useful to have examined the roots of Liu's ignorance.

It is likely, as Esmein argues, that Mao Tse-tung was critical of the personalised nature of 'ultra-left' criticism.[19] In the weeks after Ch'i Pen-yü's initial attack, this criticism reached quite savage proportions. Various leaders were accused before mass meetings[20] which, as we have seen in the case of land reform, could have some educative effect on a highly deferential population, but which could also promote factionalism if too highly personalised. In the new, highly-charged atmosphere, a whole lot of new targets appeared, among them Chou En-lai whom the 'ultra-left' felt had given unnecessary protection to Ch'en Yi and T'an Chen-lin.[21] As the number of targets increased, so the content of criticism became more trivial, focusing on things such as the dress Wang Kuang-mei wore on her visit to Indonesia and her 'shameful exhibition' of dancing with President Sukarno.[22] In such a situation, there was a great danger that the educative effect of the Cultural Revolution might be lost and that the campaign to criticise Liu Shao-ch'i's works might fail to provide a focus for Red Guard and Red Rebel unity.

Perhaps it was because they saw that one of the consequences of 'ultra-leftism' would be to strengthen the 'right' that Chou En-lai and Chiang Ch'ing were particularly active in the spring of 1967, patching up quarrels and helping to form revolutionary alliances. The press warned time and again against 'anarchism' and 'factionalism' because these deviations would cause the masses to become disenchanted with the Cultural Revolution. In February, attempts had been made to get students back into school[23] although, in the new period of ferment, the 'ultra-leftist' Ch'i Pen-yü reportedly maintained that 'to go back to classes after making revolution for six months would be an admission of defeat'.[24] But despite the exhortations of the 'ultra-left' many students did in fact go back to school where the Army busied itself organising intensive political training classes.[25] In some of the major universities, however, the Army seems to have played little role and various 'headquarters' continued to hurl insults at each other. In Peking, when the three Red Guard headquarters joined in February 1967 into a single organisation,[26] it appeared that some kind of unity had been achieved. In reality, the new Red Guard Congress was largely a creature of the Third Headquarters led, amongst others, by the Tsinghua 'hero' K'uai Ta-fu — a stalwart of the new 'ultra-left'.[27] In the universities, 'factionalism' was probably worse than ever before.

An immediate consequence of what the radicals called 'bourgeois factionalism' (which was equated with 'bourgeois parliamentarianism')[28] was that the new moderate policy towards the rehabilitation of cadres could not go into effect. It was Mao's view that a majority of cadres could, after a while, be rehabilitated.[29] But whenever one side in the universities put up a slate of cadres for rehabilitation, it would usually be vetoed by the other side and the result was chaos.[30]

It was extremely difficult to get any kind of agreement amongst students on attitudes towards the Army. The 'ultra-left' sought revenge for the events of February and persisted in their demands to 'drag out the handful'. In Peking, for example, demonstrations were held opposing the new chairman of the Red Guard Congress, Nieh Yûan-tzu, the once popular philosophy teacher who put up 'China's first Marxist-Leninist *dazibao*' but who had recently been criticised for indulging in luxuries.[31] When clashes developed, troops were sent in and the 'ultra-left' then shifted their attacks to the Deputy Commander of the PLA Peking garrison and detained some PLA cadres. In such a situation, all the leaders of the Central Cultural Revolution Group could do was convene a meeting in mid-April and chastise the 'ultra-left' for attacking the PLA and engaging in 'unprincipled civil war'.[32]

Although the above picture of China in March-April 1967 is one of increasing tension, one should note that the phenomenon of 'ultra-leftism' was largely confined to the intellectuals. In the countryside, the incidence of factional struggle seems to have declined at a time when spring planting was under way[33] and criticism within industry seems to have been confined within factories.[34] In the urban residential areas, there was considerable criticism of street cadres,[35] exacerbated in many cases by the return of young people from the countryside or the frontier regions whence they had gone during the Socialist Education Movement.[36] As urban residents' committees organised themselves into 'newspaper reading groups'[37] to formulate criticisms, they made fre-

quent contact with Red Guard organisations but do not seem to have
been greatly influenced by 'ultra-leftism'. The main problem in the
residential areas seems to have resulted from the breakdown of the
public security network and occasionally residents' vigilante groups
were formed to deal with petty crime.[38] In the spring of 1967, therefore, the main confrontation between radicals and 'ultra-left' seemed
confined to the universities and the Army. There were also the
beginnings of a decisive confrontation between intellectual 'ultra-leftists'
and Army conservatives. Convinced that these contradictions were as
yet 'non-antagonistic', the radical left strove to speed up the formation
of revolutionary committees.

As we have seen, the model for provincial-level revolutionary
committees was established in Heilungkiang on 31 January under the
leadership of the old first secretary of the Provincial Party Committee,
P'an Fu-sheng. The formation of this committee had been relatively
smooth since there was a good working relationship between P'an and
the local PLA commander and both joined the revolutionary rebels.[39]
The key to success here, it would seem, was the relative ease with which
Red Rebels identified revolutionary cadres. The Kweichow committee
was established on 12 February, again fairly smoothly because the PLA
identified clearly with the revolutionary rebels,[40] and a similar pattern
developed in Shantung where a revolutionary committee was established on 23 February.[41] In Shanghai (28 February)[42] and Shansi (22
March),[43] the new revolutionary committees grew out of 'Paris
Commune'-type organisations though, in the latter, PLA support was
not as strong as it might have been.[44] It is probable that the Shansi
revolutionary committee represented something of a model in that it
was composed of some 50 per cent Red Rebels, 25 per cent PLA and
25 per cent rehabilitated cadres. In its standing committee, however,
over half were revolutionary cadres,[45] although of course this tells us
little about their actual orientation.

By April, the radicals in Peking felt that the time had come to set up
a revolutionary committee there too, amongst other things to provide
the framework for reconciling hostile groups. At one time, Peking's
Red Guards and Red Rebels had formed an organisation called the
'Preparatory Committee for the Peking People's Commune' but,
following the promulgation of the triple alliance model in February,
attempts were made to set up a Heilungkiang-type committee under
the leadership of the Minister of Public Security, Hsieh Fu-chih.[46]
The rather questionable Red Guard Congress established in February
was the first of a number of organisational building blocks that were to

form the revolutionary committee. On 19 March, a similar Congress of
Poor and Lower Middle Peasants was formed[47] and on 25 March, with
military support, a secondary school Red Guard Congress.[48] After protracted discussions, these various congresses agreed finally on the composition of a Peking Revolutionary Committee which was established
on 20 April.[49] Of its 97 members, only 17 were soldiers and 13 revolutionary cadres. Of the remainder, 24 were workers, 20 students
(including both radicals and 'ultra-left'), 13 peasants, six members of
cultural and social organisations and four urban residents.[50] Such was
the new model which was designed to show that diverse groups could
work together. As we shall see, there were some groups who clearly
could not.

Cultural Revolution: Stage Nine — Chou En-lai and the 'Ultra Left'

Flushed with their successes in the campaign against Liu Shao-ch'i in
April 1967, the 'ultra-left' began to step up their attacks upon Chou
En-lai in early May. What provided fuel for their fire was the fact that,
in the May Day celebrations, discredited ministers such as T'an Chen-lin,
Ch'en Yi and Ch'en Yün still appeared to have retained their posts.[51]
As far as the 'ultra-left' were concerned, Chou's record in the Cultural
Revolution to date had been a whole series of actions designed to pour
cold water on the revolutionary upsurge. During the process of 'seizing
power', Chou had established a complex set of criteria which were
designed to prevent precipitate action. He had demanded that 'power
seizures' should only take place 'within systems' and not across
organisational boundaries (which made horizontal mobilisation
extremely difficult). He had demanded that power be seized gradually,
after extensive preparation from the bottom up. He had spoken much
of 'revolutionary order' and had precluded direct elections on the Paris
Commune model.[52] This, the 'ultra-left' felt, protected senior 'persons
in authority taking the capitalist road'.

Since the beginning of the year, Chou had not only protected Ch'en
Yi but also four other vice premiers including T'an Chen-lin, the alleged
architect of 'false power seizures' during the February Adverse Current.
It was only on 23 May that Chou associated himself with Red Rebel
attempts to overthrow T'an and only on 15 June that he agreed to join
in the criticism.[53] Although Chou found it impossible in the end to
protect T'an, he remained steadfast in his protection of Ch'en Yi,
whose difficulties were multiplying daily. On his return from Indonesia
on 30 April,[54] the 'red diplomat' Yao Teng-shan became the centre of
an 'ultra-leftist' faction in foreign affairs which intensified its attacks on

Liao Ch'eng-chih's Overseas Chinese Affairs Commission charged with
the 'crime' of de-nationalising overseas Chinese.[55] At a time when overseas Chinese in Indonesia were subject to savage repression,[56] these
charges seemed particularly serious. At the same time, the 'ultra-left'
criticised the 'bourgeois habits' of China's diplomats abroad and
demanded that the Cultural Revolution should apply to them also.[57]

In June and July 1967, 'ultra-leftist' pressure on the Foreign
Ministry and the inability of Ch'en Yi (and presumably Chou En-lai) to
control the situation resulted in a whole series of setbacks in foreign
relations. Faced with the growth of the revolutionary White Flag
Communist Party of Burma, the 'ultra-left' were no longer content to
offer them merely lukewarm support and still maintain 'correct' relations with Ne Win's government. Following anti-Chinese riots,
connected amongst other things with the distribution of Mao-badges,
the Chinese Government reversed its previous policy and branded the
Burmese government 'fascist'.[58] At almost the same time, Sino-
Cambodian relations soured as Sihanouk perceived (rightly or wrongly)
some connection between 'Khymer Rouge' activities and the increased
militancy of Chinese embassy staff.[59] In Kenya, Nepal and Ceylon a
similar deterioration of relations occurred partly at least as a result of
'ultra-leftist' pressure.[60]

The 'ultra-left' were not content merely to criticise Ch'en Yi's and
Chou En-lai's defence of officials they considered 'revisionist' and to
demand changes in China's foreign policy. They were concerned also
with the structure of the State Council itself. The record of power
seizures in the State Council in the first half of 1967 was hardly impressive. Officially or unofficially sanctioned power seizures had taken
place in only three of the nine state committees, 30 of the 40 ministries,
six of the 24 bureaux and none of the six staff offices. Of the 49
commissions and ministries at the core of the State Council, only one
of them — the Scientific and Technical Commission — had established a
revolutionary committee. Far from creating new organs of power in the
central government, the system of ministerial Party committees had
been re-established in February and maintained administrative continuity
throughout the turbulent period which followed.[61]

What must have been particularly galling to the 'ultra-leftists' was the
fact that the Army and certain members of the Central Cultural Revolution Group (including Ch'en Po-ta) seemed firmly behind Chou En-lai's
protection of the Central government.[62] Whatever friction might have
existed between Lin Piao and Chou En-lai, Chou enjoyed great prestige
in the Army. He attended meetings of the Military Commission,

defended the Army from 'ultra-left' attacks and at times even gave orders to the troops on his own initiative.[63]

In the period May-July 1967, the orientation of the Army was considered to be absolutely crucial by the moderate 'radical-left' leadership which Chou En-lai seemed to symbolise. In the face of 'ultra-left' provocation, the Army was under no circumstances to respond in a way similar to February 1967 and, on the anniversary of the 7 May directive, Lin Piao ordered an intensive two-week rectification campaign in the PLA to correct mistakes made in the previous period of 'supporting the left'.[64] Army units were ordered to undergo a process of self-criticism on the model of the Shantung Military District Party Committee, though even there it was revealed that the committee was reluctant to publish the results for fear that the 'ultra-left' would use them to reinforce its attack upon the military leadership.[65] Although the Army was forbidden to use force, it was not to sit passively by and watch the new series of clashes that occurred between 'radicals' and 'ultra-left' in the period after May. It was still enjoined to reconcile groups by patient persuasion although, as the summer approached, this became more and more difficult. In Yünnan, the Party first secretary, Yen Hung-yin, under attack for persecuting Red Guards and sending them to undergo reform, committed suicide.[66] In Sinkiang, Wang En-mao, who had called for an end to the Cultural Revolution, was still faced with considerable radical opposition.[67] In Szechwan, the repression of radical activity by first secretary Li Ching-ch'üan resulted in bloody clashes and his replacement by Chang Kuo-hua — the commander of troops in Tibet.[68] In Peking itself, the Minister of Public Security and chairman of the new revolutionary committee, Hsieh Fu-chih, reported that struggles in the capital were still going on and that production had declined by 7 per cent in April.[69] In such a situation, the Army could only respond with patience and issue orders forbidding armed struggle, assaults, destruction, raids and unauthorised arrests. *Liberation Army Daily* saw the only response to mass criticism as patient discussion even when the Army considered the masses to be wrong.[70] Although the Army occasionally violated the non-intervention order, one cannot but be struck by its considerable forbearance and discipline during these trying months. In the countryside (though not always in suburban communes), the Army seemed to have been remarkably successful in its use of Mao Tse-tung Thought propaganda teams to effect reconciliation and in its establishment of 'front line commands for grasping revolution and promoting production'.[71]

It was probably to test the efficacy of its orders prohibiting armed struggle, assaults and unauthorised arrests that the Centre sent to the provinces a number of investigation teams in June and July 1967. Perhaps the most famous troubleshooters of all were the Minister of Public Security, Hsieh Fu-chih, and his 'ultra-leftist' colleague, Wang Li, who were sent first to Yünnan to find out about the case of Yen Hung-yin[72] and later to Wuhan where they were to be the centre of a national crisis (see below). But a more immediate danger in early July was the convocation of the first congress of an organisation known as the 'May Sixteenth Group'.[73] Though it is said that the origins of this group go back to September 1966, it did not achieve national prominence until after 16 May 1967 when, on the first anniversary of the circular repudiating P'eng Chen's 'group of five', a 'May Sixteenth Notification' was issued attacking Chou En-lai as a 'double dealer playing with counter-revolution'.[74] The origins of the May Sixteenth group were allegedly found in the Department of Philosophy and Social Sciences in the Chinese Academy of Sciences which produced such prominent and powerful 'ultra-leftists' as Lin Chieh and Mu Hsin. The group was soon joined by Kuan Feng, Wang Li and later Ch'i Pen-yü, who held powerful positions in the Central Cultural Revolution Group and thus constituted a real threat to Chou's position. The May Sixteenth Group was joined in mid-1967 by another extreme 'ultra-left' group known as the 'June Sixteenth Group', based on the Peking Foreign Languages Institute,[75] presumably with connections with Yao Teng-shan and the 'ultra-left' in the Foreign Ministry. It was apparent, therefore, that if large-scale violence broke out in the Cultural Revolution, not only would Chou's position be in danger but the whole focus of the Cultural Revolution would be thrown in an 'ultra-left' direction with incalculable consequences for the future of any Mass Line politics. Just at this crucial point, large-scale violence did in fact break out in the city of Wuhan, where for the first time in the Cultural Revolution, a large military unit mutinied.

Cultural Revolution: Stage Ten — The Wuhan Incident and its Aftermath[76]

The Wuhan incident of July 1967 might be traced back to the beginning of that year when the military commander, Ch'en Tsai-tao, had been actively engaged in suppressing Red Rebels and had earned the reputation as something of a militarist. In the period April-June, a number of armed incidents occurred in the city and a large number of factories, including the massive Wuhan Iron and Steel Works, either suspended production for a time or were reduced to half capacity. By June, the city authorities and PLA units were co-operating with a conservative rebel formation consisting largely of industrial workers known as the 'One Million Workers' in suppressing student and worker rebels.

To rectify the situation, no less a person than Chou En-lai himself flew to Wuhan where he issued a four-point judgement declaring that the 'One Million Workers' were conservative, that the military district command should not support them and that the revolutionary workers and student organisations together with their headquarters should be rehabilitated. To help Chou sort out the situation, the now experienced troubleshooters, Hsieh Fu-chih and Wang Li, arrived in Wuhan on 14 July, whereupon Chou left them to implement his judgement. Almost immediately, however, Hsieh and Wang entered into argument with Ch'en Tsai-tao about a certain organisation that had been disbanded by Ch'en because of radical activities. Accusing Hsieh and Wang of pre-judging the case, Ch'en threatened to have the 'One Million Workers' cut off the city's water, power and transport if his verdict was reversed. Apparently, Ch'en, said to be in good standing with Lin Piao, refused to negotiate with such relatively minor personages as Hsieh and Wang and merely let them carry out inspections from 15 to 18 July. In the mean-time, however, the 'One Million Workers' continued their work of repression and by 19 July Hsieh and Wang felt they had seen enough to make a report on the situation. After hearing the report, which re-affirmed Chou's original judgement, one military commander, Niu Hai-lung, immediately mobilised his troops and, together with members of the 'One Million Workers', laid siege to Hsieh's and Wang's hotel. On the following day, when Ch'en declared that the 'One Million Workers' were beyond his control, Hsieh and Wang were seized and beaten up and the whole of the city taken over by the 'One Million Workers' backed by Niu Hai-lung's troops.

The reaction from Peking was immediate. Acting Chief of Staff Yang Ch'eng-wu ordered Ch'en to release Hsieh and Wang and escort them to Peking, ordered an airborne division, the 15th Army and five gunboats from the East Sea Fleet into action and prepared to take Wuhan by force. Chou En-lai flew back to Wuhan taking care not to land at the main airport (in order to avoid any kidnap attempt) and Lin Piao him-self went to Wuhan to assess the situation and appoint, as field commander, Yü Li-chin, the Political Commissar of the Air Force. Meanwhile, both Hsieh and Wang were either released or managed to escape and, on their arrival in Peking, were greeted by the whole of the central leadership[77] minus Mao Tse-tung and supported by several days' demonstrations in the capital. On 26 July, what was left of the Central Committee convened a special meeting to deal with the situation, dismissed Ch'en Tsai-tao and replaced him by Tseng Ssu-yü[78] and, on the following day, sent a letter of support to the PLA units now moving against the insurgents.[79] Fighting in Wuhan probably continued until 4 August, by which time Hsieh and Wang could return to the city to witness the final victory; but it was a victory won at a considerable price.

The most immediate consequence of the Wuhan incident was a violent 'ultra-left' reaction. The 'ultra-left' were now convinced that there was indeed a 'handful' in the Army taking the 'capitalist road' which they sought immediately to 'drag out'.[80] In the Army itself there were some of an 'ultra-leftist' inclination who revived the case of P'eng Teh-huai in *Liberation Army Daily* as a focus for mobilisation.[81] In the period following the Wuhan incident, a series of violent incidents occurred in over a dozen provinces.[82] The new 'hero' Wang Li returned from Wuhan immediately to join Yao Teng-shan in his bid to oust Ch'en Yi from the Foreign Ministry and topple once and for all the 'handful' there too.[83] For 14 days they were successful. Yao Teng-shan virtually appointed himself Foreign Minister and brushed the protests of Chou En-lai contemptuously aside.[84] On 11 August, the Foreign Ministry rebels held a mass rally in Peking's Great Hall of the People to denounce Ch'en and all Chou En-lai could do was to suggest smaller rallies in future.[85] Though Ch'en still continued to officiate at formal functions, policy was clearly in the hands of the 'ultra-left' who managed, in their short term of office, to alienate Cambodia,[86] deliver an ultimatum to the British government concerning the suppression of Chinese rebels in Hong Kong and, on its expiry, to burn down the British mission in Peking on 22 August.[87]

With the burning of the British mission, it was clear that the 'ultra-left' had overplayed their hand. Confident of military support, Chou En-lai was now able to issue an order restricting Red Guard activities around foreign missions[88] and, on 1 September, the Peking Municipal Party Committee reprimanded the 'ultra-left' and banned the May Sixteenth Group.[89] Red Guards were now forbidden to move around the country and were required to 'support the Army'.[90] On 5 September, Chiang Ch'ing, once a great supporter of the movement to seize power, criticised the Red Guards' attacks on the Army and the seizure of guns,[91] and her appeals were endorsed in the name of the Central Committee.[92] Now that the Army was prepared to counter 'ultra-left' violence, Yao Teng-shan disappeared from view and Ch'en Yi was reinstated. The sick Ch'en Yi was, however, never the same man again.[93]

In the weeks following the burning of the British mission, Mu Hsin, the 'ultra-leftist' editor of *Guangming Daily*, Lin Chieh, the 'ultra-leftist' editor of *Red Flag*, and Chao Yi-ya, the 'ultra-leftist' editor of *Liberation Army Daily*, were arrested and the May Sixteenth organisation rooted out.[94] At the same time, the influential Kuan Feng and Wang Li were placed under surveillance and Ch'i Pen-yü disappeared from view. As the May Sixteenth organisation was systematically dismantled, *Red Flag* suspended publication for a time[95] and, in an article criticising two books of T'ao Chu, Yao Wen-yüan signalled that those 'opportunists' who had come to power with T'ao Chu were to be carefully examined.[96] Clearly a new stage of consolidation was to begin but, unlike previous periods of consolidation, the 'radical-left' were determined that it should be consolidation on their terms.

Cultural Revolution: Stage Eleven – Consolidation

The removal of 'ultra-leftist' leaders in Peking in September 1967 deprived the 'ultra-left' of the extraordinary influence they had enjoyed over the Central government in mid-1967 but many months were to pass before this influence at lower levels was removed. In the autumn of 1967, complaints were heard that the new triple alliance organs were 'dominated by the bourgeoisie' but Mao was quite adamant that the Cultural Revolution should now be carried on relatively peacefully. In a Red Guard publication of 23 October he is quoted as saying:

> This nationwide disturbance is the last of its kind. The army is also disturbed this time. After this disturbance, the whole country will be at peace and become the regime of the revolutionary rebels. It is the Party Central Committee that allows this nationwide disturbance.[97]

Though Mao always advocated the efficacy of struggle, it was apparent that many workers and peasants had become quite alienated by the faction fighting of the 'ultra-left' and, if the Mass Line were to be effective, other groups in society must be brought into leading positions in the Cultural Revolution. If ultimately the Cultural Revolution was indeed 'proletarian', the working class organisations, which had been little affected by 'ultra-leftism', should play a much greater role.

In the autumn of 1967, Mao Tse-tung himself undertook an extensive tour of China, issuing as he went a series of 'supreme instructions', calling for the formation of 'grand alliances' and the unification of the

Communist Party.[98] With the formation of the Tsinghai Revolutionary Committee on 12 August 1967,[99] only seven of the 29 provincial-level administrative divisions had established revolutionary committees and Mao set the end of 1967 as a target for the formation of such bodies over the whole country. By the Spring Festival of 1968, the whole country was to have consolidated the new structure of power.[100]

But it proved extremely difficult to establish the necessary 'grand alliances' to form the basis of the provincial-level committees. Although the hands of the Army were no longer as tied as they had been in the period prior to the Wuhan incident, the Army was under strict orders not to allow the situation of February 1967 to recur. At that time, some military units had decided quite arbitrarily which group constituted the 'true left' that they would support and had suppressed others. We have already seen the disastrous consequences of such actions. Now the Army was still prevented from supporting particular groups but, in addition to undertaking the task of patient persuasion, the PLA could insulate certain organisations from outside contact and so prevent the influence of 'ultra-leftist' groups that cut across organisational lines.[101] Factories and schools were now to form their own alliances and then affiliate with larger bodies, rather than the previous situation where 'ultra-leftist' dominated alliances (such as the Peking Red Guard Congress) descended upon the schools and fanned into flames the already smouldering faction fighting. The Army, therefore, was to hold the ring, and to do this effectively it was required in October to undergo a new round of rectification.[102] Progress, however, was to be very slow indeed. Only one more provincial-level revolutionary committee was to be formed in 1967, that of Tientsin Municipality[103] (which was raised to provincial status early in 1967). In other parts of China, 'grand alliances' took a very long time to form. An even more difficult problem was how to reconstruct the Party. Where revolutionary committees were in existence, 'nuclear core groups' of Party members were sometimes formed but under no circumstances were the revolutionary committees allowed to appoint them. The 'nuclear core groups' were required to 'emerge from the struggle' and, as yet, not play a leading role in the revolutionary committees' policy formation.[104] The new relationship between Party and state bodies had still to be worked out.

Perhaps nowhere was the new stress on consolidation more bedevilled by 'ultra-leftist' demands than in the field of education. On 25 October, People's Daily once again put forward a plea that regular classes should be resumed, though this time according to the stipulations of Mao's May Seventh Directive.[105] Integration was to be effected between units of education and units of production. Schools were to run factories and factories to run schools. To inculcate the idea of 'revolutionary discipline', schools might be organised on a military basis with battalions and companies each with their own political instructor from the PLA. Examinations were under no circumstances to be reintroduced and recruitment was to be based on a combination of recommendation by units of production and selection by school revolutionary committees.[106] Though the reform proposals were very bold, they still did not satisfy the 'ultra-left' who rejected categorically any 'slave mentality' requiring the subordination of students to authority. They seemed to advocate nothing less than the dismantling of the formal school system, the abolition of the universities and any form of organisation based on what they called the 'three in one conglomeration'.[107]

The Shengwulian

One of the main difficulties in forming 'grand alliances' in the autumn of 1967 was the fact that the 'ultra-left' was still often quite strong in the provinces. In Hunan province in particular, there emerged in late 1967 an organisation which was unashamedly 'ultra-leftist' and which categorically rejected the policy of consolidation embarked upon in September. Though the programme of the Hunan 'ultra-leftists' might be atypical, I shall describe it here at length in order to give some idea of what an 'ultra-leftist' position was after the 'August storm'.[108]

Following Mao Tse-tung's visit to Changsha (the capital of Hunan) on 17 September, the Chairman's call for a 'grand alliance' was interpreted by the Hunan 'ultra-left' as a demand for a Paris Commune-type organisation that would reverse the drift towards the restoration of the pre-Cultural Revolution situation. The idea of the Commune was taken very seriously indeed. The Hunan Provincial Proletarian Revolutionaries Great Alliance Committee (abbreviated as *Shengwulian*), which was formed on 11 October, stated (probably wrongly), that Mao had been in favour of the original Shanghai Commune of February 1967 and were hard put to explain why he finally turned against it. Their only explanation was that the Shanghai Commune had failed to measure up to the standards of the Paris Commune of 1871, in that the proletariat had not been armed and Mao could only postpone the implementation of communes until the Cultural Revolution had truly removed the 'handful' in the Army. To this end, Mao had demanded that the People's Liberation Army 'support the left' and thus become involved in the Cultural Revolution.

As the *Shengwulian* saw it, the January Revolution had been a

glorious experience. Proletarian power had been achieved and 90 per
cent of cadres had been forced to stand aside. Since workers had shown
that they could manage factories, there was surely no need for so many
cadres to be rehabilitated. Though they did not say so in so many
words, the *Shengwulian* completely reversed Mao's statement that 90
per cent of cadres might be rehabilitated. They sympathised with Mao's
call for revolutionary committees based on the triple alliance formula,
but emphasised that such bodies were only temporary organs of power
which were to remain in existence until the Army was fully integrated
into the Cultural Revolution. Now that the Army had been so integrated, there was no reason for their continued existence and
communes and 'soviets' might be set up immediately.

The *Shengwulian* regarded it as a matter of extreme urgency that
revolutionary committees and their preparatory committees be elimi-
nated. Since the February Adverse Current, these committees had
provided an opportunity for power to be seized by a 'red capitalist
class' of whom Chou En-lai was the major representative. They had
wrested power and property away from the revolutionaries and had
imprisoned some of the Red Rebels. It was utopian to believe that such
bodies would provide the basis for a transition to communism since
they had imposed their rule from the top down and had been dominated not only by 'capitalist roaders' among the old Party cadres but
also by 'capitalist roaders' in the Army. The 'People's Commune of
China' was the only answer.

The *Shengwulian* were particularly heartened by the events of the
August storm. Looking back with nostalgia to the old days when the
Army and people maintained very close relations, they felt that the
only way this relationship could be recaptured was by an internal
revolutionary civil war such as almost developed in August. At that
time, more and more 'ultra-left' organisations seized arms from the PLA
and were convinced that many cities were in a state of 'armed mass
dictatorship'. It was the masses in arms that had provided the cement
for the old Paris Commune and this was something that the 'façade' of
the People's Militia could never achieve. What the 'ultra-left' found
most impressive about the August storm had been the extent to which
everyone had become soldiers and even primary school students had
carried out the work of communications and public security.

The *Shengwulian* firmly believed that it had been Mao Tse-tung himself who had called for the mass seizure of arms in August and they
regarded the 5 September directive ordering the surrender of arms as a
betrayal. At that time, they had launched a movement to conceal arms

from the troops in preparation for future armed struggles. The new period of consolidation launched in September was, in the eyes of the *Shengwulian*, comparable only to the situation in Russia after February 1917 where soviets had been formed but political power had been usurped by the bourgeoisie. *Their* 'October Revolution' was just around the corner and they were witnessing merely the last struggle of the 'bourgeoisie', represented in Hunan by the Preparatory Committee for the Hunan Provincial Revolutionary Committee. Hunan would perhaps see the triumph of their policy of 'victory first in one or several provinces'.

The *Shengwulian* seemed supremely confident that they would be swept to victory. They castigated those who just sat waiting for a second Cultural Revolution and believed that the revolution should be one continuous process not punctuated by stages of consolidation (though perhaps to avoid being branded as Trotskyists they did in fact make some reference to the idea of 'stages'). In the meantime, they rejected the idea of building up the Party in preparation for the Ninth National Congress by rehabilitating old cadres. What was needed was a new 'Maoist' (*Mao Zedong zhuyi de*) party (a term never used by the 'radical-left'), and not a party of the 'bourgeois reformers'.

On 24 October Lin Piao was reported to have said:

The rubbish heap of Hunan is large and the three black lines are thick and long. Hunan is a counter-revolutionary 'three in one' patchwork. Hunan has not gone through disturbances thoroughly.[109]

This speech, which I have never seen in full, was taken by the *Shengwulian* to herald a new stage in the Cultural Revolution. Similarly, speeches by Chiang Ch'ing on 9 and 12 November,[110] which called for further reforms in the field of art and literature, were taken as a signal that the period of consolidation was to be brought to an end. After all, many radical upsurges in the past had started in that field.

Whatever Chiang Ch'ing's intentions might have been in late 1967, she was most bitter in her denunciation of the *Shengwulian* programme in early 1968.[111] She was joined by K'ang Sheng[112] and Yao Wen-yüan[113] who were already engaged in a denunciation of the May Sixteenth Group. The *Shengwulian* were considered to be guilty of forming 'independent kingdoms', a 'mountain-top mentality' and above all 'anarchism'. Though it is possible that the *Shengwulian* and other organisations of an 'ultra-left' persuasion might have been committed to a coherent anarchist philosophy, it is my own view that all 'anarchism' meant in the context of early 1968 was a sectarian rejection of discipline and authority, a romantic commitment to disorder, a premature rejection of the state in all its forms and, consequently, an implied negation of the principle of dictatorship of the proletariat. Such 'anarchism' was seen by the 'radical-left' in early 1968 as a 'petty-bourgeois' deviation that negated proletarian discipline, and cadres and people were enjoined to make a class analysis of all factionalism.[114]

It has been suggested by some commentators that organisations such as the *Shengwulian* were merely radicals who had not gone along with the policy changes of September 1967; in short yesterday's 'radical-left' was today's 'ultra-left'.[115] The implication here is that had the *Shengwulian* demands been put forward earlier in the year they might have been enthusiastically applauded. It is true that, before February, some of the 'radical-left' had supported the formation of commune-type organisations and had declared that one should not be afraid of disorder. There was never, however, much enthusiasm for the removal of 90 per cent of all cadres nor a positive glorification of armed violence.

The Case of Yang Ch'eng-wu

The mounting criticism of the May Sixteenth Group and other 'ultra-leftist' organisations such as the *Shengwulian* in early 1968 led to some surprising developments in the Army. Yü Li-chin, the Air Force Political Commissar, who had commanded the PLA forces during the capture of Wuhan, and Yang Ch'eng-wu, the Acting Chief of Staff who had so promptly ordered troops into action, were removed from their posts.[116] Ch'en Tsai-tao, on the other hand, who had appeared as the hard-headed conservative military commander at Wuhan, had been treated most leniently in contrast to the 'ultra-leftist hero' Wang Li. It would be rash however to conclude, from an analysis of the Wuhan incident, that Lin Piao felt he had made a mistake and that the discrediting of the 'ultra-left' should be followed up by the removal of those who had taken a strong stand against the conservatives. Many other reasons have been put forward for Yang's dismissal. He has been accused of undue ambition and of forming his own power group to become substantive Chief of Staff, of 'bugging' the houses of Mao Tse-tung and Lin Piao and of attempting to play off 'radical-left' against 'ultra-left' to advance his own position.[117] Yang has sometimes been accused of supporting the conservatives and sometimes the 'ultra-left'.

Whatever the reasons for the removal of Yang and other senior military officers in March 1968, they cannot be disociated from a clearly conservative drift within the PLA command. Yang was replaced by none other than Huang Yung-sheng, who had been one of the more repressive commanders during the February Adverse Current, and seems to have been universally detested by 'radicals' and 'ultra-left' alike. In fact, Huang had just completed a programme of dealing with 'ultra-leftists' in Kwangtung when he was appointed. It has been argued that Huang was the representative of a powerful group of scarcely radical regional military commanders such as Han Hsien-ch'u (Fukien), Ch'en Hsi-lien (Liaoning), Hsü Shih-yu (Kiangsu) and Yang Teh-chih (Shantung) who had been opposed to Yang Ch'eng-wu's policy of centralised command and the placing of his own appointees in the provinces.[118] I am not altogether convinced by the argument. First, if the regional commanders wanted independence, why should they club together and select a former Fourth Field Army man likely to continue to enforce a policy of centralisation via the Fourth Field Army network. It must surely have been clear that the source of the military centralisation policy was in fact Lin Piao. Secondly, is it likely that regional commanders, hoping for a quiet life, would select someone who was likely to provoke an extreme reaction from what 'ultra-left' were still active? The role of Lin Piao in the events of 1968 has yet to be explained but I suspect that, if Lin was half as ambitious as he was claimed to be, the appointment of Huang Yung-sheng was his way of satisfying regional demands for a conservative appointment while still maintaining very tight control over regional appointments and thus enhancing his own position. If my guess is correct, then Lin was not much different from that other former Fourth Field Army commander, T'ao Chu, who shifted from conservative to 'ultra-left' and back again whenever his interests would be better served.

Whatever the truth in the Yang Ch'eng-wu incident, it is certainly true that the regional military played a much more important role in the formation of revolutionary committees in late 1967 and early 1968. Jürgen Domes has divided the formation of provincial-level revolutionary committees into three waves.[119] The first, as we have seen, was from January to April 1967 in which mass organisations either played a very active role or at least where the role of the military was unclear. During this period, six committees were established. During the turbulent period of mid-1967, no provincial-level revolutionary committees were established and the only committee to be established before November was in Tsinghai (12 August). Beginning in November, however, the establishment of provincial-level revolutionary committees came thick and fast — Inner Mongolia (1

November), Tientsin (6 December), Kiangsi (5 January), Kansu (24
January), Honan (27 January), Hopei (3 February), Hupei (5 February),
Kwangtung (21 February), Kirin (6 March), Kiangsu (23 March) and
Chekiang (24 March).[120] Of these committees, Domes argues, the
majority were set up under strong regional pressure from the Army. A
third wave was to begin in April and, between then and September, the
remaining 11 provincial level units set up committees, again under
strong military pressure.[121] Although it is very difficult to argue with
Domes' assertion as to the role of the military, one should beware of
coming to too hasty a conclusion as to its significance. First, although
revolutionary committees were increasingly established from above, the
conclusion shared by 'ultra-leftists' and Western élite theorists that the
mass component within them was insignificant, does not necessarily
follow. Secondly, the formation of provincial-level committees from
above tells us little about administrative units at lower levels where I
am sure the mass organisation component was greater than ever before.
One of Domes' conclusions is, however, inescapable. The ideals of the
Paris Commune had without doubt receded. Two steps may have been
taken forward, but one had certainly been taken back. Leninists should
not have been too surprised at that, but then some of the 'ultra-leftists'
who still remained active were strange Leninists.

Cultural Revolution: Stage Twelve — Renewed 'Ultra-Leftism'

March 1968 was perhaps one of the most confusing months in the
whole Cultural Revolution. In the country as a whole, a number of contradictory trends were in evidence. In the first part of the year, renewed
calls were made to 'support the Army and cherish the people',[122] aimed
at restoring Army-civilian relations and countering the growth of
factionalism in the PLA associated with the Yang Ch'eng-wu incident.
None the less, there were still many 'ultra-leftists' who were profoundly
disturbed at what they believed was a conservative drift in the Army
associated with the increased power of regional commanders. In Peking,
a number of the former marshals such as Nieh Jung-chen and Hsü
Hsiang-ch'ien achieved new prominence[123] as a focus of loyalty, and
efforts were made to reconcile the 'left' with the new military leadership.

   In the cities, a new and intensified effort was made to stress
the importance of working-class leadership. Experiments with worker
self-management were publicised[124] and examples were given of the
integration of education with productive activity. T'ungchi University,
for example, was cited as a model of how engineering faculties could be
integrated with construction engineering companies[125] and many articles

appeared showing the creativity of workers in proposing technical innovations.[126] In the countryside also, great prominence was given to the Tachai model.[127] The great slogan of the time was 'struggle, criticism, transformation' with the new stress on the third of these components.

Nevertheless, however successful the process of 'transformation' had been in the industrial and agricultural sectors, the situation in the universities was still chaotic. In late 1967 and early 1968, large numbers of 'radical' and 'ultra-left' youth were sent down to the countryside in a new programme of *xiafang,*[128] in part to dampen down their élitist tendencies but also as part of a general programme of reforming China's education system. It is probably quite understandable that some of them resented their fall in status, and it is significant that some left China for Hong Kong. Such one-time rebels have provided us with accounts (however jaundiced) of Red Guard activity[129] that have informed many studies of the Cultural Revolution. Some of these former 'little generals' were sent as far away as Sinkiang or Inner Mongolia where they were to settle down under PLA guidance to the new task of building up the frontier regions. There were, however, still a large number of disgruntled 'ultra-leftists' within the universities who continued to engage in faction fighting.[130]

The operative slogan in early 1968 had been 'support the left but not any particular faction' and, however successful this might have been in restraining those who might have wished for a repetition of the February Adverse Current of 1967, it did little to solve the problem of 'factionalism'. In Peking the 'ultra-left', still to some extent under the influence of Ch'i Pen-yü, wished to reform the Peking Municipal Revolutionary Committee and mounted an attack on its chairman, Hsieh Fu-chih.[131] Throughout March 1968, demonstrations were held in the capital both in support of and in opposition to Hsieh and in Peking University troops were called in, though seemingly to no avail.[132] In Tsinghua University (the subject of a graphic account by William Hinton),[133] strife intensified in the spring of 1968 as student organisations clashed and the Yang Ch'eng-wu incident only added fuel to the flames.

Perhaps another source of inspiration for the 'ultra-left' in May 1968 were the events in Paris and elsewhere.[134] Until that time, little attention had been paid in China to the revolutionary movements in capitalist countries. The events in Paris, however, had an immediate impact upon China and called into question once again the old foreign policy notion of the progressive nature of the 'second intermediate zone' in

which De Gaulle stood as a major figure. On 21 May, a massive rally
was held in Peking to support the 'progressive student movement in
Europe and North America' and statements were issued in support of
the French workers and students.[135] The Peking rally was followed by
similar rallies in other parts of the country and it was pointed out that
the Thought of Mao Tse-tung had had a great impact upon the development of revolutionary movements in other parts of the world.[136]
Nothing was said, however, about how this re-evaluation of the revolution in capitalist countries affected Lin Piao's 'Third World' thesis.

I am not arguing here that the Chinese attention to the events of
Europe and North America in May 1968 was merely the result of
'ultra-leftism' because clearly these events were so important that any
'radical' would have felt obliged to comment on them. It is significant
to note here that it was precisely at this time (July 1968), that Peking
felt obliged to report a French comment on the élitism of some of the
European 'new left' idols such as Régis Debray[137] (with implications
for the arch-symbol Che Guevara). The implied association between
Chinese 'ultra-left' élitism and that of Debray must surely have been
apparent.

The events in Paris, which revived once again the slogan of the Paris
Commune,[138] and the warnings of a new 'rightist' danger that came in
the wake of the Yang Ch'eng-wu incident, boosted the confidence of
the 'ultra-left'. They had been extremely heartened by statements of
Chou En-lai in March, for clearly Chou was not one of their number.

> From last winter to the present, the extreme left has been criticised
> and repudiated. Now the right has risen again, the February 'adverse
> current' has made a comeback, and the royalists have tried to
> emancipate themselves and launch a counterattack and retaliation.[139]

Now the official line seemed not to be an attack on all factionalism but
only 'bad' factionalism in accordance with the injunction to make a
'class analysis of factionalism'. In such a situation, the 'ultra-left' went
on to the offensive yet again, though their efforts were much less effective than in 1967. During this period, incidents occurred in various
parts of the country, the most serious struggle being in South China
(Kwangtung, Kwangsi and Yünnan).[140] Though fighting in Kwangtung,
in particular, was quite severe and bodies appeared floating down the
river to Hong Kong, and although much was made of the seizure and
attempted seizure of arms,[141] it is probably true that, overall, the
fighting in the spring of 1968 was less severe than in the summer of

1967. As I see it, the consolidation of 1967-8 was qualitatively different from the previous periods of consolidation in that it was carried on under essentially radical leadership and involved great experimentation and innovation at lower levels. The events of April-June 1968 were but a temporary spasm of the declining 'ultra-left'.

Though, after 28 July, the Army helped to disarm factions,[142] it was quite clear to the radicals that military action was no solution to the problem in any long-term sense. The Army intervened in February 1967 and in the summer of 1967 and had only stiffened resistance. If some new and genuine revolutionary order was to be established, the principle of working-class leadership and the study of Mao Tse-tung Thought had to be actualised and brought to bear upon the problem of 'ultra-left' factionalism. In 1967 and early 1968, it had been the PLA-led Mao Tse-tung Thought propaganda teams that had tried to bring about 'grand alliances';[143] now it was to be the *worker-peasant* Mao Tse-tung Thought propaganda teams. On 28 July, Mao Tse-tung reportedly presided over a conference of student leaders in Peking in which he said, 'You have let me down, and what is more, you have disappointed the workers, peasants and soldiers of China.'[144]

At the same time, China's first worker-peasant Mao Tse-tung Thought propaganda team was dispatched to the embattled Tsinghua University and by mid-August was achieving the impossible — discipline and reconciliation.[145] To celebrate the victory, Mao Tse-tung presented to the team a gift of mangoes that he had received from a visiting Pakistani delegation.[146] For the rest of 1968, 'mangoes' were to become the symbol of worker-peasant leadership. One of the original mangoes was preserved in formalin[147] and workshops started turning out plastic mangoes in celebration of the event. However odd such actions might seem, the symbolic importance of the mangoes was as great as that of Mao Tse-tung's Yangtze swim of 1966. Consolidation under working-class leadership and with peasant support was to be the order of the day. The 'ultra-left' were almost finished.

Cultural Revolution: Stage Thirteen — Radical Consolidation

Perhaps the most remarkable achievement of the worker-peasant Mao Tse-tung Thought propaganda teams lay in the field of education. Though considerable stress was to be given to the informal and semi-formal education system, there was now no doubt that the formal system would continue in existence and universities would continue operations. In the words of Mao Tse-tung:

It is still necessary to have universities; here I refer mainly to colleges of science and engineering. However, it is essential to shorten the length of schooling, revolutionise education, put proletarian politics in command and take the road of the Shanghai machine-tools plant in training technicians from among the workers. Students should be selected from among workers and peasants with practical experience and they should return to production after a few years of study.[148]

The Shanghai Machine-Tools Plant stressed the promotion of workers to the status of technicians after short periods of study in tertiary institutions and rejected the old system of employing graduates from the universities with little practical experience. It rejected also the 'ultra-left' utopianism that completely underestimated the role of any technicians. Now university graduates should only be employed in positions of responsibility after they had been granted a 'qualification certificate' from workers and peasants.[149] In the following period, the Shanghai Machine-Tools Plant model was extended to the whole field of university enrolment, whereby universities would not accept students until they had spent some time working in factories and communes and had been recommended by appropriate revolutionary committees.[150]

It will be evident that the stress on an integrated education system, with factories running schools and schools running factories, was but a restatement of the old *minban* idea of education which dated from Yenan days and which had been implemented once again during the Great Leap Forward. In the period of radical consolidation of 1968-9, however, many of the excesses of the Great Leap were avoided. During the Great Leap, an over-concentration on production had sometimes resulted in a concentration on educational *output* rather than the quality of inputs. Now the operative slogan was *shaoerjing* (little but well).[151] Though the Great Leap stressed informal education, institutions such as the family were not considered as important in this regard. Now attempts were made to ensure that family discussions were integrated with the activities of schools.[152] In general, however, the reforms of 1968-9 were remarkably similar to those of 1958. Modern equivalents of the old 'red and expert' universities and technical middle schools were established.[153] The expansion of the education system was assisted by a new *xiafang* of educated youth. Theoretical training was backed up by a new practical orientation in the spirit of *Kangda* (the Resist Japan University) of 1942-3[154] and a considerable amount of local initiative was fostered.

In the period 1968-9, no attempts were made to standardise the education system, for excessive standardisation and bureaucratisation had been the bugbear of the 'radicals' in 1966. Each area and each school tried to work out its own structure and programme and solve its own problems and 'advanced experiences' were propagated not as operational instructions but merely as 'reference material'.

Although these 'advanced experiences' did not have the force of directives, it would perhaps be useful to outline some of their features to give an indication of the type of education the radicals preferred. First, particularly praised were cases where more and more of the poorer peasants had been brought into the educational system; cases are cited where all sorts of problems, such as lack of classrooms and the obligation of rural children to help with farm work, were solved.[155] Secondly, schools were praised which dispensed with full-time administrators and brought workers and peasants in to help with the teaching.[156] Thirdly, communes and brigades were commended for reducing or abolishing tuition fees (though this was a very knotty problem).[157]

From an organisational point of view, it would seem the countryside was much more successful than the cities in working out a new structure.[158] Though it was relatively easy for urban factories to set up schools, it was extremely difficult for the worker propaganda teams to organise schools in residential areas where they did not exist before.[159] The main problem was availability of funds, though one might imagine that local conservatism was also significant. In the countryside, however, where peasants probably had a much clearer idea of what they wanted, 'user control' of schools was more easily effected. In the Lishu district of Kirin province, in May 1969, a programme was adopted which was given great prominence in *People's Daily*.[160] Here, secondary school revolutionary committees were to be placed under the authority of commune revolutionary committees and primary schools under the authority of brigade 'educational leading groups'. A distinction was made between policy and operations, in that only the latter was the responsibility of teachers and students. At a policy level, the triple alliance comprised (1) representatives of the poor and lower middle peasants, (2) the PLA and (3) teachers-students, but each of the first two elements in the triple alliance formula could also be involved in operations (teaching). The draft programme stipulated that school education, social education and family education should be integrated and the operation of the schools mesh in with production tasks. To this end, primary school teachers were to be paid partly as ordinary peasants

on a work-point basis, though secondary school teachers received a
salary. Priority in enrolment was to be given to the children of workers,
poor and lower middle peasants and soldiers, and age qualifications
were abolished. The number of subjects taught was reduced and excessive book learning was opposed. The old examination system was also
abolished though 'open-book tests' were permitted. Though I am sure
that many of the 'ultra-leftists' would have objected to the Kirin
scheme as a sell-out, it did represent a significantly more radical model
than anything that existed prior to the Cultural Revolution and, what is
more important, was more likely to achieve mass support than any of
the grandiose schemes of the 'ultra-left'.

The principle of 'user-control' and decentralisation was not only
applied to schools in the second half of 1968 and early 1969. Medical
services were also reorganised on a local level and integrated with
neighbourhood administration.[161] In the spirit of the Great Leap
Forward the stress was on training *more* medical workers rather than
specialised surgeons. Large numbers of para-medical works were
trained[162] who, after a short course of one or two years, could deal
with routine medical cases and were responsible for spreading China's
medical network to areas where it had hardly existed before. Such a
development, in what must surely be one of the most conservative pro-
fessions anywhere in the world, was truly remarkable, and it is perhaps
salutary to consider that many doctors were sent down into the wards
to serve for a time as nurses.[163]

The decentralisation of services in the cities was part of a general
process of urban reorganisation in which worker propaganda teams also
played an important part.[164] Despite the general reaffirmation of much
of the Great Leap Forward tradition and the fact that the model
Tach'ing oilfield had many features of the old urban commune, no
attempts were made in 1968-9 to revive the urban commune as such.
The major task, at that time, was to rebuild neighbourhood committees
(street committees and residents' groups) according to the triple combination and the old Yenan slogan of 'simple administration'. The first
residential revolutionary committees were established in Shanghai as
early as March 1967, though it took a whole year before neighbourhood revolutionary committees were set up over the whole city.[165] In
other areas, the establishment of street revolutionary committees
appears to have been undertaken a little later, though, by the second
half of 1968, progress was quite rapid. As street revolutionary committees were articulated first to military control commissions and later to
higher revolutionary committees, the number of rehabilitated urban

cadres increased and their street-level mass component decreased.[166] Nevertheless, the integration of representative bodies, formal urban administration and urban public security, which was now effected for the first time, made mass participation in urban administration much easier than ever before.[167]

By the end of 1968, many cities had established revolutionary committees at municipal ward (*qu*), sub ward (*fenqu*) and street level. Below that level, the old residents' groups had been reorganised into Mao Tse-tung Thought study groups on demographic and social rather than purely residential lines. Local public security was in the hands of 'citizens' public security enforcement teams', revived 'worker picket organisations' or bodies known as 'teams for the dictatorship of the masses'.[168] In many ways, this was a revival of the 1949 system which had been changed once the Soviet model of vertical rule had been adopted. It was, however, something more than just a reversion to 1949. The Mao Tse-tung Thought study groups were seen as having not just a control or governmental function but also an important educational function. The fusion of education with other aspects of life was rather a reaffirmation of the Great Leap Forward tradition.

Within the factories, the situation once again resembled 1949 in that the triple alliance brought together cadres (technical or otherwise), non-unionised worker representatives and PLA (or, failing that, militia representatives). In 1949, the triple alliance formula had broken down due to the low level of mass consciousness, an 'economist' union structure and the adoption of the Soviet vertical rule. Now there was a chance that when the military gave way to a reconstituted Party structure and if the unions were revived, many of the earlier mistakes could be avoided. As in urban residential administration, the pattern of administration was something much more than a reversion to 1949. The workers were much more skilled, literate and politically conscious than at the time of liberation. The 1949 forms of administration were paralleled by forms which derived from the Great Leap such as the 'two participations and triple combination' which were carried out with even greater vigour. Furthermore, the control structure (such as it was) was *internal* and not external and took the form of 'worker sentinels'. In such a situation, experiments with self-management could be continued but not along the profit-oriented Yugoslav model.

In the countryside, efforts had been directed since 1967 towards creating revolutionary committees at commune and brigade level to replace the 'front line committees' established earlier under military guidance. Like their urban counterparts, these committees differed in

composition according to when they were set up. Those that came into
being in 1967 usually had a far greater mass component than those
which came into being in 1968 when more old cadres were rehabilitated.[169] Perhaps the main reason why such was the case was that the
factional fighting in mid-1968 did have some impact on the countryside,
particularly in suburban areas where 'five category elements' were sometimes killed by fanatic 'ultra-leftists'[170] and it was felt that there was an
urgent need to regularise administration before the autumn harvest. In
the new period of consolidation, the main cadre deviation switched to
'tailism' and isolated reports came in of clan feuds[171] which many
people had considered no longer to be a major problem.

In such a situation, the Cultural Revolution in fact intensified in the
rural areas in the autumn of 1968,[172] though it was a relatively quiet
revolution with the emphasis on 'criticism and transformation' rather
than 'struggle'. In the countryside, Army influence remained strong.
PLA Mao Tse-tung Thought propaganda teams were set up and these
teams entered into the task of cadre evaluation on a grand scale.[173]
The rural teams were not, however, just latter-day versions of the old
conservative work-teams of the Socialist Education Movement, for they
were actively engaged in the task of mass mobilisation in preparation
for the new leap in agriculture. As the spirit of the Great Leap of 1958-9
was once again invoked, there was considerable discussion about
attaining higher levels in socialised agriculture[174] and even about the
partial free-supply system.[175] The new period of consolidation was
surely like none that had gone before.

In the autumn and winter of 1968, it looked as though China was on
the eve of another Great Leap Forward, though clearly much had been
learned from the Great Leap of 1958-9 and there were many mistakes
that would not be repeated. Particular attention, for example, was to be
paid to grain storage so that, if the harvests failed, China would not
suffer as she did in 1959-62. A new intensified *xiafang* movement
developed, and a tremendous amount of detailed discussion was entered
into concerning the communisation of farm machinery and how to deal
with attendant problems.[176]

One of the sources of error in the Great Leap of 1958-9 had been,
according to Mao, weak leadership on the part of cadres. In the new
Great Leap atmosphere of 1968, particular care had to be taken to see
that the 'commandist' deviations of 1958-9 did not recur. To this end,
a campaign was launched to absorb fresh blood into the Party.[177] As
more and more 'ultra-leftists' were removed from positions of responsibility, more and more cadres were rehabilitated, but care was taken to

see that such cadres had reformed. To achieve this, a particular institution was utilised known as the *May Seventh cadre school.*[178] Such schools were at first temporary creations designed to reorient cadres criticised during the Cultural Revolution but gradually became regular institutions. Cadres at different levels were required to spend a period of time in them not just studying and discussing their orientation but also engaging in productive labour.

It was in this atmosphere of radical consolidation that the process of forming provincial-level revolutionary committees was completed in September 1968[179] (nine months behind the original schedule outlined by Mao) and the Party set about organising the Twelfth (and last) Plenum of the Eighth Central Committee, which met from 11 to 31 October. At last, the Party Centre delivered its verdict on Liu Shao-ch'i:

> The report confirms with full supporting evidence that Liu Shao-ch'i, the No. 1 person in authority taking the capitalist road, is a renegade, traitor and scab hiding in the Party and is a lackey of imperialism, modern revisionism and the Kuomintang reactionaries who has committed innumerable crimes. The Plenary Session holds that the exposure of the counter-revolutionary features of Liu Shao-ch'i by the Party and the revolutionary masses in the great proletarian cultural revolution is a tremendous victory for Mao Tse-tung's thought and for the great proletarian cultural revolution. The Plenary Session expressed its deepest revolutionary indignation at Liu Shao-ch'i's counter-revolutionary crimes and unanimously adopted a resolution to expel Liu Shao-ch'i from the Party once and for all, to dismiss him from all posts both inside and outside the Party and to continue to settle accounts with him and his accomplices for their crimes in betraying the Party and the country.[180]

One might perhaps argue legalistically whether a Party body had the authority to dismiss Liu from his state posts, but by 1968 it is doubtful whether people bothered much about such niceties. Now, for the first time, 'China's Khruschev', reviled by name in hundreds and thousands of posters and Red Guard publications, could be referred to by name in the official press. It will perhaps be a long time before we know what happened to Liu after the Twelfth Plenum. At the time of writing, Liu is probably dead, but I would imagine his end was a fairly quiet one. When angry Red Guards stormed Chungnanhai (where Liu lived) in mid-1967, he was never handed over to them and probably

Mao himself prevented a public trial.[181] As for his colleagues, many
have returned and it is rumoured that even P'eng Teh-huai was last seen
living quietly in retirement in Szechwan.[182] In any case, the dismissal
of Liu formally marked the end of the 'struggle' stage of the Cultural
Revolution. The main task now was to rebuild the Party and to convene
a new Party Congress.

Czechoslovakia and the Sino-Soviet Border Conflict

In this chapter, I have avoided any lengthy discussion on Chinese
foreign policy except to describe the immediate consequences of the
takeover of the Foreign Ministry by the 'ultra-left' in August 1967. One
may summarise the whole period of the Cultural Revolution as a
general deterioration of state-to-state relationships across the board,
with the significant exception of Tanzania where China began to fulfil
her pre-Cultural Revolution undertaking to build the Tanzam Railway
in order to give Zambia an outlet to the sea other than through
Rhodesia.[183] Relations with foreign Communist parties remained very
strained[184] with the exception of Albania, Vietnam and Rumania, and
'people-to-people' relationships took the form of supporting a number
of revolutionary groups in Burma, India[185] and elsewhere. In Latin
America, upon which China had pinned high hopes for revolution, the
constant splits in the revolutionary movements presented a very dismal
prospect and, as the Cultural Revolution progressed, China became
more and more disenchanted with Cuba which she saw fast becoming a
Soviet satellite.[186]

Throughout the Cultural Revolution, Sino-Soviet relations deteriorated further especially after the Soviet Union began to give support to
Party conservatives,[187] resurrected the aged Wang Ming[188] and condemned the whole Cultural Revolution. In May 1968, China made
much of a 'Stalin group' in the Soviet Union that was determined to
combat revisionism[189] and the Soviet Party press denounced Mao
Tse-tung as un-Marxist.[190] Throughout the whole period, innumerable
border incidents occurred on the Sino-Soviet border but were probably
considered too unimportant to make the official press.[191] In August
1968, however, the Soviet Union began to emerge in a new light.

Though the Chinese heartily condemned the Dubcek leadership in
Czechoslovakia as revisionist,[192] the Soviet invasion of 20 August and
the subsequent attempt to legitimise it according to the principle of
'limited sovereignty' was unforgivable. As the Chinese saw it, the
Soviet invasion was not only an example of the Soviet Union behaving
just like the United States but was also an instance of 'great power

collusion'. 'The aggression by Soviet revisionism was carried out with the tacit understanding of U.S. imperialism.'[193] Provided the United States could do what she liked in her sphere of influence, then so could the Soviet Union.

Some analysts have suggested that the invasion convinced the Chinese leadership that the Soviet Union might be tempted to launch a pre-emptive strike against China in the knowledge that the United States would just look on, though evidence for this is doubtful. It is significant, however, that in 1967-8 a massive Soviet military build-up occurred along China's northern borders[194] which hastened the formation of the last revolutionary committees in the frontier regions.[195] It is also significant that in March 1969, the fifty-seventh border incident in the Chenpao Island area blew up into a major incident.[196]

I find it inconceivable that the Chenpao incident of March 1969 was either a prelude to a possible Soviet invasion of China in the manner of Czechoslovakia, or an example of China's revanchist wish to take back territory occupied by the Tsars. It seems more likely that what the Soviet Union was engaged in was a masking operation to hide the clampdown in Czechoslovakia which did not occur until several months after the invasion. What better distraction than a resurrection of the 'yellow peril'? From China's point of view, the border incident though disturbing, had perhaps a beneficial side. It hastened the drive towards unity after the 'struggle' stage of the Cultural Revolution and provided a patriotic motive in the rapidly developing Great Leap atmosphere. I am, of course, not arguing here that the incident was manufactured by the Chinese. It was, after all, the fifty-seventh incident in that one small spot on the map. All I am saying is that the Chinese were not reluctant to publicise it as they had been with similar incidents in the past. In my view, there was never any danger of war in 1969, though the Chenpao Island incident did serve to point up the Chinese view that the Soviet Union and the United States enjoyed equal status as enemies and it cannot be without significance that the Ninth Party Congress opened on 1 April 1969 to the cries of condemning 'The New Tsars'.[197]

The Ninth Party Congress

The Ninth Congress of the Chinese Communist Party was originally to have been held back in the early 1960s and since that time there had been constant talk of convening it, but due to the escalation of what Mao referred to in 1971 as the ninth crisis in the history of the Party it had been repeatedly postponed. With the expulsion of Liu Shao-ch'i in October 1968, however, the way was clear for its convocation and the

Twelfth Plenum discussed a draft Party constitution.[198] Though the
congress had been a long time coming, I cannot avoid the impression
that it was convened in a hurry and perhaps, like the two sessions of
the Eighth Congress, was pushed through by those of a less radical bent
in order to head off a new period of radicalism.

It was revealed in 1973 that the report to the Congress given by Lin
Piao was not his original report but had been substantially revised by
Mao.[199] The constitution of April 1969, though giving considerable
stress to the role of the military and nominating Lin Piao as Mao's
successor,[200] was much less Army-oriented than the draft document of
October 1968. Thirdly, the Congress, like its predecessors, was followed
by a new period of radicalisation which did not seem to be the result of
its deliberations. Would it be rash to suggest that the Congress had been
rushed through to stabilise the situation before a new radical offensive
was launched? Further evidence for haste is provided by the fact that
the original intention to rebuild the Party from the bottom up seemed
now suddenly to be changed to building from the top down as well as
from the bottom up.

The composition of the new Central Committee did not appear as
radical as it could have been. Though there were a few new youthful
people in its ranks, the average age (for those members whose ages we
know) was 61 as opposed to 56 in 1956. Half of the new Central
Committee came from the PLA and had a military rank between 1955
and 1965 (as opposed to 40 per cent in 1956). The percentage of cadres
in state administration went down from nearly 60 per cent to 31 per
cent which meant that the percentage of model workers and representatives of mass organisations went up considerably but did not include
many prominent Red Guard leaders.[201]

The new Party leadership elected at the First Plenum immediately
after the Ninth Congress represented a form of triple alliance. The PLA
component may be divided into two groups — regional military
commanders such as Hsü Shih-yu, Ch'en Hsi-lien and Li Teh-sheng and
a central military group headed by Lin Piao and consisting of Yeh
Ch'ün (his wife), Huang Yung-sheng (Chief of Staff, himself also a
regional commander), Wu Fa-hsien (Commander of the Air Force),
Li Tso-p'eng (First Political Commissar of the Navy), Ch'iu Hui-tso
(Director of Logistics), Yeh Chien-ying (the former marshal and vice
chairman of the Military Commission) and possibly Wang Tung-hsing
(Commander of the Peking Guard Regiment). The State administration
was represented by Chou En-lai and Li Hsien-nien (vice premier and
Minister of Finance). The radical left consisted of Mao himself, Ch'en

Po-ta, K'ang Sheng, Chiang Ch'ing, Chang Ch'un-ch'iao, Yao Wen-yüan and Chi Teng-k'uei (from Honan) and probably Hsieh Fu-chih. Finally, there was a group of Party veterans whose importance seemed to be largely symbolic — Chu Teh, Liu Po-ch'eng (a veteran marshal) and Tung Pi-wu (who, following the demise of Liu Shao-ch'i acted jointly with Sung Ch'ing-ling, the wife of Sun Yat-sen, as Head of State).[202]

I am rather doubtful whether any statistical analysis of the Ninth Central Committee tells us very much about the political orientation of its members. It is perhaps more fruitful to look at the Congress documents, which although representing something of a compromise were still quite 'radical'. The Party Secretariat was not mentioned nor the post of general secretary (though one might note that the former Party general secretary Teng Hsiao-p'ing was no longer under a cloud). The principle of 'open Party building' was adopted whereby candidates for Party membership had to be accepted not only by Party branches but also by non-Party people they worked with. It was also accepted in principle that Party members having grievances could bypass various levels of Party authority and, if necessary, appeal directly to the chairman himself and the Thought of Mao Tse-tung was given pride of place in the constitution.

The End of the Eighth Cycle

In retrospect, it would seem that Mao Tse-tung was far from happy at the tremendous power enjoyed by Lin Piao and the central military apparatus at the time of the Ninth Congress.[203] There can be no doubt, however, that he believed that the state of the rebuilt Party centre in 1969 was infinitely less bureaucratic than the one it had replaced. At the First Plenum on 28 April he declared:

> The Soviet revisionists now attack us. Some Tass broadcast or other, the Wang Ming material, and the long screed in *Kommunist* all say we are no longer a party of the proletariat and call us a 'petty-bourgeois party' . . . When they see there are many military men in our lists of personnel, they call us 'military' . . . They can say what they want. But their words have one characteristic: they avoid branding us as a bourgeois party, instead they brand us as a party of the petty bourgeoisie. We, on the other hand, say that they are a bourgeois dictatorship and are restoring the dictatorship of the bourgeoisie.[204]

Perhaps the main reason why Mao was not too disturbed that many of the radical ideals of the Cultural Revolution had only been partly achieved was that he saw the Cultural Revolution dialectically as a *process* rather than an *event*. According to Mao, there would be new periods of consolidation. Such was the core of his theory of continuous revolution'.[205] Mao held that, in any transitional society, there would always be bureaucratisation. To counter this, a whole series of revolutionary upheavals were necessary to prevent bureaucratic interests acquiring class forms. If the state were eventually to wither away, the Party should not become too institutionalised. If China's future history was to be characterised by new Cultural Revolutions, it followed that the longer the interval of time between one upheaval and the next, the more severe would that upheaval be. Perhaps as Mao saw it in 1969, the Paris Commune was not yet on the agenda but it might be at some time in the future. In the meantime, the current role of the military would be preferable to the rule of the 'bourgeoisie'. It was imperative, however, to see that military participation in civilian administration did not become institutionalised, for, in the final analysis, power should pass to the armed proletariat.

The Cultural Revolution had not resulted in instant communism but who apart from a few 'ultra-leftists' believed that it would? It had, however, created a precedent for rebellion which made the ossification of the Communist Party much more unlikely in the immediate future. The idea of 'capitalist relations' as an intrinsic form of any transitional society had been well established as was the need for constant struggle to 'transform' them. The modified Great Leap situation, which prevailed in 1969 and which had resulted from the Cultural Revolution, provided a much better framework for that struggle than the old Soviet model or its 'revisionist' transmogrification. By 1969, there was a new concentration on the importance of closing the urban-rural gap and indeed on the danger of any exacerbation of the division of labour. Education was now more clearly geared to the production of people who were both 'red and expert'. During the course of the Cultural Revolution, the people of China had experienced a profound lesson in the relationship between economic forms and political ideas and were ready to carry on where the Great Leap left off.

There were doubtless many people who were disappointed. At the end of the seventh cycle, which saw the growth of the 'ultra-left', there were many amongst the young whose hopes were perhaps too extravagant. Undoubtedly the 'ultra-leftist' activities of 1967-8 had caused considerable havoc and had led to resentments which would take a long time to heal. Even Mao had been surprised at the ferocity of their reaction and, perhaps by 1969, was still not very confident about the revolutionary consciousness of China's youth. The Red Guards were but a shadow of their former selves but, in their short period of activity, had launched a revolution which would be completed by other groups. Mao had always believed that intellectuals could be no more than a catalyst. Now as worker-peasant Mao Tse-tung Thought propaganda teams carried out basic-level leadership roles, it would appear that Mao's changing the name of the Cultural Revolution from 'Socialist' to 'Proletarian' had been justified. In future, the revolutionary potential of youth would be exercised as members of classes as opposed to a stratum defined according to education.

Doubtless the prevalence of 'economism' amongst the workers and peasants and the rise of conservative worker Red Rebel formations had also caused Mao some concern but, in the aftermath of the 1967 disturbances, it would seem that the problem had ceased to be a major one. Workers were now enthusiastically engaged in experimenting with new methods of management and the Tachai model of remuneration was actively propagated in the countryside. The new stress on collectivised agriculture in 1968-9 heralded the total discrediting of *sanziyibao* and the major impediments that stood in the way of China working out her own developmental model seemed to have been removed.

Notes

1. E.g. Domes 1973, Chapters XII and XIII, pp. 175-97.
2. *CCP.CC,SC*, Military Commission, Central Cultural Revolution Group 24 March 1967, in *URI* 1968, *CCP Documents* . . . pp. 385-7.
3. *CCP.CC* 27 March 1967, in ibid, pp. 392-5.
4. *CCP.CC* 13 April 1967, in ibid., pp. 417-19.
5. *CCP.CC* 7 May 1967, in ibid., pp. 434-8, and 16 May 1967, in ibid., pp. 443-5.
6. *SCMP* 4061, 16 November 1967, pp. 11-12.
7. Bennett and Montaperto 1971, pp. 163-5, 169, 179, 184, 188.
8. Baum 1971, p. 434.
9. Lin Chieh, *PR* 27, 30 June 1967, pp. 27-31.
10 Esmein 1973, p. 159.
11. *PR* 20, 12 May 1967, p. 7.
12. *SCMM* 652, 28 April 1969, p. 30.
13. *SCMM* 651, 22 April 1969, p. 19.
14. *PR* 17, 21 April 1967, pp. 14, 17-18.
15. *PR* 15, 7 April 1967, pp. 5-15.
16. Ibid., p. 15.
17. Liu Shao-ch'i summer 1967, in Liu 1968, pp. 365-8.
18. Compare Liu Shao-ch'i 1968, pp. 357-9 and p. 368.
19. Esmein 1973, p. 161.

20. Ibid., p. 163.
21. Robinson 1971 'Chou En-lai . . .', pp. 209-10, 219-20.
22. Daubier 1974, p. 179.
23. *CCP.CC* 19 February 1967, in *URI* 1968, *CCP Documents* . . . pp. 321-4. *PR* 11, 10 March 1967, pp. 13-15.
24. Esmein 1973, p. 130.
25. This was in response to Mao Tse-tung's 7 March directive. For text, see *PR* 11, 15 March 1968, p. 5.
26. *PR* 11, 10 March 1967, pp. 5-8.
27. Hinton 1972, pp. 117-18.
28. Ibid., pp. 115-16.
29. *PR* 10, 3 March 1967, pp. 5-9. *PR* 12, 17 March 1967, p. 15.
30. Hinton 1972, p. 112.
31. Hunter 1969, p. 153.
32. Bridgham 1968, p. 18.
33. Baum 1971, pp. 440-1.
34. Esmein (1973, p. 203) notes a decline in worker activism after the January Storm. This was rekindled in June.
35. White 1971, p. 339. Salaff 1971, pp. 295-8.
36. White 1971, pp. 338-40. Salaff 1971, p. 296.
37. Salaff 1971, p. 304.
38. Ibid., pp. 307-8.
39. Esmein 1973, pp. 220-2. Domes 1970, p. 116. *PR* 7, 10 February 1967, pp. 12-13. *PR* 8, 17 February 1967, pp. 15-17.
40. Esmein 1973, pp. 225-6. Domes 1970, pp. 117-18. *PR* 10, 3 March 1967, pp. 19-21.
41. Esmein 1973, p. 225. Domes 1970, p. 117. *PR* 11, 10 March 1967, pp. 17-19.
42. Domes 1970, p. 117. *PR* 10, 3 March 1967, pp. 10-12.
43. Esmein 1973, pp. 226-7. Domes 1970, pp. 118-19. *PR* 14, 31 March 1967, pp. 5-6.
44. Domes 1970, pp. 118-19.
45. Ibid., p. 113.
46. Esmein 1973, pp. 227-9.
47. *PR* 13, 24 March 1967, pp. 6-8.
48. *PR* 14, 31 March 1967, pp. 11-14.
49. *PR* 18, 28 April 1967, pp. 10-14.
50. Esmein 1973, pp. 228-9.
51. *PR* 19, 5 May 1967, p. 7.
52. Robinson T. 1971, 'Chou En-lai . . .', pp. 234-5.
53. Ibid., p. 221.
54. *PR* 19, 5 May 1967, p. 14.
55. Gurtov 1971, pp. 329, 332, 334-5.
56. *PR* 19, 5 May 1967, pp. 11-13.
57. Gurtov 1971, pp. 335-6.
58. *PR* 28, 7 July 1967, p. 17. See Gurtov 1971, pp. 338-44.
59. Gurtov 1971, pp. 344-6.
60. Ibid., p. 346.
61. Robinson T. 1971, 'Chou En-lai . . .', pp. 213-4, 237-8.
62. Ibid., p. 225. *CB* 844, 10 January 1968.
63. Robinson T. 1971 'Chou En-lai . . .', pp. 228-9.
64. Bridgham 1968, p. 20.
65. *SCMP* 4061, 16 November 1967, p. 12.
66. Chien 1969, p. 14.
67. Ibid., pp. 20-1.

68. Ibid., pp. 26-7.
69. Bridgham 1968, p. 21.
70. *SCMP* 3975, 7 July 1967, pp. 1-6.
71. Baum 1971, p. 440.
72. Chien 1969, pp. 15-16.
73. Robinson T. 1971 'Chou En-lai . . .', p. 223. *CB* 844, 10 January 1968.
74. Robinson T. 1971 'Chou En-lai . . .', p. 224. *CB* 844, 10 January 1968, p. 26.
75. Robinson T. 1971 'Chou En-lai . . .', p. 224. *CB* 844, 10 January 1968, p. 4 *passim*.
76. Robinson T. 1971, 'Chou En-lai . . .', pp. 239-59.
77. *SCMP* 3989, 27 July 1967, pp. 1-2.
78. Robinson T. 1971 'Chou En-lai . . .', p. 269.
79. *CCP.CC,SC*, Military Commission, Central Cultural Revolution Group, 27 July 1967, in *URI* 1968, *CCP Documents* . . ., pp. 484-8.
80. In particular Lin Chieh. For an indication of his views see his article commemorating Army Day (1 August) in *PR* 32, 4 August 1967, pp. 36-9. This article, originally published in *Red Flag*, was said to have been a factor that led to the journal's suspension in late 1967.
81. The campaign began on 16 August with the publication of the resolution of the 8th Plenum on P'eng Teh-huai. (*URI* 1968, *The Case of P'eng Teh-huai*, pp. 39-44.) Other articles from the official and unofficial press of the time may be found in ibid. For a discussion of different views on the campaign and its contemporary significance, see Esmein 1973, pp. 286-9.
82. Chien 1969, pp. 9-57.
83. Gurtov 1971, p. 347.
84. Ibid., p. 348
85. Robinson T. 1971, 'Chou En-lai . . .', p. 263.
86. Gurtov 1971, pp. 350-1.
87. For a detailed account, see Hinton 1972, pp. 132-4. See also Gurtov 1971, pp. 351-2.
88. Esmein 1973, p. 283.
89. Ibid., p. 284.
90. On 25 August, the *CCP.CC, SC*, Military Commission and Central Cultural Revolution Group issued a call to 'support the Army and cherish the people', see *CCP.CC, SC*, Military Commission, Central Cultural Revolution Group, 5 September 1967, in *URI* 1968, *CCP Documents* . . ., p. 508.
91. Chiang Ch'ing 5 December 1967, in *URI* 1968, *CCP Documents* . . ., pp. 521-33.
92. *CCP.CC* 9 September 1967, in *URI* 1968, *CCP Documents* . . ., p. 520 and *CCP.CC* General Office 6 October 1967, in ibid, pp. 543-4.
93. Ch'en was suffering from cancer and died on 6 January 1972. *PR* 2, 14 January 1972, pp. 3-5.
94. Esmein 1973, p. 283.
95. Ibid., p. 285.
96. *PR* 38, 15 September 1967, pp. 7-17. The interpretation here is that of Esmein 1973 p. 285.
97. Mao Tse-tung in *SCMP* 4075, 7 December 1967, p. 27.
98. *CCP.CC* and *CCP.CC*, Secretariat Bureau and General Office, July-Sept. 1967, in *URI* 1968, *CCP Documents* . . . pp. 550-6.
99. *PR* 34, 18 August 1967, pp. 22-3.
100. *SCMP* 4070, 30 November 1967, pp. 2-3.
101. The operative slogan in the Army was 'support the left but not any faction', *PR* 2 February 1968, pp. 8-9. Esmein 1973, p. 292.
102. *PR* 47, 17 November 1967, pp. 7-8.

103. On 6 December. *PR* 51, 15 December 1967, p. 11.
104. *SCMP* 4237, 13 August 1968, p. 9.
105. *CB* 846, 8 February 1968, pp. 15-17. The same plea was made one month later on 26 November 1967 (*SCMP* 4071, 1 December 1967, pp. 1-3)
106. Bastid 1970, p. 27, *CB* 846, 8 February 1968.
107. Bastid 1970, p. 28. The reference here is to the 'triple alliance'.
108. The following description of the *Shengwulian* is taken from *Shengwulian* autumn 1967, 21 December 1967, and particularly 6 January 1968, in Mehnert 1969, pp. 74-100.
109. *Shengwulian*, 21 December 1967 in Mehnert 1969, p. 79.
110. Text in *URI* 1968, *CCP Documents* . . ., pp. 596-601.
111. Chiang Ch'ing 21-24 January 1968, in Mehnert 1969, p. 117.
112. K'ang Sheng 21 January 1968, in ibid., p. 117.
113. Yao Wen-yüan 21-24 January 1968, in ibid., p. 118.
114. *PR* 19, 10 May 1968, pp. 3-4.
115. Such is the view of Mehnert 1969.
116. Reportedly the order dismissing them was read to a rally on 27 March by Chou En-lai (Chien 1969, p. 131).
117. For speculations on the Yang Ch'eng-wu case, see Robinson T. 1972, pp. 191-2. Esmein 1973, pp. 293-300. Domes 1973, pp. 193-4.
118. Domes 1973, p. 133.
119. Domes 1970, pp. 114-15.
120. *PR* 46, 10 November 1967, pp. 29-31 (Inner Mongolia). *PR* 51, 15 December 1967, p. 11. (Tientsin). *PR* 2, 12 January 1968, pp. 5-7 (Kiangsi). *PR* 5, 3 February 1968, pp. 11-13 (Kansu). ibid. (Honan). *PR* 6, 9 February 1968, pp. 11-12 (Hopei). *PR* 7, 16 February 1968, pp. 25-7 (Hupei). *PR* 9, 1 March 1968, pp. 5-7 (Kwangtung). *PR* 11, 15 March 1968, pp. 17-18 (Kirin). *PR* 13, 29 March 1968, pp. 10-11 and 38 (Kiangsu). *PR* 14, 5 April 1968, pp. 8-10 (Chekiang).
121. Domes 1970, p. 142.
122. This campaign started originally in 1967. On the 1968 campaign, see *PR* 4, 26 January 1968, pp. 9-10.
123. Esmein 1973, p. 298. Particularly worth noting was the fact that a number of these old marshals appeared at the 4th Congress of Activists in the Creative Study and Application of Mao Tse-tung Thought (*PR* 10, 8 March 1968, p. 12) and the subsequent reception by Mao (*PR* 11, 15 March 1968, p. 8)
124. E.g. *PR* 12, 22 March 1968, pp. 18-21.
125. *PR* 47, 17 November 1967, pp. 9-10 and *PR* 48, 24 November 1967, pp. 9-10. On the situation after 6 months, see *PR* 20, 17 May 1968, pp. 11-12.
126. E.g. *PR* 3, 19 January 1968, pp. 15-17.
127. Ch'en Yung-kuei, in *PR* 49, 1 December 1967, pp. 19-22.
128. *CCP.CC, SC,* Military Commission, Central Cultural Revolution Group 8 October 1967, in *URI* 1968, *CCP Documents* . . . pp. 560-3.
129. E.g. the subject of the biography by Bennett and Montaperto who left in November 1967.
130. Hinton 1972, pp. 145-82.
131. Daubier 1974, p. 245.
132. Esmein 1973, p. 309.
133. Hinton 1972, pp. 145-70.
134. Mehnert 1969, p. 62.
135. *PR* 21, 24 May 1968, pp. 18-19.
136. *PR* 22, 31 May 1968, pp. 9-10.
137. *PR* 30, 26 July 1968, pp. 11-12.

138. *PR* 21, 24 May 1968, p. 19.
139. Chou En-lai 21 March 1968, *SCMP* 4166, 29 April 1968, p. 2.
140. For a very confusing overview of the period, see Chien 1969, pp. 174-217. See also *SCMP* 4215, 11 July 1968, pp. 1-11.
141. E.g. *SCMP* 4215, 11 July 1968, p. 11. *SCMP* 4227, 29 July 1968, pp. 9-12.
142. *SCMP* 4266, 26 September 1968, p. 13. This account depicts students at the People's University unilaterally handing over arms to the PLA.
143. Baum 1971, p. 440.
144. Gittings in *FEER*, Vol. 35, 25-31 August 1968, pp. 377-8.
145. Hinton 1972, pp. 185-233.
146. *PR* 32, 9 August 1968, pp. 5-6.
147. Hinton 1972, p. 227.
148. *PR* 31, 2 August 1968, p. 3.
149. Ibid., pp. 9-14.
150. Hinton 1972, pp. 263-4.
151. Bastid 1970, p. 41.
152. Ibid., p. 42.
153. *SCMM* 638, 23 December 1968, pp. 10-15.
154. E.g. *PR* 2, 10 January 1969, pp. 17-20.
155. *SCMM* 638, 23 December 1968, pp. 17-18.
156. *SCMM* 647, 17 March 1969, p. 17.
157. Bastid 1970, p. 35. *SCMM* 638, 23 December 1968, p. 18.
158. Bastid 1970, p. 35.
159. Salaff 1971, pp. 314-16.
160. *SCMP* 4418, 19 May 1969, pp. 9-15.
161. Salaff 1971, pp. 316-17.
162. *PR* 5, 31 January 1969, pp. 17-18. Horn 1969, particularly pp. 135-40.
163. Horn 1969, p. 64.
164. Salaff 1971, pp. 298-312.
165. Ibid., pp. 298-9.
166. Ibid., pp. 300-1.
167. Ibid., p. 303.
168. Ibid., p. 310.
169. Baum 1971, p. 447.
170. *SCMP* 4225, 25 July 1968, pp. 12-13 and Baum 1971, pp. 448-9.
171. *SCMP* 4244, 23 August 1968, pp. 1-12.
172. Baum 1971, pp. 449-53.
173. *PR* 15, 12 April 1968, p. 27.
174. Bridgham 1970, pp. 9-10.
175. *Current Scene*, Vol. VII No. 9, 3 May 1969, p. 11.
176 *SCMM* 643, 3 February 1969, pp. 34. *SCMM* 644, 10 February 1969, pp. 40.
177. *PR* 43, 25 October 1968, pp. 4-7.
178. For a description of a May Seventh cadre school, set up in November 1968, see Macciocchi 1972, pp. 76-104.
179. *PR* 37, 13 September 1968, pp. 3-5.
180. *CCP.CC* 31 October 1968, in *PR* 44, 1 November 1968, Supplement p. vi.
181. Hinton 1972, pp. 118-22.
182. *URI* 1968, *The Case of P'eng Teh-huai*, p. 392: from unidentified Hong Kong source published in *Sing Tao Jih Pao* 16 November 1968, p. 4.
183. See Yu 1970.
184. Note, previously good relations with North Korea deteriorated after Red Guard criticisms of Kim Il-sung in February 1967, *CQ* 30 1967, p. 247.
185. *PR* 29, 14 July 1967, pp. 22-6.
186. Halperin 1967, pp. 148-51.

187. E.g. *Pravda* 16 February 1967, cited in *CQ* 30 1967, p. 244.
188. An article by Wang Ming 'China: Cultural Revolution or Counter-
      Revolutionary Coup' was published in *Canadian Tribune* 19 March 1969 and
      subsequently reprinted by the Novosti Press Agency. Cited in Schram 1974,
      p. 348.
189. *PR* 20, 17 May 1968, pp. 20-3.
190. *Kommunist* quoted in *CQ* 35 1968, p. 198.
191. *PR* 10, 7 March 1969, p. 12.
192. *PR* 6, 7 February 1969, pp. 15-16.
193. Chou En-lai 23 August 1968, *PR* 34 (Supplement), 23 August 1968, p. iv.
194. This had been going on at least since January 1967 (*CB* 892, 21 October
      1969, p. 50) when Mao noted that Soviet ground forces were on the move.
      By late 1970, Chou En-lai noted that there were over one million Soviet
      troops threatening China to the north and west (Snow 27 March 1971, p. 22.)
195. The last two provincial-level revolutionary committees were set up in Tibet
      and Sinkiang on 5 September.
196. *SCMM* 650, 14 April 1969, pp. 5-12. *PR* 10, 7 March 1969, pp. 4-12. *PR* 11,
      14 March 1969, pp. 3-21. *PR* 12, 21 March 1969, pp. 6-26, 29-31. *PR* 13,
      28 March 1969, pp. 14-26, 29-31. *PR* 14, 4 April 1969, pp. 16-27.
197. *PR* 10, 7 March 1969, pp. 6-7.
198. Text in Chien 1969, pp. 349-55 and in *CQ* 37 1969, pp. 169-74.
199. *PR* 35-6, 7 September 1973, pp. 17-18. The report is in *PR* Special Issue,
      28 April 1969, pp. 11-30 and *PR* 18, 30 April 1969, pp. 16-35.
200. Text in *PR* 18, 30 April 1969, pp. 36-9.
201. Domes 1973, pp. 208-10.
202. For a list of the new *CC*, see *PR* 18, 30 April 1969, pp. 47-8; for the new Polit-
      buro elected by the First Plenum, ibid., pp. 48-9.
203. Gayn (1973) claims that Chou En-lai informed visitors that Lin's group forced
      a reluctant Mao to name Lin his successor in 1969 (p. 305).
204. Mao Tse-tung 28 April 1969, in Schram 1974, p. 282. *Kommunist* was a theo-
      retical journal of the CPSU.
205. For a discussion of 'continuous revolution' or 'continuing the revolution' see
      Starr 1971; *PR* 46, 10 November 1967, pp. 9-16 and *PR* 39, 26 September
      1969, pp. 3-10.

9 THE TENTH CRISIS (April 1969-August 1973)

The ninth cycle in the history of contemporary China began with the Ninth Party Congress in April 1969, accelerated in the summer of that year, entered a period of consolidation in August 1970 and came to an end with the Tenth Congress in August 1973. It was dominated by the attempt of Lin Piao to hold on to and consolidate his power. Though some analysts have described the events of this period simply in terms of a power struggle, it will be quite obvious, from what has gone before, that I regard such an approach as inadequate. In the last chapter, I rejected as simplistic the notion that the central leadership changed its course, branded the radicals of the earlier period as 'ultra-left' and then imposed discipline crudely from above. I attempted to take seriously the Chinese use of the terms 'left' (or as I called it 'radical-left') and ultra-left' and to suggest that such labels had an objective referent in terms of the Mass Line. This was not to say, however, that many people were not wrongly categorised. In the last chapter I described the defeat of the 'ultra-left'. Here I am faced with a much more difficult task — that of describing the defeat of Lin Piao.

'Flying Leap'

In the period immediately after the Ninth Party Congress, it was proposed that the Party and Youth League should be built from the bottom up and rectified continuously according to the principle of 'centralised policy and divided operations'. The integration of education and production was promoted according to the *May Seventh Directive*. A new *xiaxiang* movement was under way and emphasis was given to the Mass Line. Though many of the Great Leap ideals were reiterated in this new 'flying leap', there was a certain caution and a determination not to commit once again the mistakes of 1958-9. For this reason, the radicals were adamant that what remained of the 'ultra-left' should not take the initiative.

The Chinese themselves experienced a problem in drawing the line between 'radical-left' (or, as Mao called himself, 'centre-left') and the 'ultra-left' both in the military and civilian spheres and it might be useful at this stage to suggest what the spectrum of leadership-types looked like in 1969. I have, so far, spoken rather loosely of Party conservatives committed to gradualism, Party radicals committed to the Mass Line as a practical technique of leadership, and 'ultra-leftists' committed to instant com-

357

munism and the Mass Line as a magic wand. It is reasonable to suppose that all three of these orientations might still be found after the Ninth Congress.

During the Cultural Revolution, the civilian Party conservatives associated with Liu Shao-ch'i had come under attack for their 'closed-door' mentality and their crude organisational and economic determinism. In the Army too, conservatives like P'eng Teh-huai, who saw the PLA as an elite separate from society, infused with *esprit de corps* and characterised by impeccable *organisational* discipline, had been heavily criticised. The radicals, on the other hand, were committed to a much more open Party and had ceased to regard the Party as a sacred cow which should not be criticised. As far as the Army was concerned, the radicals believed in the Lei Feng spirit of Army-mass involvement but not in a situation where the 'gun commands the Party'. The third category, the 'ultra-left', came in all shapes and sizes but its most dangerous members such as the Jacobin philosophers of 1967-8, were committed to ascetic *individual* discipline rather than *organisational* discipline.

A major problem remains: where in this categorisation do we put Lin Piao? When the Chinese first launched a campaign to criticise him in 1972, he was referred to as an 'ultra-leftist' though later the term 'ultra-rightist' came to be used. As far as I know, the Chinese have never explained what they mean by this term. In my view, the transformation of Lin Piao from 'ultra-leftist' to 'ultra-rightist' was merely a way of making the association between 'ultra-leftist' and fascist. Both tend towards individual discipline rather than organisational discipline. Both stress the power of human will and believe that history is made by great men. Both rate the 'hero' as more important than the masses and both are committed to a vague mystical ideal rather than a coherent ideology. I am, of course, not maintaining that Lin Piao was a fascist in any philosophical sense; merely that one might make a behavioural association.

In the above context, the charges that Lin Piao and others peddled the 'ideology of individual genius', in the period after the Ninth Party Congress,[1] makes sense. At that time, much was made of Lin's 'heroic' role as Mao's 'close comrade in arms and successor' (and words to that effect had been written into the 1969 Party constitution).[2] Much too was made of the 'genius' of Lin's son Lin Li-kuo,[3] whose 'heroic' qualities earned him a very high post in the Air Force.[4] Thirdly, and perhaps most important, Lin was later accused of wrongly portraying Mao Tse-tung himself as a 'genius'. Since 1966, the creator of the cult of Mao Tse-tung and the waving of the red book had been Lin Piao.

Although Mao probably did not object to being used as symbol for national unity and a rallying point for radicals, he was concerned, by 1969-70, that the cult had raised him to such an elevation that his ability to run day-to-day affairs had been hampered.[5] More galling still, the cult of Mao was turning into a cult of Lin Piao. It did not take too sophisticated a Marxist to point out that Marxists saw great men as the products of history rather than vice versa.

The Rectification and Reconstruction of the Party (Zheng Dang Jian Dang)

There was probably no disagreement between Mao Tse-tung and Lin Piao on the need to reconstruct the Party but there was probably considerable disagreement on *how* it should be done. In his speech to the First Plenum of the Ninth Central Committee on 28 April 1969, Mao made it clear that the Party and Youth League should be built from the bottom up, with renewed emphasis given to mass supervision.[6] In retrospect, his speech seems to be quite critical of the heavy hand of the Army. He noted that factory leadership was usually not in the hands of 'true Marxists', nor in the hands of the masses, nor indeed had sufficient numbers of old factory cadres been rehabilitated. If the source of bad leadership was neither the old cadres nor the masses, then surely the blame must lie with the PLA cadres sent down to 'support the left'. Mao was critical of the excessive repression that had been applied to old cadres. Some had been kept in 'cattle pens' for two years, spoke the language of two years previously and had no idea of how the Cultural Revolution had developed. One cannot be sure here whether Mao was referring to detention centres or to the new May Seventh cadre schools, which were later considered to be dominated too much by PLA leadership. Mao also seemed concerned about the way revolutionary committees had been imposed by the Army from above. Such a situation had led to resentment and the rise of 'ultra-leftists' whom some Army commanders insisted on treating uniformly as 'enemies'. Though Mao had no great love for the 'ultra-left', he considered the policy of rooting out 'ultra-leftists' everywhere as a violation of 'the correct handling of contradictions' and rebuked the Shantung military commander, Yang Teh-chih, for regarding the contradiction between himself and the 'ultra-leftist' Wang Hsiao-yü as 'antagonistic'.

If the Party was to be built successfully, in this new period of 'struggle, criticism and transformation', these who had to judge whether cadres were excessively conservative or 'ultra-leftist' were surely the masses. The mass component in the triple alliance formula, therefore, was to be given greater stress. This was important not only if a genuine 'flying leap' were to take place but also if China were to be pyschologically prepared to meet the possibility of Soviet military attack. Under no circumstances was the military to be allowed to squash that activism.

Although it is possible that I have read too much into Mao's speech of 28 April, it cannot be denied that, after the First Plenum, mass activism gained a new importance and Army representatives at lower levels of administration were often replaced by rehabilitated cadres. At the same time, however, the press continued to categorise the Army as a 'pillar of the dictatorship of the proletariat' and emphasised the way the Army continued to solve problems.[7] Though Mao would perhaps have liked to phase the PLA out of lower-level administration more quickly than actually happened, it proved to be difficult to dispense with the services of the Army, as the political climate radicalised even further in July.

By the summer of 1969, it seemed that the cautious reassertion of radical policies had given rise to a new bout of 'ultra-left' factionalism and, once again, military over-reaction. Local activists of an extreme persuasion often took the rejection of Liu Shao-ch'i's policy of being a 'docile tool' of the Party to be a licence for disruption. Serious cases of indiscipline were noted in Kweichow, Kirin, Anhui and Inner Mongolia.[8] In Shansi, in particular, the authority of Mao was invoked to put a stop to activities reminiscent of the summer of 1968.[9] In that province, disruptive elements had stolen property, opposed the triple alliance, attacked the PLA, killed soldiers, destroyed railways and bridges, occupied warehouses and banks, caused work stoppages and sabotaged production. It was even claimed that these 'ultras' had set up their own banks, though I cannot imagine what an 'ultra-left' bank might look like. In such a situation, the Centre could not but rely on the PLA to restore order and get workers back into the factories. Incidents such as these made any policy of phasing out military control very difficult to implement.

By the autumn of 1969, some progress had been made in Party rebuilding from the bottom up, but the first *xian* Party committee was not established until mid-November.[10] It was probably disatisfaction with the speed of Party rebuilding, therefore, that led to a decision to concentrate on the rebuilding of the Party at the middle levels of *xian* and municipality in the winter.[11] Here again progress was slow and, by the autumn of 1970, only 45 of the 2,185 *xian* in the country had set up Party committees.[12] One may speculate on the reasons for the slowness. One factor was undoubtedly continued factionalism[13] but another major factor might have been the unwillingness of the central military leadership (and perhaps the provincial military leadership) to allow the Army to stand aside and tolerate mass mobilisation after the disturbances of mid-1969. Mao was probably very dissatisfied.

Centralised Policy and Divided Operations

The confused process of Party rebuilding during the 'flying leap' of 1969-70 was mirrored by a similar confusion in the economy, though here, considerable successes in implementing the Yenan model were recorded. Attempts were made first to sort out the relationships between various levels of decision-making in the economy. As in 1958, greater autonomy was enjoyed at *provincial* level to which many more factories (formerly centrally controlled) were transferred.[14] In the new drive to develop local industries, the provinces were to play a major co-ordinating role. There was, of course, the ever-present danger of provincial 'localism',[15] which was perhaps made more serious by the increased power of local provincial military commanders. To counter this, demands were made that key *policy,* as opposed to operational, decisions should be taken in Peking.

Within the provinces, a considerable amount of decision-making power was transferred down to *xian* level. Here, much of the responsibility for water conservation, electrification and road building was located[16] and particular attention was devoted to industries run by *xian*-level government.[17] Within the cities, neighbourhood co-operatives were merged with street administration[18] and independent concerns transferred to local collective leadership.

In the communes there was considerable discussion concerning the basic unit of account[19] and, although attempts were made to transfer accounting of work-points from team to brigade level,[20] the policy of the central government was to retain the team as the basic accounting unit. Nevertheless, the brigades enjoyed a degree of authority far greater than at any time since the early 1960s. They could supervise team activities and most commune industry was administered from brigade rather than team level. In addition, the decentralisation of education facilities and the commercial network provided the brigades with new administrative responsibilities.[21] It seemed clear, in the radical atmosphere of 1969, that it was only a matter of time before the brigade acquired more power over the production of basic foodstuffs and it is worth bearing in mind that Tachai (the model) was a *brigade* (if only a small one) and not a team. Located at commune level were certain administrative bodies, educational facilities and also a small percentage of rural industry,[22] though in most respects the main function of the commune in 1969-70 was that of co-ordination of policy rather than operations.

The reiteration of the old Yenan pattern of 'centralised policy and divided operations' was coupled with a new stress on 'crack troops and simple administration'.[23] In Peking, the number of central ministries was reduced[24] and many cadres were transferred down to local administration or to 'the front line of production'. The dismantling of much of the bureaucracy meant that the old Yenan ideal of the 'cadre' became more important and articles appeared specifying the qualities of good Party secretaries.[25] These secretaries were required to interpret creatively generalised central policy statements and to take over the leadership of Poor and Lower Middle Peasant Associations, which were instituting reforms under PLA guidance. They were to give full play to the Mass Line, in the spirit of the Great Leap, and to avoid the 'commandist' deviations of that period. They were also to avoid the Great Leap tendency to disparage technique whilst still placing 'politics in command'.

In the new 'flying leap', the role of the cadre was difficult to fulfil for two reasons. First, he was given a large amount of operational leeway in a situation where central policy was unclear. For example, the 1965 rules on the amount of land allocated to private plots were still theoretically in force and yet, since that time, there had occurred the Cultural Revolution aimed, amongst other things, at countering privatism. Similarly, provision was still made for rural markets[26] and yet the extension of rural markets had been one of the 'crimes' of which Liu Shao-ch'i had been accused. Cadres were thus unsure as to exactly what attitude to take towards private plots and how big the free market should be.

A second source of difficulty for the cadre concerned the extent to which 'ultra-left' pressure still existed. Since the 'ultra-left' emphasised the power of human will, it was perhaps inevitable that they should have taken an extreme view of the relationship between the human factor in economic development and objective economic conditions. The Cultural Revolution made it quite clear that the crude Menshevik determinism of Liu Shao-ch'i should not be allowed to recur but then neither should there be reliance on an 'idealist' faith in human creativity divorced from reality. During the Great Leap Forward of 1958-9, it had been the conservatives who had accused the radicals of 'idealism'. In the new 'flying leap', it was the radicals who accused the

'ultra-left' of idealism,[27] but this time with probably greater justification.

In the period 1969-70, therefore, some people overestimated the
importance of the human factor in the productive process.[28] They
committed the old error of the Great Leap, inflating production goals
beyond realistic limits and then using coercion to achieve them.[29]
More seriously, their commitment to instant communism prevented the
implementation of the Mass Line. Some cadres artibrarily collectivised
private plots. They interpreted the Tachai model as a blueprint for
rural policy to be put into immediate effect over the whole country,[30]
despite the fact that certain of its features ran counter to general agricultural policy. For example, the Tachai production brigade had
instituted a partly 'communist' method of remuneration, had abolished
private plots and had amalgamated teams into the brigade organisation.
Though laudable as a radical *ideal*, to implement such a model sum-
marily over much of China would have resulted in quite impermissible
'commandist' deviations. Before such progress could be implemented,
sufficient ideological preparation had to be undertaken and such
preparation could not be enforced from above. It was out of faithful
observance of the Mass Line, therefore, that central directives on rural
transformation were somewhat cautious.

Observing that the 'Sixty Articles on Agriculture' of 1961 were still
in force,[31] the 'ultra-left' probably considered that the radical leadership of 1969-70 were repeating the errors of the conservatives of the
early 1960s, and that the new 'flying leap' was a sham. In my view, this
was incorrect and the persistence of 'ultra-leftist commandism' could
play into the hands of genuine conservatives.

Foreign Policy Reappraisal[32]

A third major field of disagreement between 'radicals' and 'ultra-left',
during the period 1969-70, concerned foreign policy, though it is very
difficult to determine just exactly when the disagreement began. As
far as Chou En-lai was concerned, the strategy based on a generalisation
of Lin Piao's People's War thesis had manifestly failed to produce any
results. In fact, during the Cultural Revolution, China's foreign policy
record was one long series of estrangements, which, however satisfying
to purist 'ultra-leftists', was neither helping China nor advancing the
cause of world socialism. Though parts of the 'world's countryside'
(such as Vietnam) were weakening the 'world's cities' (the United
States), the Third World prospect offered very little in terms of a
United Front from below. Since the Cultural Revolution began, inter-

national relations had begun to show clear signs of change. There were
distinct differences between the United States and some of its NATO
allies on the question of Vietnam. Canada, once firmly in the United
States orbit, had announced in January 1969 that it would consider
entering into diplomatic relations with China, and Italy and Belgium
were rumoured to be about to follow suit.[33] Apparently the United
States bloc was disintegrating. Similarly the Soviet Union, now placed
on an equal footing with the United States as a major enemy, also
seemed to be in difficulties.

The invasion of Czechoslovakia had weakened rather than strengthened the Warsaw Pact. Rumania was now firmly in a neutral position
and the Soviet control over other countries in Eastern Europe had
slackened. With both of the major world power blocs disintegrating,
could China still maintain a purist stand-off position?

As the Chinese radicals saw it, the Soviet Union and the United
States, in their struggle for world hegemony, oscillated between policies
of competition and collusion (when threatened from outside). It would
be foolish, therefore, to regard both of them as an undifferentiated
enemy. Rather, China should exploit the contradictions between them
and between each of them and their client states. To do this, avenues of
communication had to be kept open between China and the Soviet
Union, and reopened between China and the United States. The parallel
between 1969-70 and 1945 was immediately recalled. At that time, the
Chinese Communist Party negotiated with Chiang K'ai-shek and yet
prepared actively for the resumption of hostilities. Within two years,
clear allusions would be made to the Chungking negotiations of 1945.[34]

Though border clashes with the Soviet Union continued throughout
the summer of 1969,[35] China pursued a policy of negotiations[36]
coupled with tunnel digging and air-raid precautions.[37] Towards the
end of the year, it was decided to resume contacts with the United
States at ambassadorial level but the United States invasion of Cambodia in March 1970 made this impossible. But, as the summer of 1970
approached, it seemed that the United States might soon be willing to
talk, and China could then engage in exactly the same tactic with the
United States as she had with the Soviet Union.

It is impossible to say exactly when and how Lin Piao and the
'ultra-left' reacted to these developments, beyond the fact that Lin
Piao was said to have opposed the new foreign policy line,[38] presumably out of a crude ideological purism and more particularly since the
new strategy negated his whole generalised People's War thesis. It is unlikely, however, that things came to a head before a crisis occurred in

other fields of policy in August 1970 and ushered in a new period of consolidation.

The Crisis Develops

By the end of 1969, it is possible that most of the above areas of disagreement had been formulated and people were well aware that 'arrogance and rashness'[39] within military circles had to be combatted. It had been made clear that Army cadres could not just get away with correcting deficiencies in their 'work-style' (*zuofeng*) but had to look to their whole ideological orientation from which errors in work-style arose.[40] In retrospect, it would seem that the heightened campaign against the May Sixteenth Group at that time was a criticism of Lin Piao and the remaining 'ultra-leftist' in the Central Cultural Revolution Group — Ch'en Po-ta. After October 1969, Ch'en disappeared from view and, by the end of the year, no more reference was made to the Central Cultural Revolution Group which, in its day, had comprised most of the extreme 'ultra-leftist' leaders.

As the activities of Lin Piao and Ch'en Po-ta came under suspicion in late 1969 and early 1970, the Party was engaged in lengthy discussions in preparation for the long-awaited National People's Congress which would legitimise a new state structure. No meeting of the National People's Congress had been held during the Cultural Revolution and the state posts that existed in early 1970 (the NPC Standing Committee, the vice chairman of the People's Republic and the premier of the State Council) owed their legitimacy to a very different era. We noted that the Twelfth Plenum of the Eighth Central Committee in 1968 had taken the unconstitutional step of dismissing Liu Shao-ch'i from all his state posts. The body that was in fact constitutionally empowered to do this was the National People's Congress and if a new Head of State was to be elected, such a body would have to be convened.

This issue of Head of State was a very important one. The chairman of the People's Republic was no figurehead. Mao's resignation from that office in 1959 had caused a certain stir and it was because of his position as chairman that Liu Shao-ch'i wielded considerable power. During the Cultural Revolution, the ceremonial functions of Head of State had been undertaken by the aged Tung Pi-wu and Sung Ch'ing-ling, but it was felt, in 1969-70, that a more substantive formal chairman should be appointed. Accordingly, a draft constitution for the People's Republic was prepared[41] and circulated for comment prior to its ratification at a future meeting of the National People's Congress.

The constitution was a brief document which nominated Mao as Head of State (*yuanshou*) rather than chairman (*zhuxi*); such was apparently to the taste of Lin Piao who saw himself as substantive vice chairman and soon maybe (like Liu Shao-ch'i) the substantive chairman,[42] out-ranking Chou En-lai in *government* rank as he did in the Party. In March 1970, however, Mao Tse-tung himself recommended the removal of the post of Head of State from the constitution,[43] implying that his successors were now to be collective. Lin Piao was apparently quite angry.

In the spring of 1970, stress was laid, not so much on learning from the PLA, but on the PLA studying Mao Tse-tung's instructions on (civilian) Party building.[44] At the same time, Lin Piao's earlier criteria for Party membership which stressed ideological commitment[45] were replaced by a demand that Party members should trust the masses and undergo self-criticism.[46] Since it was clear that a full-scale attempt was being made to counter elitism, Lin Piao (like P'eng Teh-huai before him) felt that the time had come to act. The showdown came at the Second Plenum of the Ninth Central Committee which, like that similar meeting eleven years before, was held at Lushan. Clearly someone had a sense of history!

The Second Plenum and the Tenth Crisis

At the Second Plenum in August 1970, the radicals attached considerable importance to the denunciation of Ch'en Po-ta who was now linked with his Jacobin colleagues on the old Central Cultural Revolution Group, and Lin Piao resisted the denunciation. At the same meeting, Mao categorically rejected the 'theory of genius' and reaffirmed his intention to oppose the election of a new Head of State.[47] Faced with the opposition of Lin, Mao sought to bring about his demotion and the removal of his influence in the Army.

To achieve this effectively, it was evident that Party reconstruction had to be accelerated. This demanded a modification of the policy of rebuilding the Party from the bottom up or even of concentrating on *xian* and municipal-level Party committees. At provincial level, however, to which the focus of Party rebuilding was now switched,[48] power rested with revolutionary committees which did not always exhibit the right kind of balance between mass representatives, cadres and military. It could not be certain that local military commanders would associate themselves with the central government or with Lin Piao if things came to a showdown. Nor was it clear whether an acceleration of Party rebuilding at provincial level would not snuff out the policy of 'purifying the class ranks' and giving full play to mass activism. Despite the dangers, however, the Party Centre pressed ahead, in late 1970, with its new policy of *provincial*-level Party rebuilding and, in December of that year, the first provincial Party committee emerged from the Hunan Party congress.[49] In the next nine months, Party committees appeared in all 29 provincial-level units,[50] though I suspect that the whole process was too quick and mass mobilisation was not undertaken. I suspect also that the reconstruction of provincial-level congresses and Party committees was effected with some military pressure.[51] In retrospect, it does not seem that the military pressure favoured the line of Lin Piao. In fact, it is possible that the role of *local* military commanders in provincial-level Party rebuilding was such as to counter the influence of that network of trusty followers that Lin Piao had placed in positions of authority in the provinces.[52] Just as the rehabilitation of old cadres often prevented the 'ultra-leftists' squeezing out mass representatives, so the none too radical local military commanders probably prevented the complete sabotage of the Mass Line by Lin Piao's trusties.

While the process of provincial-level Party rebuilding was going on, it was probably still not clear whether such a programme was sufficient to counter the efforts of that group of military men surrounding Lin Piao, which gradually took on the appearance of a conspiracy. Mao decided, therefore, to take more decisive steps. At a meeting (work conference) in December 1970, he pressed for the reorganisation of the Peking Military Region, since if in fact there was a conspiracy to wrest supreme power, it was important that the military commanders in the capital were loyal to the Party Centre.

In January 1971, the reorganisation took place,[53] and this led immediately to the formation of a plan of action by the Lin Piao group for a military coup. In February 1971, it was reported that Lin Piao's son Lin Li-kuo (the young 'genius') was active in the Shanghai region,[54] making preparations to neutralise the Party Centre and the reorganised Peking PLA command. His efforts led, in late March, to the formulation of a document known as the '571 Engineering Outline' (*Wu Qi Yi Gongcheng Jiyao*).[55]

The words '571' (*wu qi yi*) are a Chinese pun on the words 'armed uprising' (*wuzhuang qiyi*). The conspirators, Lin Piao, Yeh Ch'ün (his wife), Lin Li-kuo (his son), Huang Yung-sheng (Chief of Staff) and the other senior military commanders (and Politburo members) Wu Fa-hsien, Li Tso-p'eng and Ch'iu Hui-tso,[56] seem to have been a rather motley collection of people united only in the belief that, if they did not immediately seize power, they would be dismissed by the forces of 'B-52' (the code-name for Mao).[57] On issues of policy, their programme reveals a hotch-potch of complaints of both a conservative and 'ultra-left' variety. For example, they condemned *xiaxiang,* in that they felt it was tantamount to labour reform; they asserted that the Red Guards had been deceived; they viewed the dispatch of cadres to May Seventh cadre schools as a form of unemployment and they demanded that the wage freeze for workers should be ended.

In their assessment of the strategic situation, the conspirators noted that they had considerable power within the Air Force. They felt also that the Soviet Union would look sympathetically upon any group that toppled Mao Tse-tung. On the other hand, they were uncertain as to what proportion of the PLA would rally to their cause and felt that some of the regional military commanders might be neutralised by the toleration of a degree of regional independence. At a tactical level, they planned to set up a training group, under the pretext of routine cadre re-education, and this group would attempt to assign to each military unit a trusty who could take over the unit when the time came. They proposed to offer favourable conditions to all old cadres who had been removed in the preceding few years, in the hope presumably of establishing a new administrative network. Finally, they chose as their centre of operations the Shanghai area whence Air Force units were to be deployed. If the worst came to the worst, Shanghai could provide a take-off point for a protracted guerrilla war, waged first of all in Chekiang province. It was crucial, therefore, that the commander of the Nanking Military Region, Hsü Shih-yu, should be watched very carefully in case he began to move against them.

The '571 Engineering Outline' was truly an extraordinary document. I still find it extremely odd that Lin Piao, famed for his venom against the Soviet Union, should have entertained the idea of Soviet support, or that such a staunch fighter against Japan should have spoken favourably of Eda Gima (the Japanese wartime naval school famous for propagating the Japanese military ethic of *bushido*).[58]

In the spring and early summer of 1971, Mao and most Party leaders were unaware of the existence of the '571 Engineering Outline'.[59] What they were painfully aware of, however, was a large-scale campaign to promote the qualities of Lin Piao, sometimes aided by provincial military commanders. Since 1969, pamphlets and articles had appeared praising Lin's achievements with unparalleled extravagance,[60] in a way reminiscent of the articles praising Kao Kang after his transfer to Peking under considerable suspicion in the early 1950s.

In the summer of 1971, it was clear that Mao had a very good idea about the impending coup and that the Nanking Military Region was a crucial area of operations. From mid-August to September 1971, the chairman undertook one of his famous tours of inspection, in which the Nanking Military Region and the Kwangchow Military Region (under the influence of Huang Yung-sheng) figured prominently.[61] It was at this time that Mao noted that the crisis had been brewing since the Second Plenum and that it was the tenth major crisis in the Party's fifty-year history.[62] It ranked, therefore, with the struggle against the lines of P'eng Teh-huai and Liu Shao-ch'i and was a 'struggle between two headquarters'. In Mao's view, however, the PLA would not follow Huang Yung-sheng into rebellion[63] and there was a remote possibility that Lin Piao's errors in line might be corrected.[64] Mao was most insistent that the three major slogans of the past few years were now inadequate. They had been: 'In industry learn from Tach'ing, in agriculture learn from Tachai, and in the whole country learn from the PLA.' Now, most significantly, he added a fourth: 'The PLA should learn from the people of the whole country.' To counter military elitism, Mao once again stressed his 'three main rules of discipline and the eight points for attention' but naturally omitted the various military slogans advanced by Lin Piao since 1959.[65]

There has been much debate as to whether an attempted coup did or did not take place in September 1971 and whether Lin did or did not attempt to assassinate Mao.[66] Whatever happened, such seems to have been Lin's intention, and on 13 September 1971, it was reported that Lin and some others died as his escape plane crashed near Undur Khan in the Mongolian People's Republic en route for the Soviet Union.[67] There is conflicting evidence as to whether Lin was in fact on board[68] and who exactly was with him, but in my view it does not much matter. By mid-September, the Lin Piao conspiracy had been squashed and Lin Piao had been officially declared dead. The Party was now determined to control 'the gun' but it was still to be a long and arduous process before the ideal Party-PLA relationship was settled. In the next few months, a large number of appointees of Lin Piao (especially in the Air Force, which had been grounded during the September crisis) were removed from their posts,[69] and a new military network built up. As things turned out, the provincial military leadership had remined loyal to Mao Tse-tung.

A New Period of Consolidation

The Second Plenum of August 1970 ushered in a new period of consolidation and brought to an end the 'flying leap'. The period which followed, like the 'flying leap' period of 1969-70, was also characterised by an intense debate on development strategy though, unlike the earlier period, the general tone of the discussions was more cautious. This fact has frequently been taken by commentators to reflect a general liquidation of the Cultural Revolution after the Second Plenum, together with the liquidation of the Cultural Revolution's major protagonists Lin Piao and Ch'en Po-ta.[70] Such a view stems from the categorisation of the protagonists in the Cultural Revolution as simply radicals and 'pragmatists'. It ignores the Chinese attempts to explain the phenomenon of the 'ultra-left'. Though clearly the defeat of Lin Piao did to some extent give rise to a strengthening of the bureaucracy (only a millennarian would believe otherwise), it is my view that most of the essential changes of the Cultural Revolution were retained. To substantiate this contention, let us examine developments in industry, agriculture and education in the period after 1970.

From Labour Discipline to Rules

The area of perhaps greatest disappointment to the radicals was industrial management but it will be remembered that this had been so even during the Cultural Revolution. In his speech to the First Plenum of the Ninth Central Committee, Mao had noted that leadership in the industrial sector was poor.[71] In the period which followed, the gradual phasing out of the military, the continued stress on the 'two participations and triple combination' and the new drive to foster technical innovations were clearly radical policies that met with some success although indiscipline continued to be a major problem.[72] While there had been continuing concern for discipline throughout the 'flying leap', in the period after the Second Plenum, this understandable preoccupation led to a stress on rules and regulations which were sometimes resisted by the workers.[73] Radicals could not have been altogether comforted by assurances that these rules and regulations were more 'rational' than those advocated by Liu Shao-ch'i.[74]

A second area of concern to radicals must surely be wages policy. The Cultural Revolution swept away piecework and large individual bonuses[75] but it did not solve that major concern of Chiang Ch'ing — the problem of temporary workers on contract. In the period of consolidation after the Second Plenum, it seems that a 24-grade salary scale was reintroduced,[76] which is less than that which existed in the 1950s but probably not much less than that which applied in the 1960s. It is unclear, however, if there have been any major changes in the differentials between grades. In 1971-2, it would appear also that a national wage rise of around 10 per cent on average[77] took place (though with a higher percentage for veteran workers on low wages). The preceding nine-year industrial wage freeze had been one of the major achievements of the radicals in preventing the excessive growth of an urban-rural gap, and one might guess that such a wage reform was not universally welcomed. It is uncertain, however, exactly how opinions divided on the issue of wage reform. According to the '571 Engineering Outline', a (rightist) criticism had been put forward that the nine-year wage freeze had constituted a form of exploitation,[78] while other accounts lay responsibility for this policy on Lin Piao.[79] A final point concerning wages policy is that, since 1970, there has been a stress on the predominance in wage grading of technical as opposed to political criteria and 'labour attitude'.[80] Of course, it is a great step from this to the growth of a technical elite but radicals might have cause to be uneasy.

A third area of concern is the policy of 'two participations and triple combination'. Although this continued to be official policy after the Second Plenum, some protests were made by technical cadres that misapplied labour was too expensive.[81] Such a comment was tantamount to saying that a radical programme of socialist transition was too expensive. Associated with this point of view is the fact that, in marked contrast to the Cultural Revolution and the subsequent 'flying leap' where large numbers of non-manual workers were returned to the shop floor, figures for the reduction of white-collar workers after 1970 do not appear to be so impressive.[82] It may be that most of the dead wood had already been cleared out, but to take that position is to ignore the dynamic nature of bureaucratisation and its cyclic character. When one considers these developments along with a decline in the active role of mass management,[83] one might surmise that some radicals would be worried.

A fourth problem for the radicals is the fact that after the Second Plenum a number of complete plants were imported from overseas[84] (though this time *not* from the Soviet Union). These plants required a sophisticated technology and, unless handled cautiously, might lead to the creation of differential wage systems applying to different sectors of the economy. The problem here is not just one of wages, however. Such plants can have a disruptive effect on national economic integration, since factory design embodies certain power relationships and (in a Marxist sense) certain relations of production which cannot be easily transferred from one society to another.

This importation of technology had a direct bearing on a debate

carried on in China since 1969, known as 'electronics versus steel'.[85]
It is possible that this debate was, in some ways, connected with the
Lin Piao case in that there was said to be people in the more technical
arms of the PLA (notably the Air Force in which Lin had considerable
power) who wished to see the electronics industry serve the needs of
national defence. Lin Piao, for all his advocacy of People's War, was
after all also a great advocate of nuclear technology and presumably also
also of missile technology which requires a sophisticated electronics
industry. But the advocates of electronics were opposed by those who
saw the effects that such an emphasis might have on industrial integration and the linkage between local technology and urban industry.
By 1973, the advocates of 'steel first' seemed to have won[86] the argument though the fact that the debate could have arisen at all, after the
developmental lessons China had learned, is surprising.

A fifth problem concerns the labour unions. During the Cultural
Revolution the unions, infected with 'economism', were considered a
hindrance to any programme of urban-rural integration. During the
'flying leap' of 1969-70, union functions at enterprise level were
managed by revamped workers' congresses[87] but, since 1973, an attempt has been made to recreate the ACFTU structure.[88] We have yet
to see what the new role of the labour unions will be.

From a radical point of view, the above picture is far from satisfactory. One should point out, however, that, contrary to what some
commentators have asserted,[89] there seems to be no return to the de
facto 'one man management' of the 1960s; the individual stress on incentive policy has not returned and the principle whereby workers can
challenge management and Party is one that cannot easily be eroded.
The revolutionary committees, though less radical than before, still
provide considerable opportunity for worker participation in decision-
making, the 'two participations and triple combination', though sometimes attenuated, are still practised and steel seems to have triumphed
over electronics. If that was all there was to the industrial balance sheet,
then radicals could indeed count the Cultural Revolution in industry a
failure. One must note two other aspects, however, which I believe are
more exciting even than the developments of 1958 — the quiet reintro-
duction of integrated urban-rural units and the accelerated development
of rural industry.

The Legacy of the Great Leap Forward in Agricultural-Industrial Integration

Although the Cultural Revolution and the subsequent 'flying leap' did not revive the name 'urban commune', any examination of the Tach'ing model reveals most of the essential features of the urban commune idea.[90] These features, moreover, were continually stressed through the period of consolidation of 1970-3. At Tach'ing, an attempt has been made to build an oil-city complex which is integrated with the total environment. In the oilfields, a cellular settlement structure has been created with central points consisting of some 300-400 households linked to small nodes of 100-200 households. Located at each central point and node are essential services and shops as well as agricultural technical stations, and the gaps between the central point and nodes consist of farmland. At Tach'ing, in accordance with the *May Seventh Directive*, oil workers are expected not only to engage in industrial pursuits, not only to help run neighbourhood services and schools but also to work part of the time as peasants. By 1970, it was claimed that Tach'ing produced a certain amount of grain, and was partly self-sufficient in meat and vegetables.[91] Discarded metals were processed into farm tools and household implements and a plant had been set up to process refinery waste into phosphate fertiliser.[92] Thus the spirit of Chengchow has been revived, and Mao is reported to have called for the extension of the Tach'ing model even to large iron and steel complexes such as Wuhan.[93]

Of course, like Tachai, the Tach'ing model cannot be transplanted holus-bolus to other areas and it will probably be a long time before we see large numbers of this type of urban-rural complex. What is important to the argument here, however, is that the deradicalisation of some aspects of industrial policy in the years 1970-3 has been more than compensated for by developments such as Tach'ing.

A second aspect of industrial policy which cannot but give considerable heart to the radicals is the development of rural industry. This has been carried on within locally (provincially) integrated economic units. The policy of 'walking on two legs' continued right through the 'flying leap' and the subsequent period of consolidation. Furthermore, there seems to have been no change in the great stress given to labour intensive industries managed from *xian* level and below. Ever since the Cultural Revolution, there has been considerable horizontal transfer of technology between *xian* and lower level economic units and care has been taken in the vertical transfer of technology between province and unit of production to prevent a one-way 'trickle-down' process.[94]

One of the most important features of rural industrial development has been fertiliser production. In 1957, China produced only some 0.63 million tonnes of chemical fertiliser. By 1971, this figure had risen to 17 million tonnes, reaching 20 million in 1972.[95] What is impressive about the 1971 figure is the fact that 60 per cent of the 17 million tonnes was produced by local (*xian* or lower level) factories.[96] The production of chemical fertiliser at a local level has aided the development of the 'Green Revolution' in which high-yielding seed strains require considerable application of fertiliser. For its part, the Green Revolution, in raising yields, makes it possible to devote more land to the production of industrial crops and this further promotes rural light industry.[97] One only has to compare parts of India where the effects of the Green Revolution have been to enrich mainly those who in the first place could afford fertiliser and costly irrigation works, to realise the significance of China's success.

What is more impressive about the policy of urban-rural integration, pursued since the Cultural Revolution, is the way in which many of the old Great Leap policies, which were not particularly successful in 1958-9, have at last borne fruit. In 1971, for example, 20 per cent of China's output of 20 million tonnes of pig iron was produced in local furnaces.[98] Though the quality is not up to the standard of the major iron and steel works, it is (unlike 1958) quite usable. The new policies seem, this time, to have been pursued quietly.

Equally impressive has been the development of the petroleum industry of which Tach'ing is particularly the model. Back in 1958, very few people would have thought that soon China would be a major oil-producing country and yet China now is self-sufficient in oil.[99] Of course the oil deposits China possesses she always possessed but what is important is that, contrary to 'expert' advice,[100] the Chinese have bothered to look for them. Here we see most clearly the importance of the dialectical interaction of man and nature in which human will is vitally important. The very concept 'resource' is inherently dialectical. Resources *are not, they become.* It is man that brings them into being and man that determines that they are in fact resources. The interaction of man and nature which creates resources cannot be simply scientific. If that were the case, the Chinese petroleum industry would have heeded expert advice and done nothing. Occasionally a Great Leap is essential and perhaps yesterday's 'utopianism' is tomorrow's commonplace. There is only one caveat; the power of human will must be geared to coming to grips with nature. Once it starts to create its own 'nature' and its own idealistic science, it can only blight human progress. This in essence, I suggest, is the crucial difference between a Marxist view (such as that of the 'radical-left') and that of the 'ultra-left'.

Decision-making in Agriculture

Although, politically, the decision to enter a period of consolidation
after the Second Plenum in 1970 was connected with the Lin Piao
crisis, one must also note that administratively, it was connected with
the Fourth Five Year Plan due to start in 1971.[101] By that time, material balance planning was being conducted in much the same way as
before[102] and higher-level planning bodies strove to prevent units mon-
opolising too great a share of resources.[103] It was, however, *policy-
making* that was tightened up rather than operational decision-making.
A high degree of provincial and *xian*-level operational autonomy was
maintained,[104] considerable flexibility was allowed to lower levels of
economic administration and contracts between production units remained extremely important.[105]

At commune level and below, one can only describe the situation as
one of flux, as confusing as the earlier period of the 'flying leap' but
exhibiting, on the whole, a greater degree of caution. A Central Committee directive of December 1971[106] noted that, though the facilities
for distrubution within the communes were excellent, there were some
which decided to 'partition all and eat all' and yet others which were
excessively 'egalitarian'. It instructed rural units to see that peasant
incomes did not suffer through excessive accumulation, condemned the
over-procurement of grain and encouraged the maintenance of sufficient
reserves. Brigades were warned not to encroach too much on the teams'
accumulation funds and higher levels could only use labour from the
teams after adequate consultation and adequate compensation had
been made. Communes were warned not to adopt arbitrarily the
methods of Tachai without consideration for local circumstances. They
were to make sure that the rations of peasants, in areas devoted to
economic crops, were not less than in adjacent areas devoted to food
grains. Finally, the Central Committee warned against the phenomenon
of 'overdrawing households' and stressed that remuneration must be
based on productivity.

The mood, therefore, was cautious and somewhat less radical than
previously. During the 'flying leap' of 1969-70, there had been much
talk of the leadership of the poor and lower middle peasants. After
1970, as the Party was rebuilt, there was more talk of the leadership of
appropriate Party committees and revolutionary committees. Many of
the mass representatives on revolutionary committees spent less time in
decision-making than they did in productive labour,[107] though communications between higher and lower levels of administration were
probably more effective than ever before.[108] Attempts to transfer the

unit of account back to brigade level were now condemned as 'ultra-leftist'[109] but brigades still retained an important role in arbitrating between teams, managing basic-level industry and organising education.[110]

Though generally less radical than previously, it is probably true that to have gone beyond the above general policy would have constituted 'ultra-leftism'. Given the rural situation in the early 1970s and the bad harvest of 1972, mass reaction to any radical transfer of power to brigade or commune level, without adequate preparation, could have generated unfavourable consequences. In some aspects, however, I cannot but feel that there were trends in the rural economy, after 1972, which can only be described as conservative. For example, there was a greater stress on family-run industry[111] and Mao Tse-tung's call for equal pay between the sexes had to be constantly restressed.[112] Peasants, however, could only sell the products of their private plots on the open market, and some guidance was given as to what ought to be grown; they could not sell landed property.[113]

It is too early to draw any conclusions concerning rural management in the period 1970-3 but we may advance a few conclusions concerning production. In 1957, grain production was some 185 million tonnes. The official figure for 1970 (after the 'flying leap') was 240 million tonnes,[114] rising to 250 million in 1971.[115] In 1972 the figure fell to about 240 million because of (worldwide) adverse weather conditions.[116] What is remarkable here is that, after probably the worst weather since the early 1960s, grain production had only declined by some 10 million tonnes. Clearly some important lessons had been learned from the earlier agricultural crisis. Moreover, the policy of grain storage[117] promised to make the impact of any future hardship years much less serious than hitherto. Various estimates have been put forward for overall agricultural growth, but what would seem to be a reasonable estimate is 4 per cent from 1963 (after the bad years) to 1971 or 3.1 per cent if one includes the bad harvest of 1972.[118] When one puts alongside this a population growth of between 1.7[119] and 2.1 per cent,[120] the situation looks hopeful, though economists tell me that a growth rate of 5 per cent would be more comfortable, given that rate of population growth. There are still problems. Some of the youth sent down to the countryside have been encouraged to settle down and have married early. Distribution within rural units still discriminates in favour of large families and the peasant ideology, which still requires a male heir, can surely not easily be eradicated. None the less, there is evidence that a major campaign has been undertaken since

1970 to restrict population growth[121] and it is likely that the already
low population growth figure (by Third World standards) will go down
even further. In the context of the development of the Third World,
China's ratio of population growth to agricultural growth, already impressive, looks like being even more so. The spectre of famine seems to
have been laid to rest.

Education and the State of the 'Two Tracks'

Although, in my view, the backtracking that has occurred in rural and
industrial policy since 1970 has been minor, there are certain features
that must have caused some disquiet. In the field of education,[122] however, apart from the complaints of the 'ultra-leftists', there is little the
radicals need worry about. Throughout the period 1969-73, the various
radical reforms in education, noted in the last chapter, continued to be
implemented. The *minban* principle was stressed, with schools being
taken to children rather than vice versa, and teachers' colleges frequently set up (often mobile) branch units to train the many new
teachers that were required. Courses were shortened and emphasis continued to be on practical subjects and the integration of theoretical
knowledge with activity in production. Literature students, for example,
were required to compose *dazibao* and write political plays. The criticism of teachers was still encouraged, though with a new emphasis on
politeness. Workers and peasants were still invited in to help teach and
lecture to students and, wherever possible, schools and colleges set up
their own production units. Admission policy to universities still
favoured mature students or those who had spent one or two years in
productive labour. Furthermore, those who had worked for a period of
five years or more continued to draw their wages at university. In
general then, the spirit of Yenan and the Great Leap was maintained.

There were, however, a number of problems which required sol-
utions that may have been distasteful to those still tainted by 'ultra-
leftist idealism'. First, the decision of mid-1968 to restore the university
system meant, in effect, that two tracks in tertiary education would
continue. In mid-1970, Peking and Tsinghua Universitities took in their
first batch of first-year students for some years and, by 1972, most
universitites were functioning 'normally'. By 1972, the requirement
that most students admitted should be from worker or poor and lower
middle peasant background was relaxed somewhat and there was a
danger that the pre-Cultural Revolution situation might, at some time
in the future, recur. In my view, however, although it would take a very
long time before a part-work part-study tertiary-level educational unit

was considered the equal of an established university, the two types of institution were closer in 1972 than at any time hitherto and it was probably a far more sensible policy to attempt to close the gap between them than simply to abolish universitites, as the 'ultra-leftists' would have wished.

At lower levels, full-time educational institutions coexisted with part-work part-study institutions and similar problems, no doubt, occurred. In the period 1969-73, there was no national policy stipulating how the two types of unit should be integrated and, in fact, standardisation had been condemned as Liuist 'bureaucratism'. Such standardisation as did occur concerned the provision of teaching material (published at *xian* level), but there was nothing like a return to the situation in 1965 where even *minban* institutions were often rigidly controlled by *xian* educational bureaux. In general, rural communes and street revolutionary committees had a major say in the administration of local secondary schools and local residents continued to sit on secondary school revolutionary committees. Primary schools, at street or brigade level, were even more closely integrated with local residential organisations and, in the rural areas, many primary school teachers continued to be paid on the same work-point basis as ordinary peasants.

The participation of local residents in school administration was not a mere formality. School revolutionary committees had the power to determine course content and to hire and dismiss teachers (formerly the prerogative of municipal and *xian* education bureaux). Such committees were an effective way of ensuring the continuance of a problem-oriented education programme so necessary in a developing (and for that matter any other) country. It is probably true, however, that some more theoretical studies suffered because of a concern with immediate practice, and the greater stress on more theoretical studies in the universitites in 1972-3 may not have been reproduced at lower levels. Perhaps at those levels, however, subjects like pure mathematics were never on the agenda.

One of the major problems affecting local schools in the early 1970s was financial. Sometimes the state would provide assistance for such schools, but generally a strict principle of 'self-reliance' was adhered to. In a situation where the state (local government) did not help schools in financial difficulties, free tuition could not always be provided. In factory-run schools, however, it was probably much easier to generate funds, though the policy of 'letting factories run schools' was only a partial solution, simply because there were too many children. In urban areas, therefore, the normal pattern of educational administration was management by street and neighbourhood revolutionary committees.

Within most schools, after 1972, there was a greater stress on open-book examinations than hitherto. Exams had been the great bugbear of the Red Guards but, as we have seen, open-book exams had returned even before the 'struggle' stage of the Cultural Revolution came to an end. Although, from the standpoint of a Western university, I person-ally find the restoration of any kind of examination unfortunate, this development and the general formality of Chinese classroom procedure is probably not very important. What *is* important is that, by 1972, China could contemplate the immediate implementation of a universal five-year programme of primary school education in rural areas, and a seven-year programme in urban areas.[123] By 1972, some places had al-ready enrolled 80-95 per cent of school-age children in schools[124] and this in itself is remarkable given the fact that in 1965 30 million chil-dren did not attend school.[125] One should also bear in mind here that I am only talking about the formal education system at a time when informal education schemes were being stressed more than ever before. Faced with this impressive achievement in a world where the gap be-between developed and underdeveloped areas is increasing alarmingly, whatever backsliding there may have been seems rather insignificant.

Foreign Policy – The Exploitation of Contradictions

The invasion of Cambodia in March 1970[126] and the suspension of the Sino-American ambassadorial talks[127] which followed, halted tempor-arily any moves the Chinese might have wished to make in opening channels of communication with the United States through third parties (such as Nikolai Ceaucescu of Rumania).[128] By the time of Edgar Snow's interviews in late 1970, it appears that the new foreign policy course had been set.[129] In April 1971, a United States table tennis team visited China[130] and, in July, Henry Kissinger flew secretly to Peking to prepare for the visit of President Nixon which took place in early 1972.[131] The Shanghai communique, following the visit, secured a United States' recognition that there was but one China with T'aiwan as a part and a promise to withdraw United States troops and military installations from T'aiwan as tension in the area diminished.[132] In the period which followed, relatively large numbers of Americans visited China and liaison offices were established in Peking and Washington,[133] in preparation for the eventual restoration of diplo-matic relations.

There has been some debate as to whether China's desire to forge

the new relationship with the United States was simply a response to
the 1.2 million Soviet troops stationed along the 11,000-kilometre
frontier. Undoubtedly the threat was very real and improved Sino-
American relations did allow China to redeploy troops to the northern
frontiers.[134] If, however, China were simply reacting to the Soviet
military build-up, one would have expected that the rapprochement
would have taken place when the build-up occurred. Sino-American
relations were established not when Sino-Soviet relations were at their
worst (early 1969) but when they were, in fact, improving (late
1970).[135] An alternative view maintains, therefore, that it was not just
Soviet strength but also American weakness in Asia that caused China
to see the possibility of driving a wedge between the super-powers.

China's second major strategy was aimed at forging some kind of
Third World identity. This was facilitated by the loosening of Soviet
and American control over a newly formulated 'second intermediate
zone' and by China's entry into the United Nations in 1971.[136] In the
period 1972-3, China devoted considerable attention to strengthening
state-to-state relations with as many countries as possible and backing
the position of Third World countries in asserting political and economic independence, such as demands for a 200-nautical-mile extension
of territorial waters[137] and various nuclear-free zones.[138] In doing this,
China has suffered some left-wing criticism from various quarters to the
effect that she has been too lavish in her praise of reactionary regimes
and has played down her support for national liberation movements in
various countries. Two instances are usually cited here – Bangladesh
and Ceylon (now Sri Lanka). China's support for Pakistan in the Bangladesh war of 1971[139] may best be seen in terms of China's concern at
being encircled by India's ally, the Soviet Union, and also by a belief
that Bangladesh independence, if imposed with Indian bayonets, might
create a state which was no more than nominally independent. I am
still at a complete loss to explain China's support for Mrs Bandaranaike's
suppression of the Ceylon rebellion of 1971.[140] Explanations both to
the effect that China was merely engaging in the game of *realpolitik*[141]
and that it was trying to forestall a right-wing coup[142] are both rather
unconvincing. It is possible that too great a concentration on what is
seen as 'the principal contradiction' with the major enemies – the
United States and the Soviet Union – might have led to too great a
neglect of national liberation movements elsewhere. As regards the
European Economic Community, which China supports,[143] it is probably true that, in the long run, Europe might constitute a power to offset that of the United States and the Soviet Union. In the meantime,

however, the European economy has been penetrated by American-based multinationals and condemned by the indigenous left.

After the American rapprochement of February 1972, a major target in China's foreign policy was Japan. During the period 1970-2, China was concerned about the possibility of Japanese rearmament[144] and that Japan might step into American shoes following a United States withdrawal from South-east Asia. But in 1972, taking advantage of the Japanese government's desire to establish diplomatic relations, Premier Tanaka was invited to Peking[145] and the issue of Japanese rearmament disappeared from the Chinese media, though I am sure not from people's minds. Following the breaking of diplomatic relations between Tokyo and T'aipei, the Kuomintang regime was more isolated than ever and, before long the old general Fu Tso-i, who had changed sides during the siege of Peking in 1949, suggested strongly the possibility of the peaceful reabsorption of T'aiwan into China.[146] I do not know if any discussions have been held since that time but it is significant to note that the new foreign policy has achieved more on the T'aiwan question than any preceding one. China is now well placed to make the most of a growing estrangement between Washington and Tokyo.

Having entered rapidly into the field of international power politics, it may be argued that China now sees herself as a major power. This the Chinese would deny categorically. The extent to which China has insisted on the 'Five Principles of Peaceful Coexistence', in particular mutual equality between nations, has been quite strict. China sees a world in which two major powers still vie with each other for hegemony and feels she cannot counter this by adopting a hegemonist policy herself.[147] The aim is to insist on equality and exploit the contradictions between various shades of enemy and friend. In the words of the Chinese themselves:

The view that all enemies are the same, that they are one monolithic bloc, is not in accord with objective reality. Moreover, with the development of the situation and the people's revolutionary forces daily expanding, the enemies' contradictions will become more and more acute. The proletariat and its party must learn to concretely analyse the situation in class struggle in the international and domestic spheres at different historical periods and be good at seizing the opportunity to 'turn to good account all such fights, rifts and contradictions within the enemy camp and turn them against our present main enemy'.[148]

The Question of Art and Literature

By 1973 there were signs that, although many of the policies of the Cultural Revolution had been continued and developed, the process of consolidation had gone too far. There commenced at that time a renewed debate on art and literature which, as we have seen in China, often heralds a new period of radicalism.

During the Cultural Revolution, there had been general agreement amongst both radicals and 'ultra-left' that all art was propaganda[149] (though clearly not all propaganda was art). Though in one's evaluation of a work of art, as Mao had stated quite emphatically in 1942, one should apply artistic as well as political criteria,[150] there was perhaps a tendency, in the mid-1960s, to overstress the political at the expense of the other. This is understandable at a time when the radicals were reacting to the elitist art of the early 1960s, which often served the political purpose of undermining the spirit of the Great Leap Forward. By 1969, however, it was possible that a more constructive debate could be entered into, similar to the great debates of the middle 1950s.

At no stage did Mao Tse-tung's formulation of policy towards literature and art ever preclude old forms or ancient themes, provided they adhered to the maxim that 'the old (must) serve the new' (*qu wei jin yong*).[151] Such a maxim was, however, much more easy to operationalise in the field of archaeology than in the field of art. During the latter stage of the Cultural Revolution and thereafter, when archaeological research made unprecedented progress in China, archaeological finds were depicted as showing the role of labour and changes in class structure over the millennia.[152] In current artistic work the problem was much more complex.

During the 'flying leap' of 1969-70, the debate in art focused, as one might have expected, on the reform of Peking opera, in which Chiang Ch'ing had played a major role. A number of model operas had been produced which were immediately subjected to criticism and revision. The revised versions, which appeared in the years 1970-2, were usually painted in terms more black and white than the earlier ones and were, on the whole, much more militant.[153] By 1972, however, when the general spirit of consolidation penetrated the sphere of art and literature, shades of grey appeared once again and, in some ways, there was a partial return to the pre-Cultural Revolution situation.[154] The literary and art worlds, once again, considered how to revive classical opera without evoking the criticism of the mid-1960s.

After 1972, the scope of official publishing activity was stepped up once again and classical novels (hardly feudal) were republished. At the same time, increased contact with the West saw visits to China of foreign artistic groups and organisations. In such a situation, criticism of Beethoven (particularly his Pastoral Symphony) occurred soon after the visit to China of the London Philharmonic (which placed the Pastoral prominently in its repertoire). In 1973, there was every indication of that kind of criticism in the literary and art world which might lead to a new radical stage in the process of continuous revolution.

In the meantime, however, we must note that although some radicals were worried about the trends in art, the period 1972-3 saw a veritable explosion in mass art and mass theatre and a new flourishing of local opera,[155] which had always enjoyed popularity, even if eclipsed in official debates by the issue of Peking opera. Such opera had always been of a mass character and the idea of a mass movement in the arts was one of the legacies of the Great Leap which did not merely survive the end of the 'flying leap' of 1969-70 but which actually accelerated after its demise.[156]

The Reopening of the Confucius Debate

Criticism in the field of literature and art was but part of a general feeling of unease, in 1973, that perhaps the process of post-'flying leap' consolidation had gone too far. By August 1972, this unease was reflected in a new stress in the media on the theory of continuous revolution, that a struggle must take place every few years.[157] There was also renewed emphasis on the need to train 'successors to the revolution'.[158] At the same time, a discussion had been initiated once again on the interpretation of Confucius. Though carried on in a very low key at first, this discussion was to be of crucial importance since, like the Wu Han debate of 1965, it was the precursor of a new period of radicalism.

The issues debated were much the same as those of 1962 and, in his article intiating the discussion in July 1972, Mao's old literary associate Kuo Mo-jo turned once again to the problem of how to periodise the history of the first millennium B.C.[159] At various times in the past, Kuo had placed the critical date of transition from slave to feudal society at around 770 B.C., 206 B.C. and 475 B.C. By 1952, however, he had settled on the last of these three dates and this he reiterated in 1972.[160] In December 1972, Yang Jung-kuo, continuing the debate,[161] adopted a broader period of transition but focused on the issue of Confucius who lived in this transitional period. As Yang saw it, Confucius attempted to block progress towards the more advanced feudal society, based on the private ownership of land, and adopted a conservative position regarding the various slave revolts which took place at that time. The contemporary relevance of Yang's contention was quite apparent, since much had been made, at that time, of slaves as the creators of history[162] rather than (Lin Piao's) 'heroes'.

I must confess that I am still very puzzled about the contemporary significance of Yang Jung-kuo's December 1972 article. One might suggest three possible explanations. The first (and most improbable) was that Yang's position was 'ultra-leftist'. According to this view, Confucius was a Chou En-lai[163] committed to 'government by ritual' (*lizhi*), the importance of benevolence (*ren*), a priori knowledge (knowledge predetermined by birth), the 'rectification of names' (keeping people in their place), a dislike of military virtues and a desire to restore the old system.

A second possible interpretation was that Yang's position was conservative.[164] This view is based not so much on Yang's denunciation of Confucius as his extolling those enemies of the Confucian school, the 'legalists' (*fajia*) and the First Emperor of Ch'in, who unified China in the third century B.C. Knowing full well that Lin Piao had painted Mao as a tyrannical First Emperor of Ch'in,[165] Yang felt obliged to praise the First Emperor, but did so with tongue in cheek, hoping to capitalise on a conventional wisdom that the First Emperor, who burned books and buried scholars, was a despot. What Yang was really trying to do was to advance certain features of legalist philosophy associated with the First Emperor in order to reinforce the current tendency towards conservatism in China's domestic policy. Yang, therefore, only selected those features of the legalist position that supported a conservative political position and neglected other features such as their harsh administration. If Yang were really committed to the legalists, he would have attempted to justify their harshness. Such a task would not have been difficult since there had been much discussion to the effect that one should not shy away from the fact that the dictatorship of the proletariat was, in fact, *dictatorship*.

In my view, the above explanation of Yang's position seems very farfetched and a third view, which I tend to support, is simply that Yang was an ambivalent radical. Despite the fact that he was once an admirer of Mo Tzu, who believed in universal love transcending classes, Yang's position in 1972 was to condemn the idea of a universal human nature and the assertion of Ch'en Po-ta that communism was the manifestation of humanism in its highest form.[166] He was in favour of the policies of the Cultural Revolution (and therefore supported the burning of *some* books by the Ch'in Emperor). He condemned 'independent kingdoms' (and therefore supported the unification policies of the Ch'in Emperor) but opposed the imposition of harsh rule from above (and hence did not mention this aspect of the Emperor's policies). He opposed 'idealism' and the excessive power of 'virtue' (Confucian values as well as 'ultra-leftist') and was committed to a cautious rehabilitation of men of talent (as were the legalists and Mao Tse-tung). Finally, it is possible that one can even establish a parallel between the strong unified state of Ch'in, surrounded by great disorder amongst the feudal states in the period before the creation of the Ch'in Empire, and the contemporary world situation also characterised by 'great disorder' in which China sought to exploit contradictions. If this view of Yang Jung-kuo's article is correct, then an association of the criticism of Confucius with the recategorisation of Lin Piao as an 'ultra-rightist',[167] in late 1972, might be made.

Move Towards Radicalism 1973

By the spring of 1973, criticism of Lin Piao intensified, under the code name of 'other political swindlers[168] of the Liu Shao-ch'i-type', and the achievements of the Cultural Revolution were stressed with renewed vigour. The 'socialist new things' praised were:

> the creation and popularisation of model revolutionary theatrical works, enrolment of worker-peasant-soldier students in universities and colleges, settling of educated city youth in the countryside, participation of cadres in productive labour, development of cooperative medical services and emergence of 'barefoot doctors' in the rural areas (and the) shifting of medical workers to the countryside.[169]

As the January storm of 1967 was assessed in positive terms,[170] the newly re-established labour union organisations were urged to pay attention to the struggle against 'economism'.[171] More articles appeared in the press dealing with educational reforms[172] and the *xiaxiang* of youth.[173] By the spring of 1973, therefore, there was a considerable amount of evidence that a debate was in progress on whether to promote a new period of radicalism.

In the summer, the debate intensified. By August, the failure to celebrate Party Day (1 July) and Army Day (1 August) had surely convinced most people that the Lin Piao issue (of which, I am told, most people were well aware) was, in fact, a major one of political line. At that time, the Confucius debate switched into higher gear,[174] the Great

Leap Forward, the people's communes[175] and political consciousness
in industry[176] received renewed stress and, on 18 August (the anniversary of the famous rally of 1966), the achievements of the Red
Guards were once again praised.[177] The slogan 'never forget the class
struggle' was most prominent and articles warned against bourgeois
representatives who sought to undermine socialism.[178] Despite the
increasingly radical atmosphere, there were still some trends about
which the radicals might have felt uneasy. Most of these have been
mentioned before but there is one that needs reiteration. The rebuilding
of the Party and Youth League had resulted in the rehabilitation of a
number of cadres who had come under attack in the Cultural Revolution. No less a person than Teng Hsiao-p'ing himself, once branded as
'the number two person in authority taking the capitalist road', reappeared as vice premier in April 1973[179] and in August, T'an Chen-
lin, the architect of the 'February Adverse Current', and Ulanfu, the
former head of the Nationalities Commission accused of fostering
narrow nationalism, were reinstated.[180] It is Mao's view that people's
political orientation may change and clearly these rehabilitated cadres
would hardly pursue the same policies as they did in the 1960s. One
might suspect, however, that until these men actually demonstrated a
changed attitude, some people would be uneasy.

In August 1973, therefore, it seemed that a new period of radicalism
would shortly be under way, yet at the same time attempts were being
made to strengthen the central government and rehabilitate cadres. In
such an atmosphere, the Party held its Tenth National Congress.

The Tenth National Congress of the Chinese Communist Party (August 1973)

I have suggested earlier the hypothesis that the Party Congress tends to
occur at the end of a period of consolidation when conservatives try to
head off more extreme radical measures.[181] By 1973, however, the old
conservative Party establishment had been dismantled and Lin Piao's
challenge had been beaten off. None the less, I would still maintain that
attempts were made at the Congress to prevent too radical an explosion
in late 1973 and 1974.

The evidence for this is that first, the Congress was called suddenly,
without a preparatory plenum and seemingly to stabilise the situation
before a movement of nationwide proportions got under way. Secondly,
there was a contradiction between radical policy statements and
cautious measures taken to strengthen the Party leadership. Prominence
was given to the principle of continuous revolution and Mao's statement

in 1966 that revolutionary upsurges will occur every seven or eight years[182] (in fact seven years had elapsed). The official treatment of the Lin Piao affair (now formally made public) was that it was a continuation of the struggle against 'revisionism'.[183] On the other hand, it was announced that the National People's Congress would soon be convened,[184] rehabilitated ministers received Party posts, and Chang Ch'ing and the Shanghai radicals received a slight demotion in favour of somewhat less radical figures.[185] If, in fact, another movement of nationwide proportions was to be launched, why was there a need to stabilise Party structure and predetermine the leadership? Thirdly, the decline in the overall proportion of Central Committee members whose first identification was with the PLA did not lead, as far as we know, to a marked increase in activists who had distinguished themselves in the Cultural Revolution.[186] If a mass movement was to be launched to produce 'revolutionary successors', would it not have been better to have readjusted the leadership after it had shown some results?

Although the Tenth Congress was said to be a continuation of the Ninth Congress[187] (at which the influence of Lin Piao was said to have been removed in time and his report replaced by another one),[188] there were a number of significant differences between them. The Ninth Congress had nominated a single successor to the Chairman. Now, leadership was to be collective. Two sorts of triple alliance were actualised. The first of these consisted of (1) Army (regional military commanders who had demonstrated their opposition to Lin Piao) and a much smaller central military leadership headed by Yeh Chien-ying;[189] (2) old cadres headed by Chou En-lai, and (3) new blood represented in particular by Wang Hung-wen who became, quite suddenly, Party Vice Chairman.[190] Wang had, at one time, been a worker in the Shanghai Number 17 Cotton Mill, had risen to prominence in the Cultural Revolution and had been responsible for ensuring that No. 17 Cotton Mill was the first factory in Shanghai to form a Party committee after the Ninth Congress.[191] Unlike the previously more prominent Shanghai radicals, Yao Wen-yüan and Chang Ch'un-ch'iao, Wang had been predominantly a *local* leader in the Cultural Revolution and was something of a model activist. There was also a second form of triple alliance which is equally signficant, that of the old, the middle-aged and the young. The old included some national leaders such as Tung Pi-wu, who still served as Acting Head of State and who was, by 1973, an octogenarian[192] and Mao himself, who was almost eighty. The former Shanghai radicals were not particularly young, neither were the senior military commanders. Wang Hung-wen, however, was in his thirties and was a symbol of the rising generation. The future leadership, therefore, seemed to be collective. In state affairs, considerable influence continued to be exercised by Chou En-lai, joined now by Teng Hsiao-p'ing, whereas in the Party efforts were made to see that no one man exercised particular power.

Unlike the Ninth Congress, the Tenth gave great prominence to the new foreign policy of exploiting contradictions[193] and the works of Mao were to be studied together with the Marxist classics.[194] If there was to be a new mass movement, it was to be one based on study and not merely on book-waving.

It will probably be some time before we know exactly what differences there were in the policies thrashed out before and during the Tenth Congress, but one only has to look at the different emphases in the speeches of Wang Hung-wen and Chou En-lai[195] to know that a considerable debate must have preceded it. As things turned out, the National People's Congress was not held until 1975 and a new period of radicalism got under way, once the campaign to criticise Confucius explicitly centred on the 'Confucian' policies of Lin Piao. The Tenth Congress, therefore, failed to prolong the period of consolidation and, by the autumn of 1973, a tenth cycle had begun.

The End of the Ninth Cycle

The period following the Ninth Party Congress has sometimes been looked upon as one in which the Cultural Revolution became institutionalised. I have tried to demonstrate, in this chapter, that Mao's view is that one can never institutionalise a revolution. There was some backsliding in industrial management and rural administration and perhaps also in the policy towards literature and art. Similarly, in foreign policy, it may be true that China's aid to national liberation struggles has declined but the evidence is sparse.

Though I concede the above, I have tried to demonstrate that whatever backsliding occurred has been more than offset by some remarkable achievements — victory over famine, moves towards the univeralisation of education and a degree of mass participation unequalled in the 1960s. Perhaps most important of all, China has demonstrated the efficiency of a consciously *political* management of the process of modernisation, defined not in technical terms but in terms of a Marxist concern with overcoming the division of labour. The process of rural industrialisation is extremely impressive and the Tach'ing model offers us an exciting vision of urban-rural integration.

The period of consolidation, at the end of the eighth cycle in 1969, saw a reiteration of many of the organisational features of the Yenan model and the Great Leap shorn of some of its more utopian elements. It was, however, a somewhat artificial situation in that the Party structure had been imposed from the top down and the Army was perhaps too powerful. In the period which followed, 'mistakes' were made both of a 'leftist' and then a 'rightist' variety but, in general, the overall framework for reform continued. At the point where that framework seemed in danger, a new period of radicalism began. Its contours are still very blurred and it is premature to attempt an evaluation here.

NOTES

1. *Issues and Studies,* September 1972, p. 67.
2. *PR* 18, 30 April 1969, p. 36.
3. *CCP. CC., Zhong fa* (1972) 12, 17 March 1972, in *Issues and Studies,* September 1972, p. 71. Mao here refers to a 'super genius' in his twenties. This is clearly a reference to Lin Li-kuo.
4. Lin Li-kuo became Deputy Director of Operations in the Air Force at the age of 24 (Burchett 1973, p. 24).
5. Van Ginnekan 1972 (from Burchett) describes this as part of a plot. Snow (10 April 1971) describes Mao's unease about the cult.
6. Mao Tse-tung 28 April 1969, in Schram 1974, pp. 282-9.
7. *SCMM* 664, 2 September 1969, pp. 1-23.
8. *CQ* 40, 1969, p. 171 (from *SWB* III FE/3129).
9. *CCP.CC,* 23 July 1969, in *Issues and Studies,* Vol. VI, No. 1, October 1969, pp. 97-100.
10. Domes 1973, p. 215.
11. Ibid.
12. Ibid.
13. *China News Analysis* 799, 1 May 1970, p. 6.
14. Bastid 1973, pp. 183-4.
15. On the importance of provincial power in the economy, see the two essays by Donnithorne 1972. I disagree with many of her conclusions.
16. Bastid 1973, p. 181.
17. E.g. *SCMM* 650, 14 April 1969, pp. 37-40.
18. Bastid 1973, p. 174.
19. *Hongqi* 2, 27 January 1969, p. 29.
20. *CQ* 49, 1972, p. 186.
21. Bastid 1973, pp. 177-80.
22. Ibid., p. 180.
23. *SCMM* 654, 12 May 1969, pp. 28-33.
24. Snow 27 March 1971 (from Chou En-lai), p. 21. In late 1970 there were only 26 departments under the central government compared with 90 in the past. In recent years, however, some have been added.
25. Bastid 1973, p. 185.
26. Bastid 1973, p. 173: i.e. private plots were permitted but should not exceed 5 per cent of land under cultivation. The extent of free markets during this period should not be overestimated. In 1969, for example,

moves were undertaken in some areas to restrict the private trading in pigs. (*China News Analysis* 778, 17 October 1969, p. 5.)

27. Yang Jung-kuo, *SCMP* 5456, 15 August 1973 and *PR* 45, 6 November 1970, pp. 4-5.
28. Bridgham 1973, from *FBIS* 17 December 1971, p. F2.
29. Ibid., from *NCNA*, 24 January 1972, in *FBIS*, 2 February 1972, p. G2.
30. Ibid., from *FBIS*, 21 December 1971, p. D.1.
31. Tseng Ssu-yü's speech on Wuhan Radio, 18 January 1973 (*SWB* III FE/4202), cited in *CQ* 54, 1973, pp. 411-12.
32. I am grateful here for the assistance of G. O'Leary and have drawn upon his unpublished work.
33. *CQ* 38, 1969, p. 189.
34. Certain direct quotes from Mao's essay on the Chungking negotiations were made in a much publicised essay discussing Mao's 'On Policy' written not long after the visit of Henry Kissinger to China in 1971, *PR* 35, 1971, pp. 10-13 and *Hongqi* 9, 2 August 1971, pp. 10-17.
35. E.g. *PR* 28, 11 July 1969, pp. 6-7; *PR* 33, 15 August 1969, p. 3 and 7; *PR* 34, 22 August 1969, pp. 4-5, 8-10.
36. An agreement to maintain the *status quo* on the border pending further negotiations was concluded by Chou En-lai and Kosygin on 11 September 1969 (Snow 27 March 1971), p. 23).
37. Goodstadt L., *The Times*, 1 December 1969, p. 5.
38. *CQ* 52, 1972, p. 768. *PR* 27, 2 July 1971, p. 21, notes that the new foreign policy line was attacked from the 'left' as well as the 'right'.
39. *PR* 12, 21 March 1969, p. 4.
40. *PR* 46, 14 November 1969, pp. 5-6.
41. Text in *Studies in Comparative Communism*, Vol. 4, No. 1, January 1971, pp. 100-6.
42. *Issues and Studies*, September 1972, p. 67.
43. CCP. CC. *Zhong fa* (1970) 56, 12 September 1970, in *Chinese Law and Government*, Vol. V, Nos. 3-4. Fall-Winter 1972-3, p. 69.
44. Bridgham 1973, p. 433.
45. Bridgham 1967, p. 25.
46. *PR* 27, 3 July 1970, pp. 10-11.
47. *Issues and Studies*, September 1972, pp. 66-7, May 1972, p. 78. This was confirmed by reports of unpublished speeches made in 1972. Personal information.
48. Domes 1973, p. 215.
49. *RMRB*, 14 December 1970, p. 1.
50. For a list, see Domes 1973, pp. 224-5, Note 47.
51. Domes (1973, pp. 215-6), I think, grossly overstates the case. Though I am sure the role of the military was excessive, an impressive list of military affiliations suffers from the classic flaw of all elite studies. It tells you little about actual behaviour.
52. Joffe 1973, pp. 456-8.
53. *Issues and Studies*, May 1972, p. 78.
54. Ibid., p. 79.
55. Partial text in ibid., pp. 79-83.
56. Ibid., p. 78.
57. Ibid., pp. 80-1.
58. *Issues and Studies*, May 1972, p. 82.
59. Apparently the document was seized after Lin's coup failed. It was found on a helicopter arranged by Lin to remove incriminating evidence. Personal information.

60. The most remarkable pamphlet circulated in June 1969 has been translated in *CB* 894, 27 October 1969. This extravagant praise continued into 1971 (Bridgham 1973, p. 437).
61. Bridgham (1973, p. 438) specifies the Kwangchow and Nanking regions.
62. *CCP, CC, Zhong fa* (1972) 12, 17 March 1972, in *Issues and Studies*, September 1972, p. 65.
63. Ibid., p. 69.
64. Ibid., pp. 67-8.
65. Ibid., p. 70.
66. For one account of the assassination attempts, see Burchett 1973. Bridgham's account (1973, pp. 440-1) doubts whether Lin ever attempted to carry out his plan to assassinate Mao. According to unpublished speeches made by Chinese leaders in 1972, several attempts were made to assassinate Mao both before and during a quite horrific train journey made by Mao from Shanghai to Peking. Personal information.
67. Chou En-lai 24 August 1973, *PR* 35-6, 7 September 1973, p. 18.
68. According to Salisbury (1973, p. 273), there were at least three Soviet versions as to the people on board the crashed Trident aircraft. One said no one of Lin's age was aboard. Another said the bodies had been too badly burnt to be identified. A third positively identified Lin through dental work done in the Soviet Union.
69. Bridgham 1973, pp. 442-3.
70. Such is the view of Bridgham 1973.
71. Mao Tse-tung 28 April 1969, in Schram 1974, pp. 283-4.
72. E.g. *SCMP* 4510, 6 October 1969, pp. 6-9.
73. E.g. *SWB FE/4080/B* 11/13, 31 August 1972.
74. *SCMP* 5076, 18 February 1972, p. 66.
75. Howe 1973, p. 251.
76. Meisner 1972, p. 731.
77. Howe 1973, p. 251.
78. *Issues and Studies*, May 1972, p. 80.
79. Howe 1973, p. 252 (from *SWB* III FE/4090).
80. Meisner 1972, p. 731.
81. Howe 1973, pp. 249-50 (from *SWB* III FE/4145).
82. Howe 1973, p. 250 *SCMP* 5187, 2 August 1972, p. 107.
83. See, for example, *SWB FE/4135/B* 11/4, 3 November 1972. Bettelheim 1974 (based on visit made in 1971) paints a much more optimistic picture.
84. Some plants were, in fact, imported before 1970 though not in such quantity. *China News Analysis* 809, 24 July 1970, pp. 5-6.
85. See the discussion in Sigurdson 1973, pp. 227-32 and Cheng 1973, pp. 2-3. *SCMP* 5045 3 January 1972. Goodstadt, *FEER* 40, 2 October 1971 (on the military link).
86. According to Cheng, the advocates of steel gained the upper hand after 1970. (Cheng 1973, p. 2).
87. Meisner 1972, p. 726.
88. Beginning April 1973. *PR* 17, 27 April 1973, pp. 13-15.
89. Domes (in *FEER*) 1973, p. 6.
90. See Broadbent 1972, pp. 49-51.
91. *PR* 53, 31 December 1971, p. 8.
92. Ibid., p. 8.
93. *Hsinhua Selected News* 5, 29 January 1973. This is one of a series of five articles on Tach'ing. The remaining four can be found in ibid., pp. 21-2 and *CB* 979, 2 March 1973, pp. 4-15.
94. Sigurdson 1973.

95. The 1970 figure was 14 million tonnes (Snow 27 March 1971, p. 20).
    PR (2, 14 January 1972, p. 7.) speaks of a 20 per cent increase, making 17
    million tonnes. *PR* (I, 5 January 1973, p. 13) speaks of a 20 per cent
    increase, making approximately 20 million tonnes.
96. *PR* 2, 14 January 1972, p. 8.
97. Sigurdson 1973, p. 205.
98. Ibid., p. 208.
99. Snow 27 March 1971, p. 20
100. *PR* 1, 1 January 1971, p. 11.
101. The first announcement of this was made by Chou En-lai on the eve of
     national day 1970. *PR* 41, 9 October 1970, p. 16.
102. Bastid 1973, pp. 168-72.
103. Kuo Chien-wei, *SCMP* 5159, 22 June 1972, pp. 126-33.
104. Bastid 1973, pp. 181-4.
105. *SCMP* 5078, 23 February 1972, pp. 57-61.
106. *CCP.CC. Zhong fa* (1971) 82, 26 December 1971, in *Issues and Studies*,
     Vol. IX, No. 2, November 1972, pp. 92-5.
107. Bastid 1973, p. 186.
108. Ibid.
109. *CQ* 49 1972, p. 186.
110. Bastid 1973, pp. 179-80.
111. Bastid 1973, pp. 173-4.
112. Ibid., p. 181. This problem was noted in *CCP. CC. Zhong fa* (1971) 82, in
     Issues and Studies, Vol. IX, No. 2, November 1972, p. 94.
113. Bastid 1973, pp. 172-3.
114. Snow 27 March 1971, p. 20 (from Chou En-lai).
115. *PR* 1, 5 January 1973, p. 13.
116. Ibid., p. 12.
117. According to Chou En-lai, grain reserves were some 40 million tonnes in
     1970 (Snow 27 March 1971, p.20).
118. Perkins 1973, p. 4.
119. UN figure (1970-5), cited in Orleans 1972, p. 18.
120. U.S. Bureau of Census (1970-5) figure, cited in Orleans 1972, p. 18. Note,
     the figure given by Chou En-lai in 1973 was 1.9 per cent, *Ta Kung Pao*
     (HK), 14 May 1973 (reference unchecked).
121. This was but the acceleration of a campaign dating from 1962 (Orleans
     1972). According to Snow, the campaign suffered somewhat in the
     Cultural Revolution due to Red Guard mobility (Snow 1 May 1971, p. 21).
122. The following section on education is a summary of the excellent article
     by Gardner and Idema 1973.
123. Robinson 1973, p. 17.
124. Gardner and Idema 1973, p. 263.
125. *SCMP* 3475, 11 June 1965, p. 14.
126. On events in Cambodia see *PR* 13, 27 March 1970, pp. 13-28, *PR* 14, 3
     April 1970, pp. 16-33, *PR* 15, 10 April 1970, pp. 31-5, *PR* 16, 17 April
     1970, pp. 17-27, *PR* 17, 24 April 1970, pp. 26-8. *PR* 18, 30 April 1970,
     pp. 25-9. *PR* 19, 8 May 1970, pp. 14-24. *PR* 20, 8 May 1970, pp. 6-25.
     PR Special Issue, 23 May 1970, pp. 1-24. In particular, Mao Tse-tung 20
     May 1970, in Special Issue, pp. 8-9.
127. China refused to take part in the next session of the talks scheduled for
     20 May. A meeting of liaison personnel took place on 20 June with the
     promise that talks would resume at an appropriate time.
128. An account of these steps may be found in Nixon 1972, pp. 327-31.
129. Snow 27 March 1971, pp. 22-3.

130. *PR* 16, 16 April 1971, p. 3.
131. *PR* 7-8, 25 February 1972, pp. 6-9.
132. *PR* 9, 3 March 1972, pp. 4-5.
133. On 22 February 1973. *PR* 8, 23 February 1973, p. 4.
134. Lu Yung-shu 1971, pp. 898-906 – an account of military redeployment.
135. O'Leary, unpublished paper.
136. On the restoration of China's seat, *PR* 45, 5 November 1971, pp. 6-8.
137. Kuo Chi-tsu, *PR* 1, 5 January 1973, pp. 18-20.
138. Ch'iao Kuan-hua 24 November 1971, *PR* 49, 3 December 1971, p. 15.
139. *PR* 50, 10 December 1971, pp. 6-15. For a very jaundiced view from the left, see Addy 1972. See also the correspondence on his article in *Journal of Contemporary Asia,* Vol. 3, No. 3, pp. 321-49. In the polemic much has been made of a letter from Chou En-lai to Yahya Khan, reprinted in ibid., Vol. 4, No. 1, p. 138.
140. See letter from Chou En-lai to Mrs Bandaranaike reprinted in *Journal of Contemporary Asia,* Vol. 4, No. 1, 1974, p. 139.
141. Addy 1972, pp. 410-11.
142. Muthiram 1973, p. 339.
143. For a discussion of China's relations with the EEC, see Wilson 1973.
144. *SCMP* 4827, 17 January 1971, pp. 101, 104, *SCMP* 4849, 20 February 1971 1971, pp. 120-1. *SCMP* 4868, 30 March 1971, pp. 82-3.
145. For an account of the Tanaka-Chou initiative see Hsiao 1974. See also *PR* 40, 6 October 1972, pp. 12-13.
146. *PR* 10, 9 March 1973, p. 11 and 21.
147. Significantly the key slogan for the New Year 1973 was 'dig tunnels deep, store grain everywhere and never seek hegemony', *PR* 1, 5 January 1973, p. 10.
148. *PR* 35, 27 August 1971, p. 12. Italics in original – a quotation from Mao Tse-tung 27 December 1935, SW I, p. 159.
149. Hsin Wen-t'ung *SCMP* 4674, 11 June 1970, pp. 73-82.
150. Mao Tse-tung May 1942, in *SW* III, *p. 89.*
151. Chung An, *SCMM* 730, 5 June 1972, p. 85.
152. E.g. *PR* 34, 20 August 1971, pp. 8-9. *PR* 32, 11 August 1972, p. 11. *PR* 4, 26 January 1973, pp. 13-16.
153. To illustrate the importance of these models some were reprinted in *Hongqi* (No. 5, 1970, pp. 23-46) (English: in *SCMM* 681, 22 May 1970, pp. 1-42) (*The Red Lantern*); (No. 2, 1972, pp. 22-48) (English: in *SCMM* 723, 28 February 1972, pp. 23-73) (*On the Docks*); (No. 3, 1972, pp. 36-62) (English in *SCMM* 725, 3 April 1972, pp. 37-92) (*Ode to Dragon River*). These three operas and the revisions made to them are discussed in Mackerras 1973, pp. 484-91. He notes that, in these latter two operas, the role of the single hero is not so important which may reflect the contemporary concern about heroes (pp. 490-1). On the hero of *The Red Lantern,* see *SCMM* 681, 22 May 1970, pp. 43-54.
154. Mackerras 1973, p. 509 (specifically here on the theatre).
155. Ibid., pp. 493-4.
156. Ibid., pp. 496-506.
157. Ch'i P'ing, *PR* 33, 18 August 1972, p. 8.
158. Ch'ing Yen, *SCMP* 5240, 24 October 1972, pp. 1-5.
159. Kuo Mo-jo, *SCMM* 734, 8 August 1972, pp. 70-8.
160. Ibid., p. 71.
161. Yang Jung-kuo, *Hongqi* 12, 1 December 1972, pp. 45-54.
162. *RMRB,* 7 November 1971, p. 1.
163. In the view of Robinson (1974), the movement was probably aimed at Chou.

164. This is the view of Moody 1974,pp. 332-4.
165. Ibid., p. 317.
166. Ibid., p. 313.
167. Jao Ko, *Hongqi*, No. 12, 1 December 1972, p. 12.
168. E.g. *PR* 17, 27 April 1973, p. 11.
169. Chi P'ing., *PR* 19, 11 May 1973, p. 6.
170. *PR* 17, 27 April 1973, p. 11.
171. Ibid., p. 13.
172. Chu Yen, *PR* 38, 21 September 1973, pp. 19-21. *PR* 39, 28 September 1973,pp. 10-11. *SCMP* 5442, 23 August 1973, pp. 112-14 (a letter written on the back of an examination paper in protest against quantitative assessment by a student, Chang T'ieh-sheng).
173. *SCMP* 5437, 16 August 1973, pp. 136-9.
174. Yang Jung-kuo, *SCMP* 5436, 15 August 1973, pp. 106-15.
175. T'ien Ch'e, *SCMP* 5439, 20 August 1973, pp. 15-16 and ibid., pp. 17-24 (on the Ch'iliying People's Commune visited by Mao on 6 August 1958).
176. Yu T'ung, *SCMP* 5447, 31 August 1973, pp. 134-40.
177. *SCMP* 5444, 28 August 1973, pp. 8-9. *SCMP* 5445, 29 August 1973, pp. 39-46.
178. Li Chien, *PR* 34, 24 August 1973, p. 4.
179. *PR* 16, 20 April 1973, p. 4. Teng appeared at a banquet celebrating Samdech Sihanouk's return from the liberated areas of Cambodia.
180. *PR* 35-6, 7 September 1973, p. 9.
181. This point is made with reference to the 10th Congress by Bradsher 1973, p. 993.
182. Wang Hung-wen 24 August 1973, in *PR* 35-6, 7 September 1973, p. 30.
183. Chou En-lai 24 August 1973, in *PR* 35-6, 7 September 1973, pp. 19-20.
184. Ibid., p. 25.
185. For a discussion of leadership changes see Wich 1974, pp. 234-9.
186. Ibid., pp. 238-9.
     There was, however, a marked increase in the representation of mass organisations. Approximate composition of the 195 members and 124 alternates is as follows:

	1969	1973
	%	%
Military	44	32
Party and government cadres	27	28
Rev. masses	29	40

Robinson 1974, p. 3.
187. Chou En-lai 24 August 1973, *PR* 35-6, 7 September 1973, p. 18.
188. Ibid., pp. 17-18.
189. Yeh appeared to have taken over the Ministry of Defence.
190 For a short profile of Wang, see Chang 1974, pp. 124-8.
191. Wich 1974, p. 235. Note, many factory-level Party branches had been reconstituted before the 9th Congress.
192. Tung Pi-wu died in 1975.
193. Chou En-lai 24 August 1973, *PR* 35-6, 7 September 1973, pp. 22-4.
194. Ibid., p. 24.
195. *PR* 35-6, 7 September 1973, pp. 17-25. 29-33.

CONCLUSION

The Models

Bearing in mind the caveat about the use of models made in the preface, I have attempted here to examine two models of development that were employed in China in the 1940s and 1950s and modified thereafter.

The Yenan model, articulated in 1942-3, consisted of a process of rectification whereby leaders learned how to apply Marxism-Leninism to a concrete environment and were made to answer for their conduct in the field. In this process, a new leadership type was prescribed — the cadre — committed to change within a network of human solidarity and with an orientation which was both 'red' and 'expert'. The cadre operated in a situation where a distinction was drawn between policy and operations, according to the principles of the Mass Line, whereby central policy was reconciled with mass sentiments. Administration was organised according to a principle of dual rule and political campaigns were effected by horizontal mobilisation under the leadership of local Party branches. To prevent a growing division of labour between leaders and led, a programme of *xiaxiang* (later called simply *xiafang*) was introduced whereby cadres engaged for periods of time in manual labour and helped peasants construct an informal or semi-formal *minban* educational system. Throughout this whole process, units (both civilian and military) were encouraged to become self-sufficient and competent at both production and other duties. Rural co-operativisation, therefore, was by no means merely an agricultural programme and attempts were made to integrate agriculture, industry, administration, education and defence, in so far as wartime conditions allowed.

In the early 1950s, faced with the problems of administering large urban as well as rural areas, the general inexperience of cadres, the Cold War and economic blockade, decisions were taken to implement a model of adminstration that derived from the contemporary Soviet Union. As an imported model, it was not very applicable either to the objective situation in China in the early 1950s not to the tradition of the Chinese Communist Party. The Soviet model, which was often implemented dogmatically, tended to prescribe a leadership type which was more managerial than that of the cadre — committed to change but within a network of technological solidarity. In a situation where both policy and operational decision-making were centralised, the commitment of leaders was more to 'expertise' than to political values and the notion of 'virtue' (or 'red') was interpreted increasingly in technological terms. The culture-hero increasingly became the engineer and model worker rather than the political activist and the powers of local Party branches tended to be eclipsed in a centrally-organised vertical bureaucracy. In such a situation, *xiaxiang, minban* education and the Mass Line became less important, a slow programme of co-operativisation tended to be run from the top down and the Army became separated from the rest of society.

The Soviet model was, however, only imperfectly implemented and, by the mid-1950s, certain of its features were under attack. By the Great Leap Forward of 1958-9, the model was dismantled and many features of the Yenan tradition adapted to the changed situation. The original Yenan model had been formulated in a period of moderate radicalism. In 1958-9, however, the political climate was much less relaxed and, occasionally, an excessive concern with production and 'ultra-left' idealism resulted in 'mistakes'. The great debates of the early 1960s focused on the extent of these 'mistakes', and the division in the Chinese Communist Party between radicals and conservatives became sharper.

The debates of the early 1960s were complicated by two important developments. First, China was plagued by three very bad harvests and an economic crisis. This, the conservatives attributed to the policies of the Great Leap Forward while the radicals felt that the Great Leap Forward had been a success as far as it had gone and ought, therefore, to be revived. Secondly, a profound split had developed between China and the Soviet Union over the question of 'revisionism' both on an international level and domestically. The Chinese radicals felt that, although central power in the Soviet Union under Stalin had been too strong, the decentralisation measures of the late 1950s had resulted in the atomisation of individual production units which were now linked not so much by the plan as by the market. With the growth of market relationships, a number of economists had come forward to justify the situation. They talked of the importance of market socialism and the profit motive and had been encouraged by an elitist leadership cut off from the masses. By the late 1950s, the Chinese were to talk of the 'restoration of capitalism' in the Soviet Union[1] though this should be interpreted not as a *state* but as a *process*. Internationally, the Chinese saw the Soviet Union behaving more and more like a great power which desired to contend with the United States for influence and collude with the United States when the interests of both of them were threatened. The invasion of Czechoslovakia in 1968 was seen, therefore, as essentially an *imperialist* venture, designed to preserve the Soviet Empire in Eastern Europe as an area to be exploited.

It is clear, from the above, that the Chinese radicals considered that, within the Soviet Union, the Soviet model of the 1950s had metamorphosed into one conducive to the restoration of capitalism. But, amongst the conservatives within China, there were many who advocated the adoption of some of the features of this Soviet model, and to a very large extent the Cultural Revolution was a battle between these conservatives and the radicals.

By no stretch of the imagination did the Cultural Revolution constitute a developmental model. The terms of the battle, which was waged in 1966-9, had already been set in the period following the Great Leap Forward. The 'ultra-left', however, which emerged at that time, did seek to put forward a programme which, if adopted, would have probably spelt doom to any attempt to implement Mass Line politics. Though there were many different kinds of 'ultra-left', it is possible to abstract from their writings something approaching a model which negated the leadership of the Party. Though the Party structure was dismantled in the Cultural Revolution, the principle of Party leadership was consistently maintained by the radicals. The 'ultra-left', on the other hand, saw China consisting of a number of 'Paris Commune'-type organisations run by popularly elected assemblies subject to immediate recall. There was a suspicion of all formal leadership and all formal education and administration. Their model prescribed neither vertical rule nor dual rule but autonomous segmental organisations in which the Army was eventually to be replaced by the 'people in arms'.

By 1968, the influence of the 'ultra-left' had been checked and attempts were made to restore some of the features of the Yenan model, in preparation for a new 'flying leap'. By the Second Plenum in 1970, however, a far more important problem was on the agenda — Lin Piao's alleged attempt to launch a military coup. Efforts to counter the influence of Lin Piao seemed to result in much more conservative policies after 1970 than before, though there was not, in my view, any large-scale return to the policies of 1965. After the Tenth Congress in 1973, a new period of radicalism began and this still continues. It is much too early, at this stage, to evaluate its results. I suspect, however, that there has been yet another reaffirmation of many of the principles of Yenan though of course modified according to the experience of the Great Leap, the Cultural Revolution, the 'flying leap' of 1969-70 and the struggle against Lin Piao.

In my view, an appreciation of the Yenan model, the Soviet model, and their transformations is absolutely vital to understanding the events of the past thirty years in China's domestic politics. With regard to China's foreign policy, however, it is much more difficult to construct models. Perhaps the most useful approach in this direction has been made by Peck and, in general, I have used his scheme in this book. In the period up to 1950, one can only describe China's foreign policy as one of ambivalence. With the outbreak of the Korean War, however, foreign policy tended to adhere to the principle of 'leaning to one side'. This is not to say that the Soviet Union and China constituted a monolithic bloc and there is considerable evidence of differences between the Soviet Union and China right through the early 1950s. Nevertheless, the paradigm within which China's leaders saw the world was one which placed the 'socialist camp' at the centre.

By the middle 1950s, China began to establish more and more contacts with the newly independent countries of Asia and Africa. In this Bandung period of diplomacy, however, the 'socialist camp' paradigm still remained and only began to crack after the development of the Sino-Soviet polemic in the late 1950s. In the 1960s, a second model began to develop which Peck has called 'revised Soviet internationalism'. Attempts were made to create a new Marxist-Leninist socialist camp and Marxist-Leninist Communist parties began to spring up in many countries in opposition to Soviet 'revisionism'. At the same time, China renewed its attempts to foster Third World solidarity.

A whole series of rightist coups which occurred in 1965, in particular in Indonesia, together with the war in Vietnam, called into question the efficacy of the 'Liuist' model, and it was replaced by the generalisation on a world scale of Lin Piao's essay *Long Live the Victory of People's War*. According to this model, the world's countryside was surrounding the world's cities and China should adopt a policy of maximum verbal support for wars of national liberation and maximum hostility towards imperialism. At the same time, it was stressed that wars of national liberation were the concern of the countries themselves and any kind of global strategy was out of the question. As such, it has been argued, this foreign policy model was a recipe for passivity and did not do much beyond isolating China diplomatically.

A final model, which emerged in the early 1970s, was very different from this. Now, attempts were made to drive wedges between the contending hegemonic powers and between them and their client states and the Third World in general. To do this effectively, channels of com-

munication had to be opened between China and the United States and
kept open between Peking and Moscow. This final model, which has
fundamentally altered the world's balance of power (if that term has
any meaning nowadays), has caused much heartache amongst the 'left'
in many countries. It has been charged that China has toned down her
support for wars of national liberation and is increasingly behaving like
a Great Power. In my view, it is much too early to make any judgement.
The evidence that China has, in fact, toned down her support for wars
of national liberation is inconclusive and most accounts do not provide
us with any operational framework within which to evaluate the global,
the international and the intra-national.

The Theories

During the course of this book, I have outlined three theories developed
by Mao as to the nature of the transitional period through which China
is passing — 'people's democratic dictatorship', the 'correct handling of
contradictions among the people' and 'continuous revolution'. The
first of these, 'people's democratic dictatorship' stipulated that, after
liberation, China was experiencing not a socialist revolution but a 'new
democratic' revolution, during which time a 'four class' bloc would
jointly eradicate the comprador and bureaucratic bourgeoisie and the
landlords. This theory, which held during the 1950s, saw development
as a linear process and held that socialist relations would be built and
consolidated after the bourgeois revolution was completed.

In the mid-1950s, there was much discussion of the idea of 'uninterrupted revolution' (buduan geming lun) and, as I suggested in Chapter 4,
there has been much argument as to the extent to which this theory of
Mao's was similar to that of Trotsky's 'permanent revolution'.[2] The
argument rests on the extent to which Mao saw the various revolutionary stages (bourgeois democratic, socialist and communist) growing
over one into another. As Mao saw it:

> I advocate the theory of uninterrupted revolution. You must not
> think that this is Trotsky's theory of uninterrupted revolution. In
> making revolution, it should be like striking while the iron is hot,
> one revolution to follow another . . . without interruption.[3]
> Trotsky advocated that socialist revolution be undertaken even
> before the democratic revolution was accomplished. We are not like
> that. For example, the 1949 Liberation was followed immediately
> by land reform. After the conclusion of land reform, mutual aid
> teams were launched, then were followed by primary co-operatives

and later by higher co-operatives. In seven years, co-operativisation
has been accomplished and productive relations have changed. This
was followed by the launching of rectification and after that by the
technological revolution.[4]

In Mao's view, therefore, there should be an uninterrupted process of
revolution *within* historical stages but not *between* historical stages, and
hence lies the difference between his view and Trotsky's.[5] One might
also point out that Trotsky's permanent revolution was seen as taking
place on a world stage whereas Mao's was definitely within one country.

It is true, however, that during the euphoria of 1958 there was much
talk of the socialist revolution growing over into communism. This
view was much closer to Trotsky's though I am not sure just how far it
is directly attributable to Mao. What is perhaps more to the point here
than the transition to communism, however, is that by the time of the
Great Leap one seems no longer to be contemplating a bourgeois democratic revolution but uninterrupted revolution within the socialist stage
of development. By that time, the socialist transformation of agriculture
and industry had been, in the main, completed and even though the
concept of the 'four class bloc' remained, future references to the continuous nature of revolution applied to revolutionary leaps within a
single stage of development.

Between the Great Leap Forward and 1962, Mao developed a new
theory of socialist transition which became known later as 'continuous
revolution' (*jixu geming lun*). The starting point for this theory was his
1957 speech 'On the Correct Handling of Contradictions among the
People' in which he drew the distinction between contradictions among
the people (internal contradictions), which might be solved by peaceful
means, and contradictions between the enemy and oneself (antagonistic
contradictions), which could only be solved through struggle. What is
of major relevance here is Mao's contention that each kind of contradiction could transform itself into the other and, therefore, that the
revolution could go backwards. By the time of the Socialist Education
Movement and the publication of the essay 'On Khruschev's Phoney
Communism . . . ', it was quite apparent that such was the case. Earlier,
in 1962, Mao had pointed out the importance of class struggle in
socialist society and he was grasping for a formulation explaining the
restoration of capitalism and the methods one should use to prevent it.

The theory forumulated during the Cultural Revolution, reaffirmed
the persistence of mutually transforming contradictions and, therefore,
class struggle within socialist society. It warned against a tendency for

political power to be concentrated in the hands of an elite which might become cut off from the masses and take on bourgeois characteristics. Thirdly, it stressed the reciprocal nature of an economic base and ideological superstructure and the importance of parallel changes in both areas. In my view, the theory of 'continuous revolution' was an acknowledgement that status differences and power differentials in society might grow over into class differences unless countered by a continuous process of revolution within the socialist stage. Such was the genesis of Mao's view that upheavals must occur every few years, and that new socialist men are born in the process of participating in revolution, rather than *after* a revolution in the economy has been undertaken by someone else. Hence his injunction that radicals should 'go against the tide' when that tide was moving towards institutionalisation and the formalisation of status and power relationships. It is significant, therefore, that the principle of 'going against the tide' was stressed in the documents of the Tenth Party Congress of 1973.[6]

I might suggest one corollary to Mao's theory of continuous revolution. In 1967, Mao made it quite clear that he saw the current Cultural Revolution as only the first of many:

The present great cultural revolution is only the first; there will inevitably be many more in the future. The issue of who will win in the revolution can only be settled over a long historical period. If things are not properly handled, it is possible for a capitalist restoration to take place at any time. It should not be thought by any Party member or any one of the people in our country that everything will be all right after one or two great cultural revolutions, or even three or four. We must be very much on the alert and never lose vigilance.[7]

The corollary, therefore, is that the longer the interval of time between Cultural Revolutions or revolutionary upheavals, the more acute is the struggle likely to be. The above quotation from Mao should be required reading for all those who see progress in China as purely incremental.

The Cycles

In rejecting, as Mao does, an incremental view of progress towards socialism within China, I have divided this book into nine cycles (up to August 1973). Each of these cycles is characterised by a period of moderate radicalism, then accelerated radicalism and finally a period of consolidation. The first cycle (1942-50) saw victory in the Civil War and the establishment of a transitional form of government. The second cycle (1950-54) saw the stabilisation of government according to the Soviet model and the growth of bureaucratism. The third cycle (1955-6) saw attempts to counter that bureaucratism and the generalisation of the Yenan heritage (though not, one must add, in a mechanical sense). The fourth cycle (1957-9) saw an attempt to go beyond the Yenan model in a Great Leap Forward. The fifth cycle (1959-62) saw deteriorating economic conditions in which there was a distinct danger that many of the achievements of the mid-1950s might be lost. The sixth cycle (1962-5) saw an intensifying struggle, both within China and internationally, between the radical policies put forward by Mao and 'modern revisionism'. The seventh cycle (1965-7) — the Cultural Revolution — saw the implementation of Mao's theory of continuous revolution and the eighth cycle (1967-9) was its continuation. During the eighth cycle, the major protagonists were not so much the Party radicals and the conservatives but the radicals and the 'ultra-left' whose policies, Mao felt, could have finished up with much the same kind of result as those of the conservatives. The ninth cycle (1969-73) was a direct consequence of the eighth and focused on the attempted coup of Lin Piao. Finally, in late 1973, a tenth cycle began in the form of a 'Movement to Criticise Lin Piao and Confucius', the dimensions of which must await a revised version of this book.

Each of the above cycles, is, in the Chinese idom, 'saddle shaped' (*maanxing*) and it was hoped that the period of consolidation that terminated each cycle represented a step nearer the realisation of socialism. With the exception of the fifth cycle, China's radicals would argue that such has been the case. Progress then, is seen not incrementally but dialectically. The criterion of socialism, against which this progress is measured, is also not a static goal representing a stage of economic development or a behavioural constant, but a process where the division of labour contracts or, more specifically, where Mao's three great differences between leader and led, town and country and mental and manual labour decrease.

As I suggested in the preface, several other models have been put forward to explain changes in Chinese politics. I have rejected the notion of 'compliance cycles' on the ground that they presuppose a manipulative view of politics. Similarly, I rejected the 'pendulum model', where policy seems to alternate right and left of a fixed point. We have seen that what constituted the mid-point between left and right must shift according to objective conditons. This is not, however, to support the view which maintains the Mao switches to a leftist position from time to time and back to a rightist one when he finds his policies have not worked. Clearly certain leftist policies such as the local steel campaign of 1958 were retracted by Mao once they were seen not to be very successful *at that time*. Nevertheless, it is my view that the remarkable success of the Chinese Communist Party in such mammoth undertakings as collectivisation have only been possible because the central leadership, and Mao in particular, have been unwilling to push policy too far ahead of mass consciousness. In general then, Mao's self-characterisation as a 'centre-leftist' is probably correct and the fact that, for most of the time, he has been left of the Party Centre only reflected the influence of the bureaucrats after the adoption of the Soviet model.

The Crises

Four of the ten major crises in the history of the Chinese Communist Party, which Mao singled out in 1971, have occurred in the period under review. One must note, however, that when Mao spoke of them he referred not to 'crises' but 'line struggles'.

The first of these (and the most obscure) centred on Kao Kang, the arch-advocate of the Soviet model who was said to have had good relations with the Soviet Union. The second centred on P'eng Teh-huai, who was similarly charged. The third involved Liu Shao-ch'i, who was supported, probably much to his embarrassment, by the Soviet press during the Cultural Revolution. A similar charge was made concerning Lin Piao — the object of the fourth crisis, though we do not know to what extent it can be substantiated.

A common thread linking each of these crises, therefore, is the allegation of association with the Soviet Union and the applicability of a discredited foreign developmental model. Secondly, there is evidence that each of them attempted to create an 'independent kingdom' — regional in the case of Kao Kang and organisational in the case of the others. There have been many people who have advocated policies sharply diverging from those of Mao (such as Ch'en Yün and T'an Chen-lin) but who have been subsequently rehabilitated. Kao, P'eng, Liu and Lin have all, however, brought institutional pressure to bear on the Party Centre and have thus threatened to split the Party. In his talks of 1971, Mao seemed to characterise 'line struggle' as antagonistic once an attempt was made to specify two Party centres.

I do not propose here to go into any detailed discussion of the extent to which Kao, P'eng, Liu and Lin contributed to a 'capitalist restoration'.[8] Such would be a major study in itself and would require a considerable amount of work, evaluating to what extent each of them was consciously on the right of left of the Party. Suffice it to say that each of them symbolises a potential danger to any revolution – the creator of a highly centralised, modernised region at the expense of the whole country (Kao), a military technocrat (P'eng), a Party organisation man dedicated to 'orderly' development (Liu) and an erratic 'hero' (Lin).

The Movements

During the whole period of the history of the Chinese People's Republic, Republic, there have probably been over a hundred political movements. movements. In the preceding pages, I have outlined only those I have considered to be the most important, however interesting such movements like the one devoted to the eradication of sparrows might have been. I have attempted to divide the movements into two types; those from the top down and those involving mass mobilisation and a degree of spontaneous generation from below. Clearly the Yenan model prescribed movements of the latter type and the Soviet model the former. In terms of our cycles, movements at the beginning of a cycle tend to be from the top down, those in the middle require mass mobilisation and those in the consolidation stage are once again from the top down. The Party and union rectification movement of 1950, the movement to create a responsibility system in 1953 and *Sufan* were from the top down and the Three and Five Anti Movements, co-operativisation (after 1955) and the Great Leap Forward were movements involving considerable mass mobilisation.

By the early 1960s, however, it was extremely difficult to speak of any movement being one thing or the other. The Socialist Education Movement, as we have seen, was really two movements in one – one from the top down led by work-teams and one from the bottom up led by the Poor and Lower Middle Peasant Associations. Similarly, in the early Cultural Revolution, the same dichotomy might be found. In such a situation, one type of movement might tend to counteract the effects of the other and thus intensify struggle. As to exactly what the nature of the Movement to Criticise Lin Piao and Confucius, is, I am not sure, and probably my inability to understand its dynamics stems from the fact that, after the lessons of the Socialist Education Movement and the Cultural Revolution, movements have taken on a new form. I am tempted to suggest that again there are two movements, one aimed at criticising Lin Piao (from the top down) and another aimed at criticising Confucius with considerable mass mobilisation. At the time of writing, the movements seem to have joined but it is perhaps too early to say whether the effects of such a junction will be as explosive as in similar junctions in the early and middle 1960s.

In this short conclusion, I have summed up the models, the theories, the cycles, the crises and the movements. One would like to finish by outlining the situation in early 1975. This I am unable to do, for events are once again in a state of flux as indeed they must be, so long as the theory of continuous revolution is adhered to. I put down my pen with only one certain prediction. All I have written will soon be out of date and reincorporated into a new paradigm.

Notes

1. *PFLP 1968, How the Soviet Revisionists . . .*
2. Schram 1963.
3. Mao Tse-tung 28 January 1958, *Chinese Law and Government,* Vol. 1, No. 4, winter 1968-9, pp. 13-14.
4. Ibid., p. 14.
5. Starr 1971, p. 613.
6. *PR* 35-6, 7 September 1973, p. 26.
7. *PR* 22, 26 May 1976, p. 38.
8. Such an exercise has been undertaken, in the case of Liu Shao-ch'i, by Dittmer 1974, pp. 214-93.

BRIEF BIOGRAPHICAL DATA

Chang Chih-i (1905-

One of the Party's foremost spokesmen on national minority affairs. 1950-4 secretary general Central South Military and Admin. Committee and vice chairman of its nationalities committee. 1952-4 vice chairman GAC Nationalities Commission. 1955-9 deputy director CCP.CC United Front Work Dept. Held a number of senior posts in the Chinese People's Political Consultative Conference until the Cultural Revolution when he was severely criticised.

Chang Ch'un-ch'iao

Until the Cultural Revolution engaged in Party and government work in Shanghai (mainly concerning propaganda). 1966 deputy head of Central Cultural Revolution Group. 1967 leader of Shanghai People's Commune and later chairman of the Shanghai Municipal Revolutionary Committee. 1969 member Politburo. 1971 first secretary CCP Shanghai, 1973 member Politburo Standing Committee. 1975 vice premier; delivered important report on the revision of the state constitution, director PLA General Political Dept.

Chang Kuo-hua (1907-72)

A veteran military commander. 1952 appointed commander Tibet military region. 1955-9 second vice chairman Preparatory Committee for Tibet Autonomous Region. 1959 became ranking vice chairman. 1965 first secretary Tibet CCP. 1967 transferred to Szechwan, becoming chairman Szechwan Revolutionary Committee.

Chang Kuo-t'ao (1897-

A founder member of the CCP. 1931 vice chairman Chinese Soviet Republic, commander Fourth Front Army. 1935 broke with Party leadership on strategy of the Long March. 1938 expelled from Party and moved to 'white areas'. 1949 began long retirement in Hong Kong.

Chang Wen-t'ien (1898-

1931 member of Politburo closely associated with Wang Ming. 1933 director CCP Propaganda Dept. 1950 head of Chinese delegation to

United Nations. 1951-5 ambassador to Moscow. 1954 vice foreign
minister. 1956 demoted from full to alternate member of CC. 1959
removed from post in foreign ministry. Last seen 1962.

Ch'en Chia-k'ang (1911-

Important for his long tenure as ambassador to Egypt (1956-65).

Ch'en Hsi-lien (1913-

Veteran military commander. Early 1950s held a number of important
posts in south-west. 1959-73 commander Shenyang military region.
1968 chairman Liaoning Revolutionary Committee. 1969 member Politburo
(re-elected 1973). 1971 first secretary CCP Liaoning. 1973 commander
Peking military region. 1975 vice premier.

Ch'en Po-ta (1904-

1930s-1950s active in Party propaganda work. 1949 deputy director
CCP Propaganda Dept, vice chairman GAC Culture and Education
Committee. 1956 alternate member Politburo. 1958 first editor *Red Flag*.
1966 member Politburo Standing Committee, 1966 head Central Cultural
Revolution Group. 1970 criticised at 2nd plenum of 9th CC. Has not
been seen since.

Ch'en Tsai-tao (1908-

Commander PLA units in Wuhan during incident of 1967. 1974 deputy
commander Foochow Military region.

Ch'en Yi (1901-72)

1941 acting commander of New Fourth Army. 1949 commander East
China military region, mayor of Shanghai. 1954 vice premier. 1956
member Politburo. 1958-72 Foreign Minister (although he was not
very active in this role during the last few years of his life).

Ch'en Yün (c. 1900-

An early CCP labour leader. 1949 one of four vice premiers of GAC
and chairman of its Finance and Economics Committee. 1949-50
minister of heavy industry, 1954 vice premier of State Council. 1956
vice chairman of the CCP.CC. 1956-8 minister of commerce; adopted
position contrary to Great Leap Forward strategy. In 1960s and 1970s
somewhat eclipsed but remained in central leadership. 1975 vice chairman National People's Congress.

Ch'en Yung-kuei

1963 Party secretary Tachai production brigade. 1967 vice chairman Shansi Revolutionary Committee. 1969 member CCP.CC. 1971 secretary CCP Shansi. 1973 member Politburo. 1975 vice premier.

Ch'i Pen-yü. (C. 1900-

1966 member Central Cultural Revolution Group, deputy editor-in-chief of *Red Flag*. 1967 associated with May Sixteenth Group. 1968 criticised as 'ultra-leftist'.

Chi Teng-k'uei

Before the Cultural Revolution an alternate secretary of CCP Honan provincial committee. 1968 vice chairman Honan Revolutionary Committee. 1969 alternate member Politburo (1973 full member). 1971 secretary CCP Honan.

Chiang Ch'ing (c. 1914-

One time actress (Lan P'ing), wife of Mao Tse-tung. 1948 head of Film Office of CCP.CC Propaganda Dept. 1963-4 started reform movement in Peking opera and ballet. 1966 first deputy head of Central Cultural Revolution Group, PLA advisor on cultural work. 1969 member Politburo (re-elected 1973). 1975 vice premier.

Chiao Yü-lu (1922-64)

1965 model Party secretary.

Ch'ien Wei-ch'ang (1910-

Prominent leader of China Democratic League. Held a number of important posts in Academy of Sciences and other scientific bodies. In mid-1950s designated a 'rightist' and uncapped in 1960.

Ch'ien Ying (1907-

Best known as minister of state control 1954-9.

Ch'iu Hui-tso

Veteran military commander. 1967 deputy director PLA Cultural Revolution Group. Director of logistics PLA. 1969 member Politburo. Associated with Lin Piao plot in 1971.

Chou En-lai (1898-1976)

One of the most prominent Chinese leaders in the twentieth century.

Involved in founding the Red Army in the 1920s and a member of the
Politburo since 1927. 1949 premier of GAC. 1954 Premier of SC.
1955-69 vice chairman of CCP. 1973 again vice chairman CCP.

Chou Hsiao-chou (c. 1912-

1953-9 Hunan first Party secretary. 1959 associated with P'eng
Teh huai; dismissed.

Chou Yang (c. 1908-

Until 1966 the principal Party spokesman on cultural policies, referred
to by his critics as the 'literary tsar'. 1951-66 deputy director CCP.CC
Propaganda Department. Sharply criticised in early Cultural Revolution;
dismissed.

Chu Teh (1886-1976)

'Father' of the Red Army and commander-in-chief of the PLA on its
foundation. 1954 vice chairman of People's Republic. 1959 chairman
of standing committee of National People's Congress. 1973 member
Politburo Standing Committee. 1975 re-elected chairman standing
committee National People's Congress.

Feng Pai-chü (c. 1901-

In 1930s a guerrilla leader in Hainan Island. 1951 chairman Hainan
Military and Administrative Council. 1953 vice governor Kwangtung.
1956 alternate member CCP.CC 1958 removed from office for
'localism'.

Feng Yu-lan (1891-

Veteran professor of philosophy. 1923 Ph.D Columbia. Before 1949
professor at various universities. In 1950s held senior posts in China
Democratic League. Criticised in mid-1950s and Cultural Revolution. In
1970s his self-examination figured importantly in campaign to criticise
Confucius.

Han Hsien-ch'u (1909-

Veteran military commander. In 1960s commander of Foochow
military region. 1968 chairman Fukien revolutionary committee. 1971
first secretary CCP Fukien. 1973 commander Lanchow military region.

Ho Ch'i-fang (1910-

Writer and poet. Held many posts in All China Federation of Literary

and Art Circles. 1960 member of secretariat Chinese Writers Union.
1966 dismissed from all posts along with Chou Yang.

Ho Lung (1886-

Veteran military commander. Late 1920s and early 1930s commanded
Red Army troops on Hunan-Hupei border. 1950 commander South-
west military region, vice chairman South-west Military and Admin.
Committee. 1952 secretary CCP.CC South-west bureau. 1956 member
Politburo. 1961 vice chairman Military Commission. 1966 for a time
marshal of the Red Guards. Soon attacked as 'conspirator'. Now
believed to be dead.

Hsieh-Fu-chih (1907-72)

Veteran PLA political commissar. In 1950s held a number of senior
posts in South-west. 1959 minister of public security. 1963 commander
PLA public security forces. 1966 alternate member Politburo. 1967
chairman Peking Municipal Revolutionary Committee. 1967 captured
during Wuhan incident. 1969 member Politburo.

Hsü Hsiang-ch'ien (1902-

Veteran military commander. 1948 Deputy Commander North China
military region, 1949 chairman T'aiyüan Military Control Commission.
1949-54 chief of staff People's Revolutionary Military Council. 1955
one of ten Marshals of PLA. 1967 member Politburo, vice chairman
Military Commission, member Cultural Revolution Group. 1975 vice
chairman National People's Congress.

Hsü Shih-yu (c. 1906-

Veteran military commander 3rd Field Army. 1949-55 commander
Shantung military district. 1955 commander Nanking military region.
1956 alternate member CC. 1959 vice minister of defence. 1968 chairman Kiangsu Revolutionary Committee. 1969 member Politburo (re-
elected 1973). 1971 first secretary CCP Kiangsu. 1973 commander
Kwangchow military region.

Hsüeh Mu-ch'iao (c. 1905-

Economist and statistician. 1949-52 secretary general Finance and
Economics Committee GAC. 1952-9 director State Statistical Bureau.
1954 vice chairman State Planning Commission. 1958 vice chairman
State Economic Commission. Criticised during Great Leap but reappointed vice chairman of State Planning Commission in 1960. 1963

director National Commodity Price Commission.

Hu Feng (1903-

Literary critic and writer. 1949 member standing committee All China Association of Literary Workers (áfter 1953 Chinese Writers Union). 1954 criticised by Party. 1955 designated 'counter-revolutionary'.

Hu Yao pang (c. 1913-

In 1930s and 1940s associated with CCP Youth League activities. 1949 member of New Democratic Youth League CC. 1949-54 director political department 18th Corps, 2nd Field Army. 1952 secretary New Democratic Youth League. 1953-9 vice chairman World Federation of Democratic Youth. 1956 member CCP.CC. Criticised for maintaining élitist Youth League in Cultural Revolution. 1972 reappeared.

Huang Hua (c. 1910-

In 1930s student leader. 1954-9 head Foreign Ministry West European and African Affairs Dept. 1960-6 ambassador to Ghana. 1966 ambassador to United Arab Republic (the only ambassador to remain at his post during the Cultural Revolution). 1971 ambassador to Canada. 1971 ambassador to United Nations. 1973 member CCP.CC.

Huang Yung-sheng (c. 1905-

Veteran military commander. 1953 commander South China military region. 1954 deputy commander 4th Field Army. 1956 commander Kwangchow military region. 1958-62 temporarily replaced as Kwangchow commander. 1967 actively involved in suppressing Red Guards. 1968 chairman Kwangtung Revolutionary Committee. 1968 chief of staff PLA. 1969 member Politburo. 1971 involved in Lin Piao conspiracy.

Jao Shu-shih (c. 1901-

In 1920s a labour organiser in Wuhan. 1945 member CCP.CC. 1949 political commissar 3rd Field Army. 1949 chairman East China Military and Admin. Committee. 1954-5 associated with Kao Kang in constructing an 'independent kingdom'.

K'ang Sheng (c. 1899-1975)

In 1920s a labour organiser in Shanghai. In 1930s and 1940s director CCP Social Affairs (Security) Dept. 1949-55 governor Shantung. 1950s and early 1960s concerned with higher education and liaison with foreign Communist Parties. 1956 alternate member Politburo. 1966 member of P'eng Chen's group of five. 1966 adviser to Central Cultural Revolution Group. 1969 member Politburo Standing Committee. 1973 vice chairman CCP. 1975 vice chairman National People's Congress.

Kao Kang (c. 1902-c. 1954)

In 1930s one of the organisers of a soviet government in Shansi. In 1940s one of principal leaders of Shen Kan Ning Border Region. 1949-54 secretary CCP North-east bureau, commander N.E. military region, chairman N.E. People's Government (after 1953 N.E. Admin. Committee), Vice chairman Central People's Government Council. 1951 vice chairman People's Revolutionary Military Council. 1952-4 chairman State Planning Commission. In early 1950s probably the most influential leader in China after Mao Tse-tung. 1954 criticised for trying to set up an 'independent kingdom'; suicide.

K'o Ch'ing-shih (1902-65)

In 1920s and 1930s active in CCP underground in East and North China. 1955-65 ranking secretary Shanghai bureau of CC. 1958-65 Mayor of Shanghai. 1958 member Politburo. 1965 vice premier.

Kuo Mo-jo (1892-

One of China's principal literary figures. 1927-37 in exile in Japan. 1949 Chairman All China Federation of Literary and Art Circles, vice premier GAC, chairman Culture and Education Committee GAC, chairman China Peace Committee. 1954 vice chairman National People's Congress Standing Committee. 1958 readmitted to CCP membership. 1950s to 1970s active in all the important literary and ideological debates. 1975 vice chairman National People's Congress.

K'uai Ta-fu

1967-8 student leader at Tsinghua University, associated with 'ultra-left'.

Kuan Feng

Philosopher. One time teacher at Peking University and editor of *Philosophical Studies* and *Red Flag*. 1966-7 an influential member of the Central Cultural Revolution Group. 1967-8 associated with 'ultra-left'.

Lai Jo-yü (1910-58)

1952 secretary general All China Federation of Labour (All China
Federation of Trade Unions).

Lei Feng (1939-62)

Model soldier whose exploits were published after 1963.

Li Ching-ch'üan (c. 1906-

In 1940s active in South-west China. 1950 chairman Ch'engtu
Military Control Commission. 1952-5 governor Szechwan. 1952-65
ranking secretary Szechwun CCP committee. 1958 member Politburo.
1961 first secretary CCP.CC South-west Bureau. 1967 criticised during
Cultural Revolution and dismissed. 1973 re-elected to CCP.CC. 1975
vice chairman National People's Congress.

Li Fu-ch'un (1899-1975)

Economic administrator. In 1940s deputy director CCP.CC Finance
and Economics Committee. 1950 vice chairman Finance and Economics
Committee GAC. 1950-2 minister of heavy industry. 1954 vice premier,
chairman State Planning Commission. 1956 member Politburo. 1966
member Standing Committee, Politburo. Remained as vice premier
throughout Cultural Revolution.

Li Hsien-nien (c. 1907-

Party economic specialist. 1954 minister of finance, vice premier. 1956
member Politburo. 1962 vice chairman State Planning Commission.
1969 and 1973 re-elected to Politburo. 1975 reappointed vice premier.

Li Hsüeh-feng (c. 1906-

In early 1950s held a number of important posts in Central South
region. 1955 director of Industrial and Communications Work Dept. of
CCP.CC. 1963 first secretary North China Party Bureau. 1966 succeeded
P'eng Chen as first secretary of Peking Party Committee. 1968 chair-
man Hopei provincial revolutionary committee. 1969 alternate member
Politburo.

Li Li-san (c. 1899-

In 1920s major labour organiser. 1930 *de facto* leader of CCP.CC
responsible for 'Li Li-san line'. 1930-45 remained in Moscow. 1946-9
member CCP North-east bureau. 1948 first vice chairman and *de facto*
head of All China Federation of Labour. 1949 minister of labour. 1953

criticised for 'economism' and dropped from most posts. 1956 deputy director CCP.CC Industry and Communications Work Dept. 1962 secretary CCP.CC North China Bureau.

Li Ta-chao (1888-1927)

At time of May Fourth Movement professor at Peking University. 1921 co-founder of CCP. Executed.

Li Teh-sheng (1914-

Military commander. 1968 chairman Anhui Provincial Revolutionary Committee. 1969 alternate member Politburo, director PLA General Political Dept. 1971 first secretary CCP Anhui. 1973 member Politburo Standing Committee, commander Shenyang military region. 1975 vice premier.

Li Tso-p'eng (1916-

Military commander. 1963 deputy commander Navy. 1969 member Politburo. 1971 associated with Lin Piao conspiracy.

Li Tsung-jen (1890-1969)

Former Kwangsi military commander. 1938 led KMT troops at battle of T'aierhchuang. 1948 vice president National Government. 1949 acting president. 1949 retired to United States. 1965 returned to China.

Liao Ch'eng-chih (1908-

Japan and Overseas Chinese expert. 1949-64 held a number of important posts in Youth League. 1949-59 vice chairman Overseas Chinese Affairs Commission (chairman after 1959). Criticised during Cultural Revolution, later reinstated. 1973 member CCP.CC, adviser to Foreign Ministry.

Liao Mo-sha (1907-

1961-6 director United Front Work Dept. CCP Peking Municipal committee. Associated with Wu Han and Teng T'o in criticism of Great Leap. 1962-5 vice chairman Peking Municipal Committee. 1966 denounced in Cultural Revolution.

Lin Li-kuo

Son of Lin Piao. Given major posts in PLA before conspiracy of 1971.

Lin Piao (1907-71)

In 1940s commander of 4th Field Army. 1950-4 chairman Central
South Military and Admin. Committee. 1954 vice premier. 1955 member
Politburo. 1958 vice chairman of Party. 1959 minister of defence. 1966
referred to as Mao Tse-tung's 'close comrade in arms'. 1969 Party vice
chairman and nominated as successor to Mao Tse-tung in Party constitution. 1970 sought to have himself nominated Head of State. 1971
engaged in conspiracy, died en route for Soviet Union.

Liu Ch'ang-sheng (1904-67)

Held a number of important posts in Shanghai and the All China
Federation of Labour (Trade Unions).

Liu Po-ch'eng (1892-

Veteran military commander. 1932 chief of staff Central Revolutionary
Military Council. In late 1940s commander 2nd Field Army. 1950-4
chairman South-west Military and Admin. Committee. 1951-7 president
PLA Military Academy. 1956 member Politburo. In 1960s member
Standing Committee Military Commission. 1969 and 1973 re-elected to
Politburo. 1975 vice chairman National People's Congress.

Liu Shao-ch'i (1898-

In 1920s labour leader. 1931 member Politburo. 1948-57 chairman All
China Federation of Labour. 1949-53 vice chairman World Federation
of Trade Unions, chairman Sino-Soviet Friendship Association. 1954-9
chairman Standing Committee National People's Congress. 1956 vice
chairman CCP. 1959 chairman of People's Republic of China (Head of
State). Denounced in Cultural Revolution. 1968 stripped of all posts.
Now believed to be dead.

Lo Jui-ch'ing (c. 1906-

1949-59 minister of public security. 1950-9 commander PLA public
security forces. 1959-65 chief of staff of PLA and vice minister of
defence. 1965 criticised and later denounced in Cultural Revolution.
1975 reappeared.

Lu P'ing (c. 1910-

Best known as chancellor of Peking University 1960-6. Closely
associated with P'eng Chen. 1966 removed at beginning of Cultural
Revolution.

Lu Ting-i (c. 1901-

A long history (from 1930s) of involvement in propaganda. 1945-66 deputy director (later director) of CCP.CC Propaganda Dept. 1956 alternate member of Politburo. 1959 vice premier. Replaced in early Cultural Revolution, 1966.

Mu Hsin

Journalist. In 1960s member standing committee All China Journalists Association. 1963 deputy editor-in-chief (and in 1965 editor-in-chief) *Guangming Daily*. 1967 vice chairman All China Journalists Association. 1968 criticised as 'ultra-leftist'.

Nieh Jung-chen (1899-

Veteran military commander. 1949-54 deputy chief of staff People's Revolutionary Military Council (mostly acting chief of staff). 1954 vice chairman National Defence Council. 1956 vice premier. 1959 chairman Scientific and Technological Commission. 1967 member Politburo. Vice premier throughout Cultural Revolution. 1975 vice chairman National People's Congress.

Nieh Yüan-tzu

Lecturer in philosophy Peking University. 1966 put up famous *dazibao* critical of Lu P'ing. 1966 chairman Peking University Cultural Revolution Committee. 1967 vice chairman Peking Municipal Revolutionary Committee. 1969 alternate member CCP.CC.

Niu Hai-lung

Military commander active in Wuhan incident 1967.

P'an Fu-sheng (1905-

1953 first secretary CCP Honan, political commissar Honan military district. 1956 alternate member CCP.CC. 1958 criticised as 'rightist' and removed from Honan posts. 1962 reappeared. 1963 chairman All China Federation of Supply and Marketing Co-ops. 1966 first secretary CCP Heilungkiang. 1967 chairman Heilungkiang Provincial Revolutionary Committee.

P'eng Chen (c. 1962-

1945 member Politburo. 1951-66 mayor of Peking. 1954 vice chairman National People's Congress Standing Committee. 1956 second ranking secretary Central Party Secretariat. 1966 criticised in early Cultural Revolution and removed from posts.

P'eng Teh-huai (1898-

Veteran Military commander. 1948 commander North-west military region. 1950-4 chairman North-west Military and Admin. Committee. 1950 commander Chinese People's Volunteers in Korea. 1954 vice premier and minister of defence. 1959 criticised Great Leap at Lushan Plenum; removed from office. Early 1960s retained some nominal posts. 1966 attacked in Cultural Revolution.

Su Yü (c. 1908-

Veteran military commander. 1945-56 alternate member CCP.CC. 1949-51 chairman Nanking Military Control Commission. 1949-54 vice chairman East China Military and Admin Committee. In early 1950s considered to be the obvious appointment to command troops for the liberation of T'aiwan. 1954-8 chief of staff PLA. 1959 vice minister of defence (retained post in early 1970s).

Sun Yeh-fang

Economist. In early 1950s held a number of posts in East China. 1954-61 deputy director State Statistical Bureau. 1958 acting director (later director) Institute of Economics, Academy of Sciences. 1966 denounced as a follower of Liberman.

Sung Ch'ing-ling (Soong Ching-ling)

Widow of Sun Yat-sen. 1920s-40s associated with left wing of KMT. 1949 vice chairman Central People's Government Council, honorary chairman All China Federation of Democratic Women. 1950-2 bureau member World Peace Council. 1954-9 vice chairman Standing Committee of National People's Congress. 1959-75 vice chairman People's Republic of China. 1975 vice chairman National People's Congress.

T'an Chen-lin (1902-

In 1930s and 1940s held various military posts. 1949-52 active in Chekiang province. 1950-4 chairman East China Land Reform Committee. 1952 governor Kiangsu province. Early 1950s director Huai River Harnessing Commission. 1958 member Politburo, active in promoting Great Leap Forward in Yellow River Basin. 1959 vice premier. 1962 director Agriculture and Forestry Office of State Council, vice chairman State Planning Commission. 1967 held to be responsible for

'February adverse current', disappeared. 1973 rehabilitated and re-
elected to CCP.CC. 1975 vice chairman National People's Congress.

T'ao Chu (c. 1906-
1949-54 vice chairman (later chairman) Wuhan Military Control
Commission. 1952-4 secretary South China Sub-bureau CCP. 1953-5
vice governor Kwangtung. 1955 governor Kwangtung. 1957 political
commissar Kwangchow military region. 1961-5 first secretary CCP
Central South Bureau. 1964 vice premier. 1966 director CCP.CC
Propaganda Dept., member Standing Committee Politburo. 1966-7
criticised and dismissed posts in Cultural Revolution.

Teng Hsiao-p'ing (1904-
1920s-40s military commander, political commissar 2nd Field Army.
1949-54 member Central People's Government Council, People's
Revolutionary Military Council. 1950 vice chairman South-west
Military and Admin. Committee, chairman South-west Military and Admin.
Committee, Finance and Economics Committee. 1952 vice premier
GAC, member State Planning Commission. 1953 minister of finance.
1954 vice premier SC. 1954-6 secretary general CCP.CC. 1955 member
Politburo, 1956 general secretary CCP.CC. Denounced in Cultural
Revolution as 'No. 2 person in authority taking the capitalist road'.
Reinstated 1973 as vice premier. 1973 re-elected to CCP.CC. 1975 vice
chairman CCP, chief of staff PLA.

Teng T'o (c. 1911-
Journalist. 1930s and 1940s edited various Party newspapers. 1950-7
deputy managing director and editor in chief *Renmin Ribao* 1956-9
vice chairman International Organisation of Journalists. 1957 managing
director *Renmin Ribao*. In early 1960s published articles criticising the
Great Leap Forward. 1966 denounced in early Cultural Revolution.

Teng Tzu-hui (1895-1972)
Party specialist in economic affairs. 1945 political commissar Central
China military region. 1949-54 member Central People's Government
Council, People's Revolutionary Military Council. 1952 held a number
of important posts in Central South Military and Admin. Committee.
1953 director Rural Work Dept. CCP.CC. 1954-65 vice premier SC.
After Great Leap lost influence and was replaced as chief agricultural
spokesman by T'an Chen-lin. 1969 re-elected to CCP.CC.

Ts'ao Ti-ch'iu

1955-65 vice mayor of Shanghai. 1965-6 mayor of Shanghai. 1966-7 denounced in Cultural Revolution.

Tsêng Ssu-Yü(1907-

In early 1960s a high-ranking military commander in Shenyang military region. 1967 took over Wuhan units after disgrace of Ch'en Tsai-tao. 1968 chairman Hupei Provincial Revolutionary Committee. 1969 member of CCP.CC. 1971 first secretary CCP Hupei. 1973 commander Tsinan military region.

Tung Pi-wu (1886-1975)

A founding member of the CCP. 1945 member delegation to founding conference of United Nations. 1948 chairman North China People's Government Council. 1949-54 vice premier GAC, chairman Political and Legal Affairs Committee GAC. 1954-9 Chief Justice Supreme Court. 1955 secretary CCP Control Commission. 1959-75 vice chairman People's Republic of China. 1970-5 acting chairman of People's Republic after dismissal of Liu Shao-ch'i.

Wang Chen

Veteran military commander, commander of the famous 359th brigade at Nanniwan. 1951-3 commander and political commissar Sinkiang. 1954 commander and political commissar PLA Railway Corps. 1956 Minister of State Farms and Land Reclamation. 1975 vice premier.

Wang Chin-hsi

('Iron Man Wang') Famous as team leader at the Tach'ing oil field in the early 1960s. 1968 vice chairman Tach'ing oil field Revolutionary Committee. 1969 member CCP.CC. 1970 died.

Wang En-mao

Famous querrilla leader from 1920s. 1952 first secretary CCP Sinkiang sub-bureau. 1954 political commissar Sinkiang military region. 1956 commander Sinkiang military region. 1956 alternate member CCP.CC. 1958 full member CCP.CC. 1964 secretary CCP North-west Bureau. 1967 resisted introduction of Cultural Revolution in Sinkiang. 1968 vice chairman Sinkiang Revolutionary Committee.

Wang Han

1954-8 vice minister of State Control. 1957 capped as 'rightist'.

Wang Hsiao-yü

1967 chairman Shantung Provincial Revolutionary Committee. First political commissar PLA Tsinan units. 1969 member CCP.CC. 1973 deputy commander Ninghsia military district.

Wang Hung-wen (1941-

1967 founder Shanghai Workers Revolutionary General HQ. 1968 vice chairman Shanghai Revolutionary Committee. 1971 secretary CCP Shanghai. 1973 vice chairman CCP.CC. 1975 vice premier.

Wang Jen-chung (c. 1906-

1949-52 vice governor Hupei. 1954 first secretary Hupei Party committee. 1958 alternate member CCP.CC. 1961 second secretary CCP.CC Central South Bureau. 1966 first secretary CCP.CC Central South Bureau. In Cultural Revolution associated with T'ao Chu; disappeared.

Wang Kuang-mei

Wife of Liu Shao-ch'i. 1946 worked in Foreign Affairs section of CCP.CC. 1957 executive member All China Women's Federation. 1966 member work-team to direct Cultural Revolution in Tsinghua University; denounced.

Wang Li (1918-

1945-54 engaged in propaganda work in various CCP committees. 1954-64 member CCP.CC Propaganda Dept. 1958-66 vice governor Hopei. 1966 leading member Central Cultural Revolution Group. 1967 sent with Hsieh Fu-chih to sort out situation in Yünnan and Wuhan, associated with May Sixteenth Group, dismissed from all posts.

Wang Ming (Ch'en Shao-yü) (1904-75)

1930, as leader of 'the 28 Bolsheviks' returned to China. 1931 acting general secretary CCP. 1933-4 gradually took over leading role in Kiangsi Soviet. 1935 subordinated to Mao Tse-tung at Tsunyi Conference. In 1940s gradually deprived of power. 1949 vice chairman Political and Legal Affairs Committee GAC. 1954 stripped of all government posts. From mid-1950s lived in exile in Soviet Union and in late 1960s took part in Sino-Soviet polemic on Soviet side.

Wang Tung-hsing

1949 captain of guards GAC. 1955-8 vice minister of public security.

1958-60 vice governor Kiangsi. 1962 vice minister public security. 1967 director administration office CCP.CC. 1969 alternate member Politburo (1973 full member).

Wu Fa-hsien (1914-

1950 director Political Dept. PLA. 1952-5 deputy political commissar PLA Air Force. 1955-71 political commissar PLA Air Force. 1965-71 commander PLA Air Force. 1969 member Politburo. 1971 associated with Lin Piao conspiracy.

Wu Han (1909-

1937-46 professor of history Yünnan University. 1947-66 member standing committee China Democratic League. 1949-66 vice mayor of Peking. 1959-62 wrote a series of pieces critical of Great Leap Forward. 1966 denounced in early Cultural Revolution.

Wu Leng-hsi (c. 1915-

1949-50 editor in chief *Xinhua News Agency*. 1950 deputy director *Xinhua* (after 1952, director). 1957 editor-in-chief *Renmin Ribao*. 1960 chairman All China Journalists Association. 1966 criticised in Cultural Revolution. 1972 reported to be working once again in *Renmin Ribao* directorate.

Yang Ch'eng-wu (c. 1912-

1949-53 commander Tientsin garrison. 1954 member National Defence Council. 1956 alternate member of CCP.CC. 1959-66 deputy chief of staff PLA. 1966-8 acting chief of staff PLA. 1968 criticised and removed from post. 1974 reappointed deputy chief of staff.

Yang Hsien-chen (c. 1899-

Philosopher. 1953-early 1960s vice president Higher Party School. 1964 denounced for advocating theory of 'two combine into one'.

Yang Jung-kuo

Philosopher. 1949 member of China Democratic League CC. 1961 head of philosophy dept. Zhongshan University, Kwangchow. In 1970s active in campaign to criticise Confucius.

Yang Teh-chih (1910-

1951-3 chief of staff Chinese People's Volunteers in Korea. 1955 commander CPV. 1956 alternate member CCP.CC (full member 1969).

1958 commander Tsinan Military region. 1967 first vice chairman Shantung Revolutionary Committee. 1971 first secretary CCP Shantung. 1973 commander Wuhan military region.

Yao Teng-shan

Diplomat. 1954-7 counsellor Finland. 1957-62 counsellor Ceylon. 1966-7 chargé d'affaires *ad interim* Indonesia. 1967 returned to China and engineered takeover of the Foreign Ministry, associated with 'ultra-left'.

Yao Wen-yüan

1965 published criticism of Wu Han launching the Cultural Revolution. 1966 leading member Central Cultural Revolution Group. 1967 editor-in-chief *Renmin Ribao*. 1969 member Politburo (re-elected 1973). 1975 vice premier.

Yeh Chien-ying (1898-

Veteran military commander. 1949 chairman Peking Military Control Commission, held a number of the most senior posts in Kwangtung. 1952 acting commander Central South Military Region. 1954 vice chairman National Defence Council. 1961 member standing committee Military Commission. 1966 member Politburo. 1971-5 seemed to act as minister of defence following Lin Piao conspiracy. 1973 vice chairman CCP. 1975 vice premier and minister of defence.

Yeh Ch'ün

Wife of Lin Piao. 1967 member of PLA Cultural Revolution Group. 1969 member Politburo. 1971 associated with her husband's plot.

Yen Hung-yin (1908-67)

In 1950s held a number of important posts in Szechwan. 1969 first secretary CCP Yünnan. 1967 accused of persecuting Red Guards; suicide.

Yü Li-chin

1959 commander PLA Nanking Air Force units. 1965-8 political commissar PLA Air Force HQ. 1967 member PLA Cultural Revolution Group. 1967 commanded forces putting down Wuhan rebels. 1968 removed from post with Yang Ch'eng-wu. 1974 reappeared along with Yang Ch'eng-wu.

BIBLIOGRAPHY

Addy, P., 'South Asia in China's Foreign Policy — A view from the Left', *Journal of Contemporary Asia*, Vol. 2, No. 4, 1972, pp. 403-14.

Adie, W., 'Chou En-lai on Safari', *CQ* 18, 1964, pp. 174-94.

Andors, S., 'Revolution and Modernization: Man and Machine in Industrializing Society, the Chinese Case', in Friedman and Selden 1971, pp. 393-444.

Andors, S., 'Factory Management and Political Ambiguity 1961-63', *CQ* 59, 1974, pp. 435-76.

Barnett, A., *China on the Eve of Communist Takeover*, New York, Praeger 1963, 371 pp.

—— (ed.), *Chinese Communist Politics in Action*, Seattle and London, University of Washington Press, 1969, 620 pp.

Barrett, D., *Dixie Mission: The United States Army Observer Group in Yenan 1944*, Berkeley, Center for Chinese Studies, 1970, 96 pp.

Bastid, M., 'Economic Necessity and Political Ideals in Educational Reform During the Cultural Revolution', *CQ* 42, 1970, pp. 16-45.

——, 'Levels of Economic Decision Making', in Schram 1973, pp. 159-97.

Baum, R., 'China Year of the Mangoes', *Asian Survey*, Vol. IX, No. 1, January 1969, pp. 1-17.

——, 'Revolution and Reaction in the Chinese Countryside: The Socialist Education Movement in Cultural Revolutionary Perspective', *CQ* 38, 1969, pp. 92-119.

——, 'The Cultural Revolution in the Countryside: Anatomy of a Limited Rebellion', in Robinson 1971, pp. 367-476.

——, 'Elite Behaviour under Conditions of Stress: The Lesson of the "Tang-ch'üan P'ai" in the Cultural Revolution', in Scalapino 1972, pp. 540-74.

——, and Teiwes, F., *Ssu-Ch'ing: The Socialist Education Movement of 1962-1966*, Berkeley, California, University of California, Center for Chinese Studies, 1968.

Beal, J., *Marshall in China*, Toronto, Doubleday, 1970, 385 pp.

Belden, J., *China Shakes the World*, New York and London, Monthly Review Press, 1970, 524 pp.

Bennett, G., and Montaperto, R., *Red Guard: The Political Biography of Dai Hsiao-ai*, New York, Doubleday 1971, 267 pp.

Bernstein, T., 'Leadership and Mass Mobilisation in the Soviet and Chinese Collectivisation Campaigns of 1929-30 and 1955-56: A Comparison', *CQ* 31, 1967, pp. 1-47.

——, 'Problems of Village Leadership after Land Reform', *CQ* 36, 1968, pp. 1-22.

——, 'Cadre and Peasant Behaviour Under Conditions of Insecurity and Deprivation: The Grain Supply Crisis of the Spring of 1955', in Barnett (ed.) 1969, pp. 365-99.

Bettelheim, C., *Cultural Revolution and Industrial Organisation in China*, New York, Monthly Review Press, 1974, 128 pp.

Bowie, R. and Fairbank, J., *Communist China 1955-1959: Policy Documents with Analysis*, Cambridge,Mass, Harvard University Press, 1965, 611 pp.

Bradsher, H., 'China: The Radical Offensive', *Asian Survey*, Vol. XIII, No. 11, November 1973, pp. 989-1009.

Bridgham, P., 'Mao's Cultural Revolution', *CQ* 29, 1967, pp. 1-35, *CQ 34, 1968, pp. 6-37, CQ* 41, 1970, pp. 1-25.

——, 'The Fall of Lin Piao', *CQ* 55, 1973, pp. 427-49.

Broadbent, K., 'The Transformation of Chinese Agriculture and its Effects on the Environment', *International Relations*, Vol. IV, No. 1, 1972, pp. 38-51.

Brugger, W., *Democracy and Organisation in the Chinese Industrial Enterprise*, Cambridge University Press, 1976, 374 pp.

Buck, J., *Land Utilisation in China: A Study of 16,786 Farms in 168 Localities and 38,256 Farm Families in Twenty-Two Provinces in China 1929-1933*, New York, Paragon Book Reprint Corp. 1964, 494 pp.

Burchett, W., 'Lin Piao's Plot — the Full Story', *FEER*, Vol. 81, No. 33, 20 August 1973, pp. 22-4.

Burki, S., *A Study of Chinese Communes 1965*, Cambridge, Mass, Harvard University, East Asian Research Center, 1970, 101 pp.

Burton, B., 'The Cultural Revolution's Ultra Left Conspiracy: The May 16th Group', *Asian Survey*, Vol. XI, No. II, November 1971, pp. 1029-53.

Carr, E.H., *The Bolshevik Revolution*, Vol. I, Harmondsworth, Penguin, 1966, 448 pp.

Chai, W., *Essential Works of Chinese Communism*, New York, Pica Press, 1970, 464 pp.

Chang, P., 'Research Notes on the Changing Loci of Decision in the Chinese Communist Party', *CQ* 44, 1970, pp. 169-94.

——, 'Political Profiles: Wang Hung-wen and Li Teh-sheng', *CQ* 57,

1974, pp. 124-31.

Chao Kuo-chün, *Economic Planning and Organisation in Mainland China: A Documentary Study* (1949-1957), Cambridge, Mass, Harvard University, East Asian Research Center, 1963, Vol. I, 273 pp., Vol. II, 184 pp.

Chassin, L. (trans. Osato and Gelas), *The Communist Conquest of China' A History of the Civil War 1945-49*, London, Weidenfeld and Nicolson, 1966, 264 pp.

Chen, C. and Ridley, C., *Rural People's Communes in Lien-chiang: Documents Concerning Communes in Lien-chiang County, Fukien Province, 1962-1963*, Stanford, Hoover Institution Press, 1969, 243 pp.

Ch'en, J., *Mao and the Chinese Revolution*, London, Oxford University Press, 1965, 419 pp.

—— and Tarling, *Studies in the Social History of China and South East Asia*, Cambridge University Press, 1970, 424 pp.

Chen Kuang-sheng, *Lei Feng, Chairman Mao's Good Fighter*, PFLP, 102 pp.

Cheng Chu-yuan, 'China's Machine Building Industry', *Current Scene*, Vol. XI, No. 7, July 1973, pp. 1-11.

Cheng, J., *The Politics of the Chinese Red Army: A Translation of the Bulletin of Activities of the People's Liberation Army*, Stanford, Hoover Institution, 1966, 776 pp.

Cheng Tsu-yüan, *Anshan Steel Factory in Communist China*. Hong Kong, Union Research Institute, 1955, 88 pp.

Cheng, Y.K., *Foreign Trade and Industrial Development of China*, Washington D.C., University Press, 1956, 278 pp.

Chesneaux, J., *The Chinese Labour Movement 1919-1927*, Stanford, Stanford University Press, 1969, 574 pp.

Chiang K'ai-shek, *China's Destiny and Chinese Economic Theory*, New York, Roy Publishers, 1947, 347 pp.

Chien Yu-shen, *China's Fading Revolution*, Hong Kong, Centre of Contemporary Chinese Studies, 1969, 405 pp.

Clark, G., *In Fear of China*, Melbourne, Landsdown Press, 1967, 219 pp.

Cohen, J., 'Drafting People's Mediation Rules', in Lewis, 1971, pp. 29-50.

Compton, B., *Mao's China: Party Reform Documents 1942-44*, Seattle and London, University of Washington Press, 1966, 278 pp.

Cowan, C. (ed.), *The Economic Development of China and Japan*, London, George Allen and Unwin, 1964, 255 pp.

Crankshaw, E., *The New Cold War Moscow v. Peking*, Harmondsworth,

Penguin, 1965, 175 pp.

Dallin, A., *Diversity in International Communism*, New York and London, Columbia University Press, 1963, 867 pp.

Daubier, J., *A History of the Chinese Cultural Revolution*, New York, Vintage Books, 336 pp.

Dittmer, L., 'The Structural Evolution of "Criticism and Self-Criticism"', *CQ* 56, 1973, pp. 708-29.

——, *Liu Shao-ch'i and the Chinese Cultural Revolution: The Politics of Mass Criticism*, Berkeley, University of California Press, 1974, 386 pp.

Djilas, M., *Conversations with Stalin*, Harmondsworth, Penguin, 1969.

Domes, J., 'The Role of the Military In the Formation of Revolutionary Committees 1967-68', *CQ* 44, 1970, pp. 112-45.

—— (trans. Rüdiger Machetzki), *The Internal Politics of China 1949-1972*, London, Hurst & Co., 1973, 258 pp.

——, 'A Rift in the New Course', *FEER*, 1 October 1973, Supplement, pp. 3-8.

Donnithorne, A., *China's Economic System*, London, George Allen and Unwin, 1967, 592 pp.

——, *The Budget and the Plan in China: Central-local Economic Relations*, Canberra, Australian National University Press, 1972, 19 pp.

——, 'China's Cellular Economy: Some Economic Trends Since the Cultural Revolution', *CQ* 1972, pp. 605-19.

Dreyer, J., 'China's Minority Nationalities in the Cultural Revolution', *CQ* 35, 1968, pp. 96-109.

Eckstein, A., 'Economic Growth and Change in China: A Twenty-Year Perspective', *CQ* 54, 1973, pp. 211-41.

——, Galenson, W. and Liu Ta-chung, *Economic Trends in Communist China*, Edinburgh University Press, 1968, 757 pp.

d'Encausse, H. and Schram, S., *Marxism and Asia*, London, Allen Lane, The Penguin Press, 1969, 404 pp.

Erasmus, S., 'General de Gaulle's Recognition of Peking', *CQ* 18, 1964, pp. 195-200.

Esherick, J., 'Harvard in China: The Apologetics of Imperialism', *Bulletin of Concerned Asian Scholars*, Vol. 4, No. 4, December 1972, pp. 9-16.

Esmein, J. (trans. W. Jenner), *The Chinese Cultural Revolution*, New York, Anchor Books, 1973, 346 pp.

Etzioni, A., *A Sociological Reader on Complex Organisations*, 2nd edition, New York, Holt, Rinehart and Winston, 1969, 576 pp.

Feuerwerker, A., *China's Early Industrialisation: Sheng Hsüan-hua (1844-1916) and Mandarin Enterprise*, Cambridge, Mass, Harvard University Press, 1958, 311 pp.

——, 'China's Nineteenth Century Industrialisation: The Case of the Hanyehping Coal and Iron Company Limited', in Cowan, 1964, pp. 79-110.

Fokkema, D., 'Chinese Criticism of Humanism: Campaign against the Intellectuals', *CQ* 26, 1966, pp. 68-81.

——, *Report from Peking*, Sydney, Angus and Robertson, 1971, 185 pp.

Fong, H.D., *Industrial Organisation in China*, Tientsin, Nankai University, Institute of Economics, 1937, 88 pp. (Originally in *Nankai Social and Economic Quarterly*, Vol. IX, No. 4, January 1937, pp. 919-1006.)

Friedman, E., 'Problems in Dealing with an Irrational Power: America Declares War on China', in Friedman and Selden, 1971, pp. 207-52.

—— and Selden, M. (eds.), *America's Asia: Dissenting Essays on Asian-American Relations*, New York, Vintage Books, 1971, 458 pp.

Funnell, V., 'The Chinese Communist Youth Movement, 1949-66', *CQ* 42, 1970, pp. 105-30.

Gardner, J., 'The Wu-fan Campaign in Shanghai: A Study in the Consolidation of Urban Control', in Barnett, 1969, pp. 477-539.

——, 'Educated Youth and Urban Rural Inequalities', in Lewis, 1971, pp. 235-86.

—— and Idema, W., 'China's Educational Revolution', in Schram (ed.), 1973, pp. 257-89.

Garthoff, R., *Sino-Soviet Military Relations*, New York, Praeger, 1966, 285 pp.

Gayn, M., 'Who After Mao', *Foreign Affairs*, Vol. 51, No. 2, January 1973, pp. 300-9.

Gelder, S. and R., *The Timely Rain, Travels in New Tibet*, London, 1964.

Gittings, J., *The Role of the Chinese Army*, London, New York, Toronto, Oxford University Press, 1967, 331 pp.

——, *Survey of the Sino-Soviet Dispute: A Commentary and Extracts from the Recent Polemics, 1963-1967,* London, New York, Toronto, Oxford University Press, 1968, 410 pp.

——, 'The Great Asian Conspiracy', in Friedman and Selden, 1971, pp. 108-45.

Goldman, M., 'Hu Feng's Conflict with the Communist Literary Authorities', *CQ* 12, 1962, pp. 102-37.

——, 'The Unique "Blooming and Contending" of 1961-62', *CQ* 37, 1969, pp. 54-83.

Gongren Chubanshe, *Wusan Gongchang Gonghui Gongzuo Jingyan (The Experiences of Labour Union Work in the Wusan Factory)*, Peking, 1953, 188 pp.

Gravel (ed.), *The Pentagon Papers: The Defence Department History of United States Decisionmaking on Vietnam*, Vol. II, Boston, Beacon Press, 834 pp.

Gray, J., *Modern China's Search for a Political Form*, London, Oxford University Press, 1969, 379 pp.

——, 'The High Tide of Socialism in the Chinese Countryside', in Ch'en and Tarling, 1970, pp. 85-134.

——, 'The Two Roads: Alternative Strategies of Social Change and Economic Growth in China', in Schram (ed.), 1973, pp. 109-57.

Guillermaz, J., 'The Nanchang Uprising', *CQ* 11, 1962, pp. 161-8.

Gurtov, M., 'The Foreign Ministry and Foreign Affairs during the Cultural Revolution', in Robinson, T., 1971, pp. 313-66, (also *CQ* 40, 1969, pp. 65-102).

Halperin, E., 'Peking and the Latin American Communists', *CQ* 29, 1967, pp. 111-54.

Harper, P., 'The Party and the Unions in Communist China', *CQ* 37, 1969, pp. 84-119.

Harrison, J., 'The Li Li-san Line and the CCP in 1930', Pt. I, *CQ* 14, 1963, pp. 178-94; Pt. II, *CQ* 15, 1963, pp. 140-59.

Hinton, H., *Communist China in World Politics*, London, Melbourne, Macmillan, 527 pp.

Hinton, W., *Fanshen: A Documentary of Revolution in a Chinese Village*, New York, Vintage Books, 1966, 637 pp.

——, *China's Continuing Revolution*, London, China Policy Study Group, 1969, 33 pp.

——, *Hundred Day War: The Cultural Revolution at Tsinghua University*, New York, Monthly Review Press, 1972, 288 pp.

Ho Kan-chih, *A History of the Modern Chinese Revolution*, PFLP, 1959, 627 pp.

Ho Ping-ti, *The Ladder of Success in Imperial China: Aspects of Social Mobility 1368-1911*, New York and London, Columbia University Press, 1962, 385 pp.

Hofheinz, R., 'The Autumn Harvest Uprising', *CQ* 32, 1967, 37-87.

Horn, J., *Away With All Pests*, New York and London, Monthly Review Press, 1969, 192 pp.

Howe, C., *Employment and Economic Growth in Urban China*

1949-1957, Cambridge University Press, 1971, 170 pp.

——, *Wage Patterns and Wage Policy in Modern China 1919-72*, Cambridge University Press, 1973, 171 pp.

——, 'Labour Organisation and Incentives in Industry, before and after the Cultural Revolution', in Schram (ed.), 1973, pp. 233-56.

Hsiao, G., 'The Sino Japanese Rapprochement: A Relationship of Ambivalence', *CQ* 57, 1974, pp. 101-23.

Hsiao Tso-liang, 'Chinese Communism and the Canton Soviet of 1927', *CQ* 30, 1967, pp. 49-78.

Hsieh, A., *Communist China's Strategy in the Nuclear Era*, Englewood Cliffs, NJ, Prentice Hall, 1962, 204 pp.

Huadong Renmin Chubanshe, *Tewu Pohuai Gongchang de Zuixing* (*The Crimes of the Special Agents who Sabotage Factories*), Shanghai, May 1951, 55 pp.

Hudson, G., Lowenthal, R. and MacFarquhar, R., *The Sino-Soviet Dispute*, London, *The China Quarterly*, 1961, 227 pp.

Hunter, N., *Shanghai Journal*, New York, Praeger, 1969, 311 pp.

Institute of International Relations, *Collected Documents of the First Sino-American Conference on Mainland China*, Taipei, 1971, 952 pp.

International Commission of Jurists, *Tibet and the Chinese People's Republic: A Report to the International Commission of Jurists by its Legal Inquiry Committee on Tibet*, Geneva, International Commission of Jurists, 1960, 345 pp.

Isaacs, H., *The Tragedy of the Chinese Revolution*, Stanford, California, Stanford University Press, 1961, 392 pp. *Note:* this is not the original text.

Israel, J., *Student Nationalism in China 1927-1937*, Stanford, California, Stanford University Press, 1966, 253 pp.

——, 'The Red Guard in Historical Perspective: Continuity and Change in the Chinese Youth Movement', *CQ* 30, 1967, pp. 1-32.

Joffe, E., 'The Chinese Army after the Cultural Revolution: The Effects of Intervention', *CQ* 55, 1973, pp. 450-77.

Johnson, C., *Communist China and Latin America 1959-1967*, New York and London, Columbia University Press, 1970, 324 pp.

Johnson, C., *Peasant Nationalism and Communist Power*, Stanford, California Stanford University Press, 1962, 256 pp.

——, 'The Two Chinese Revolutions', *CQ* 39, 1969, pp. 12-29.

Kallgren, J., 'Nationalist China's Armed Forces', *CQ* 15, 1963, pp. 35-44.

Kamenka, E. and Tay, A., 'Beyond the French Revolution: Communist Socialism and the Concept of Law', *University of Toronto Law*

Journal V, 21, 1971.

Khruschev, N., 'On Peaceful Coexistence', *Foreign Affairs*, Vol. 38, No. 1, October 1959, pp. 1-18.

Klein, D. and Clark A., *Biographic Dictionary of Chinese Communism 1921-1965*, Cambridge, Mass, Harvard University Press, 1971.

Laodong Chubanshe Bianshenbu, *Qiye Guanli Minzhuhua (The Democratisation of Enterprise Management)*, Shanghai, July 1951 94pp.

Larkin, B., *China and Africa 1949-1970: The Foreign Policy of the People's Republic of China*, Berkeley, Los Angeles, London, University of California Press, 1971, 268 pp.

Lee, C., *Communist China's Policy Toward Laos: A Case Study, 1954-67*, Lawrence, Kansas, Center for East Asian Studies, 1970, 161 pp.

Lee, R., 'The Hsia Fang System: Marxism and Modernisation', *CQ* 28, 1966, pp. 40-62.

Levy, M., *The Family Revolution in Modern China*, Cambridge, Mass, Harvard University Press, 1949.

Lewis, J. (ed.), *The City in Communist China*, Stanford, California, Stanford University Press, 1971, 449 pp.

——, 'Commerce, Education and Political Development in Tangshan 1956-69', in Lewis, 1971, pp. 153-79.

Lieberthal, K., 'Mao Versus Liu? Policy Towards Industry and Commerce', *CQ* 47, 1971, pp. 494-520.

——, 'The Suppression of Secret Societies in Post-liberation Tientsin', *CQ* 54, 1973, pp. 242-66.

Lifton, R., *Revolutionary Immortality*, London, Weidenfeld and Nicolson, 1968, 178 pp.

Lin Piao, *Long Live the Victory of People's War, PFLP*, 1965, 69 pp.

Lindsay, M., 'The Taxation System of the Shansi-Chahar-Hopei Border Region 1938-1945', *CQ* 42, 1970, pp. 1-15.

Liu Shao-ch'i, *Collected Works*, Vol. 2 (1945-57), 484 pp., 1969; Vol. 3 (1958-67), 405 pp., 1969; Hong Kong, Union Research Institute.

——, *On The Party, PFLP*, 1950, 206 pp.

——, *et al.*, *Xinminzhuzhuyi Chengshi Zhengce (New Democratic Urban Policy)*, Hong Kong, *Xinminzhu Chubanshe*, 1949.

Liu Ta-chung, 'Quantitative Trends in the Economy', in Eckstein, Galenson, and Liu, 1968, pp. 87-182.

Lo Jui-ch'ing, *The People Defeated Japanese Fascism and Can Certainly Defeat U.S. Imperialism Too, PFLP*, 1965, 30 pp.

Lu Yung-shu, 'Preparation for War in Mainland China', in Institute of

International Relations, 1971, pp. 895-920.

Macciocchi, M., *Daily Life in Revolutionary China*, New York and London, Monthly Review Press, 1972, 506 pp.

MacFarquhar, R., 'Problems of Liberalization and the Succession at the Eighth Party Contress', *CQ* 56, 1973, pp. 617-46.

Mackerras, C., 'Chinese Opera after the Cultural Revolution (1970-72)', *CQ* 55, 1973, pp. 478-510.

Mao Tse-tung, *Selected Works*, Vol. 1, 347 pp; Vol. 2, 468 pp; Vol. 3, 340 pp; Vol. 4, 459 pp, *PFLP*, 1965.

——, *Quotations from Chairman Mao Tse-tung, PFLP*, 1966, 312 pp.

——, *Selected Readings, PFLP*, 1971, 405 pp.

——, *Muqian Xingshi he Women de Renwu* (*The Present Situation and our Tasks*), *Jiefangshe*, November 1949, 188 pp.

Maxwell, N., *India's China War*, Harmondsworth, Penguin, 1972, 546 pp.

Mehnert, K., *Peking and the New Left: At Home and Abroad*, Berkeley, California, Center for Chinese Studies, 1969, 156 pp.

Meisner, M., *Li Ta-chao and the Origins of Chinese Marxism*, Cambridge, Mass., Harvard University Press, 1967, 326 pp.

Meisner, M., 'The Shenyang Transformer Factory', *CQ* 52, 1972, pp. 717-37.

Moody, P., 'Policy and Power: The Career of T'ao Chu 1956-66', *CQ* 54, 1973, pp. 267-93.

——, 'The New Anti-Confucian Campaign in China: The First Round', *Asian Survey*, Vol. XIV, No. 4, April 1974, pp. 307-24.

Moore, B. Jnr., *Social Origins of Dictatorship and Democracy: Lord and Peasant in the Making of the Modern World*, Boston, Beacon Press, 1967, 559 pp.

Moseley, G., 'China's Fresh Approach to the National Minority Question', *CQ* 24, 1965, pp. 15-27.

——, *The Party and the National Question in China*, Cambridge, Mass., The MIT Press, 1966, 186 pp.

Munro, D., 'The Yang Hsien-chen Affair', *CQ* 22, 1965, pp. 75-82.

Muthiram, T., 'China's Policy in South-East Asia', *Journal of Contemporary Asia*, Vol. 3, No. 3, 1973, pp. 335-44.

Myers, R., *The Chinese Peasant Economy, Agricultural Development in Hopei and Shantung, 1890-1949*, Cambridge, Mass., Harvard University Press, 1970, 394 pp.

Nee, V., *The Cultural Revolution at Peking University*, New York and London, Monthly Review Press, 1969, 91 pp.

Neuhauser, C., 'The Chinese Communist Party in the 1960s: Prelude to the Cultural Revolution', *CQ* 32, 1967, pp. 3-36.

Nixon, R., 'Report to Congress', 9 February, 1972, *Department of State Bulletin*, 13 March, 1972, pp. 313-418.

Oksenberg, M., 'Communist China, A Quiet Crisis in Revolution', *Asian Survey*, Vol. VI, No. 1, January 1966, pp. 1-11.

Orleans, L., 'China: The Population Record', *Current Scene*, Vol. X, No. 5, 10 May, 1972, pp. 10-19.

Patterson, G., *Peking Versus Delhi*, London, Faber and Faber, 1963, 310 pp.

Peck, J., 'Why China's "Turned West" ', *Socialist Register*, 1972, pp. 289-306.

PFLP, *The Marriage Law of the People's Republic of China*, Peking, 1950, 44 pp.

PFLP, *The Electoral Law of the People's Republic of China*, Peking, 1953, 48 pp.

PFLP, *Eighth National Congress of the Communist Party of China*, 3 Vols (328 pp., 387 pp., 262 pp.), Peking, 1956.

PFLP, *Second Session of the Eighth National Congress of the Communist Party of China*, Peking, 1958, 95 pp.

PFLP, *Long Live Leninism*, Peking, 1960, 106 pp.

PFLP, *Constitution of the People's Republic of China*, (20 Sept. 1954), Peking, 1961, 45 pp.

PFLP, *The Sino-Indian Boundary Question*, Peking, 1962, 133 pp.

PFLP, *Workers of All Countries Unite, Oppose Our Common Enemy*, Peking, 1962, 27 pp.

PFLP, *Training Successors for the Revolution is the Party's Strategic Task*, Peking, 1965, 59 pp.

PFLP, *The Polemic on the General Line of the International Communist Movement*, Peking, 1965, 586 pp.

PFLP, *The Diary of Wang Chieh*, Peking, 1967, 96 pp.

PFLP, *How the Soviet Revisionists Carry out All-Round Restoration of Capitalism in the USSR*, Peking, 1968, 73 pp.

PFLP, *Down With The New Tsars*, 1969, 44 pp.

PFLP, *Important Documents on the Great Proletarian Cultural Revolution in China*, Peking, 1970, 324 pp.

PFLP, *The Seeds and Other Stories*, Peking, 1972, 193 pp.

PFLP, *Taching: Red Banner on China's Industrial Front*, 1972, 46 pp.

PFLP, *Three Major Struggles on China's Philosophical Front (1949-64)*, Peking, 1973, 66 pp.

Perkins, D., 'Industrial Planning and Management', in Eckstein, Galenson and Liu, 1968, pp. 597-635.

——, 'An Economic Reappraisal', *Problems of Communism*, Vol. XXII, No. 3, May-June 1973, pp. 1-13.

Pien Hsi, 'The Story of Tachai', in *PFLP, The Seeds and Other Stories*, 1972, pp. 166-93.

Powell, R., *Politico-Military Relationships in Communist China*, U.S. Dept. of State, External Research Staff, Bureau of Intelligence and Research, 1963, 21 pp.

Price, R., 'The Part-Work Principle in Chinese Education', *Current Scene*, Vol. XI, No. 9, Sept. 1973, pp. 1-11.

Pusey, J., *Wu Han: Attacking the Present through the Past*, Cambridge, Mass., Harvard University Press, 1969, 84 pp.

Rádvanyi Janos, 'The Hungarian Revolution and the Hundred Flowers Campaign', *CQ* 43, 1970, pp. 121-9.

Rees, D., *Korea: The Limited War*, London, Macmillan, 1964, 511 pp.

Riesman, D., Glazer, N., Denney, R., *The Lonely Crowd*, Garden City, New York, Doubleday, 1953, 359 pp.

Rigby, T., *The Stalin Dictatorship*, Sydney University Press, 1968, 128 pp.

Riskin, C., 'Small Industry and the Chinese Model of Development', *CQ* 46, 1971, pp. 245-73.

Robinson, J., *The Cultural Revolution in China*, Harmondsworth, Penguin Books, 1969, 151 pp.

Robinson, T. (ed.), *The Cultural Revolution in China*, Berkeley, Los Angeles and London, University of California Press, 1971, 509 pp.

——, 'Chou En-lai and the Cultural Revolution in China', in Robinson, 1971, pp. 165-312.

——, 'Lin Piao as an Elite Type', in Scalapino, 1972, pp. 149-95.

——. 'China in 1972: Socio-Economic Progress Amidst Political Uncertainty', *Asian Survey*, Vol. XIII, No. 1, January 1973, pp. 1-18.

——, 'China in 1973: Renewed Leftism Threatens the New Course', *Asian Survey*, Vol. XIV, No. 1, January 1974, pp. 1-21.

Rossanda, R., 'Mao's Marxism', *Socialist Register*, 1971, pp. 53-80.

Rue, J., *Mao Tse-tung in Opposition 1927-1935*, Stanford, California, Stanford University Press, 1966, 387 pp.

Salaff, J., 'The Urban Communes and Anti-City Experiment in Communist China', *CQ* 29, 1967, pp. 82-109.

——, 'Urban Residential Communities in the Wake of the Cultural Revolution', in Lewis, 1971, pp. 289-323.

Salisbury, H., *The Coming War Between Russia and China*, London, Secker and Warburg, 1969, 200 pp.

——, *To Peking and Beyond: A Report on the New Asia*, London, Arrow Books, 1973, 312 pp.

Scalapino, R. (ed.), *Elites in the People's Republic of China*, Seattle and London, University of Washington Press, 1972, 672 pp.

Schram, S., *Documents sur la Théorie de la 'Révolution Permanente' en Chine: Idéologie Dialectique et Dialectique du Réel*, Paris, Mouton, 1963.

——, *Mao Tse-tung*, Harmondsworth, Penguin, 1966, 352 pp.

——, 'Mao Tse-tung and the Theory of the Permanent Revolution 1958-69', *CQ* 46, 1971, pp. 221-44.

Schram, S. (ed.), *Authority Participation and Cultural Change in China*, Cambridge University Press, 1973, 350 pp.

——, *Mao Tse-tung Unrehearsed*, Harmondsworth, Penguin, 1974, 352 pp.

Schurmann, H., 'China's "New Economic Policy" — Transition or Beginning', *CQ* 17, 1964, pp. 65-91.

——, *Ideology and Organisation in Communist China*, Berkeley and Los Angeles, University of California Press, 1966, 540 pp.

Schurmann, H.F. and Schell, O., *China Readings 2, Republican China* (382 pp.); *China Readings 3, Communist China* (647 pp.), Harmondsworth, Penguin, 1968.

Schwartz, B., *Chinese Communism and the Rise of Mao*, Cambridge, Mass., Harvard University Press, 1966, 258 pp.

Selden, M., *The Yenan Way in Revolutionary China*, Cambridge, Mass., Harvard University Press, 1971, 311 pp.

Seybolt, P., 'The Yenan Revolution in Mass Education', *CQ* 48, 1971, pp. 641-69.

Shanghai (no publisher stated), *Jiefanghou Shanghai Gongyun Ziliao* (*Materials on the Shanghai Workers Movement after Liberation* [*May-December 1949*]), Hong Kong, reprint, no date, 254 pp.

Shanghai Zonggonghui Wenjiaobu (Shanghai General Labour Union Cultural and Education Department), *Gongchang zhong de Xuanchuan Gudong Gongzuo* (*Agitprop Work in Factories*), Shanghai, *Laodong Chubanshe*, October 1950, 196 pp.

Shewmaker, K., 'The "Agrarian Reformer" Myth', *CQ* 34, 1968, pp. 68-81.

Sigurdson, J., 'Rural Industry and the Internal Transfer of Technology', in Schram (ed.), 1973, pp. 199-232.

Simmonds, J., 'P'eng Te-huai: A Chronological Re-Examination', *CQ* 37, 1969, pp. 120-38.

Skinner, G., 'Marketing and Social Structure in Rural China', *Journal of Asian Studies*. Vol. XXIV, No. 1, November 1964, pp. 3-43 (Pt. 1); No. 2, February 1965, pp. 195-228 (Pt. II); No. 3, May 1965, pp. 363-99 (Pt. III).

—— and Winckler, E., 'Compliance Succession in Rural Communist China: A Cyclical Theory', in Etzioni, 1969, pp. 410-38.

Smedley, A., *The Great Road: The Life and Times of Chu Teh*, New York and London, Monthly Review Press, 1972, 460 pp.

Snow, E., *Red Star Over China*, New York, Grove Press, 1961, 529 pp.

——, 'Interview with Mao', *The New Republic*, 27 February 1965, pp. 17-23.

——, 'The Open Door', *The New Republic*, 27 March 1971, pp. 20-3.

——, 'Aftermath of the Cultural Revolution', *The New Republic*, 10 April 1971, pp. 18-21.

——, 'Population Care and Control', *The New Republic*, 1 May 1971, pp. 20-3.

Solomon, R., *Mao's Revolution and the Chinese Political Culture*, Berkeley, Los Angeles, London, University of California Press, 1971, 604 pp.

Starr, J., 'Conceptual Foundations of Mao Tse-tung's Theory of Continuous Revolution', *Asian Survey*, 1971, pp. 610-28.

State Statistical Bureau, *Ten Great Years: Statistics of the Economic and Cultural Achievements of the People's Republic of China*, Peking, 1960, 223 pp.

Stone, I., *The Hidden History of the Korean War*, New York and London, Monthly Review Press, 1970, 368 pp.

Strong, A., *When Sergs Stood Up in Tibet*, Peking, New World Press, 1965, 320 pp.

Swarup, S., *A Study of the Chinese Communist Movement*, Oxford, Clarendon Press, 1966, 289 pp.

T'ao Chu, *The People's Communes Forge Ahead, PFLP*, 1964, 37 pp.

Teiwes, F., 'The Purge of Provincial Leaders 1957-8', *CQ* 27, 1966, pp. 14-32.

Teng T'o (pseud. Ma Nan-t'un), *Yanshan Yehua*, Peking, *Beijing Chubanshe*, 1963, 546 pp.

Thomas, R., 'China in Transition: Society and Criminal Law', *Flinders Journal of History and Politics*, Vol. IV, 1974, pp. 14-60.

Tsou Tang, *America's Failure in China 1941-50*, Chicago, University of Chicago Press, 1967, 2 vols., 614 pp.

Tuchman, B., *Sand Against the Wind: Stilwell and the American Experience in China*, London, Macmillan, 1970, 621 pp.

URI, The Case of P'eng Teh-huai, Hong Kong, 1968, 494 pp.

URI, CCP Documents of the Great Proletarian Cultural Revolution 1966-67, Hong Kong, *URI* 1968, 692 pp.

URI, Tibet 1950-1967, Hong Kong, 1968, 848 pp.

URI, *Communist China 1967*, Hong Kong, 1969, 226 pp.

URI, *Documents of Chinese Communist Party Central Committee*, Hong Kong, 1971, 838 pp.

Van Ginnekan, 'The 1967 Plot of the May 16 Movement', *Journal of Contemporary Asia*, Vol. 2, No. 3, 1972, pp. 237-54.

Vogel, E., 'From Revolutionary to Semi-Bureaucrat: The "Regularisation" of Cadres', *CQ* 29, 1967, pp. 36-60.

——, *Canton Under Communism: Programs and Politics in a Provincial Capital 1949-1968*, New York, Harper and Row, 1971, 448 pp.

Walker, K., 'Organisation of Agricultural Production', in Eckstein, Galenson and Liu, 1968, pp. 397-458.

Waller, D., *The Government and Politics of Communist China*, London, Hutchinson, 1970, 192 pp.

——, *The Kiangsi Soviet Republic: Mao and the National Congresses of 1931 and 1934*, Berkeley, Center for Chinese Studies, 1973, 116 pp.

Watson, A., 'A Revolution to Touch Men's Souls: The Family, Interpersonal Relations and Daily Life', in Schram (ed.), 1973, pp. 291-330.

Wheelwright, E. and McFarlane, B., *The Chinese Road to Socialism*, New York and London, Monthly Review Press, 1970, 256 pp.

White, L., 'Shanghai's Polity in Cultural Revolution', in Lewis, 1971, pp. 325-70.

——, 'Leadership in Shanghai 1955-69', in Scalapino, 1972, pp. 302-77.

Whiting, A., *China Crosses the Yalu: The Decision to Enter the Korean War*, Stanford, California, Stanford University Press, 1968, 219 pp.

Whitson, W., 'The Field Army in Chinese Communist Military Politics', *CQ* 37, 1969, pp. 1-30.

Wich, R., 'The Tenth Party Congress: The Power Structure and the Succession Question', *CQ* 58, 1974, pp. 231-48.

Wilbur, C., 'The Ashes of Defeat', *CQ* 18, 1964, pp. 3-54.

Wilhelm, H., 'The Reappraisal of Neo Confucianism', *CQ* 23, 1965, pp. 122-39.

Wilson, D., *A Quarter of Mankind: An Anatomy of China Today*, Harmondsworth, Penguin, 1968, 333 pp.

——, *The Long March, 1935*, London, Hamish Hamilton, 1971, 331 pp.

Wilson, D., 'China and the European Community', *CQ* 56, 1973, pp. 647-66.

Winnington, A., *The Slaves of the Cool Mountains*, London, Lawrence and Wishart, 1959, 223 pp.

Wright, M., *The Last Stand of Chinese Conservatism: The T'ung-chih Restoration 1862-1874*, Stanford, California, Stanford University

Press, 1957.

Wylie, R., 'Red Guards Rebound', *FEER*, Vol. LVII, No. 10, 10 September 1967, pp. 462-6.

Yahuda, M., 'Kremlinology and the Chinese Strategic Debate 1965-66', *CQ* 49, 1972, pp. 32-75.

Yu, G., *China and Tanzania: A Study in Cooperative Interaction*, Berkeley, California, Center for Chinese Studies, 1970, 100 pp.

Zagoria, D., 'Khruschev's Attack on Albania and Sino-Soviet Relations', *CQ* 8, 1961, pp. 1-19.

——, *The Sino-Soviet Conflict, 1956-61*, New York, Atheneum, 1966, 484 pp.

——, *Vietnam Triangle: Moscow, Peking, Hanoi*, New York, Pegasus, 1968, 286 pp.

Zhonghua Quanguo Zonggonghui Shengchanbu (All China Federation of Labour: Production Department), *Shengchan Gongzuo Shouce (Production Work Handbook)*, Vol. I, Peking Gongren Chubanshe, May 1950, 265 pp.

Zhonggong Yanjiu Zazhi she, *Liu Shaoqi Wenti Ziliao Zhuanji* (A Special Collation of Materials on Liu Shao-ch'i), T'aipei 1970.

Zhongguo Minzhu Tongmeng Zongbu Xuanchuan Weiyuanhui (China Democratic League, General Office, Propaganda Committee), *Zengchan Jieyue Fan Tanwu Fan Langfei Fan Guanliaozhuyi (Increase Production and Practise Economy: Oppose Graft, Waste and Bureaucratism)*, 1951, 132 pp.

INDEX